The Second Archives of Bertrand Russell

Bertrand Russell tearing up his Labour Party card over Vietnam during speech to Youth CND, London, 15 October 1965 (*Sport and General*)

A DETAILED CATALOGUE OF THE SECOND ARCHIVES OF BERTRAND RUSSELL

By
Kenneth Blackwell
&
Carl Spadoni

Archives and Research Collections
McMaster University Library

THOEMMES PRESS

Published in 1992 by
Thoemmes Press
85 Park Street
Bristol BS1 5PJ
England

ISBN 1 85506 162 7

British Library Cataloguing in Publication Data

Blackwell, Kenneth
Detailed Catalogue of the Second
Archives of Bertrand Russell
I. Title II. Spadoni, Carl
192

ISBN 1-85506-162-7

Table of Contents

List of Illustrations .... *page* viii
Schedule of Document Numbers ix
Introduction xi
Russell's Chronology, 1960–70 xxiii
List of Abbreviations xxv

*100 ANCESTRAL PAPERS

*111 Lord John Russell 3
*112 Lady John Russell 3
*113 Rachel Russell 3
*132 Kate Amberley 3

*200 MANUSCRIPTS

*210 Book Manuscripts 7
*220 Article Manuscripts 9
*221 Embargoed Manuscripts 20
*240 Pocket Diaries 20

*300 THE BERTRAND RUSSELL PEACE FOUNDATION

*315 General Political Correspondence 23
*316 Financial Correspondence Relating to Politics 87
*320 World Affairs 93

*330 Political Prisoners 120
*340 Civil Rights 133
*350 Bertrand Russell Peace Foundation Offices 141
*360 Miscellaneous Politics 151
*371 International War Crimes Tribunal: Members' Correspondence 157
*372 IWCT: Refusals 158
*373 IWCT: Investigation Teams and Witnesses 160
*374 IWCT: French Office 161
*375 IWCT: Working Correspondence with Vietnamese 162
*376 IWCT: General Correspondence on Vietnam 164
*377 IWCT: General Correspondence (by Country) 169
*378 Visa Campaign for Vietnamese 176
*379 Vietnam Solidarity Campaign 178
*380 British-Vietnam Committee 180
*381 British Council for Peace in Vietnam 181
*382 World Vietnam Committee 182
*383 Vietnam—Correspondence with Newspapers 183
*384 IWCT: Essays, Meetings and Reports 184
*385 IWCT: Printed Material 186
*390 IWCT: Members' Correspondence on Czechoslovakia 192

*400 PUBLISHING CORRESPONDENCE

*410 Publishing Correspondence 195

*500 POLITICAL ORGANIZATIONS TO 1955

*510 Women's Suffrage 247

*600 NUCLEAR DISARMAMENT

*630 Nuclear Disarmament Campaigns 251

*700 PERSONAL AND FAMILY CORRESPONDENCE

*710 Personal Correspondence 255
*710 Personal Correspondence (Embargoed) 276
*712 Miscellaneous Personal Documents 284
*720 Miscellaneous Correspondence 285
*721 "Cranks" 286
*724 90th Birthday Tribute 287

*725 95th Birthday Letters 290
*726 Condolences on Russell's Death: Answered by Lady Russell 292
*727 Condolences on Russell's Death: General 294
*728 97th Birthday 301
*730 Frank Russell and Bertrand Russell 303
*735 Frank Russell 303
*736 Russell Relatives 303
*737 Stanley Relatives 304
*740 Invitations 305
*750 Russell's Dictation 306
*751-4 Embargoed Financial Correspondence 307
*753 Financial and Legal Correspondence (Embargoed) 308
*760 Legal Correspondence (Embargoed) 309
*761 1935 Divorce Documents (Embargoed) 312
*762 Later Legal and Business Correspondence 313

*800 LEGAL CORRESPONDENCE

*811 Legal Actions: City College of New York 317

*900 WORKS BY OTHERS, FILMS, TAPES, PHOTOGRAPHS, CLIPPINGS, ETC.

*910 Works by Others 321
*930 Films 340
*940 Tape Recordings 341
*950 Photographs 343
*970 Obituaries 344
*971 Newsclippings 344
*972 Odds and Ends 344
*973 Archival Lists 344
*974 Photocopied Documents 344
*975 Mimeographed Statements 344

ADDENDA 349

Index of Names 357

Illustrations

Bertrand Russell tearing up his Labour Party card over Vietnam during speech to Youth CND, London, 15 October 1965. (*Sport and General*) .... *frontispiece*

1 Russell to his Granny, the Dowager Countess Russell, 1 May 1892 .... *page* 2

2 Russell's revisions to his article "Free World Barbarism" (1964) 6

3 Heinz Brandt, East German political prisoner, to Russell, 28 November 1964, and cartoon from *Metall*, 9 March 1964 22

4 Letters from Russell to Sir Stanley and Lady Unwin, 4 August and 15 October 1968 194

5 Copy in Alys Russell's hand of Russell's resignation letter of 25 November 1909 to Marion Phillips, Secretary of the National Union of Women's Suffrage Societies 246

6 Manuscript of statement by Russell on his dispute with Canon L. John Collins over the compatibility of CND and the Committee of 100 250

7 Father F.C. Copleston to Russell, 18 May 1962 254

8 Letter to *The Times*, 3 Dec. 1964, re *Penthouse* 316

9 Russell's revisions on an anonymous typescript, "The Queen of Sheba's Damnation" (1930) 320

10 First leaf of notes on "Oscillations of Four Particles under Attraction & Repulsion" (*c.*1897). Found in Russell's copy of J. L. Lagrange's *Mécanique analytique* 348

Schedule of Document Numbers

Inclusive Numeration	Class	Number of Documents
.100001–.100187	*751	187
.100188–.100476	*752	289
.100501–.100566	*754	66
.101001–.102160	*760	1,160
.102501–.102678	*753	178
.103001–.107260	*710 (Embargoed)	4,260
.107261–.107276	*712	16
.108001–[.108018]–.108021	*111	20
.108018	*113	1
.108022	*132	1
.108101–.108105	*730	5
.108106–.108119	*735	14
.108120–[.108173]–.108219m	*736	112
[736].108173	*112	1
.108220–.108339	*737	140
.110001–.112657	*710	2,657
.113001–.113252	*762	252
.113253	*811	1
.115001–.116435	*740	1,435
.117001–.117498	*724	498
.117501–.117635	*725	135

.118001–.118108	*726	108
.119001–.119732	*727	732
.119733–.119781	*728	49
.120001–.132656	*720	12,656
.132701–.132740	*750	40
.133001–.133924	*760	924
.133925–.134005	*761	81
.135001–.136195	*721	1,195
.137001–.137836	*910	836
.140001–.147060	*410	7,060
.147501–.147509	*210	9
.148001–.149111	*220	1,111
.149301–.149717	*630	417
.150001–.158566	*315	8,566
.159107–.162198	*316	3,092
.163001–.164009	*385	1,009
.170001–.170825	*371	825
.170826–.171181	*372	356
.171182–.171691	*373	510
.171692–.172149	*374	458
.172150–.172461	*375	312
.172462–.173314	*376	853
.173315–.174724	*377	1,410
.174725–.174921	*378	197
.174922–.175248	*379	327
.175249–.175309	*380	61
.175310–.175348	*381	39
.175349–.175420	*382	72
.175421–.175753	*383	333
.175754–.175907a	*384	155
.175908–.176049	*390	142
.177001–.183284	*320	6,284
.183301–.184392	*340	1,728
.184901–.184931	*510	31
.185001–.188353	*330	3,353
.189001–.192296	*350	3,296
.192001–.193519	*360	1,519
.199000–.199635	*340 Addenda	636
Total number of documents		72,200

Introduction

I. CONTENTS OF THE SECOND ARCHIVES

The archives of the philosopher and political activist Bertrand Russell (1872–1970) came to the McMaster University Library by means of two purchases; together they form a vast trove of documentation for one of the most prolific authors of the century. The catalogue prepared by Lord Russell's literary agent, known as the Feinberg catalogue, describes the documents in the first acquisition, or Archives I. The present catalogue describes those in the second acquisition, or Archives II. It does not describe documents, and copies of documents, acquired independently of Lord Russell and his Estate.[1]

As the scope and magnitude of Archives II revealed themselves during the years that it took to sort, classify, catalogue and microfilm the papers, I was led to wonder what other archives of the 1960s might be comparable to them. It is likely that some institutional archives—e.g., those of governmental intelligence agencies and U.N. Secretaries-General—are comparable, and they would contain far more documents than accumulated by Russell and his secretariat. But aside from official archives, I can think of only two private persons who may have amassed archives comparable to Russell's—they are Linus Pauling, winner of the Nobel Peace Prize in 1962, and Jean-Paul Sartre, a fellow winner (with Russell) of the Nobel Prize for Literature. It is indisputable, as this catalogue shows, that those who wish to study world politics in the 1960s have, in the second Russell

[1] For these acquisitions, see the reports in *Russell: the Journal of the Bertrand Russell Archives*, nos. 1–40 (1971–80), n.s. 1– (1981–).

Archives, an extraordinarily rich collection of documents generated to a large degree by a single man in his attempt to influence the disastrous trend of events in the nuclear age.

Why, exactly, the second Russell Archives? McMaster University Library has a family of Russell Archives and related collections. There is Archives I, purchased from Lord Russell in 1968, covering his life (with the exclusion of certain private papers) until 1966. There are the collections of original documents, photocopies and microfilms we have acquired independently of Russell and, after his death on 2 February 1970, his Estate. There are the files of printed Russelliana and the supporting library formed to back up the manuscripts of his articles and essays. There are the collections of cognate papers—those of Lady Constance Malleson, Rupert Crawshay-Williams, C.K. Ogden, Edith, Countess Russell, and Dora Russell. But second only in importance to the original Russell Archives is the mass of papers purchased from the Bertrand Russell Estate in 1972. Its size is indicated by the number of microfilm frames it occupies—some 175,000. The present catalogue lists 72,200 documents and indexes about 14,000 names.

Archives II covers a great deal more than the political activities of 1960–70, and private affairs before that period. That is because Russell never spent much time ordering his old papers, although he certainly weeded them until his fourth marriage, to Edith Bronson Finch. Having done biographical research herself,[2] she knew the value of private papers and seems to have discarded nothing of Russell's above the level of grocery lists. The chronological division between the first and second Archives cannot be made precisely. Five years after the delivery of Archives II, Russell's last secretary, Christopher Farley (who succeeded Ralph Schoenman in 1966), found several additional boxes of old letters in the back of Russell's basement at Plas Penrhyn, Penrhyndeudraeth, Wales, where he spent his last years. And we found that the political correspondence of Archives II contains quantities of 1962 correspondence whose omission from Archives I had not been apparent.

The scope of Archives II can best be conveyed by considering it from three different aspects: the personal, the philosophical, and the political. Archives II contains several thousand personal documents belonging to earlier years of Russell's life. There is correspondence with all of his

[2] She published biographies of Carey Thomas and Wilfred Scawen Blunt. For the inventory of her papers, see Sheila Turcon, "The Edith Russell Papers", *Russell*, n.s. 12 (1992): 61–78.

wives, and two principal lovers, Lady Ottoline Morrell and Lady Constance Malleson. The omission from Archives I of some letters from the last two was, I believe, an oversight; the omission of the correspondence with his last three wives was deliberate. As Russell wrote in the Preface to Feinberg's *A Detailed Catalogue of the Archives of Bertrand Russell*: "Many of the letters which I have written on behalf of the Bertrand Russell Peace Foundation are not included here; nor are letters which are confidential" (p. 7). The last three women who married him were all living when Archives II arrived at McMaster. Even now the correspondence with one of them remains under embargo. The embargo on Edith Russell's letters was lifted in January 1983, five years after her death, and that on Dora Russell in May 1991, five years after hers. In addition, the embargo on the correspondence with his son John Conrad Russell, the fourth Earl Russell, will be lifted in December 1992. Among the personal papers are a very lengthy legal correspondence over the divorce from his second wife, and correspondence between Russell and his children and grandchildren (under embargo, except for that between Russell and the late Lucy Russell). There is a certain amount of correspondence with other relatives (not embargoed). And there are Russell's later financial papers, useful for a study of his authorial career. In conjunction with the personal papers, including the many letters from friends and acquaintances, I should mention the photographs, the tribute letters that came on Russell's ninetieth and ninety-fifth birthdays, and the very absorbing condolences—often filled with remembrances of Russell or assessments of his character—and the files of obituaries and newsclippings.

Straddling the personal and the political is Russell the author—the man who published seventy books and some 2,500 papers. There is a huge publishing correspondence here—the description occupies forty-nine double-column pages. The category has been interpreted widely and includes many good replies to biographical and bibliographical inquiries. The daunting characteristic about this class is how Russell usually managed without a literary agent until he was ninety-four, when he engaged Mr. Anton Felton of Continuum 1 Ltd. It was Continuum that negotiated the sale of both Archives to McMaster University.

Books represented in manuscript or typescript in Archives II include *Unarmed Victory*, *War Crimes in Vietnam*, and the second and third volumes of the *Autobiography*. The third volume is remarkable for the uncharacteristic revisions on the earliest extant typescript. *Dear Bertrand Russell* is also present, although Russell did not compile it. Among the articles is "Stalin's Legacy". Russell said in his *Autobiography* (III: 20)

that he wrote a piece on the death of Stalin in 1953 for the BBC, but that it never went on the air. There was no such piece in Archives I, although there was one on a cognate topic titled "A New Russian Policy?", dated the week of Stalin's death. There was naturally some doubt—now put to rest—of the existence of "Stalin's Legacy".

There is some philosophical content to Archives II. Most of it was created before the 1960s and for various reasons was not included with Archives I. There is manuscript material for the revised (French) edition of *An Essay on the Foundations of Geometry* (1897) and for the first edition of *Principia Mathematica* (1910–13). The latter file includes the only surviving page of marked proof, lists of unused propositions, and calculations of the length of the manuscript. The philosophical content in the correspondence exists entirely in letters replying to other philosophers and to students of philosophy. Russell wrote no philosophical books during his last decade. He would say that he was busy working for the survival of the human race so that the class of readers of his past philosophical works would not be null. In class ***220** Article Manuscripts there are a number of leaves containing early philosophical notes removed from books in Russell's library.

The politics of Archives II have a definite leftward slant. While Russell's anti-Bomb activities were designed to appeal to right, left and centre—since the issue was simply human survival—his campaigns of the middle and late sixties were different. On the Vietnam War, Russell considered the Americans only another in the succession of invading imperialist countries whose actions threatened to involve China and precipitate a nuclear war.

Russell's politics of the sixties were carried out through the instrument he created—the Bertrand Russell Peace Foundation. The launching of the BRPF took place on 29 September 1963; the preparations are documented in Archives I, ****311–312** and ****313–314**. The latter classes cover the first two full years of the BRPF. Its concerns were, in practice, threefold: (1) political prisoners, (2) campaigns in various countries, (3) Vietnam.

The BRPF's concern with political prisoners was world-wide and often successful. As Russell wrote in his *Autobiography, 1944–1967*:

> To gaol a man merely for his political views, however tempting it may be, is more likely to spread than to stop the dissemination of those views. It adds to the sum of human misery and encourages violence, and that is all. In recent years I have become, as I have

> said, more and more involved in work against the incarceration and persecution of individuals and groups because of their political and religious opinions. I have received a continually increasing number of written appeals for help from individuals and organizations all over the world and almost daily visits from representatives of the latter. (P. 146)

Russell could rarely make public his successes in this sphere, but the second Archives allow many different cases to be traced in detail. See particularly class ***330** Political Prisoners. Among well-known cases that Russell took up were those of Ahmed Ben Bella, Hugo Blanco and Heinz Brandt. There were hundreds of others.

Russell's involvement in political campaigns in various countries ranged from his efforts to prevent the election of Republican Senator Barry Goldwater to the U.S. Presidency in 1964 and campaigns for democracy in Greece in the early 1960s, to proposals for solving the Sino-Indian conflict in 1962–63 and opposing the Soviet invasion of Czechoslovakia in 1968. These campaigns are to be found particularly in ***320** World Affairs, ***340** Civil Rights and ***360** Miscellaneous Politics.

Partly because of Russell's own public efforts in the 1950s and early 1960s through the Russell–Einstein Manifesto, the Pugwash Conferences, the Campaign for Nuclear Disarmament and the Committee of 100, the danger of nuclear war has abated. As Ronald Clark comments in *The Life of Bertrand Russell*,

> [Russell] was not yet an optimist, but the world had drawn back from the brink, and it was possible to believe that the threat of nuclear war had diminished. However small the improvement might be, it did allow him to redeploy his forces and turn to other parts of the international scene where he felt he could set the world on the path he believed it should go. (P. 602)

Beginning in the spring of 1963, Vietnam absorbed the greater part of Russell's energies and financial resources until nearly the end of his life. He supported the goals of the South Vietnamese National Liberation Front. The papers documenting his involvement are classified in ****371–390**. While aspects of the International War Crimes Tribunal injured his reputation at home and in North America, there is evidence in Archives II that in many countries, by opposing the war, Russell's reputation took on heroic dimensions. Very little has been written on this period of his

life, but an essential reference is Ralph Schoenman's "Bertrand Russell and the Peace Movement", in George Nakhnikian's collection, *Bertrand Russell's Philosophy*. The papers described in this catalogue will be instrumental in assessing of the politics of Russell's later years. The Selected Bibliography on pages xxi–xxii should be of assistance.

II. ORGANIZATION OF THE SECOND ARCHIVES

Archives must be organized. While an index would suffice to refer staff to an arbitrary shelf location for each letter and manuscript, for ease of research and retrieval the documents must be sorted and grouped. The second Archives were already in some obvious groupings upon their arrival in June 1973.[3] The papers had been preceded by a twenty-page "Schedule of Material in the Second Archives", drawn up by Barry Feinberg on behalf of the Bertrand Russell Estate. The schedule was sent to William Ready, McMaster's University Librarian, in April 1971. As a sales catalogue the schedule emphasized those parts of the Archives likely to attract buyers. For example, the schedule listed in considerable detail the correspondence with wives and family, with enclosures noted. Other sections were treated more summarily. An example is Political Prisoners and Civil Rights (****330** and **340**), which was said to have 6,000 items (as catalogued here, the two classes have 5,079 items). A political class entirely missing from the schedule was ***315** General Political Correspondence. As catalogued, it has 8,566 documents. It was created at McMaster out of files that had no definite place in the sales catalogue scheme.

Feinberg's schedule was classified initially according to the original classification of the Feinberg catalogue. When Archives I arrived at McMaster that classification was refined and a new, more flexible numbering system substituted, based on a three-digit class number. This system was applied to Archives II upon its arrival. The main classes are as follows:

***100** Ancestral Papers
***200** Manuscripts
***300** The Bertrand Russell Peace Foundation
***400** Publishing Correspondence
***500** Political Organizations to 1955

[3] See the report in *Russell*, no. 10 (summer 1973): 2–4.

***600** Nuclear Disarmament
***700** Personal and Family Correspondence
***800** Legal Correspondence
***900** Works by Others, Films, Tapes, Photographs, Clippings, etc.

The present catalogue follows the same classification.

The largest main class is ***700**, which has the 12,656 documents of ***720** Miscellaneous Correspondence. That class has little priority for Russell studies and was not inventoried until the advent of BRACERS (see below). The next largest main class is ***300**, which contains most of the political correspondence of Archives II. The total number of documents in Archives II, 72,200 (excluding late insertions), is distributed among 68 classes, plus three new ones needed in the Addenda.

The initial task upon the arrival at McMaster was to decide whether to integrate the second Archives with the first. Integration was rejected on the following grounds: the documents of the first Archives had all been assigned individual document numbers, and had been microfilmed in document number order; it was significant sometimes what Russell had withheld from Archives I, and to integrate the two would have obscured provenance; no matter how the Archives were organized, only staff may retrieve and refile documents, so that retrieval ultimately depends on supplying researchers with good indexes; and in fact the greater part of the two Archives do not overlap in respect either of correspondents or activities covered. (The greatest area of overlap is the Miscellaneous Correspondence.) Once the decision was made to treat Archives II as a unit, the problem remained of sorting and ordering the documents in the most effective order for retrieval and research, while at the same time respecting the order (such as it was) given the documents by Russell, Edith Russell, and his staff.

Each document was assigned a number that is a composite of a class number and a serial document number. For example, **737**.108221 is the number of a letter from Russell to Dorothy Henley, his niece through his mother's sister, Rosalind Howard, Countess of Carlisle. **737** is the class. The number to the right of the decimal point is the document number and is stamped on the document. The Schedule of Document Numbers on pages ix–x identifies the class to which a given document belongs. In Archives I each document number began with 0. It will be noted that all document numbers in this catalogue begin with 1. That identifies the document as part of Archives II. All independent accessions begin with 2 or 3. The document numbers have proved very useful in facilitating

exact scholarly reference and in computerizing our control of the collection.

The Addenda (see pp. 349–54) arrived from the Russell Estate too late for incorporation in the page proofs at the points at which they belong. The Addenda are fully indexed in the Index of Names.

Archives I and II are now served by their own catalogues, the latter more fully than the former. But to cover the more than 1,100 independent acquisitions of Russell's correspondence and manuscripts, and to provide a comprehensive access tool to the contents of Archives I and II, an integrated, computerized catalogue was launched in 1988. Known as BRACERS, the Bertrand Russell Archives Catalogue Entry and Retrieval System catalogues all the individual documents on a detailed basis. At the time of writing, 34,000 entries had been made in BRACERS. At the present pace, we will be into the twenty-first century before BRACERS is comprehensive, although it is already useful.[4]

III. TYPES OF CATALOGUE ENTRIES

There are two approaches employed in this catalogue to arranging and describing the contents of the files: the alphabetical and the chronological. Some classes (e.g., ****315, 710** and **910**) naturally lend themselves to the alphabetical approach because in such classes researchers' interests lie in particular correspondents and their relationships with Russell. These classes are inventoried in summary, or folder-level, form. Letters are organized chronologically within the files. In the catalogue entry every document is accounted for in the totals of letters to and from Russell, plus enclosures and other correspondence, if any. Consider the following entry from page 65:

Pugwash Continuing Committee	
(J. Rotblat) **8**	1963–9
To RS **2**	1962–3
Encl: circular, 1. to *The Observer*, essay, reports, form 1.,1. from ER to RS	
ER to **2**	1960–1
RS to **3**	1962–5
RSt. to	1963

[4] See my "BRACERS", *Russell*, n.s. 10 (1990): 158–64.

CF to 1965
BR to **7** 1966–9

As the parentheses indicate, Professor Rotblat was the person corresponding on behalf of the Pugwash Continuing Committee. The bold figures are the numbers of letters; no number indicates the presence of a single letter.[5] Rotblat wrote eight letters (to Bertrand Russell) over the years 1963–69, and two more to Ralph Schoenman. Rotblat's two letters include several enclosures, as listed. To Rotblat there are letters from Edith Russell, three from Schoenman, single letters from Russell Stetler, Jr., and Christopher Farley, and seven from Bertrand Russell. (The List of Abbreviations on p. xxv provides the key to the initials of persons appearing frequently in the catalogue.) All of the correspondence listed here forms a single chronological sequence. Elsewhere in the catalogue a simpler form of alphabetical listing will be encountered—as in ***376** IWCT: General Correspondence on Vietnam. This form is explained below.

The overall chronological approach is suitable to distinct kinds of documents: diverse manuscripts by a single author, and what we call working files. Class ***220** is a good example, though not the only one (see also the addenda section at the end of ***340**), of documents ordered chronologically. Given the topical, political nature of Russell's writing during the 1960s, his articles, press statements and letters to the editor are most accessible when they are filed in the order in which they were written. In the case of working files, Russell and his staff corresponded with many persons on a given topic. Researchers want to examine the documents as they were created, one after another, as one led to another. Take, for example, class ***375** Working Correspondence with Vietnamese. Most of the relationships of scholarly interest are best studied with the correspondence arranged in chronological order. To be sure, there will be researchers interested in individual correspondents or sub-topics. Those interested in the former will be well served by the comprehensive name index; those interested in the latter will need to examine the files as they are anyway.

Manuscripts are catalogued individually; other classes of documents

[5] Because of the great number of documents and the subject-oriented nature of researchers' interests in them, no distinction is drawn between typed and holograph letters, signed and unsigned, or original and facsimile forms. There are, in fact, a number of letters from prominent individuals that are represented only by photocopies. The originals did not accompany Archives II, and their whereabouts are unknown.

are not. A new method had to be devised for files arranged chronologically but not deserving of document-by-document description, for there was not enough space for the description of each document in the political classes. An example of exhaustive description can be seen in Classification x of the Feinberg catalogue. Given the restriction on space, I decided that it was sufficient for the chronological files to record the first occurrence of a correspondent's name, regardless of how many letters he sent or received. Since the list of names under each heading is chronological, the list should be read as recording the place, relative to other first appearances, of the first appearance of each correspondent in the file. Other kinds of documents in the sequence are recorded as well. The rest of the file will have to be searched to discover whether it contains further correspondence with that person; but this approach was the alternative, in the circumstances, to no listing at all.

Limited subject access to the documents is provided by the classification. Sometimes (as in ***320** World Affairs) subject access is assisted by bold sub-headings. To some extent the political classes overlap, and use of the Index of Names is recommended.

IV. ACKNOWLEDGEMENTS

Over the years of compilation several well-trained staff contributed to the task. Initial sorting and assistance in classification were provided by Darlene Booth, Archival Assistant. Graham R. Hill as Director, and his successor Charlotte A. Stewart-Murphy, of the William Ready Division of Archives and Research Collections in the Mills Memorial Library, seconded staff from other collections to aid me in ordering, classifying and filing the papers. Terry Smart and Dallas Bagby both helped from Research Collections. Diane M. Kerss, then the Russell Archives secretary, utilized her phototypesetting skills to keyboard the handwritten cards. The typesetting was completed by Cheryl Walker, Archival Assistant. The final stages of compilation and document-stamping were carried out with the help of Hilary Turner, Alan Siaroff, Don Ross, Ben Zipursky and David Harley. Diane Kerss, Karen Zizzo and Myrna-Gail McDonald drafted the Index by alphabetizing the original catalogue cards.

Richard A. Rempel, John G. Slater and Charlotte A. Stewart-Murphy kindly commented on the Introduction. Any errors in the catalogue, however, remain the responsibility of the authors.

Funds to prepare the catalogue were provided by McMaster University, through the University Library (the late William Ready and Graham R. Hill, Librarians) and the Office of Research Services (Alan C. Frosst, Assistant

Vice-President). The Bertrand Russell Archives Advisory Board (Alwyn Berland, Chairman) actively supported the catalogue's compilation.

Throughout the major phases of the work my co-author was Carl Spadoni, then Assistant Russell Archivist and now Research Collections Librarian at McMaster. Sheila Turcon, Russell Archives Cataloguer, in a position funded through time released by a grant to me from the Social Sciences and Humanities Research Council of Canada, drafted recent corrections, many of which she also initiated. They were typeset by Arlene Duncan of the Bertrand Russell Editorial Project.

The letter chosen to be reproduced in facsimile on page 2 has since been transcribed, introduced and annotated in *The Selected Letters of Bertrand Russell*, Vol. 1: *The Private Years (1884–1914)*, edited by Nicholas Griffin (London: Allen Lane the Penguin Press; Boston: Houghton Mifflin, 1992).

April 1992 Kenneth Blackwell
Russell Archivist

SELECTED BIBLIOGRAPHY

Blackwell, Kenneth. "The Second Russell Archives: a First Report". *Russell*, no. 10 (1973): 2–4; illus. p. 24.

——. "BRACERS: the Bertrand Russell Archives Catalogue Entry and Retrieval System (1)". *Russell*, n.s. 10 (1990): 158–64.

——, "The Finding-Aids of the Russell Archives". *Russell*, n.s. 5 (1985): 66–71.

——, and Harry Ruja. *A Bibliography of Bertrand Russell.* 2 vols. London: Routledge, forthcoming 1992.

Clark, Ronald W. *The Life of Bertrand Russell.* London: Jonathan Cape and Weidenfeld & Nicolson, 1975; New York: Alfred A. Knopf, 1976.

Coates, Ken, ed. *Czechoslovakia and Socialism.* Nottingham: Bertrand Russell Peace Foundation, 1969.

——, Peter Limqueco, and Peter Weiss, eds. *Prevent the Crime of Silence: Reports from Sessions of the International War Crimes Tribunal Founded by Bertrand Russell.* London: Allen Lane the Penguin Press, 1971.

Duffett, John. *Against the Crime of Silence: Proceedings of the Russell International War Crimes Tribunal [in] Stockholm [and] Copenhagen.* New York and London: Bertrand Russell Peace Foundation / O'Hare Books, 1968. Rev. ed., New York: Simon and Schuster, 1970.

Farley, Christopher. "Bertrand Russell: Reminiscences and Reflections". In J. E. Thomas and Kenneth Blackwell, eds., *Russell in Review: the Bertrand Russell Centenary Celebrations at McMaster University, October 12–14, 1972.* Toronto: Samuel Stevens, Hakkert, 1976.

Feinberg, Barry, ed. With P.M. Fisher, D. Ash, K. Blackwell and R. Kasrils. *A Detailed Catalogue of the Archives of Bertrand Russell*. London: Continuum 1 Ltd., 1967.

——, and Ronald Kasrils. *Bertrand Russell's America: 1945–1970*. Boston: South End Press, 1983.

——, and ——, eds. *Dear Bertrand Russell ... a Selection of His Correspondence with the General Public 1950–1968*. London: Allen & Unwin; Boston: Houghton Mifflin, 1969.

Harley, David, and Carl Spadoni. "Bertrand Russell's Library". *The Journal of Library History*, 20 (1985): 25–45.

Hayhurst, Stephen. "Russell's Anti-Communist Rhetoric before and after Stalin's Death". *Russell*, n.s. 11 (1991): 67–82.

Lackey, Douglas P. "Russell's Contribution to the Study of Nuclear Weapons Policy". *Russell*, n.s. 4 (1984): 243–52.

Lewis, Albert C. "Some Computer-Produced Finding-Aids". *Russell*, n.s. 7 (1987): 167–70.

Moorehead, Caroline. *Bertrand Russell: a Life*. London: Sinclair-Stevenson, forthcoming 1992.

Russell, Bertrand. *The Autobiography of Bertrand Russell*, Vol. III: *1944–1967*. London: Allen and Unwin; New York: Simon and Schuster, 1969.

——. *The Collected Papers*. 7 vols. to date. London: [various publishers, now Routledge], 1983–.

——. *War Crimes in Vietnam*. London: Allen & Unwin, 1967; New York: Monthly Review Press, 1967.

——, and Sidney Hook. "The Nature of Liberal Civilization". *Russell*, n.s. 5 (1985): 5–13.

Ryan, Alan. *Bertrand Russell: a Political Life*. London: Allen Lane the Penguin Press; New York: Hill and Wang, 1988; London: Penguin, 1990.

Schoenman, Ralph. "Bertrand Russell and the Peace Movement". In George Nakhnikian, ed., *Bertrand Russell's Philosophy*. London: Duckworth; New York: Braziller, 1974.

Seckel, Al. "Russell and the Cuban Missile Crisis". *Russell*, n.s. 4 (1984): 253–61.

Shibata, Shingo. "The Significance of the Bertrand Russell International War Crimes Tribunal". Chapter III of his *Lessons of the Vietnam War: Philosophical Considerations on the Vietnam Revolution*. Amsterdam: B. R. Gruner, 1973.

Spiegelberg, Herbert, ed. "The Correspondence between Bertrand Russell and Albert Schweitzer". *International Studies in Philosophy*, 12 (1980): 1–45.

Stone, I.F. "Bertrand Russell as a Moral Force in World Politics". *Russell: the Journal of the Bertrand Russell Archives*, n.s. 1 (1981): 7–25.

Taylor, Richard, and Colin Pritchard. *The Protest Makers: the British Nuclear Disarmament Movement of 1958–1965, Twenty Years On*. Oxford: Pergamon Press, 1980.

Turcon, Sheila. "The Edith Russell Papers". *Russell*, n.s. 12 (1992): 61–78.

Russell's Chronology, 1960–70

1960 Debates with Bahba and Teller on the nuclear threat on CBS (Feb.). Awarded the Sonning Prize for Contribution to European Culture (19 April). Meets Ralph Schoenman (July). Addresses CND meeting at Trafalgar Square (24 Sept.). Becomes President of Committee of 100 (Oct.). Resigns from CND (5 Nov.). Publishes *Act or Perish* (advocating mass civil disobedience) and *Bertrand Russell Speaks His Mind.*

1961 Leads mass sit-down demonstration outside Ministry of Defence (18 Feb.). Speaks twice to Youth CND in Birmingham (March and April). Speaks in Trafalgar Square at conclusion of Aldermaston March. Speaks at Hyde Park demonstration on Hiroshima Day (Aug.). Sentenced with Edith Russell to two months imprisonment for civil-disobedience activity, reduced to one week for reasons of health (Sept.). Speaks in Trafalgar Square (29 Oct.) and at Cardiff (2 Nov.). Schoenman becomes his secretary (Nov.). Demonstrates at US air base at Wethersfield (9 Dec.). Publishes *Fact and Fiction*, *The Basic Writings of Bertrand Russell* and *Has Man a Future?*

1962 Celebrates 90th birthday with luncheon at the House of Commons, musical tribute at Festival Hall, and evening dinner in his honour at Café Royale (18 May). Has discussions with U Thant about international nuclear and disarmament policies. Acts as intermediary in the Cuban Crisis (Oct.) and the Sino-Indian border dispute (Nov.–Dec.). Publishes *Essays in Skepticism.*

1963 Resigns from Committee of 100 (Jan.). Presented with Tom Paine Award by American Emergency Civil Liberties Committee (Jan.). "Bertrand Russell Committee of 100" formed in Greece (April). Receives the Carl von Ossietsky Medal (May). Speaks in Trafalgar Square on behalf of political prisoners in Greece (July). Launches the BRPF and the Atlantic Peace Foundation (Sept.). Publishes *Unarmed Victory*.

1964 Returns the Carl von Ossietsky Medal to East Germany in protest of imprisonment of Heinz Brandt (Jan.). Becomes President of the British "Who Killed Kennedy?" Committee (Aug.). Sends Schoenman and Farley to Vietnam to investigate the war (Nov.).

1965 Speaks at London School of Economics on Labour Party (Feb.). Resigns from Labour Party, tearing up his membership card during speech to Youth CND in London (Nov.).

1966 Decides to publish his *Autobiography* (April). Addresses founding of the Vietnam Solidarity Campaign (June). Decides to sell his archives (*c.* June). Addresses preparatory meeting of the International War Crimes Tribunal and its press conference (Nov.).

1967 Stockholm session of International War Crimes Tribunal (May). Publishes *War Crimes in Vietnam* and Vol. 1 of *The Autobiography of Bertrand Russell*.

1968 Sells his archives to McMaster University (March). Protests Soviet invasion of Czechoslovakia (Aug.). Publishes Vol. 2 of his *Autobiography* and *Mr. Wilson Speaks Frankly and Fearlessly on Vietnam to Bertrand Russell*. *Against the Crime of Silence* published.

1969 Writes "Private Memorandum concerning Ralph Schoenman" (8 Dec.). Publishes Vol. 3 of his *Autobiography* and *Dear Bertrand Russell*.

1970 Dictates message (31 Jan.) on the Middle East Crisis, read on his behalf to the World Congress of Parliamentarians in Cairo (3 Feb.), the day after his death.

List of Abbreviations

c.	card or *circa*
ch.	chapter
cs.	cards
ed.	edited by or edition
Encl:	enclosure (usually followed by a description of item enclosed)
l(s).	letter(s)
mimeo	mimeographed document
ms(s).	manuscript(s)
n.d.	no date
newsl.	newsletter
no(s).	number(s)
n.s.	new series
p.c.(s)	post card(s)
s(s).	statement(s)
trans.	translated by, or translation
ts(s).	typescript(s)
tscc.	carbon copy of typescript
tsscc.	carbon copies of typescript

AY	Alaistair Yule (BRPF)
BR	Bertrand Russell
BRPF	Bertrand Russell Peace Foundation
CE	Charles Ellis (BRPF)
CF	Christopher Farley (BR's secretary)
CND	Campaign for Nuclear Disarmament

DN	Diane D. Nair (BRPF)
DR	Dora Russell (née Black, later Grace, BR's 2nd wife)
ER	Edith Russell (née Finch, BR's 4th wife)
HR	Heather E. Richardson (BRPF)
ID	Ian Dryden (BRPF)
IWCT	International War Crimes Tribunal
NJ	Nicholas Johnson (BRPF)
NLF	National Liberation Front
PJ	Pat Jordon (BRPF)
PR	Patricia Russell (née Spence, "Peter", BR's 3rd wife)
PW	Pamela Wood (BRPF)
RS	Ralph Schoenman (BR's secretary)
RSt.	Russell Stetler (BRPF)
UN	United Nations

*100
Ancestral Papers

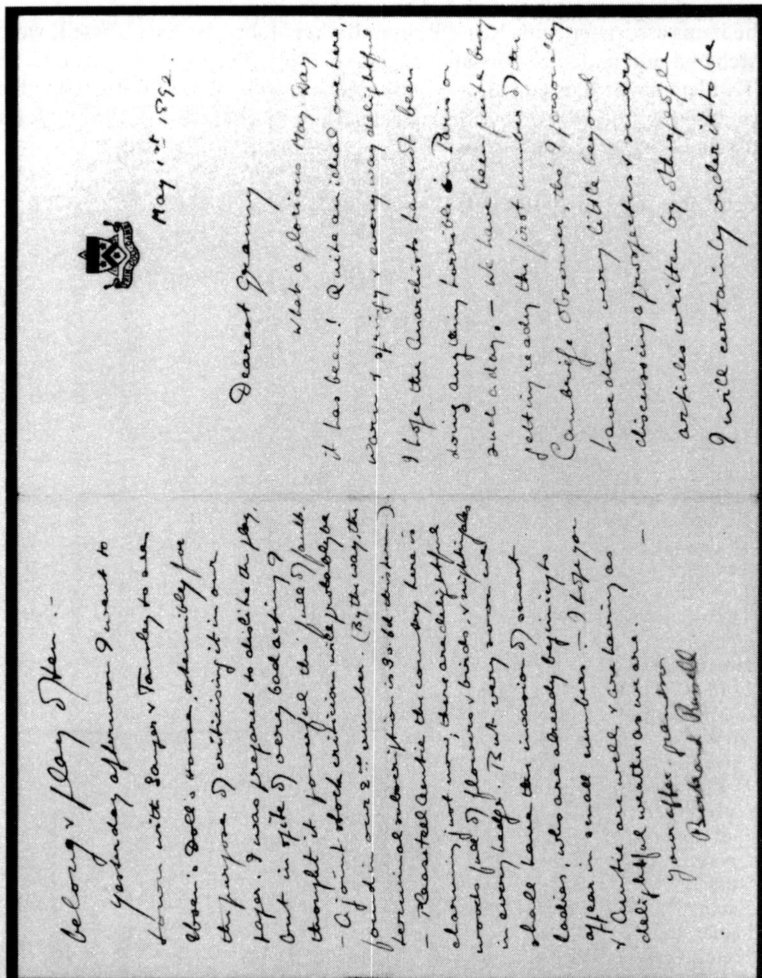

May 1st 1892.

Dearest Granny

What a glorious May Day it has been! Quite an ideal one here, warm & springy & every way delightful. I hope the Anarchists haven't been doing anything horrible in Paris on such a day. — We have been quite busy getting ready the first number of the Cambridge Observer, tho' I personally have done very little beyond discussing a prospectus & reading articles written by other people. I will certainly order it to be [illegible] Yesterday afternoon I went to town with Sanger & Tawney to see Ibsen's Doll's House, ostensibly for the purpose of criticising it in our paper. I was prepared to dislike the play, but in spite of very bad acting I thought it powerful tho' full of faults. – A joint stock criticism will probably be found in our 2nd number. (By the way, the terminal subscription is 3s. 6d. [illegible]) – [illegible] the country here is charming just now; there are delightful woods full of flowers & birds, & nightingales in every hedge. But very soon we shall have the invasion of [illegible] ladies, who are already beginning to appear in small numbers. – I hope you & Auntie are well, & are having as delightful weather as we are. –

Your affec. grandson
Bertrand Russell

Plate 1 Russell to his Granny, the Dowager Countess Russell, 1 May 1892.

**111–113, *132 Russell Family

The items associated with Russell's grandfather, John, 1st Earl Russell, were purchased and added to Russell's papers in 1966. (See the letter from C. & I. K. Fletcher Ltd. listed below.) The copies of two letters from Russell to his grandmother, the Dowager Countess Russell, were sent to him in 1969 by John Russell Lloyd, grandson of Russell's paternal uncle, Rollo Russell.

Documents *111.108001–[.108018]–.108021; *113.108018; *132.108022

*111 Lord John Russell

Russell, Lord John,
to Queen Victoria 2 ... 1837-65
To William Lynch 1834
To Philip Crosbie (envelope address) 1834
To ? 2 1832-7
To Bishop of Durham (copy) 1850
Note on Ireland .... 1833?
Lord and Lady Russell to Mr. Shapiro .... n.d.
To William G. Hunt (envelope address) 1833
J. W. Addington to (with reply on verso) 1850
J. M. to .... n.d.
2 portraits of Lord John Russell .... 1837-n.d.
Encl: bookseller's or cataloguer's notes; C. & I. K. Fletcher Ltd. to Michael Lester (who was on BR's secretariat), re sale of ls. from Lord John Russell 1966

*112 Lady John Russell

Russell, Lady John,
BR to (copies) 2 1892-5
Filed with ls. to Rollo Russell (*736.108173)

*113 Rachel Russell

Receipt 1706

*132 Kate Amberley

Amberley, Kate (notebook of teacher's attendance record) 1859

*200
Manuscripts

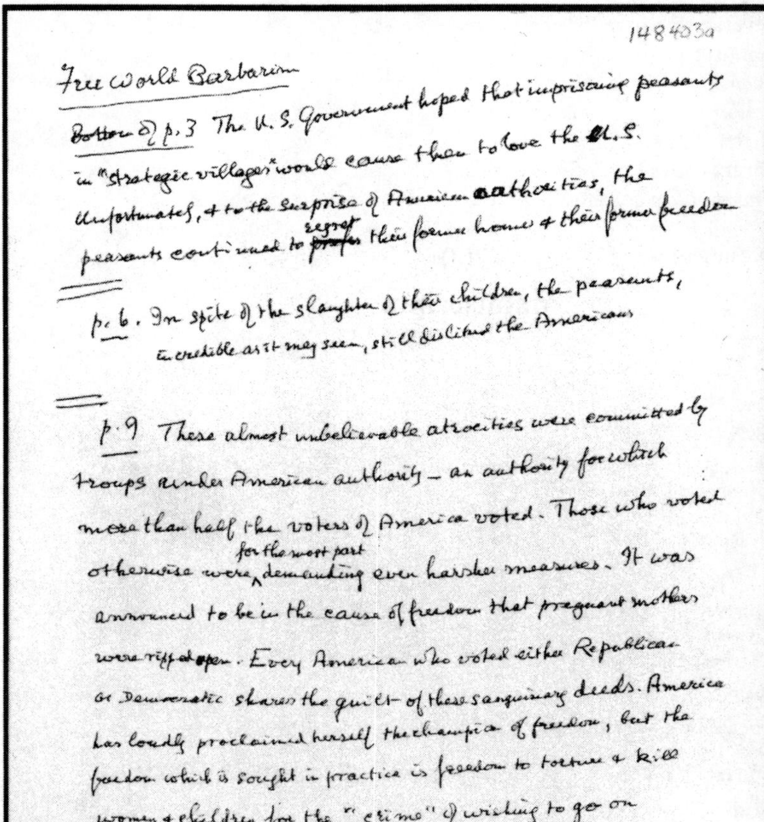

148403a

Free World Barbarism

Bottom of p. 3 The U.S. Government hoped that imprisoning peasants in "strategic villages" would cause them to love the U.S. Unfortunately, & to the surprise of American authorities, the peasants continued to ~~prefer~~ regret their former homes & their former freedom

p. 6. In spite of the slaughter of their children, the peasants, incredible as it may seem, still disliked the Americans

p. 9 These almost unbelievable atrocities were committed by troops under American authority — an authority for which more than half the voters of America voted. Those who voted otherwise were, for the most part, demanding even harsher measures. It was announced to be in the cause of freedom that pregnant mothers were ripped open. Every American who voted either Republican or Democratic shares the guilt of these sanguinary deeds. America has loudly proclaimed herself the champion of freedom, but the freedom which is sought in practice is freedom to torture & kill women & children for the "crime" of wishing to go on living in their homes. Is it surprising that the rest of the world looks coldly on American professions?

Plate 2 **Russell's revisions to his article "Free World Barbarism" (1964).**

*210 Book Manuscripts

Several of Russell's books are represented in a major way. There are the manuscript additions for the French edition of *An Essay on the Foundations of Geometry*, the manuscript of "The Perplexities of John Forstice", a typescript of *War Crimes in Vietnam* and several versions of the second and third volumes of the *Autobiography*. Included also are documents removed from Russell's library copy of the first edition of *Principia Mathematica*. The papers relating to *Unarmed Victory* should be consulted in conjunction with those in Archives I.

Documents .147501–.147509 (See also Addenda, p. 349.)

1897

[*An Essay on the Foundations of Geometry*.] Preface to the French Edition [and other notes and changes]. Ms. 4 leaves. Also notes on Cremona, possibly for the thesis or 1897 version. Ms. 4 leaves. Removed from BR's library copy of L. Cremona's *Elements of Projective Geometry*, 2nd ed. (London, 1893).

1912

The Perplexities of John Forstice. Ms. 97 leaves. Removed from BR's library.

1920

Errata in "Practice and Theory of Bolshevism". Ms. 1 leaf. Removed from BR's library copy (London, 1920).

c.1922

Corrections in "Analysis of Mind". Ms. 3 leaves. Removed from BR's library copy of this book.

Desire & Purpose. Ms. 3 leaves. Removed from BR's library copy of *The Analysis of Mind*.

c.1923

Corrections in PM from Mr Boscovitch. Ms. 1 leaf. Removed from between pp. 14-15 of BR's library copy of *Principia Mathematica*, I (1910).

Unused props. Ms. 1 leaf. Removed from between pp. 64-5 of BR's library copy of *Principia*, I (1910).

[Tabulation of ms.? pp. in *PM*.] Ms. 1 leaf. Removed from between pp. 64-5 of BR's library copy of *Principia*, I (1910).

Props used in *359·44 and *356·33 [and] ... *350·62. Ms. 10 leaves. Removed from between pp. 64-5 of BR's library copy of *Principia*, I (1910).

Additional Errata to Volume I. Proof sheet dated 20 Nov. 1911. Removed from before the fly-leaf of BR's library copy of *Principia*, I (1910).

1934

Freedom and Organization*. Ms.; 1 leaf in PR's hand sketching the materialist theory of history. Partially used on p. 219. Removed from BR's library copy of F. Engels' *Socialism: Utopian and

Scientific (London, 1925; reprint of 1892 ed.).

1954

Nightmares of Eminent Persons. Proofs of illustrations.

1963

Unarmed Victory. Ts.; tscc. and ms. (ER's hand). Corrected partially by BR but mainly in ER's hand. Ms. of 2 tentative tables of content, of end to Ch. IIIc, and of outline of Sino-Indian dispute.

1967

War Crimes in Vietnam. Drafts of ts.; tscc. and photocopy. Partial corrections in RS's hand.

1968

Mr. Wilson Speaks "Frankly & Fearlessly" on Vietnam to Bertrand Russell. Tscc. and photocopy (corrected in part in CF's hand).

The Autobiography of Bertrand Russell, 1914-1944. 4 boxes of galley proofs; tss.; photocopies of tss.; and photocopies of ls. for the appendices. The tss. comprise various stages of BR's text, including the extensive revisions of 1967. There is a file of comments by Lady Constance Malleson in Box 4 on the pages concerning her which had been sent to her by BR. See also the tss. in Archives I.

1969

The Autobiography of Bertrand Russell, 1944-1969. 3 boxes of revised tscc. and photocopies; galley proofs of illustrations and text; corrected galley of index (corrections not in BR's hand). There is also a large number of photocopied ls. considered for inclusion in Vol. III.

Dear Bertrand Russell. Ts.; tscc. Corrected by the editors.

*220 Article Manuscripts

Most of the manuscripts (and typescripts and mimeographed documents) in this class date from the mid- to late 1960s. But many supplement the collection from the early 1960s in Archives I, and some are even earlier. The earlier items tend to be sheets of notes which Russell made on books he was reading. They have been removed from those books, which are in his library, now in the Russell Archives.

Documents .148001–.149111 (See also Addenda, pp. 349-50.)

1895?

Abstract of Lobatchewsky. Ms. 5 leaves. Removed from opening pp. of Russell's copy of G. B. Halsted's trans. of N. Lobatchewsky's *The Theory of Parallels*, 4th ed. (Austin, 1892).

1901?

MacColl. Ms. 1 leaf. Removed from between pp. 158-9 of an offprint of S. MacColl's "La Logique Symbolique et Ses Applications", bound up with other offprints (mainly by MacColl) in a volume in Russell's library titled on the spine *Symbolic Logic*.

1902-3?

Frege. Ms. 4 leaves. Removed from between pp. XVIII-XIX of Russell's library copy of G. Frege's *Grundgesetze der Arithmetic*, Vol. I (Jena, 1893).

Frege Vol. II. Ms. 1 leaf. Removed from between pp. 162-3 of Russell's library copy of Frege's *Grundgesetze der Arithmetik*, Vol. II (Jena, 1903) (which is bound with Vol. I).

1912

Schiller. Ms. 3 leaves. Removed from between pp. 184-5 of Russell's library copy of F. C. S. Schiller's *Formal Logic* (London, 1912).

1913

The Proposed Change in the Ordination Service. *Cambridge Magazine*. 22 Nov. 1913, *et seq.* Tear sheets of the controversy, including what is perhaps the first published caricature of BR.

1914?

Wiener. Ms. 5 leaves.

1919

Moore. Ms. 7 leaves. Notes on the comments on the reading of BR's "On Propositions: What They Are and How They Mean". Sewn into BR's library copy of *Problems of Science and Philosophy*, Aristotelian Society, Vol. II (1919), just before BR's paper.

1923?

What is meant by "A believes *p*"? Ms.

2 leaves. Removed from BR's copy of Wittgenstein's *Tractatus Logico-Philosophicus*.

1930?

Conversations with Men. Tscc. Unsigned, but ascribed to BR on the basis of style and the presence of revisions in his hand.

1934

Notes/B.A.W.R. Ms. notebook. Including notes for use in "Thomas Paine", *Great Democrats*.

1945?

[Notes on] Reichenbach, *Experience and Prediction*, and *Probability*. Ms. 1 leaf. Removed from between pp. 302-3 of Russell's library copy of H. Reichenbach's *Wahrscheinlichkeitslehre* (Leiden, 1935).

[Notes on] Reichenbach, *Warhscheinlichkeitslehre*. Ms. 2 leaves. Removed from between pp. 302-3 of Russell's library copy of Reichenbach's *Wahrscheinlichkeitslehre*.

1948

Culture and the State. Sept. 1948. Tscc.

1952

Bertrand Russell and the U.S.A. *Manchester Guardian*. 12 Jan. 1952. Ms.; clipping.

[L. to *Manchester Guardian*]. 27 Feb. 1952. Tscc. With 2 tscc. of another person's l. in *Guardian* of 11 Feb. 1952.

1953

Stalin's Legacy. Ts.

A New Russian Policy? 8 Mar. 1953. Tscc.

1954

What India Can Do for Mankind. Ts.

Where Will Britain Stand in 2000 A.D.? Men and Women in 2000 A.D. Education in 2000 A.D. The State in 2000 A.D. For *Everybody's*. 14-22 Oct. 1954. Tsscc.

Man's Peril from the Hydrogen Bomb. New tscc.

1956

Introduction to C. Lamont's *Freedom Is as Freedom Does*. Ts.

1957

[Review of M.P. Sharp's *Was Justice Done? The Rosenberg-Sobell Case*]. Reprinted from *The University of Chicago Law Review* by The Committee to Secure Justice for Morton Sobell.

1958

Inconsistency? Tscc.

1960

After the Four Minutes? 4 Mar. 1960. Tscc. For *Sunday Dispatch*; revised for *Coronet*.

Peace? and Freedom? *New Leader*. 9 May 1960. Tearsheets (together with tearsheets of Sidney Hook's rejoinder).

A Reply to Dr. Hook's Rejoinder. Tscc.

Speech for Federal Union. 2 June 1960. Tscc.

Great Britain as a Neutral. *Manchester Guardian*. 14 July 1960. Tscc.

Statement for *Sanity or Suicide*. 14 July 1960. Tscc.

Press Statement by BR and Michael Scott. 30 Sept. 1960. Ts.

The Cold War & the Income Tax: A Protest by Edmund Wilson. 6 Oct. 1960. Tscc.

Joint Statement by the President and Chairman of the Campaign for Nuclear Disarmament. 6 Oct. 1960. Mimeo ts.

[Lord Simon of Wythenshawe:] l. to *The Guardian*. 10 Oct. 1960. Tscc.

Polaris. 12 Nov. 1960. Tscc.

The Case for Neutralism. Tscc.; pamphlet.

[S. for recording for CND]. 2 tss.

1961

Statement by Bertrand Russell—February 25, 1961—Trafalgar Sq. Ts.

Thermonuclear War: Battle of the Experts. *New Republic*. 3 Apr. 1961. Tearsheet.

Human Life Is in Danger. 29 Apr. 1961. Ts.

Speech for Committee of 100. 2 July 1961. Tscc.

The Two K's *Versus* Mankind. 31 July 1961. Tscc.

Speech by Bertrand Russell for Hyde Park (made in Trafalgar Square). 6 Aug. 1961. Ts.

To the Editor of *The Daily Mail*. 19 Aug. 1961. Ts. Encl: *Daily Mail* (William Hardcastle) to BR.

Notes on the Berlin Crisis. 23 Aug. 1961. Mimeo ts.

The Requirements of World Leadership Today. 24 Aug. 1961. Tscc. For *Today*.

Trafalgar Square Meeting. *The Times*. 26 Aug. 1961. Tscc.

To the Conference of Uncommitted Nations at Belgrade, 1961. 28 Aug. 1961. Also signed by Michael Scott. Mimeo ts. (on verso of "Notes on the Berlin Crisis" above).

Statement for Press Conference: September 9th Demonstration. Tscc.

To the Editor of *The Guardian*. 28 Sept. 1961. Tscc.

Speech for Nonesuch Records Limited, 25 October, 1961, by Bertrand Russell. 18 Oct. 1961. Tscc.

Speech by Bertrand Russell for Meeting at Cardiff, 1 November, 1961. 21 Oct. 1961. Tscc.; mimeo ts.

Speech by Bertrand Russell for Trafalgar Square Meeting, 29 October, 1961. 2 tscc; mimeo ts.

The Role of Neutrals in Dissolving the East-West Deadlock. 11 Nov. 1961. Mimeo ts.

Speech for Foyle's Literary Luncheon, 23 November, 1961. Mimeo ts.

Whose Victory? Dec. 1961. Tscc.

Memorandum from Bertrand Russell. 15 Dec. 1961. Mimeo ts.

Memorandum from Bertrand Russell to the Members and Supporters of the Committee of 100. 22 Dec. 1961. Mimeo ts.; ts.; tscc.

To My Japanese Readers [of *Has Man a Future?*]. Removed from l. to Ikki Hitaka, dated 30 Dec. 1961.

Prison Sentences. 2 tscc.

Birmingham. Ms. notes.

1962

Statement for *Revolución*, Habana, Cuba. 3 Feb. 1962. 2 tscc.

Statement by Bertrand Russell concerning the trial at the Old Bailey of six members of the Committee of 100. 12 Feb. 1962. Mimeo ts.

[Letter to Professor Ichiro Moritaki]. 30 Mar. 1962. Mimeo ts.; also Japanese version.

Statement from Bertrand Russell. 26 Aug. 1962. Ts.

To Avoid Nuclear War. 30 Aug. 1962. *Atlantic Monthly* galley proofs. Encl: *Atlantic Monthly* (Louise Dsaulniers) to BR.

Speech for the Tenth Pugwash Conference. 5 Sept. 1962. Tscc.

Recorded Statement for Zengakuren re: 5-10-62. 26 Sept. 1962. Tscc.

Press Statement [etc., 22-8 Oct. 1962]. Mimeo ts. of messages sent by BR during Cuban Crisis. Ts.

Message from Bertrand Russell. 23 Oct. 1962. Leaflet. Tscc.

To London C. 100. 26 Oct. 1962. Ts.; tscc.

[S. on war over Berlin]. Removed from l. to Comité d'Organisation du Colloque International (Henri Longier). 14 Nov. 1962. Tscc.

[Message to Conference]. 26 Nov. 1962. Tscc.; encl. in l. to Socialist Party of Japan (Jotaro Kawakami).

To President Gamal Abdel Nasser and the People of the United Arab Republic. Dec. 1962. Tscc.

Statement to Young Japanese World Federalists. Statement to Young Japanese from the President of the Committee of 100 in Britain. 12 Dec. 1962. Tscc. Encl: Ikki Hitaka to BR; BR to Hitaka.

Answers to two queries. 28 Dec. 1962. Tscc.

Nuclear War: An American Expert's Forecast. Ts.

1963

Message to the People of Cuba from Bertrand Russell, January 1963/ Draft. 2 tscc. Encl: CF to BR.

Message to the Conference on "World Government" to be held on January 26, 1963, at the University of London Union. Tscc.

A Decent Way to Live. Feb. 1963. Tscc. Encl: *Toronto Star Weekly* (Ray Gardner) to BR; tscc.

[Statement on Rossi's *The Third World*]. 11 Feb. 1963. Photocopy of ts.

[To the editor of the *New Statesman*]. 22 Feb. 1963. 4 tsscc.

Message to the Continental Congress of Solidarity with Cuba. 21 Mar. 1963. Tscc.

Russell's Appeal to Heads of States. Apr. 1963. Mimeo ts.

Message for Nobel Dinner. 8 Apr. 1963. Ts.; tscc.

Statement on Easter Demonstrations. 16 Apr. 1963. Tscc.

To the Editor of *The Times*. 20 Apr. 1963. Tscc.

Statement for Meeting on "Spies for Peace". 28 Apr. 1963. Ts.; 4 tsscc.

[S. on obstructing Secret Service telephone lines]. 13 May 1963. Ts.; 7 tsscc.

[S. on Regional Headquarters in Brecon]. 14 May 1963. Tscc.

To the Editor of *Peace News*. 16 May 1963. Ts.; 8 tsscc.

[S. on death of Pope John]. 7 June 1963. 2 tsscc.

[Message]. Encl. in l. to Mrs. P. Andrews. 22 July 1963.

[Message to Ninth World Conference against Atomic and Hydrogen Bombs]. Encl. in l. to Japan Council against Atomic and Hydrogen Bombs (Kaoru Yasui). 23 July 1963.

To the Editor of *The Guardian*. 30 July 1963. Tscc.

Sequel to the Test-ban Treaty? Aug. 1963. Tscc.; 3 tsscc.

China and the Test Ban Treaty. 9 Aug. 1963. Ms. (ER).

[S. for Czech News Agency]. 9 Aug. 1963. Tscc.

To the Editor of the *New Statesman, et al.* 12 Aug. 1963. Re test-ban treaty. Tscc.

Statement on The Test Ban Treaty for The Soviet Press Agency. 15 Aug. 1963. Tscc.

To the Editor of *The Guardian, et al.* 16 Aug. 1963. Re Adlai Stevenson. Tscc.

To the Editor of *The Guardian*. 23 Aug. 1963. Re K. H. W. Hilborn's l. 4 tsscc.

[S. on the American Negro]. 26 Aug. 1963. Ts.

[Message]. Encl. in l. to Yoshiyuki Tsukaguchi. 18 Sept. 1963.

Part II. 18 Sept. 1963. Tscc.

[Untitled article]. 18 Sept. 1963. Tscc.

[S. on wars]. 22 Sept. 1963. Ts.

Message for Rome Conference on Soviet Jews of October 1. 30 Sept. 1963. Tscc.

[Message honouring Thomas Merton]. Encl. in l. to PAX (Martin Peretz). 17 Oct. 1963.

Message for International Student Week for Peace and Friendship. 11 Nov. 1963. 2 tsscc. Encl: BR to International Union of Students (Zbynek Vokrouhlicky).

Statement by Bertrand Russell: November 30, 1963. 2 tsscc.

Press Release [re Soviet Jews]. 2 Dec. 1963. Mimeo ts.

[Message]. Encl. in l. to Youth Peace Campaign (Marnie Siggers). 5 Dec.

1963.
My View of the Cold War. 12 Dec. 1963. Tscc.
[Message to Schools' Conference]. Encl. in l. to Andrew Papworth. 19 Dec. 1963.
War and Peace in the Nuclear Era. For *Paese Sera*. 27 Dec. 1963. Tscc.; 2 tsscc.
Message to the People of Rumania from Bertrand Russell. 29 Dec. 1963. Ts.; 4 tsscc.
Blurb for *Political Ideals*. Tscc.
The Imminent Danger of Nuclear War. Ts.
The Myth of American "Freedom". 2 tsscc.
Pacem in Terris. Tscc.
Pope John XXIII. Ts.
Suggestions for an article "What is a good newspaper? For *New York Times*. 3 tsscc.
Suggestions for Atlantic Peace Foundation part of Russell Conference. Ts.; tscc.
Why India's Belligerence? Tscc.
My Idea of a Good Newspaper. For *New York Times*. Tscc.

1964

My View of the Cold War. *The Minority of One*. Jan. 1964. Ts.; 3 tsscc.
Statement from Bertrand Russell to the Conference of the International Confederation for Disarmament and Peace. Jan. 1964. 4 tsscc.
To the Editor of *The Times*. 2 Jan. 1964. 5 tsscc.
Semantics and the Cold War. *Playboy*. 5 Feb. 1964. Tscc.
[Message]. In l. to Unitarian Church of Calgary (David B. Craig). 5 Mar. 1964.
[Message for conference]. Encl. in l. to American Humanist Association (Roger Williams). 11 Mar. 1964.
A New Approach to Peace. 28 Apr. 1964. Tscc.; mimeo ts.
[L. to President Johnson]. 5 May 1964.
[L. to *The Scotsman, et al.*]. 5 May 1964. Tscc.
Anomalies of the Cold War. 7 May 1964. Photocopy of ts.; 3 tscc.; mimeo ts.
Statement on "The Face of War". 11 May 1964. 3 tsscc.
To the Editor of *The Times*. 29 May 1964. Ts.; tscc.
[S. on Vanessa Redgrave's recording of songs against apartheid]. In l. to Topic Records (G. Sharp). 19 June 1964.
[S. on the suspension of Dr. Ozmon and Dr. Taylor]. 23 June 1964. Tscc.
Message [to Conference for the Denuclearisation of the Mediterranean both at sea and on land]. July 1964. Tscc.; mimeo ts.
To the Editor of *The Guardian*. 20 July 1964. Tscc.
To the Editor of *The Observer*. 20 July 1964. Ts.; 4 tsscc.
To the Editor of the *Sunday Times*. 22 July 1964. Tscc.
Statement for Novosti Press. 28 July 1964. 3 tsscc.
Statement for TASS on Test Ban Treaty. 28 July 1964. 2 tsscc.
Africa and the Movement for Peace. 28 July 1964. 2 tsscc.; mimeo ts.
[S. on Goldwater]. Aug. 1964. Mimeo ts.
[S. on the Cold War]. 5 Aug. 1964. Tscc.
Statement on the Attacks on North Vietnam. 7 Aug. 1964. Mimeo ts.
To the Editor of *The Observer*. 5 Aug. 1964. Ts.; 3 tsscc.
To the Editor of *The Observer*. 7 Aug. 1964. 2 tsscc.
Answers to Questions of *At-Tarik Review*. 13 Aug. 1964. Tscc.
[Message to Youth Forum]. In l. to TASS (E. Egorov). 13 Aug. 1964.
Statement to the Vena. 14 Aug. 1964. 2 tsscc.
To the Editor of the *New Statesman*. 15 Aug. 1964. 2 tsscc.

Replies to Questions for the *Sun* and the *Journal*. 16 Sept. 1964. 3 tsscc.
[Replies to questionnaire]. 1 Oct. 1964. Tscc. Sent to Abidine Dino, 2 Oct. 1964.
[L. to *Sovietisch Heimland*]. 29 Oct. 1964. Mimeo ts.
Cold War and World Poverty. *Africa and the World*. Nov. 1964. Also *Mainstream*.
Prospects for Peace in 1965. Sent to *British-Soviet Friendship*. 18 Nov. 1964. Tscc.
[Message on danger of war]. In l. to Wilhelm Ude. 20 Nov. 1964.
Message to Conference in Opposition to the War in Vietnam, Hanoi. 25 Nov. 1964. Ts.
War and Atrocity in Vietnam. Tscc. Page proofs.
The Ethos of Violence. Photocopy of ts.
Free World Babarism/The Great Sin in Vietnam. Ts.; 2 tsscc.
Tribute to Nehru. Ts.; ts.; part of l. from BR to *The Minority of One* (M. S. Arnoni); tear sheet from *Illustrated Weekly of India*.
16 Questions on the Assassination. Mimeo ts.

1965

Statement for Australian WILPF. 8 Jan. 1965. 2 tsscc. Encl: E. Christiansen to RS; RS to Christiansen.
Press Statement. 2 Feb. 1965. Ts.; tscc.
Press Statement. 8 Feb. 1965. Ts.; tscc.
Statement by Bertrand Russell. 8 Feb. 1965. Tscc.; 2 mimeo tss.
Emergency Statement on Vietnam to be Delivered Before Full Address. 15 Feb. 1965. Mimeo ts.
Statement on *Dark Ghetto* by Kenneth Clark. 18 Feb. 1965. Tscc.
To: Martin Key, Youth Against War and Fascism. 18 Feb. 1965. Tscc. Encl: RS to Youth Against Fascism and War (Martin Key).
Press Statement by Bertrand Russell on International Conference. 21 Feb. 1965. Tscc.
Statement Made March 8, 1965, and given to Mrs. Ghosh. Ts.
Message from Bertrand Russell to the Conference Against Repression in Spain, London, Sunday, 28th March 1965. Ts.
Press Statement. 26 Mar. 1965. Tscc.
[S. re American government actions in Vietnam]. Removed from l. to *The Week* (Ken Coates). 8 Apr. 1965. Tscc.
[S. re selection of targets in China for bombing by U.S.]. 29 Apr. 1965. Ts.
Danger in South-East Asia. May 1965. Leaflet; Xerox of ts.
[S. re President Johnson and Vietnam]. 9 June 1965. Ts.
Statement by Bertrand Russell for Rally on Vietnam at Trafalgar Square of Y.C.N.D. 3 July 1965. Ts.
Statement by Bertrand Russell for World Conference of Peace at Helsinki. 8 July 1965. Ts.; 3tscc.; Xerox of tscc.
[Message to Martin Peretz re Harvard teach-in]. 12 July 1965. Tscc. Encl: Martin Peretz to BR.
Statement by Bertrand Russell on William Warbey. 30 July 1965. 2 tsscc.
Statement for World Congress for Peace in Vietnam. 4 Aug. 1965. Mimeo ts.
The Negro Rising. *The Minority of One*. 22 Aug. 1965. Mimeo ts.
Message for the Anniversary of Independence of the Democratic Republic of Vietnam. 27 Aug. 1965. Tscc.
Press Statement on Visa Campaign. 1 Sept. 1965. Xerox of ts.
[On the Indo-Pakistani situation]. 23 Sept. 1965. Mimeo ts.
Message [for Cyprus]. 1 Oct. 1965. Tscc. Encl: RS to Z. Tofallis.

Statement for Soviet Peace Fund. Nov. 1965. Mimeo ts.
[S. re American imperialism]. Removed from l. from *The Statesman*. 6 Nov. 1965. Tscc.
Statement [on the arrest of Madalyn Murray]. 4 Dec. 1965. Tscc.
[S. on the rising in Harlem]. 6 Dec. 1965. Tscc.
Press Statement [on 2 U.S. soldiers]. 30 Dec. 1965. 2 tss.; tscc.
Appeal on behalf of National Liberation Front representatives. Tscc.
Broadcast I. Broadcast II. Broadcast III. Tscc.
The Cold War: A New Phase. Ts.
Message from Bertrand Russell to the Welsh Council for Peace in Vietnam. Tscc.
Notes for Speech at Mahatma Gandhi Hall. Tscc.
Statement by Bertrand Russell. Ts.

1966

Press Statement to *Daily Worker* on Vietnam Bombing. 31 Jan. 1966. Ms. (not in BR's hand); ts.; tscc.
Vietnam and American Opinion. *The Minority of One*. 21 Feb. 1966. Tscc.
South Vietnam; Broadcast by Bertrand Russell for Political Union Board of Stanford University. 1 Mar. 1966. Ts.
[S. re. American government and Vietnam]. 23-6 Mar. 1966. Ts.; 2 tsscc.
Press Statement. 14 Apr. 1966. Ts.
The Only Honourable Policy in Vietnam. 28 Apr. 1966. Tscc.
Statement Sent to Berkeley, Cal. 11 May 1966. 2 tsscc.
Message from Bertrand Russell to the People of Vietnam on Radio Hanoi. 24 May 1966. Ts; 2 tscc. 5 mimeo tss.
Message from Bertrand Russell to the People of South Vietnam on the Radio of the National Liberation Front. 24 May 1966. Ts.; 2 tsscc.
Speech by Bertrand Russell on Radio Hanoi to American Soldiers Serving in South Vietnam. 24 May 1966. 2 tss.; tscc.; 6 mimeo tss.
Speech by Bertrand Russell to V.S.C. Conference. June 1966. Ts.; 3 tsscc.; mimeo ts.
Statement by Bertrand Russell. 17 July 1966. 2 tss.; 3 tsscc. Re Sen. Richard Russell.
Press Statement. 20 July 1966. Ts. Re USSR airforce.
Press Statement. 20 July 1966. Ts.; tscc. Encl: BR to Kosygin (cable).
Press Statement. 20 July 1966. Ts.; 3 tsscc.
[Mr. Thompson's unawareness of nuclear weapons]. 21 July 1966. Ms. in ER's hand.
Press Statement [re Ronald Ramsey]. 26 July 1966. 2 tsscc.
Text of Tape-Recorded Message for Hiroshima Day, 1966. 26 July 1966. Ts.; 9 tsscc.
Tape recorded message for U.S. 26 July 1966. Ts.; tscc.
[Comments on the Vietnam war]. In l. to Cecil Woolf. 27 July 1966.
Press Statement [re Nguyen Huu Co's visit]. 10 Aug. 1966. 2 tss.; 2 tsscc.
[S. on medical aid for Vietnam]. 10 Aug. 1966. Tscc.
[Statement re Saigon embassy]. 11 Aug. 1966. Ts.
Press Statement [re USSR air force]. 15 Aug. 1966. 2 tss.; 3tsscc.
Press Statement [re Stokely Carmichael]. Ts.; 3 tsscc.
[Press s. re President Johnson and IWCT]. 28 Aug. 1966. Ts.
Cable to Linda Dannenberg [re Fort Hood Three]. 5 Sept. 1966. Tscc.
Speech by Bertrand Russell to T.U.C. Conference in Blackpool. 6 Sept. 1966. Tscc.
Statement on "Elections" in South Vietnam. 9 Sept. 1966. 2 tss.; tscc.
Press Statement [re Stokely Carmichael's imprisonment]. 12 Sept. 1966. 2 tscc.
Un Mensaje de Bertrand Russell a los Americanos de Vietnam. *Siempre*.

14 Sept. 1966.
[Cable sent to l'UNEF]. 16 Sept. 1966. Ts.
Press Statement. 26 Sept. 1966. Tscc.
[Answers to questionnaire]. Encl. with l. to *Der Spiegel* (H. G. Alexander). 28 Sept. 1966.
Message from Bertrand Russell to American Negro Soldiers in Vietnam. 30 Sept. 1966. 2 tss.; 4 tsscc.
The Choice before Us over Vietnam. Oct. 1966. 2 tss.; tscc.
[Message to IWCT national committee in Japan]. 5 Oct. 1966. Tscc.
Le Tribunal. *Le Monde*. 15 Oct. 1966. Tscc.
A Message to the Peoples of the Third World from Bertrand Russell. 19 Oct. 1966. Ts.; 3 tsscc; tear sheet from *Marcha*, 18 Nov. 1966.
Message from Bertrand Russell for Teach-In to be Held in Stockholm. 19 Oct. 1966. 2 tsscc.
Press Statement [re Filipino demonstrators]. 26 Oct. 1966. Tscc.
Preface to *Vietnam North* by Wilfred Burchett. 30 Oct. 1966. 2 tsscc.
Message to Japanese Students and School Children. Nov. 1966. 2 tsscc.
Message for a Teach-in at the University of Pennsylvania on Chemical and Germ Warfare and the War in Vietnam. Nov. 1966. Tscc.
The Western Press and U.S. War Crimes. Nov. 1966. Mimeo ts.
Message from Bertrand Russell to Grand National Convention on Vietnam. 11 Nov. 1966. Tscc.; mimeo ts.
Speech to First Meeting of Members of the War Crimes Tribunal. 13 Nov. 1966. Tscc.
Statement by Lord Russell on Resignation of Sponsors of the Bertrand Russell Peace Foundation. 13 Nov. 1966. Ms. in ER's hand; mimeo ts.
Message to Scottish National Conference from Bertrand Russell. 18 June 1966. Ts.; mimeo ts; pamphlet.
Speech by Bertrand Russell to Press Conference Called by International War Crimes Tribunal. 16 Nov. 1966. Ts.; mimeo ts.
[Answers to questionnaire]. Encl. with l. to Kyodo News Service (Ikuo Kanmuri). 24 Nov. 1966.
Cable [for demonstration]. Encl. with l. from Sozialistischer Deutscher Studentenbund. 28 Nov. 1966.
[Message to Finland]. Encl. with l. to Vietnam Friendship Committee (Pentti Järvinen). 30 Nov. 1966.
Message to Turin Vietnam Committee. 21 Dec. 1966. Ts.
Addendum to Lord Russell's Report. Mimeo ts.
The Case against Negotiations in Vietnam. Ts.; tscc.
An Appeal to the American Conscience from Bertrand Russell. Ts.; mimeo ts.; pamphlet.
Post Script: To the Conscience of Mankind. Ts.; tscc.; mimeo tss.; pamphlet; tear sheet from *Karachi Leader*.
Un Secondo Tribunale per i Crimini di Guerra. *Il Paese Oggi*. Mar. 1966.

1967

Message to the Demonstration in Zurich on February 4 1967. 30 Jan. 1967. Encl. with l. to Komitee gegen den Krieg in Vietnam (Jean-Louis Simmen); Simmen to BR.
Replies from Bertrand Russell to Mr. Armando Rodrigues Suarez for Latin American News Agency. 19 Feb. 1967. 2 tscc.
Press Statement (unsent). 28 Feb. 1967. Ts.; 3 tsscc.
Statement in Support of John Harris. 1 Mar. 1967. Xerox of tscc.
[S. re President Johnson's resuming of the bombing of North Vietnam]. 2 Mar. 1967. Ts.; tscc.
[Message to Spanish opposition to American involvement in Vietnam]. 2 Mar. 1967. Encl. with CF's l. to H. B. Martin. Encl: Martin to BR; Martin to Deirdre Griswold; Gris-

wold to Martin; John L. Dins to BRPF.
Message from Bertrand Russell to the Meeting at the University of Toronto, March 11, 1967. Encl. with l. to Canadian Committee for the International War Crimes Tribunal (Kenneth Warren). 7 Mar. 1967.
Message from Bertrand Russell, March 14, 1967. Encl. with l. to Comitato per la Settimana di Agitazione per il Vietnam. 14 Mar. 1967.
Statement from Bertrand Russell to the Osaka Rally, March 18, 1967. Encl. with l. to Takeo Shimizu. 14 Mar. 1967.
Les Américains sont-ils des Criminels? *Temoijnage Chrétien*. 16 Mar. 1967.
An Appeal to Trade Unions from Bertrand Russell. 4 Mar. 1967. 2 tsscc.
[Message for *Aktiv*]. 20 Mar. 1967. Encl. with l. from RS to Aktion für Frieden und Abrüstung (Helmut Kramer). Encl: Kramer to RS.
Introduction to pamphlet containing report from S.N.C.C. and speech by Stokely Carmichael. 30 Mar. 1967. Ts.
Message to the People of Okinawa. Apr. 1967. Tscc.
Recorded Message for Spring Mobilisation. 7 Apr. 1967. Ts.
May Day Message to the Cuban People. 7 Apr. 1967. Ts.
Message to the First National Youth Conference for Solidarity with Vietnam. 10 Apr. 1967. Ts.; tscc.; 12 mimeo tss.
The International War Crimes Tribunal and the Nature of the War in Vietnam. 12 Apr. 1967. Ts.; tscc.
Statement. 4 May 1967. Ts.; tscc.
Answers to *Expressen* (Stockholm), May 4, 1967. Encl. with l. to *Expressen* from CF.
Statement Given to *The Times*. 9 May 1967. Ts.; tscc.
Tribunal—Closing Statement. 10 May 1967. Tscc.; 2 Xeroxes of tss.
Message to Cuba; Answers to Marta Rojas. 13 May 1967. Signed tscc.
Press Statement [re Howard Levy]. 21 May 1967. 2 tscc.
Press Statement [re Mohammed Ali]. 23 May 1967. Ts.
Press Statement (not sent) [re Soviet air force]. 24 May 1967. Ts.; 3 tsscc.
Replies to Questions by Cuban Journalists. July 1967. Tscc.
Views on Vietnam. In l. to Leonard Brown. 4 July 1967.
Statement for Czech Radio from Bertrand Russell. Aug. 1967. Tscc.
Statement by Bertrand Russell to the Japan Council against Atomic and Hydrogen Bombs, World Conference. Aug. 1967. Tscc.
Message from Bertrand Russell to the Anti-Imperialist March, Stockholm. 27 Aug. 1967. Tscc.
Message from Bertrand Russell to the Tokyo Tribunal. 28 Aug. 1967. 2 tsscc.
[On George Brown]. Oct. 1967. Tscc. Written for *London Bulletin*.
Questions and Answers for *Aftonbladet*. Oct. 1967. 3 tsscc.
Bertrand Russell Replies to Questions from *Granma* on the War in Vietnam. Oct. 1967. Ts.; tscc.
Statement to the International Mobilisation, October 21-22, 1967. Ts.
[S. re Portugal and Jose Bernardino]. 27 Oct. 1967. Xerox of ts.
To the Editor, *The Times*. 1 Nov. 1967. Tscc.
Closing Message to the Copenhagen Session of the International War Crimes Tribunal, 1 December, 1967. Tscc.; Xerox of ts.
Press Statement [re bombing of Hanoi]. 16 Dec. 1966. 2 tsscc.
[Message on Vietnam]. For Newslimited of Australia. Tscc.
Appeal for Financial Support. Leaflet.
Declaration of Members of the International War Crimes Tribunal. Bertrand Russell *et al.* Tscc.
Message from Bertrand Russell to the

International War Crimes Tribunal. Mimeo ts.
Memorandum from Bertrand Russell regarding First Public Session. Xerox of ts.
Opposing Fascism in Greece. Tscc.
1967. Ms. 4 leaves. Sent to McMaster by ER in Apr. 1977.

1968

Message from Bertrand Russell to the Conference in West Berlin. 12 Feb. 1968. 2 tsscc.
[Message to President of the Sussex University Union]. 25 Feb. 1968. Ts.; tscc.
[Message on Vietnam]. 28 Feb. 1968. Ts.
Statement by Bertrand Russell [on British racial discrimination]. 28 Feb. 1968. Photocopies of ts.
Message from Bertrand Russell to the Trafalgar Square Rally on Vietnam. 17 Mar. 1968. 2 tsscc.
Message to the Workers' Control Conference at Nottingham. 30-31 Mar. 1968. Photocopy of ts.
Statement by Bertrand Russell, released to Reuters April 5 1968, concerning the death of Martin Luther King. Tscc.
Message from Bertrand Russell to CND's Easter March. 10 Apr. 1968. Tscc.
Introduction to *Against the Crime of Silence*. May 1968. Tscc.
Message from Bertrand Russell to the Meeting on May 3, 1968 for the Late Dr. Martin Luther King. Tscc.
[On American deserters]. 20 May 1968. 3 tsscc.
Message from Bertrand Russell to the Stockholm Conference on Vietnam to be Held December 13-14. Dec. 1968. Encl. with l. to Peter Limqueco.
Bertrand Russell on Vietnam. *Interstate*. n.d.

1969

Czechoslovakia. *The Times*. 19 Aug. 1969. 2 tscc.
Bertrand Russell's Statement on the Death of Ho Chi Minh. 4 Sept. 1969. Ts.; tscc.
Labour's Goldwater. 23 Nov. 1969. Tscc.
Coming Czech Trials. *The Times*. 5 Nov. 1969. 3 tscc.
Press Statement [re l. to U Thant]. 1 Dec. 1969. Ts.; tscc.
The Entire American People Are on Trial. 8 Dec. 1969. 4 tsscc.

1970

Message from Bertrand Russell to the International Conference of Parliamentarians in Cairo, February 1970. 31 Jan. 1970. Ts.

Undated

Insertions for Russian article for journal *Religion and Science*. Ts.
Notes for Propaganda/New Thoughts for Changing Conditions. 3 tsscc.
Spare page 2 for Zamindar Statement. Tscc.
Addition to Frontier article: *The Menace to Human Survival*. Tscc.
A Statement by Bertrand Russell. Tscc.
Will Man Survive? Ts.; tscc.
Violence in the Young. Ts.; 3 tsscc.
World Instability and the American Imperium. Ts.
Suggested Corrections to *Playboy* article. Tscc.
Suggested questions for tape. Ts.
Press Statement—Rainbow Blast. Ts.; tscc.
Governments and Mass Murder. *Strike*. Mimeo ts.
[Draft l. on nuclear testing]. Ts.
The Problem for Nuclear Disarmers. Tscc.
A Suggestion for the Avoidance of War. Tscc.
Nuclear Tests. 2 tsscc.
The Need for Non-Alignment. 2 tsscc;

mimeo.
What British Unilateralists Want. Tscc.
Mythology and the Cold War. 2 tsscc.
Scientists and World Peace. 3 tsscc.
Oppression in South Arabia. Mimeo ts.
On Civil Disobedience. Tscc.
The Menace to Human Survival. Ts.; 2 tsscc.
Text of Bertrand Russell's statement for Moscow Radio. Tscc.; Xerox of ts.
[Appeal for War Crimes Tribunal]. Tscc.
[S. re U.S. policy]. Ts.; Xerox of ts.
Press Statement [re bombing of Hanoi and Haiphong]. Ts.
Press Statement [re "Family of Man" award to President Johnson]. Ts.; tscc.
[S. on South East Asia with J.D. Bernal *et al.*]. Tscc.; 30 mimeo tss.
[S. re IWCT]. Tscc.
Message to Japan. 2 tsscc.
[S. re film on Vietnam]. Ts.; 3 tsscc.
[S. re Vietnam]. Ms. in RS's hand.
[S. re American misunderstanding of U.S. policy]. 5 mimeo tss.
Foreword to the Hebrew edition of *Unarmed Victory*. 3 tsscc.
A Plea for Neutral Action. 4 Tsscc. For Jerome Davis, *Building Peace in the Atomic Era*.
Special Preface for the Swedish Edition of *Has Man A Future?* Ts.; 3 tsscc.
Statement for recording for Conference of World Freethinkers. Ts.; 2 tsscc.
Advice to Prospective Suicide. Ms. in ER's hand.
Interview with *Compass and Fleet*. Mimeo ts.
The Increase of American Violence. 2 tscc.
Statement for future use by S.O.S. Photocopy of ts.
To prevent nuclear war. Ms. notes.
Civil Disobedience. Ms. notes.
How to prevent nuclear war. Ms. notes.
West'r Speech. Ms. notes.
Notes for Propaganda. Ts.
3 files of miscellaneous notes and jottings, particularly on nuclear disarmament.

*221 Embargoed Manuscripts

The contracts between McMaster University and Lord Russell and his Estate specify that any documents concerning his last three wives are to be embargoed until the survivor of Russell and the wife in question has been dead for five years. (See also **751–754, *760 and *761.)

Documents .149201–.149203

1919

"The present state of affairs is lamentable...." Ms. 2 leaves.

"The present situation is unstable...." Ms. 1 leaf. 8.10.19.

1949?

"The trouble started...." Ts.; 2 tscc. 2 leaves. Undated. Filed as 710.106144.

1955

Private Memoirs. 26 Dec. 1955. Ms. in ER's hand. 11 leaves. Tscc. corrected by BR; Xerox of this tscc. Also partial ts. and tscc., the latter with insertions by BR and ER. Encl: l. to Sir Stanley Unwin from BR, 1956.

*240 Pocket Diaries

This class includes Russell's Cambridge Pocket Diaries from 1953 to 1970. These diaries record not only his appointments but also his income as an author. Shelved with this class are the diaries that came with Archives I.

Documents .107501–.107553

The Cambridge Pocket Diary for the following years:
1950-1951 to 1968-1969 (inclusive)

The BBC Diary for the following years:
1951 (not used)
1952 (not used)

Appointments. 7 May–30 June 1967. Ts. with additions in ER's hand. 1 leaf.

*300
The Bertrand Russell Peace Foundation

Heinz Brandt
Frankfurt am Main
Kohlederstr. 19

Frankfurt, den 28.11.64

185432

The Earl Russell, O.M., F.R.S.
Plas Penrhyn,
Penrhyndeudraeth,
Merioneth.

Sehr verehrter Lord Bertrand Russell!

Wir haben Ihnen schon in unserem Brief vom 6. Juli 1964 mitgeteilt, daß meine Frau und ich zum Tag der Menschenrechte am 10. Dezember auf Einladung von Amnesty International in London sein werden. Wir haben uns sehr über Ihre freundliche Aufforderung gefreut, Sie während unseres London-Aufenthaltes aufsuchen zu können. Sie wissen, verehrter Lord Russell, daß ich Ihnen vor allem meine Freiheit verdanke, und wie sehr ich Ihre Leistungen für atomaren Frieden und das persönliche Beispiel, das Sie geben, schätze.

Gestern erfuhr ich von Ihrem bewegenden Appell an Präsident Johnson und Ihrer Warnung an die amerikanische Regierung, durch militärische Abenteuer in Vietnam die Welt in den atomaren Krieg zu führen. Ich hoffe, daß Ihnen in all Ihren Aktionen der gleiche offenkundige Erfolg beschieden sei wie das im Kampf um meine Befreiung der Fall war, wenn es auch jetzt um weitaus größere Dinge geht, als um einen einzelnen Menschen.

Meine Frau und ich treffen am 9. Dezember gegen 10 Uhr in London ein. Am 10. Dezember, dem Tag der Menschenrechte, ist am Nachmittag die Feierstunde von Amnesty International, am günstigsten für uns wäre der 11. Dezember, an dem wir völlig frei sind. Wir wissen natürlich gar nicht, wie es um Ihre Zeit bestellt ist. Am 12. Dezember fliegen wir morgens zu meinem Freund und Verwandten Prof. Erich Fromm, der uns nach Mexico eingeladen hat. Wir möchten von uns aus alles tun, um eine Begegnung mit Ihnen zu ermöglichen.
Sollte Ihnen, verehrter Lord Russell, keiner der oben genannten Termine recht sein, dann würden wir einen Tag früher nach London kommen, sodaß wir Sie evtl. am 8. oder 9. Dezember aufsuchen könnten.

Es wäre sehr freundlich von Ihnen, uns Ihre Entscheidung baldmöglichst wissen zu lassen, und wir hoffen mit großer Freude auf eine Begegnung mit Ihnen.

Mit recht freundlichen Grüßen
Ihr dankbarer
Heinz Brandt

Herzliche Grüße
Ihre
Anneliese Brandt

"Metall", 9-3-1964.
185401

Russel: Kein Bedarf an DDR-Orden, solange Brandt im Zuchthaus.
MK

Plate 3 Heinz Brandt, East German political prisoner, to Russell, 28 November 1964, and cartoon from *Metall*, 9 March 1964.

*315 General Political Correspondence

The chief criteria used in forming this class were the independence of the correspondents from governmental bodies, and their independence from the specific campaign organizations with which Russell was involved. The correspondence ranges in date from 1962 to 1970. Russell's messages to demonstrations are often included in the contents.

Documents .150001–.158566

A

Anonymous 5 1962-8
To RS .... n.d.
To RSt. .... n.d.
To Tom? 1962
To PW .... n.d.
To ? 1961
BR to 1964
Aall, Cato, BR to 1963
Abayavardena, Hector,
BR to 1967
Abdel-Malek, Anouar 1964-9
To RS 1965-7
Encl: clipping
RS to 1964
BR to 3 1964-9
DN to 1967
Abdulle, Mohommed 1966
To RS 1965
RS to 1965
Aber, Joel, to RSt. and
Sue Stetler 1968
BR to 1966
RSt.? to 1968
Aberdeen Students Campaign
for Nuclear Disarmament
(Marion H. Maclennan) 2 . 1959
Aberman, Sidney 1962
BR to 1963

Abhoy Ashram (Nripendra
Nath Bose) 1963
CE to 1963
Abraham, Rudy 2 1967
CF to 1967
RSt. to 1967
Action Civique Non-Violente
(Jean-Pierre Lanvin) 1965
BR to 1965
Ad Hoc Committee for an
Anti-Wallace/Le May
Demonstration (Flo
Kennedy) 1968
Adams, G. Howard 1963
BR to 1963
RSt. to 1964
Adelakum, D. G. 1965
CF to 1965
Aden Trades Union
Congress 2 1965
Khalid Zaki to 1965
Adkins, Edward R. 1968
Encl.
RS to 1964
BR to 1968
Adkins, Warren D. 1966
Adler, Marvin 1966
BR to 1966

Ady, D. Howard **11** 1952-68
To RS 1966
To IWCT (Karen Wald) ... 1967
To DH 1968
To DN 1968
To RSt. **2** 1968
Encl: D. Howard Ady to Ambassador to the UN (Warren Austin) 1952
photos, articles, essays, Xerox of clippings
BR to **5** 1963-7
RS to 1966
RSt. to **2** 1967-8
CF to 1968
Afro-Asian Solidarity Committee of Burma (U Hla Gyaw), BR to 1966
Afroasian Youth Organization (Ishaque Sobani) .... n.d.
Agarwal, Chandra Prakash ... 1968
Agudas Israel World Organisation (M. R. Springer) 1967
Encl.
CF to 1967
Ahimsa Shodh-Peeth (Bool Chand) 1963
Encl.
BR to 1963
Ahmed, Mrs. J. E. 1965
Encl: journal sheets
PW to 1965
Aitch, K. 1962
Encl.
BR to 1962
Aitchison, Keitch, CF to 1968
Ajiboye, Emmanuel Ola, to CF 1965
CF to 1965
Aktionsgemeinschaft gegen die atomare Aufrüstung der Bundesrepublik (O. Vetter) **3** 1962
Encl.
Alberti, Nicholas 1964
Encl.
AY to 1963
BR to 1964
Albrecht, Herbert O., RS to 1964
Aldouby, Z. H. 1969
CF to 1969
Aldred, Guy 1962
Encl: newspapers
BR to **2** 1962
Alexander, Cynthia 1968
CF to 1968
Alexander, K. J. W., to RS 1964
RS to 1964
Alhadeff, Boaz I. 1967
BR to 1964
Ali, F. 1966
Ali, S. B., RS to 1964
Ali, S. Hamid, BR to 1966
(returned)
Ali, Syed Ashraf 1962
BR to 1962
Ali, Tariq **2** 1964-5
CF to **2** 1965
Allen, Donna, BR to 1964
Allen, Emily A. 1958
BR to 1958
Allen, Lloyd M. 1966
Allen, Seawillow 1967
Allen, Steve (secretary, Donna Zink) 1965
BR to **2** 1964-5
Allen, Jr., Charles R., BR to 1966
Alliance for Jobs or Income Now (Frances Witlin) 1964
Encl: Xerox of clipping, essay
BR to 1964
Alliance in Action for the Federal Elections of 1969 (Warner Hofmann) 1968
Encl.
Allison, Michael H. G., BR to **2** 1963
Alloy, Evelyn and Jack .... n.d.
Almogy, Saul 1967
DN to 1967
Alonso Rivera, Luis, to RS .. 1965
CF to 1965
al-Sulh, Kadhim, BR to 1964
Alvarez, Osvaldo Paredes, CF to **2** 1968
Amancio, Luis Ricardo Barata 1964

Ambatielos, Betty, to AY 1963
Ambrose, David D. 1963
Encl: David D. Ambrose to *The Guardian* 1963
BR to 1963
Amdur, Irving 1964
Encl.
RS to 1965
American Committee on Africa (Albert J. Lutuli and Martin Luther King, Jr.) 1962
Encl.
The American Council for Judaism (Michael Selzer, Bill Gottlieb, Norton Mezvinsky) **4** 1965-7
BR to **2** 1966-7
CF to **3** 1967
PW to 1967
American Embassy (David Bruce) 1962
BR to **2** 1962-3
American Friends Service Committee (Mary L. Davis) to BRPF 1966
PW to 1966
American Servicemen's Union (Andrew Stapp), CF to 1969
Americans Want to Know (Ava Helen Pauling, Dagmar Wilson) 1967
Encl: booklet, *Is Cambodia Next?*
BR to **2** 1964-7
Encl: s. by BR
Amnesty International (Peter Benenson *et al.*) **5** 1963-9
To BR and ER 1963
To BRPF .... n.d.
To CF 1963
To Bill Kaye 1964
To RS 1965
Encl.
BR to 1963
CF to 1969
PW to 1969
Anand, J.K. 1969
CF to 1969
Andersen, H. 1962
AY to 1962
Anderson, Bo 1968
CF to 1968
Anderson, Bruce, BR to 1967
Anderson, L. S., BR to 1964
Anderson, Martha, BR to 1964
Anderson, Perry, CF? to 1965
Another Mother for Peace (Barbara Avedon) (form l) .... n.d.
Anstey, J. H., BR to 1964
Encl.
The Anti-Apartheid Movement (S. Abdul *et al.*) **5** 1963-5
To RS 1964
Encl: form ls., invitations, political literature, "Appeal on Sanctions" by Nelson Mandela
BR to **2** 1963-4
RS to 1965
PW to 1965
CF to 1968
Antonis, Paulette 1963
To CF 1968
Encl: articles
BR to 1963
CF to 1968
Aoyama World Federation Society (Yoshio Chilba), BR to 1963
Apcarian, S.H. **7** 1966-8
Encl: United Nations (C. N. Geccato) to S. H. Apcarian 1967
United Nations (Stephen Landau) to Apcarian 1968
BR to 1966
Appeal for Amnesty in Spain (Eileen Turner) **2** 1967-8
Encl: political literature
CF to 1968
The Arab Lawyer Union (Shafik Arshidat) 1967
Ardeleanu, N. **2** 1967-9
To DN 1968
Encl: clippings, greeting card
Arley, Niels 1963
To AY 1964
Encl: essay
BR to 1963

CE to 1964
Armstrong, David, to RS 1964
[RS] to **2** 1964
Armstrong, Noel, *et al.* 1968
Encl.
Armstrong, R., to *The Calgary Herald* (A. Parker Kent) ... 1963
Arrau, Claudia, BR to 1966
The Arts and Professions Committee for the Defense of Bill Epton (Wendy Nakashima) 1966
Asadullah, M., BR to 1963
Asahigaoka Senior High School, Pen Friend Club 1962
BR to 1962
Asambla Nacional por la Libertad de los Presos Politicos y la Derogacion del Delito de Disolucion Social (Emilo Abreu Gomez) .... 1965?
Encl: pamphlet
Asamblea Unica Mundial to BRPF 1968
Encl.
Ash, David (on behalf of Michael Ash), to RS 1965
RS to 1965
Ash, Michael 1965
Ashby, Graham 1965
Ashton, David, to CF? 1964
CF to 1964
Ashton, G. J. **2** 1965
PW to **2** 1965-6
Ashton, Robert W. 1962
BR to **3** 1962-4
Ashworth, Brian, BR to 1964
Assembly of Captive Europeans Nations (Stefan Korbonski) 1966
CF to 1966
Assis, Maria de Lourdes, to BRPF 1967
Association contre le Danger Radiologique (Jean Pignero) 1964
Encl: form ls., pamphlet
Association des Combattants pour la Liberte et Demokratie (Henryk Matysiak) 1967
BR to 1967
Association for International Co-operation and Disarmament (G. R. Anderson, D. Gietzelt) to BRPF **2** 1965-6
To PW 1966
Encl: press s.
PW to **3** 1965-6
Association of Victims of Nazi Persecution (Elizabeth Dales) **2** 1963-9
BR to 1963
Association pour le Développement du Droit Mondial (André Bossin) 1963
Encl: pamphlet, clipping
BR to 1963
Atkinson, Ralph B. 1962
BR to 1962
Atlantic Peace Foundation (s. of objectives) .... n.d.
Atwood, Thomas 1969
CF to 1969
Auchinleck, Field Marshal Sir Claude **2** 1964
To CF 1965
To RS **7** 1964-6
BR to **6** 1964
RS to **9** 1964-5
CF to **2** 1965
Encl: RS to White Elephant Club (Leslie Linder) 1964
Auckland Hiroshima Day Committee, 1966 (L. Reid) 1966
RS to 1966
Austin, George 1962
BR to 1962
Austin, Jonathan, to BRPF ... 1965
Australian & New Zealand Congress for International Co-operation & Disarmament (Sam Goldbloom) **3** 1965-6
Encl: political literature, form l.
BR to 1965
RS to 1965
PW to **2** 1965-6
Australians and New Zealanders

against the Vietnam War
(John Roberts and Michael
Taussig) 1967
RSt. to 1968
Avanzada Nacionalista de
Venezuela (Mireya
Blanco) 1963
BR to 1963
Avila, Horacio 1968
Avorn, Jerry L. 1965
RS to 1965
Axelbank, Albert **3** 1964-8
To CF 1968
Encl: Joseph Rotblat to
Victor Purcell? 1964
articles
BR to **2** 1964-6
RS to 1966
CF to **2** 1968
Axon, Gordon, V. 1966
BR to 1966

B

Back, E. W., to BRPF 1964
RS to 1964
Baer, Walter 1965
To PW 1966
PW to **2** 1966
Beartling, Olle, BR to 1966
Bailey, Maisie 1965
PW to 1965
Bailey, Shirley 1963
BR to 1963
Baker, Peter Shaw 1962
Encl: clipping
Balcombe, Rosalyn .... n.d.
To CF 1967
CF to **2** 1965-7
Baldwin, C., to BRPF 1963
CF to 1963
Ball, Adrian, BR to 1962
Ballin, Ruth, to BRPF 1965
PW to 1966
Bandhu, Bhadra 1966
Banfield, Alan, to BRPF 1965
PW to 1966
Banks, Stan, to BR and ER 1964
Encl: petition
BR to 1964
Bao, Luyi 1968
Barbajosa, Gil **3** 1964-5
To RS **5** 1964-6
To PW **2** 1965-6
To PW and RS 1965
Encl: essays
BR to **2** 1964
RS to **2** 1964-5
CF to 1965
PW to **4** 1965-6
Barbasevich, Vyacheslav
Yanovich 1963
BR to 1963
Barclay, Gary M. 1968
CF to 1968
Barlovatz, A. 1963
Encl: A. Barlovatz to Lord
Boyd Orr 1966
Lord Boyd Orr to RS 1966
BR to 1963
Barratt-Brown, Michael,
Daniel Coleman to 1964
Barrett, J. F., to BRPF 1965
HR to 1965
Barrett, Lynda, to PW 1969
Barron, Zelda 1965
BR to 1965
Barton, Hugo R., to BRPF 1968
CF to 1968
Basaran, Ayhan, BR to 1966
Basham, W. R. **2** 1962
BR to 1962
Bassi, J. J. 1962
BR to 1962
Bastion, Charlton 1962
BR to 1962
Baxter, Rosemarie 1965
PW to 1965
Bay, Christian **2** 1962-8
Encl: Christian Bay to
*New York Times
Magazine* **2** 1962-8
BR to **2** 1962
CF to 1968
Bay, John G. 1962
BR to 1963
Baylis, N., to BRPF 1966
PW to 1966
Bazaar, Mona 1964

BR to 1964
Bearman, Ronald 1963
BR to 1963
Beasley, Alec C., to
BRPF **4** 1963-5
To RS **8** 1963-7
Encl: Alex C. Beasley to
Peace News 1963
clippings
CF to **2** 1963
RS to **7** 1963-7
BR to **3** 1964
Beaton, Leonard,
BR to **2** 1964
Beauregard, Laurent
A. **2** 1965-7
Encl: clippings
BR to **3** 1965-7
Becker, Moshe 1967
RSt. to 1967
Beeton, P. D. 1963
BR to 1963
Belcher, C., CF to 1969
Belfast Young Socialists of
the North Ireland Labour
Party (Cyril Toman) to G.
Coggan 1967
Belilos, Leon 1958
Belland, Christopher C. ..... 1963?
BR to 1963
Bellavista, Luciano 1968
CF to 1968
Belous, Charles, BR to 1963
Belton, Henry, BR to 1963
Belton, Howard 1964
Bench, Peter G. H. 1964
Ben-Gurion, David, to Enrico
Pratt 1961
Benjamin, D. J. 1964
Encl.
RS to 1964
Benjamin, Jack **99** 1962-8
To BRPF 1964
To CE 1964
To CF **8** 1964
To RS **21** 1965-7
To AY **2** 1963
Encl: *Progressive World*
(Hugh Robert Orr) to
Benjamin 1963
Benjamin to *The New
York Times* (C. L. Sulzberger,
John B. Oakes) **2** 1965-7
The New York Times (Marie
Dairett) to Benjamin 1967
Benjamin to *Look* 1967
Look (Anne Celli) to
Benjamin 1967
BR to **19** 1962-6
CF to **15** 1962-8
AY to 1963
CE to 1964
RS to **12** 1964-7
PW to **2** 1965-7
Benn, S. Edwin, BR to 1963
Bennett, W. C., PW to 1967
Benney, Robyn, CF to 1969
Bent, John A. 1966
To PW **2** 1966
PW to **3** 1966
Bentley, Jerry H., CF to 1968
Bergol, Alexander 1968
PW to 1968
Bergstrom, David Lawrence .. 1962
BR to 1962
Berlin, Isaiah 1969
CF to 1969
Bernadotte, Sigvard 1964
Bernal, J. D. 1962
Encl: form ls. from J. D.
Bernal Peace Library, text
of cable by Bernal to UN
BR to 1965
Bernal, Margaret, NJ to 1962
Bernardino, Luis, BR to 1967
Berry, William A. 1970
Encl.
BR to 1970
Bevan, Yolande 1966
Encl: ls. on Vietnam to the
British Medical Journal
RS to 1966
Bevis, B. Cecil, to RS **2** 1962
To CE 1963
RS to **2** 1962
CE to **2** 1963
Bhat, A. N. **2** 1962
Encl: cartoons
BR to 1962
AY to 1962

Bhatnager, V. M. 1968
CF to 1968
Bhatt, Govind 1962
To ER 1964
BR to 1962
Bhutto, Zulfikar A.,
BR to 2 1968-9
Bierich, Marcus 1952
Binch, Paul, CF to 1969
Binding, D. C., to BRPF 1969
RSt. to 1969
Birmingham Indian
Association 1968
Bishop, Daphne E. 1964
BR to 1964
Black, Paul 3 1962
BR to 2 1962
NJ to 1962
Blackett, P. M. S., BR to 1964
Blackett, P. M. S.?, Szilard,
L.?, Pamm, ?, and
Bullard, ? 1961
Blake, Robert, RS to 1964
Blankenship, Ben F. 1963
Encl: l. to *Saturday*
Evening Post 1963
poem
BR to 1963
Blindell, Walter R. 1966
PW to 1966
Blond, Neville 1964
BR to 1963
Blood, A. 1967
PW to 1967
Bloom, John, BR to 1963
The Blue Rag (Peter Grundy)
to PW 1966
Encl: issue of journal
PW to 1966
Bluhm, Walter, to RS 2 1964
RS to 1964
Blumberg, Irving Samuel 1968
To CF 1969
CF to 2 1969
Blum, William, RS to .... n.d.
Bocu Music Ltd. (A. Fraser
White) 1965
Encl.
BR to 1965
Bofman, Robert 1964
Encl.
Bögholm, K., to BRPF 1965
RS to 1965
Boissenot, M., BR to 1963
The Bomb-Test Suits (Ralph B.
Atkinson) (form ls.) 1963
Bonetti, Alberto 1968
Bonnett, F. M., to BRPF 1965
RS to 1965
Bonnevie, Carl 2 1963
Encl.
BR to 2 1963-4
Bornschein, Earl J.,
to BRPF 1964
BR to 1964
Bornstein, Steven A. 1965
BR to 1965
Borra, Yvon 1968
DN to 1968
Borsook, Eve 1967
Janet Viney to 1967
Bos, José Martin-Chico,
to BRPF 1968
Bos, Marianne 1969
CF to 1969
Boukema, H. J., to BRPF 1967
RSt. to 1967
Boulding for Congress
(Edward Geffner) 1966
Encl: political literature
RS to 1966
Bourdet, Claude, BR to 1964
Bourne, H. E. 2 1962
BR to 1962
Bovard, René, BR to 2 ... 1962-3
Boxer Indemnity Advisory
Committee (Chancellor of
the Exchequer, James
H. Hudson) 1924
Dickinson, G. Lowes, to
BR 2 .... 1924?
Foreign Office (Nevile Butler,
B. L. Newton) to 2 1924
Waterlow, Sidney, to
BR 3 1924
Encl: ts. of BR's "Memo-
randum on the Boxer
Indemnity"
Boyd, Frances 2 1965
PW to 1965

Boyd Orr, Lord **5** 1962-3
Encl: petitions
BR to **9** 1962-7
RS to **2** 1962-3
boyFrank, Manuel 1966
CF to 1966
Bozic, Sreten N. 1968
CF to 1968
Brahms, Flemming 1968
CF to 1968
Branko, Rudolf, BR to 1966
Bratby, John, BR to 1966
Bray, Barbara, BR to 1964
Break-Through to Disarmament (Avis Hutt) 1963
Brennan, James **8** 1962-5
To BRPF 1964
To CF **2** 1963-4
To RS 1965
Encl: James Brennan to *The Guardian* 1964
poem ("Sage of Plas Penrhyn"), summary report of the Nottingham Test Campaign
BR to **10** 1962-5
CE to 1963
CF to **3** 1964
RS to **2** 1964-5
Brewer, Colin, BR to 1965
(not sent)
Encl: BR to *The Times* 1965
(not sent)
Brier, Bob 1965
PW to 1965
Brigade der Deutsch-Sowjetischen Freundschaft (Seidenschur and Könnecke) to PJ 1968
Encl: political literature
Brighton Defence Fund (Renate Prince) to PJ 1967
Brighton Peace Action Group (K. M. Stodden), BR to 1966
Brindley, Terry, BR to 1966
Bring the Troops Home Now Newsletter, BR to 1966
The Brisbane Professionals for Peace (Robert Smith) 1965
RS to 1965
Bristol Vietnam Concert Committee (Sylvia Argyle) **2** 1968
Encl: leaflet
The British Association for World Government (Jon Skinner) 1968
Encl: pamphlet, conference agenda
CF to 1968
British Broadcasting Corporation (extract from news bulletin) 1961
British Campaign for Peace in Vietnam (Dick Nettleton) (form ls., political literature)
British Committee for Portuguese Amnesty (Patricia M. Steadman, Audrey Wagner) 1967
CF to 1967
British Council for Peace in Vietnam (Amicia M. Young, Sheila Thiles) to BRPF 1968
To ER 1965
To CF 1965
Encl: leaflets, petitions, form ls., press releases, political literature
CF to 1965
British Council for World Government (Charles Coyne) 1965
Encl.
PW to 1965
British-Cuba Committee (form ls.) 1962
British Humanist Association (A. J. Ayer, H. J. Blackham, *et al.*) **8** 1963-8
To BRPF 1967
Encl: form ls., issue of journal, annual report, etc.
BR to **6** 1963-8
CF to 1969
British Movement for Freedom in Russia (Gavin (Harris) (form l., pamphlet) 1969
The British Peace Committee (Colin Sweet) **8** 1962-7

To RS 1966
Encl: invitation, form
l., invoice, leaflet
BR to **5** 1962-6
RS to **3** 1964-7
HR to 1965
RSt. to 1967
British Poster Advertising
Association (H. H. Mallatratt)
to BRPF 1964
British Soviet Friendship
Committee (Colin
Williams) 1962
Britten, Benjamin,
BR to 1966
Brock, ?, BR to 1959
Brockway, Fenner,
Lord **16** 1931-69
To RS **3** 1962
To PW 1969
Encl: David Boulton
to CF .... n.d.
draft l. entitled "Opposition
to World War I" by Fenner
Brockway and BR, essay by
Maurice Soleillet, invitation,
circular
DR? to 1931
BR to **8** 1962-70
RS to 1962
AY to **2** 1962
CF to **2** 1962-8
BR and ER to 1968
PW to 1969
Brody, L. B. 1963
Bromley Technical College
Students' Association (Richard
Clarke) 1965
Brook, Judy, to BRPF 1964
To RS 1966
RS to 1966
CF to 1969
Brooks, Jeremy 1958
Brothers to All Men (Michael
Pickett) to BRPF 1969
Brown, Mrs., RS to 1965
Brown, Harrison (form l.),
to A. V. Topchiev 1962
Brown, Warwick D. 1968
CF to 1968
Brownbill, Eric J. 1964
CF to 1964
Brownlow, Donald G. **3** .. 1963-5
BR to **3** 1963-4
ID to 1965
RS to 1965
Bruck, Elsbeth to
BRPF **4** 1967-8
Encl: poem
BR to 1966
RSt. to **2** 1968
Brunner, Sir Felix 1964
BR to 1964
Buchbinder, Heinrich 1963
BR to 1963
Burchett, Wilfred G. **2** 1969
Encl: petition
Bureau Africain d'Information
(M. Boujasson), BR to 1964
Burhop, E. H. S.,
to J. Rotblat 1967
Burke, Kenneth 1966
BR to 1966
Ed Burnett, Inc., Lists (Ed
Burnett) to CE **2** 1964
CE to 1964
Buro, Andreas (political
literature) 1962
CF to 1962
Burris, Barbara, BR to 1966
Busby, H. Duane 1966
Butler, Joyce, RS to 1964
Butt, Joyce R. 1964
CE to 1964
Butters, John H., BR to 1964
Buxton, Jane, ER
to **2** 1961-2
Bynner, Bill **3** 1963-6
To CE 1964
Encl: Maurice ? to Bill
Bynner 1966
petition
BR to **3** 1963-5
CE to **2** 1964

C

Calder, Alexander, BR to 1966
Calder, Ritchie 1964

BR to 1964
Caldwell, Julius A.,
to BRPF 1965
To CF 1967
CF to 1967
Encl: list of foreign branches of BRPF
Caldwell, Malcolm 1967
To RS 1966
[RS] to 1966
BR to 1967
Callado, Antonio 1967
RSt. to 1967
Calverd, Alan 1963
BR to 1963
Cambridge Free Front (Frank Gawthrop) to BRPF (form l.) .... 1968?
CF to 1969
Cambridge University Campaign for Nuclear Disarmament (Richard Porter) to Jonathan Tinker 1962
RS to 1962
Cameron, Louis-Jacques 1964
BR to **2** 1964
RS to 1964
Camey, Elizabeth Ann 1962
Campagna per Disarmo Nucleare 1965
Campaign for a World Constituent Assembly (M.R. Cosyn) **5** 1963-4
To RS 1964
To CF 1965
Encl: form l., political literature, minutes
BR to **4** 1963-4
CF to 1965
HR to 1965
Campaign for Peace in Vietnam (D.T. Healey) 1968
Encl: political literature
CF to **2** 1969
Campbell, Craig S. 1962
BR to 1962
Campbell, Douglas K. 1966
PW to 1966
Campbell, Jock, BR to 1963
Campbell-Purdie, Wendy,
BR to 1963
Canadian Campaign for Nuclear Disarmament (F.C. Hunnius), BR to 1962
Canadian Peace Research Institute (N.Z. Alcock), NJ to 1962
Cañaveral, M. Parra, and Carroquino, J., to BRPF ... 1969
CF to 1969
Cardenas, Lazaro, BR to 1966
Cardiff Peace Committee (T.N.W. Bush) **4** 1963-5
To BRPF 1964
CF to 1965
PW to 1966
Carlson, Chris 1969
PW to 1969
Carroll, Jane, to BRPF 1966
PW to 1966
Carter, Michael J., to BRPF 1964
Casa della Cultura e della Ricreazione (Gastone Gimignani) to BRPF 1967
RSt. to 1967
Casals, Pablo, BR to 1962
Encl: clipping
Center for the Study of Armament and Disarmament (Marjorie Jensen) to BRPF 1969
Center for the Study of Democratic Institutions (Hallock Hoffman) 1964
Centre Liegeois d'Action pour la Non-Violence (Arno Hamers) **4** 1964-7
Encl: l. to Groupe de Recherche et d'Action pour le Règlement du Problème Palestinien 1967
essays, clippings, newsls.
BR to **4** 1963-4
RSt. to 1967
Centro Studie Iniziative per la Piena Occupazione (Mary Taylor) to BRPF 1963
CERGE (William McAdoo), BR to 1965
Cerveny, F.M. 1965

Encl: l. to *Montreal Star*
(Boyce Richardson) 1965
CF to 1965
Chagall, Marc, BR to 1966
Chakotin, Serge, BR to **2** ... 1963
Chamungwana, G. M. 1968
CF to 1968
Chapman, F. M., to CE 1963
BR to 1963
Chapman, Meg, to BRPF 1965
Chatroussat, Jet S. (form
l.) 1962
Chattopadhyay, S., BR to 1966
Chauvin, Jean René,
to [RS] 1966
RS to 1966
Chen, John P. H., BR to 1963
Cheney, Howard **2** 1962-3
BR to **2** 1962-3
(l. dated 1962 not sent)
Chiba, Hideo, BR to 1964
Chingford Nuclear Disarmament
Committee (Mrs. J. Royall)
to CF 1963
Encl: Serge Chakotin
to BR .... n.d.
political literature
CF to 1963
Chislehurst Constituency Labour
Party (W. J. Gilroy) 1962
BR to 1962
Chitty, Christopher,
to BRPF 1964
Cholewa, Kazimierz, BR to ... 1964
Chorley, Lord 1969
BR to 1969
Chowdhury, Ambikagiri
Roy 1962
Christiansen, Elspeth,
to RS **3** 1965
RS to **3** 1965
CHURCH (Viv Broughton,
Janette Hammond and
John Careswell) 1968
Encl: leaflet
Citizens' Committee for
Disarmament (Tom
Brewer) **8** 1963-4
Encl: articles, essays, poems,
journal issues, clippings, etc.
BR to **7** 1963-4
PW to 1965
Citizens for Governmental
Restraint, Inc. (James
Malcolm Williams) 1968
BR to 1968
Clark, George **2** 1962-4
To RS 1964
To BRPF 1965
Encl: extract from trial
transcript, political literature
Clark, Grenville 1963
BR to 1963
Grenville Clark Institute
for World Law (George
C. Holt) (form ls., declaration,
newsl.) 1966-8
Clark, Len 1956
Encl: re Suez meeting
Clifford, Harry W. 1965
BR to 1965
RS to 1965
Coates, Ken, BR to 1966
CF to **2** 1965-6
Cockburn, Alex, CF to **2** ... 1968
Encl: CF to the Bulgarian
Embassy (? Alexander) 1968
note on Alex Cockburn
Coggan, Geoffrey, BR to 1966
CF to **3** 1966
Colaabavala, F., BR to 1964
Coleman, Daniel 1965
RS to 1965
Collins, Marjory, to RS **5** ... 1965
RS to **2** 1965
Collins, Jr., F. Warren,
to BRPF **2** 1965
Colne, Judith, to PW 1966
Encl: clippings
Combined Universities
Campaign for Nuclear
Disarmament (Michael Craft
and John Gittings) .... n.d.
Il Comitato della Pace di Pesaro
e Urbino .... n.d.
Comité d'Action pour
l'Exposition (Anne Barbey)
(form l.) 1966
BR to 1966
Comité Senegalais de Soutien

au Vietnam (Philip Langley)
to BRPF 1967
Committee Against the Blockade
of Cuba (Mike Miller) .... 1962?
Committee for Biafran Artists
(Miriam Reik) 1969
CF to 1969
Committee for Democratic
Rights in the U.S.A. (Helen
Bastable) 2 1962-3
To RS 1963
To AY 1963
BR to 2 1962-3
AY to 1963
RS to 1964
Committee for GI Rights
(Shirley Jolls, Eddie Oquendo,
Maryann Weissman) 2 ... 1967
BR to 2 1967
Committee for May 10th
Demonstration (David
McReynolds) 1962
Encl: political literature
Committee for Nonviolent Action
(Mary Mergs, A. J.
Muste) .... 1962?
Encl: form ls., reprint of
ls. of BR re Everyman III
Committee for Nuclear Disarma-
ent of the Arab-Israeli
Region (Yehuda Ben-Moshe),
RS to 1966
The Committee for Solidarity
with the Victims of Re-
pression in Peru (John
Edmunds) to BRPF 2 1967
To RS 2 1967
RS to 2 1967
RSt. to 1968
Committee of Americans
Abroad for an Honorable
Foreign Policy (Allen Young)
(petition) .... n.d.
Committee to Aid the Monroe
Defendants, BR to 1963
Committee to Defend the
French Students (Helena
Hermes), BR to 1968
Communist Party of Great
Britain (Reuben Falber,
John Gollan) 1965
BR to 1965
The Communists (Stock-
holm) 1967
Concerned Citizens (Douglas
Mattern) 1966
Concord Films Council (Eric
Walker) (form ls.) 1965-6
BR to 1966
CF to 1968
Congress for Cultural
Freedom 1956
Encl.
Congress for Disarmament and
International Cooperation
(mimeo) 1958
The Congress of Scientists
on Survival (Hector J.
Ritey) 1962
Encl: conference report,
questionnaire
BR to 1962
Conseil Federal Espagnol
(Salvador de Madariaga)
(form l.) 1962
Contemporary Press (P.
Watter) 1962
Encl: essay
BR to 1962
Cook, E. O. 1958
Cook, Fred J., BR to 1963
Cookson, Sybil, to RS 2 .. 1963-5
RS to 2 1963-5
Co-operative Bookshop
Ltd. .... n.d.
Coordinating Committee for
International Service (W.
Martin Dyas) to RS 2 1965
Encl: information documents
re Committee programme
RS to 1965
Corbet-Milward, Commander
N. R., CF? to 1964
Corneliani, Gaetana E. 2 1962
BR to 1962
Corridon, Juliana M. 2 1962
BR to 2 1962
Cosmopolitan Institute of
Public Affairs (Shiv
Prasad Muflis) 1964

RS? to 1964
Costello, Christopher 1968
PW to 1968
Courouclis, Evangelos 1962
BR to 1962
Cousins, Frank W. 1964
Crankshaw, Edward 1964
Craver, W. T., to BRPF 1969
CF to 1969
Crichton, Dorothy 1962
BR to 1962
Crocker, Ruth 1967
Encl: political literature
RSt. to 1967
Cropper, Frank, CF to 1967
Crosser, Paul 1963
BR to **4** 1963-4
Csendes, Francis E. 1962
BR to 1962
Cuban Embassy (Federico de Cordova Castro) 1962
BR to 1962
Cukurs, Andris 1965
PW to 1965
Cuu Quoc Weekly (Nguyen Van Sao, Pham Duc Thanh, and Nguyen Linh Qui) (form l.) 1968

D

da Costa Doria, João A., to RS 1964
Encl.
da Curba, Miguel Luis C. 1969
Dadvar, J. **2** 1965
HR to 1965
Daković, Predrag, BR to 1966
Dale, Rowland 1966
RS to 1966
Daly, Lawrence 1969
To CF 1969
Encl: l. to *The Times* 1969
BR to **2** 1967
CF to 1969
Danek, Cyril, and Dankova, Olga **2** 1969
Darling, E. W. 1962
BR to 1962
Darr, Jr., John W. 1965
To RS 1965
Encl: form l. from Peace Research Project, outline of a book
CF to 1965
da Silva, F. H. Lopes 1962
Davidson, Angus 1962
BR to 1962
Davidson, Donald, to BRPF 1964
Davies, Jeffrey, CF to 1968
Davies, John, BR to 1963
Davies, Mansel **15** 1958-69
To AY 1963
To ER 1967
To CF 1969
Encl: l. to Donald F. Horig 1967
Horig to Davies 1967
"Comments on the 17th Pugwash Conference", "Protest and Proposition for 1970"
BR to **11** 1963-9
AY to 1963
ER to 1967
CF to **3** 1963-9
Davis, Jerome **3** 1963
BR to 1966
Dawley, Robert P., to BRPF 1965
de Almeide, Pedro Bieira 1966
BR to 1966
de Arrocha, Angela Delli Sante 1967
Debbaut, Pierre, BR to 1966
Encl: Jean-Luc Vernal and Claude Vanderhaeghen to BR 1966
de Brioni, Marie-Louise K., RS to 1965
Decrez, Laurette, CF to 1968
Defence Committee for Victims of Nazi Persecution (Elizabeth Dales) 1963
To AY 1963
Encl: form ls.
BR to **2** 1963-4

AY to 1963
Defenders of 3 against HUAC (Martha W. Dudley) (form l., Xerox of clippings) 1966
BR to 2 1966
de Jager, E., to BRPF 1965
de la Torre, Haye, to CF 1962
CF to 1962
NJ to 1963
de Lippe, Jürgen 1963
BR to 1963
De Los Toyos, Alberto, BR to 1966
De Marco, Clara Hermann 2 1962
BR to 1962
Demos, Kathleen 1966
BR to 1966
de Oliveira, Raimundo Bezerra 1962
Deppenwiese, Manfred 1966
RS to 1966
Derrick, Jonathan M. 1964
PW to 1964
Derricourt, Robin M. 1964
To Bill Kaye 1965
To RS 1965
BR to 1964
RS to 2 1965
Deutsch, Alex T. 1966
To CF 1966
CF to 1966
RS to 1966
Deutsche Friedensgesellschaft (Gottfried Wandersleb, August Bangel) (form ls.) 2 1965-7
BR to 1964
Deutscher, Isaac, BR to 1966
Deutscher, Tamara 1967
To ER 1966
BR to 1967
Encl: press s. by BR on the death of Isaac Deutscher
Dev, Vasu 1968
CF to 1968
Diaz, Marisa Olive, to BRPF 1968
PW to 1968
Dickie, James 1969
CF to 1969
Dino, Abidine, BR to 1966
Direct Action Committee (receipt) 1958
BR to (G. Jannor) 1959
Encl: clippings
Dissent (Irving Howe) (form ls.) 2 1963-4
Divine Light Mission (R. S. Yogi) 1962
BR to 1962
The Divorce Law Reform Association (I. B. Burnett) 1969
The Divorce Law Reform Union (Charles Skilton, R. V. Banks) 1963
Encl: form ls., speech
Dixon, George H., to Pat Pottle 1963
Pat Pottle to 1963
Dixon, Ian .... n.d.
Dixon, Mary W. 2 1963-5
To BRPF 1963
To RS 1965
BR to 1963
AY to 1963
RS to 2 1965
Dolan, Joe 1963
To RS 2 1963
BR to 1963
RS to 1963
Dolci, Danilo 3 1962-3
(Robin Dixon on behalf of Danilo Dolci Trust) to BR 1962
To RS 2 1963
Encl: Associated-Rediffusion Ltd. (Marjorie Sullivan) to RS? 1962
political declarations, form ls., newsl., note
BR to 4 1962-4
RS to 1963
BR to Robin Dixon 1962
Encl: s. by BR re David Mitchell case
Dominican Committee of Wives and Families of Political Prisoners .... n.d.

Donat, Ilon, to RS 1962
Encl: Ilon Donat to
The Guardian 1962
RS to 1962
Doran, E.C. 1967
To CF 1969
CF to 1969
Doukhobor Society of Canada
(John J. Chernenkoff)
to CF 1963
To AY 1963
Encl: Doukhobor Society of
Canada (John N. Postnikoff
and John J. Chernenkoff)
to UN (U Thant) 1963
BR to 1964
AY to 1963
CF to .... n.d.
Drexel, Helen Carter,
BR to 1963
ER to 1964
Dundas, Malcolm 1967
RS to 1967
Dundas, Malcolm,
and Abelman, Jane 1966
BR to 1966
Dundee Humanist Group (E.C.
Macfarlane) **3** 1965
Encl: l. to Colonial Office
(Mr. Bottomly) 1965
newsl., leaflets
RS to 1965
PW to **2** 1965
Dunham, W.R. **2** 1967
Encl: *The Sunday Times*
(Derek Humphry) to W.R.
Dunham 1967
CF to 1967
Dunne, R. 1962
BR to 1962
Durham Colleges Labour Club
(Ian Taylor) 1963
BR to 1963
Duriaud, François 1965
CF to 1965
Duve, Arne (form l.,
essay) 1963
BR to 1963
Dyer-Bennett, Miriam 1962
BR to **2** 1962-3

E

Eaby, Christian, to BRPF .... 1966?
PW to 1966
Eaton, Anne **2** 1963
BR to 1963
Eaton, Cyrus **15** 1962-9
(Betty Royon **10** 1966-70
(N.R. Comiskey) **2** 1966-9
Encl: articles, issue of *Toronto
Star Weekly*, clippings,
form ls.
BR to **9** 1962-9
RS to **3** 1962
Ebbert, George C. 1963
BR to 1963
Eberhart, Roland F. 1963
Eco Contemporaneo (Miguel
Grinberg) 1966
Edenborough, Alan 1969
CF to 1969
Edginton, J.D. 1962
BR to 1962
Edmonds, Laurie, to CF 1965
HR to 1965
Edwards, ? 1963
Edwards, Bob 1964
Edwards, George **2** 1962
BR to 1962
Edwards, H., BR to 1963
Effendi, Aslam **11** 1963-9
To RSt. 1968
Encl: Khyber Express Ltd.
(Khawayah Ahmad Din) to
Effendi 1967
State Bank of Pakistan (A.S.A.
Mulla) to Effendi **2** 1967
The London Book Co.
(Rahman Mani) to
Effendi 1968
Classic (Agha Amin Hussam)
to Effendi 1968
BR to **10** 1963-7
RS to 1964
RSt. to 1968
CF to **2** 1968-9
Egall, Peter 1968
Encl.
Egbimike, Ken A., CF to 1968
Egwu, Igbo N. **2** 1967-8

Encl: Xerox of ls., articles, etc., re Biafra
Ehrem, Prince Mohmed 1964
BR to 1964
Eilam, Aviva 1967
RS to 1967
Eisenstein, Anatol **4** 1964-6
BR to **2** 1964
RS to 1966
Elisabeth of the Belgians, Queen **2** 1962
BR to **3** 1961-2
Elliot, Elsie **3** 1966
To PW 1966
Encl: memorandum
BR to 1966
Elliot, J., to BRPF 1967
RSt. to 1967
Elliot, Jeff M. 1967
CF to 1968
Ellis, Charles R. **16** 1962
RS to **17** 1962-4
CF to **2** 1962-5
Encl: note by BR re Ellis
Ellis, Nathalie, RS? to 1963
Ellis, R. A. 1963
BR to 1963
Ellman, Michael 1966
RS to 1966
CF to 1968
Ellscheid, Robert 1964
Emeruwa, John N. 1963
BR to 1963
Emmanueli, Antonio 1969
PW to 1969
End the Draft Committee (Sheldon Jacoby) to RS 1966
Eng, Aw Say 1969
Erickson, Arthur W. 1967
Encl: clippings, political literature
Erlich, Reese W., to DH 1968
RSt. to 1968
Essex, M., BR to 1963
Evan-Thomas, Katharine, to Jack Singleton 1962
Evans, Avril M., to BRPF 1965
Evans, Gwynfor 1967
Encl: *Hansard Parliamentary Debates* for 21 April 1967
BR to 1967
Evans, W. Houghton 1961
Evensen, Lars 1969
Everyman III (Jeffrey Hurford, Barnaby Martin) **2** ....
Encl: form ls. (containing BR's ls. re Everyman III), political literature
Ewén, Stud. Gõrtn, to BRPF 1969
Ex-Service Movement for Peace (S. Knight) 1964
To PW **2** 1965-6
Encl.
Ezzell, F. 1967
PW to 1967

F

Fabsic, Jiri, CF to 1969
Fackler, Ernest C. **3** 1963-5
BR to **2** 1963-4
RS to 1965
Factory for Peace (T. McAlpine, Jim Evans) 1962
Encl.
CF to 1965
Fahy, Julian 1965
Encl: l. to *Washington Post* 1963
BR to 1963
Fairbrass, F. C. 1965
To CF **2** 1965
Encl: F. C. Fairbrass to the Receiver of the Metropolitan Police 1965
CF to 1965
HR to 1965
RS to 1965
Fakhrutdinova, S. B., BR to .. 1963
Fallin, Richard **3** 1961-3
BR to **4** 1962-3
RS to 1964
Fardoonii, M. S. 1965
RS to 1965
Faredoon, Mahmood, BR to 1966
Farr, A. F. **2** 1964-7
To CF 1967

BR to 1964
Farrington, B. 1954
Fast, Howard 1966
Fawcett, John T., to
BRPF 1963
CE to 1963
F.C.I. News Agency (Josef
Josten), CF to 1968
Fearing, Mrs. Bruce 1964
BR to **2** 1964
The Federal Council for the
Advancement of Aborigines
and Torres Strait Islanders
(Mamie Smith) 1967
Federal Union (David
G. Allen) 1958
Encl.
BR to 1958
The Federated Gas Employees'
Industrial Union (L. H.
Thompson) **2** 1964-5
BR to **3** 1964-8
Encl: "An Appeal on the
Danger of the World of
Goldwater's Policies"
Fédération Internationale des
Résistants (Jean Toujas)
(form l., appeal, greeting
c.) 1963
Fédération Nationale des Jeunes
Gardes Socialistes (Fajersztajn
Albert) to RS 1966
RS to 1966
Feied, Frederick 1965
BR to 1965
Feigenbaum, Stan A.,
BR to 1964
Fein, Louis 1962
Encl: essay
BR to 1962
Fekete, Paul **3** 1962-3
To RS 1962
Encl: Paul Fekete to *London Forum* (Muriel Howlett) ... 1963
Feldman, Edwin *et al.* **2** 1962-5
Encl: l. to Kennedy
and Khrushchev 1962
Edwin Feldman to Lyndon
B. Johnson 1965
BR to 1962
RS to 1965
Feldman, Victor 1965
BR to 1965
RS to 1965
Fellowship of Reconciliation
(H. Williams *et al.*) **3** ... 1962-4
To CF 1964
Encl: political literature
BR to 1962
The Fellowship Party (James
Haigh) **2** 1965
To BRPF **3** 1965
To CF 1965
To PW 1965
Encl: leaflets
PW to **2** 1965
Ferguson, Alan 1964
To RS 1964
RS to 1964
Ferris, A. 1967
Encl: essay
RSt. to 1967
Ferzan, Abdul Karim 1965
CF to 1965
Field, Elsie 1964
RS to 1964
CF to 1965
Field, S. S. 1968
BR to 1968
RS to 1968
Fields, F. Herbert 1964
BR to **2** 1964
Fiesta Cultural Association ... 1966
CF to 1967
Fifth Ave. Vietnam Peace Parade
Committee (Dave Dellinger,
Virginia Ruffulo) **2** 1966-7
RS to 1967
Filho, Antonio de Deus Teles,
to BRPF 1969
PW to 1969
Filho, Noronha Rodrigues ... 1966
Encl: Xerox of clipping
RS to 1966
Filippov, Ivan, RS to 1963
Finberg, J., RS to 1964
Finch, P. W., to Pat? 1966
Firth, Hugh, to RS **2** 1965
RS to 1965
Fishell, John M. 1964

Encl: BR l. in *St. Louis Post-Dispatch*
BR to 1964
Fisher, Brian, to David Robinson 1967
Encl: tributes to Isaac Deutscher
RSt. to 1967
Encl: David Robinson to RSt. 1967
Fisher, Carol, to RS 1964
Fisher, Ralph 1963
Encl: article
BR to 1963
Fishwick, Colin 1962
BR to 1962
Fitch, Ana Norma Bazúa 1968
Flamm, Irving H. 1964
Encl: l. to *The Minority of One* 1962
l. to Center for the Study of Democratic Institutions (W. H. Ferry) .... 1962?
CF to 1963
BR to **2** 1964-7
Encl: *The Minority of One* (Eric Norden) to BRPF 1963
CF to *The Minority of One* (Eric Norden) 1963
Fleischmann, Miriam, to BRPF 1967
RS to 1967
Flug, Ewald 1959
Encl: Sittliche Manifestation
Focus on Soviet Jewry (Joel Cang) **2** 1969
Encl: booklet
CF to **2** 1969
Foot, Michael, to RS **2** ... 1962-4
NJ to 1962
RS to 1964
CF to 1964
Forbes, David 1966
To PW 1966
PW to 1966
The Foreign Office, HR to ... 1965
Foreign Office course on Communism (schedule of lectures) 1951
Forest, James to CF 1964
Encl: brochure
Forman, Hilda S., BR to 1963
Fox, Phil, to BRPF? 1966
PW to 1966
Fox, Philip, to RS 1962
Fraidenraich, N., BR to 1963
Frampton, Geoffrey, ER to ... 1961
Encl: Frampton's l. in *Manchester Guardian*
Frank, Jerome D. 1964
To BRPF 1964
Encl: articles
BR to 1965
Frankel, Charles 1962
Frederick, Harry 1966
Frémont, Jean **2** 1962
To CE **4** 1963-4
To CF 1965
To PW 1965
Encl: form l., new address c., memoranda
BR to **2** 1962
CF to 1963
CE to **4** 1963-4
RS to 1964
PW to **2** 1965
Freney, Denis 1966
RS to 1966
Freud, Arthur 1963
To RS 1965
Friedell, Morris F. 1963
BR to 1963
Friedensrat der Deutschen Demokratischen Republik (Walter Friedrich) 1966
Friedlander, Zelda **2** 1963-4
BR to **2** 1964
RS to 1964
Friedman, Thomas B. 1969
CF to 1969
Friel, Patrick, to BRPF 1968
RSt. to 1968
Friends Service Council (William E. Barton), CF to 1968
Friendship Universal (Emmanuel Petrakis) to BRPF 1964
Encl: form l., questionnaire
CF to 1964
Fullerton, Hamish 1968
Encl: l. to *The*

Guardian 1968
CF to 1968
Fulljames, R. 2 1962-3
Encl: form ls., ss.
BR to 2 1963-4
Fuse, T., BR to 1966

G

Gaess, Roger 1962
BR to 1962
Galitzine, Theo, to BRPF 1965
HR to 1965
Gallois, André, BR to 1963
Gambert, Stephen R.,
to BRPF 1966
RS to 1966
Gamble, Marie 1969
To BRPF 1967
RSt. to 1968
Gandy, J. K. 1962
Encl: clipping
BR to 1962
Garfield, Allan 1968
BR to 1968
Garner, Roy, CF to 1968
Garnett, Tony (form ls.) 1968
BR to 1968
Garst, Jim, to RS 2 1962
RS to 1962
Garvard, Timothy F. 1964
Gastón, Nilita Vientós,
to BRPF 1966
PW to 1966
Gaughey, Andrew D. 2 1966
To ID 1967
Geering, Ken, CF 1969
Geisendorfer, James V. 5 ... 1963-6
To PW 1965
BR to 5 1963-4
RS to 1965
PW to 1965
General Strike for Peace
(Roy Lofstedt) (form l.,
leaflets) 1963
Geneva Reception and Information
Centre for Deputations to
Conferences Concerned with
Disarmament (René
Bovard) 3 1962
Encl: form ls., declarations
BR to 2 1962
Genschel, Rudolf 1964
BR to 1964
Genteman, Paul 1967
BR to 1967
Genthner, James 5 1965-8
Encl: clippings
BR to 2 1965-6
CF to 1965
RS to 2 1965
Gerard, David L. 1966
Encl: Xerox of clipping
PW to 1966
Gerst, Karl 2 1962-3
Encl: l. to Radio Frank-
furt 1962
BR to 1962
Getz, Andrew 2 1962
To BRPF 1964
BR to 1962
CE to 1964
Ghanacom 1963
Gibor, Aharon 1963
Encl: l. to President
Kennedy 1962
BR to 1963
Gidwani, M. M. 1962
BR to 1962
Gilbert, Mary 1964
Encl: clipping
RS to 1965
Gill, J. S., BR to 1963
Gladwyn, Lord 2 1964-9
RS to 1964
BR to 1969
Glasgow Vietnam Solidarity
Campaign (D. S. Riddell) .. 1967
RSt. to 1968
Glass, Bentley 1963
BR to 1963
Glenfield, William R. 1966
Glenn, John R. 3 1963
BR to 1963
Glick, Ira 1967
Encl: clipping of article by
C. L. Sulzberger, "Foreign
Affairs: Corpse on Horseback"
Global Books (Jean

Kransdorf) **3** 1965
Glover, Jake 1964
BR to 1964
Goddard, Don 1969
To RS **2** 1962
To [RS] **2** 1962-4
To CE **2** 1963
To PW **3** 1966
RS to .... n.d.
PW to **3** 1966-9
Godwin, George 1962
Encl: George Godwin to *The Guardian*
BR to 1962
Goldberg, Arthur J. 1969
Encl: s.
CF to 1969
Goldfarb, Samuel **2** 1965
To RS **7** .... n.d.
Encl: Good Neighbor Publications, Inc. (Gilbert Waters) to BR 1964
Goldfarb to Melvin Dubinsky .... n.d.
To Mohammed Hassanein Heikal **2** 1964
To Isaac Wolfson 1964
S. N. Behrman to Goldfarb 1964
Pearl Buck to 1964
Jimmy Durante to .... n.d.
Harry Emerson Fosdick to 1964
Paul Hunter to 1964
Fanny Hurst to 1964
Theodore R. McKeldin to 1964
Wilfred A. Peterson to 1964
Samuel Sobel to 1965
Louis E. Wolfson to 1964
clippings, book jacket
Goldhammer, Joachim 1962
Goldman, David, to BRPF ... 1965
CF to 1965
Goldreich, Abraham Jacob, *et al.* 1967
Goldstone, Julian S. **2** 1966
BR to 1967
Goodman, Peter, CF to 1969
Gordon, Haim 1967
To PJ 1967
PW to 1967
Gordon, Jeffrey 1968
CF to 1968
Gordon, Joseph **2** 1963
To RS? 1963
To ER 1964
RS to 1963
ER to **2** 1964
Gordon, Michael 1963
BR to 1964
Gordon, Mitchell 1962
BR to 1962
Gordon, Ronald W. 1968
Gordon, Sam, CF to 1969
Görög, I. 1969
Encl: proposal
CF to 1969
Gosse, Keith 1965
RS to 1965
Goswamuy, Shyam 1966
RS to 1966
Goyal, Narendra, BR to 1963
Graeff, Thomas L. **2** 1964
Encl: leaflet
RS to 1964
Grant, Allen Frederick 1962
BR to 1962
Grant, Edmund 1962
Encl: l. to *The Guardian* 1962
RS to 1962
Graves, John 1963
Encl: photo, clippings
BR to 1963
Gray, Camilla 1963
Encl: invitation
BR to 1963
Gray, Guy W. S. **2** 1968
CF to **2** 1968
Gray, J. O. D. G., BR to 1966
Grayson, Jeffrey 1962
BR to 1962
Greek Society for Nuclear Disarmament, Bertrand Russell (Michael Peristerakis) 1966
Encl: form l., appeal
BR to 1966
Green, Anthony **2** 1962
BR to **2** 1962

Green, S.W. 1963
Encl: pamphlet, Green to National Council for the Abolition of Nuclear Weapons Tests (Mrs. Jones), draft leaflet
BR to 1963
Greene, Felix, BR to 1963
Greene, Graham, BR to 1968
Greet, Dr., BR to 1964
Gregor, Norman, BR to 1964
Gregory, C. C. L., to BRPF ... 1964
RS to 1964
Gregory, Frank, CF to 1968
Gregory, M., to BRPF 1968
DN to 1968
Griffen, William L. .... n.d.
Encl: leaflet
Griffith, David 1958
BR to 1958
Grigoletto, Getulio G. 1969
PW to 1969
Griicrush 1962
Grooms, John, RSt. to 1967
Gross, William F. 1965
To RS 1965
RS to **2** 1965
Grosser, Willi 1962
BR to 1963
Encl: note by BR
Grunbaum, M. 1967
Encl: clipping
RS to 1967
Grupo Cultural Melchor Ocampo (greeting c.) 1968
Guerin, M., BR to 1966
Guha, A.K. 1963
BR to 1963
Guillaume, A. 1962
BR to 1962
Guimarães, Murilo Humberto de Barros 1964
Guppy, Nicholas, ER to 1963
Gupta, Anirudha 1965
PW to 1965
Gupta, Shri Prakash,
RS? to 1962
Gutman, Jeremiah S. 1969
CF to 1969
Guttman, Simon,
CF to **2** 1968

H

Hachenberger, Werner,
BR to 1966
Hacopian, Roland, to
BRPF 1966
RS to 1966
Hadje, ?, BR to 1959
Hagerty, Jr., Mr. and Mrs. H. R., BR to 1966
Hague, T.E. 1962
BR to 1962
Hahn, Mrs. Joseph **2** 1964-5
BR to 1965
PW to 1965
Hahn, Kurt 1967
Encl: literature concerning Rudolf Hess, booklet
CF to 1967
Hailsham, Lord 1962
BR to 1962
Hainsworth, Malcolm,
to RS 1965
RS to 1965
Hajda, Joseph **9** 1962-7
Encl: essays, postcards
BR to **4** 1962-4
CF to 1965
PW to 1967
Halfhill, Robert
Wakefield **4** 1962-9
Encl: clipping
BR to **2** 1962-3
RS to **2** 1966-9
CF to 1969
Halifax, Lord 1941
BR to 1941
Hall, W. J., BR to 1966
Hallgren, Carl, to BRPF 1965
RS to 1965
Hamai, Shinzo, to RS 1962
Encl.
BR to 1963
Hameed, S. A. 1964
Hamlin, Jerome **3** 1962-5
BR to **3** 1962-4
RS to **2** 1963-5

Hammer, Mrs. Anselm 1965
BR to 1965
Hammer Film Productions (Dennison Thorton) to Michael Randle 1961
Hancock, Bertram (form l., leaflet) 1965
PW to 1965
Hankinson, Wendy 1962
To BRPF 1963
BR to **2** 1962-3
CF to 1963
Hansden, Martin 1965
Hansen, Aslak 1969
Hansler, W. D. 1963
CE to 1963
Harcourt, J. T. **5** 1962-3
Encl: leaflet, clipping
BR to **3** 1962-3
Harding, Neville, to RS 1962
To ER **2** 1964
RS to 1962
CF to 1964
Harlem Youth Opportunities Unlimited, Inc. (K. B. Clark), RS to 1964
Harlowe, Marie 1965
RS to **2** 1965
Harman, C. L. 1966
Harman, W. R., BR to 1964
Harod, H. 1963
Harries, Morfudd, PW to 1965
Harris, H., CE to 1963
Harris, John Robert 1964
To CF 1964
BR to 1964
CF to 1964
Harris, Judith 1968
Encl: Xerox of clipping
CF to 1968
Harris, Morgan 1967
CF to 1967
Harrison, III, Bradford 1962
BR to 1962
Hart, Alex, to *The Times* 1969
Harvard-Radcliffe Committee to End the War in Vietnam (John Barzman) 1966
BR to 1966
Hauber, W. J. R.,
BR to **2** 1964
Hawkes, Anthony 1969
CF to 1969
Hawkins, Dora 1962
BR to 1962
Hawkswell, Marjory L. 1967
BR to 1967
Hayes, Bryan, to CF 1965
CF to 1965
Head, Viscountess Dorothea **3** 1966
To BRPF 1966
BR to **4** 1966
RS to 1966
Encl: note
Healey, Albert, to BR *et al.* 1968
Heckstall-Smith, Hugh W. ... 1958
Encl: questionnaire
BR to 1958
Encl: replies to questionnaire
Heelas, Terence 1963
To RS 1964
BR to **2** 1963-4
RS to 1964
Heidelberger, Michael 1964
BR to 1964
Heilmann, Albert 1955
Encl.
Heiner, Gianni A. 1963
BR to 1963
Heiser, Bryan M. 1963
CE to 1963
Heisler, Francis **3** 1958-69
To RS 1962
BR to **2** 1958-69
Heller, Howard 1967
To BRPF **4** .... n.d.
BR to **2** 1964
CF to 1964
HR to 1965
RS to 1965
PW to 1967
Hendricks, Henry W. 1963
Encl: transcripts of court proceedings
BR to 1963
Hendrix, P. 1967
RS to 1967
Heney, John **4** 1966-8

To RS 1967
RS to 2 1966-7
BR to 2 1966-8
Henry, Maurice, to RS .... n.d.
Henry, Rondel D. .... n.d.
Henson, Barbara 1962
Encl: note
BR to 1962
Herbath, J. V. 1965
CF to 1965
Hermenau, Herman P. 1965
PW to 1965
Herneck, Friedrich 2 1966
BR to 3 1963-4
RS to 1966
Herrington, Richard A. 1963
BR to 1963
The Alice Herz Peace Fund
(Shingo Shibata) 1967
Encl: Vietnam Women's Union
Standing Committee (Phan
Thi An) to Shibata 1966
essay, chapter of book
BR to 2 1966-8
Herz, Hermann 1967
RSt. to 1967
Hess, Wolf Rudiger 1967
Encl: petition concerning
Rudolf Hess
Hester, Hugh B. 1963
Encl: l. to *The Times*?
BR to 1967
Hewgil, John, to RS 2 1966
RS to 1966
Hewitt, David, to BRPF 1968
PW to 1968
Heyn, Herman M. 2 1966
BR to 1966
Hickerson, George H. 1963
Encl: form ls.
BR to 1963
Hickey, Helen, and
Finucan, Michael 1969
CF to 1969
Hicks, Calvin, BR to 1966
Hicks, N., CF to 1968
Higgs, G., to BRPF 1969
CF to 1969
Highams, S. 1963
BR to 1963
Highsmith, D. J. 1964
RS to 1964
Hijner, C., and Groen, H. 1969
CF to 1969
Hilburn, John E. 1964
Hilgart, Arthur 1967
Hill, L. 1962
BR to 1962
Hill, Marion S. 1968
Hill, Maurice 1969-70
BR to 2 1963-4
CF to 1969
Hill, W. W. 1963
To BRPF 1964
AY to 1963
RS to 1964
Walter Hill's Poster Advertising
Co. Ltd. (N. H.
Gardner) 2 1962
Hintze, Mrs. Edward,
to BRPF .... 1965?
Hirfan, S., to BRPF 1965
PW to 1965
Hiroshima Day Committee (J.
Baggen) 1965
RS to 1965
Hiroshima House Foundation
(Ira Morris) .... n.d.
Encl: form ls., brochure
Hirsch, Roland A.,
BR to 1963-4
Hirsch, Sigismundo 1962
Encl: Xerox of clippings,
booklet, l. to President Kennedy
BR to 1962
Hitchens, Christopher 3 .. 1966-7
BR to 1966
CF to 1967
RS to 1967
Hoashi, Kei (curriculum
vitae, photos) .... n.d.
BR to 1966
Hodgkin, Dorothy 2 1967
BR to 2 1967
Hodgkin, Thomas 1967
BR to 1967
Hoegler, Michael 1962
BR to 1962
Hoffer, Frances M. (page from
newsl.) 1963

Hoffman, Paul G., BR to 1964
Hoffman, Richard C. 1962
Encl: l. to Senator Paul Douglas
BR to 1962
Hofstatter, Moritz 1968
Encl: essays, clipping
Hoggart, David, RS to 1965
Holdershaw, C. 1966
CF to 1967
Hollis, F. R., to BRPF .... n.d.
Holt, Julian 1966
PW to 1966
Home Office (L. S. Finerly) ... 1962
BR to 1966
RS to 1966
The Homosexual Law Reform Society (A. J. Ayer *et al.*) (form ls., annual report) 1963-6
Hone, Basil 1969
Honey, P. J., BR to 1963
Hooper, Denis E., BR to 1963
Hooper, R. G. 1966
CF to 1966
Hope, Karen 1969
To CF 1969
CF to 2 1969
Hopkins, Peter 1966
BR to 1966
Horak, Jan 1968
Encl: s.
Horbatiuk, Peter 1965
RS to 1965
Horn, Mrs. Rae P. 1967
To RSt. 1968
RSt. to 1968
Horne, Geoffrey M. .... 1964?
CE to 1964
Horne, John G., to BRPF 1965
CE to 1964
RS to 1965
Hornstein, D. 1963
BR to 2 1963
Hosegood, J. Edmund, to BRPF 1964
Hoult, T., BR to 1967
House of Commons (copy of *Hansard*) 1968
The House of Free Speech (Nicholas Selvablancos) (form l.) 1966
House of Lords (form ls. re leaves of absence, cheque receipt, writ of summons to Parliament) 1961-6
BR to Lord Lucan 1961
Housing Ad Hoc Committee (form l., leaflet) .... n.d.
Hovell, Harry 2 1968
To CF 1968
BR to 1968
CF to 1968
Howes, Kenneth 1963
BR to 1963
Howland, Larry 1964
RS to 1964
Howson, Joan 1962
Encl: magazine page
Huang, Wen-Shan, to RS 1965
RS to 1965
Hubbard, John H. 1967
CF to 1967
Huddleston, Jr., James L. ... 1963
BR to 1963
Hughes, Cyril 1965
BR to 2 1964-5
Hughes, John 1963
BR to 1963
Hughes for Senate (Jerome Grosseman) .... n.d.
BR to .... n.d.
Human Relations and Communications Today (Quintin Whyte) 1962
Encl: extract from l.
Humphrey, J. H. 1962
Encl: petition
BR to 1962
Humphrey, Terence J. 1967
To CF 1967
CF to 2 1967
Hunnius, F. C., to CF 1962
To BRPF 1964
Encl: change of address c., brochure
CF to 4 1962-3
Hunt, Helen, to BRPF 1968
PW to 1968
Hunt, R. A., to BRPF 1965

PW to 1965
Hunter, Anne 1963
BR to 1963
Hunter, Coll M., to BRPF ... 1964
Hurtado, Jose Arata (note by CF) 1969
Hurwitz, Leo, BR to 1966
Husein, Ahmed, RS to 1964
Huston, Ervin L. 1965
BR to 1965
Hutchings, J. F. 1955
Encl.
Hutchinson, Royal D., to BRPF 1968
CF to 1968
Hutchison, Jean 1965
BR to 1965
Huxley, Christopher V., to BRPF 1967
Huybrechts, Paul, to BRPF .. 1968
RSt. to 1968
Hyland, Matthew P. **4** 1961-3
Encl: l. to Senator Michael J. Mansfield, clipping, brochure
BR to **4** 1963-4

I

Illyas, H. M. 1968
CF to 1968
Les Indépendants Republicains Yéménites (Mohamed Said Al-Attar) to RS 1967
Encl.
RS to 1967
Independent Labour Party (Alistair Graham, Wilfrid Wigham, Harry Mukherjee) **3** 1962-5
To BRPF 1965
Encl: form l.
BR to 1962
CF to 1962
HR to 1965
The Independent Nuclear Disarmament Election Committee (Michael Craft, N. Feltz, J. Gittings, Richard Gilbert) **3** 1963-5
Encl: leaflet, form l.
BR to **4** 1963-4
RS to **2** 1964-5
The Indonesian Organization for Afro-Asian Peoples Solidarity (Masao Kitezawa and Yoko Kitazawa) to Osmon Blackburn 1966
Encl: appeal
RS to 1967
Infeld, Leopold 1955
The Institute for Strategic Studies (Leonard Beaton, Y. Streatfield) 1964
BR to 1964
RS to 1964
Institute for Training in Non-Violence (Fred H. Blum) to BRPF 1965
Encl.
RS to 1965
The Institute of National Planning (I. H. Abdel-Rahman) to RS 1963
The Intelligentia Committee of Karachi (Hasan Rijni) 1968
CF to 1968
International Balzan Foundation (Ulisse Mazzolini) 1963
To RS **3** 1964
Encl.
BR to **3** 1963-4
RS to **3** 1964
The International Children's World Peace Crusade (Elsa Hicks), BR to 1963
The International Club 1965
BR to 1965
International Confederation for Disarmament and Peace (Kenneth Lee, Gerry Hunnius) **2** 1963-4
To CF 1965
Encl: brochure, form l.
BR to **4** 1963-4
HR to 1965
International Congress of Mathematicians (Mischa Cotlar) **2** 1962
BR to 1962

Institut für Weltwirtschaft an der Universität Kiel (Dr. Muziol, Hildegard Weichert) **2** 1964
BR to 1964
International Fellowship of Reconciliation (E. Philip Eastman) to PW 1964
Encl: form ls., petition
BR to 1962
International Institute for Peace (S. W. Molodtsov, V. Duncan Jones, F. Vigne, A. A. Pellizzari) (form l., petition) **2** 1958-68
International League Against Conscription (Charles R. Manning, Jr.) 1967
Encl: leaflet
CF to 1967
International League for Peace and Universal Brotherhood (Gabriel Ruiz Jaime), BR to 1963
International Learning Systems Corporation Limited (M. Langford) 1969
International Liaison Committee of Organisations for Peace (Niels Mathiesen) to RS **4** 1963
To CF 1963
CF to 1963
RS to 1963
International Literary Agents (John Wolfers), CF to 1967
International Peace March (E. P. Menon) 1962
Encl: leaflet with BR quote
BR to 1962
International Registry of World Citizens (Patrick Armstrong *et al.*) **4** 1966-8
Encl: leaflets, declaration
BR to 1966
International Review Service (A. G. Mezerik), CF to 1969
International Union of Students (Zbynek Vokrouhlický) **5** 1963-6
RS to 1966
Internationale der Kriegsdienstgegner (Ossip K. Flechtheim, Alois Stoff, Christa Clausen) **3** 1963-5
To David Prassah 1963
To AY 1963
Encl: form l., political literature
BR to **4** 1963-6
AY to 1963
RS to 1964
PW to 1965
The Iona Community (Lord MacLeod of Fuinary) 1967
BR to 1967
Iowa Socialists League (Donald L. Barnett) to CF 1965
PW to 1965
Iranian Students Scholarship Fund (K. Chakeri) to BRPF 1966
PW to 1966
CF to **2** 1967
The Irish Democrat (C. Desmond Greaves) 1966
Encl: p.c.
Isenberg, Howard 1966
BR to 1966
Islam, M. S. 1966
Encl: Jamel N. Islam to BR 1966
RS to 1966
Islam, Tajul **2** 1965-7
To RS **2** 1964-6
To PW 1965
Encl: article
RS to **3** 1964-6
PW to 1965
BR to 1967
Ispahani, M. A. H. 1966
Encl: booklets
BR to 1966
Issel, Karl-Heinz, BR to 1964
Italian Communist Party .... 1966?
Encl: form ls., journal
Italian Peace Committee 1965
Ivory, Paul, *et al.*, to BRPF 1966
BR to 1966

J

Jackson, D. E. 1962
Encl: clipping
BR to 1962
Jacobson, S. 1962
To AY 1963
BR to 2 1962-3
CF to 1963
Jaeger, Friedrich, to BRPF ... 1965
RS to 1965
Jaffer, Ahmed E. H. **3** 1966-8
Encl: greeting card, clippings, page from journal, form ls.
BR to **7** 1966-8
The Jaffna Thirukkural Cultural Society (C. Navaratnam) 1961
Encl.
BR to 1962
Jagoda, Ilsnen? 1967
Jahnke, Peter, to BRPF **2** .... 1967?-8
CF to 1968
RSt. to 1968
Jaikervi, Altaf H. 1966
Encl: essay
RS to 1966
James, Bert 1962
NJ to 1962
James, N. 1968
Jamieson, G. L., to BRPF **2** 1964-5
To CE 1964
To PW **2** 1965
CE to **2** 1964
BR to 1964
PW to 1965
RS to 1965
Janjua, M. K. 1967
CE to 1964
BR to 1967
CF to **3** 1968-9
The Japan Council Against Atomic and Hydrogen Bombs (Kaoru Yasui, Ichiro Moritaki, Yoskikiyo Yoshida) **6** .. 1962-9
To RS 1962
Encl: clippings, conference proceedings, report, article
BR to **4** 1962-9
Japan "Peace for Vietnam!" Committee, BR to 1966
Javsicas, Gabriel 1957
Encl: re Milovan Djilas
Jaydvidya, C. 1961
BR to 1962
Jehali, Hussain .... 1963?
BR to 1963
Jemmett, J., to BRPF 1967
To RSt. 1968
CF to 1968
Jenkins, C., PW to 1966
BR to 1966
Jensen, Erik Vagn, BR to 1966
Jepson, Charles A., to BRPF? .... n.d.
RS to 1965
Jerome, A., to BRPF? 1969
Jersey Association for Nuclear Disarmament (John E. Gale and Reginald C. Statt) 1962
BR to 1962
Joe, Calypso, to RS **2** 1963
Encl: songs
RS to **2** 1963-5
Johansen, Ivar, to BRPF 1969
John, Brian, to BRPF 1965
To PW **2** 1965
PW to **2** 1965
Johnson, Albert P. **2** 1962
BR to 1962
Jones, Thomas A. **2** 1962
BR to **2** 1962
Jones, Walter Benton, BR to 1964
Jopling, L. A. 1965
Encl: note
RS to 1965
Jordan, Joseph .... n.d.
NJ to 1962
Jordan, Patrick, to ER .... n.d.
CF? to 1967
Josephson, Eric .... n.d.
CF to 1967
Jowett, Harold Uttley 1962
To CF 1962
CF to **2** 1962
Jumabhoy, Amur, to RS? 1962
BR to 1962
Juzwiak, C., *et al.* 1962
BR to 1962

K

Kahane, W. **4** 1963-5
To RS? **2** 1963-5
To AY 1963
BR to **3** 1963-5
AY to 1963
RS to **3** 1965
Kahn, J. M. 1964
BR to 1964
Källberg, Sture, BR to 1966
Kampagne für Abrüstung Ostermarsch der Atomwaffengegner (Andreas Buro, Klaus Vack) 1964
Encl: form ls., leaflets, political literature
Kampagnen mod Atomvåben (Carl Scharnberg, Steffen Larsen) 1961
Michael Randle to 1961
BR to 1961
Kane, John F., BR to 1963
Encl: cartoon
Kaplan, Albert **2** 1963-7
To RSt. **4** 1967-8
Encl: articles
BR to 1963
RSt. to **4** 1968
Kaplan, Howard S. 1965
To RS **2** 1965
RS to **2** 1965
Kapluck, Manfred, BR to 1966
Karalasingham, V. 1968
CF to 1968
Kashmir Committee for Afro-Asian Peoples Solidarity (Amanullah Khan) 1966
BR to **2** 1966
Kassebaum, Robert G., BR to 1963
Kastler, A., CE to **2** 1963
Kaston, Maryna 1963
AY to 1963
Katayama, Kazuo 1967
Encl: petition, clipping
BR to 1967
Katzman, Eleanor and Sam . . . 1967
BR to 1967
Kaylon, Charles 1964
RS to 1964
Keats, Mark 1966
BR to 1966
Keck, Alan J. 1969
PW to 1969
Keeler, W. S., to DN? 1968
PW to 1967
RSt. to 1968
Keet, D. L. 1965
CF to 1965
Keister, John R. 1963
To AY 1963
To the British Who Killed Kennedy? Committee 1968
Encl: note to *Peace News*, article, Xerox of journal page
BR to 1963
AY to 1963
CF to 1968
Keith, Jr., Carl, to CE **2** 1963
CE to **2** 1963
Keller, Hans, to RS 1962
The John F. Kennedy Foundation (Joseph K. von Arb) 1964
Kepper, Douglas 1969
To Vietnam Solidarity Campaign 1966
PW to 1964
CF? to 1966
Kern, Coralee, to BRPF 1965
Kertesz, D. 1962
Ketzalkoatl (J. A. Bautista Orozco) 1968
To BRPF 1965
Encl: deed of covenant, leaflet
Key, Theo, to RS . . . . n.d.
Khanji, A. J. **7** 1963-9
Encl: l. to *Times of India*, l. to President of India, l. to International League for the Rights of Man, 3 ls. to President of U.N.O., appeal p.c.s
BR to 1963
Khindaria, B., to BRPF **2** . . 1965
RS to 1965
Kiefer, Christie W. 1963
BR to 1963
King, Cecil, BR to 1964
King, Fergus 1963
BR to 1963

CF to 1964
King, J. 1964
Kirsch, Ida, BR to 1963
Kirsch, Irving 1963
BR to **3** 1963
Kirschenbaum, Walter L. 1963
CF to 1963
Kinsey, Richard 1965
RS to 1965
Kissinger, Jr., William G.,
to BRPF .... n.d.
Klein, James **3** 1963-6
BR to **2** 1963-5
CE to 1963
Klüber, Theodor **4** 1962-7
Encl: leaflet, form ls., p.c.
BR to **3** 1962-7
RS to 1964
Knapp, Gertrude M.,
to RS **3** 1962-3
Encl: clipping
RS to 1964
Kneller, Glenn S. **3** 1965-6
BR to 1966
PW to **2** 1966
Knobel, Jakob 1964
To RS 1965
To BRPF **2** 1966-8
To RSt. **2** 1967
Encl: clippings
RS to 1964
RSt. to **4** 1967-8
Knottenbelt, Martin J. 1966
To BRPF? 1966
To DN **3** 1968
Encl: clippings, essays, form ls., l. to A. Dubcek, l. to *The Australian*
BR to **2** 1966
CF to 1966
CF to 1968
Koach, K.H. 1962
Encl: clipping
CF to 1962
Koch, Otto 1968
CF to 1968
Koekenbier, J. 1968
Encl.
BR to 1968
Koelling, Sidney 1968
Encl: declaration
Koffman, Josephine **5** 1963-7
To RS **3** 1965-7
To PW 1966
To RSt. **2** 1967
To BR and ER 1969
To CF **3** 1969
Encl: l. to Alistair Cooke, l. to Miss Sharp, ls. to *London Bulletin*
BR to 1963
PW to **2** 1966
RSt. to **4** 1967-8
CF to 1969
Kohlberg, Alfred 1958
Encl.
Kohls, Stanley 1966
BR to 1966
RS to 1966
Kohn, Phil, and Krinski, Beth,
to *New Statesman* 1963
BR to 1963
Kolko, Gabriel, BR to 1966
Komitee der Hundert (Fritz Meinicke) 1962
Komitee der Iranischen National-Front (B. Gharahbeiglu),
BR to 1963
Komitet do Spraw Radia i Telewizji (E. Uzdánski) 1962
Encl: booklet
BR to 1962
Kondor, Judith 1966
RS to 1966
Korbin, Kenneth **7** 1964-9
To BRPF .... n.d.
To CF 1965
BR to **4** 1964-6
CF to **4** 1965-9
Kreuzschule Dresden,
BR to 1966
Kreves, Eugene W. 1966
BR to 1966
Krishnan, O.N. 1963
To RS 1964
BR to **2** 1963
Kropp, Werner 1962
Encl: political literature
BR to 1963
Kuno, Osamu, CF to 1968

Kusin, Mr. **4** 1962-4
Encl: calling c., photo
BR to **2** 1963-4
Kyoto Buddhist Association .. 1966
Encl: political literature

L

Labadie Collection of Social Protest Literature (Edward Weber) to Who Killed Kennedy? Committee 1965
PW to 1965
The Labour Party (A. L. Williams *et al.*) **7** 1916-65
Encl: form ls., petition, booklet, annual report, Leeds agenda (1917), l. to Vietnam Solidarity Campaign (Faris Glubb), etc.
BR to 1965
RS to 1965
The Labour Peace Fellowship (Frank Allaun, Emrys Hughes *et al.*) **3** 1962-5
To RS 1962
Encl: form l., leaflets, annual report for 1969, note
RS to **2** 1962-5
CF to 1965
Lacasa, B. 1962
BR to 1963
Laguna, Jair R. Peixoto, to BRPF 1969
PW to 1969
Lambert, Eric 1963
Encl: clipping
BR to 1963
Langstone, G. A., to BRPF ... 1966
PW to 1966
Larnach, John 1966
BR to 1966
Lau, Philip, to BRPF 1969
PW to 1969
Launags, Freds 1962
BR to 1962
Laurin, Jean Mac. 1967
Encl: l. to UNESCO
DN to 1967
Lawford, Evelyn L. 1968
To CF **2** 1969
BR to 1968
CF to **2** 1969
Lawyers Committee on American Policy Towards Vietnam (Joseph Crown) 1967
BR to 1967
League for Democracy in Greece (Diana Pym, Frank Cropper) 1962
Encl: form ls., essay, petition
BR to 1962
Leary, Frank 1962
BR to 1962
Leavitt, Frank J. 1967
Encl: l. to IWCT
Lees, Thomas 1969
Leet, Don, and Schrag, Philip 1962
Encl: calling c., clipping
BR to .... n.d.
Leicester Secular Society (G. A. Kirk) 1953
Encl: BR's l. on Syngman Rhee
Lemilchama Wetipul Behazalet Rechush Yehudy (S. Webman) 1969
Encl: calling c., l.
Le Mouton, R. 1963
BR to 1963
Lenton Ward Labour Party (A. D. Gardiner) 1962
BR to 1962
Levi, Moise Victor, to The International League for the Rights of Man 1963
Levick, R. B. M. (political literature) .... 1965?
Lewis, Ed 1962
Encl: essay
BR to 1962
Lewis, Florence **2** 1968
To BRPF 1968
RSt. to **3** 1968
Leyden, Peter, to RS 1966
Encl: essay
Liberi e Svizzeri 1965
Light, Peter 1962
BR to **2** 1962-3

Ligue Belge pour la Défense des Droits de l'Homme (A. Walters) to BRPF 1965
Ligue Mondial pour la Paix (Georges Dejean) 1963
Likan, Barbara, to RS 1966
Encl: clipping
RS to 1966
Lim, Leng Soon, CF to 1969
Lima, Osorio 1963
BR to 1963
Lindeman, David B., to BRPF .... n.d.
Linden, F.C. (form l.) .... n.d.
Linsell, L. A. C., to BRPF ... 1968
Lippold, Kay 1964
BR to 1964
Little, R. P., to *Reader's Digest* and reply 1962
Little River High School (Jacquelyn Whitten) (form l.) 1969
Litvinoff, Emanuel, to RS 1963
To PW 1965
Encl: l. trans. by Litvinoff
BR to 1963
RS? to **2** 1964
CF to **4** 1964-7
PW? to **4** 1965-7
The Living Word Islamic Propagation Centre (Farouk Flowers) to BRPF **2** 1965
CF to 1965
Lobb, Warwick, to BRPF 1968
CF to 1968
Local Forum (Jerry Rothman) 1966
RS to 1966
Lock, Desmond 1962
RS to 1962
Loeber, R. M., BR to 1966
Logan, Mr. and Mrs. Jimmy, RSt. to 1967
Lolan, N. R., CF to **2** 1965
Lomax, Sir John 1963
Encl: essay
BR to 1963
The London Association for the Protection of Trade, CF to 1968
The London Committee for the Armenian Cause (Yedvard Gulbekian) 1965
BR to 1965
London Students' "Peace in Vietnam" Committee (Derek Boothman) 1965
CF to 1965
London Trade Union Peace Committee (Sam Butter) ... 1962
BR to 1962
Long, Rodney, to BRPF 1969
CF to 1969
Longstaff, D., CF to 1965
Longton, Denzil **2** 1964-6
BR to **3** 1964-6
Loots, W. 1968
Lopez, Ann 1962
BR to 1962
Lord, David **2** 1963-9
To BRPF **3** 1965-8
To CF 1969
To AY .... 196?
Encl: l. to *The Nation* (Cary McWilliams), l. to S. L. Holland, l. to National Committee for a Sane Nuclear Policy, l. to Jerome Frank, l. to Christianity and Crisis, calling c.
BR to **3** 1963-9
BR to 1966
CF to **5** 1968-9
Lord, F. M. 1964
Lorda Alaiz, F. M. 1958
BR to 1958
Loubeh, Silvio, to BR and DN 1969
To PW 1969
PW to **2** 1969
Loveman, Lenore **2** 1962-4
Encl: leaflet
BR to **2** 1962-4
Lubelska, Anna .... n.d.
RSt. to 1968
The Lucanian Fellowship, Ltd. (Colin Whillier) 1967
Encl: political literature
Luchins, Daniel 1965
PW to 1965
Lumsden, Malvern M., to

BRPF 1964
RS to 1964
Lurcy, Reine 1967
Luscombe, Leslie H. 1969
To PW 1969
Encl: l. to L. J. J. Nye, l. to W. J. H. Harris, synopsis of book
PW to 2 1969
Lustig, Jeremy, BR to 1966
The Albert Lutuli Rectorial Campaign (David Miller) 1962
Lutzenberger, Jose 1963
BR to 1963
CF to 1963

M

Maas, Elton R., to BRPF 1968
Maasing, Ulo 1967
MacDonald, J. Ramsay 1923
Mackenzie, Compton,
CF to 1964
MacLachlan, T. R.,
BR to 1966
Magalhães, Manuel Barbedo de 1969
Magarinos, Sophie 1969
CF to 1969
Maglione, Michael C. 1968
Mahdi, Molvi Ghazanfar 1967
RSt. to 1967
Mahida, Ebrahim Mahomed 1966
CF to 1966
Majumdar, Mukunda Bihar 1967
Encl: essay, leaflet
Mäkitalo, Arto 2 1966-8
Encl: speech
Malay, Steve, RS to 1964
Malhas, Lufti 1966
Encl: essay
Malhotra, A. K. 1962
BR to 1962
Malhotra, D. N. 1962
BR to 1962
Mall, Mahmood 7 1963-6
To NJ 1962
Encl: circulars, press releases
NJ to 1962
BR to 5 1963-5
PW to 1965
Encl: l. from PW to CF
Mallalieu, E. L. 1964
BR to 1964
Maloff, Peter 1966
Encl: speech
CF to 1966
Maltby, Veronica and Brian 1962
BR to 1962
Manacorda, Eduardo 1962
BR to 1962
Manas Publishing Company 1962
Encl: clipping
BR to 1962
Mandel, Ernest, to RS 1966
RS to 1966
Manes, Hugh R., to RS 1966
RS to 1966
Mann, Erika 1965
BR to 1965
Mann, Golo 2 1964
BR to 2 1964-5
Mannine, Alice 1967
Encl: poem
Manuel Navarre Luna Literary Workshop 1966
RS to 1967
Manwell, Clyde .... n.d.
Maraghee, Mrs. Farangees, to UN (U Thant) 1967
Maragides, Steve 1967
CF to 1967
Marák, V. 1968
March on Washington for Jobs and Freedom (Bayard Rustin) to RS 1963
RS? to 2 1963
March 16th Mobilization Committee (J. H. Cuthbert and Dave Galeshan) (form l.) .... n.d.
Encl: leaflet
Marchant, Kelly .... n.d.
Marchesi, Claudio, and Artioli, Mauro 1967
CF to 1967
Marchok, Michele 1964
RSt. to 1964
Marica, John 2 1962

Encl: form l., essay, circulars
BR to **3** 1962-3
Marin, John 1963
Encl: Christmas c.
BR to 1963
Markovitch, Micheal 1967
Encl: poem
Markus-Verlag GMBH
(form l.) 1967
Maroney, Jr., James N. 1968
Marques, Cândido 1963
BR to 1963
Marshall, Mildred H.,
to RS **3** 1965-6
Encl: petition, poem
RS to **2** 1965
Marston, Howard E. 1965
Encl: l. to Edward M. Kennedy
BR to 1965
Martin, Barnaby, to RS 1962
Encl: report
Martin, Betty Jean, CF to 1967
Martin, D., BR to 1963
Martin, George William 1963
Martin, Henry A., to
L. B. Johnson 1965
Martin, I. C. 1964
Martinet, Mme. Marcel,
BR to 1966
Martinez, J. M. (leaflet) ...... n.d.
Martinez, Sabastián
Murcia **2** 1962-8
BR to 1962
Martionetti, Thomas 1962
BR to 1962
Mashiach, Lea, BR to 1967
Mason, John J. 1962
CF to 1962
Matheson, P. C. .... n.d.
RS to 1965
Matthews, Florence 1962
BR to 1962
Matthews, John, CF to 1969
Matthews, R. D. .... n.d.
BR to 1962
Matthews, Richard .... n.d.
Matthews, Thomas M.
(circular) 1962
BR to 1962
Mauriac, François, BR to 1966
May, Andrew .... n.d.
May, Stephanie **10** 1962-5
Encl: l. to *Washington Evening Star*, l. to A. Stevenson, clipping
BR to **5** 1962-5
AY to 1962
Mayfield, Martin, to
BRPF **2** 1965
CF to 1965
RS to 1965
Mazzawi, Musa, to BRPF 1967
CF to 1967
McCabe, Michael, to BRPF .. 1966
RS to 1966
McClellan, Hugh D. 1969
McClure, David E. 1963
BR to 1963
McColl, Charles P. 1962
Encl: thank-you note
BR to 1962
McCormick, Carson, BR to ... 1963
McCormick, Thomas W.,
to BRPF 1969
PW to 1969
McFarland, Lilian C. **5** ... 1963-8
BR to **2** 1963-4
PW to 1965
McGlynn, T. R.,
to RS **4** 1965-7
Encl: envelope, l. from Austrian fascist organization to *New York Times*, fictionalization of post-World War II Axis victory
RS to **3** 1965-7
McIntosh, E. C. **3** 1962
Encl: l. from Dr. Breit to McIntosh, McIntosh's treatise on "The Apparent Expansion of a Universe of Constant Size"
BR to **3** 1962
McIntyre, Lindsay, BR to 1966
McKenzie, Patricia Anne 1962
BR to 1962
McLaughlin, John J. 1962
McManus, M. J., to BRPF ... 1964
RS to 1964
McNally, C. V., to RS? 1962

RS to 1962
McShane, Philip 1964
McWhirter, Norris, to RS 1964
Meally, Victor 1964
Encl: clippings
BR to 1963
Mechoulam, Alberto 1968
Medical Aid Committee for Vietnam (leaflets, reports, financial ss., newsls., invitations, tickets, advertisements) 1966-9
Medical Aid for Biafra Committee (H. M. Warby) 1969
BR to 1969
Meister, Zinovet Filipovich **2** 1963
BR to 1963
Melman, Seymour (l. from Alexander Kiefer, clippings) 1962
Menon, E. P. **3** 1962-3
To RS 1964
BR to **3** 1962-3
RS to **2** 1964
Merioneth Labour Party (Owen Edwards) 1960
Encl.
Merki, E. (leaflet) 1964
BR to 1964
Merle, Robert, to BRPF **2** 1966
Mertens, André 1962
Encl: circular, essay
Mertens, M. S. .... n.d.
Métraux, Daniel, Roper, Wilfred, and Sweeney, William 1965
RS to 1965
Meyer, I., BR to 1966
Meyer, Sarah 1967
RSt. to 1967
Mezerik 1969
Encl: l. from Postmaster, Portmadoc (J. Bulkeley)
Michaels, Cyrus 1964
To RS 1964
Encl: clipping
RS to **2** 1964
Middle East Non-Intervention Committee (circular) 1967
Midorikawa, Toru 1966
BR to 1966
Mielke, Lloyd L., to Xuan Thuy 1969
Mikhailusenko, Igor **17** ... 1962-9
Encl: clippings, p.c.s, photos
To CF 1968
To RS **2** 1962
BR to **4** 1962-3
RS to **2** 1963
CF to **2** 1968
Miklos, Szabo 1967
CF to 1967
Miliband, Ralph, to RSt. 1967
To CF 1968
RSt. to 1967
The Militant (George Lavan) .. 1963
BR to **2** 1963-6
Millar, Haldis 1962
BR to 1962
Miller, Frederick J. **3** ... 1969-70
Miller, Robert 1962
BR to 1962
Millett, Mervyn **13** 1962-9
To AY 1963
To RS **11** 1964-8
To CF **4** 1965-8
To Deirdre Griswold 1967
Encl: essay, circular, clippings, photos, l. to *Knoxshire and Mountain District Free Press*, l. from J. J. Leibler
BR to **8** 1962-6
AY to 1963
RS to **6** 1964-5
CF to **5** 1964-8
PW to 1965
Milne, John E. 1969
CF to 1969
Milton, Barry, AY to 1963
Minke, Fritz, BR to 1962
Minojetti, Luigi, to BRPF ... 1969
Minorsky, V. 1965
Minskers, Advokats J. 1966
Encl: envelope, mailing list, open l.—all concerning alleged Latvian war collaborators living in the West
BR to 1967
Miranda, Alvaro, to CF 1965

Encl: circular
CF to **2** 1965
Mirelman, José 1968
Encl: s.
Miro, Joan, BR to 1966
Miroslav, Subrt 1966
BR to 1966
Mirza, Akhtar 1965
Mission of the Malayan National Liberation League (P. V. Sarma) 1966
BR to 1966
RS to 1966
Mitchell, David, BR to 1967
Miyata, Matakatsu (circulars) 1962
Mkparu, E. C. 1968
Mobilisation Committee, Sydney (John Deer), RSt. to 1967
Modemann, Richard, *et al.* ... n.d.
Mohamed, Audrey 1968
CF to 1968
Mohan, Brij 1962
BR to 1962
Mohile, S. D. 1963
BR to 1963
Monaghan, L. W. 1964
To RS 1964
Encl.
RS to 1964
Mongar, J. L., to BRPF (essay) .... n.d.
RS to 1963
Monjardino, J., BR to 1966
Monod, Michel, BR to 1963
Monro, Jack 1964
Encl: leaflet
RS to 1964
Montenegro, Ilson Falcone, to BRPF 1967
RS to 1967
Montgomery, Lawrence 1963
BR to **2** 1963
Monti, Mario, to CF 1967
Monti, Raffaello **5** 1962-5
Encl: l. from Silvio Monti, invitation, advertisement
CF to 1964
RS to 1965
PW to 1965
Moody, Roger 1966
To RS **2** 1965
Encl: circular
RS to **2** 1965-6
PW to 1966
Moore, Henry, BR to 1966
Moore, J. T. 1966
RS to 1966
Moore, Lillian, to ER 1967
Morais, V. L. 1969
Encl: open l.
CF to 1969
Morgan, Ada M. 1963
BR to 1963
Morgan, Dorothy P., CF to 1963
Morgan, Patricia, to CF 1965
RS to 1965
Morgan Guaranty Trust Company (Sidney G. Butler) 1964
Moritaki, Ichiro (booklet, *New Morality for the Atomic Age*) .... n.d.
BR to **2** 1962-6
Morland, Simon 1968
CF to 1968
Morrell, Roy 1967
Encl: l. to *The Listener*
Morris, Edita 1958
Encl: essay on the effects of radiation poisoning
Mortada, Mary S. 1967
RSt. to 1967
Morton, B. D. 1965
BR to 1965
Encl: list of names
Moseley, Lorraine 1962
BR to 1962
RS to 1962
Moss, David **3** 1966-8
BR to 1966
CF to 1968
Moss, Norman, to RS **3** 1962-3
RS to **2** 1962-3
CE to 1963
Mount Roskill Citizens for Peace (Hilda M. Parry), BR to ... 1963
Mouvement contre l'Armement Atomique (Paris) (C.

Desnoyers, C. Bourdet) to
BRPF 2 1964-7
Mouvement de Jeunesse, Nice
(Jacques Vecker) 1965
Movement for Colonial Freedom
(Peggy Saunders, John Eber,
Barbara Haq) **4** 1967-8
To CF 5 1965
To RSt. 1967
Encl: leaflets, circulars
HR to 1965
PW to 1965
CF to 5 1965-8
RSt. to **3** 1967-8
BR to 2 1968
Movement for Human Rights
(K. Murad Bey) 5 1967
Encl: booklet, essay
BR to 1967
CF to 1967
Movement for the Liberation
of Portugal (Frente de
Libertação Nacional e
Colonial) (A. Norohna-
Rodrigues) 1967
RSt. to 1967
Movement of Support for the
Peoples of Angola and Other
Portuguese Colonies (M.
Heimann and M. Biolly),
CF to 1968
Movimento Cristão Brasileiro
pela Paz (Raimundo
Bezerra) 1962
BR to 1962
Movimento por la Paz y la
Soberania de los Pueblos
(Juan Marinello), BR to 1963
Mowshowitz, Israel, to RS ... 1965
RS to 1965
Moxon, Oliver 1966
BR to 1966
Moyer, Edward P. 1966
BR to 1966
Mukherjee, S.K. 1968
Muller, H.J. 1962
BR to 1962
Munk, Arthur W. 2 1962
BR to **3** 1962-4
Muñoz, Lorenzo
Garcia 2 1962-3
Encl: clipping
BR to 2 1962-3
Munro, Kenneth 2 1962
BR to 1962
Muret, André, BR to 1968
Murphy, T.M. 1962
CF to 1962
Murray, Alan, to BRPF 1965
PW to 1965
Murray, F. 1966
Murray, S.M. 1966
PW to 1967
Museum of Modern Art
(Mr. Hulton), BR to 1966
Musgrave, James L. 1965
RS to 1965
Musri, G.N. 1962
BR to 1962
Muste, A.J. **4** 1962-3
To CF 2 1962
Encl: l. to *New York Times*,
form l.
CF to **4** 1962
BR to **4** 1962-6
RS to 1963
Muta, Sueo, BR to 1964
Myers, Alvin 1967
Myers, G., to BRPF 1964
CF to 1964
Myrdal, Gunnar 2 1964
BR to 1964

N

NAACP (National Association
for the Advancement of
Coloured People) (form ls.,
brochures, return
envelope) 1967-8
Naeve, Virginia 2 1963-4
Encl: leaflets
BR to 2 1963-4
Encl: form l.
Nagar, D.S. 1966
The Nagasaki Council Against
A. and H. Bombs (Atsushi
Sugimoto) 1962
Encl: leaflet

BR to 1962
Nagel, Julian, to BRPF 1964
RS to 1964
Naheem, Abbas (l. to U Thant, l. in response from UN) 1967
Nahum, Hector 1962
Narayan, Jayaprakash, and Bhave, Vinoba, BR to 1962
Nanavaty, P. C. **4** 1962
Encl: text of an appeal to Kennedy and Khrushchev
BR to **2** 1962
Encl: form l.
Nash, Edward F. 1965
Nassis, J. 1962
Encl: s., poem
BR to 1962
Nathan, Abe 1965-8
Encl: pamphlet
BR to 1965
CF to 1966
National American Party (form l.) 1966
National Campaign for the Abolition of Capital Punishment (L. John Collins) 1969
BR to 1969
National Committee for the Control of Radiation Hazards (Hugh Keenleyside), BR to 1961
National Coordinating Committee to End the War in Vietnam, BR to 1966
National Council for Civil Liberties (Martin Ennals, Tony Smythe, Barry Cox) **5** 1962-8
To CF 1968
Encl: circular, invitation
BR to **3** 1963-8
RS? 1964
CF to **3** 1968
National Farmers Union (James Patton), BR to 1964
National Guardian (Gerald Long), BR to 1964
RSt. to 1968
National Mobilization Committee to End the War in Vietnam (circular) to BRPF .... n.d.
National Peace Council (George Delf) 1963
To BRPF 1963
Encl: advertisement
BR to 1963
National Tunisian Opposition (I. Tobal), BR to 1966
National Youth Conference (pamphlet reprinting BR's writings) .... n.d.
Neal, Charles E. **3** 1964-7
To BRPF 1965
To RS **3** 1965-7
Encl: petition
BR to **2** 1964
CF to **2** 1964-7
RS to **4** 1964-7
Nedelcovic, Bosco, to BRPF 1963
Encl: form l.
CE to 1963
Negro Advancement Council (form l.) 1967
CF to 1967
Neighbors, E. Laverne 1964
RS to 1964
Nelson, Floyd B. 1969
Nemoto, Chie, to AY 1963
AY to 1963
Neo-Marxist Movement (circular) .... n.d.
Neruda, Pablo, BR to 1966
Nettleton, Dick (poster) .... n.d.
CF to 1969
Nevers, Robert Allison 1968
Encl: résumé, leaflet, essay
Nevins, George 1963
BR to 1963
Nevo, Eviatar 1967
To CF **2** 1963
To RS 1967
To RSt. **3** 1967
CF to 1963
BR to 1964
RSt. to **3** 1967
New South Wales Humanist Society (W. G. Weeks, N.

Stenning) 1965
To CE 1964
To BRPF 1965
BR to 1963
CE to 1964
CF to 1964
PW to 1965
New York Committee for the General Strike for Peace (Rey Lofstedt?) (leaflet, form l.) .... n.d.
New York Federation of Anarchists 1966
BR to 1966
New Zealand Campaign for Nuclear Disarament 1963
Encl: leaflets
Newens, Stan 1966
BR to 1966
Newman, Sol 1962
Encl: poems, essay
BR to 1962
Nho, U (l. to Arnold Toynbee, open l. to "Intellectuals de Tous les Pays", cartoon, short essay) 1968
Niaz, S. D. 1966
Niazi, M. A. K. 1965
PW to 1965
Niblock, Tim 1967
Nice, Lester A. 1965
Nii, Masashi 1968
Encl: p.c., open l.
CF to 1968
Nike, William G. 2 1962
BR to 1963
Nimitz, Mildred 1962
BR to 1962
No Arms for Nigeria Campaign (advertisement, petition) ... 1969
Non-Violent Action in Vietnam (G. V. Vasudev) 1967
Encl: leaflets
CF to 1967
Nordahl, Bjorn .... n.d.
Norris, Gordon .... n.d.
BR to 1967
Norris, R. M., to BRPF 1965
North American Coalition for Biafran Relief (Peter Colasante), CF to 1969
Norvell, Daniel R., to CE 1965
PW to 1965
Norwood, Woody 1964
RS to 1964
Notario, Luis Arranz, to BRPF 1967
RSt. to 1968
Novak, Betty Jones 1962
BR to 1962
Nuclear War Information Centre (Stephen King-Hall) 1962
Encl: form l., charter of organisation
RS to 1962
Nunn, A. C. 1964
Encl: essay
BR to 1964
Nutley, Jack K. 1968
To CF 1968
CF to 1968

O

Obrenavic, Milan, CF to 1968
O'Brien, Conor Cruise, to RS 1967
PW to 1967
O'Brien, M. **3** 1963-7
Encl: ls. to Prime Minister Wilson, response from Political Office (J. Claessens)
To BRPF 2 1967-8
CF to 1967
RSt. to 1968
Ockels, John and Kay, to BRPF 1964
O'Connell, Pat 1962
BR to 1962
O'Connor, Donald M. 1963
BR to 2 1963
O'Connor, Jessie Lloyd and Harvey 1968
Encl: brochure
BR to 1968
Ofer, Ludwig .... 196?
Ofstad, Harald, BR to 1963
Ogbourne, John, Warpiuk,

Douglas, *et al.* 1965
BR to 1965
Oglesby, Leslie E.,
to BRPF 1964
O'Halloran, M. V. 1962
O'Hanlon, F. 1965
To RS 1965
Encl: p.c.
RS to **2** 1965
O'Hara, Coral, to BRPF 1968
Ohye, Mrs. Saburo 1964
BR to 1964
Oji, Ihejika Sam, BR to 1966
Okamoto, Tatsuo 1966
BR to 1966
Okishio, Nobuo, to RS 1965
RS to 1965
Oldhage, Hans **2** 1968-9
CF to 1969
Olinky, Oded 1967
One World Council
(James F. Ferrand) 1958
O'Neill, James P. 1966
To RS 1966
Abercrombie Mafufnik
(pp CF) to 1966
RS to 1966
O'Neill, William
Michael **2** 1969
Encl: address
CF to **2** 1969
Ong, T. S., to BRPF 1964
Ontario Institute for Studies in
Education (Anthony
Barton) 1970
CF to 1970
Operation Outrage (The North
American Coalition for
Biafran Relief) 1967
Encl: form ls., newsl.,
clippings
Operation Truth .... n.d.
Encl: leaflets, booklet
Oppenheimer, Ernest Kant
(circular) 1966
Oppenheimer, Frank 1965
Encl: course outline
PW to 1965
Oppenheimer, Paul .... 196?
RSt.? to 1968
Organisation des Nations Neutres
(Frédéric Fortoul) 1965
Encl: essay
RS to 1965
Orozco, J. A. Bautista de,
to BRPF 1965
RS to 1964
Orr, A., to BRPF 1966
PW to 1966
Osman, M. A. 1962
BR to 1962
RS to 1966
Ostermarsch der Atomwaffen-
gegner (A. Buro) to CF 1962
Encl: leaflets
CF to 1962
BR to 1963
Otter, Laurens, BR to 1963
CF to 1969
Oussedik, Maitre, BR to 1962
Encl: BR to Roger Briottet
Overseas Development Institute
Ltd. (William Clark) 1964
BR to 1964
Owen, Bob 1958
BR to 1958
Owen, O. W. 1969
Encl: pamphlet
CF to 1969
Oxford Committee for Famine
Relief **2** 1964-9
To CE **2** 1964
To CF **3** 1965-7
Encl: form ls., l. to J.
Nyerere, booklet
BR to 1964
CE to 1964
RS to 1965
CF to 1969
Oxon, Jennifer, to BRPF 1966
RS to 1966
Ozan, Evnur, to BRPF 1965
PW to 1965

P

Pacem in Terris (Jacob Greenberg,
Jean Caullet) **3** 1964-9
Encl: petition, circulars,

booklet, stickers, l. to College of Cardinals, clipping
BR to 1966
Paco (F. J. Rodriguez) .... n.d.
Page, Robert R. 1962
Pahor, Boris 1963
BR to 1963
Painter, Colin (translator) **2** .... 1962-?
To RS **2** .... n.d.
To AY 1963
Encl: p.c.
BR to **6** 1962-3
RS to **4** 1962-4
Pak-China Friendship (cable) 1966
Pakhtoon, Ganesha Singh **2** 1964-6
Pakistan National Oils Limited (Qazi Abdul Qadir) 1969
Pal, Yash, to *Times of India*
BR to **2** 1962-4
Palestine Liberation Organization (Youssef Azmeh) 1968
Palfreman, M. J., to BRPF 1965
CF to 1965
Pálosi, Catherine 1966
BR to 1966
Panakal, Thomas **5** 1963-7
To PW 1966
BR to **2** 1963-4
RS to **2** 1963-4
PW to 1966
Papworth, John 1965
To CF **2** 1965
To RS 1965
Encl: essay, list of suggestions for BRPF fund-raising
CF to **2** 1965
RS to 1965
PW to 1965
Encl: l. from BR to "To whom it may concern", 1963
Paranagama, D. M., to BRPF 1968
RS to 1968
Pare, Mrs. Eugene 1969
PW to 1969
Parera, Francisco
Abad **2** 1962-3
BR to **2** 1962-3
Parish, David P. 1967
Parivar, Ali, to RS 1964
RS to 1964
Parker, Dave?, to PW 1965
PW to 1965
Parker, Elsie 1966
BR to 1966
Parker, Howard Marion (political literature) .... n.d.
Parliamentary Group for World Government (P. Armstrong, W. Hildred) **4** 1958-69
Encl: circulars, Memorandum to the Prime Minister, receipt
CF to 1969
Parmar, S. S. 1962
BR to 1962
Parmenter, Enid 1962
BR to 1962
Parmer, Devore 1967
La Parole de Popolo to Socialist International and Asian Socialist Conference (draft l.) 1966
Pasternak, Aleksander,
BR to **2** 1963-6
Patel, B. V., BR to 1964
Paterson, J. Craig 1969
Patterson, Mark **2** 1965
To PW 1966
Encl: ls. to L. B. Johnson, H. Humphrey, Ho Chi Minh; bibliography, photo
PW to 1966
Pattinson, R. C., to BRPF ... 1964
RS to 1964
Pauling, Linus 1963
To RS 1963
Encl: l. from Pauling's lawyer (Heisler & Stewart), cablegram, ls. from Pauling and BR to Khrushchev
BR to **3** 1963
Paull, Thomas Eggington 1967
Paynter, W., CF to 1965
Peace and Freedom Party of California (Fred Bunnell, Clifford Humphrey) (form

l.) ... 1968
Encl: position paper
Peace Association (Kutlay Ebiri) **3** ... 1966
To RS ... 1966
BR to ... 1966
RS to **2** ... 1966
Peace Council of the German Democratic Republic (Heinz Willman, K. Hälker) ... 1962
To CF ... 1965
Encl: memoranda, form l.
BR to ... 1962
Peace in Vietnam Committee (Socialist Society) ... 1965
The Peace Lodge of the Theosophical Society (H. Redfern) to BRPF ... 1964
The Peace Movement in Linköping (Christer Fellman) ... 1967
RSt. to ... 1968
Peace Pledge Union (Bernard Withers) ... 1964
Encl: leaflets
Peace Publications Limited ... 1965
Encl: note, p.cs., book list
Peace Research Institute (Oslo) (questionnaire filled in by BRPF) ... 1964
Pearson, C. J. ... 1967
Pearson, Frances, to BRPF ... 1963
CF to ... 1963
Peat, Sidney H. ... 1966
Encl: note to *The Minority of One*, clipping
CF to ... 1966
Pehkonen, Elis ... 1964
BR to (form l.) ... 1964
Pelegri, Antoni ... 1962
Pellegrini, Anne, BR to ... 1968
Pellegrini, Gesualdo ... 1968
Penberthy, Tom ... 1967
CF to ... 1967
Pence, Joseph A., to BRPF ... 1962
Pence, Walter, BR to ... 1964
People's Co-operative Bookstore Association (William Philipovich) to BRPF ... 1966
PW to ... 1966
Percikow, Henri ... 1965
Encl: poem
RS to ... 1965
Perlman, Nathan D. **3** ... 1962-3
Encl: questions, leaflet, photos, note
BR to ... 1962
AY to ... 1963
Perlongo, Robert, BR to ... 1966
Peters, Charles R., to BRPF ... 1965
RS to ... 1965
Petruzzellis, Joseph, and Davey, Mark A. ... 1962
BR to ... 1962
Pettyjohn, Bob, to BRPF ... 1967
Pezzagno, Bramante ... 1966
RS to ... 1966
Pflug, Raymond J. ... 1963
BR to ... 1963
Phelps, Jon ... 1965
To BRPF ... 1965
BR to ... 1965
RS to ... 1965
Phillips, Glyn O. ... 1964
BR to ... 1964
Phinney, W. P., to L. B. Johnson ... 1967
Pic, Roger, RSt. to ... 1968
Pierce, C. S. ... 1967
Pierce, David ... 1969
CF to ... 1969
Pierce, S. H. ... 1962
BR to **2** ... 1962-3
Pillow, Woll, to BRPF ... 1967
Pipon, H. C. P. **3** ... 1963-4
Encl: l. to *The Times*
BR to ... 1963
RS to ... 1964
Plá, Manuel ... 1962
BR to ... 1963
Plant, E. N. ... 1964
BR to ... 1964
Playford, John, to BRPF **2** ... 1966
RS to **2** ... 1966
Pleas, David R. ... 1962
BR to ... 1962
Pliskina, E. T. ... 1963
BR to ... 1963
Plochmann, Carolyn G. ... 1963

Encl: photos, clipping, resumé
BR to 1963
Plogstedt, Sibylle, to BRPF ... 1965
RS to 1965
Ploog, Jürgen, to and from
Allen & Unwin Ltd. 1965
PW to 1965
Plum, Niels Munk,
BR to 2 1964
Plummer, Howard 1968
Encl: essay, Xerox articles
from *The Progressive*
Poger, Ruth, BR to 2 1964
Poggioli, Yves, BR to 1963
Poldy, Franzi 1966
PW to 1966
Polish Cultural Fund (Count
Zamoyski) (form l.) 1969
Polk, David C. 1970
CF to 1970
Pollio, Armando, to BRPF ... 1962
Polonkey, C. James, to AY ... 1962
AY to 1962
Pomeroy, William J. and
Celia 1964
To RS 2 1966-7
BR to 1964
CF to 1964
RS to 2 1966-7
PW to 1967
Ponte, Lowell 1969
Poorman, Roy T. 2 1962-5
Encl: s. for distribution
in England
BR to 1962
RS to 1965
Popp, F. C., BR to 1964
Poremsky, V. 1969
Encl: Western scientists' response
to Sakharov's 1968 memo
Portele, Gerhard, and
Stallwitz, Walter **3** 1963
Encl: demonstration plan
BR to **4** 1963
Portuguese Students Association
Committee in Great Britain
(Jose Laranjo) to BRPF 1966
Encl: conference s.
RS to 1966
Potter, D. F. 1962
Pottle, Pat, *et al.* from
prison 1962
To RS 1962
RS to 1962
Encl: note re Pottle by
BR 1963
Powell, C. F. 2 1967-8
Encl: paper, form l.
BR to 2 1967-8
Powell, Joan 2 1964
CE to 1964
Encl: form l. (from BR, 1963)
Powell-Evans, John 1963
Encl: text of article, clipping
BR to 1963
Powers, C. A. 1962
Powers, F. 1965
Encl: l. to *The Guardian*
RS to 1965
Pownall, A. 1965
PW to 1965
Pozniak, Richard A., BR to .. 1966
Prain, Ronald L. 1964
BR to 1964
Prakash, Marcia 1966
Prasad, C. S. 1962
Prasad, V. V. 2 1966-7
Encl: leaflet, ls. from and to
Prasad's employer
BR to 2 1966-8
Pratap, Raja Mahendra 2 ... 1962
Encl: leaflet, circular
BR to 1963
Premananda, M. 1964
Prescott, Cornelia 2 1964
BR to 1964
CE to 2 1964
Presidencia de la Republica,
México, El Secretario Privado
(Humberto Homero) 1964
Presmont, John 1962
BR to 1962
Pressman, Gillian (poem) 1962
Prewett, J. Neill, to RS 1966
Encl: leaflets
RS to 1966
Price, Anthony, to
BRPF 2 1965
HR to 1965
PW to 1965

Priestley, Jaquetta 1958
Primeklles, Leon, to BRPF ... 1962
Pringle, Frank E. 1963
BR to 1963
Prismon, Donald, to RS 1966
BR to 1966
Prison Reform Council (Ella Salthouse) **2** 1963
Encl: leaflets, reports
BR to 1963
Prisoner of Conscience Library (A. Braithwaite) 1966
Pritchard Jones, Hugh, to BR and ER **3** 1962-3
To ER 1961
Encl: l. to newspaper(?), essay
BR to **2** 1963
ER to **2** 1964
Pritchard, W. D. N., to BRPF 1966
PW to 1966
Probyn, Brian, CF to **2** ... 1962-3
Project Unilat (H. A. J. Martin) 1964
Encl: leaflet
Pronina, N. I. 1962
BR to 1963
Propaganda Voor Federale Wereld-regering (H. A. C. v. d. Kraan) 1966
BR to 1966
Protest Movement Against the Plan for Nuclear Missile Sites in South Eastern France 1965
Encl: circular
Prunair, Jacques, to BRPF **2** 1968
PW to 1968
Ptacek, Paul **6** 1963-5
BR to **3** 1963
Pugwash Continuing Committee (J. Rotblat) **8** 1963-9
To RS **2** 1962-3
Encl: circular, l. to *The Observer*, essay, reports, form l., l. from ER to RS
ER to **2** 1960-1
RS to **3** 1962-5
RSt. to 1963
CF to 1965
BR to **7** 1966-9
Pullium, Jr., Ray 1965
RS to 1965
Pullrick, G. F., to BRPF 1964

Q

Quail, Bernard, to NJ 1962
To RS 1962
NJ to 1962
RS to 1962
Quaker Action Group (circular, leaflet) 1968
Quaker Group, Wellingborough (cable) 1968
Quebec-Washington-Guantanamo Walk for Peace (Mary Suzuki) to CF 1964
Queensland Peace Committee for International Co-operation and Disarmament (Mrs. N. Chalmers) 1963
BR to 1963
Quintanilla, Luis **4** 1967-9
BR to 1967
CF to 1969
Qureshi, Muhammad Siddique 1966

R

R., U. P. 1962
Encl: open l. to world leaders
Rabelo, Genival 1968
Encl: manifesto, clipping
Racherbäumer, Jürgen H., to *The Observer* 1963
Racy, R.F. 1961
To RS 1961
Rada, Jirí, and Dinda, Joseph 1963
BR to 1963
Radcliffe, J. M. **2** 1958
BR to 1958
Radford, Jim (mimeos) .... n.d.
Radical Alliance (M. Craft, K. Burdon, Richard

Gott) 5 1965-6
Encl: newsls.
BR to 965
RS to 1966
PW to 1966
Radical Education Project (Ted
Steege) to BRPF 2 .... n.d.
RSt. to 1967
Radice, Francis W. .... n.d.
RS to 1966
Radio Free Zimbabwe Committee
(G. Matatu) 3 1969
CF to 3 1969
Raffles, G., RS? to 1964
Raj, V. S. Durai 1968
Raja, S., to Secretary-General
of UN 1966
Rajagopal, A. (leaflets) .... n.d.
Rajagopalachari, C., to the
Swarajya, Madras
BR to 1962
Ramaswamy, K. 2 1966
Ramat Gan Students Council
(R. Lieber) 2 1967
DN to 1967
Ramello, Catone 2 1962
Encl: Jon Tinker to Alan ?
Ramírez, Jorge A., to
BRPF 1969
PW to 1969
Rampal, Mr. 1962
Encl: essay
BR to 1962
Ramsey, Ronald B. 3 .... n.d.
BR to 1964
RS to 1964
Rand Corporation
(B. W. Haydon) 2 1964-9
BR to 1964
PW to 1969
Randall, J. 1963
BR to 1963
Randle, Michael 2 1962-8
BR to 2 1962-8
Rao, K. Venkata 1966
CF to 1966
Rao, Nageswara 1966
PW to 1966
Rao, R. Srihari 1966
PW to 1966
Rao, Suresh 1962
BR to 1962
Rapi, Eugene S.,
to BRPF 2 1965
To HR 2 1965
HR to 3 1965
Encl: form l. 1967
Rasker, Albert J. 1966
Rasmussen, Hans Kaalund .... n.d.
Rasmussen, Lauritz H. 2 ... 1962-5
To BRPF 1966
Encl: clipping
BR to 1962
PW to 2 1965-6
Rastogi, A. K. 1962
BR to 1962
Rastrong, Hans Petter,
NJ to 1962
Ratcliff, A. R. N. 1967
Encl: clipping
Rathore, K. P. D. 4 1962-6
BR to 2 1962-6
CF to 1966
Rattansey, Salima 1962
BR to 1962
Rautenstrauch, Mrs. Walter .. 1963
BR to 1963
Raven, Mr. 1962
BR to 1962
Rawlins, David B. 1969
CF to 1969
Read, Bert 1965
To PW 1965
Encl: l. to L.B. Johnson
RS to 1965
PW to 2 1965
Read, R. M. 1962
Encl: leaflet
BR to 1962
Reading and District Coordinating
Committee for Disarmament
(Frida Knight) 1963
Encl: conference report
BR to 1963
Redman, L., to HR 1965
Redston, F. S. 1964
Reed, Adolph L. 1962
BR to 1962
Reed, Gordon, to BRPF 1963
CE to 1963

Reed, Jr., Mrs. Henry Hope .. 1962
Encl: l. to H. Applebaum
BR to 1962
Reed, Richard L. **2** 1968
Rees, Tom 1965
RS to 1965
Regelson, Leon 1965
Encl: essay
PW to 1965
Registani, B.P.N. 1965
PW to 1965
Registre International des
Citoyens du Monde **2** 1968-9
Encl: leaflets
Reid, John V. 1966
Encl: essay
Reid, Joseph 1969
Reid, Ralph 1963
BR to 1963
Reimann, Max 1966
Encl: essay
Relvani, K.N. **6** 1962-8
Encl: index, ls. to *The Times* of India, U Thant, S. Radhakrishnan, Chairman of Press Council of India, Union Finance Minister, New Delhi
BR to 1962
Renow, Lilly, CF to 1969
Renwick, M., RS to 1964
Rerabek, Jaroslav, to BRPF .. 1966
Encl: l. to Czech P.M., list of publications, list of book reviews
Resistance (John Hutchinson, Marilyn Smith) 1963
Encl: poem, form l.
Reston, Jr., James 1968
CF to 1968
Reto, Roberto 1968
Rety, John, RS to 1964
Revolutionary Workers Party (Trotskyist) (John L. Davis) 1968
Encl: leaflets
BR to 1968
Reynolds, Barbara, to CF
CF to 1962
Riazuddin, Akhtar .... 196?
Ricci, Cesare, BR to 1966
Rice, C. Edward, to CF 1967
CF to 1967
Rice, Charles E. 1969
Rice, Donald 1962
BR to 1962
Richards, Colin, to Vietnam Solidarity Campaign 1966
Encl: l. to Harold Wilson
BR to **2** 1964-6
Richards, D.H., BR to 1963
Richards, Gordon, to CF 1962
CF to 1962
Richardson, M., to BRPF 1969
PW to 1969
Richmond Council for Peace Education (James C. Rogers) to RS 1966
Encl: newsl.
RS to 1966
Richter, Sviatoslav,
BR to **2** n.d.-1966
Rickards, ? 1962
Rickards, David A. 1963
Encl: clipping
BR to 1963
Ridley, Walter **2** 1963
BR to 1963
Riley, A., RSt. to 1967
Ringer, G.J. 1966
Encl: abstract
Riochet, Margaret .... n.d.
CF to 1962
Ríos, José (*Mi Articulo*) (clipping of article on BR) .. 1966
Riposanu, Pamfil, and Lipsig, Harry 1968
Encl: petition, pamphlet
CF to 1968
Risch, ? 1966
Risholm, Olle 1969
BR to 1969
CF to 1969
Rix, Leo, BR to 1964
Rixwani, Shakir 1969
Ro Jai Ho (*The People's Korea*) 1966
BR to 1966
Roback, A.A., RS to 1963
Roberts, Carol 1962
BR to 1962

Roberts, G. R. 1965
Encl: open l.
PW to 1965
Roberts, Glyn, CF to 1968
Roberts, John C. H. 1964
Encl: essay
BR to 1964
Robertson, Grady F. 1965
BR to 1965
PW to 1965
Robertson, Margaret 1963
BR to 1963
Robinson, Aileen, to RS 2 1965
RS to 2 1965
Rocca, Sr., Bernard T. 2 ... 1964
BR to 6 1964-7
CF to 1967
Roche, Stephen R. 1962
BR to 1962
Rode, Margarethe .... n.d.
Encl: leaflet, open l.
Rodenberg, Ludwig (printed open l. to BR) .... n.d.
BR to 2 1963
Rodger, R. 1962
BR to 1962
Rodriguez, Daniel 1962
BR to 1963
Rodriguez, Eddie 1964
Rodriguez, Enrique I., to BRPF .... n.d.
To RSt. 1968
RSt. to 1967
Rodríguez, Hernán 2 1963
To AY 1963
To CF 1965
BR to 1963
CF to 2 1963-5
Roger, Hedebouw, to BRPF 1968
Rogosin, Lionel 6 1962-5
To NJ 1962
Encl: photo, leaflets, clippings, reviews, open l.
BR to 3 1962-5
NJ to 1962
Rolfs, William C. 1964
Rooum, Donald, to RS 3 ... 1962
RS to 2 1962
Roper, Raymond H. 1963
BR to (form l.) 1963
Rosenberg, Naomi 1962
BR to 1962
Rosenfeld, Herbert T., to RS 1963
BR to 1963
RS to 1963
Encl: form l.
Rosenthal, Stanley 2 1969
CF to 1969
Rosenwald, Peter J., to RS ... 1964
RS? to 1964
Rosenwald, Ruth F. 2 1965-6
Encl: l. to *Rome Daily American*
PW to 2 1966
Ross, Jerry 1965
Encl: diagram
Ross, John A. 1965
To RS 1965
RS to 2 1965
Ross, Larry 2 1963-4
Encl: l. to *New York Times*, essay, open l. to "Members of Parliament and others"
BR to 8 1963-8
RSt. to 1967
Rossi, Roberto 1969
Encl: leaflet
Roston, Michael 2 1966
Encl: leaflet
BR to 1966
RS to 1966
Rotblat, J. 1953
Encl: syllabus
Roth, Edith P. 1963
BR to 1963
Rowlson, Tom 1967
BR to 1967
Roy, Manojit (Committee to Fight U.S. Imperialism) 1967
BR to 2 1967
Roy, Sukhen, open l. to *New York Times* 1967
Rozsypal, H. and I. J. 1968
BR to 1968
Ruark, Robert, BR to 1964
Rubbra, F., ID to 1965
Rubinstein, Charles 1966
BR to 1966
Rubinstein, Christopher 1968

Encl: leaflet
Ruda, Harris 1966
PW to 1966
Ruf, Hannes 1963
BR to 1963
Rugiles?, O. R., to BRPF ... 1967
Ruiz, Marino 1965
PW to 1965
Rush, Catherine 1964
BR to 1964
Rushlight (Denis Knight) 1965
Encl: issue of journal, leaflet
Rusin, Michele 1969
Russell, B. (form l.) 1962
Russell, Gustavo
Cabrera **2** 1963-8
BR to 1963
Russell, Jr., David, BR to 1963
Russell, Robert W. 1969
Encl: clippings (incl. BR's lunar article from *Asahi Evening News*)
Bertrand Russell Peace Foundation,
BR to RS *et al.* 1963
ER to CF *et al.* 1964
RS to BRPF 1963
Encl: press releases, form l.
Bertrand Russell Peace Foundation,
Queensland Branch
(W. J. H. Harris) 1967
Encl: booklet, *Verdict of the Stockholm Session*
RSt. to 1967
Russo, Serofino, BR to 1962
Rutecki, John F. .... 1963?
BR to 1963
Rutherford, Jan, and
Haunaer, Karen 1962
BR to 1962
Ryan, N. F. M. 1962

S

S., M., to Committee of
100 .... n.d.
Saar-Freundeskreis des Albert Schweitzer-Spitals in Lambarene-e.V. (Günther Heipp) 1963
Sachs, Mendel **3** 1966-7
BR to 1966
CF to 1967
Sacks, Lawrence R. 1966
RS to 1966
Sacks, William M., BR to 1963
Sadler, Mark David 1963-7
Encl: clipping
BR to 1963
RSt. to 1967
Sadosky, Manuel, to BRPF ... 1965
PW to 1965
Sagall, Joseph, and Mrs.,
CF to 1964
BR to (form l.) 1968
St. Andrews, Arthur 1962
St. George, George 1965
St. John, M. Gregory 1969
CF to 1969
St. John, Ortega 1964
Encl: poems
BR to 1964
St. Kitts Prisoners' Defence Fund
(Diana M. Prior-Palmer) ... 1968
Encl: open l., leaflets
St. Pancras Building Society
(Eric Bales) (report) 1963
BR to 1964
Saito, Tsuruko **5** 1963-9
Encl: photos, c., clipping
BR to **12** 1963-9
Sakurai, K. 1969
CF to 1969
Saldana, F., BR to 1966
Salomon, Sarah 1966
BR to 1966
Salt, Liz, to CF **2** 1968
CF to **2** 1968
Saltman, David B. 1967
Salton, Harold G. **2** 1967
Encl: magazine article, leaflets
BR to 1963
CF to 1967
Salvadori, Max **3** 1966
BR to 1966
RS to 1966
Sampson, Ronald V. 1965
To RS 1965
To CF 1969
CF to 1969

San Jacinto High School (Mack Godwin) (form l.)
to BRPF .... n.d.
Sanchez Porras, Julian Antonio 1969
PW to 1969
Sanctuary, the 1969
Encl: leaflets
CF to 1969
Sandén, Bertil 1962
To CF 3 1963
BR to 1962
CF to 2 1963
Sandperl, Ira 1964
Sandy, Clive 1966
BR to 1966
SANE (Norman Cousins, Homer Jack) 2 1958-64
To CF 2 1962
Encl: reports, leaflets, form ls., membership form
CF to 2 1962-3
Santhanam, K. (biographical article, clipping) 1962
Santhi, S. 1966
Encl: poem
Santillan, Juan Alberto Camilo,
to RS 1966
RS to 1966
Sapin, R. 3 1963-6
Encl: form ls., circulars, c.
BR to 3 1963
RS to 2 1964-6
Sao, Nguyen Van, BR to 1968
Sarferaz, R. M. 1968
Sarfrazahmad, Mian 1965
PW to 1965
Sarja, Mamie, to RS 1962
NJ to 1962
Sarjit, ?, RS to 1965
Sarley, W. N. and Lois M. ... 1962
BR to 1962
Sartre, Jean-Paul *et al.* (petition) .... n.d.
Sarva Seva Sangh (Radhakrishna) (form ls.) 1966
Sassella, Leo, to Tom Kinsey 1963
CE to 1964
Sattler, Jim, RSt. to 2 1967
Saunders, David,
CF to 2 1967
Save Our Sons (Anne Gregory)
to BRPF 1965
RS to 1965
Sawyer, H. 1967
Saxena, Mathura Prasad 2 1962-3
BR to 2 1962-3
Scamell, E. D., to BRPF ..... n.d.
BR to 1962
Scanlon, Hugh, BR to 1968
Scarborough New Left Club (Peter Baines) 1965
PW to 1965
Scarry, John 1966
BR to 1966
Schenck, Marie 2 1964-5
Encl: open l., receipts
CF to 1965
RS to 1964-5
Robert Scher Community for New Politics 1967
Schermer, H., to U Thant (open l.) 1966
Schick, Alan S., to BRPF 1964
CE to 1964
Schiefelbein, Anita 1967
To RS 1967
RS to 1967
Schirmer, Sergio, RSt. to 1967
Schlesinger, R. A. J.,
BR to 2 1966
Schmidt, Hans-Joachim 1963
Schmidt, Siegmund 5 1962-5
Encl: clippings, leaflet, open ls. to U Thant, L. B. Johnson, Field Marshall Montgomery, Barry Goldwater, British Secretary of State, Robert Kennedy, Sir Quaison Sackey; ls. from Gamal Abdel Nasser, H. Weibringhaus, Keith Holyoake, Basil Capella, T. Panayides
BR to 2 1963-4
PW to 1966
Schneider, Dorothy L. 1969
Encl: l. to U Thant, l. in response

CF to 1969
Schöchlin, Raoul 2 1962-9
Encl: photo
BR to 3 1963-4
Schönholzer, Ernst 1968
Encl: photo, leaflets
School of Living (Mildred J. Loomis) to RS 1964
Encl: book summary, leaflet
RS to 1964
Schott, Guenter 1962
Schrag, Philip G. 1963
BR to 1963
Schreiber, Isabelle Georges 2 1963
To AY 1963
BR to 2 1963
Schroll, Susannah 1966
Encl: pamphlet
RS to 1966
Schwarz, Günther, to BRPF 1964
BR to 1964
CF to 1964
RS to 1964
Schwartz, J. A. 1964
BR to 1965
Schwartz, Laurent 1962
BR to 2 1962-6
CF to 1966
Encl: declaration
Schweig, Bruno 1962
BR to 1962
Schweiger, Walter 2 1966
Encl: resolutions, leaflet
Schweizerische Bundeskanzlei (Chan. Oser) 1967
Scott, Edward J. 2 1963
BR to 1963
Scott, G. Michael 5 1961-8
Encl: clippings, leaflets, essay
BR to 6 1962-9
CF to 1963
Scott, Joan 1965
Scott, William R., CF to 1969
Scott Bader Commonwealth (Scott Bader, Godric E. S. Bader) 1968
To RS 1963
To CE 1964
To CF 1964
Encl: calling c., leaflet, clipping
CE to 1964
RS to 1964
CF to 2 1964-5
BR to 1968
Scwell, Frances, CF to 1968
Sears, M., CF to 1969
Seary, William J. 1963
Encl: essay
BR to 1963
Seattle Peace Information Centre (Ann Stadler, Mrs. Alex Gottfried) to CF ..... n.d.
Encl: l. from SANE (Homer Jack), clipping
BR to 1962
Encl: essay
CF to 1962
Seeley, John R. 1965
To PW 2 1966
PW to 2 1966
Segal, Allen, ... n.d.
Segaram, G. S. 1969
Sel, Yilmaz 1969
Selby, D. A., to RS 1962
RS to 1962
Sen, B. R., BR to 1964
Senkovic, Predrag 2 ..... 1962?-7
Encl: poems
BR to 1962
Setina, Vladimir 1969
Encl: open l.
CF to 1969
Seward, M., CF to 1968
Shaber, Milton B. 1966
Shackleton, James ..... n.d.
Shaffer, Mrs. Robert, to BRPF (note, clippings) 1967
RSt. to 1967
Shah, F. P., to BRPF 1965
RS to 1965
Shaikh, Z. H. 1968
Shanin, Teodor, RSt. to 1967
Shank, Paul 1966
Shapiro, Mark A. ..... n.d.
Shapiro, Pauline W. 1968
Encl: poem
BR to 1969
Sharma, Kusum 1962
BR to 1962

Sharp, Gene, CF to **2** 1962-3
Sharp, Jack 1964
BR to 1964
Shaw, Anne, to CF 1965
CF to 1965
Shaw, H. C. W. 1962
BR to 1962
Shealy, Jr., Edwin A. 1963
BR to 1963
Sheikhmous, O., BR to 1963
Sheldon, W. F. 1962
Encl: clipping
BR to 1962
Shepherd, Jack, to CF **2** ..... 1962-?
Encl: leaflet
CF to **2** 1962-4
Shereshevsky, Simon (articles) 1969
Sherman, Elna 1963
Encl: clipping
BR to 1963
Shima, Yasuharu **6** 1962-6
To RS 1964
Encl: clippings, photo
BR to **3** 1963-6
RS to **2** 1964-5
CF to **2** 1964-6
Shimabuko, Eduardo, *et al.*, BR to 1962
Shloimovitz, Marcus **2** 1963
RS to 1963
Shlonsky, Avraham, *et al.* 1967
Shodunke, M. O. **2** 1965
RS to **2** 1965
Shoner, Sarah 1966
Encl: article
BR to 1966
Shore, Donald P. 1969
CF to 1969
Shrapnell, Mike, to RSt. 1967
RSt. to 1967
Shukla, Shyam 1962
BR to 1962
Shura, Shames, BR to 1964
Siebens, Henry C. 1962
BR to 1962
Sieff, John Henry **2** 1962-3
BR to **2** 1962-3
Siegel, Eli (poem to President Johnson) ..... n.d.
Sierra, Francisco Díaz 1969
PW to 1969
Sigg, Walter 1963
BR to 1963
Sil, Arun Kumar **4** 1962-3
Encl: outline of book, *If Winter Comes*
BR to **2** 1962-3
CF to 1963
Sillars, James 1965
To RS 1965
CF to 1965
RS to 1965
Silver, Michael M. 1965
To BRPF **2** 1966
PW to **2** 1965-6
Silverman, S. J., to BRPF 1965
PW to 1965
Silvers, Stuart **2** 1967-9
Simich, Milutin 1967
DN to 1967
Simmonds, Aubyn L., to RS 1963
RS to (form l.) 1963
Simmons, Donald, BR to 1963
Simmons, James R. 1962
BR to 1962
Simon, Charles 1963
RS to 1963
Simpson, John C. 1965
BR to 1965
Simpson, M. 1962
BR to 1962
Simpson, Mary W. 1967
Simpson, Roger A., BR to 1966
Sims, B. J., to BRPF 1964
CF to 1964
Singer, D., to BRPF ..... n.d.
RS to 1965
Singer, Stanley **3** 1962-3
Encl: essays
BR to **3** 1963
Singh, D., to BRPF? 1965
RS to 1965
Singh, P. P., to BRPF 1965
RS to 1965
Singh, Shambhri N. **2** 1968-9
BR to 1964
Singhgill, Dhanwant 1962

BR to 1963
Sinh, Aditya V. 1965
PW to 1965
Sinha, K. K. 1962
Encl: clipping
BR to 1962
Sinha, Murari 1963
BR to 1963
La Sinistra (G. Cavell)
to CF 1968
Sirc, Ljubo 1970
Encl: clippings
CF to 1970
Sixth Hungarian Peace
Conference 1963
Skarzynski, Janusz 1966
RS to 1966
Skerl, Valerie **2** 1964
Encl: circular
BR to **2** 1964
RS? to 1964
Skinner, M. B. .... n.d.
RSt.? to 1969
Skoglund, Bo 1966
RS to 1966
Skolnick, Sol **2** 1964
RS to 1964
Skorpil, P. R., BR to 1966
Slanson, J. Sayne 1962
CF to 1962
Sleep, Philip 1965
BR to 1965
Sloan, Edward M. (form l.) ... 1969
CF to 1968
Slocombe, Charles H. A. 1962
BR to 1962
Smart, Michael **3** 1966
Smedley, Frederic C. 1962
Encl: l. to Bernard Lovell,
l. to Philip Jessup, l. to
New York Times
BR to **2** 1962-3
Smith, Gloria, to RS 1966
RS to 1966
Smith, J. Michael,
BR to 1963
Smith, Jack, BR to 1966
Smith, Mrs. P. **2** 1964
BR to **2** 1964
Smith, Peter 1964
RS to 1964
Smithback, John B., BR to ... 1966
Smolski, Theresa L. 1968
Snelling, Richard 1968
CF to 1968
Sobel, Joseph 1964
RS to 1964
Sobell, Morton 1969
Encl: clipping
BR to **2** 1969-70
Social Research and Development
Programs (James C.
Rogers) 1965
RS to 1965
Socialist Society, Borough
Road College, Isleworth
(H. Kahn) 1958
Socialist Union of Central-Eastern
Europe 1963
Encl: leaflet
CF to 1963
Socialist Workers Party (Priscilla
Ring, Jack Barnes) **2** 1966
Encl: clipping, press release
Socialist Zionist Party-Napam
(D. Billis), CF to 1969
Socialistika Förbundet (Christer
Hogstedt) 1967
Encl: leaflet
BR to 1967
Sociedad Humanista (Fermín
Torres) 1962
Encl: leaflet
BR to 1962
Sociedade Amigos de Cuba
(Luiz Gonzaga de Oliveira
Leite) **3** 1962-3
Encl: form l.
BR to 1963
Société Internationale de
Prophylaxie Criminelle (V. V.
Stanciu, H. Baruk) 1966
RS to 1966
Society for Aiding Victims of
Miscarriages of Justice
(F. B. Russell) 1962
Encl: leaflet
BR to 1962
Society for Anglo-Chinese
Understanding (Joseph

Needham *et al.*) 1965-7
Encl: leaflets
CF to 1965
Society for Cultural Relations with the USSR (M. Wainwright) .. 1962
To AY 1963
Encl: l. from "Studio Kievnauch-film"
AY to **2** 1963
Society for the Cause of Mother's Lineage (leaflets, c.) .... n.d.
Society of Friends Peace Committee (Jack Mongar *et al.*) **2** .. 1963-5
To RS **2** 1964-5
CF to 1962
BR to 1963
PW to 1965
Solidarité Fraternelle Mondiale (Edwin de Robillard) (leaflet) 1967
Solomon, Deborah,
BR to 1966
Solstad, Ken 1969
Somerville, M. J, to BRPF ... 1965
RS to 1965
Sommer, M. Lloyd 1965
RS to 1965
Somoza, Jose Antonio, to BRPF 1968
PW to 1969
Sorensen, R. W. 1964
BR to 1964
Sorlie, Wayne, to BRPF 1968
CF to 1968
Sosialistik Ungdomsforbund (Erik R. Selmer, Vigdis Vollset) to BRPF 1967
RSt. to **2** 1967
Sosnen, Samuel, to RS 1966
Soubeyran, Charles 1962
Soucek, Sylvia 1969
CF to 1969
Soumar, Robert B. 1962
Encl: clippings
South Africa Protest (Mamie Smith) 1964
South African Defence and Aid Fund, Victoria (Ian D. Aiken) 1963
South Place Ethical Society (Harry G. Knight), RSt. to 1967
South Wales Nuclear Disarmament Campaign (Emrys P. Roberts) (form l.) 1958
BR to 1958
Southon, R. M. 1964
BR to 1964
RS to 1964
Soviet Peace Committee (Nikolai Tikhonov, Michael Kotov, Yuri Zhukov) **5** 1962-7
Encl: text of *Pravda* article, New Year's greeting, form ls.
BR to **6** 1962-7
Soviet Peace Fund (V. Kalinin)
Encl: New Year's c.
BR to 1964
RS to 1964
Sow, Alfâ Ibrâhîm 1966
PW to 1966
Sowerby, G. S., BR to 1963
Soyinka, Wole, RS to 1962
Spanel, Abram N.
Encl: clippings, leaflet, business c., copies of ls. to Spanel
BR to 1963
Spaziani, L. 1965
RS to 1966
Spencer, Ann 1964
Spieole, M., RS to 1965
Spillman, Martin, to BRPF 1965
RS to 1965
Spilman, Ramona, to BRPF 1969
PW to 1969
Spooner, Heather, to BRPF 1967
PW to 1967
Sprecher, Max 1966
RS to 1966
Squires, Vera M. (clippings, circulars) .... n.d.
BR to **2** 1963
Squitieri, Neal Paul 1968
Srenaski, Denis 1964
RS to 1964
Stack, Jim, BR to 1964
Stahl, Donald, to BRPF 1965
BR to 1963

HR to 1965
Stake (Joseph Meyer) 1963
BR to **2** 1963-4
Stalder, Fred, to BRPF 1965
Encl: chart
RS to 1965
Ständiger Arbeitsausschus für Frieden ... (E. Engel, *et al.*) (circular) 1965
Standish, Peter R. 1963
BR to 1963
Stanford, John W. 1964
Encl: leaflet
BR to 1964
Staniger, W. L. 1968
Encl: leaflet
CF to 1968
Stanković, Petar J. 1961
BR to 1963
Stanley, Pamela, CF to 1968
Stanton, Charles E. **2** 1966
BR to 1966
Re Kennedy assassination
Stanton, Nile, ID to 1965
Starcke, Viggo 1967
Encl: clippings
Starrs, Robert J. **7** 1963-5
To RS **2** 1964
Encl: ls. to L. B. Johnson, J. F. Kennedy, Prof. Molodtsov; l. from Prof. Molodtsov, l. from Nedville E. Nordess, l. to Peace Committee USSR
BR to **3** 1962-7
RS to **3** 1964
Steel, Antony 1969
CF to 1969
Steen, Otto A., to BRPF 1965
RS to 1965
Steffens, Jr., Henrick,
BR to 1963
Steiner, Rudolf, BR to 1966
Steinfelder, Frank 1963
Encl: poem
BR to 1963
Steinweg, Gernot, to RSt. 1967
RSt. to **2** 1967
Stell, Karl H., to RSt. 1967
To RS **2** 1967-8
RSt. to **2** 1967
Stephens, Bette 1964
BR to 1964
Stephens, Kenneth, BR to ... 1963
Stewart, W. M. (form l.) 1962
BR to 1963
Stibbs, Timothy 1966
CF to 1966
Stichting Anti Atoobom Actie (G. A. de Bock) to RS 1962
Stichting J'Accuse (Harry Wielek, Marian v. d. Bergh-v. d. Meer) **2** 1969
CF to 1969
Stichting Werkgroep Wereldunie **4** 1967-8
Encl: circulars, l. to Mr. Von Thun
Stieger, Mr. and Mrs. 1962
BR to 1962
Still, Joseph W. 1965
Encl: form l., clipping, l. to *Africa and the World*
BR to **2** 1963-4
RS to 1965
Stirling, Ian, to *The Guardian* and *New York Times* 1962
BR to 1962
Stjärnskog, Hans 1968
CF to 1968
Stockholm International Peace Research Institute (R. R. Neild) (form l.) 1969
Encl: yearbook summary, handbook
Stockwood, Mervyn **2** 1958
BR to 1958
Stoke Newington and Hackney North Young Socialists (Alec Spencer) to BRPF 1964
CE to 1964
The Stoke Newington Liaison Committee for Women's Peace Groups (M. Morten) to CF 1965
Stommel, Edeltrud 1966
Encl: photo
BR to 1966
Stone, M. K., to RS **2** 1967
RS to 1967
Stonor, C. R. P. 1963

Encl: "Memorandum to the Governments of the Nuclear Nations"
BR to 1963
STOP-WAR-VIP-TRIP (E. A. Bierdrager) 1968
CF to 1968
Storch, Vergel Cook 1962
BR to 1962
Storey, John A. 1964
Stovicek, Iva, and Kidrica, Aleja B. 1967
Stowell, Robert F. 1964
RS to 1964
Strassburg, Richard C., to BRPF 1967
PW to 1967
Stricker, O. 1962
BR to 1962
Stuart, Maxine, to BRPF 1965
Stuber, Ernst 1967
Encl: pamphlet, leaflet, l. to U Thant
Student Mobilization Committee Benefit Fund (form l.) 1968
Student Peace Movement (Philip Altbach, A. J. Muste, *et al.*) **2** 1962-5
To RS 1965
To PW 1965
Encl: declaration, form ls., discussion bulletins
BR to 1963
RS to 1965
PW to 1965
Encl: form l.
Student Peace Union (Irving Kirsch, James Silver) **3** 1964-6
BR to **2** 1963-6
RS to 1964
Students for a Democratic Society (E. Jennings) ..... n.d.
BR to (Everett C. Frost) 1966
Stupin, Karl, BR to 1966
Sturla, Ana Maria 1965
PW to 1965
Stüttgen, Wolfgang 1967
CF to 1967
Subramanyam, B. K. 1963
Encl: form l.
BR to 1963
Sucupira, N. A. **5** 1962-7
BR to **2** 1962-3
RS to 1965
PW to 1965
Suirez?, to RS 1966
Sullhau, Hari Krishan **2** 1962-8
BR to 1962
Sullivan, Christopher J. ..... n.d.
Sullivan, Vicki M., BR to **2** 1966
Sunday Sun, New Delhi (hand-copied extract) 1967
Sundra, Triska 1963
To CE 1964
BR to 1963
CE to 1964
Surridge, L. 1963
Encl: poem
BR to 1963
Suryaprakasarao, P. ..... n.d.
Encl: clippings
PW to 1965
Sutcliffe, Sara ..... n.d.
Encl: photos, poem
BR to **2** 1963-4
Svoboda, I. Lubor 1969
Swain, G. W. (essay) 1968
Swann, Robert **2** 1962
Encl: leaflet
BR to **2** 1962
Sweeny, Kim, BR to 1963
Swindley, R. D. H., to BRPF 1964
RS to 1964
Symons, Janice **3** 1962-4
BR to **3** 1962-4
RS to 1965
Szondy, G. A. 1963
Encl: essay
BR to 1963
Szpakowski, Slawomir 1962
Encl: l. to Khrushchev, Kennedy, *Pravda*, *New York Times*

T

Tacchi-Morris,

Kathleen **12** 1962-9
BR to **4** 1962-3
Tahri, Mohammed, BR to 1966
Taikan, Rosa 1967
Takata, Toyozo **5** 1965-7
Taluka, D. D. 1962
BR to 1962
Tampoe, Bala, BR to 1967
Tapies, Antonio 1962
BR to 1962
Tarrow, William 1968
Encl: essay
CF to 1968
Tarry, Paul B., *et al.*,
to CE 1963
Encl: essay
CE to 1968
Tarsis, Valery, BR to 1966
Tate, Brian, BR to 1963
Encl: James Brennan to
BR 1963
Tate, Ernest (open ls.) 1966
Encl: clipping
BR to 1966
CF to 1968
Tate, Robert S. **3** 1968
CF to 1968
Taylor, Brian D. 1964
BR to 1964
Taylor, David K., to CF 1965
To BRPF 1967
CF to **7** 1964-9
Taylor, G. 1962
Taylor, George R. **2** 1962-3
BR to **2** 1962-3
Taylor, Isabel 1969
Encl: clipping
Taylor, Kathleen 1964
CE to 1964
Taylor, Norman 1969
Encl: clipping
PW to 1969
Taylor, Stuart 1965
Teichman, C. Joseph **2** 1967
BR to 1967
CF to 1967
Teimourian, Hazhir 1968
Encl: leaflets
BR to 1969
Teitelbaum, Isidor 1963
Encl: essay
BR to 1963
Telephone House, BR to 1964
Telford, Michael, *et al.* 1962
BR to 1962
ten Cate, L. O. 1962
BR to 1962
Testro, Rex C. 1962
BR to 1962
Thanning, Niel S., CF to 1969
Tharaldsen, Mary Ann, to
Freedom Press 1965
Thetford, Philip Henry 1966
CF to 1966
Thier, Karl-Heinz,
to BRPF 1964
To RS 1965
Encl: l. to Mr. von Zircz
Thing, Bob 1962
Thirring, Hans (l. from Arthur
Schlesinger Jr., Special Asst.
to the President) 1962
BR to 1964
Thomas, A. 1962
Thomas, Alfred J. **2** 1964
BR to 1964
Thomas, Bruce (outline
of book) .... n.d.
Thomas, Norman **2** 1964
BR to 1964
Thompson, David F. M. 1969
Thomsen, Alexander, to
RS **2** 1965
Encl: essay, leaflet
RS to 1965
Thornhill, C. .... 1962?
Thorogood, Maura 1969
Encl: clipping
Thouroude, Jean-Claude 1968
BR to 1963
Tibor, Asher 1967
Tierney, J. C. 1966
RS to 1966
Tierney, Penelope, BR to 1960
Encl: Tierney's l. in
Manchester Guardian
Till Eulenspiegel (William
Ostfeld) (form l.) 1962
Encl: issue of magazine
Timpany, Frederick P. 1965

RS to 1965
Tinner, Dale R. 1969
BR to 1969
Encl: l. from BR to Tinner's draft board
Titchenor, ?, RS to 1967
Tiwar, Shesh Narayau, to BRPF 1965
PW to 1965
Tofallis, Zannetos **8** 1962-8
BR to **2** 1963
CF to **2** 1963-8
Tokkie, Rik 1966
CF to 1966
Tokyo Conference of Scientific Technique Study (Hiroo Ochiai Executive Committee) 1964
BR to 1964
Tomlin, Ian 1966
BR to 1966
Topchiev, A. V. (form l.) 1962
Re World Congress for General Disarmament and Peace
Torres, Edelberto, to RSt. ... 1968
Townroe, Christopher, to BRPF 1968
PW to 1968
Tracy, I. I., BR to 1963
Trajtenberg, Mario 1963
Encl: clipping
BR to 1963
Transport and General Workers' Union (H. Nicholas, F. Cousins) 1963
BR to **2** 1966
Trent Park College Socialist Society (R. Turpin) **2** 1967
BR to 1967
Tricontinental Magazine (Ramon Echevarria, Jose Peréz) to *London Bulletin* 1968
RSt. to **2** 1968
Tripp, Mrs. Leslie M. **2** 1966
Tristram, M. P. W., CF to 1968
Trivedi, Purushottam N. 1967
Trivedi, Sudhir 1968
Trondheim Student Union (Unn Laukvik) 1967
Trotta, Avv. Arveno,
BR to 1966
Tsigmond, Anna 1962
BR to 1962
Tsurushima, Setsure, RS? to 1966
Tucker, Bill, Salveson, Christopher, and Hunter, Charlotte 1958
Tucker, O. R. 1963
BR to 1963
Turk, M. A. **2** 1966
PW to 1966
Turnbull, Arthur (open l.) 1962
Turnbull, Eddie **3** 1963-5
BR to 1964
PW to 1965
Turnbull, Frances 1964
RS to 1964
Turner, Margaret, BR to 1963
Turpin, C. C., BR to 1964
Tutino, Saverio, CF to 1969
Twin, Tom L. 1967
RS to 1967
Twinn, Stephen, CF to 1966
Tyler, Mary 1967
RSt. to 1967
Tynemouth CND 1962
Tyrrell, Barbara 1958

U

Ueda, Teiji 1966
Encl: essay, l. to L. B. Johnson, photo
RS to 1966
Uffelmann, Erika **2** 1963-4
Encl: clipping
BR to 1963
RS to 1965
Umlandt, Wolf-G. **2** 1962-6
BR to 1966
Unidade Democratica Portuguesa (Ruy Luiz Gomez *et al.*), RSt. to 1967
Union de Escritores y Artistas de Cuba (Argeliers Léon) to RS 1962
RS to 1962

Union d'entraide en favour de l'hopital due Dr. A. Schweitzer, BR to 1964
Union des Architectes du Vietnam (Hoang-Linh) 1963
BR to 1963
Union of American Exiles in Britain (Howard Engelskirchen, Harry Pincus) 1969
Encl: leaflets, advertisement
CF to 1969
Union of Australian Women (Freda Brown, A. M. Hughes) 2 1965-6
BR to 1965
RS to 1966
Union of Democratic Control (Arthur Ponsonby, H. M. Swanwick, Charles Trevelyan) ... 1924
Re E. D. Morel Memorial Fund
BR to (Mrs. Jean Orton) ... 1963
Union of Shop, Distributive and Allied Workers (David Thomas) 1965
BR to (A. W. Allen) 1966
Unitarian Extension Movement in Australia (H. Forrest) ... 1968
Encl: l. to BBC
CF to 1968
United Federation of Teachers (Marvin Adler) ... 1964
BR to 1964
United Nations (U Thant) 1962
BR to 2 1962
United Nations Association, Highgate (Derek D. Bannister) to BRPF 1964
Encl: agenda
CF to 1964
United Nations Association, London (circulars) 1967
United Nations Technical Assistance Board (David Owen), BR to 1964
RS to 1964
United Peace Front Party (Michael Dansey) to RS 1967
Encl: clippings, circular
United World Federalists (James Mundstock) to PW 1965
Universal Brotherhood (leaflets) .... n.d.
Universal Peace Festival (Hayri Eroglu) 1967
Universidad Javeriana (Battle Smith) to BRPF 1963
Urdu Digest (A. H. Qureshee), BR to 1966
Urrego Agudelo, Antonio M. .. 1969
PW to 1969
Usborne, Henry 1958
Encl: *The Road to Peace?*
US News and World Report (Joseph Fromm) 1967

V

Vaishnavi, Rugho Nath 1963
BR to 1963
van Bösllager, Ada? 1965
BR to 1965
The Vancouver Viet-Nam Day Committee (R. D. Burns), RS to 1966
Van den Heuvel, Walter 1962
To BRPF 1965
BR to 1962
PW to 1965
Vanderhaeghen, Claude 1967
Encl: l. to U Thant
Van Do, Xuan .... 196?
Encl: clipping
Vane, Raymond R., *et al.* 1963
Encl: note
BR to 1963
van Heesch, C. A. 1965
Encl: poems
PW to 1965
Van Meter, Jr., Robert H., CF to 1969
van Stolk, C. R. A. 1963
BR to 1963
Van Twyl, Myrth
Encl: l. to *Los Angeles Times*
Van Wormer, Mrs. 1964
BR to 1964
Vargas, Philip, to BRPF 1965
Varughese, P. N., to RS 1967
RS to 1967
PW to 1967

Vaughan, Edward **2** 1962
BR to 1962
RS to 1962
Vaughan, James W. K., to RS 1962
Encl: note to CF, ls. to and from "The Accra Assembly—the World Without the Bomb"
CF to 1962
Vaughn, Sue A., to Ho Chi Minh 1967
The Vedanta Movement (Swami Avyaktananda *et al.*) **2** 1965-9
To CE **2** 1965-9
Encl: leaflets, ls. to U Thant, political literature
BR to **2** 1963
CE to 1963
Verband der Kriegsdienstverweigerer (Klaus Vack, Wilhelm Peters) **4** 1962-5
CF to 1962
RS to 1965
Verma, Gurdial 1962
BR to 1962
Verma, R. P. **2** 1962-4
Encl: essays
BR to 1962
RS to 1964
Vernon, Hilda, to BRPF 1965
To HR 1965
HR to 1965
Verona, Sergiu 1968
Veroz, L. (essay) .... n.d.
Vesper-Triangel, Bernward, to BRPF 1966
RS to 1966
Vetter, Hermann, to BRPF ... 1966
RS to 1966
Victoria Humanist (J. L. Brereton) 1965
Encl: magazine
RS to 1965
Vietnam Day Committee, BR to 1966
Vietnam Peace Movement, Oxford (Jennifer Hinton) to BRPF **2** 1966
RS to 1966
PW to 1966
Vietnam Solidarity Campaign (Pat Jordan) (circulars, c.s) 1967
Villamil, Ricardo Bergoa 1962
BR to 1963
Viola, C. R., to BRPF **2** 1969
Encl: clipping
CF to 1969
V.I.P. Newsletter Management Guide, BR to 1964
Vishva Manav Mandal 1968
Vlahov, Ivan S. 1966
Encl: l. to A. Momigliano
BR to 1966
Voice of the Unions (Richard Fletcher) to RSt. **2** .... n.d.
Encl: essay (by Ken Coates?)
RSt. to 1968
Voice of Women (Judith Cook) **5** 1962-3
Encl: circulars, l. to J. F. Kennedy
BR to **6** 1962-4
Vollrem, Kaare, BR to 1963
Volunteers' Organizations for World Disarmament (Christian Kier) 1965
Encl: leaflets, l. from Philip Noel-Baker, l. from Eduard Hambro
PW to 1965
von Ardenne, Manfred 1956
von Schwarze, Klaus E. R., BR to 1962
von Westphalen, Karl 1968
BR to **2** 1965-8
von Winthofen, Alexander, BR to 1966
Votes for Youth Campaign (J. M. Honfield) to BRPF 1963
Encl: circular, petition
BR to 1963

W

Wade, Margaret 1964
RS to 1964
Wadhams, Jack 1965

Encl: ls. to and from "Pendennis"
RS to ... 1965
Wadia, H. R. ... 1962
Encl: essay
BR to ... 1962
Waerland, Ebba **2** ... 1962
Encl: magazine article
To RS ... 1962
BR to ... 1962
Wagunyanya, J. G., to
RS **2** ... 1966
RS to **2** ... 1966
PW to ... 1966
Waih, Elisabeth ... 1966
Waite, Tom, BR to ... 1964
Wajdani, Malik H. ... 1965
Wald, George **2** ... 1969
Encl: speech
BR to ... 1969
Wales Against Apartheid (R. A. Coates) **2** ... 1969
CF to ... 1969
Wales Rejects Apartheid Co-Ordinating Committee (form l.) ... n.d.
Walker, Claire ... 1963
BR to ... 1963
Walker, Jan ... 1966
Walker, Samantha, to
BRPF ... 1965
RS to ... 1965
Walker, T. ... n.d.
Wallis, R. G. ... 1965
PW to ... 1965
Walter, Nicolas, to
BR and ER ... 1966
To CF ... n.d.
To RS ... 1965
Encl: questionnaires
CF to **3** ... 1962-5
Walters, Margaret, to
BRPF ... 1968
CF to ... 1968
Walton, E. H. H. ... 1967
CF to ... 1967
Wantuck, Julius O. ... 1962
BR to ... 1962
War Resisters' International (Tony Smythe, Devi Prasad, *et al.*) **2** ... 1966-9
To RS **4** ... 1962
To PW ... 1962
To CF **2** ... 1962-8
Encl: magazines, circulars
RS? to ... 1962
CF to **4** ... 1962-9
PW to ... 1966
War Resisters League (David McReynolds) to CF **3** ... 1964
Encl: circular
CF to **3** ... 1964-5
Warbey, William, CF to ... 1965
Warburg, James P., to *New York Times* **2** ... 1964-6
Encl: essay
Ward, Michael D., to
RS **2** ... 1965
HR to ... 1965
RS to **2** ... 1965
RSt. to ... 1967
Ward, Robert ... 1962
CF to ... 1962
Ward, Shirley ... 1963
BR to ... 1963
Warda, Samuel S. ... 1967
To RSt. ... 1967?
Encl: clippings
RSt. to ... 1967
Warth, Derek ... 1962
BR to ... 1962
Washington, Walter ... 1967
CF to ... 1967
University of Washington Vietnam Committee (Calvin Winslow) ... 1968
Watkins, Peter R. ... 1964
To CE ... 1964
CE to ... 1964
Watson, Dean? ... 1967
Watson, Gordon ... 1963
Encl: l. to *The Statesman*
BR to ... 1963
Watson-Watt, Sir Robert ... 1962
To CF ... 1962
To RS **2** ... 1962
Encl: l. to Joseph Rotblat, clipping
BR to ... 1962
RS to **2** ... 1962

CF to **2** 1962-3
WBAI-FM Radio (Frank Millspaugh), RS to **2** 1966
Weaver, Anthony (circulars) .. 1967
CF to 1967
Webb, Colin 1967
CF to 1967
Weber, Neil 1969
Weener, Martin, to RS .... n.d.
Encl: advertisements, c.
RS to 1966
Wegodsky, R. 1964
BR to 1964
Weidner, Hansgeorg 1962
Encl: magazine
BR to 1962
Weil, Robert, CF to 1968
Weiler, Heinrich,
CF to 1969
Weinberg, Mindy 1964
BR to 1964
Weir, Ian G. **10** 1962-7
Encl: clipping, diagram, l. to "F. D."
BR to **2** 1963
Weisberg, Harold 1966
BR to 1966
RS to 1966
Weiss, Peter, Takman, Jan, and Limqueco, Peter 1967
BR to **3** 1966-9
Wellborne, J. E. de Montfort, to CE 1963
BR to 1963
Wells, Donald R. 1964
RS to 1964
The Welsh Party (Plaid Cymru) 1958
BR to 1958
Weltert, Christopher 1969
PW to 1969
Wenk, Juerg, to BRPF 1969
Werner, R. .... 196?
West, E. G. .... 196?
West Birmingham Youth CND (John K. Boler) to BRPF ... 1963
To CF 1963
CF to **2** 1963
West European Conference for Amnesty Portuguese Political Prisoners and Exiles (H. Ward) 1962
West Indies Guiana Socialist Union (Sydney Burnett Alleyne),
BR to 1964
West Indies News Bulletin (press release, resolution, leaflet) 1965
West Pakistan College Teachers Association (Hasnain Kazmi) 1965
BR to 1965
Western Institute for Advanced Study (D. M. Morandini),
PW to 1966
Weston, Mary 1963
Wheeler, John, to RS? 1965
RS to 1965
Whisson, M. E. **2** 1969-70
Encl: l. to *New Scientist*
White, Louis A., BR to 1963
White, Merit P. (open l. to Jacob Malik, Soviet Ambassador to UN) 1968
White, Robert Tyner 1967
Encl: leaflet
The White Cross Movement for Infantile Paralyses (M. H. Amswych) **5** 1962
Encl: note, form l., leaflets, l. to *Peace News*, note from *Peace News* to BRPF
BR to 1962
RS to 1964
Whitehead, N. .... 196?
Whlie, Thomas D., BR to 1963
Wickens, Keith, BR to 1963
Wicks, John **2** 1964
To RS **5** 1964-6
To PW 1966
RS to **4** 1964-5
PW to **2** 1966-7
Wiggs, Richard 1963
To BRPF 1964
To CF 1964
Encl: form l., essay
CF to 1964
RS to 1964
Wighton, Charles 1963
BR to 1963
RS to 1963

Wijesena, P. K. D. 1964
BR to 1964
Wildbolz-Dorman, Moura ... 1968
CF to 1968
Wiley, John C. 1963
Wilhelmy, Jerry 1962
BR to 1962
Wilkes, Mr. and Mrs. Owen,
BR to 1966
Wilkes, R. G. **3** 1964-9
BR to **2** 1964
CF to **2** 1969
Wilkinson, M. G. 1962
BR to 1962
Willcox, Bertram F. 1966
BR to **2** 1966
Williams, Anne M., BR to ... 1964
Williams, Bennett L. (ls. to John Peet, J. F. Kennedy, L. B. Johnson) 1963-8
BR to **4** 1963
Williams, Bryan 1965
BR to 1965
Williams, Bryce, BR to 1963
Williams, Charles St. E. **2** .. 1966
Encl: magazines
BR to 1966
Williams, Eva **2** 1966-7
Encl: l. to *New York Post*, clippings
RS to **2** 1966
Williams, Neville V. **2** ... 1955-62
BR to 1962
Williams, Richard **2** 1968-9
CF to 1969
Williams, Robert L. **2** 1968
Williamson, J. H., BR to **2** 1964
Wills, Michael .... n.d.
Wills, T. T. 1964
RS to 1964
Wils, Ingrid, to BR and ER 1963
Wilson, ? 1965
Wilson, G. H. 1968
Encl: clipping
Wilson, M. H., to BRPF 1965
PW to 1965
Winchester, Gail, to BRPF ... 1965
Winiawsky, Clemens 1967

Wink, Walter 1968
CF to 1968
Winkel, Victor W., BR to 1963
Winslow, Hank 1962
BR to 1962
Winston, James, to *The Guardian* 1965
Winter, Ella, to RS .... n.d.
Encl: petition
RS to **2** 1962-4
BR to 1967
Winwood, A., to CF 1963
Encl: poem
Wirtanen, Atos 1966
Encl: clipping
Witchell, John B. 1962
Encl: l. to Jon Tinker, clipping, affidavit
RS to 1962
AY to 1962
Witlin, Frances **2** 1964
Encl: leaflets
BR to 1964
RS to 1964
Wittig, Georg 1966
Wittkamp, William T. 1965
Wivel, Ole, BR to 1967
Wobbe, Charles C. 1965
RS to 1965
Wober, J. M. (leaflet) .... n.d.
Wolf, Professor, and Bittrich, Professor, BR to 1966
Wolin, Ron, RSt.? to 1968
Wolkowska, Ruth A. 1962
BR to 1962
Women Against War (Eileen Bernal) 1962
To ER **2** 1963
To RS 1965
Encl: leaflets
BR to 1962
ER to 1963
CF to 1965
PW to 1965
Women for Peace (Anna Vroland, Gloria Feldman) 1965
To BRPF 1963
Encl: leaflets
BR to 1963
CE to 1963

Women Strike for Peace (Dagmar Wilson *et al.*) **3** 1964-5
To CE 1963
Encl: petition, note
RS to 1963
BR to **4** 1964
Women's Association for Radiation Information (Pauline Phillips *et al.*) 1963
To RS 1962
Encl: leaflet
NJ to 1962
BR to 1963
Women's International League for Peace and Freedom (Sue Rose *et al.*) **10** 1961-9
To ER 1964
To BRPF **2** 1964
To RS **2** 1964
Encl: flyer, pamphlets, leaflets, clipping, form ls., newsl., l. to de Gaulle
BR to **4** 1962-4
RS to **5** 1964
PW to 1969
NJ to 1961
Wood, G., BR to 1963
Wood, Herbert 1962
BR to 1962
Wood, Marilyn Rose and Stuart L. 1963
BR to 1963
Wood, Roman Kenneth, BR to 1964
Woodley, William L., BR to 1963
Woods, R. A. 1969
CF to 1969
Woodward, M., BR to 1963
Woodworth, Richard H., to George Allen & Unwin 1967
PW to 1967
Worcester College for the Blind (Michael Beck *et al.*) (circular) 1966
Workers Committee for the Defence of Freedom of Press and Freedom of Speech (circular) 1968
Working Group World Union (circular) 1968
World Academy of Art and Science (Hugo Boyko) 1965
World Affairs Club, Tarsus (Cengiz Çandar and Can Saydam) 1965
To PW 1966
PW to **2** 1966
World Assembly for Peace (H. Elamin, M. Husseini) .. 1969
CF to 1969
World Association of World Federalists (Tokutaro Kitamura, Ichi Morita) 1963
Encl: circulars
BR to 1963
Encl: short essay
CF to 1968
PW to 1968
World Committee for a World Constitutional Convention (Philip Isely) **9** 1963-8
Encl: form ls., leaflets, agenda, l. to President Nkrumah, Prime Minister Kaunda, President Ayub Khan
BR to **5** 1963-6
RS to 1965
World Conference Against A [and] H Bombs 1968
BR to **2** 1968
World Congress for World Federation 1966
Encl: ls. to Prime Ministers of Singapore, Malaysia-Indonesia, Foreign Ministers of Burma, Thailand, Japan, Ceylon, Nepal, Cambodia, Afghanistan; leaflets
RS to 1966
World Congress of Women (Bess Marsh, Joan Carritt) to ER **2** 1963
Encl.
ER to **2** 1963
BR to 1964
World Council of Peace (J. D. Bernal *et al.*) **7** 1962-3
To BRPF **2** 1965

Encl: leaflets, clippings
BR to **3** 1963
World District Agency
(A. Von Samson, J. de
Castro) **2** 1964
Encl: leaflets, calling c.
BR to **3** 1964-5
World Federalists of Canada
(Ruth McFarlane) 1967
World Forum (journal) 1967
World Government League
(R. Kishore) 1969
CF to 1969
World Government of Youth
(David Arnold) .... n.d.
Encl: leaflet
BR to 1962
World Institute for World Peace
(J. Weingarten) 1964
BR to **3** 1964
World Internationalists
(Richard Daly) to BRPF ... 1967
World Muslim Congress
(Inamullah Khan) to CF ... 1967
CF to 1967
World Peace Association
(Alexander Winthofen) 1969
CF to 1969
World Peace Brigade (Suresh
Ram, Max Maxwell, A. J.
Muste) **7** 1962-3
To CF 1963
To RS **2** 1963
Encl: leaflets
BR to **3** 1962-3
CF to **2** 1963
RS to **2** 1963-4
The World Peace Research
Association (H. F.
Tung) **2** 1963
To RS **2** 1962-3
Encl: applications for certifi-
cates of identity, photos, form l.
BR to 1963
RS to 1963
World Union of Freethinkers
(C. Bradlaugh Bonner) 1963
Wormald, Michael **2** 1959
BR to 1959
Worrall, Michael 1968
Worrall, T., to CND 1965
PW to 1965
Worthy, William, NJ to 1962
RS to **2** 1965-6
Encl: l. from NJ to Taylor Adams
Wrightson, Graham 1965
To RS **3** 1965-6
RS to **4** 1965-6
Wrightson, Rodger, to
BRPF 1965
Wyatt, Winifred L. **2** 1967
CF to 1967
Wyly, III, L. David 1964
BR to 1964
Wyly, L. T. 1966
Encl: l. to Senator Fulbright,
clipping
Wyman, Daniel 1963
BR to 1963

Y

Yamada, Setsuo **2** 1967-8
Encl: Hiroshima Peace
Declarations 1967-8
BR to 1967
Yan, Law Wai 1966
To RS **5** 1966
RS to 1966
PW to 1966
Yapa, C. S., to Chief Justice of
the American Judiciary 1967
Yeager, Ruth G. .... n.d.
PW to 1965
Yeakel, Jesse .... n.d.
RS to 1966
Yelland, Leslie F. 1968
CF to 1968
Ying, Seto Kwok **2** 1963
BR to **2** 1963
Yoshida, Micko, BR to 1964
Young, Denis 1967
Young, Edgar P. .... n.d.
CF to 1969
Young, Fredric .... n.d.
CF to 1968
Young, L. C., to BRPF 1967
Young, Tony, to RS 1967
Young European Left (Fred
Sawbridge) 1968

Encl: leaflet
Young Men's Progressive Association (S. M. Joshi) ... 1962
Encl: s.
Youth Action for Peace (Margaret Laver) 1963
BR to 1963
Youth Against War and Fascism (Deirdre Griswold),
BR to 1966
RS to 1966
Youth Peace Campaign (John Goldschmidt) to BRPF ..... n.d.
Yueff, Mike, to BRPF 1969
CF to 1969
Yule, Alastair, to RS and Pat Pottle 1963

Z

Zajícek, Oldrich 1962
Encl: form l., s.
BR to 1962
Zaman, A. 1966
PW to 1966
Zamindar, N.C. **4** 1962
To NJ? 1962
Encl: poem
BR to **2** 1962
NJ to 1962
RS to 1963
ER to 1964
Zamir, Shalom 1968
To BRPF 1969
Encl: open l. to President Nasser, open l. to UN delegates, s.
Zandee, Pieter, CF to 1968
Zaninovic, Lucas Seperiza,
BR to 1964
Zasler, Bob 1967
BR to 1966
Zia-un-Nabi, Syed 1965
PW to 1965
Ziegler, Antoinette 1965
RS to 1965
Zilliacus, Konni 1963
Encl: l. to *New Statesman*
BR to 1963
Zinner, A. 1966
Zivanović, Milisav M. 1969
Encl: l. to President Tito, l. to U Thant, response from UN
Zook, Douglas-Paul, to
BRPF 1969
CF to 1969
Zuby, Ozzir 1966
Encl: reproduction of painting
BR to 1966
Zunic, Radovan **3** 1964-9
Encl: plans for a new organ of the UN
BR to 1964
CF to 1969
Zuno Arce, Andrés, to
BRPF 1968
To PW 1969
PW to 1968
Zusman, Salomon 1965
Encl: l. from European Commission of the Rights of Man, l. from Malayan lawyer

*316 Financial Correspondence Relating to Politics

The Bertrand Russell Peace Foundation was financed partly through donations and partly through Russell's own resources. The former were very important to the BRPF, as they were a demonstration of popular support for the Foundation's work. Such correspondence begins, however, in 1962, when Russell's political work first received the financial support of others interested in it. The class also includes business correspondence on topics such as Russell's frequently interrupted telephone service.

Documents .159107–.162198

Angela Abbott
Acton Society Trust (Roy Manley)
Marion Adams
Pam Adams
Laird Addis
Bernard Ades
Esther H. Adler
M. G. Akhurst
James L. Allison
Ambassade de Belgique
Thomas Amneus
Amsterdam-Rotterdam Bank (re Mevrouw G. Angeloff-Hoefsmit)
Apeco Ltd. (B. E. Hood)
Archangel Agency
Ashfords & Sons
Associated Insurers (British Electricity) Management Committee
Atlas Photography Ltd.
J. E. Bailey
Bank of London and South America
Banque Nationale de Belgique
Barclays Bank
B. Barr
Martin Bayer
O. K. Bazaars (Sam Cohen)
Beach & Beach, Solicitors
E. Beckman
Ralph P. Bell
John Bell and Croydon (Mr. Lambert)
Henry Beloch?
Anthony Wedgwood Benn
John Berryman
Emma M. and Lester Bigg
B. M. Birla
P. S. Bland
Baron P. Bonvoisin
Brighton Kemp Town Labour Party (Gillian C. A. Steer)
British Aid to Algeria Committee
British Eagle International Airlines
British European Airways
British Insurance Association
British Motor Corporation
British Olivetti Ltd. (G. Fei)
W. J. Brook
Olga Brooks
E. H. Brooks & Sons
Clara Browder
G. Bulkeley
Burroughs Corporation (Dan P. Lutzeier)
Jane Buxton
Edward Cammack
Paolo Cavara
A. P. Cavendish
Lloyd Chandler
Elizabeth Goucher Chapman (Mrs. B.

Burgoyne Chapman)
Chester Telephone Area
Jean Christie
Webber D. Clark
C. R. A. Clarke
Clyne Radio Ltd.
K. D. Cole
Collet's Holdings Ltd.
William L. Collier
Albert L. Colloms
Committee to Aid the Bloomington Students (Joyce De Groot)
Conn, Goldberg & Co., Solicitors
Cooperative Retail Services (P. J. Parsons)
Roy Coupal
Coventry Cathedral (H. C. N. Williams)
Coward, Chance & Co. (L. P. Tylor)
Ephraim Cross
Gertrude B. Cuneo
J. W. Dafoe Foundation, University of Manitoba (D. Chevrier)
Daimler Hire Ltd.
Daimler-Benz Aktiengesellschaft
Dartmouth Street Trust
Brian Darwent
Mr. and Mrs. ? Davis
Peter Dawnay Publishers
Defence and Aid Fund (Rica Hodgson)
Irene Den Bok
E. De Rango
Thomas C. Desmond
O. Detoman
Diablo Press Ltd.
The Diner's Club
H. L. Dixon
Ian Dixon
Nita Dixon
N. Dopsin
Louise Jackson Doyle
A. Drachman
John A. Duggan
Duncairn Divisional Labour Party (D. Murphy)
Dunlop Rubber Co. Ltd.
Greta Duschinsky
M. Eady
George D. Edwards
Hugh Edwards
English Electric Company
Sven Erixson
Rosalie Ernest
Charles Evans
G. Evans
Evening Standard (R. C. Parrett)
Douglas N. Everingham
Marvin Fallgatter
Family Trustee Company Ltd. (P. R. Smith)
P. Farley
Paul J. Feder
Sergiu Feldman
Giangiacomo Feltrinelli
Fiat Societa per Azioni
Anthony Filton
Stella Fisher Bureau
B. M. Foley
James Foley
Ford & Son
Paul T. Forrer
E. French
Darrell N. Garwood
General Guarantee Corporation Ltd. (R. L. Sendles)
Peter Gessner and Robert Kramer
Glyn-Mills and Co. (Childs)
Goodwin Press Ltd. (L. Cooke, Hugh Brock)
Donald V. Graham
Evan D. Griffin (encl: Frank [Hempl?] to CF)
Fuller Griffith
Gujarat University, India
Calouste Gulbenkian Foundation, Lisbon (J. C. Thornton)
Arthur ap Gwynn
Gypsy Council Liaison Committee (Grattan Puxon)
M. Hacker
Halford, Henry, Montefiore & Co.
Theodore Hall
Molly Hallett
Hambros Bank Ltd.
Hammond and Champness Ltd.
Sonia Harrison
The Hatfield Press Ltd.
Roy Heimbach
L. J. Heistek

John Hendrickson
Norman Henry
Hepburn & Ross Ltd.
Mary Herman
Hertz Drive Yourself Stations of Ontario Ltd.
Hertz Rent a Car
Hickson, Lakeman & Holcombe
C. F. L. Hill
Margo Strange Hill
H. M. Stationery Office
Hodge Unit Trust Managers Ltd. (K. M. Roberts)
M. Holmes
Rexford Holmes
A. S. Horsley
Houses of Parliament Sports and Social Club
Elmina Huddy
Jane Huff
Phillip Hugh-Jones
Mrs. Bill Hughes
Hungarian Sports News (Paul Zelenka)
June Hunt
M. Hussey
Indian Students Hostel
Inland Revenue
Inner London Telephone Centre
Inspector of Taxes
International Conference of Youth and Students for Disarmament, Peace, and National Independence (Shoichiro Hatsuoka)
Iranian National Front
William Jackson Books Ltd.
Alice Jenkins
C. D. Jenkins
J. Jennisen
Victor Jensen
The Jewish Chronicle
Jewish Observer & Middle East Review
Jiffy Packing Company
Arnold Johnson
Mr. and Mrs. David Johnson
Warren Russell Johnson
D. A. Johnston
Emrys Jones
H. A. Jones
W. M. Jones (Mansel Davies)
George Joy
K. K. L. Executors and Trustees Co. Ltd.
Robert Kahn
Randall P. Kane
Kay Laboratories
Lorin E. Kerr
R. W. King
King, Wood & Company, Auctioneers, Surveyors & Valuers
Kjøbenhavns Telefon Aktieselskab
Jon Kraus
Irving F. Laucks
M. Leslie
Benn W. Levy
Bernard Lee Lifshutz
Liverpool School of Tropical Medicine (D. White)
Lloyds Bank Ltd. (J. C. Halsall)
Lloyd's Bookshop
Lockheed Missiles and Space Company (J. W. Brandon)
London Electricity Board
P. Maastgleugen
Dwight Macdonald
H. E. Madams
Frank Maguire
Manila Banking Corporation
Judd Marmor
F. M. Martin
Ubiratan R. Mascarenhas
Margery Mason
Julien Masseron
William McGovern & Co. Ltd.
Susheela Mehra Memorial Hospital (C. L. Anand)
Heinrich Meng
Mercantile Bank Ltd.
M. J. Metcalfe
Methodist International House (Clifford Cook)
Joseph Meyer
David H. Miller
F. Eugene Miller
Ian Miller
Dan Molony
Monthly Review (Paul M. Sweezy)
Elizabeth and Geoffrey J. Morrow
Andrew R. Morton
R. W. Muladore
R. Myall

National Hotel, Bedford Way
National Institute for Social Work Training (J. M. Hunt)
Nefa Services: J.L. Printing and Stationery Supplies
Pietro Nenni
B. H. Neumann
New Left Review (Quintin Hoare)
New York Herald Tribune (J. Glockman)
Wayne H. Nielsen
Gwen Lloyd Noad
Northfield and Mount Hermon Schools
Nu-Swift International Ltd.
Walter Fraser Oakeshott
Keith Osborne
Osborne King & Megran
"Our Dogs" Publishing Co. Ltd.
Christine Overy
Percy W. Oyler
W. Pace
Pan American World Airways
Thomas Parry
Tom Parry & Co.
Pavilion Hotel, Scarborough (W. M. Reid)
Harry H. Payne
P. J. Payne
Peace Seals (Jeremy M. Palmer)
People's Co-operative Bookstore (C. Rush)
Lyman L. Petersen
P. E. Peterson
Bernard Phillips & Co.
Suzanne Picot
Gerard Piel
Leopoldo Pirelli
The Portland Finance Company (M. Essex)
Portmadoc Waterworks Co.
John Powles
Prime Minister's Secretariat, India (K. L. Gupta)
Lea Provo
A. J. Prust
Purdue & Greenhill
Salvatore Quasimodo
Enrique Raab
Louis M. Rabinowitz Foundation (Victor Rabinowitz)
Edward Randall
Jean Redman
Rufus H. Reed
W. R. Rodger Reid
Arnold E. Reif
Beatrice Reilly
William Reimbold
S. Reizin
Marcel Renard
Reserve Bank of India
Reserve Bank of New Zealand (G. Wilson)
David Robinson
F. Robinson
David Rockefeller
The Rockefeller Foundation (J. Kellum Smith, Jr.)
Rosemarie Röder
E. Rodker
Rodney Youth Centre, Liverpool
Rolls Prestcold Appliances Ltd. (Harvey Langer)
Dennis Rosen
Martin Rosen
Roth-Warren Pharmacists (Saul Roth)
Andrew Rothstein
Rowen Onllwyn Ltd. (Frank Gregory)
Royal National Institute for the Deaf
Royal Naval Association (F. Jones-Hughes *et al.*)
Royal Sportsman Hotel (C.P. Grimsell)
Margaret Russell
Robert Ryan
Joseph C. Sabbeth
Ben Sackheim
St. Saviours Church (Francis Anderson)
Arnold Saltzman
Helen G. Saran
Oliver Scallan
Joseph K. Scarlett
Edward Schindtler
Blanche Schlick
Michael Schmidt
Georgia H. Schneider
Morris D. Schneider
Schott & Co. Ltd. (Ian Kemp)
Belle W. Schulz

Scientists Appeal for Vietnam (C.F. Powell)
Cyril Scott Presentation Fund
Gerald Seaman
V. Sels
T.W. Seragg
M. Seyler
Ben Shahn
The Shakespeare Exhibition (The Earl of Harewood)
Farid Shanti
Denis Shaw
F.A. Sheppard
George Shields
Daniel Shively
A.D. Shroff
John H. Sieff
Siemans-Schuckertwerke A.G. (F. Bauer)
Albert Siggs
Ruth B. Simon
D. Simpson
E.L. Simpson
Esther Singer
Julia Smailes
Peter Smith
L. Soiseth
Solicitors' Law Stationery Society, Ltd.
R.W. Sorensen
Spanish Refugee Aid, Inc. (Hannah Arendt *et al.*)
The Spastics Society (James Loring)
Armin Speegel
Wolf Spoerl Ltd.
Bernard R.J. Staines
W.G. Standen
John Steadman
Anne Steinmann
The Lawrence Sterne Trust (Kenneth Monkman)
Dorothy Stewart
Lily Strobl
Studio Neue Literatur (Gundrun Esslin)
Graham Sutherland
Swiss Credit Bank (J.J. Kurz)
Kent Sym
Ruth Symonds
Leon Szur
R.H. Tagett
Tarrant & Frazer Ltd.
W.H. Temple
C. Thompson
Werner Thönnessen
J.E. Tonnies
Trans World Airlines Inc.
Trust House Services Ltd.
Tuborg Breweries Ltd. (Viggo J. Rasmussen)
Horikoshi Tunemi
Judith M. Turner
Bert Tuttle
Unitarian Universalist Association
United Association for the Protection of Trade (London Branch) (A. Smith)
United Nations Student Association (Edwin H. Cox)
United Nations Association in Canada, Hamilton Branch (D.M. Davies)
United Tobacco Company (K.M. de Villiers)
Universal Friendship Organisation
Universal Medical Assistance (Nicola Manessis)
Universities Fight for Economic Development (Clive Jordan)
Ingegerd Uppman
William V. Vitarelli
Voice of Women (Kathleen Macpherson)
Christopher Wade Ltd.
Aileen Walker
L.R. Walker
Derek Wallace
Harry A. Warner
Y. Washi
"Watamu Expedition", University College of North Wales (W.F. Humphreys)
Doris W. Waters
Julyan A. Watts
Herr Weisbart
Arnold and Rita Weiss
John Weiss
Rollin Webber
Ellen C. Weight
Dorothea Weitzner
K.J. Weller

R. C. West
John Westergaard
Westminster Bank Ltd.
George White (Stationer)
G. Whitman
Wicken Fen Appeal (Charles Mitchell)
John J. Wielon
P. Wigham-Richardson & Co.
Helen Wilkes
R. Williams
Archie M. Winckworth
Robert E. Wise
Woburn Trust
Wolfe and Hollander, Ltd.
Miles D. Wolpin
William M. Woods
Ethel Woolf
K. R. Wootton
World Citizens Information Communication Centre
World People's Television Offices (Nicholas Wardey)
Tom Xynides
Natasha Yakovleva
E. R. Yarham
Douglas Young
Young Women's Christian Association of Great Britain (Myfanny Evans)
Susie Younger Korean Trust
Richard Zatloukal-Williams
Frank P. Zeidler
A. Zerfas

*320 World Affairs

Included here is Russell's correspondence with heads of state and governmental bodies. The correspondence starts as early as 1955 and ends in 1970s. Press statements by Russell are also to be found here. The catalogue lists the correspondents' names under each country chronologically *according to the first appearance of that correspondent in the file*.

Documents .177001–.183284

Aden 1965

Aden Trades Union Congress (Deputy General Secretary)

Afghanistan 1964-6

Faiz Ahmad Zikria
Zahir Shah
Ambassador of Afghanistan

Albania 1965-9

Ambassador to France (Kritaq Misha)
Enver Hoxha
Albanian Peace Committee (Petraq Pojani)
Albanian Peace Committee (Thanas Nano)
Le Monde
The Times
Jean-Paul Sartre
Laurent Schwartz

Algeria 1957-69

Ritchie Calder, L. John Collins, Benn W. Levy
Ahmed Ben Bella
Mouvement Algerian Paix (Souiah Haouari)
Algiers Appeal
Abdelaziz Bouteflika
Houari Boumedienne
Tunisian National Opposition (Ibrahim Tobal)

Australia 1964-7

BR, s., "A Warning to the People of Australia and New Zealand"
Australian Women's Project Against French Tests in the Pacific (Sybil Cookson)
South Coast Peace Committee (M. Nixon)
Australia and New Zealand Congress for International Co-operation and Disarmament (Denny Martin)
The Federal Council for the Advancement of Aborigines and Torres Strait Islanders (Mamie Smith)

Austria 1961-9

Oesterr Gewerkschaftsbund
Niederösterreichischer Badminton-Verband (Walter Annerl)
Günther Anders
Alfons Gorbach
Christian Broda
Austrian Ambassador (Joseph Schroenen)
E. Hochleitner

Bahrain 1965

Bahraini Students (Mohammed Naserallah)
Bahraini Students in Beirut (A. Rahman Nuasami)

Belgium 1961-9

La Conférence des Sommets (Dino Vastapane)
Queen Elisabeth of Belgium
Baron Jean van den Bosch
Le Directeur, Palais de Justice (L. Raymaekers)
Ligue Belge pour la Défense des Droits de l'Homme (G. Aronstein)

Bolivia 1967-70

BR, s.
I. F. Stone's Weekly
Le Monde
New York Herald Tribune
The Times
Siempre
Rene Barrientos Ortuno
Christopher Logue
BR, press s.
Siles Salinas
Jean-Paul Sartre *et al.*
Alfredo Ovando Canvia
Mariano Baptista Gumcio
Monthly Review Press
New Left Review (David Fernbach)
Ideologie (F. Rossi-Landi)
Saverio Tutino
Woodfall Films Ltd. (Tony Richardson)
Brian Darling

Brazil 1964-5

Joao Belchior Marques Goulart
Castelo Blanco
João A. da Costa Doria
BR, s. entitled, "Message to the Continental Congress of Solidarity with Cuba"

Bulgaria 1965-8

Todor Zhivkov
Embassy of the People's Republic of Bulgaria (L. Zhelyaskov)
Peter Voutov
Mrs. ? Alexander
BR, s. entitled "Message from Bertrand Russell to the Sofia Youth Festival"
The Times
Le Monde

Burma 1964-6

U Hla Maung
Ne Win
Tin Pe
V. H. Binh

Cambodia 1964-70

Norodom Sihanouk
So Nem
Hing-Ear and Ngeth-Sophy
Chan Youran
Hong Hoeung Doeune
Samdech Chef de L'Etat au Parlement
Chef du Cabinet, Cambodia
Charles Meyer
Chau Seng
Norodom Phurissara
Pho Bopin
? Margain
Lon Nol
Lawrence Daly *et al.*
Ung Mung
Sihauouk, s. on IWCT
Nguon Chhay Kry
Nguon Pytoravuth
s. of discussions with Cambodians

Cameroons 1965

Ahmadou Ahidjo

Canada—Political Prisoners and Civil Liberties 1963–5

John R. Glenn
Canadian Campaign for Nuclear Disarmament (Abraham L. Feinberg)
Copy of D. Stanley, *The Red Rabbi*

Canada 1958–63

Brian E. Johnston
Aubrey J. Halter
Beatrice Ferneyhough
Canadian Institute of International Affairs (Anna Solomcoe)
Toronto Daily Star
Clive Neumann
Lester B. Pearson
Alec Beasley
Alma Mater Society of the University of Victoria (Gordon R. Pollard)
BR, ts. p.4 only, re Canada's role

Ceylon 1963–9

High Commissioner

A. T. Moorthy
Sirimavo Bandaranaike
B. P. Tilakaratna
D. S. Senanayake

Chile 1963-8

The Royal Institute of International Affairs (Claudio Veliz)
BR, s. entitled "Message to the People of Chile and Latin America"
Salvador Allende
Eduardo Frei
Teusaca (Fernando Vélez)

China 1955-70

Andrew Boyd, Denis Mathews, D. M. Ross
***People's Daily*, Peking (C. H. Yeh)**
Hsinhua News Agency
Chou En-lai
Office of Chargé d'Affaires of the People's Republic of China in the United Kingdom (Hsiung Hsiang-hui; later, Hsieh Chi-mei, Shen Ping)
Press s.
***Unarmed Victory*, 2 ts. pp.**
Li Chu-wen
Anna Louise Strong
Kuo Mo-jo
J. D. Bernal, s.
Li Shon-pao
Ping-po
Society for Anglo-Chinese Understanding (Derek Bryan, Hugh Trevor-Roper *et al.*)
BR, ts., "The Yellow Peril?"
Mao Tse-tung
***La Sinistra* (Giulio Savelli)**
C. A. Watts & Co.

China—Political Prisoners 1968

Jeffrey Gordon
Anita Gordon

Congo (Brazzaville) 1964-8

Text of testimony to United Nations Security Council
***Africa and the World* (RS's article with K. Zaki)**
Zahir Shar, Afghanistan, and all other heads of state (form ls.)
Embassy of the Republic of the Congo in the United Kingdom (J. A. Kabemba, Chargé d'Affaires)
Daily Telegraph
Alphonse Massamba-Débat
Mobutu

Cuba 1960-70

Cuban Embassy in Great Britain (Sergio Rojas Santamarina, Federico de Córdova Castro, Luis Ricardo Alonso, *et al.*)
***Tribune* (Sheila Noble)**
Michael Callinan
Syndicalist Workers' Federation (Ken Hawkes)
***I. F. Stone's Weekly* (I. F. Stone)**
Fidel Castro
BR, message to the Continental Congress of Solidarity with Cuba
BR, s.
John Wicks
Osvaldo Dorticos Torrado
BR, message to rally in Havana
Latin American Congress of Solidarity with Cuba and the Right of the Peoples to Self-determination (Victorio Casartelli, Elena Ruglio)
BR, press s.
BR, press s.; message to Solidarity Conference; message to the people of Cuba
Tana de Gámez
Casa de las Americas
Alba Antonia Griñán Núñez
Tri-Continental Committee in Support of Vietnam (Cardinas)
BR, "Message to Cuba, Answers to Marta Rojas"
Comité Cubano de Solidaridad con Viet-Nam del Sur
Herbert Read
Comité Organizador de la Organizacion Latinoaméricana de Solidaridad (Haydée Santamaria)
Jorge Bolaños
BR, message to the Organization of Solidarity of the Peoples of Asia, Africa, and Latin America
BR, message to the Havana Cultural Conference
BR, ss.
Ken Coates, O.L.A.S. speech (with s. by BR)
Text of interview with Ken Coates in *Juventud Rebelde*

Press release
Señor Manolo
Cultural Congress of Havana (José Llanusa Gobel)
Dagens Nyheter **(article on Che Guevara by Peter Weiss)**
Alois Grohs
Cuba Sixtyeight (Russell Stetler)
Osvaldo Paredes Alvarez
Juan Aguilar
International Youth Camp
London Bulletin**, no. 5**
Movement for Colonial Freedom (Barbara Haq)
Jean-Claude Garot
L'Organisation de Solidarité des Peuples d'Afrique, d'Asie et L'Amérique Latine (P. Jorge)
Nick Beeton
Instituto del Libro (Eduardo H. Gispert)
Britain-Cuba Association (Sheila Van Bloemen)
Cuba: Alegre Como Su Sol (with signatures of Vietnamese)
BR, *A la Consciencia de la humanidad*

Cyprus 1956-69

Cyprus Conciliation Committee
Greek Alumni Associations of Cyprus (Phoebus S. Christis)
Listowel
Movement for Colonial Freedom (Helen Bastable, John Eber)
United Democratic Youth Organisation of Cyprus (P. Peonides)
Zannetos Tofallis
National Cypriot Committee
Archbishop Makarios
F. Kuchuk
Prime Minister of Greece
Ismet Inonu
The Guardian
Mayor of Cavala (Mr. Tsolakis) and the Chairman of the Municipal Council (Mr. Baharis)
Cyprus High Commission (A. Cleanthous)
Swaziland Progressive Party *et al.*
Anglo-Cypriot Friendship Council (Manuela Sykes)
K. Papademetriou *et al.*

Czechoslovakia—Civil Liberties 1963-7

Leo B. Hieblinger
Edna Mayo
Vojtech Seidler
Irma Ehrlich
Eva Lukesh
Joseph Lenart
Jaroslav Hospodka

Czechoslovakia—Statements I 1968-9

New Statesman (Paul Johnson, Kingsley Amis)
The Times
The Guardian
Vecerni Praha (Jiri Has)
The Scotsman
BR, message to the Stockholm Conference on Czechoslovakia
Declarations of the Russell Conference on Czechoslovakia
The Irish Times
BR, l. to newspapers
Declaration of Members of the International War Crimes Tribunal

Czechoslovakia—Correspondence with Lenart and the Czech Embassy 1962-8

Head of Consular Department
M. Jiráska
Czechoslovakian Ambassador to the United Kingdom (Zdenek Trhlik, M. Růzek)
Mr. Czerny
Joseph Lenart
Frantisek Hruza
M. Glozar

Czechoslovakia—Correspondence with Novotny 1962-7

Antonin Novotny
Jaroslav Hospodka

Czechoslovakia—Correspondence with UN representative 1964-5

Permanent Representative of the Czechoslovak Socialist Republic to the United Nations (Jirí Hájek)

Czechoslovakia—Statements II 1968-70

Ss., appeals, press releases
Declaration of the Russell Conference on Czechoslovakia
Jiri Müller, Karel Kovanda and Lubos Kolacek
Alexei Kosygin

Czechoslovakia—Statements III 1968

BRPF appeal
International War Crimes Tribunal declaration
BR, s.

Dahomey 1965

Migan Apithy

Denmark 1964-6

C. O. Gjerløv-Knudsen
Jens Otto Krag
Knud Jespersen
Christen Amby
BR, s. on Vietnam

Dominican Republic 1967

Francisco Caamano

Ethiopia—Political Prisoners 1969

Ethiopian People's Movement Council
Arne Thing Mortensen
Jørg. Jørgensen

Ethiopia 1963-5

Haile Sellassie
Berhane Deneke
Yohannes Kidane Mariam
Ethiopian Ambassador to U.K. (Haddis Alemayehu)
British Ambassador (John Russell)
Menassie Haile

Finland 1964-9

Urho Kaleva Kekkonen
Kurt Westerholm
Richard Tötterman

Formosa—Political Prisoners 1968

Clippings re Chen Yu-hsi
Aiko and John Reinecke

Formosa 1968

Francis W. Chang

France—Political Prisoners 1969

Annuaire Internationale des Prisonniers Politiques
François Maspero

France 1958-68

J. Recht *et al.*
France-Observateur
Jean Chauvel
Jean Foyer
Fédération pour le Respect de l'Homme et de l'Humanité (André Gros)
BR, s. "Statement for French Radio"
Georges Pompidou
Roger Frey
BR, press s. re Mehdi Ben Barka
Charles de Gaulle
Paris-Match
François Mauriac
Mohamed Tahri
Consulat Général de France (P. Poli)
L. de Braulaycourt
Committee to Defend the French Students (Helena Hermes)

Gabon 1965

Leon M'Ba

Germany–*Foreign Affairs Bulletin* and Defence Committee for Victims of Nazi Persecution 1963-5

Defence Committee for Victims of Nazi Persecution (Elizabeth Dales)
Maurice Bolle
Foreign Affairs Bulletin

Germany—Nazi Documents 1964-8

Maurice Lichtig
Fédération Internationale des Résistants (Renato Bertolini)
Elizabeth Dales
Commission D'Histoire de la Fédération Internationale des Resistants
Defence Committee for Victims of Nazi Persecution
New Women's and Mothers' Pilgrim-

age to Rome for Peace
Information Service of the Peace Council of the German Democratic Republic
Comité Belge contre la Préscription des Crimes Nazis

Germany—Nazis (Heinz Reinfarth)

Central Commission for the Prosecution of War Crimes in Poland (Czeslow Pilichowski)
Photographs of Nazi documents

Germany—Correspondence re Nazis 1963-7

T. Immer and K. Linke
Komittee zum Schutze der Menschenrechte (E. Doller and F. Malter)
Defense Committee for the Victims of Nazi Persecution (Elizabeth Dales)
Fladung Defence Committee
? Morris
Aleksander Cichoski
O. Crautzfeldt
Kurt Hälker
Maurice Lichtig
Charles Wighton
German International
Bei Veroffentlichung in Ihrem Pressedienst
Conseil National des Victimes Spoliés d'Allemagne
Peter Foges
Carl Marzani
Women Strike for Peace (Miriam Levin)
Heinz Wilmann
Anita Zander
Lena M. Klein
Peace Council of the German Democratic Republic
Czechoslovak Radio (Kvetoslav Faix)
The Memorial Committee (L. Douglas)
Joseph Hajda
Maurice Bolle
BR?, s. "Extension of Deadlines on War Crimes"
Internationale Föderation der Widerstandskämpfer (Renato Bertolini)
Fraternelle des Amicales de Camps Verbroedering van de Vriendenkringen der Kampen (M. Bolle)
Internationales Treffen der Vertreter der Jugend und Studenten
Organisationsburo des Internationalen Jugendtreffens
Rita Eschefeld
Daily Telegraph
Wolfgang Knoper?
British Humanist Association (H. J. Blackham)
Carlheinz Stiller
Otto Schönfeldt
Association des Combattants pour la Liberté et la Democratie (Henryk Matysiak)

Germany (East)—Political Prisoners I 1962-7

Sigrid Gräßner
Hellmut Vogel
W. Shaw
Werner Gaida
Walter Thieme
Herbert Satter
Stefan Ammer
Paul Ptacek
"Groups for Three"
Amnesty International (P. Benenson, Christel Marsh)
Werner Strinitz
E. W. Wagstaff
Johannes Schillbach
Albert Lionel Colloms
Hellen Battle
Kurt Hahn

Germany (East)—Political Prisoners II 1965-70

Amnesty International (M. Pentreath, Paddy M. Coyle, Bruce Laird)
Hans J. Baer
Anneliese Nebauer
Mary Anne White
Liesbeth Henschel
Karl Stüpin
Horst Hock
D. D. Naird
Herbert Zajonz
Gotthard and Anita Böhme

Germany (East) 1962-8

Gerald Götting, Representative of the President of the Council of State of the German Democratic Republic
Joachim Hindemith
German Democratic Republic: Chancellory of the Council of State, Protocol and Organisation Department (Herr Streller)
Peace Council of the German Democratic Republic (Walter Friedrich, Kurt Hälker)
Walter Ulbricht
Daily Worker (George Matthews)
Blaetter fuer Deutsche und Internationale Politik
Herr Gotsche
Arvid von Nottbeck
Allgemeiner Deutscher Nachrichtendienst
Komittee zum Schutze der Menschenrechte (Friedel Malter)
BR, s. on Heinz Brandt
BR, s. to German Metal Workers' Union
I. G. Metall (Werner Thoenessen)
Stadt Frankfurt-am-Main, Oberbürgermeister Bockelmann
Ministry of Justice, German Democratic Republic (Hilda Benjamin, Richard Jaeger)
Communist Party of Germany (Max Reimann)
Minister of the Interior, German Democratic Republic (Friedrich Dickel)
Hellmut Vogel
Walter Thieme
Komitee der Antifaschistischen Widerstandskämpfer (Waldemar Schmidt)
CF, note on Hellen Battle, *Every Wall Shall Fall*
Attorney-General of the German Democratic Republic (Dr. Streit)

Germany (West)—Civil Liberties 1968

G. Schachter
World Jewish Congress (F. L. Brassloff, Emanuel Litvinoff)
Rozalia Schenker

Germany (West) 1954-68

Sozialistische Jugend Deutschlands (Lorenz Knorr)
K. Saller
Fritz Helling
Berliner Arbeitsausschuss "Gegen den Atomtod" (Ansgar Skriver)
Verband der Kriegsdienstverweigerer e. V. (Wilhelm Keller)
Deutsche Friedens-Union (L. Knorr)
Deutsche Friedensgesellschaft (Max Stierwaldt, Helmut Hertling, Erna Heitmann)
The Guardian
Defence Committee for Victims of Nazi Persecution (Elizabeth Dales)
The Observer
Maurice Lichtig
Embassy of the Federal Republic of Germany, Press Department (Hans Scherer)
Saar-Freundeskreis des Albert Schweitzer-Spitals in Lambarene-e.V. (Günther Heipp)
BR, press s.
West German Ambassador (Hasse von Etzdorf)
Minister of Justice of the Federal Republic of Germany (Ewald Bucher)
Ludwig Erhard
Der Chef des Bundeskanzleramtes (Dr. Osterheld)
Minister of Justice for Lower Saxony (Arvid von Nottbeck)
Der Präsident des Schleswig-Holsteinischen Landtages (Dr. Rohloff)
Der Ministerpräsidenten des Landes (Franz Meyers)
Heinrich Lübke
Bundespräsidialamt (Dr. Meyer)
Generalbundesanwalt
Der Bundesminister des Auswärtigen (Herr Arnold)
Albert L. Colloms
Kurt Hubrig
Rosel Lohse-Link

Wolfgang Wilhelm
Jürgen Horlemann
Lothar Menne

Germany (West)—Statements 1962-8

***Elan* clipping**
Text of interview in *Saur*
? s.
Florence Knepler
The Guardian
The Observer
Defence Committee for Victims of Nazi Persecution (Elizabeth Dales)
Richard Weyl
Message to Allgemeiner Deutscher Nachrichtendienst
Margaret Lloyd
Deutsche Volkszeitung (Fritz Hollstein)
Hamburger Komitee zur Wahrung Demokratischer
The Count of Westphalen
Kampagne für Abrüstung Ostermarsch der Atomwaffengegner (Andreas Buro)
Bayerische Staatszeitung (Dr. Lange)
BR, ss. on the German Peace Union and on Emergency Legislation
Klaus Vack
Bundesjustizministerium (R. Jaeger)
Friedrich Hund (including BR's introduction to the Born-Einstein book)

Germany (West)—Nazis 1963-7

BR, s.
Peace Council of the German Democratic Republic (Kurt Hälker)
Pamphlets
Defence Committee for Victims of Nazi Persecution (E. Dales)
Charles R. Allen, Jr.
Helmut Ridder

Ghana 1962-6

The Accra Assembly for the World Without the Bomb (Julie Medlock [many ls.], F. E. Boaten)
High Commissioner for Ghana (Kwest Armah)
University of Ghana (Conor Cruise O'Brien)
The Times
Press s.
The Guardian
Antony Steel
Shirley ?
Deputy Secretary to the Cabinet (T. K. Impraim)
Johnnie J. Mensah
Augustus D. Sackey
Ghana Peace Council (J. S. A. Stephens)
"Memorandum on the Congo and Southern Rhodesia"
BR, mimeo'd ts., "Africa and the Movement for Peace"

Greece 1962-8

"Bertrand Russell" Committee of 100 in Greece (M. Peristerakis)
T. Doganis
Jean Passalides
Diana Pym
Youth Society for Nuclear Disarmament "Bertrand Russell" Committee of 100
Greek Youth "Bertrand Russell" Committee for Nuclear Disarmament
Nicos Constandopoulos
BR, s., "Message from Bertrand Russell to the 'Bertrand Russell' Committee of 100 in Greece"
Pat Pottle
Greek Ambassador
Papayotis Pipenelis
Tom Swaine
Lady Peake
George A. Papandreou
Michel Melas
Comité Hellenique pour la Detente Internationale et la Paix
Association de Parents des Expatriotes Politiques Grecs à Angleterre (Maria Hadjiandreou)
Stephanos Stephanopoulos
[Thetis] Kotsaki
Committee of Fifth Marathon March for Peace (K. Pyromaglou)
Harold Wilson
George Papadopoulis

League for Democracy in Greece

Greece—Political Prisoners, etc. 1964-70

Athens Association of Political Exiles and Prisoners (Thetis Kotsaki)
Emily C. Moore
League for Democracy in Greece (Diana Pym)
World Federation of Democratic Youth (message from Mikis Theodorakis)
Amnesty International (Paul J. Lyons)
Democratic Committees of Resistance (B. Bladimiros, K. George)
Greek Committee Against Dictatorship *et al.* (Raphael Papadopoulos)
A. Hamilton
The Greek Relief Fund (E. E. Jordan)
Comité Central des Réfugiés Politiques de Grèce
Conseil Central des Comités Antidictatoriaux Grecs
Paul J. Guthrie
Free Greece Campaign
Fourth Marathon March Committee (M. Nikolaides) [This and the following documents are interspersed among the statements below.]
The Guardian
The Observer
The Times
Union of Greek Democrats of Great Britain (C. Zissimos)
The Sunday Times
BR, ss.: "Message from Bertrand Russell to the 'Bertrand Russell' Committee of 100 in Greece"; "Message to the Hiroshima Day Demonstration in Athens"; "To the General Assembly of the United Nations"; "Statement Concerning Deportation of My Secretary from Greece"; "Statement on the Death of Dr. Gregory Lambrakis, M.P., 27 May, 1963"; "Statement by Bertrand Russell to the *Sunday Times*"; "The Ethics of the *Sunday Times*"; "Answers to Questions from *Athinaki*"; "Message to Marathon Peace March"; "Message to the Greek Committee for Nuclear Disarmament"; "Message from Bertrand Russell to the Trafalgar Square Rally, April 1968"

Guatemala—Political Prisoners and Civil Liberties 1966

Enrique Peralta Azurdia

Guinea—Political Prisoners 1964

Alfa Ibrahim Sow
Sekou Touré

Guinea 1964-9

Sekou Touré
Kwame Nkrumah

Guyana—Political Prisoners 1962

Committee for the Release of the Detainees in British Guyana (Margaret Stanton)

Guyana 1968-9

Bob Edwards
Secretary-General to the Prime Minister's Conference
Cheddi Jagan

Haiti—Political Prisoners

Comité Haitien Dominicain de Solidarité

Hong Kong—Political Prisoners 1967-8

D. R. Holmes
Elsie Elliott
Eastern Horizon Monthly Review (Lee Tsung-ying)

Hungary—Political Prisoners 1964-8

Zoltan Laffers
Janos Kadar
Private Secretary to the Prime Minister of Hungary (Peter Márkanys?)
G. Medgyesi
P. Várkonyi
Amnesty International (Stella Sweetman, Martin Enthoven)
L. Logodi
Ivanne Wellisch
Steve Strowski

Hungary 1964-8

The Murder of an Idea: The Execution of Imre Nagy
Hungarian Ambassador
Janos Kadar
Private Secretary to the Hungarian Embassy
Jenö Incze
Peter Janos
Gyula Kallai
World Federation of Democratic Youth (Francis Le Gal)
Mihaly Korm

Iceland 1965

Bjarni Benediktsson

India—Correspondence with Heads of State 1962-9

Sarvepalli Radhakrishnan
Zakir Hussain
V. K. S. Iyengar
Jawaharlal Nehru
N. B. Menon
K. L. Gupta
Indira Gandhi
Lal Bahadur Shastri
Jivraj N. Mehta
Rajeshwar Prasad

India—Correspondence with High Commission 1962-6

Kewal Singh
V. Subramanian
Manjit Singh
U. S. Bajpai
Jivraj N. Mehta
P. N. Haksar
R. C. Shukla

India—Statements 1962-5

Rajkumari Amrit Kaur
Jawaharlal Nehru
Vanita Maha Vidyalaya (Mr. Raess)
BR, ss. (some tear sheets): "Statement for International Use to N.C. Zamindar"; "India and World Peace"; "Our Debt to Nehru"; "With Bitterness Towards None"; 2 untitled ss.

India—Political Prisoners 1969

Mohammad Lateef Dar

India 1962-70

P. Shaw Baker
Rajkumari Amrit Kaur
Loka Shikshana Trust, Hubli (R.R. Diwakar)
P.C. Nanavaty
Charochandra College Teachers' Council (Asim Kumar Chaudhuri)
Govind N. Deodhekar
V.V. Ramana Murti
P. Cadogan
Om Prakasha Kahol
All India Peace Council (Diwan Chaman Lall *et al.*)
P.C. Chadha
Gandhi Smarak Nidhi [Gandhi Peace Foundation] (R. R. Diwakar)
K.S. Rangappa
Mahendra Nadkarmi
Gandhi National Memorial Fund
Naga National Council (A.Z. Phizo)
Committee of Indian Parliamentarians for Peace (Diwan Chaman Lall)
World Peace Brigade (Siddharaj Dhadda)
Suresh Ram (enclosing printed interview with BR)
Rabindranath Basu
Delhi Gandhi Smarak Nidhi (C.A. Menon)
M.N. Mehra
Sundar Ghosal
War Resisters' International (Devi Prasad)
Air-India (J. Beart, I. Lobo)
Loyn Moon
Mir Nasrullah
International Conference Against War Danger (V.K. Krishna Menon)
Mohammed Lateef Dar
Dinsh Singh

Indonesia 1962-7

Achmed Soekarno
Burhanudin M. Diah
Suyoto Suryo-di-Puro

Secretary to the Charge d'Affaires Indonesian Embassy
Utami Suryadarma
Kiapma Consolidation Bureau
R. Sukartiko
New Left Review (Perry Anderson)
Youth Against War and Fascism (Deirdre Griswold)
Ken Larbuck
A. M. Hanafi
Organisasi Indonesia Untuk Setiakawan Rakjat Asia-Afrika (Ibrahim Isa)

Indonesia—Statements 1966-70

The Guardian
Deirdre Griswold
BR, ss.: "The Second Biggest Crime of the Century", "American Murder Über Alles", 1 untitled press s.
A. M. Hanafi

Iran 1964-9

Mohammed Mossadegh
BR s., "Bertrand Russell on Iran"
Shah of Iran
Iranian Students Society in Great Britain
BR, press s.

Iran—Political Prisoners 1967-9

Mansoor Meshgin-Poosh
Organisations Européenes du Front National Iranien (M. Rassekh)
Iranian National Front Organisation in England
Confederation of Iranian Students (M. Bozorgmehr)
Françoise Anvar
Action for Human Rights in Iran
The Iranian Committee for the Defence of Political Prisoners
Shah of Iran

Iraq—Government Correspondence 1962-9

Naji al-Asil
Abdul Karim Kassem
Abdul Salem Mohammed Aref
Fouad Al-Rawi
Abdul Rahman Al-Bazzaz
International Students Committee
Abdulla Saloom Al-Sammare'e
Kadhim M. Khalaf

Iraq 1964-8

Iraqi Students' Society in the U.K. (L. M. Abbawy, N. K. Bayati)
Iraqi High Committee
Barzani Mosrafa
Khalid Zaki
Kufa University Founding Organization (Mohammed Makiya)
Tabitha Petran
Elizabeth Dodds

Iraq—Political Prisoners 1966-9

High Committee for the Defense of the Iraq People (Rahim Ajina)
Board of Deputies of British Jews (Sir Barnett Janner)
Abraham J. Marks
President Aref of Iraq
BR, ss.: "Recorded .. for Millenary Tribute to al-Kindi and the City of Baghdad", "Message to Iraqi Students' Annual Conference and Spring Festival", "Message to the Iraqi Students' Society"; 2 untitled ss.
Iraqi Students' Society in the U.K. (H. K. Ahmed)
BR and CF ss. on the death of Khalid Zaki
The Guardian
The Times

Ireland 1965

Sean F. Leamass

Israel 1962-9

Aubrey Hodes, note on press reports of Jerusalem prize award to BR
Hodes' ts., "The Arab Refugees: A New Approach"
BR, tscc., foreword to the Hebrew edition of *Unarmed Victory*
Mapam
New Outlook (Shmuel B'ari)
Ezra Talmor
Hodes, trans. from *Maariv* of Rafael Bashan's "Russell Shocked by Anti-Semitic Poster"
Israeli Ambassador to London (Arthur Lourie)
Hodes, trans. of Bashan's "The English Philosopher's Jewish Secretary"
NER (Simon Shereshevsky)
Embassy of Israel (E. Evron)
David Ben-Gurion
RS, reply to Bashan interview
I. Navon
Embassy of Israel (E. Kaufman)
Israel Loeff
Martin Buber

The Third Force Central Committee (M. Stein)
Hodes, trans. of Y. Finkelstein's "Russell Sends Letters to Israeli and Arab Leaders"
Avner Falk
Socialist Zionist Party—Mapam of Great Britain and Ireland (A. Yaari)
New Outlook (Simha Flapan)
Jacko Farqui
Eviatar Nevo
Ts. of press conference with Prime Minister of Israel
Al Hamishmar (Jacob Rabinovitz)
Golda Meir, s.
Adbul Aziz Zu'bi
Levi Eshkol
Photocopy of ts., "Address by the Prime Minister and Minister of Defense Mr. Levi Eshkol at Overseas Press Club"
Ts., "Address by Levi Eshkol, Prime Minister of Israel to the World Affairs Council, Los Angeles"
Israeli Ambassador to Washington (Avraham Harman)
Leaflet by Abba Eban, *The Arab Refugees*
United Workers Party of Israel—The Central Committee (Meir Yaari)
Al-Ard Co. Ltd., mimeo ts., "Memorandum on the Arabs in Israel"
Committee for Nuclear Disarmament of the Arab-Israeli Region (Yehuda Ben-Moshe)
Joseph Netzer
Embassy of Israel (Binyamin Peled)
London Committee of 100 (Douglas Kepper)
Yaakov Herzog
Abe Nathan
Sarah Salomon
Embassy of Israel (Aharon Remez)
M. Machover
J. Nikola
Maxim Ghilan
Soviet Peace Committee; Israel Peace Committee
Israel Shahak

Israel—Political Prisoners, etc. 1969

The Israel Socialist Organization, Students' Committee (A. S. Bober)
Jerusalem Liberation Committee (Mr. Gaillard)
International Red Cross, Geneva

Israel—Statements 1965-8

Abba Eban s. entitled, "The Arab Refugees"
A. B. Nathan Firshman
Haolam Hazeh
Jerusalem Post
Haaretz
Jean-Paul Sartre *et al.*
Israeli Socialist Organisation, Students' Committee (A. S. Bober)
Israel Imperial News

Italy 1963-9

Rosa Bianca Panvini
Pietro Nenni
Giorgio La Pira
International Confederation for Disarmament and Peace (Aldo Capitini)
Partito Communista Italiano (Luigi Longo)
BR, article in *Il Ponte*, 1966, s. for *Corriere della Sera*

Ivory Coast 1965

Felix Houphouet-Boigny
Siméon Aké

Japan 1957–69

Japan Council Against Atomic and Hydrogen Bombs (Kaoru Yasui)
Tetsuzo Tanikawa
BR, ss.: "Message to the People of Okinawa", "Message to the Survivors of Hiroshima", "Message to the Conference of the Japan Council Against Atomic and Hydrogen Bombs", "On the Atomic Bombing of Japan"; and untitled s.
Japan Council of Organizations of Atomic Bomb Victims (Ichiro Moritaki)
Martin Knottenbelt
Shigetoshi Iwamatsu
Bunri Shoin, International Division (Ikki Hitaka)
Ichio Maruyama
The People's Korea **(Son Jin Hyung)**
Shingo Shibata
Misuzo Shobo Publishing Co. (Toshito Obi)
Japan "Peace for Vietnam" Committee (Makoto Oda)

Raimo Bärlund
Albert Axelbank
Japan Civil Liberties Union (Koichi Nishida)
Committee of Seven to Appeal for World Peace
The Third Kyoto Conference of Scientists
Maruki Gallery for the Hiroshima Panels
City of Hiroshima (Setsuo Yamada)

Jordan 1963-9

King Hussein I
Zaid Rifa
Jerusalem Liberation Committee (Suleiman Nabulsi)
Auropa Public Relations Agency (Mustafa Jaber)
Arab Tourist Union (Abdullah Tai)

Kashmir—Statements 1965

BR, s. "On Indian-Pakistan War and Kashmiri Situation"

Kenya—Statements 1964-8

Jomo Kenyatta
O. A. Fakih
BR? statement entitled "Confidential Memorandum on the Crisis in Vietnam for the Attention of President Kenyatta"
Sarjit?
Oginga Odinga

Kenya 1965-8

Jomo Kenyatta
Ajuma Oginga Odinga
E. W. Mathu

Korea 1964-6

The 1919 Independence Revolutionary Elders' Club (Lee Jung Band *et al.*)
Kim Il Sung

Kuwait 1963-5

Abdullah Al Salim Al Sabah
Khalid M. Jaffar
Hassan Ali Dabbagh

Laos 1964-5

The Laotian Embassy
Souvanna Phouma
Bureau of the International Conference for Solidarity with the People of Vietnam against US Imperialist Aggression and for the Defence of Peace

Latin America—Political Prisoners, etc. 1967-9

U.S. Committee for Justice to Latin American Political Prisoners (Richard Garza)
Tri-Continental Information Centre (Michael Myerson)
Studie en AktieKomitee Camilo Torres (Walter De Bock)
North American Congress on Latin America (Michael Klare)
BR, 4 untitled press ss.

Lebanon 1962-8

As-Safa (Salim Nassar)
Sa-ab Salem
Rashid Karame
Kadhim Al-Sulh
Anwar Habaybeh
League of Arab States, London Office (S. B. ElBarky)
Talib El-Shibib
BR, s., "Message to the Conference on Human Rights in the Middle East"

Liberia 1965

William Tubman
Embassy of the Republic of Liberia, London (J. D. Lawrence)

Libya 1964-9

BR, s., untitled
Moamer al Kadhafi

Malawi 1964-7

Hastings Banda

C. Lurb? (Deputy Chief Immigration Officer) to Audrey Khan

Malaysia 1965-9

Royal Federation of Malaya Police (D. F. Sundra Raj)
Malayian National Liberation League (P. V. Sarma)
Mission of the Malayan National Liberation League in the People's Republic of China
Indonesian Embassy, Peking
Tunku Abdul Rahman
Dr. Ismail

Malaysia—Political Prisoners, etc. 1968-70

Anonymous Malaysian
Amnesty International (Paula ?)
Federation of United Kingdom and Eire Malaysian and Singapore Student Organizations

Mali 1964-6

Modibo Keita

Malta 1963-4

Dom Mintoff

Mexico 1963-70

Mexican Ambassador to the U.K. (Antonio Armendáriz, Eduardo Suárez)
Humberto Miguel Jiménez
Alberto Lumbreras
Adolfo Lopez Mateos
Gustavo Diaz Ordaz
C. Jefe del Departamento de Prevencion
BR, ss.
Frente Internacional de Derechos Humanos (Benjamín Laureano Luna)
National Strike Committee of Mexico
Angel Caamaño Uribe
BR and Jean-Paul Sartre, s.
Direccion General de Gobierno (Cuauhtémoc Santa Ana)
BRPF, press ss.
Consejo Nacional de la Publicidad (Antonio Menendez, Ladislao Lopez Negrete)

Middle East Conference (Proposed) 1964-5

Lists of invitees
At-Tarik Review (Antoine Tabet)
Ahmed Ben Bella *et al.* (same ls. to many addressees)
Anouar Abdel-Malek
The Governor of Cairo (Salah Dessouki)
Arab Socialist Union (Kamal Rifaat)
Abdul Rahman Shoukair
Maxime Rodinson
Abidine Dino
Conference pour la Denuclearisation du Bassin Méditerraneen sur Mer et sur Terre (Genziz Kevenk)
A. H. Mehryar
Behice Boran-Hatko
The Workers' Party of Turkey (Mehmet Ali Aybar)
Sadun Aren
The Centre for Group Studies (Richard Hauser)
Niyazi Agirnasli
Sabri Esat Siyavuşgil
Çetin Özek
Milliyet (Cetin Altan Abdi Ipekçi)
Necat Erder
Sabahattin Eyuboglu and Vedat Günyol
Karim Sanjabi
M. Hashtroodi
K. Djanab
Ali Shayegan
Ghulam-Hossein Sadighi
Nadir Nadic
European Organizations of the National Front of Iran (T. Tchubinè)
C. Bozkus
Al Ahram (**Muhammed Hasanein Heikal**)
Confederation of Iranian Students (Khosrow Shakeri)
Giorgio La Pira

Middle East 1964-9

Israeli Consul General (Binyamin Peled)
Israeli Ambassador to the U.K. (**Arthur Lourie**)

Committee for Nuclear Disarmament of the Arab-Israeli Region (Yehuda Ben-Moshe)
Pat Jordan
Council for the Advancement of Arab-British Understanding (Michael Adams, Grania Birkett)
Palestine Democratic Front
Ethel M. Minor
The Arab Lawyer Union (Shafik Arshidat)
Démocratique Palestinien
Movement for Human Rights (Kanburzada Murad Bey)
Al Fatah: Palestine Liberation Movement
Charles Bettelheim and Maxime Rodinson
Eric Rouleau
"Middle East Report"
Giulio Savelli
The American Council for Judaism (Michael Selzer, Bill Gottlieb)
Congres des Droits de l'Homme (Abdelhalek Hassouna)
Harry Ruja
Labour Union Associations of Jordan (Hani Dahleh)
League of Arab States (Talib El-Shibib, S. B. El Barky)
The General Union of Arab Students (Nouri Al-Bahrani, M. S. Shaalan)
Anouar Abdel-Malek
Fawwaz Trabulsi
Arthur J. Goldberg
"Free Palestine"
Y. Alexander
A. Orr
Jerusalem Liberation Committee
Israel Palestine Committee

Middle East—Statements 1963-70

Message to *Al Hamishmar*
Open l. to Arab intellectuals
A. Orr and M. Machover
Press s. on Dr. Soebandrio
BR, ts., introduction to *The Palestine Problem*
Press ss.
Ad Hoc Middle East Non-Intervention Committee
Pointer, Autumn 1967
Palestine Solidarity Campaign *et al.*
International Conference of Parliamentarians on the Middle-East Crisis
General Union of Arab Students
BR, ts., "Message from Bertrand Russell to the International Conference of Parliamentarians in Cairo, February 1970"

Middle East—United Arab Republic 1962-70

Governor of Cairo (Salah Dessouki)
Gamal Abdel Nasser
United Arab Republic Peace Council (Khaled Mohieddin)
Said El Naggar
United Arab Republic Ambassador to the U.K. (Mohammed el-Kony, Mohamed Hafez Ismail, Ahmed Hassan El-Feki)
***Al Ahram* (Hasanein Heikal)**
Kamal Rifaat
Mahmoud El-Gayar
F. Noris
Peace Council (Khaled Mohey El Din)
Lotfi Al Kholi
Afro-Asian Peoples' Solidarity Organization (Youssef Elsebai)
The Arab Lawyer Union (Shafik Arshidat)
Consul General, High Commission of Pakistan (A. F. M. Mahboub)
Al Talia Review
Mohammed Sid Ahmed
Nabil Othman
Fenner Brockway
Embassy of the United Arab Republic, **Chargé d'Affaires (M. Samir Ahmed)**
International Conference of Parliamentarians on the Middle-East Crisis (Kamal Eddine El-Hennaoui)

Monaco 1964

Martin A. Dale
The Prince of Monaco

Mongolian People's Republic 1965

Yumzhagiin Tsendenbal

Morocco 1963-6

Mustapha Al Alaoui
King Hassan II

New Zealand 1965

K. J. Holyoake

Niger 1965

Hamani Diori

Nigeria 1964-9

Abubakar Tafawa Balewa
Ihejika Sam Oji
Yakubu Gowon
Save Biafra Committee (Ken A. Engbrincke?, Nadia Fowler)
E. C. Mkparu
Simon Guttman
Eric Heffer
BR, s. on Biafra
Movement for Colonial Freedom (Barbara Haq)
Markpress, Biafran Overseas Press Division (H. William Bernhardt)
Fenner Brockway
Fédération Internationale Terre des Hommes (Edmond Kaiser)
The South Swedish Biafra Committee
Operation Outrage: North American Coalition for Biafran Relief (Peter Colasante)
Paulette Antonis
Basil Antonis
Medical Aid for Biafra Committee

Norway 1956-65

Det Norske Studentersamfund (Brita Brandtzæg)
Walter Wolfgang
Norwegian Campaign for Nuclear Disarmament (Norah Farstad)
Einar Gerhardsen
Norwegian Embassy (Arne Skaug)

Pakistan 1962-9

Kamrul Islam
Aslam Effendi
Ahmed E. H. Jaffer
Rugho Nath Vaishnavi
Sardar Surjit Singh Majithia
M. K. Janjua
Mohammed Ayub Khan
Mssrs. T. Islam, K. Majlis, S. Ahmed and Shafindden
Mansur Ahmad
Ministry of Foreign Affairs (Shahid M. Amin)
Zulfikar Ali Bhutto
Audits and Accounts Office, Office of the High Commissioner for Pakistan
Baquer Ali
Afzal Iqbal
M. A. H. Ispahani
Fazlun Huq
State Bank of Pakistan
A. Kosygin
Pakistan Council for World Government (Ahmed E. H. Jaffer)
Jammu and Kasmir Plebiscite Front (Amanullah Khan)
The Pakistan Association of World Federalists
The Pakistan Islamic Council for International Affairs
Asrar Ahmad
Minhaj Barna
Abdullah Malik
Anis Hashmi
Movement for the Preservation of Pakistan, ss.
The Spectator
Andrei A. Gromyko
The Economist
The Pakistan Parliamentary Group for World Government
J. A. Rahim
S. M. Yusuf
Noor Mohammed
Students' Front against Aggression, Lahore (M. Amanullah Khan)
Mazhar Kazi
Q. Lohani, Abdul Kassem, Fareed Javed
East Pakistan Students Union (Shamsuddoha)
Mahmoud A. Haroon
Pakistan High Commission (Agha Hilaly)
Tasadduq Ahmed

Pakistan—Statements 1962-8

BR, press s.: ts.
The Statesman (M. Owais)
Pakistan Times (Zahid Chaudhuri)
Frontier (incl. BR on Pakistan)
BR, ts. for Pakistan *Morning News*
BR, "Background to Tashkent" (tear sheets)
BR, articles on
BR, press ss.; s. entitled "On the Rann of Kutch Dispute"; 1 untitled s.

Panama 1964

Roberto Chiari

Peru—Political Prisoners, etc. 1968-70

Jacqueline de Lobaton
Giselle Halimi *et al.*
Rosa Alarco
U.S. Committee for Justice to Latin American Political Prisoners
The Latin American Committee (John "Juan" Edmunds)
Comité Français de Solidarité avec les Victimes de la Repression au Pérou; Jean-Paul Sartre
Solidarité Pérou
Gerald Suberville
Amnesty International (Inger Fahlender)

Peru 1966-70

Militant Labour Forum (Priscilla Ring)
BR, s., "On the Persecution of Latin American Revolutionaries"
H.E. Cardinale (Apostolic Delegation)
Belaunde Terry
BR, 4 press ss. re Hugo Blanco
Juan Velasco Alvarado
Gustavo Silva Aranda

Philippines 1965-8

Diosdado Macapagal
Thomas C. Benitez
The Manila Times (José Luna Castro)
Manila Chronicle (I.P. Soliongco)
BR, press s.
Republic of the Philippines, Department of Justice, Board of Pardons and Parole (Crispina L. Ang)
Republic of the Philippines Senate (Juan R. Liwag)
Peter Limqueco, interview and photo with BR (*Philippines Free Press*, 1968)
Ferdinand E. Marcos

Poland 1964-9

Wladyslaw Gomulka
Josef Cyrankiewicz
Jan Choroszewski
Polish Peace Committee
Jon Sliwka
Jerzy Morawski
CF, Memorandum of Meeting of Emanuel Litvinoff and CF
Elzbieth Kolankowska
? Trepczynski
Polish Western Press Agency (Jan Moszczeński)
George Zyzak
Group of (Anonymous) Polish Intellectuals
Adam Chiolkosz
The Times
BR, press s.
Alfred Jaroschek
Institute of Jewish Affairs (S. J. Roth)
BR, s. entitled "On Anti-Semitism in Poland"
Günter Maczioch

Portugal 1965-9

Portuguese and Colonial Bulletin (R. Ferreira)
John Matthews
International Socialist Journal (Lelio Basso)
Shakuntala Miranda
Unidade Democratica Portuguesa (Manuel Moura)
Frente de Libertacao de Mocambique (Frelimo) (Jorge Rebelo)
BR, s. entitled "Message from BR to the Conference on Portugal held in Lausanne, February 1968"
Comité Portugal Libre (W. Rios?)
Mouvement de Soutien aux Peuples de l'Angola et des Autres Colonies

Portugaises (Jean-Pierre Heimann, Gerard Henriod, and Michel Boilley)
M. C. H. da Silva
Frente de Libertacao National e Colonial
Mozambique Liberation Front
Committee for Freedom in Mozambique
Voz de Portugal (Benedito Teixeira Vaz)
Amnesty International (Martin Enthoven)
The Guardian

Rhodesia 1968

The Anti-Apartheid Movement (Ethel de Keyser)

Rumania 1963-9

Alexandre Missirliu
Johann Lupul
Moritz Cohn-Michel
Victoria Danziger
Rosa Goldschläger
Berthold Mihali
Leon Hamburger
D. B. Spalding
Bella Hamburger
Eleonora Koffler
Bernard Berl
Elisabeth Cahane
H. Miutzer
Clara Moscovici
Leiba Ceauşu
Uta Purice
Lazar Pesa
David Aharonovicz
Ernestina Feldman
Rozalia Schenker
Horia Tanasescu
Mircea Tanasescu
Anna Tanasescu Morelli
Maximilian and Sidonia Weisselberg
Simona Toren
Gheorghe Gheorghiu-Dej
A. Lazareanu
Ion Gheorghe Maurer
M. Ghibernea
E. N. G. Maurer
Vasile Pungan
Nicolae Ceausescu

Rumania—Civil Liberties (Jews) 1959-69

World Jewish Congress (E. Litvinoff)
Joachim Goldhammer
Ignatz Goldschlaeger
Nicolae Bageac
Clara Brauner
Iancu Segal
Leon Weidenfeld
O. Roza
Beti Basch

Rwanda-Urundi 1964-5

BR, s.
Theodore Ntihinyurwa
Haile Selassie I
Gregoire Kayibanda

Saudi Arabia 1965

King Faisal ibn Abdul Aziz

Senegal 1964-6

United Towns Organisation (K. Fournier)
Leopold S. Senghor
Leon Boissier-Palun
Aldou Diouf
G. Etcheverry
Lyndon B. Johnson

Sierra Leone date?

Albert Margai
Milton Margai

Sino-India Conflict 1962-3

Atulananda Chakrabarti
BR, ss.
Mimeographed texts re Cuban Crisis
J. Nehru
Chou En-lai
Herbert Read
Chaudrakaut J. Desai
Peace News (Michael Randle)

Somali Republic 1965

Abdirazak Hagi Hussen
Mr. Lawaha
The Director-General, Ministry of Foreign Affairs

South Africa 1966-9

Comité d'Action pour l'Exposition

(Anne Barbey)
South Africa Protest and Defence and Aid (Mamie Smith)
Manuscript Exhibition Appeal Committee (Raymond Kunene)
Anti-Apartheid Movement (Ethel de Keyser)
Preparatory Committee for Khartoum Conference on Southern Africa (K. Dube, P. Katjavivi and R. Kunene)

South Arabia 1964

BR, ls. to *Guardian*, *Daily Telegraph*
Al Ahram (Hasanein Heikal)
BR, ts., "Oppression in South Arabia"
Salah Dessouki
Arab Socialist Union (Kamal Rifaat)

Soviet Jews n.d.-1970

Lize Dorfman
Eidea Drubetzky
Fany Yakovlevna Granirer
Eugenia Grimberg
S. Lewin
Esther Israelit
Atara Stern Granik
Benzion Gurwitz
Socialist Zionist Party—Mapam (D. Billis
Elka Kedari
A. Kosygin
Emanuel [Litvinov?]
Risa Gordina
S. Karbi
Perl Fischberg
A. Soldatov
I. Palkovitch
J. Pecht
Gizella Auslaender
Ana Rozen
Fania Perelmutter
Mania Rosenzweig
Bluma Shinar
Isaiah Berlin
Sara Friedenthal
Klara Roll
Sarah Salomon
Raissa O. Russineks
David Schuster
Devorah Lipshitz
Josef Schwartz
G. L. Shabsovitch
Chaim and Ester Frenk
Haim Smickowitch
Musya Kaplan
Rebecca Liskovsky
J. Stenzler
Teodoro and Susana Werbitzky
Mrs. I. Ostroumoff
Mira Gerz
I. Zilinski
Aron Fogelman
Baruch Fogelman
Estonian Aid, Inc.—Eesti Abi (Erich Park)
Mihkel Vaab
Emma Usdin
Paul Wechselblatt
Leah Dershowitz
Erika Semenass
Dvora N. Gottesman
Izvestia (Alex Adzhubei)
Adrian Sunshine

Soviet Jews—Statements, etc. 1963-4

BR, ss.
Izvestia
Clippings, photostats
Sovietish Heimland
Literaturnaia Gazetta
Emanuel Litvinoff

Soviet Jews—Miscellaneous Correspondence 1963-9

Nikita Khrushchev
[V?] Gollancz
Nicholas Jacobs
The Board of Deputies of British Jews (C. D. Rappaport, A. G. Brotman)
Emanuel Litvinoff
Society for Cultural Relations with the USSR (H. Campbell Creighton)
A. A. Roback
C. P. Snow
A. Dragoli
Radio Free Europe (Talbot Hood)
Student Struggle for Soviet Jewry (Jacob Birnbaum)
Agudas Israel World Organisation (M. R. Springer)
New Fraternal Jewish Association

(Beth Silburt)
J. Klein
Jewish Daily Forward (David Liberson)
Mandel A. Terman
Parti Communiste Français (W. Waldeck-Rochet)
World Union of Jewish Students (Michael Hunter, Susan Chaplin)
David Cohen
Jewish Book Centre (Alfred Jason)
Focus on Soviet Jewry (Joel Cang)
Itta and Lupu Schwartz
Luigi Longo
The Wiener Library, Department of Contemporary Jewish History (Walter Laquer)
The Polish Ambassador (Jerzy Morawski)
D. A. Deason
Cleveland Council on Soviet Anti-Semitism (Herbert S. Caron)
World Jewish Congress, British Section (Jack Winocour)
Inter-University Jewish Federation of Great Britain and Ireland (Alan Gold)
Jewish Community Centre of Milwaukee (Frances Peltz, Rodney S. Eglash)
Chief Rabbi of Israel (Isser Yehuda)
Iser J. Unterman
Mrs. Michal Grunberg
H. Hoekstra
Knud Jespersen
Cambridge Opinion (Jonathan Lewis)
Universities' Committee for Soviet Jewry (Gordon Hausmann, Malcolm Lewis)
Conference of Study of the Situation of the Jewish Minority in the USSR (Belisario Betancur *et al.*)
2 files of documents

Soviet Jews—General Correspondence and Statements 1963-70

BR, s.
Press s.
Message for World Union of Jewish Students' Conference
Summaries of cases
Zena Weisman
Pierre Mendès France
Jewish Daily Forward (David Liberson)
Jean-Paul Sartre
C. P. Snow
Report on the "Situation of Jews in the U.S.S.R."
Arnold Wesker
The Soviet Ambassador (A. A. Soldatov)
Yevsei Yevrienov
Nikita Khrushchev
Sovietish Heimland (Aron Vergelis)
World Jewish Congress, Department of International Affairs
Jona Rodinov
Mr. Vassev
Paul Wechselblatt
Conference on the Situation of Jews in the Soviet Union (Daniel Mayer)
Soviet Writers' Union
Literaturnaia Gazeta
The Times
The London Committee for the **Armenian Cause (M. Alexanderian, P. Gulbenkian)**
Parti Communiste Français (W. Waldeck-Rochet)
Scandinavian Conference on the Situation of Jews in the Soviet Union (Torgny Segerstedt)
A. N. Kosygin
World Jewish Congress, British Section (Jack Winocour)
Mexican Committee for Soviet Jews (Martin Luis Guzman)
Jews in Eastern Europe
Jonathan Lewis
Rouben Chublarian
Flemish Action Committee for Eastern Europe (Victor van Brantegem)

Soviet Jews—Addendum 1964-70

T. I. Glazer
Mr. & Mrs. Gordon Leizer
Jehezkiel Altman
E. Alterovici
Jacov Beilis

Srul Birnberg
Israel-Maushovits Blecher
Aliza Shapiro
Lea Kaliska
Shevach & Zinaida Borshchevsky
Esther Reznik-Fishman
Rachel Broide
Regina Cahn
Mosche Edilman
Elka Edelman [*sic*]
Isidor, Rosa, and Leo Fang
T. Feigin
Habiba Retig
Aviva Karni
Eva Goldenberg
I. Gordin
Rachel Weiner
Ber Glezer & Paulina Glezer
L. Slovin

Spain 1964-9

José María Vega
Amadeo Alaez
Gretel Rieber
Camilo Alonso Vega
BR, "Message to the Paris Conference on Spain"
Institute for Workers Control (Ken Coates)
Spanish Workers' Defence Committee
The Spanish Ambassador to the U.K.
Alberto López Herce
Minister of Justice (Antonio Maria de Oriol)
The Guardian

Sudan 1964

Ferik Ilbrahim Abboud
El Khatim El Khalifa

Sweden 1962-9

Mrs. Wenner Gren
G. Olson
Peter Lorentzon
Olle Hallström
Morten Grindal
Kampanjen Mot Atomvapen (Bertil Svahnström)
Tage Erlander
Svenska Träindustriarbetareförbundet (Yngve Persson)
BR, ts. of interview with *Aftonbladet* (same as in *Philippines Free Press*)
Swedish Communist Party Congress (Mr. Hermanson)
International Institute for Peace
Göran Therborn
Olaf Palme
BR, s.

Switzerland 1963-7

C. E. Zeller
Heinrich Buchbinder
Hans-Peter Tschudi
Ch. Oser

Syria 1962-9

M. Radwan Hamwi
Salah Bitar
Marguerite Gebran Majdalany
Leah Mashiach
Yossif Zeayen
Ibrahim Makous
Ambassador Istiwani
Mowaffak Allaf
Nureddin Atassi

Tanzania 1964-7

Sebyeza Gabriel
Julius K. Nyerere
Joan E. Wicken
Tanzania High Commission (Mr. Mtingwa)
Oscar S. Kambona
Dora Taylor

Thailand 1966-7

Committee for Afro-Asian People's Solidarity of Thailand
Office of the Representative Abroad of the Patriotic Front of Thailand
Mr. Sebai

Togo, Republic of 1965

Nicholas Grunitsky

Trinidad/Tobago 1964

Eric Williams

Tunisia 1968

Nouri Boudali
Movement for Colonial Freedom (Barbara Haq)

Taieb Ammar
Msika & Taieb

Turkey 1964-8

Mr. A. Dino
The Golden Horn (Richard Reid)
Turkish Teachers' Union Revolutionary Education Council (Fakir Baykurt)

Uganda 1964-5

Martin F. Aroma
Milton Obote
Shafiq Arain
S. entitled "Confidential Memorandum on Overall Strategy for the Attention of Dr. Milton Obote"

United Arab Republic 1956-65

BR, untitled s. for *Reynolds News*; another s. for Suez meeting
Jeremy Brooks
Kenneth Cottman
Al Ahram (Hasanein Heikal)
Arab Socialist Union (Kamal Rifaat)

United Kingdom 1962-70

Queen Elizabeth II (summons to Parliament)
Act or Perish
Michael Scott
London Committee of 100
Labour Peace Fellowship (Len Nicholas)
BR?, s. entitled "Appreciation of Isaac Deutscher"
P. F. de Zulueta
National Committee of 100 (Helen Allegranza)
Accidental War ... The Mershon Report
Morning Star
Sunday Times
The Guardian
Harold Wilson
Earl Attlee
Michael Foot
Private Secretary to the Postmaster General
Hugh Foot
Frank Soskice
The Under Secretary of State
J. E. Cable
BR, mimeo, speech entitled "The Labour Party's Foreign Policy" (later, pamphlet)
BR, press ss.
E. Shinwell
W. J. Vole
Jennie Lee
Michael Stewart
Olwen Wright
? Walston
BR, ts. entitled "Broadcast concerning Einstein"
BR, ts. entitled "Introduction to a Programme on the Webbs"
BR, s. for freethinkers
BR, ts. (for the Third Programme) about CND
BR, s. on Coates
BR, s. on the seamen's strike
The Home Office
M. Hill
H. Fawcett
Guild Gazette (P. L. Smith) (interview with BR)
Roy Jenkins
RS, s. on break and entry at Shavers Place
David Robinson
Students Union, London School of Economics
Lord Brockway
D. H. Andrews
J. A. Chilcot
Gwynfor Evans
Coventry Centre for Socialist Education (Jack Knight)
Frederick Herbert Gamble
BR, s.; ts. and galley proof of article, "Nato Forever?" (1968)
BR, various ss. (including one on his archives, 1968)
Ernie ?
The Sun
Students' Union President, Essex University
Robert Byng
A. J. Topham
National Council for Civil Liberties (Tony Smythe)
Ken Coates
The Times
National Secular Society (William McIlroy)
Amnesty International (International

Secretariat) (Martin Ennals)
BR, s.
London School of Economics and Political Science (Lord Robbins)
Harry Nicholas
J. E. C. Macrae
Lord Robbins
Friedrich Hund (including BR's introduction to the Born-Einstein correspondence)
Ben Whitaker
Len Nicholas
Lord Chorley
BR, tear sheet of lunar article from *The Times*, 1969; s. on *L.S.E.* by Hoch and Schoenbach
Stanley Newens
BR, ts. entitled "Labour's Goldwater"
Russell Kerr
Marius Goring
Post Office Corporation (Viscount Hall)
BRPF, press s.

United Nations 1962-9

U Thant
The Security Council of the UN
The General Assembly of the UN
Paul G. Hoffman
Food and Agricultural Organization (B. R. Sen)
Technical Assistance Board (David Owen)
UN London Information Centre
BRPF, press s.
BR, press s.

Uruguay 1965-8

ER, ms. note from BR to CF
Comité National Coordinador del Apoyo a la Revolución Cubana
Luis Giannatasio
Ambassador of Uruguay
Hector Luisi
Carlos Maria Velazquez
BR, ss.

U.S.A. 1960-64

New York Times
BR, ss. entitled "Message of Greeting to the Meeting in Madison Square Garden", "The Myth of American Freedom", press s., "Sixteen Questions on the Assassination"
The Nation
The Times
The Guardian
Hubert H. Humphrey
Daily Telegraph
New Statesman
Mark Lane, "The Warren Commission Report and the Assassination"
BR, tss., introduction to *Accidental War*, "The Yellow Peril?", s. on John Harris
Socialist Workers Party (Jack Barnes)
Ramparts, March 1970 (containing a BR s.)
Goldwater Appeal [see section ***313** of Archives I]
List of names of people to be contacted
BR, unsent form ls.
Form ls.
Chesapeake & Ohio Railway Company (Betty Royon)
Niels Mathieson
Alberto Baltra-Cortés
Communist Party of Great Britain (John Gollan)
Corliss Lamont
I. F. Stone
The Minority of One (M. S. Arnoni)
Ella Winter
Heinrich Buchbinder
Bertil Svahnström
C.P. Snow
John Gollan
Linus Pauling
Stephanie May
Alex Comfort
Mary Clarke
Hideo Chiba
Trisko Sundra
D. A Talbot
The Accra Assembly
Benjamin Greenbaum
Barbara Wootton
Lance Dallalien
Ted Willis
Lord Walston
C. Spiess
John and Florence Paton
Clerical and Administrative Workers' Union
J. Chuter Ede
C. A. Coulson
Frank Allaun
V. Tamshead

Kathleen Taylor
New Statesman (John Freeman)
Barbara Hepworth
J. Strong
F. Sanger
Alan Sillitoe
John Silkin
The Earl Attlee
Helen Sellar
National Union of Public Employees (Edna Hamly)
Richard W. Marsh
Kingsley Martin
The Bishop of Llandaff
Emrys Hughes
Iris Murdoch
Cecil Northcott
Kenneth Tynan
Bertil Sanden
Ira Morris
Mervyn Millett
Norman Langford
Erik Kästner
Arthur Henderson
Sonja Schilling
Lloyd Chandler
Isabel Bethwite-Thomson
form ls.
Percy Collick
Helmut Ridder
Leonard Berkeley
Wolfgang Weyrauch
Lord Willis
De Algemene Centrale (Dore Smets)
Dickson Mabon
Carl Iverson
Heinz Hierest?
Gerald Gardiner
John Arlott

U.S.S.R. 1957-69

U.S.S.R. Embassy, London (V. Vassev)
I. Nyman
Jas. Braud
Isaak and Sophia Livshitz
Elka Bronshtein
Aiziks Schneider
Mordechai Rosenberg
Sima Zacz
Sara Arik
Esther Labanovsky
Yigal Lossin
Sara Frida Metrgar
Rafael Misroch
Galina Ulanora, *et al.*
Nikita Khrushchev
Andrei A. Gromyko
A. Kosygin
I. Saprykin
Yuri Zhukov
A. A. Soldatov
V. M. Vassev
V. I. Kalinin
Leo Kostenko
Soviet Peace Committee (Nikolai Tikhonov)
Pavel Litvinov
L. Brezhnev

U.S.S.R.—Political Prisoners/Civil Liberties 1963-9

Mervyn Matthews
June Bergman
The Postmaster General
Phyllis Sara Fishberg
Curt Bergström
Grani
Valeriy Tarsis
Eva Sardin
Arts et Progrès (T. Basquin)
Derek Deason
USSR Company for Foreign Travel "Intourist"
Lord Sorensen
George Thomson
A. M. Wood
J. H. Osborn
Ronald Buxton
Jennie Lee
Michael Stewart
Eirene White
V. Zemskov
A. J. Ayer
Camilla Gray
Stefan Themerson
Comité International pour la Défense des Droits de l'Homme (E. Beaujard)
N. Whitehead
George Katkov
Georges Nivat
Lord Dundee

Luba Pendzey
Amnesty International (Stella Sweetman, Peter Benenson, Jean Kitching)
Rosa Kagan
Klimentiy Voroshilov
Emanuel Litvinoff
John Jay
Mary Ayarian
Karapet Boghos Kiragosian
Israel Moshowitz
Lize Dorfman
A. A. Soldatov
Anastas I. Mikoyan
P. Medwedyk
E. Youde
Hans-Georg Nußbaum
Jews in Eastern Europe
Mrs. E. Bushkoff
J. H. Sexton
M. D. Whitehouse
Gunnel Hausler
Alice Kröger
Rudolph Schlesinger
Ligue Belge pour la Defense des Droits de l'Homme (A. Wolters and G. Aronstein)
Lew Shulgasser
The Minority of One (M. S. Arnoni)
The New York Times (Harrison E. Salisbury)
New York Times, London Bureau (Anthony Lewis)
Anthony de Meeûs
Alexander Sergeevich Esenin-Volpin
Michael Ellman
Nathan Zbrijer
Elizabeth Hoey
Susan Poole
Michael Beckley
Robert Dwyer

U.S.S.R.—Statements 1957-68

Sovietisch Heimland (Aron Vergelis)
Press s.
Nikita Khrushchev
Alexei Kosygin
I. Shishkin
The British Broadcasting Corporation (M. B. Latey)
Encounter (Stephen Spender)
BR, 2 press ss.
BR, s. entitled "Statement for Soviet Peace Fund", "Message for World Union of Jewish Students Conference", "Anti-Semitism in Eastern Europe", s. for the Russian section of the B.B.C.
A. Soldatov, Soviet Ambassador

U.S.S.R.—Visas for Soviets (Boris Polevoi, Victor Shnjakine, and Nikolai Matkovskiy) 1964-65

Soviet Peace Fund Delegation (Michael Kotov)
Frank Soskice
Joyce Butler
Home Office (R. M. Morris)
BRPF press s.
Harold Wilson
D. J. Mitchell

Venezuela—Correspondence 1964-7

Luis Durán
BR, press s.
Marta Borell
John Calder
Jonathan Cape Ltd. (Tom Maschler)
Mariano Baptista Gumucio
André Deutsch Publishers (Piers Burnett)
George Allen & Unwin Ltd.
Roberto Sosa Fernández
Raul Leoni

Vietnam—Free Speech Campaign 1965

John J. Mendelson (with encl. for information and signature; returned, "gone away")
Mimeos
Some correspondence with signators
Printed materials
Many petition signatures; newspaper advertisement

Vietnam—YCND Meeting 1964

National Youth Campaign for Nuclear Disarmament (Mervyn Rice)

BR, ts. entitled "On the Labour Government's Foreign Policy"
Daily Telegraph

Vietnam—Printed Material 1965

British Vietnam Committee; *Vietnam Bulletin*
RS, s. on American involvement in Vietnam
Clippings and mimeos
"Extract of Data Compiled on War in Vietnam"
The Minority of One
BR, untitled press s.
BR, ms., "S. Viet-nam" (an outline)
Stanford University Peace Caucus (Cheryl Arnold and Richard Such)
S. titled: "Summary of Facts Concerning the War in Vietnam"
New York Herald-Tribune

Vietnam—Correspondence 1964-6

Philadelphia Daily News
Philadelphia Evening Bulletin
American Humanist Organization (Roger Williams)
Stanford University Peace Caucus (Cheryl Arnold and Richard Such)
British Vietnam Committee (Hilda Vernon)
Toronto Star Weekly (Ray Gardner)
Unitarian Church of Calgary (David B. Craig)
National Liberation Front Central Committee (Nguyen Huu Tho)
Tran Viet Dung
Russell Dearnley Stetler, Jr.
Citizens' Committee for Nuclear Disarmament, San Francisco (Tom Brewer)
Clara Urquhart
Committee of Struggle Against U.S. Imperialists (Nguyen Xien)
BR, press s.
Movement for Colonial Freedom (John Eber)
Nguyen Van Hieu
Cuu Quoc Weekly (Tran Viet Dung)
Jean-Paul Sartre
The Guardian
The Times
U Thant
Soviet Peace Committee (Nikolai Tikhonov)
Press ss.; report of meeting with U.S. ambassador
David Bruce
Nguyen van Hieu
William Warbey
BR, many press ss.
New York Herald Tribune
Chicago Tribune
Central Committee of S. Vietnam National Liberation Front (Nguyen-thi-Binh)
BRPF, press s.
David Horowitz
SANE (Donald F. Keys)
Graham Greene
The May Second Movement (Jeffrey S. Gordon)
L. B. Johnson
BR, taped s. on Vietnam war
J. E. Cable
BR, press ss.
Security Council of the United Nations
BR, s.
Sunday Times (Peter Hiley)
BR, s.
The Observer
Fellowship of Reconciliation (Robert B. Shaw)
BR, ss.
Frank Soskice
BR, ts. of taped s.
BR, s.
The Week (Ken Coates)
BR, s.
The White House (Chester L. Cooper)
E. Shinwell
BR, ms., "Forms of Protest"
Women for Peace (Gloria Feldman)
Hanoi s.
BR, "Message for the Women's Institute"
Fenner Brockway
John R. Osborne
BR, s. for Warbey; ms. outline
BR, s.
South Vietnam Liberation Red Cross

(Phung Van Cung)
BR, s.
Christian Science Monitor et al.
BR, s. for French Radio
T. Schoenman
BR, many ss.
J. W. Fulbright
Mordecai Briemberg
BR, ss.
Dagens Nyheter
BR, ts. of recorded s.
Cecil Woolf

Yemen 1963-7

Assayed Abdul Wahab Al-Shamy
Mr. and Mrs. G. B. Simmons
Mohamed Said Al-Attar
Yememi Revolutionary Front
Hussain Ali Bayoomi
Comité de Solidarité a la Révolution Yémémite

Yugoslavia 1963-70

BR, s.
Josip Broz Tito
Srdja Prica
Vladimir Dedijer
Ivo Sarajcic
The Times
Le Monde
J. P. Sartre
Laurent Schwartz
Milan Zupan
Marko Vrhunec

Zambia 1964-6

Kenneth Kaunda
Council of African Organizations
D. Talmage
Simon Katilungu
Simon B. Zukas

*330 Political Prisoners

This class reflects the concern of Russell and the Peace Foundation to free political prisoners, whatever their nationality. Of necessity many of the negotiations with foreign governments had to be conducted with the strictest secrecy. The frequent successes could not be publicized, but the background to each can be ascertained in these files. The files are catalogued on the basis of the first appearance of a given correspondent in a given file. It is only in these files that we learn of Russell's connections with certain organizations—e.g., his honorary presidency of the Spanish Workers Defence Committee. Public statements and messages are also to be found here.

Documents .185001–.188353

Algeria 1964-8

Comité pour la Défense d'Ahmed Ben Bella
Mohammed Chebila
Algerian Peace Committee (Haouari Souyiah)
Ahmed Ben Bella
Algerian Ambassador
World Festival of Youth and Students for Solidarity, Peace and Friendship
Abdelaziz Bouteflika
Houari Boumedienne
Maurice Jardot
Robert Merle
BR, s. on Ben Bella
Akhdar Ibrahimi
Jean-Jacques de Félice
Madeleine Lafue-Véron
Jacques Berque

Argentina 1964

Miguel Grinberg

Armenians 1965

London Committee for the Armenian Cause (M. Alexanderian, P. Gulbenkian)
Bibliography

Basques 1964

Mouvement Révolutionnaire Basque de Libération Nationale E.T.A.

Belgium 1966-7

Jean-Luc Vernal and Claude Vanderhaegen
Pierre Debbaut
Mahmud Jaghbir
Michel Mahnaoui
Ernest Mandel
Pierre Le Grève

Brazil 1964-6

Li Chu-wen
Phelippe Nagi Haddad
Amnesty International (Andre Mann)
Salomão Tabak
Alzira Rudge
RS, s.

Burma 1964

Amnesty International (Peter Benenson)

Cameroons

Popular Union of the Cameroons (Charles M. Bog)
Tribune de la Jeunesse
The Guardian (A. Hetherington)

Ceylon 1964

Carmen Serrano

China 1965-6

Leo K.T. Yen
R.O. Hall (Bishop of Hongkong)
Chou En-lai
Gertrude Woker
Karl Detter
Art Sharon

Congo 1965-8

Arthur Worth
Pamfil A. Riposanu and Harry H. Lipsig

Cuba 1964-7

Michael Callinon
Venezuela's Cuban Exiles (Felix Mondejar, José Marti)
Rene Pelleya

Czechoslovakia 1962-7

Herman Davis
Edna Mayo
Frantisek Klemens
Socialist Union of Central-Eastern Europe (Vilem Bernard)
"Background to Czechoslovakia" (essay)
Embassy of the Czechoslovak Republic in London (Z. Thrlik)
Vojtech Seidler
Eugen Stefka
Jaroslav Rerabek
Labour's Call
Miroslav Hloch
Amnesty International (Bruce Laird)
United Nations (G. N. Ceccatto)
Mary Tyler

Dominican Republic 1965

Federacion de Mujeres Dominicanos Comision Familias Prisoneros Constitucionalistas
The Latin American Committee of the Movement for Colonial Freedom (A. Quintero)

Ethiopia 1964-6

Amnesty International (Eileen Kay)
Organisation of African Unity (Diello Telli)

France 1962-8

Maitre Oussedik
M. Briottet
P. Coursault
Amnesty International (Peter Benenson, Robert Swann)
The Olympia Press (Maurice Girodias)
British Embassy
Frank Allaun (documentation re Lucien Taieb and Jean-Ange Msika)
Charles de Gaulle and Louis Lecoin

Germany—London Agreement 1963-9

Pamphlets
Lorenz Knorr
Karl Graf von Westphalen
'arl Attlee
Viscount Montgomery of Alamein
Pierre Mendes-France
Edgar Faure
Klimentiy Voroshilov
Lord Shawcross
Vincent Auriol
Associazione Italiana Giuristi Democratici
Deutsche Friedens-Union (Arno Behrisch *et al.*)

Germany (East) 1962-4

R. F. Lambert
Erich Fromm
Clara Urquhart
Mr. Gotsche
file on Heinz Brandt
Ossip K. Flechtheim
Wolfgang Abendroth
Otto Brenner
N. S. Khrushchev
Lord Fenner Brockway
German Socialist Student's Union (Eberhard Dahne)
Naturfreundejugend Deutschlands
Verband der Kriegsdienstverweigerer
Committee "For Freedom of Heinz Brandt"
Walter Ulbricht
The President of the Moscow Conference on Disarmament
S. F. Kissin
Daily Worker (George Matthews)
Werner Thönnessen
Annelie Brandt
War Resisters' International (Harold F. Bing)
Johanna Andersen Nexö
Verband der Kriegsdienstverweigerer-Gruppe Westharz (Günter Bleisch)
Thoemetten I. G. Metall
Jim Brennan

Germany (West) 1962-6

Dr. Trabert and J. A. Herles
Klaus E. R. von Schwarze
Elfriede Kautz and Gertrud Schröter
Johannes Kautz and Rudolf Schröter
Frank Werkmeister *et al.*
German and International Youth Information Service
Lorenz Knorr
BR s. on Knorr
Karl Graf von Westphalen
E. Turnbull
Peter Benenson

Hannelore Nowak
Ernst Aust
T? Wiffin?
David Fisher to *The Observer*
Richard Weyl to *The Observer*
Charles Wighton
? Gralmann
Ingrid Wils
Defence Committee for Victims of Nazi Persecution (Elizabeth Dales)
Bella Seginer (ls. to Dr. Muller and Dr. Flechtheim)
W. Ammann
Komitee zum Schutze der Menschenrechte
Jewish Chronicle (Geoffrey D. Paul)
Peter A. Danning
Dr. Willms (l. to O. Creutzfeldt)
T. Stelzenmüller
Hans Fladung
Margaret Lloyd
Dorothy Thornycroft
Embassy of the Federal Republic of Germany (Hans Scherer)
Renate Riemeck (open l. to H. Fladung)
Martin Niemoller
W. Abendroth
Fladung Defence Committee (l. to T. Stelzenmuller)
Ruth F. Rosenwald
Elmar Herterich
Justizoberinspektor
Dietrich Günther
Stefan Meyer
Gustav Wyneken
E. Bucher
Bill Kaye
Committee for Human Rights (Mr. Foreberger)
Klaus Rose
Daily Telegraph
Karl Otto
Salomon Seginer
Klara Schabrod
Justizminister des Landes Nord-rhein-Westfalen
Irene Jakobi
Fritz Meinicke
Committee for the Protection of Human Rights
Georg Jakobi
Gerhard Böhm
Morton Lange
BR, s. "The Political Prosecution of Lorenz Knorr"
Heinrich Lübke
Gerda Kahler
Bernward Vesper-Triangel
Wolf Rüdiger Hess
Carlheinz Brück

Ghana 1964

Charles M. Bog
W. Bolkan
Industrial Aids Limited
A. Potts
Patrick Marlowe
Antony Steel
Royal Moroccan Embassy (Abbas El Mokri)
G. Levy
Mme. Richard Wright

Greece—Miscellaneous Correspondence 1962-6

Constantinos D. Constantinou
Athens Association of Families of Political Exiles and Prisoners (Tassia Glezou *et al.*)
Costas Varnalis
Andréas Dambassis
P.B. Richardson
Conference for a General Amnesty for the Detainees and Political Exiles and for the Rights of Man in Greece (Andre Leroy)
Constanten Tsamantanis
Ellen E. H. Collins (poem)
Michael Peristerakis
Chambers
Gregory Hatjistephanidis
British Embassy in Athens
Westlands Committee of 100
Nikos G. Daskalopoulos
Encl: poem
Greek Ambassador to London
Comite Asopes (Marie Kyriakidou)
Gunnar Alkahammar
Evangelos Courouclis
Hellenic Committee for International Détente and Peace (Andreas Zakkas)
Second German Television Corporation (Werner Rulf)
The Guardian
The British Peace Committee
Frank Hill
John N. Dragoumis
Thetis Kotsaki
Amnesty for Greek Political Prisoners (Marcus Lipton)
Committee for the Release of Greek Political Prisoners
BR, s. on Dr. Lambrakis
E.F. Patterson

The Charlotte Observer
G. Ronald Guast?
The General Confederation of Greek Labour
The Private Secretary to the Prime Minister
Ronald L. "Pervert"
Rik Evans
George Donnbassis
L. B. Brody
Political Prisoners' and Exiles' Families' Association (Thetis Kotsaki, Marie Kyriakidou)
The Nation (Carey McWilliams)
Amnesty International (Albert Lodge)
The Anglo-Greek Luncheon (Catherine, Lady Peake)
Lilian Cook McFarland (l. to Maria Kyriakidou)
Political Prisoners in the Aegina Prison (Anthony Ambatielos *et al.*)
Theodore Xirotagaros
Nikandros Kepesis
Mr. Zis
Clara Urquhart
Mr. Ferentinos
Association of Greek Democratic Lawyers
Betty and Tony Ambatielos
Democratic Youth "Gregory Lambrakis" (Mikis Theodorakis)
League For Democracy in Greece (Diana Pym)
Costis Moskoff
Fédération Internationale des Droits de l'Homme
Judy Brook
Fourth Marathon March (Melis Nikolaides)
Greek Society for Nuclear Disarmament "Bertrand Russell" (Michael Peristerakis, Nikos Kiaos)

Greece 1962-7

negatives of BR and Betty Ambatielos
League for Democracy in Greece Relief Committee (Betty Ambatielos)
Doukakis Vasilios
Giannis Katsantonis
The Guardian (A. Hetherington)
Diana Pym
BR, s. on the Celebration of "October 28th 1940"
notes by CF
Greek National Resistance (Nikandros Kepesis *et al.*)
Maria Kyriakidou
Political Detainees of Chalkida Prison (Stathis Zareifis and Giannis Katsantonis)
Institute for Research and Development of Vocational Rehabilitation of Disabled (Maria Kypraioy)
West European Conference for an Amnesty for Greek Political Prisoners and for a Return to a Normal Democratic Life (Compton Mackenzie *et al.*)
Costas Varnalis
The Observer
BR, message re amnesty for Greek political prisoners
N. Kepessis, G. Potiris and M. Siganos
Amnesty for Greek Political Prisoners (Benedict Birnberg)
BR, s. to General Assembly of the United Nations
John Kalogiannis
"Bertrand Russell Committee of 100" (M. Peristerakis and N. Costantopoulos)
BR, message on leaflet
BR, several ss.
The Times (Geoffrey Woolley)
M. Nicolaides
BR, cable and s.
The Greek Ambassador
BR, s. re death of Gregory Lambrakis
Political Prisoners of AMFISSA
N. Kostodoros, G. Manolakas and V. Grammatikakis
World Council of Peace, Presidential Committee
BR, message on leaflet
BR, several ss.
The Times (Colin MacLean)
Papayotis Pipenelis
Peace News
Private Secretary to Queen Elizabeth II
Marcus Lipton
The Sunday Times
BR, s. paying tribute to Dr. Lambrakis
BR, s. to *Sunday Times*
Henry Brooke
Home Office (G. G. Otton)
BR, s.
Save Greece Now
General Confederation of Greek Labour
Michael Adeane, Secretary to Queen Elizabeth II
BR, s. on Greek demonstrations
Organization of Families of Greek Political Prisoners
Foreign Office (Lord Home)
Athinaki
BR, message to Hiroshima Day Demonstrators, Athens
Daily Worker (George Matthews)
The Minority of One (M. S. Arnoni)

Thetis Kotsaki
Daily Telegraph
The Word
Kostas Vasalos and Giannis Potiris
Political Prisoners in the Aegina Prison (Anthony Ambatielos *et al.*)
George A. Papandreou
list of prisoners
Association d'Athens des Familles des Exiles et Prisonniers Politiques (Elli Ionnidou *et al.*)
Tasopoulos Dimos *et al.*
Zannetos Tofallis
George Lavrides
Political Prisoners of Trikala Prisons (Christos Kasiouras *et al.*)
BR, s.
Michel Melas
Comité Central des Réfugiés Politiques de Grèce (Jannis Nocolopoulos)
Prime Minister's Office, Athens, Greece
Provisional Committee of the Association of Released Political Prisoners
BR, s. re Papandreou and political prisoners
G. Lis
Lambros Florakis *et al.*
George Koutroukis, Stefanos Papayianis and Kostas Filinis
Manolis Siganos
T. Doganis
photos of protest marches
biographies of women political prisoners
British Delegation to Paris Conference
Alekos Matheopoulos
Emily C. Moore
Andreas Lentakis
BR?, s. re members of the Greek Youth Association for Nuclear Disarmament
N. Kiaos
London Committee of 100 (Sue Abrahams)
Mr. Kostopoulis
War Resisters' International
Bertrand Russell Peace Foundation of Australia
Comité Hellenique pour la Détente Internationale et la Paix
Union of Relatives of Greek Political Refugees Abroad (Irene Papadimitriou and Maria Hodjiandreou
The Central Committee of the Repatriation of the Greek Refugees (D. Papademetriou)
André Leroy
BR, s. to *The Morning Star*
Union of Greek Political Refugees in Poland (Kostas Stfosis)

Hungary—Separated Families and Political Prisoners 1958-67

Cyrus Eaton
Ferenc Munnich
The Times
Hungarian Writers' Association Abroad (Paul Ignotus)
Hungarian Chargé d'Affaires (István Molnár)
A. J. Ayer *et al.* (l. to Janos Kadar)
Leslie Budai
Janos Kadar
Michael Csaba
Jean R. Bewley
P. Várkonyi
BRPF (record of activities on behalf of political prisoners)
Eva Laffers
Hungarian Ambassador (Jeno Incze)
Istvan Molnar
Attila Stersky (Szterszky)

India 1963-6

D. M. Kolhatkar
Jawaharlal Nehru
Lal Bahadur Shastri
Indian Workers Association, Great Britain (J. Joshi)
The Pakistan Association of World Federalists (Ahmed Jaffer)
Tariq Abdullah
Ranjana Ash
Indira Gandhi

Indonesia 1965-6

Norman Thomas
Dr. Sukarno
Mission of the Malayan National Liberation League in the People's Republic of China (P. V. Sarma)
BR, s. on Dr. Subandrio
E. P. Quigly

Iran 1963-6

Committee of the Iranian National Front in West Berlin (B. Gharahbeiglu)
The Shah of Iran
Iranische Studentenvereinigung
Le Ministre de la Cour
Iranian National Front Organisation in Great Britain
Executive Committee of Iranian National Front Organization in Great Britain (A. Taghizadeh)
Parviz Edalat-Manech (l. to M. le Président de la Cour d'Appel Spéciale)
Ingénieur Oboudyat (l. to M. le Procureur Général)

BR, message to the Iranian Students' Society
Confederation of Iranian Students
Congress of the Confederation of Iranian Students (Hassan Massali)
Iranian Student Society in Great Britain
BR, s.
Iranian National Front Organisations in Europe
Facts on Iran no. 7 (containing s. by BR re the royal tour of the Shah)
Imperial Iranian Embassy (N. Shirzad)
summary of Iranian facts
Ardeshir Zahedi
F. Sahabi
A. H. Mehryar
Mohammed Reza Pahlevi
A. H. Mehryar and K. Zaki
Encl: tss. by BR, "Oppression in South Arabia", "Freedom in Iran"
Dr. Osterheld
League of Iranian Socialists in Europe (H. Khani)
The International League for the Rights of Man (Jan Papanek and Roger Baldwin)
Verein Iranischer Studenten in Wien (l. to Ayatulah Shirazi)
Mr. Nehryar
Mr. Djahansuz
INF Information (containing BR's "Freiheit im Iran")
Martin Spillman
Iranian Students Union of Freiberg
Iranischer Studentenverein (Ahmad Farrokhi)
list of expelled Iranian students
Verein Iranischer Studenten
Fred J. Cook
Iranian Students Defence Committee (report)
Iranische Studentvereinigung Stuttgart
Iranian Committee for the Defence of Imprisoned Graduates (Françoise Anvar)
K. Shakeri
Iranian Students Association in the USA (Ali Barzegar)
Farman Yusufzai
K. Chakeri
BRPF, s. "The Iranian Students Scholarship Fund"
Ette La'at (list of accused and court proceedings)
Human Rights Commission of the UN (John P. Humphrey)
Parviz Nikkhah (court proceedings)
Iranian Students in Moscow
Iranian Committee in London for the Defence of Political Prisoners in Iran
The Blue Rag
Leeds University Union Conservative Association (P. Grundy)
Confederation of Iranian Students, Hamburg
Organisation of Iranian Students
Iran Report
Le Comité Iranien de Défense à Bucharest
Iranian Committee for the Defence of Political Prisoners in Iran

Iraq—Political Prisoners: Statements 1963-6

National Iraqi Defence Committee, Budapest
Nationalist Kurdish Movement in Europe (J. T. Nebez)
Iraqi News
"Kurdish and Arab students of Iraq"
Iraqi Students Society in U.K. *et al.*
International Society Kurdistan (Silvio E. van Rooy)
R. D. Lewis
Kurdish Students in Europe (O. Sheikhmous)
Mostafa Barzani
H. K. Ahmad
Committee for the Defense of the Kurdish People's Rights
Comité de Solidarité à la Révolution Kurde (Michel Hoang) (communique, memorandum from Moustafa Al-Barzani)
Movement of Defending Iraqi People
The Kurdish Students Society in Europe and The Iraqi Students Society in U.K.
The General Representation Abroad of the Kurdish Revolution
Amnesty International (Charles Medawar)
Jean-Pierre Viennot
Kurdish Facts West-Asia

Iraq—Conference on Iraqi Political Prisoners 1963-6

Report from Iraq
Iraqi High Committee
International Amnesty Meeting for Political Prisoners in Iraq
BRPF, s. re Ba'ath Party
BR, s. re death sentences
BR, speech to the International Conference on General Amnesty for Iraqi Political Prisoners
notes on the conference and lists of supporters and delegates
Arab Students Union in U.K. and Ireland

Prisoners in the Hilla Prison
information sheets on Iraqi political prisoners
Appeal to the UN Movement for Colonial freedom (A. A. Karin)
mimeo ss. and communiques
Abdul Salem Aref
National Libertion Front in Bahrain
Ligue Française pour la Défense des Droits de l'Homme et du Citoyen (Pierre Couteau, Daniel Mayer)
The Congress of Canadian Women (V. Dewhurst)
E.H.S. Burhop
Ethel Mannin
V. Manuel Gutiérrez G.
H.M. Zahir Shah *et al.* (form l.)
Association Internationale des Juristes Démocrates (Solange Bouvier-Ajam)
BR, s.

Iraq 1962-6

Committee for the Defence of the Iraqi People, Leipzig (H. Ramadan)
Iraqi Students Society in the U.K. (N. Mufti)
"Bratislava Conference"
Antoine Tabet
As-Safa (S. Nassar)
The Movement of Defending Iraqi People (Mohamad Mahdi Al Jawahiri)
British Committee for the Defence of Human Rights in Iraq
The Committee for the Defence of the Iraqi People (Ralph Stather, Falah al-Khawaja)
Ahmed al-Haj Ali al-Mirza (appeal)
The High Committee for the Defence of the Iraqi People
British Committee for the Defence of Freedom in Iraq (Lord Chorley, Ethel Mannin and Will Griffiths)
National Iraqi Defence Committee, Budapest
World Federation of Democratic Youth
Yehya G. Roomi Al-Washi
Hadi al-Mirza
"Kurdish and Arab students on hunger strike"
John Platts-Mills
M. Hashimi
International Amnesty Meeting for Iraqi Political Prisoners
various leaflets and booklets
Sunday Telegraph (B.R. Roberts)
Committee for the Defence of the Kurdish People's Rights (Ismet Cheriff Vanly)
The Revolution of Iraki Kurdistan
Movement for Colonial Freedom (John Eber)
H.K. Ahmad
"Political prisoners in Al Hila Central Prison"
Khalid Zaki
General Assembly of International Permanent Committee for Amnesty for Political Prisoners and the Respect of Human Rights in Iraq
Union of Australian Women (B. Miller)
Society for Defence of Law and Liberty in Iraq (N.K. El-Amir)
Comité International pour l'Amnistie aux Détenus Politiques et le Respect des Droits de l'Homme en Irak (Jacques Couland)
Building Workers' Industrial Union of Australia (E. Boatswain)
Amnesty International (Charles Medawar, Ann Clark)
Amnesty for Iraqi Political Prisoners (International Committee)
Comité de Solidarité à la Révolution Kurde
General Representation of the Kurdish Revolution
N. Nirvan
H. Khaibawi

Ireland 1964-5

Report of the Commission on Itinerancy
Charles J. Haughey
Itinerant Action International (Grattan Puxon)
Northern Branch Itinerant Action (Patrick Lynch)
P. Robertshaw
Irish Ambassador
World Romany Community, Canada (Ronald Lee)
M.G. Brazil
Noel Brown
J.J. Brown
M. Lennon
Seamus Kerr
Dominique Santiago

Israel

Haaretz
Haolam Hazeh
Jerusalem Post

Italy 1962-6

Danilo Dolci
Centro Studi e Iniziative per la Piena Occupazione (Diana Fussell)
Amedeo Cottino
Judith Colne

Japan 1964-7

Central Standing Committee of General Association of Korean Residents in Japan (Han Duk Su)
The People's Korea (Kim Min Hua, Ro Jai Ho)
Formosan Committee for Liu's Human Rights

Kenya

Denis Akumu *et al.*

Korea (South) 1965-7

Ian D. Aiken
Amnesty International (Robert Swann)
W. Skupnik
Stella Joyce

Lebanon 1965

Embassy of Israel (Benyamin Peled)

Malaysia 1965-8

Tunku Abdul Rahman
Dato Nik Daud
N.R. Lolan
Mission of the Malayan National Liberation League in the People's Republic of China (P.V. Sarma)
Committee of Families of Political Detainees in Muar and Batu Gajah Detention Camps
United Malaysian and Singaporean Students' Action Front

Mexico 1963-70

Embajada de México en Inglaterra (Antonio Ármendáriz)
Sociedad Mexicana de Geografía y Estadística (Roberto Monsivais Aguilar and Juan Pablo García)
American Dialogue (Walter Lowenfels)
Alberto Lumbreras
Adolpho Gilly (excerpts from l. to Leo Huberman and Paul Sweezy)
Agapito Pozo
Eduardo Ferrer McGregor
John L. Davis
Gustavo Diaz Ordaz
Julio Patiño
Revolutionary Workers' Party (John L. Davis)
BR, s.
Daniel Camejo Guanche *et al.*
Frente Internacional de Derechos Humanos (Benjamín Laureano Luna)
Comite de Defensa de los Presos Politicos en México
Alejandro Lincona G.
The Campaign for the Liberation of the Trotskyists Jailed in Mexico
Eli de Gortari
Red Flag
? Jacobi
U.S. Committee for Justice to Latin American Political Prisoners (Richard Garza)
European Committe for the Freedom of Mexican Political Prisoners
Joanna Wickenden

Morocco 1963-4

British Aid to Algeria Committee (René Catroux)
King Hassan
BR, s.
National Union of Popular Forces
Amnesty International (Peter Benenson)

Nigeria 1964

Margaret Nandy
Abubakar Tafewa Balewa
Alahji Abdul Maliki
Nigeria High Commission
E.N. Oba
Marxist Society (H.J. Dudderdge)

Pakistan 1964-9

National Awami Party of Pakistan
Hari Krishan Sullhan
Ayub Khan
Deputy Secretary to the President (A. Waheed)
Amnesty International (Monica Jackson)
Asad Aid Committee (S.M. Shariff)

Peru 1965-7

Jacqueline de Lobaton (essay: "Le Cas Guillermo Lobaton")
Union de Peruanos en Cuba (Hilda Gadea)
Pakistan/China Friendship
Belaunde Terry
Militant Labor Forum (Priscilla Ring)
BR, s. "On the Persecution of Latin American Revolutionaries"
Committee for Solidarity with the Victims of Repression in Peru (John Edmunds)
Gisela
Pope Paul II
Hugo Blanco
Peruvian Committee for Human Rights, Havana
BR, s. re Guillermo Lobaton
BR, s. re dictators of Latin America
United Secretariat Fourth International (Diego)
Millie van Gelderen
BR, s. re Hugo Blanco
Rosa Alarco
Jean-Paul Sartre *et al.* (cable to Belaunde Terry)

Philippines 1963-6

William J. Pomeroy
Diosdado Macapagal
Manila Chronicle (Benjamin Defensor)
Embassy of the Philippines (Marcial P. Lichauco)
Crispina L. Ang
Tiburcio Baja
Ferdinand Marcos
The Manila Times
The Weekly Graphic
Chief Justice of the Supreme Court, Manila

Portugal 1962-8

Brigid Brophy *et al.*
Amnesty International (Peter Benenson)
West European Conference for Amnesty (H. Ward)
F.H. Lopes de Silva and J.P.V. Monjardino
British Committee for Portuguese Amnesty (H. Ward)
Jane Dyball
Antonio de Oliveira Salazar
German Bleiberg
Minister of the Interior
W.H. Auden *et al.*
list of political prisoners in Peniche Fortress
Amaro Coelho Nunes
Manuel Ferrajota Rocheta
Secreteriado Nacional da Informação, Cultura Populare Turismo (Ramiro Valadão)
Tribune
Portuguese and Colonial Bulletin
The Week (Ken Coates)
Companhia Carris de Ferro de Lisboa (R.D. Wyatt)
list of forthcoming trials
list of women political prisoners
Fédération Internationale des Droits de l'Homme (S. Collette-Kahn)
R. Ferreira
Pamphlets
Front Patriotique de Liberation Nationale de Portugal
Nicolas Jacob
Jean Mettas
National Union of Mineworkers (W. Paynter)
Portuguese Students Association Committee (Alvaro de Miranda)
International Socialist Journal (Lelio Basso)
BR, message to Italian Conference on Portuguese Political Prisoners
R. Hodgetts
Associacao de Estudantes de Instituto Superior Tecnico
João Monjardino
Portuguese Amnesty Conference (G.V. Kimball)
Amnesty International (Robert Swann, Maureen Teitelbaum)
Alberto Antonio Noronha-Rodrigues
Home Office (Maurice Foley)
BR, s. on the Portuguese situation
Unidade Democrática Portuguesa (Ruy Luiz Gomez *et al.*)
Frente de Libertação Nacional e Colonial (A. Noronha-Rodrigues)
Portuguese Canadian Democratic Association (Estevão Gago)
Luis Bernardino
Audrey Wagner
BR, s. re José Bernardino
Secretariat of the Meetings of Portuguese Students Abroad (António Barreto)
Manuel Moura
Table Ronde pour les Libertés au Portugal (Olivier Pavillon)
Martin Enthoven
Jonas Negalha
Inger Fahlender

Rumanian Jews—Closed Cases 1963-5

Rumanian People's Republic Legation

Ignatz Goldschlaeger
Wilhelm Kahane
Simon Grunberg
Gheorghe Gheorghiu-Dej
A. Lazareanu
Alda Ilana Goldschläger
BR, message to the people of Rumania
Emanuel Litvinov
Melanie Aldea
Gheorghe Maurer
J.C. Gordon

Rumanian Jews—Embassy and Head of State Correspondence 1962-7

G. Gheorghe-Dej
Ilya Siniansky
list of prisoners
A. Lazareanu
Wilhelm Kahane
Elie Siniansky
Alda Ilana Goldschläger
BR, message to the people of Rumania
Iris Festenstein
Joachim Goldhammer
Eleonora Koffler
J. Nussen *et al.*
BRPF (chronology of correspondence, list of names)
Ion Gheorghe Maurer
Amnesty International (Robert Swann)
A. Missirliu
Vasile Pungan

Rumanian Jews 1962-7

J. Goldhammer
Leon Staar
G. Gheorghiu-Dej
Josef Nussen
Clara Schoenfeld
Peter Kloos
Israel Geller
The Jewish Chronicle (J. Finklestone)
Willy Israilovici
Frida Lazarescu
Ernestina Feldman
Lidia Marculescu
Siegfried Schenker
Rebecca Gillon
Helen Apostolescu
Clara Moscovici
Luigi and Golda Solomon
Vlasceanu Constantina
Amnesty International (Robert Swann)
Encl: l. from A. Missirliu, l. to Alexandre Missirliu
Elka Kedari
Anglo-Rumanian Refugee Committee (E. Iliescu)
Rozalia Schenker

South Africa 1962-6

Sharad N. Desai
BR, s. re the sale of Buccaneer Bombers to South Africa
Oliver Tambo
The Anti-Apartheid Movement (Dorothy Robinson)
S. Abdul
BR, s. re Nelson Mandela
BR, s. re the Union of South Africa
Amnesty International (Peter Benenson)
S. Jacobson
BR, s. on South Africa re letter of S. Jacobson
The Times (Colin MacLean)
Daily Telegraph
Nancy Brooke
Barbara Castle (with note from BR asking for reply and message to be drafted)
International Conference on Economic Sanctions against South Africa (Ronald Segal)
Max Born
BR, s. for Anti-Apartheid March
Christian Action
World Campaign for the Release of South African Political Prisoners (Jeremy Thorpe)
South African Defence and Aid Fund, Victoria (Ian D. Aiken)
Zelda Friedlander
The Lord Provost
Committee of Afro-Asian and Caribbean Organizations
Iraqi Students Society in the U.K.
BR, ts. of "Speech made in Trafalgar Square on Sunday, 14 June, 1964"
Rosalynde Ainslie
Draughtsmen's and Allied Technicians' Association
World Campaign for the Release of South African Political Prisoners
South Africa Protest (Mamie Smith)
Transport and General Workers Union (Frank Cousins)
Alexander Defence Committee (Connie Kirkby)
Hilliard Festenstein
Foreign Affairs (article by Charles A.W. Manning)

World Campaign for the Release of South African Political Prisoners (S. Aller, Dick Taverne)
The Stoke Newington Liaison Committee for Women's Peace Groups (M. Morten)
BR, s. for Anti-Apartheid
Amnesty International Swedish section
Appeal for release of Albert Lutuli (George de Hevesy *et al.*)
Africa and the World
The British Alexander Defence Committee
Barry Desmond and Ernest Wood
Scholarships Committee of South Africa (I. Yusef)
Amnesty International, Stockholm (H. G. Franck)
South African Coloured Peoples Congress (Barney Desai)
Arnold Salomon
Pamphlets and clippings
Ethel de Keyser

South Arabia 1964

Bulletin of the People's Socialist Party

Southern Rhodesia 1964

Movement for Colonial Freedom (B. Haq)
Ivor Williams

Spain 1962-7

The Spanish Ambassador
Appeal for Amnesty in Spain (Eileen Turner)
International Brigade Association and Friends of Republican Spain (Alec Digges)
BR, s. on execution of Julian Grimau and message to the House of Commons
The Word
Spanish Workers' Defence Committee
R. H. Casad
G. Baldelli
Pamphlets
Anti-Franco Appeal Fund (Gladys Martin)
Federacion Iberica de Juventudes Libertarias
Vanderbilt University (Germán Bleiberg)
Paco Pendas Labra
London Committee of 100 (Douglas Kepper)
National Committee Syndicalist Workers' Federation
Foreign Office (R. A. Butler)
BR, ss. re Stuart Christie and Fernanda Carballo
José Perez
Spanish Intellectuals in the U.S.S.R.
Michael Polanyi
National Confederation of Labour of Spain in Exile
BR, message to Conference Against Repression in Spain
Francisco Franco
Workers' Trade Union Alliance of Spain (A. Roa)
Radio Cologne, Germany
Gretel Rieber
Camilo Alonso Vega
Revolutionary Workers Party (Trotskyist) (John L. Davis)
Ligue Belge pour la Defense des Droits de l'Homme
Maria Cecilia Vidigal Fernandez *et al.*
Rui Galapez Gomes
Frente Patriotica de Libertaçáo Nacional
A. Lazaro
Contemporary Films Ltd. (L. Steinhart)
Secretariat of the Meetings of Portuguese Students Abroad
Abidine Dino
Robert Edwards
Front (Denis Berger)
Daniel Guerin
Movement for Colonial Freedom (Barbara Haq)

Sweden 1966

Dagens Nyheter

Switzerland—Political Freedom 1958

President of the Swiss Confederation

Syria 1965-7

Amin al-Hafidh
Marguerite G. Majdalany
Lea Mashiach

Tanzania 1964-5

Muhammed bin Abdulla Uzdi
Julius K. Nyerere

Tunisia 1967

Groupe d'Etudes et d'Action Socialiste Tunisien (M. Chaabi)
Encl: l. from Daniel Guerin, transcript of interview with Laurent Schwartz

Turkey 1963-4

Y. Kemal
Nikmet Alkilic
Perihan Çambel
Ismet Inönü

United Arab Republic 1962-6

The Isis (Geoff Varley)
list of prisoners
"Communists, Democrats and Trade Unionists, UAR"
Gamal Abdel Nasser
Amnesty International (Peter Benenson, Albert Lodge)
Kenneth Cottman
I. Simonsui
Mohamed el-Kony
Federation of Students Islamic Societies in UK and Eire
Pour les Indépendants Républicains Yéménites (Mohamed Said Al-Attar)

United Kingdom 1958-69

National Council for Civil Liberties
Pamphlets
Hampstead Group, Committee of 100 (Andrew Papworth)
World Jewish Congress, British Section
National Federation of Pakistani Associations
Home Secretary
Samuel Afful
Peace News (encl: ts. by BR, "Prison Sentences")
BR, s. re trial at the Old Bailey of six members of the Committee of 100
Japan Council Against A and H Bombs
The Honourable Society of the Middle Temple (R.H. Williams)
Pat Pottle
BR (transcript of BR's testimony at trial, n.d., ss. on trial proceedings)
B. McKenna (encl: s. by BR)
Fenner Brockway (memorandum)
Martin Ennals
Amnesty International (Albert Lodge)
Campaign Caravan Workshops
BR, press s.
Emmanuel Petrakis
Humanist Group Action (Gordon England)
Peacemakers
Social Surveys (Stuart Bowes)
BR, message for Westminster Amnesty Group Meeting
Desmond A. Robinson
Wood, Costa & Harty
Kaiser Bauxite Company
Alcan Jamaica Ltd.
Prison Reform Council (Margaret Turner)
The Observer
Civilian Establishment and Pay Office
K.H. Roome
D.G. Braund
Army Apprentices School (J.R. Paddington)
Homosexual Law Reform Society (A.J. Ayer)
Prison Reform Council (newsl.)
Bert Bensen
J. Finberg
E. Turnbull
Itinerant Action International (Grattan Puxon)
National Secular Society (W. McIlroy)
Jim Radford
Graham Whettam
Hans Keller
BBC (Frank Gillard)
Juan Martinez de León
BR, s. re legislation against immigrants
Lewisham Council for Community Relations (Anthony Goodman)
Elizabeth Scott
Tony Smythe
Committee for the Defence of Obi B. Egbuna (Connie W. Harris)
National Joint Action Campaign for Women's Equal Rights (F. Blake)
Victor J. Schoenbach
Laurette Decrez
University of London Vice-Chancellor (B.W. Windeyer)
Mr. Downes
Charles Forte
Eric Hartwell
Heald, Johnson, Garton & Co. (J. Black)

Uruguay 1966-8

Marcha (Pedro Scaron)
Revolutionary Workers Party (Trotskyist) (John L. Davis)

U.S.S.R. 1964-6

Morgen Freiheit (extract)
Emanuel Litvinoff (encl: trans. of BR s. from various newspapers)
Alice Kröger
R. A. J. Schlesinger
A. N. Kosygin
Gunnel Hausler
V. E. Johnstone

Venezuela 1963-7

National Liberation Front (London Committee)
Romulo Bentacourt
BR, s.
Pamphlet
Committee for the Release of Political Prisoners in Venezuela (A. Quintero)
Conferenza Europea per l'Amnistia dei Detenuti Politica e per le Libertà Democratiche in Venezuela
Edmundo Chirinos
Aberto Moravia
Roberto Sosa Fernández
Raul Leoni
BR, ss.
Hilda Gadea

Vietnam (North) 1963

P. J. Honey
Ho Chi Minh

Vietnam (South) 1964-5

Vietnam Afroasian Committee Solidarity (Phung Van Cung)
Nguyen Xien
Représentation du Front National de Liberation du Sud Vietnam en Tchécoslovaquie (Nguyen Van Hieu)
Lyndon B. Johnson
Nguyen Khan
BR, s.

Yugoslavia 1964-7

War Resisters' International (Devi Prasad)
Yugoslavian Ambassador (Srdja Prica)
Peter Sedgwick
Josip Broz Tito (Bogdan Crnobrnja)
Valery Tarsis

*340 Civil Rights

This grouping of files overlaps somewhat with *330, in that it contains papers dealing with both Soviet Jews (who wished to leave the U.S.S.R.) and Soviet political prisoners. Many of the latter were also Jewish. These files, and especially those dealing with the United States, contain many statements by Russell and even typescripts of articles as early as "Using Beelzebub to Cast Out Satan", published in the *Manchester Guardian* on 30 October 1951. There is also considerable printed material. Attention is drawn in particular to the "U.S.A. Addenda", valuable material that had to be catalogued separately (pp. 136ff.) due to its late arrival at McMaster. It appears in chronological order.

Documents .183301–.184392; Addenda .199000–.199635

Morton Sobell 1966

Including copies of court documents
Aaron Katz
Citizens' Committee of Inquiry (Steven J. Burton)

Soviet Jews 1962-9

Nikita Khrushchev
Foreign Office (Lord Dundee)
C. Crane-Robinson
H. Husslein
Anna Rauchwerger-Wechselblatt
Paul Wechselblatt Benowicz
Amnesty International (Peter Benenson, Martin Enthoven)
Österreiche Botschaft in der UdSSR
D. N. Ciotori
Rabinowitz & Boudin (Leonard B. Boudin)
Mr. and Mrs. Black
Embassy of the United States (David Bruce)
World Jewish Congress (I. M. Rodinov)
Jean Srednicki
McGill Debating Union (Daniel Lowe)
U. Weinelberg
Jews in Eastern Europe (E. Litvinoff)
Valery Tarsis
Mihajlo Mihajlov
A. F. Gorkin
Iser J. Unterman
Genia Haitin
Elka Bronshtein
Josef Ramai-anasi Tschernobilski
Baruch Fogelman
Regina Cohn
Aleksandrovitch Bentsion

Soviet Jews Appeal 1963-7

Emanuel Litvinoff
Martin Luther King
N. Khrushchev
Lord Boyd Orr
Linus Pauling
Giuseppe Ungaretti
Riccardo Lombardi
Martin Buber
Norman Thomas
Otto Nathan
Albert Schweitzer
Pierre Mendès France
Hewlett Johnson
Danilo Dolci
C. P. Snow
Reidar Larsen

Soviet Jews—General Correspondence 1963-4

BR, "Draft for Cable to Premier Kosygin"
Nikita Khrushchev
Martin Buber
Fakhrutdinova Sugda Berkhanovna
Joseph Shainkman
E. Shudarsky
Mrs. Jules Zimmerman
Jews in Eastern Europe (E. Litvinoff)
Board of Deputies of British Jews (Marcus Shloimovitz)
Lev Zonshtein
V. Bobrishchev-Pushkin
Maya Glozman
Mrs. Rumashevskaia
Josef Weil
Mr. Ushakov
Georgiev Ivan Dmitrievna
A. B. Shtaadze
John H. Sieff
Maksim Brakarenko
Agudas Israel World Organisation (M. R. Springer)
Izvestia
D. L. Barron
The Hall Syndicate, Inc. (Victor Riesel)
A. A. Roback
Israelitische Kultus-Geminde Innsbruck
The Minority of One (M. S. Arnoni)
A. T. Usakov
Anatoli Ilych Shlyk
BR, s., "Message from Bertrand Russell"
Arthur Willey
Jewish Minorities Research (M. Decter)
Vincenzo Arangio Ruiz
BR, s., "Message for Rome Conference on Soviet Jews of October 1"
Nicholas Jacobs
Cleveland Committee on Soviet Anti-Semitism (Herbert S. Caron)
World Council for the "Righteous Gentiles" at the World Jewish Congress (L. Bernstein and A. Reiss)
BR, s., "Message for World Union of Jewish Students' Conference", dated 25 Feb. 1966
BR, message for Student Debating Union of McGill University

Soviet Jews—Political Prisoners 1963-7

Nikita Khrushchev
Morris, Mollie and Joanna Block
G. L. Shabsovitch
David Bruce
K. E. Voroshilov
Joseph Cwietkowicz
Mina Piller
A. A. Soldatov
Becker Carol
H. Sirota
Jonis Israel Ahron
Babanskaja Shmeli
Joseph Hurvitz
Mina Katz
Simon Schnapp
Ricardo Zugaro
Anton Penkaitis
Cilla Shmueli
Esther Berry
James L. Tull
C. Crane-Robinson
Ida Burgin
Comité International de la Croix-Rouge (Anton Penkaitis)
S. Roshchin
Joel Kaganowicz
Hava Goldblatt
M. Zacielsky
E. Karstadt
UN: Division of Human Rights (Stephen Landau)
Amalie Z. Karlin
S. Kuppeshmidt
I. Liwschitz
L. Migneau
Amnesty International (A. B. H. Lumley)
Miriam Avram
Simon Rubinstein
Johannes Schillbach
Elka Futerman

Eve and Michal Grinberg
R. M. Guriel
A. Pillokat
Elieser Karstadt
Feiga Barash
Herzl Amikam
? Stenzler
Musia Breslau
Zvi Segal
Alexi Kosygin
Chana Koilman
I. M. Lerman
M. Kretchmer
Gita Giladi
Petah Tekva
Tova Suleimanova
Devorah Lipshitz
L. Soleyman-Irani
T. Sirota
M. Zacielsky
Elie Goberman
Elie Siniansky
Ligue Belge pour la Defense des Droits de l'Homme (Adrien Wolters and Georges Aronstein)

Soviet Jews—Press Clippings and Documents 1960-7

2 files

U.S.A. 1951-67

New Leader
BR., ts., "Using Beelzebub to Cast Out Satan"
Eugene H. Bird
Mr. Brennan
Mr. Burton
Mrs. Osborn
Mr. Reitman
American Committee for Cultural Freedom
BR, ts. of Introduction to Corliss Lamont's *Freedom Is as Freedom Does*
The Times
Committee for Democratic Rights in the USA (Helen Bastable)
BR, article, "What Does America Offer Humanity?"
Emergency Civil Liberties Committee (Clark Foreman)
BR, revised ts. of ss.
Magazines and pamphlets
American Federation of World Citizens (Mary H. Weik)
Washington Post
Frontier: the Voice of the New West (Philip Kerby)
The Menard Time (Paul Bolte)
New York Times
Leonard Schwartzburd
George Williams
BR, s. on the American Negro
American Committee for the Protection of the Foreign Born (Annette Provinzano)
The Minority of One (M. S. Arnoni)
James Boggs
Louis Todd
The Education Journal (Marvin Adler)
Emergency Civil Liberties Committee (Phillip Abbott Luce)
David K. E. Bruce
War Resisters' International (Tony Smythe)
Becky Dorheim
The Thomas Paine Foundation (Joseph Lewis)
American Civil Liberties Union (Walter Bergman)
Jake Glover
Afro American Students in Cuba (Charles Simmons, III)
BR, s. on Negro unrest in America
Mauri Russell
Daily Telegraph
New York Herald Tribune
New Statesman
Jean Dameron Felber
Reina Hamilton
Victor Rabinowitz
Independent Negro Committee to End Racism and Ban the Bomb (Gwendolyn Mallett)
Fred J. Cook
The Nation (Carey McWilliams)
Milton Elbogen
Jerome R. Johnson
CERGE (Nat Barnett)

Young Socialist Alliance
BR, ts., "The Negro Rising"
BR, ts., "The Increase of American Violence"
Enlightened Citizens Committee
Muhammad Ali

U.S.A.—Political Prisoners 1963-5

End the Draft Committee
Jean-Paul Sartre and Simone de Beauvoir, s.
David Henry Mitchell (court brief, statements, circulars)
Rabinowitz and Boudin (Leonard B. Boudin)
David Mitchell
Geoffrey Reed Conklin
National Guardian
Vladimir Dedijer
Günther Anders
Josué de Castro
Max Born
Alberto Moravio
Arnold Toynbee
François Mauriac
Danilo Dolci
End the Draft's Downdraft
Martin Boksenbaum
Peter Weiss
Lazaro Cardenas
Isaac Deutscher
Pablo Neruda
International Committee to Defend Eldridge Cleaver (Clive Goodwin)
Organization of Afro-American Unity (Malcolm X)
BR, press s. on murder of Malcolm X
Citizens Committee of Inquiry (Mark Lane)
Clippings
Grace Lee Boggs
Pamphlets and press clippings: 3 files
The Texas Observer (Ronnie Dugger)
Freedomways (Norma Rogers and Esther Jackson)
Ramparts
BR, s. on Mohammed Ali
Calvin Winslow

U.S.A. Addenda (catalogued separately because of its late arrival at McMaster)

N.d.

Bomb-test suits

1955

Jacob Mindel
Federal Parole Board

1956

Corliss Lamont
Sidney Hook

1957

Norman Thomas
BR, s., *New Leader*

1958

BR in *New Leader* debate with S. Hook

1960

Linus Pauling
BR, s., *New York Times Magazine*

1962

James G. Fulton
BR, s., "Bertrand Russell on Peace", *New America*, 15 June 1962
Clipping re William Worthy
New York Times
John F. Kennedy
Taylor Adams (William Worthy case)
Committee for Nonviolent Action (A. J. Muste)
Soviet Peace Committee (N. Tikhonov)
Mimeo ts. of BR's cables during Cuban Crisis
Clipping
BR, s. [inspection of nuclear test sites], *New York Times*, 25 Nov. 1962
Asociacion por la Responsabilidad Social del Investigator Cientifico (Mischa Cotlar, T. Buch)
Ss., "Imprisonment in 1961"; "Bertrand Russell's work for peace"

1963

New York Times (Marion Underhill, Heather Bradley)
Trade Union Committee for Defense of Maurice Paul (E. H. Paul)
BR, s. re Maurice Paul
Fernando Barreto e Costa
Harper's Magazine (John Fischer)
BR, s., "The Myth of American Freedom", *Frontier*, Apr. 1963
BR, "The Myth of American Freedom". Reprinted from *The Minority of One*, May 1963
BR, "Notes and Comment", *The Minority of One*, June 1963
Heisler & Stewart (Francis Heisler)
The Bomb-Test Suits (Ralph B. Atkinson)
BR, "The Doctrine of Extermination", *The Texas Observer*, 28 June 1963
BR, s., "On The Rationality of the Arms Race", *The Minority of One*, July 1963
BR, "Chemical Warfare", *The Nation*, 6 July 1963
Thomas Lawson Clark
Methodist Federation for Social Action (Mark A. Chamberlin)
BR, s. re Hamish MacKay and William Mackie
Committee for the Freedom of William Worthy (Vernel Olson)
Monthly Review (Leo Huberman, Paul Sweezy)
James G. Fulton
York Gazette and Daily
BR, s. re Adlai Stevenson, *New York Herald Tribune*, 18 Aug. 1963
David W. Edmunds
Andrew Feldmar
BR, s., "Statement on William Worthy", 3 Sept. 1963
Herald Tribune (Dwight Sargent)
I. F. Stone
Stephanie May
BR, s. re Reverend Ashton Jones
Emergency Civil Liberties Committee (Clark Foreman)
Harry Steinmetz
S. re Ashton Jones
The Texas Observer (Ronnie Dugger)
Committee to Uphold the Right to Travel (Jeffrey Sheppard Gordon)
BR, s. re travel in Cuba
BR, s., *Esquire*, 18 Sept. 1963
BR, s., *Alarman* [?] 18 Sept. 1963
John W. Stanford, Jr.
BR, s., "World Needs Free Access to News", *New York Herald Tribune*, 29 Sept. 1963
BR, "Courage to Work for Survival", *The Minority of One*, Oct. 1963
The Minority of One (M. S. Arnoni)
John F. Kennedy
BR, s., "My View of the Cold War". For *Esquire*
James Boggs
Kenneth B. Clark
BR, pamphlet, *Bertrand Russell on the War in Vietnam*
BR, s. [treatment of the American Negro]
BR, "The Conflicting Ideologies of East and West", *Playboy*

1964

Lyndon B. Johnson
The New York Times (H. Liebowitz)
John W. Stanford, Jr.
Committee to Honor Dr. Willard Uphaus (Grenville Clark *et al.*)
BR, s. re Dr. Willard Uphaus
BR, s., "Semantics and The Cold War", 5 Feb. 1964
Varsity
Robert Leckie, "The Forgetful Lord", *Country Beautiful*
Barbara Likan
New York Herald Tribune
Committee to Aid the Bloomington Students (Jim Bingham)
The Paterson State College Beacon (G. F. Cronk)
BR, "The American Empire", *The Minority of One*, May 1964
BR, s., "A U.S. 'Blind Spot'", *The Washington Post*, 13 May 1964
BR, s., "A Briton's View of U.S. Cuba Policy", *The Philadelphia Inquirer*,

13 May 1964
BR, s., "Would Halt U.S. Flights over Cuba", *Chicago Tribune*, 14 May 1964
BR, s., "U.S. Cuban Attitude Questioned by Russell", *Los Angeles Times*, 16 May 1964
St. Louis Post-Dispatch (Robert Lasch)
BR, s., "Legality in Cuba", *St. Louis Post-Dispatch*, 17 May 1964
San Francisco Chronicle (Carolyn Fisher)
BR, s., "Cuba and the U.S.", *San Francisco Chronicle*, 21 May 1964
BR, s., "The US, the USSR, and Cuba", *The New Republic*, 23 May 1964
James G. Fulton
Corliss Lamont
BR, s. re Drs. Camon and Taylor
David L. Evans
The Guardian
New Statesman
Dick Gregory
A. J. Muste
Arthur Steuer
BR, s. re Dick Gregory
Wayne Morse
BR, s., "Statement for Delivery By Senator Morse in the Senate"
James V. Geisendorfer
Fred J. Cook
1 file re Kennedy Assassination; BR, pamphlet, "16 Questions on the Assassination", reprinted from *The Minority of One*, Sept. 1964; *Inquiry*, Dec. 1964; mimeo tss.; clippings
Hubert H. Humphrey
Governor A. Stevenson (Clayton Fritchey)
Miscellaneous notes
BR, ss., *Frontier*, *New York Herald Tribune*

1965

Murray Newsletter (Madalyn Murray)
Madalyn Murray O'Hair
Clippings re Madalyn Murray
Barbara Likan
BR, s. re Madalyn Murray
Parent's Defense Committee For Berkeley Students (Adele Erenberg)
BR, s. re demonstrations by Berkeley students
David K. E. Bruce
Lyndon B. Johnson
Chester L. Cooper
BR, s., "Vietnam", *Frontier*, Sept. 1965
SVN Peace Committee (Dr. Phung van Cung)
BR, s. re Dominican Republic
Organization of Afro-American Unity (Malcolm X)
BR, "Statement on *Dark Ghetto* by Kenneth Clark", 18 Feb. 1965
Defenders of 3 Against HUAC (Miriam Levin, Martha W. Dudley)
BR, s. re Defenders of 3 Against HUAC
Clippings re HUAC
Women Against War (Eileen Bernal)
CERGE (William McAdoo, Wendy Nakashima, Nat Barnett)
BR, s. re Bill Epton, 31 Mar. 1965
The Nation, 15 Nov. 1965
BR, s. re Bill Epton, 6 Dec. 1965
Progressive Labor Party (form l.)
Mimeo tss.
ID?
The Week, 10 Mar. 1966
"The Case of Bill Epton"
Mimeo tss.
Martin Luther King, Jr.
Kenneth B. Clark
James G. Fulton
P.c. re Dagmar Wilson, Donna Allen and Russell Nixon
Amnesty International (Peter Benenson)
Documents re Merv Griffin interview; mimeo tscc.; clippings
The Merv Griffin Show (Bob Shanks)
Elizabeth Ramsden Eames
Steven A. Borstein
BR, s., "The Negro Rising", Oct. 1965
BR, s. re persecution of two American soldiers, 30 Dec. 1965
Rabinowitz & Boudin (Leonard B.

Boudin)
Advocate General, American Army
Deirdre Griswold
"The Campus and the Constitution", mimeo ts.
Transcript of "People of the State of Michigan v. David Lee Bloom"
BR, s., "Anomalies of the Cold War"

1966

Mimeo ts.
BR, ss. re House Committee on Un-American Activities, 10 Aug. 1966; 16 Aug. 1966
Defenders of 3 Against HUAC (Martha W. Dudley)
BR, s. re Defenders of 3 Against HUAC
Emergency Civil Liberties Committee (Joe Pool), mimeo ts.
The Minority of One (M. S. Arnoni)
BR, s., "A Century of General Civil War", *The Minority of One*, 8 Feb. 1966
Michigan Free Speech Defence Committee (John O'Malley Burns, Fred W. Janvrin)
BR, s. re Michigan Free Speech Defence Committee, *The Paper*, 12 May 1966
Allen M. Krebs
Ann Arbor Defense Fund (Jeremy Lustig)
Vietnam Peace Parade Committee (A. J. Muste)
BR, s. re Ann Arbor Defense Fund
Linda Dannenberg
Sidney Hook, "Lord Russell and the War Crimes 'Trial'", *New Leader*, 24 Oct. 1966
Fort Hood Three Defense Committee (A. J. Muste, Staughton Lynd)
BR, "Statement in Support of John Harris", 1 Mar. 1967
International Anarchist, mimeo list of buttons and bumper stickers
BR, s., "Bertrand Russell's Appeal to the American Conscience on Vietnam". Reprinted from *National Guardian*, 30 July 1966
Lyndon B. Johnson
Simone de Beauvoir
BR, s. re Stokely Carmichael, 12 Sept. 1966
The Minority of One, Dec. 1966
BR, s., "Nuclear War: An American Expert's Forecast"
BR, s. re Nuremberg trials?

1967

BR, s. re Bill Epton, 6 Dec. 1965
SNCC Newsletter, mimeo tss.
Mohammed Ali
Mimeo tss., clippings
Student Nonviolent Coordinating Committee (Ethel H. Minor, James Forman, Julius Lester *et al.*)
Committee for G.I. Rights (Shirley Jolls, Eddie Oquendo, Maryann Weissman)
Committee to Defend the Rights of P.F.C. Howard Petrick (Caroline Lund)
Press release re Dick Gregory
South Carolina SHICK (Sandi Sellers)
Pamphlet, *What Would it Profit a Man*
Flora Lewis
James Cameron
David Mitchell
BR, s. re Mohammed Ali, 23 May 1967
Arnold Toynbee
Rudolf Carnap
Jim Garrison
BR, s., "Message From Bertrand Russell to American Negro Soldiers in Vietnam"
BR, s., "Statement by Bertrand Russell, Released to Reuters April 5 1968, concerning the death of Martin Luther King"
Leonard Boudin
BR, "Statement by Bertrand Russell, April 18 1968", re persecution of Black Panther Party
The Washington Post (Karl E. Meyer)
BR, s., "The Presidential Candidates: A Comment for *The Washington Post*", 20 May 1968
BR, s. re Howard Levy, 21 May 1967
Corliss Lamont

BR, s. re Corliss Lamont's book, 18 June 1968
Stephanie May
New Statesman, forwarding Honeywell ad
Ernest J. Sternglass
Noam Chomsky
American Ambassador to Britain
BR, s., "The International War Crimes Tribunal and the Nature of the War in Vietnam"

1968

Contemporary Issues (A. Maxwell)
Leonard Liggio
BR, "Message From Bertrand Russell to the Meeting on May 3, 1968 for the Late Dr. Martin Luther King"
Jonathan Cape Limited (Susan Oldman)
James Forman
Union of American Exiles in Britain (Howard Engelskirchen, Harry Pincus)
Clipping
International Committee to Defend Eldridge Cleaver (Robert Scheer)
National Association of Black Students (Gwendoly M. Patton); pamphlet

1969

Morton and Helen Sobell
BR, s., "The Entire American People Are on Trial"

*350 Bertrand Russell Peace Foundation Offices

Grouped here are the Peace Foundation files of incoming correspondence (with carbons of replies) from its offices around the world. There are also files dealing specifically with conferences sponsored, the Foundation's directors and advisers, its executive officers (Christopher Farley and Ralph Schoenman), and efforts to win the Nobel Peace Prize for Russell. In one file (London School of Economics meeting, 1965) there is a reading text in Edith Russell's hand of Russell's speech entitled "The Labour Party's Foreign Policy". In another there is the *Foundation Bulletin*, Vol. 1, no. 1 (Feb. 1966), with various pre-publication versions. The contents of the files are listed on the basis of the first appearance of a given correspondent in a given file.

Documents .189001–.192296

Argentina 1964-8

H. Almada Sapriza
BR, s. in *Gacetilla Austral*, 1964
Eco Contemporaneo (M. Grinberg)
Youth Movement (Hilda Miasf)
Enio Viterbo
Grupo Joven
Francisco Sforsa
Juan Luis Hogan
Acelo Marcus do Amaral
Pamphlet on BRPF in Spanish
Carlos Cossio
Association por la Responsabilidad Social del Investigador Cientifico (Mischa Cotlar)
Ney de Araripe Sucupira
RSt., ts., "John William Cook Talks to the *Bulletin*"
Ricardo Rojo
Julio Notta
Noe Jitrik
Carlos Portantiero
Maria Rosa Oliver
Antonio Caparros

Australian Branch 1967-70

BRPF Queensland Branch (W. J. H. Harris)
BRPF Australia and New Zealand Branch (Lawrence F. J. Ross)
Manchester Guardian
United Nations (U Thant)
Peace, Power and Politics in Asia Conference
Roy Garner
Newsls. and other printed materials

Bolshoi Ballet 1965

Newsclippings
Michael Foot
Royal Albert Hall (C. R. Hopper)
The Guardian (W. Harford Thomas, A. Hetherington)
Jennie Lee
N. Summers
The Daily Telegraph
Foreign Office (Michael Stewart)
Wimbledon Town Hall

Bulletins 1964-66

1 file of BRPF bulletins
Lawrence F. J. Ross
Draft ts. of *Foundation Bulletin*, Vol. 1, No. 1: Feb. 1966

Danish Branch 1963-4

Elias Bredsdorff
C. O. Gjerlov-Knudsen
Niels Munk Plum
Torkel Weis-Fogh
H. C. Branner

Dedijer Conference 1964-5

Vladimir Dedijer

David Horowitz
BR, s. on International Conference dated February 21, 1965
Julio Alvarez del Vayo
Japan Postal Workers' Union (Minoru Akiyama)
Look Magazine (Dan Chapman)
Alice Wheelwright
P. M. Worsley

Directors and Advisers 1962-7

The Bomb-Tests Suits
Linus Pauling (including RS to BR)
Bulletin of the Atomic Scientists (Ruth Adams)
The Minority of One (M. S. Arnoni)
BR's message to Herbert T. Rosenfeld, Reception Committee, Aero Institute, dated November 30, 1963
Maila E. Lamb
Jock Campbell
BR, s. on Linus Pauling dated January 2, 1964
Heisler and Stewart (Francis Heisler)
Estate of Albert Einstein (Otto Nathan)
The Institute for Strategic Studies (Leonard Beaton)
Gerard Piel
Russell Brain
Giorgio La Pira
Victor Purcell
OXFAM (Lulu Kuhling *et al.*)
Leslie Kirkley
Caspar John
Conor Cruise O'Brien
Amnesty International (Peter Benenson)
Michael Foot *et al.* (form ls.)
Joe Playhill?
C. F. Powell
Günther Anders
Giangiacomo Feltrinelli
Seymour Melman
Martin C. D'Arcy
Leopold Infeld
Il Vice Presidente dei Consiglio dei Ministri (P. Nenni)
Claude Bourdet
Charles R. Allen, Jr.
Lord Silkin
Hideki Yukawa
Fred J. Cook
Centre International pour le Développement (Josué de Castro)
Abdus Salam
Joseph Rotblat
James R. Newman
Michael Scott
D. Martin Niemöller (Ingrid Zachäi)
Lord Gardiner
George Catlin
Herbert Read
Hugh Beaver
The Chesapeake & Ohio Railway Co. (Betty Royon, N. R. Comisky)
Kampagne für Abrüstung Ostermarsch der Atomwaffengegner
Vladimir Dedijer
The Observer (Colin Legum)
C. Allen-Ocho Cuarto
Fenner Brockway
Glyn Phillips
George Allen & Unwin (Stanley Unwin)
M. L. Oliphant
A. L. Curtis
Paul Hoffman
Hugh Foot
Rabinowitz & Boudin (Leonard B. Boudin, Michael Standard)
Department of State, Washington (Frances G. Knight)
Adlai Stevenson
Sigvard Bernadotte
Ritchie Calder
Robert Watson-Watt
Bertil Bernadotte
Peter Rosenwald
Women against War (Eileen Bernal)
Mr. and Mrs. Gardner
Seymour Melman
Peter Burns
William L. Shirer
RS, speech, 1965
P. M. S. Blackett
Babu *et al.* (form ls.)
Ho Chi Minh
The Royal Society
Lewis Silkin & Partners
Heald, Johnson, Garton & Co.
RS, speech, 1966

RS, photocopies of notes from Bolivia?
Posters for memorial meeting for BR

Christopher Farley 1962-70

Clare?
David Aspinwall
Auropa Public Relations Agency (**Mustafa Jaber**)
Beas World Travel Agency Ltd. (Michael Beasley)
John Bowden
Caravel Press
John Roy Carlson
Roger Caulkett
Celebrity Bulletin (J. F. Hoshins)
John Chambers
Judy Chambers
G. R. H. Chase
Chemins de Fer Britanniques (H. C. Talbot)
John Conway
The Ambassador of the Republic of Cuba
Dagenham Motors Ltd. (P. D. Bligh)
Daily Express (F. J. Tyler)
Ann Davidson
Robin Davis
Ernest Dowson
Anton Felton
F. I. R. Geschichtskommission (Renato Bertolini)
Brian Fitzgerald
Flying Magazine
The Ford Film Library
S. Gerrosi
Robert Glazer
Faris Glubb
A. E. Hall Dairy
New Left Books Ltd. (Jon Halliday)
Hampstead Borough Council
Harman Healy & Co.
Jan Hawly
Audrey Harris
Connie Harris
Ronald F. Harvey
Claudine Henry
Richard Hobin
David Hogget
Mrs. Holder
Iraqi Society, Leeds University (M. V. Ibrahim)
Isle of Thanet Constituency Labour Party (R. Sankey)
John Jervis
Jerusalem Liberation Committee
Nicholas Johnson
Russell Johnson
Niels Jonassen
Bill Kaye
Keesings Publications Ltd.
William Kempner Ltd. (re proofs of "The Labour Party's Foreign Policy")
Pat Kirby
Jack Knight
Clemens Kuby
Eileen Lee
Liberation (Dave Dellinger)
Liverpool Road Pottery Ltd. (C. P. Baskeyfield)
Richard Mabey
W. MacDonald
Metropolitan Police Central Ticket Office (E. O'Mara)
Harry Mister
Jeff Nuttall
H. A. O'Brien
Pitmans College
Report
D. Robin
R. S. Rogers
BR
ER
Arnold Salomon
Edie Schoenman
Ralph Schoenman
Gene Sharp
J. Allen Skinner
Ken Tarbuck
Mieko Tarumoto
Dora Taylor
Noel Taylor
Edward Thompson
Tidsignal (Bo Hammar)
Towry Law (General Insurance) Ltd. (J. A. Taylor)
Transworld Circulation Co.
N. Tamarin (Maryann Weissman)
Ken Weller
Wells Street Magistrates' Court
George Whitman

(Ex-) German Branch 1964-5

Vorgänge (article entitled "Die

Bertrand-Russell-Friedensstiftung"
Marcus Bierich
Günther Schwarz
H. J. Hopf
Verlag Schnelle
Renate Poeschel
Verband der Kriegsdienstverweigerer (Alfred Riedel)
Günther Heipp
J. Schneider
Carl Backhaus

(Ex-) Indian Branch

1 file of printed material (including *Should India Make an Atom Bomb? Bertrand Russell Answers* and *Bertrnad Russell Journal for India*)

(Ex-) Italian Branch **1965**

BR, s. re the Italian Council of the BRPF
Danilo Dolci
Joyce Lussu
Printed documents, clippings, photos

Japan—Miscellaneous
Politics 1952-68

Information Bulletin, The Fourth World Conference Against A & H Bombs and for Disarmanent
Shigetoshi Iwamatsu
"Japan's Tragedy"
Yukiko Iinuma
Tsuruko Saito
A-bomb photos
Masahiro Okada
Shuzo Yajima
Ritsumeikan University Caravan Club
The Japan Council Against Atomic and Hydrogen Bombs (Kaoru Yasui)
Chie Nemoto
Hideki Yukawa
Seirin Ishido
Zengakuren (All Japanese Federation of Student Autonomies) (Toru Kurokawa)
Konkokyo Church of Izuo (Toshio Miyake)
Daigakusha Co.
The Nagasaki–Hiroshima Pilgrimage for Peace (Seikichi Yonekawa)
Keisui Takemura *et al.*
Tokyo Junior Chamber of Commerce (Masanori Miyairi)
Hakumon Herald (Kenji Nakadate)
Eleventh Congress World Association of World Federalists (Iwao Ayusawa)
Union of Mutual Prosperity Headquarters (Toshio Miyake)
City of Hiroshima (Shinzo Hamai)
Jotaro Kawakami
Jasuharu Shima
Sojiro Okaya
Russ Nixon
Zenshin
Iwanami Shoten (Genzaburo Yoshino)
Orizuru-kai
Haruo Iimura
Junichi Aomi
Kooko Iimima
Albert Axelbank
Yamagishi-kai (Rokuzo Murakami)
Mr. Ohkawa
Koji Mori
World Conference in Hiroshima and Nagasaki (B. Sano, Ichiro Moritaki, Kaoru Ohta)
Le Comité National des Artistes du Japon (N. Morita)
Ichiro Moritaki
Shuken Suzuki
Yohio Nagai
Tsutomu Makino
Japan Revolutionary Communist League (Toru Kurokawa)
Japanese Section of the British Broadcasting Corporation (T. Leggett)
CF to RS
Masao Kunihiro
Minoru Vezumi
Tanaka Yasunebu
Kanichi Nishimura
Friendship Centre (Barbara Reynolds)
General Council of Trade Unions of Japan (Hiroshi Wakabayashi)
Shimpei Fujimaki
Sekai (Toru Midorikawa, Yohane Shimamura, Ryosuke Yasue)
Sadao Morita
Mainichi Daily News (Koji Mori)
Mieko Tarumoto
Kiyoshi Saito
Gakken Co. (Hiroyuki Takeda)
Obunsha Co. Ltd. (Kimihiro Torii)
CF? to BR and ER
The Three-Penny Review (I. Shigeo)
Japan Socialist Party (Nobuyuki Kato)
Kanichi Nishimura
Shinichiro Tomonaga
Shigeru Nambara
Seiji Kaya
Kazuo Hirotsu
Rokuro Hidaka
Yoshio Nakano

Hyoe Ouchi
Ikutaro Shimizu
Shoichi Sakata
Toshiyuki Toyoda
Kiyoko Takeda
Shinzo Tajima
Shigeto Tsuru
Tamaki Uemura
Tetsuzo Tanigawa
Dr. Tsuneto
Yasunari Kawabata
Osamu Kuno
Tano Jodai
Yasuo Miyake
Masao Maruyama
Fujiko Isono
Tomoji Ave
Kiyoshi Saito
Bank of Japan (Masamichi Yamagiwa)
Yoshio Kato
Lu Hsing
Kinnosuke Otsuka
Kazuteru Hitaka
Teiji Ueda
Yasuharu Shima
S. Yoshioka
Toshiko Tsushima
Yukiko Funai
Soshyu Nishikawa
Tadashi Asano
Hiroshima-Nagasaki (Tomin Harada, Takuo Matsumoto, Barbara Reynolds)
The General Association of Korean Residents in Japan (Han Duk Su)
Y. Katayama
Yujiro Hayashi
The Manufacturers Hanover Trust Co.
Maéhata Norihiro
Fumitaka Kawasaki
Hiroshima House Foundation (Edita and Ira Morris)
Kenji Nakamura
Kazunaga Suzuki
Hakumon Herald (Hidenao Tomimori)
Japan Congress against A- and H-Bombs (Ichiro Moritaki)
BR, ts. for *Hakumon Herald*
Yoshio Arai
Muta Sueo
Charles E. Tuttle Co., Inc. (Y. Katahira)
Kobun Sha Ltd. (K. Suzuki)
S. Yoshioka
Yutaka Yano
Japan Lawyers International Liaison Association
CBA International (Yusuke J. Matsumura *et al.*)
Oda
Beheiren—Japan "Peace for Vietnam!" Committee (Ichiyo Muto)
Memorandum on Japanese peace movement
BR, ss.
21st Atomic Bombing Anniversary International Conference
Faris Glubb
The Alice Herz Peace Fund (Shingo Shibata)
Japanese Civil Liberties Union (Shinkichi Unno)
Kaoru Ishido
Yoshihiko Irie
Loving Peoples of World Sohyo (Toshikatsu Horii)
Ichio Maruyama
City of Hiroshima (Setsuo Yamada)
Okinawa Prefecture Council Against Atomic and Hydrogen Bombs
Ikki Hitaka
Koichiro Tanabe

Japan Information Centre of BRPF 1968-9

Tsuruko Saito
Shigetoshi Iwamatsu

Job Vacancies 1963-9

London Region CND (Peter Simmons)
Philip Seed
Jack Shepherd
Robert Fromer
John Gare Pitt
Dorothy Losey
Aubrey Hodes
John Gittings
Roy Smith
J. Z. Kedzierski
F. P. W. Wyer
John N. Dragoumis
Liliana Munzi
Marjorie E. Taylor
Gerald Strickland
Brenda Stanway
Hans Koningsberger
S. C. Ghosh
Richard Wiggs
Vlad. Pazourek
Wendy H. M. Hankinson

Brenda Stanway
George C. Ebbert
Benno Wasserman
Jose Cherrez Chiriboga
New Statesman
Margaret Bates
Hans Hammerschmidt
John L. Sears
Joseph Meyer
Philip B. Braithwaite
Hugh Cherry
T. Manuilow
B. Paul
Kenneth D. Kefford
Sheila Cooper
John Rose
Vargis Panaveli
Eleanor Hinton
Jane Schnobel
T. C. Price
Blaine Greensand
O. M. Hickey
M. Mitchell
K. Rink
G. H. Main
E. Hill
A. B. Horowitz
Gertrude A. Kuehl
B.M. Shepherd
E. C. Doran

London School of Economics Meeting 1965

Printed documents on Labour policy
BR's ts., untitled (re the Labour Government), n.d.
"Short-list of Labour Government Iniquities"
"Failure of Labour Government to Keep Pre-election Promises"
London University Socialist Society (Fuman Nuresh)
LSE Labour Club (Mr. Golder, Jim Clarke)
Sunday Times, *et al*. (form ls.)
BR, ts. and hand-lettered copy (in ER's hand) entitled "The Labour Party's Foreign Policy", dated 10 Feb. 1965; "Emergency Statement on Vietnam" (also in ER's hand); mimeo ts.
Abidine Dino
Björn Hällstrom
G. Fanti
? Trofimenko
Cum Quoc Weekly (Nguyen Van Sao)
Newsclippings (some on James Baldwin)
Sanity

Manchester Meeting 1964

James Robertson-Justice
Robert Maxwell
Free Trade Hall (Harold C. Lighten)
Robert Bolt
Mr. and Mrs. K. Taylor
Dick Nettleton
United Nations Association (D. Kirshaw-Grigg) *et al*.
YWCA of Great Britain (Christina McClellan)
Mike Johnson
B. Abhyankar
The Guardian (Frank Wolsencroft)
Socialist Leader
Central Police Headquarters, Manchester
New Statesman, *et al*. (form ls.)
Emrys Hughes
John Roper
A. S. Horsley
City of Manchester Conservative Association (A. Bowen-Gotham)
Manchester Poster Services Ltd. (R. M. Standen)
BR, ts. entitled "The Cold War and the Bertrand Russell Peace Foundation", dated 28 April 1964
Leaflet advertising meeting
The Times
Rodney S. Elliot
Nottingham Evening Post (James Brennan)
Notes

New Zealand Branch 1964-8

Printed New Zealand Branch documents primarily on Vietnam
Alec C. Beasley
Lawrence F. J. Ross (letters, articles, newsclippings)
New Zealand Listener
Christchurch Star
Christchurch Press
Ian Ballantyne
Wayne Morse
Newsweek
Shirley?
Kay Jackson
Jon Pearce
Mervyn Millet
J. K. Hunn
K. J. Holyoake

National Council of Churches of New Zealand (D. M. Taylor)
Bruce Barnitt
William James Hall
Jon Pearce
U Thant
Hans J. Morgenthau
The Minority of One (M. S. Arnoni)
Mimeographed ss. issued by branch; clippings
Arthur A. Calwell
The Australian
Robert Menzies
Jean Prust
Douglas N. Everingham
The New Zealand Rationalist and Humanist
E. H. Richardson
Outlook (Helen G. Palmer)
David K. R. Hodgkin
D. Bendick
Barry Mitcalfe
Mrs. Atkinson
Mr. Oneill
Mrs. Palmer
Weekly News
Eric Herd
Bill?
Mr. Moore
Peace Action in Australia (Geoff Broadhead)
Clarence Hansen
Mr. Morrison
L.R. Bedggood
Keith Sinclair
The Press
I. G. Walker
New Zealand Assistance to the Republic of Vietnam
Lyndon Baines Johnson
BR, s. re formation of branch
Marlene Jensen
New Zealand Broadcasting Corporation
The Great Debate on Vietnam: Holyoake and Hanan v. Ross
Rod?
R. Clegg
S. K. Lipski
New Zealand Social Credit League (P. E. Devcich)
New Statesman
Corliss Lamont
J. William Fulbright
National Liaison Committee for New Zealand Committee on Vietnam
New Zealand Broadcasting Corporation (Douglas N. Eckhoff)
Life
Australian Broadcasting Corporation
New Zealand Press Association Ltd. (H. L. Verry)
Henry Cabot Lodge
D. R. Chapman
Philip Isely
National Guardian
Center for the Study of Democratic Institutions
Lawyers Vietnam Committee
William L. Standard
Kenyon Moore, Jr.
Mr. Grove
Mrs. Davis
N. E. Kirk
Mrs. Wilkinson
Shigetoshi Iwamatsu
Bert James
D. Charles
Mr. and Mrs. Owen Wilkes
Margaret Holmes
The Progressive
Z. During
John Larnach
Mark?
W. H. Ferry
list of BRPF members and donors
Committee on Vietnam
Harold Holt
William Warbey
Harold Wilson
W. Harris
Wolfgang Rosenburg
W. B. Sutch
Roy Garner
H. G. Kilpatrick

Nobel Peace Prize and Nehru Peace Prize 1962-4

Gunnar Jahn
Nobel Institute (August Schou)
Lester B. Pearson
U Thant
Michael Nir
Julius Nyerere (Joan E. Wicken)
United Nations (Ralph J. Bunche)
Edvard Hambro
Tss. (by RS and others) detailing BR's work for peace
Arne Naess
Clyde R. Cameron
R. G. Menzies
Walter Millis
N. J. C. M. Kappeyne van de Coppello
Linus Pauling
Morten Grindal
Herbert T. Rosenfeld
Ts., "Bertrand Russell, *Curriculum Vitae*"
India Council of Cultural Relations
Cecil Miller

Philippines 1964–5

Ramon Carter Suzara

The Manila Banking Corporation
Many printed documents and news-clippings
William N. Gan
Allen L. Tan
Carlos P. Romulo
The Sunday Times (J. V. Cruz)
William J. Pomeroy
Copy of *Africa, Asia, Latin America*
Hernando J. Abaya
Teodoro Lansang
Raquiza, Llacar & Associates (Perfecto E. Llacar)
Balbino G. Sablad
Philippine Committee for Freedom in South Vietnam (Ricardo S. Malay)
National Federation of Labour Unions (Rolando M. Olalia)
Francisco Nemenzo
Peter Limqueco

Russell Foundation 1963

1 file of printed material re aims and sponsors of BRPF, including list of possible questions at first press conference

Russian Revolution—50th Anniversary 1967

Tony Topham
David Horowitz
Hamish Henderson
John Saville
Stuart Hall
S. C. Newens
Tamara Deutscher
John C. Daniels
Len Deighton (Ellenor Handley)
Royden Harrison
Mr. and Mrs. Peter Weiss
E. H. Carr
Laurent Schwartz *et al.* (form ls. containing s. to be signed)
James Dickens
Malcolm Caldwell
Rodney H. Hilton
Sydney Bidwell
Eric S. Heffer
Joan Robinson (Wesley J. Bowes)
National Union of Mineworkers (Lawrence Daly)
Terry Lacey
Neil Carmichael (Elaine Strachan)
Stan Mills
Michael Shrapnell
Naw Milton
Tony Bunyan
Herbert Bell
Albert Booth
Alvaro Miranda
N. M. Perera
Voice of the Unions (Walter Kendall)
Leslie Goonewardene
Raymond Cuallinor
Ken R. Johnston
Petition paying tribute to Che Guevara

Ralph Schoenman

RS, s., 1968
Anonymous ls.
Edith M. Adlam
Tarik Al-Zoubaidi
The Baghdad Hotel (H. Killu)
James A. Baldwin
S. B. Bensen
Benedict Birnberg
Eric Blumenson
Joseph Boudin
Leonard Boudin
Chester Telephone Area
Victor Cullen & Sons
Chris Farley
Gene Feingold
Frank Feldinger
Michael Fife
Robert Fink
Robert Finn
Robert Fisher
Peter F?
Julie Gaitskell
Theodore Goddard & Co. (Blanche Lucas)
Eric Gordon
Arne Bjerring Hansen
Ronald and Audrey Harvey
Jim Haynes
International Socialist Journal (Jon ?)
Iraqi Airlines (J. Johnson)
Hans Isaksson
Stephen Dean Jakobs
Ricardo Jaluat
Stella Johnson
Mary Jonas
David Kaye
Audrey Khan
Slater H. King
King Screen Productions (Charles Horman)
Peter Kingshill

Kodak Ltd.
Eric Lubbock
Neil Macmillan
C. A. Menon
J. J. Mensah
Peter Merriton
Joe Meyer
Elliot G. Mishler
John Morris
Aaron Mutiti
Nicholas ?
Francis Noble
R. G. Phillips
Pointer (Peggy Lang)
Bob Rehder
Nathan Riley
Arnold A. Rogow
Peter Rosewall
Alan Ross
BR
ER
CF
PW
Carmen Serrano
Colin Smart
Michael Standard
Pauline Swindells
I. B. Tabata
? Talaat
Ann Tompkins
United Nations (Margaret McAfee)
Robert Watson-Watt
H. H. Wilson
Alistair Yule

Sponsors of the BRPF 1962-70

Albert Schweitzer
Pablo Casals
Centro Studi e Iniziative (Danilo Dolci)
Max Born
Lord Boyd Orr
Royal Netherlands Embassy (Baron Adolph Bentinck)
Vanessa Redgrave
Duke of Bedford
Linus Pauling
Queen Elisabeth of the Belgians
S. Radhakrishnan
The Albert Schweitzer Fellowship (Emory Ross)
BR, ss.
Walter Friedrich
Gustav Born

United Arab Republic Branch 1965-6

Ts., "Bertrand Russell's efforts for peace ..." (8pp.)
"Addendum to Memorandum on Bertrand Russell Institute for Advanced Political Studies"
"Memorandum on Bertrand Russell Institute for Advanced Political Studies in Cairo"
Lofti Al Kholi
Mohamed Hafez Ismail
Al-Ahram (Hasanein Heikal)
Gamal Abdel Nasser
El Katib (Kamal Rifaat)
National Council for Peace U.A.R. (Khaled Mohey El Din)

Uruguayan Branch 1966–8

Marcha (Pedro Scaron)
R. L. M. Synge
Sección Uruguaya de la BRPF (Raúl Cariboni and Raúl I. Acuña)
Nelson Minello
Bank of London & South America Ltd. (Gordon A. Pair)

U.S.A. Office 1963–9

Louis M. Rabinowitz Foundation Inc. (Victor Rabinowitz)
Frank J. Angeloff
Vo-Thanh-Minh
Henry Cabot Lodge
Frances Damon
Alice Mary Hilton
Corliss Lamont
John Darr
Paul Henshaw
Harold Taylor
Frieda Diamond
I. F. Stone
Simon and Schuster, Inc. (M. Lincoln Schuster)
Estate of Albert Einstein (Otto Nathan)
David Susskind
American Humanist Association, Minnesota Chapter (Bette Chambers)
D. I. Kurth
List of people to see on U.S. trips

New York Times
National Farmers Union (James G. Patton)
Mr. and Mrs. Theodore Schoenman (from and to RS)
American Humanist Association, New York Chapter (Joseph Ben-David)
James Arnold Bond
Youth Against War and Fascism
Robert W. Minor
Lee Stern and Horace Champney
Eugene S. Rapi
The Militant
James V. Geisendorfer
The Peacemaker
Students for a Democratic Society
Michael B. Standard
American Humanist Association (Rober W. McCoy)
The New American Library, Inc. (Sally Belfrage)
Norman Sturgis
Marjory Collins
BR, ts. entitled "Broadcast I" (for Norman Sturgis) dated 21 August 1965
American Academy of Chinese Culture, Inc. (Wen-shan Huang)
BR, s.
Joseph Meyer
Ignacio Sved
Harry W. Clifford
National Educational Television (Don Davis, Ben Sweet)
Community Television of kSouthern California (James Case)
Fieling Davis
Conor Cruise O'Brien
Bertrand Russell Humanist Club
Kathleen Cruise O'Brien
H. H. Wilson and Cora Wilson
William Worthy
KPFK (Ben Sweet)
D. Goddard
War Resisters' International (Devi Prasad)
John ("Tito") Gerassi
James Boggs
Staughton Lynd
James Forman
Warren Miller
John Lewis
American Liberation League (Gerald Long)
Ralph Nader
Daily Telegraph (W. S. K. Thompson)
Manley Thompson
David Horowitz
Russell D. Stetler, Jr.
Michael Roston
U.S. Committee for Justice to Latin American Political Prisoners
David Blum
The International Whitsun March
Leonard P. Liggio
Stephen Spender
Dan Kendall (enclosing biography of Norbert Wiener)
The Artists Civil Rights Assistance Fund

*360 Miscellaneous Politics

This class contains a variety of specific files that do not fit well into any other political classification. The files date from 1962 (the Cuban Missile Crisis) to correspondence in the India file from 1970. Some files concern specific campaigns such as the South-East Asia Appeal or the Committee of 100. The first file reveals an unsuccessful attempt at fund-raising through the offer of the use of Bertrand and Edith Russell's names on commercial products.

Documents .192001–.193519

Advertising: BR & ER 1964

Fribourg and Freyer (R.H. Bridgman-Evans)
Hepburn & Ross Ltd. (Alan Marshall)
Elizabeth Arden Ltd. (Moya Nixon)

Algiers Conference on Denuclearization of the Mediterranean Basin 1964

Emil Abdul Kader
Comité Algérien de la Paix (Louahla Tehami)
Ben-Gurion Speaks (pamphlet)
BR, s. to Conference (+ mimeos)
List of delegates
RS, address to Conference (+ mimeos)
Programme
Le Problème Palestinien (mimeo)
Ali Hussein El Kadi, s. entitled "Address of the Delegation of Aden"
Speech of the Albanian Delegation
RS, notes
Speech of the Algerian Delegation
World Council of Peace (J. D. Bernal)
T. Schönfeld
Ethiopian Delegation, s.
French Delegation (M. Boudouresque), s.
British Delegation (Michael McGahey), s.
Eugenie Cotton, s.
Jusuf M. Dadoo, s.
German Democratic Republic Delegation (Walter Friedrich), s.
Peter A. Adjei, s.
Greek Delegation, s.
Italian Delegation (Lucio Luzzato), s.
Libyan Delegation, ss.
Rumanian Delegation (Miron Nicolescu), s.
Senegal Peace Movement (N'Dene N'Dao), s.
Spanish Delegation (Enrique Lister), s.
Tunisian Delegation (Mahmoud Mamouri), s.
UAR Delegation, s.
Accra Assembly, Ghana (F. E. Boaten), ss.
"Final Communiqué"
"Algiers Appeal" (s.)
Djennrdi Djaffr
Haouari Souyiah

Biafra 1968–9

3 files of printed material, incl. trans. of (1969) "Perspectives: Biafra" conference (Stephen Lewis, Andrew Brewin, D. McDonald, F. Brockway *et al.*)

Campaign against Imperialism 1966

draft programme for seminar
New Left Review (Robin Blackburn)

Committee of 100—Fund-raising

BR, article in Bogota newspaper
BR, "The Social Responsibilities of Scientists" (*Science* offprint)
John B. Witchell
Shelagh Delaney
List of letters to be typed
Form 1.
Vera Brittain
Alex Comfort
Hugh MacDiarmid
John Osborne
Arnold Wesker
John Braine
George Melly
Benjamin Britten
Martin Hyman
Alan Sillitoe
Robert Bolt
Edith Sitwell
John Arden
Herbert Read
Compton Mackenzie
Helen Sellar
Sonia McGuinness
Michael Tippett
Summary of contributions
Iris Murdoch
Michael Scott (with mimeo s.)
Welsh Committee of 100 (David Mathias)
London Committee of 100 (Laurens Otter)

Congo (Leopoldville) 1964-5

BR, s. entitled "Preface to *Death and Pillage in the Congo*"
Carol Fisher
R. Alway
A. Barlovatz
Ligue Belge pour la Défense des Droits de l'Homme (A. Wolters)
RS, ts. and notes for "Death and Pillage in the Congo"
1 file of printed material

Cuban Crisis 1962-5

Revolucion
British-Cuba Committee (Stanley Mayne)
Norteamericanos Amigos de Cuba
British-Cuba Committee
Cuban Embassy (Federico de Córdova Castro *et al.*)
New York Times
ER, blurb for *Unarmed Victory*
BR, press s. given out before Kennedy's speech, 22.10.62
Linus and Ava Helen Pauling
John F. Kennedy
U Thant
Nikita Khrushchev
Harold Macmillan
P. F. de Zulueta
Hugh Gaitskell
D. V. Glass *et al.*
Robert W. Everett, Jr.
Radio WMCA Editorial
Fidel Castro
Aberdeen CND
World Council of Peace Presidential Committee (Vivien Pixner)
Cuban Movement for Peace and Sovereignty of Peoples (Juan Marinello)
Communist Party of Great Britain (John Gollan)
Thank You, Bertrand Russell (Penrhyndeudraeth leaflet)
The Observer (David Astor)
Carole McMillan
A. J. Muste
Max Born
Continental Congress of Solidarity with Cuba (Ruiz Gonzaga de Oliviera Leite)
Pravda (Y. Zhukov)
B. Y. Barbasevich
Movimiento por la Paz y la Soberania de los Pueblos
Tore Hokanson
Luis Ricardo Alonso
News from Cuba
Cuba Hurricane Relief Fund (L. Levy)
Alec C. Beasley
Magdalene de Rodriguez

L'Express (Denise Servan-Schreiber)
Embassy of Soviet Union
Izvestia (M. Mikhailov)
Amnesty International
2 fat files of clippings (including interviews with BR)

Factory Scheme 1963

Factory for Peace (Tom McAlpine)

Helsinki Conference 1965

World Council of Peace Presidential Committee (J. D. Bernal)
Printed documents and addresses
s. by BRPF on Report by American Delegation
conference programme
Representatives of the South Vietnam National Liberation Front
Delegation of the Peace Movement of South Vietnam of the Helsinki Congress (Dinh Ba Thi *et al.*)
British-Vietnam Committee (Hilda Vernon)
Soviet Embassy (Leo Kostenko)
Günther Anders
International Institute for Peace
Bulletin of the World Council of Peace (C. Marcucci)
Morse Economic Consultant Service (Elsa Peters Morse)

P. J. Honey 1964

Vietnam controversy in *The Times*
The Times (Geoffrey Woolley, A. P. Ryan, *et al.*)

David Horowitz 1966

Leslie Stewart
Marzani & Munzell Publishers (Carl Marzani)
George Kennan
Isaac Deutscher, ts. of "Myths of the Cold War"
BRPF, ts. "Plan for the Progressive Neutralization and Unification of Europe"
Studies in the Cold War, prospectus

Indian Correspondence 1964–70

H. K. Sullhan
Christian Service Association (V. C. Mathew Vettikattumetom)
Mr. Harma Rajan?
Neela Chandvadkar
Asok Kumar Roy
Chittaranjan Sarkar
Rameshwar Nath Rai
Chakravarthi Srinivasan
Debaprased Mahapatra
Santosh Kumar Pillai
R. N. Vaish
S. C Diwaker
D. Kishan Rao
G. R. DeSilva
Kaj Pal Bagai
BR, s.
Nrisinha Prasad Bhattacharyya
Rashid Khan
C. D. Deshmukh
T. V. Srinivasan
K. P. Sinha
C. M. J. Gilbert
Shalam Light
S. H. Apcarian
B. Malhotra
Jitendra Kumar Roy
V. S. Nipankal
M. M. Abdullah
Akmal Ahson *et al.*
V. B. Gopinatha Menon
Prem Dayel Gupta
K. N. Relvani
G. L. Mehta (enclosing articles on BR)
Alokemay Sen
A. Daili
Apurva J. Mehta
S. Ahmad Adhi
K. M. Joseph

Indian Press 1964

Hindustan Times
National Herald
Times of India
Hindu
Statesman
Evening News of India
Mail
Herald

Indonesia-Djakarta Conference For the Liquidation of Foreign Military Bases 1965

International Conference against Foreign Military Bases (Arudji Kartawinata, E. A. Martalogawa)
Printed documents and speeches
K.L.M. Royal Dutch Airlines (C. H. Swinkels)
BR, s. re conference
RS, ts. of speech
Women Strike for Peace (Mrs. Stein)
All India Peace Council (Chitta Biswas)
Film negatives

Iraqi Statements 1963-4

The Movement of Defending Iraqi People (Mohamad Mahdi Al Jawahiri)
Faisel El-Samir and Aziz Al Haj
BR, draft of s.
Abdul Salem Mohammed Aref
BR, "Message to the Iraqi Students' Society"
John Platts-Mills
British Committee for the Defence of Human Rights in Iraq (Ethel Mannin)
Movement for Colonial Freedom (Fenner Brockway)
BR, s. dated 9 April 1964
Printed material, mainly in Arabic

Japan

Signatures of the Japanese People (CBA International) Suggesting BR's Appeal or Indictment of Johnson etc. as War Criminals (13,316 signatures), 1 box

London School of Economics Fight 1967

Court of Governors, LSE (Sidney Caine *et al.*)
H. Kidd
Weth Adams

Middle East Nuclear Appeal 1958–64

Jewish Newsletter (William Zukerman)
Prevent World War III
Josip Broz Tito
BR, ts. of appeal to Heads of State re Arab-Israeli relations
E. Nevo
New Outlook
Embasssy of Israel (Arthur Lourie)
Society for the Prevention of World War III, Inc. (Albert Simard and Isidore Lipschutz)

"Miscellaneous"

BR, *The Faith of a Rationalist*
The Yorkshire Post (1934)
Voltaire Society (Frank Cioffi) (1950-53)
CND North-West Regional Committee (notice of public meeting)
Lywood & Sons (Builders and Decorators)
London Library ticket
Glyn, Mills & Co.
Anonymous poem, "Sea Life"
Publisher's Announcement
Chamberlaine Brothers & Edwards (Auctioneers, Land Agents, Surveyors, and Valuers)
List of titles and awards bestowed upon BR, 1908–1960
Committee of 100 pamphlet
Silver Pears Trophy for Achievement (card)
Dust-jacket of *Human Society in Ethics and Politics*
BR, l. of introduction for Anthony J. Topham
Independent Labour Party pamphlet
Clipping of BR on George Brown in *Tribune*
Notes re Khrushchev correspondence
Corliss Lamont
Accra Assembly (Frank Boaten)
Clippings (on RS)
Tidsignal (containing article on RS's arrest in Bolivia)
New Left Review (David Fembul)

Thomas G. Buchanan article (enclosing l. and interview with Jim Garrison)
National Youth Campaign for Nuclear Disarmament (David Swaffer)
BRPF, summary of work accomplished
s. re *Limited Bombing* by Peter Weiss and Gunilla Palmstierna-Weiss
Renate Riemeck
Colin Painter
Anonymous l. from USSR on nuclear warfare
RS, speech at Algiers Conference
RS, s. re Brazil
Sunday Telegraph
The Guardian
N. Khrushchev
P. F. de Zulueta
New York Review of Books
Sanity (David Boulton)

Nuclear and Conventional War— Miscellaneous Publications

Linus Pauling, "Would Civilization Survive a Nuclear War?" (article from *The Minority of One*)
Proceedings of the 4th annual Tri-Service Council
Printed material and newsclippings
Arms Control and Disarmament
World Assembly for Peace (circulars)
Institute for Strategic Studies pamphlet, *The Military Balance*
E. J. Sternglass, "Can the Infants Survive?", "Infant Mortality and Nuclear Tests", "Evidence for Low-Level Radiation Effects on the Human Embryo and Fetus"
Bulletin of the Atomic Scientists, April 1969
Handwritten notes by RS?
Lauris Norstad, "The Control of Nuclear Weapons"
Richardson Institute Newsletter
The Unesco Courier
Rapacki Campaign
Notes from *Window on the World*
Soviet Scientists on the Danger of Nuclear Tests
Philip Noel-Baker, *The Way to World Disarmament–Now!*
A. J. Brown, *The Economic Consequences of Disarmament*
Booklets: *An Imminent Danger to Peace*; *Break the Nuclear Monopoly, Eliminate Nuclear Weapons*
Four Lights
Notes, RS?
BR, mimeo ts. "Africa and the Movement for Peace"
Youth Campaign for Nuclear Disarmament newsl.
To Scientists and Engineers in Great Britain, s. by BR *et al.* (reprinted from *The Guardian*)
Nuclear Information
Ralph E. Lapp, "The Strategy of Overkill"
"Biological and Chemical Warfare"
Defence Market Digest, s.
Women's International League for Peace and Freedom, pamphlet
Clippings
Scientist and Citizen, Oct. '64

Nuclear and Conventional War

Ernest J. Sternglass
Peter Foges
Glyn O. Phillips
C. W. Griffin, Jr.
American Federation of World Citizens (Mary H. Weik)
J. William Fulbright
Wayne Morse
Donald Sashin
Ernest J. Sternglass *et al.*, "Strontium-90: Evidence for a Possible Genetic Effect in Man"
J. Rotblat
Bulletin of the Atomic Scientists (Merry Selk)
Tony McCarthy

Nuclear Disarmament

Essay on nuclear weapons
Ss., some by BR?
"Book Unreview" essay by Arnoni
Committee of 100 (Peter Cadogan), s.
CF to RS
Robin Davis

Peace News
New Statesman
CF, review of *Second Wind* by George Clark (copy of pamphlet attached)
"Against All Bombs" (C100 mimeo)

Poland 1965–9

Amnesty International (Eileen Quilter)
Jean Srednicki
mimeo
Chairman of the Council of Ministers (Josef Cyrankiewicz)
Wladyslaw Gomulka
clippings
World Union of Jewish Students (Gordon Hausmann)
mimeo
Robert Weil
European Jewish Publications Ltd. (Emanuel Litvinoff)
Fourth International, s.
Alfred Jaroschek
Günter Maczioch

Public Meetings 1967–9

Marcel-Francis Kahn
Caxton Hall
Movement for Colonial Freedom (Barbara Haq)
Program for Che Guevara meeting
Alicia Merrett

Rocca file 1964–5

Report of the Committee to Explore Trade Possibilities with the People's Republic of China
Bernard T. Rocca, Sr.

South-East Asia Appeal 1964

World Council of Peace (J. D. Bernal)
V. K. Krishna Menon *et al.* (form l.)
BR and Bernal, s.
BRPF, ss. re BR's meeting with American Ambassador
The Times
Nguyen Van Hieu *et al.*
Charles de Gaulle (Henri Coury)
The Guardian
D. Martin Niemöller (Ingrid Zachäi)
Linus Pauling
V. Krishna Menon
Comité Algérien de la Paix (Souiah Haouari)
Vladimir Dedijer
Polish Peace Committee (Stanislaw Kulczynski)
Max Born
Kuo Mo-jo

United Arab Republic— Correspondence 1965

Al Ahram (Hasanein Heikal)
U.A.R. Peace Committee (Khaled Mohey El Din)
Kamal Rifaat
BR, l. re Khalid Ah'med Zaki
Gamal Abdel Nasser
Akhbar El Yom Organization (Khaled Mohieddin)
Embassy of the U.A.R.

U.S.A. 1957-62

Washington Newsletter
Heisler & Stewart
Stewart W. Hurlbut
James P. Warburg, pamphlets
SANE–U.S.A., vol. 1, no. 1 (1958)
Felix Greene
Mr. Bramel
The Peninsula Committee for the Abolition of Nuclear Tests
Let There Be A World (by Greene)
Charles O. Porter
Monthly Review
Ruth C. France
Walk for Peace Committee (leaflet)
Underdog (David Cowlishaw)

Vietnam

2 files of press clippings and other printed documents mainly on Vietnam

Who Killed Kennedy? Committee 1964

The Guardian
Sunday Times
Articles by Mark Lane: Inquiry of the President's Assassination The Warren Report: A First Glance, etc.
Mimeo tss. of ls. to newspapers
Playboy, interview with Jim Garrison, 1965

*371 International War Crimes Tribunal: Members' Correspondence

The names listed below appear in chronological order in the correspondence between Russell and his staff and various persons who were members of the Tribunal. The files reveal that the idea of the Tribunal was first put forth in 1965. The correspondence ends in 1968 with Russell still hopeful for peace in Vietnam. He wrote to Günther Anders: "The present generation of Americans is, after all, the first to challenge the fundamental premises of the Cold War. The resurrection of critical thinking in the American universities offers some promise for the future" (26 Jan. 1968).

Documents .170001–.170825

Undated notes, draft telegrams
Amado Hernandez
Dang Chan-Lieu
Vladimir Dedijer
Dave Dellinger
Kinju Morikawa
Wolfgang Abendroth
Mahmud Ali Kasuri
Laurent Schwartz
International Socialist Journal (Lelio Basso)
Mehmet Ali Aybar
Student Non-Violent Coordinating Committee (Stokely Carmichael)
Simone de Beauvoir
Jean-Paul Sartre
François Mauriac
Isaac Deutscher
Lázaro Cárdenas
Peter Weiss
Martin Penetz
Günther Anders
Josip Vidmar
André Puig
Mahmud Ali Kasuri
Shoichi Sakata
Danilo Dolci
Kurt Steinhaus
Harvard University (William M. Pinkerton)
Slobodan Princip-Seljo School
Instituto Croata Latinoamericano de Cultura (Milan Blazeković)
James Baldwin
Lawrence Daly
Student Non-Violent Coordinating Committee (Elizabeth Sutherland)
Carl Oglesby
Sadun Aren
Gösta Wennström
Ivar Werner
Yngve Persson
Ha Van Lan and Phan Ngoc Thach
BR, s., "An Appeal to Trade Unions"
E. Eagan
David A. Leeming
Students of Nagaya University
Comité Cubano de Solidaridad con Viet Nam del Sur (Melba Hernández)
Verlag Kurt Desch GMBH (H. J. Mundt)
Tamara Deutscher
Student Non-Violent Coordinating Committee (Ethel H. Minor)
Peter Limqueco
Russell Stetler
International Literary Management (John Wolfers)

*372 International War Crimes Tribunal: Refusals

The success of the Tribunal depended partly on the personages who would agree to serve on it. Of particular interest are the reasons given by those listed below for declining to serve. Many supported the purpose of the Tribunal, but considered themselves too partisan to be of use.

Documents .170826–.171181

Bo Y. Åkerrén
R. W. Apple, Jr.
Jacabo Arbenz Guzman
The Earl of Avon
H. M. Bao-Dai
Ayhan Başaran
Zulfiquar Ali Bhutto
Homer Bigart
P. M. S. Blackett
Donnell W. Boardman
Max Born
Leonard B. Boudin
Juan Mari Brás
George B. Bronfen
Wilfred Burchett
Amilcar Cabral
James Cameron
A. R. Cornelius
Maurice Cornil
Courtland Cox
M. P. Damdin
Josué de Castro
Jacques Decornoy
Danilo Dolci
Donald Duncan
A. Elliot
Karl Evang
Abraham L. Feinberg
Georges Fischer
James Forman
Celso Furtado
Hilda Gadea
Graham Greene
Ernesto Guevara
Benjamin Halevy
Philip Harvey
Carl Hirsch
D. M. C. Hodgkin
Henrik Hoffmeyer
Gunnar Inghe
Russell Johnson
Lipmann Kessel
Tran Buu Kiem
V. K. Krishna Menon
Moshe Landau
Jack Langguth
Jose Lansang
Oscar Lewis
Kathleen Lonsdale
Antonio Daríe López
Staughton Lynd
Herbert Marcuse
Michio Matsuda
François Mauriac
Floyd McKissick
Pierre Mendès France
Arthur Miller

Khaled Mohey El Din
V. M. Molotov
Alberto Moravia
Mohammed Mossadegh
Lewis Mumford
Ngo Dinh Nhu
Martin Niemöller
Pak Il Guon
Hans Palmstierna
Linus Pauling
Faustina Perez
Pablo Picasso
Luis Quintanilla
Anatol Rapoport
Yitzhak Raveh
Hussain Riadh
Joan Robinson
José Rodriguez
Henri Rolin
? Rudenko
S. Sakata
Harrison Salisbury
Jobita Salonge
Stanley K. Scheinbaum
S. Sevitt
Sydney Silverman
Lotfallah Solaiman
Prince Souphanouvong
Benjamin Spock
John Stanton
I. F. Stone
Mohammed Suleiman
Utami Suryadarma
R. L. M. Synge
? Talabani
Oliver Tambo
Lorenzo M. Tañada
Elizabeth Topley
Arnold Toynbee
Kenneth Tynan
Vietnamese lawyers
K. W. Wedderburn
Tom Wicker
Ole Wivel
Yevgeni Yevtushenko
Hideki Yukawa

Lists of correspondents

*373 International War Crimes Tribunal: Investigation Teams and Witnesses

These files are of great importance for their first-hand reports of conditions in Vietnam. Many were never published. The background correspondence demonstrates the difficulties of preparing the major investigative effort which was the Tribunal.

Documents .171182–.171691

Tariq Ali
Dr. Behar
Martin Birnstingl
Medical Aid Committee for Vietnam
C. Brightman
Malcolm Caldwell
Marcelo Cini
Donald Duncan
Stanley Faulkner
Stephen H. Fritchman
Japan Committee for the Investigation of U. S. War Crimes in Vietnam (Yoichi Fukushima)
John Gerassi
Gisèle Halimi
Axel Höjer
Yves Jouffa
Francis Kahn
Gabriel Kolko (who writes RS: "Archival work is perhaps the most straining activity of all.")
Joyce Kolko
Jean-Michel Krivine
Hugh R. Manes
Léon Matarasso
J. B. Neilands
International Association of Democratic Lawyers (Joë Nordmann)
Roger Pic
John Takman
Oliver Tambo
Gustavo Tolentino
Setsure Tsurushima
Le Dinh Tham
Jean-Pierre Vigier

*374 International War Crimes Tribunal: French Office

The French office and the Bertrand Russell Peace Foundation experienced difficulties in cooperating in the multi-national Tribunal. Letters, memos, and notes in this single file record some of the difficulties—as well as the achievements.

Documents .171692–.172149

Jean-Marie Vincent
Abidine Dino
? Guerin
Denis Berger
Charles Bettelheim
Claude Cadart
Lily (Claude)
Jane Cheng
Peter Weiss
Victor Rabinowitz
Madeleine Garaudet
Ligue les Etats Arabes (Al-Joundi, A. M. Naggar, A. Shammout, A. Amer)
Laurent Schwartz
Jean-Pierre Vigier
Japan Committee for the Investigation of U. S. War Crimes in Vietnam (? Narita)
Colette Thach
Jean-Paul Sartre
Vladimir Dedijer
Juliette Minces
Comité Viet Nam National (Denis Berger)
Notes (some in ER's hand)
International Socialist Journal pamphlets on Vietnam

*375 International War Crimes Tribunal: Working Correspondence with Vietnamese

This correspondence is arranged in chronological order, beginning in 1963. The earliest item from Ho Chi Minh is dated 10 August 1964. The thick files indicate the symbolic importance of Russell's solidarity with the Vietnamese struggle for independence. The correspondence continued after Ho's death in 1969 until Russell's death in 1970.

Documents .172150–.172461

Miscellaneous cards and notes
John Takman
Comité Action Intellectuals Vietnamiens (Nguyen Xien)
Pham Ngoc Thach
Trantrong Quat
Vietnam Afroasian Solidarity Committee
Cuu Quoc Weekly (Tran-Viet Dung *et al.*)
National Liberation Front Central Committee (Nguyen Huu Tho)
Committee of Struggle against U.S. and Henchmen's Persecution of Intellectuals in South Vietnam (Nguyen Xien)
National Representation of the National Liberation Front of South Vietnam in the Socialist Republic of Czechoslovakia (Nguyen Van Hieu)
Ho Chi Minh
Nguyen Van Sao
Vietnam Peace Committee (Nguyen Duy Tinh)
Chef Adjoint de la Représentation Permanente du Front National de Libération du Sud Vietnam en URSS (Nguyen Van Dong)
Xuan Thuy
General Khanh
BR, ts., "Urgent Memorandum for the Attention of President Ho Chi Minh on the Crisis"
Mai Van Bo
Cu Dinh Ba
Bureau of the International Conference for Solidarity with the People of Vietnam (Nguyen Duy Tinh)
Pham Van Chuong
Ts., "Memorandum" (re OXFAM) dated August 13, 1965
BR, ts., "Confidential Memorandum to President Ho Chi Minh from Bertrand Russell on the Subject of the International War Crimes Tribunal"
RS, memo on discussions with NLF in Prague and Budapest
summary report of meetings between the NLF and the BRPF
Pham Van Dong
Albert Axelbank
Représentation Commerciale de la République Démocratique du Viet-Nam en France (Vo Van Sung)
Tariq Ali
Vietnam Committee for the Defense of World Peace (Le Dinh Tham)
South Vietnam National Front for Liberation in Budapest (Dinh Ba

Thi)
Vietnam Peace Committee (Xuan Oanh)
Association des Juristes Vietnamiens (Pham Van Bach)
RS and RSt., ts., Report of meetings with Ho Chi Minh
Cam Pham Ngoc Thuan
BR. ts., "Confidential Memorandum from Bertrand Russell to President Nguyen Huu Tho"
Commission on US War Crimes (Ha Van Lau)
Tran Buu Kiem
Fidel Castro
Dorothy Hodgkin
RS, memo on discussions with Le Huu Van of the NLF
South Vietnam Peace Committee (Nguyen Van Hoa)
Tham Van Chuong, "Observations"
Commission for Investigation of the U.S. Imperialist War Crimes in Vietnam (Pham Van Bach)
Mai Lam
The Information Bureau of the P.R.G. of the Republic of South Vietnam in Paris

*376 General Correspondence on Vietnam

This class groups miscellaneous correspondence with individuals and organizations on the subject of the Vietnam War. The correspondence is international in scope and is organized alphabetically. This is the principal file for requests made to Russell to participate in anti-war activities sponsored by others.

Documents .172462–.173314

Cartoon of BR as March Hare, 1968
Anonymous *or* "An American Who Loves his Country"
Susan Stanich Abrams
Action pour Une Assemblée Constituante Mondiale (Maurice R. Cosyn)
D. Howard Ady
Afro-Asian Peoples' Solidarity Organization (Yousef Elsebai)
Miguel Alcobendas
Aldermaston March Committee (Andrew Papworth)
Tariq Ali
Donna Allen
American Deserters Committee (Bill Jones and Donald Williams)
American Friends Service Committee
Amnesty International (Robert Swann)
Richard M. Andrews
Anglo-French Vietnam Weekend
Anti-Vietnam-Draft Co-ordinating Committee
Anti-Vietnam War Demonstration, BRPF ts.
Sylvia Argyle
Artists' Protest
Arts Festival
Association Juristes Vietnamiens (Pha Nanh and Tran Cong Tuong)
Lisa Aumack
Albert Axelbank
Cu Dinh Ba and Mr. Sao
Phan Van Bach
R. Balcombe
Nguyen Ba Bao
Luis Gomez Baquero
Donald L. Barnett
Luis Barreiros
Ademir de Moraes Barros
José Miguel Barthe
Jasmine M. Beadle
Beheiren: Japan "Peace for Vietnam" Committee (Ada Makoto)
Alan Bell
? Berger
J. D. Bernal
Peter Bischoff
William Blum
Boots the Chemists
Roberto William Borges
Terry Brindley
British Artists' Protest
British Campaign for Peace in Vietnam
British Council for Peace in Vietnam (Pat Clarke)
British Peace Committee (Colin Sweet)

British Universities' Ad Hoc Committee on Vietnam
Gordon Brooks
André J. Bruwer
Wilfred Burchett
Adilcio Caldorin
Malcolm Caldwell and John Westergaard
California State College Teach-In (Stuart Silvers)
James Cameron
Campaign for Nuclear Disarmament (Dick Nettleton)
Campaign for Peace in Vietnam (D. T. Healey)
Catholic Peace Fellowship (Tom Cornell)
Centro di Studio e Documentazione sul Vietnam e Il Terzo Mondo (Giampiero Cotti-Cometti)
Bette Chambers
Chemical and Biological Warfare Group (Frances Knight)
Jean Chesneaux
Chester Council for Peace in Vietnam (Jean Brunsdon)
Jorge Chirinos
Ma Thi Chu
Citizens for Governmental Restraint (James Malcolm Williams)
Citizens Protest (Tom Brewer)
Robert S. Cohen
Collectif Intersyndical pour la Paix au Vietnam (S. de Brunhoff, Jean Chesneaux)
Comitato per la Settimana di Agitazione per il Vietnam
Comité d'Action des Intellectuels Pour les Etudiants (Sonia Orwell, Richard Wollheim, and Rupert Crawshay-Williams)
Committee for April 17 March Against the War in Vietnam (Hugh Fowler)
Committee for Cultural Relations with Foreign Countries, Information Department, Hanoi (Thu Cuc)
Committee for the English Publication of *Vietnam–A Voice from the Villages* (Reiko Ishida)
Committee of Americans Abroad for an Honorable Foreign Policy (Allen Young)
Committee of 100, London (Douglas Kepper)
Committee on Vietnam (Adrian Webster)
Concerned Citizens of Palo Alto (Douglas Mattern)
Conference Internationale de Solidarité avec le Peuple Vietnamien (R. Wollast)
Council of African Organizations (Sam King)
Covietnamex
Danish Whitsuntide March (Christen Amby)
William C. Davidson
Ademir de Moraes Barros
Democratic German Report (John Peet)
Kamrudin Dhalla
John W. Dower, *et al*.
W. E. B. Dubois Clubs of America (Mike Meyerson)
Peggy Duff
Cyrus Eaton
John Edmonds
Emergency Action Conference, Stockholm Conference on Vietnam
Ex-Service Movement for Peace (S. Knight)
Faustino Aroca Fabregat
José Carlos T. Fialho
Finchley Central Ward, Labour Party (Mavis Norrie, Phoebe Pole)
Zbynek Fiser
Richard Fletcher
Henry Francia
Free Speech Petition on Behalf of the South Vietnamese National Liberation Front
Denis W. Freney
Gandhi and Man in Evolution (T. K. Mahadevan)
Nguyen Ngoc Giao
John Gittings
Felix Greene
Graham Greene
Dick Gregory
Edmundo Guerra Theilheimer, *et al*.
Otto Hahn
Halifax Vietnam Council (T. Enright)

Hemispheric Conference to End the Vietnam War (Edward Martin Sloan)
Miguel Gomez Hervia
Thomas Ford Hoult
Ruben Angel Icardi
Independent Labour Party (Hira Mukherjee, John Downing)
Institute of Commonwealth Studies, Oxford University
International Institute for Peace (E. Wojtaszek)
International Politics Society, University College of Wales, Aberystwyth (J. Lynton Jones)
International Union of Students
Internationale der Kriegsdienstgegner (Alois Stoff)
Det Internationale Krigsforbrydelses-Tribunal (Ole Strandberg)
Israeli Socialist Organization (Matspen)
? Jackson
K. G. Jackson
Japan Committee for the Investigation of US War Crimes in Vietnam (Saburo Kugai, Kinju Morikawa)
Japanese Civil Liberties Union (Masao Ohno)
Japanese Scientists' Mission for the Investigation of US. War Crimes in Viet Nam
Nadine Jensen
Nic Johnson
Paul Jones
Alfred Kagan
W. Kahane
Kansas City Area Committee to End the War in Vietnam (L. Howard)
Bill Kaye
Ida Kirsch
Christopher Koch
Gabriel Kolko
Nguy-Nhu-Kontum
Marc Kravetz
V. K. Krishna Menon
Dick Krooth
David Kuhrt
Labour Party, East Midlands Regional Council
Labour Peace Fellowship (B. Feder)
Corliss Lamont
Abel Alexis Latendorf
Lawyers Committee on American Policy towards Vietnam (Joseph H. Crown)
Leicester University Students' Union (Keith Osborne)
John Russell Lloyd
Jimmy and Judy Logan
Riccardo Lombardi
Phillip Abbott Luce
Staughton Lynd
Ricardo Malay
Manchester and District Young Fabian Group (Phillip S. Bland)
March for the Maimed (Ben F. Blankenship, Tom Brewer)
C. J. Martin
Eddie Martin
Monty Martin
William J. Martin
Alberto Martinez
Michio Matsuda
May 2nd Committee (Robert Fitch)
Vashti and Dan McCollum
Stewart J. McCulloch
James C. McGovern Jr.
Medical Aid Committee for South Vietnamese Peoples (E. Salisbury)
Medical Aid for Vietnam Committee (Joan K. McMichael, Joan Carritt)
Stephen Merrett
Merton Council for Peace in Vietnam
Merton Friends of China
Ian Miller
Mobilisation Committee, Sydney (John Deer)
Monash University Anti Conscription Society (John Conway)
"Mothers" (Karen Wald, P. Larsen)
Movement for Colonial Freedom (A. R. Karim, Barbara Haq, John Eber, Fenner Brockway)
Geoff Muirden
A. J. Muste
National Coordinating Committee to End the War in Vietnam (Duane Allen)
National Union of Mineworkers (Joe

Whelan)
National Youth Campaign for Nuclear Disarmament
Charles E. Neal
Colleen Neitzke
New Society
Newton Park College Socialist Society (Denise G. Lawrence)
Nguyen Phu
David Nicholson
Wayne H. Nielsen
Martin Niemöller
D. E. Noel
North Herts Youth for Peace (Dick Mealia)
Forlio Ulo Oliano
M. L. Oliphant
José Maria Albaigés Olivart
Oregon Mobilization to End War in Vietnam (Roger Sterchi)
Orpington C. N. D. (Rex Phillips)
John Osborne
John R. Osborne
OXFAM (Malcolm Harper)
Oxford University Humanist Group (Tony Lambert)
Oxford Vietnam Committee (Fred Halliday)
Oxford Vietnam Peace Movement (J. Edinton, P. Sedgwick)
Partito Socialista Italiano di Unità Proletaria (Pino Tagliazucchi)
E. F. Paterson
Peace News (Theodore Roszack, Bob Overy)
Philadelphia Resistance (Eva Gold, Dina Portnoy)
Philadelphia University Committee to End the War in Vietnam (Joel Aber)
Martin Peretz
Nguyen Phu
Juan Luis Pozo
Quaker Action Group (George Willoughby, Lawrence Scott)
Jim Radford
Radical Education Project (Donald McKelvey)
Ron Ramsey
Regmarad (Reginald Piggott)
Grady F. Robertson
Alan Rooney
Vicky Rooney
Steven Rose
Herbert T. Rosenfeld
J. Rupoz
Justo Silvestre Sancha
SANE (Donald F. Keys)
Jean-Paul Sartre
J. E. Schild
Albert Schrut
Georg Schwarzenburger
Leonardo César Schweid
Scientists' Appeal for Vietnam (C. F. Powell)
Scientist's [*sic*] Committee to End Chemical Warfare in Vietnam (J. B. Neilands, E. B. Pfeiffer)
Sheffield University Students' Union (Jake Empson)
Shephall Labour Party (Bill Brown)
Yasuharu Shima
Marta Sierra and Héctor Prividera
Takari Simizu
Jo Sinclair
Samuel Sosnen
Agustina Sourále
South Vietnam Liberation Red Cross Society (Phung Van Cung)
South Vietnam National Front for Liberation
Southampton University Students Union (Philip Dangerfield)
Soviet Peace Committee (Nikolai Tikhonov)
Robert J. Starrs
R. W. Steer
Rudolf Steiner
Gloria Stewart
Stockholm Conference on Vietnam (Bertil Svahnström)
Student Mobilization Committee to End the War in Vietnam (Carol Lipman, Mike Maggi)
Student Mobilizer (Syd Stapleton)
Students to Organize for Peace (Margaret J. Cashman)
Students' Union (Autonomous), Calcutta University (Ranapriya Moulik)
Richard Such and Cheryl Arnold

University of Sussex Joint Faculty-Student Committee on Vietnam (E. Lilley)
Ernie Tate
Tax Payers Against War
David K. Taylor
Third World Organizing Committee (J. B. Fletcher)
Dale R. Tinner
Arne Tiselius
Tokyo Tribunal on U.S. Crimes of Agression and War in Vietnam
Tricontinental Committee
Feyzi Ulus, Ilhan Tezel and Munir Cerid
Unified Buddhist Church of Vietnam (Thich Thien-Hoa)
United Coalition to Avert Pandemic and Biocide (Thomas J. Mooney)
United Nations Student Association (Peter Mansfield)
U.S. Committee to Aid the National Liberation Front (Walter D. Teaque, III)
Raymond R. Vane
Pedro E. Muñoz Vargas
Bill Vester
Vietnam Action Group (Mike O'Brien)
Vietnam Commitee for the Defence of World Peace
Vietnam Day Commitee (Jerry Rubin, Jaimey Allen)
Vietnam Federation of Trade Unions (Hoang Quoc Viet)
Andres Solari Vincente
University of Virginia (Howard Ozmon)
Karen Wald
War Resisters' International (Devi Prasad)
William Warbey
Sam Warda
Eric Watkins
Welsh Council for Peace in Vietnam (R. S. Saxton)
Arnold Wesker
West Australian University Labour Party
George Wheeler
Paul M. Whitaker
Raymond Williams
Wimbledon Young Socialists (Jasmine M. Beadle)
Ella Winter
University of Wisconsin Student/Faculty Committee to End the War in Vietnam (Lowell Bergman)
Le Roy Wolins
Women's International League for Peace and Freedom, New South Wales branch (Lorraine Moseley)
Workers of the World Party (Sam Marcy)
World Congress of Women, British Delegation (Joan Carritt, Bess Marsh)
World Council of Peace, Presidential Committee (J. D. Bernal)
World Federation of Scientific Workers (C. F. Powell)
World Youth Campaign of Action (S. Chakraborty)
William Worthy
Peter Wyncoll
Xunhasaba (Nguyen Huu Dinh and Ngo Duc Mau)
Mr. and Mrs. Leo K. T. Yen
York Vietnam Group (Anita Hess)
Youth Against War and Fascism (Key Martin)
Youth for Peace in Vietnam (Mervyn Rice)
Vesna Zidovec and José Dovis

*377 International War Crimes Tribunal: General Correspondence (by Country)

Whereas *376 is organized in one alphabetical sequence, Russell and his Foundation had the following material organized by country. There is considerable overlap in content between *376 and *377. *377 unaccountably ends with Japan—unless it be supposed that *376 contains the correspondence that should have comprised the remainder of *377.

Documents .173315–.174724

Argentina 1966-9

Daniel Brauer
Jorge Sanchez de Bustamante
Luis Armando Carello
Libreria Editorial Jorge Alvarez S.R.L. (Maria C. Saenz)
Leon Ferrari
Richard A. Frondizi
Juan García Elorrio
Adalberto Srokola
Eduardo Iacomuzzi
Carlos Rogelio Moreno

Australia 1966-9

Pamphlets and clippings relating to BR
Society of Democratic Action (Queensland University) (Laurette Ooms)
Women's International League for Peace and Freedom (Australian Section) (Lorraine Moseley)
James Bennett Pty. Ltd.
Christine Murray
Bruce Anderson
Vietnam Action Committee (Bob Gould)
Elizabeth Goucher Chapman
Elspeth Christiansen
Vietnam Study Group (John Layfield)
M. J. Knottenbelt
Erica Lloyd Jones
Douglas Everingham
St. Kilda-Brighton Peace Action Group (K. M. Stodden)
B. B. Chapman
S. C. Sopote
John Beghetti
Mobilisation Committee (John Deer)
Mervyn Millett
Noel Hume
Sheelagh Aherne
Building Workers' Industrial Union (female staff)
Commercial Bank of Australia (B. W. Cramb)
Man Stewart
John W. Old
L. J. J. Nye
G. D. Jenkins
O. Snelling
A. Flatow
Department of the Parliamentary Library, Canberra (H. L. White)
A. C. Jackson
Association for International Cooperation and Disarmament (G. Anderson)

"Bring the Boys Home" Newsletter (Gus Horowitz)
Anthea Eyres
Bruce G. Downie
J. M. Bray
M. E. Outhred
Rex Mortimer
Walter Slaghuis
Raymond Griffith
Reg Harrison
Committee for Vietnam Protest (Alexandra Freeley?)
Marjorie Thompson
New South Wales Humanist Society (W. G. Weeks)
Ian Martin
Brisbane Friends of the United Nations (J. Hill)
Gray's Point-Sutherland Communist Party (B. Foden)
Stewart MacInnes
Union of Australian Women (Barnes)
Sydney "Save Our Sons" Movement (Alma Scarpbrook)
Manly and Pittwater Newspapers Ltd. (Richard H. Bruce)
The Rationalist Association of N.S.W. (L. N. Briot)
G. W. Abrams
Roy Garner
Commonwealth Trading Bank of Australia (W. A. Simson)
John Heney
Building Workers' Industrial Union of Australia, Queensland Branch (G. M. Dawson)
Peter Wesley Smith
Christopher Harding
Congress for International Co-operation and Disarmament (S. Goldbloom)
C. P. Harding
Norman Taylor
Rob Blackwell
Adelaide University ALP Club (Richard Anderson)
University of Hanoi Student Aid Fund (John Powles, Chris Owens)
Reflex (B. M. Fitch)
Rowan John Cahill
Lawrence F. Bullock
Frances Newell
John E. Fletcher
The Federated Gas Employees' Industrial Union (L. H. Thompson)
Vietnam Co-ordinating Committee (Gwen Lloyd Noad)
Warwick Lobb
Geoff Muirden
E. J. Wilson
Robyn Benney
James E. H. Sim

Austria 1966-7

Karl H. Hiller
Pastor Erwin
International Institute for Peace
Union of Socialist Students of Austria (Anton Baier and Helmut Steiner)
Sensen-Verlag (Ernst Schwarcz)
Herbert Hönel
Hans Günther
Herbert Leirer
Salzburger Nachrichten
Frank Zwillinger

Belgium 1966-8

Roger Berck
Conference Internationale de Solidarité avec le Peuple Vietnamien (R. Wollast)
International Association of Democratic Lawyers (Joë Nordmann)
Noel Cuesmes
Laurette Ooms
Jacques Grippa
Ernest Mandel
Sara van de Sande
Baron Jean van den Bosch
Art Sharon
Louise Struelens *et al*. (form ls.)
Philip Folk
Comité de Solidarité Belgique-Vietnam (Antoine Allard, Stéphane Struelens, and Xavier Relecom)
A. Allard
Federation Nationale des Jeunes Gardes Socialistes (F. Albert, D. Neyens)

Mrs. C. E. Raven
Fédération Générale du Travail de Belgique (J. Yerna)
C. Van Damme
Jean-Pierre Gallet
Marcel Thibaut
Vietnam Solidarity Campaign (Megan Sharp)
R. Bonny
Fernand Tanghe
Laurette Decrez

Brazil 1967-8

L. Y. Correa
Maria Bernardo Ramos Maderia
José Wanderley Quevedo de Ávila
Alfredo Guí Ferreira
Maria Lucia Bacaleinick
Jarbas Barbeitos
Jairo Messias Monteiro
Wolfgang W. Hablitschek
Sebastiao Matos
Luis Barreiros
Ubiratan R. Mascarenhas
Jaime Diniz
Carlos Alberto Dória
Gilda Shimizu
Ronald Fucs
Venerando Carlos Martins
Pedro Soares Valente
C. O. Corrêa de Castro
Gilberto Jugend
Ida Maria Moretzsohn Brandi
Jerome A. Lafferty
Sociedade Amigos de Bertrand Russell (Mario Negreiros dos Anjos and Marçal Oliveira dos Anjos)
Valmir Gentil Aguiar
Líton Lanes Pilau
Julio Toro Lozano
Carlos Rogério Barleze
Luiz Carlos Sachs
Nino Gariglio Júnior
João Jose Sady
Idelberto F. Gurgel
Arno Francisco de Souza
Admario Gama

Bulgaria 1966-7

Ivan Stefanov Vlahov
Dimitar Kostov
September Flag (Tzvetan Gizdou)
Bulgarian Peace Committee (George Pirinsky)

Burma 1966

Afro-Asian Solidarity Committee of Burma (U Hla Gyaw)
copy of *VNA News Bulletin*

Cambodia 1966-8

Wilfred Burchett
Hotel Le Royal, Phnom Penh
International Control Commission (Om Prakash)
Ministry of Information
"Americans Want to Know" (Dagmar Wilson)

Canada 1965-9

Eugene Kurz
The Hellenic Postman of Canada (John Kambites)
Phil Gamester
J. O. D. G. Gray
John V. Reid
Ross Dowson
Stephen J. Scheinberg
O. and L. Martin
John B. Thompson
John P. Liebe
Henry Hui
Elizabeth Briemberg
Canadian Dimension
Keith Sutherlands
York Committee to End the War in Vietnam (B. Bryant)
James Steele
Canada Vietnam Newsletter (Jeffrey White)
Jean Chattillon
The Vancouver Viet Nam Day Committee (Ray Burns)
Kenneth Warren
Maloff's Research Library (Peter Maloff, Sr.)
Abraham L. Feinberg
W. J. Koochin

Carole Oleniuk
L. C. Green
Lucien Aubin
Young Socialist Forum (John Riddell)
Alma Mater Society of the University of Victoria (Gordon R. Pollard)
Claire Dowson
Gordon E. Martin
Elma C. Larsen
Tom Middlebro'
Paul K. Hoch
William A. Johnstone
Canadian Committee for the International War Crimes Tribunal (Kenneth Warren)
Tom Penberthy
A. F. Ries
R. H. Carlin
BR, message for meeting at University of Toronto
Stephen Preston
Christian Bay
Robert K. F. Clark
Gordon Selman
P. D. McTaggart-Cowan
Marjory L. Hawkeswell
Bill Russell
R. H. Patmore
W. Clyde Houston
BR, "An Appeal to Canadians" (message on back of leaflet)
Geoff Coggan
The Edmonton Journal
Dennis S. W. Prendergast
G. N. Forst
Beatrice Reilly
Congress of Canadian Women (Hilda Murray)
Paul Genteman
Duncan Graham
Ron Day
Humanist Fellowship of Victoria (M. N. Sherman)
Homer Gibson
O. Detoman
Marilyn Granten
Ralph Schippanoski
John and Isabelle Harris
W. M. Gough
John Ecclestone
W. Lee
R. O. Lettesge?
John G. Slater
George Robbins
Susan Lichtman
Connie Harris
Jean-Pierre Pellenin
Peter Mitchell
New York Times Magazine
Michel Pellerin
Jeannette McCullough
C. E. Kunelius
G. Noble
Edward Wener

Ceylon 1966-7

G. Rathnapala de Silva
Ceylon Rationalist Association (Abraham T. Kovoor)
Gisela Ernest
Hector Abayavardena
Osmund Jayaratne
Bala Tampoe
Democratic Workers' Congress (M. Jaya Ram)
Afro-Asian Solidarity Association of Ceylon (A. Aziz)
Sri Lanka Anti-Imperialist Youth Front (Padmavarna Wijayatilake)

Chile 1966

Jorge Albornoz Tobar
Ricardo Zabala Caussin
José Rodríguez Elizonde
Pablo Neruda
Federacion Estudiantes Universidad Tecnica Estado Chile (Alejandro Yanez)

China 1967

Mohammed B. Dada

Columbia 1967

Juvenal González Moreno

Cuba 1966-8

BR, miniature pamphlet, *To the Conscience of Humanity*
Martha Dodd and Alfred Stern
Alois Grohs
Fidel Castro
Alberto de los Toyos

Hilario Molina Vega
Robin Blackburn
Tricontinental Committee (? Cardenas)

Czechoslovakia 1966-8

Maria Banajsová
Eva Krásová *et al.*
Brno District Manifestation for Peace
Benjamin B. Page
Miroslav Subrt
Joseph Hajda
Cyril Danek
Karel Kyncl
Martha Dodd Stern
Ivo Sramek
Gleb Lub
Faix Kvetoslav
Jaroslav Zourek
Osvaldo Paredes Alvarez

Denmark 1966-9

Den danske Forberedelseskomité (Hans Hansted Poulsen)
Johan Mowinckel
Ole Wivel
World Association for International Friendship, Peace, and Security (Alexander von Winthofen)
Werner B. Andreasen
Mich. O'Cleary Todd
Harold M. Kock
Theatret Fiol (Henrik Holm Hansen)
Hans Lyngby Jepsen's trans. of "Krigsforbryderproces mod praesident Johnson?"
Gunnar Jensen
Kasper Neergaard
Vietnam-aktion (Peter Bangsvej)
Henrik Sidenius
Kai Moltke
Ebbe Reich
Erik Vagn Jensen
Niels Erik Nielsen
Julian [Trevelyan]
Asger Pilegaard
Richard Frederiksen
Janice Campbell
Dansk Bertrand Russell Rad
Steen Jacobsen
Ellen Brun
War Resisters' International
Karsten Hald Nielsen
Niels Henrik Arendt
Vagn Søndergard
Mark Vandel
"Danske Forberedelseskomité"
Flemming Brahms
Niels-Henrik Gertung
Linda Harrison
Mogens Errboe
Det Internationale Krigsforbrydelses Tribunal (Ole Strandberg)
Politisk Revy (Ellen Brun)
Niels Thanning

Finland 1966-7

Arto Mäkitalo
Janko Laiho
Aarne Fårsten
Asko Mattila
U. M. Wahlberg

France 1966-8

Sandu Missirliu
Gilbert Krausener
Denis Freney
Robert Blum
Joë Nordmann
Association pour le Désarmament Général et le Progrès Social (Guy Desson)
Pierre-Marie Laurent
J. Diedisheim
Muriel F. MacSwiney
Conseil National du Mouvement de la Paix (Michel Langignon)
Daniel Guêrin
José Lenzini
Jean-Yves Erhel
Jean Chesneaux
Cornelia Wallis Honchar
Michael R. Marrus
Ilse Meyer-Heine
Austryn Wainhouse
L'Evenement (Emmanuel d'Astier)
Jean Heinemann
Ronald Ramsey
Georges Savelli
Renée Martinet
Eugénie Cotton
Ray L. Miley
D. R. Dorrance
Comité de Solidarité à la Révolution

Kurde (N. Nirvan)
Paese Sera (Giorgio Fanti)
Les Amis de la Fondation Russell (Lily Cheng)
Claude Roy
Maison de la Mutualité (J. Demars)
Terre des Hommes (J. Lenzini)
François Maspero
Alexis Cary
Roland Thibaut
Aziz N. Kurtha
Mme. Libertad Piconnell de Molinero
Dick Bard
Bernard Lucas
Geneviève Robert
Fédération Internationale Terre des Hommes (Edmond Kaiser)
Marianne Littman
Jean Pierre Clauet
Jean-François Courquin
Nigel Hazeldine
Mr. and Mrs. Christian Gaven
Harold M. Koch
Comité Vietnam de Toulon (Care Marcel)
Barbara Mathey
Odile Hélier
Abdul G. Khan
(Mr. & Mrs.) Granelle
Ligue des Etats Arabes, Bureau de Paris (Al-Joundi, A. M. Naggar, A. Shammout, A. Amer)
Pablo Casals
Frank Zwillinger
Philippe Giard
Cercle Laique d'Etudiants de Grenoble
Michel Geoffrey
Bernard Guillet
Mme. Avon
Jean-Paul Tran-Thiet

West Germany 1966-8

Marie Greve
Gerd Klotsch
Pro-Contra (Walter Rathgeber)
Helfried Schreiter
Gina Schönbauer
Roland Herzog
Edeltrud Stommel
Elan (Rolf J. Priemer)
Jennifer Schon
Wolf-G. Umlandt
Elsbeth Bruck
Leonhard Wienhold
George Allen & Unwin Foreign Rights Department (A. Dadlez, re Hugo Freund, *Archiv für universelle Entwicklungspolitik*)
Bayerischer Rundfunk (André H. Carbe)
Internationale der Kriegsdienstgegner (Alois Stoff)
R. L. Hidden
Der Spiegel (H. G. Alexander)
Joachim Joesten
Bernward Vesper-Triangel
Hugo Freund
Horst Mahncke
Ilona H. Gira
Hervé Masson
Mannheim Lindenhof
Women's International Democratic Federation (Rosa Jasovich-Pantaleon)
European Organizations of the National Front of Iran (Hassan Massali)
Stefan Heym
Hilde Bentele
Deutsche Volkszeitung (Walter Bloch)
Gerhard Schoenberner
Theodor Riexinger
Sozialistischer Deutscher Studenbund (Peter Gäng)
Abend Zeitung (Osmund Schwab)
Friedrich-Martin Balzer
Hubert Detzner
Anna Haag
Jürgen Eidam
Robert Smith
George Heisig
Otto Schönfeldt
Graham Wrightson
Renate Dörner
Midland Bank
Peter R. Smith and John McC. Mor-

gan, Jr.
Nasser Towhidi
Kampagne für Abrustung (Wolfgang Wirsig)
Robert J. Smith
Archiv-Dienst (G. Ziegler)
Informations-Dienst zur Notstandsgesetzgebung (Günther Heipp)
Klemens Tilmann
Paul Gebliast
Jens Alber
Staatliches Sinfonie Orchester
Michael Hamm *et al.*
Peter Tautfest
James Sattler
Dr. Rausse
Annaluise Plate
Heinrich Weiler
Leopold Bayerl
Pieter Zandee
Dieter Schmidt
José Bosch
W. Thomas Craver
Jürgen Horlemann
H. Lohaus
Tribunal de Grande Instance de la Seine
Gunnar Krone

German Democratic Republic 1966-7

Werner Hachenberger
Friedensrat der Deutschen Demokratischen Republic (W. Friedrich)
Gerd Gruber
Elsbeth Bruck
Illustrierte Zeit im Bild (Werner Kluge)
Gerold D. Voigt
Friedensrat (Kurt Hälker)
Kreuzschule Dresden (Norbet Botril *et al.*)
Dr. Wolf and Dr. Bittrich
Werner Ruempel
Rosemarie Brotke
Peace Council of the German Democratic Republic (Renata Miltke)
VEB Hochbauprojektierung, Schwerin (Seidenschnur *et al.*)
? Kawan
Frank Erler
Members of the Collective of the Metal Workers Industry in the Institute for Data Processing, Dresden (R. Philipp *et al.*)
Leo Regener

Greece 1966-7

Stella Mindaki
Samuel P. Fay

Hong Kong 1966-7

Brian Fisher
J. F. C. Carrington
Maxwell Brem
I. V. Sheratte

Hungary 1967

K. Govinda Pillai
Kossuth (Andor Berei)

Japan 1967-9

Kei Hoashi
Shinkichi Unno
Japan Committee for the Investigation of U.S. War Crimes in Vietnam (Kinju Morikawa, Yoichi Fuku shima, Saburo Kugai)
Investwar
Setsure Tsurushima
BR, s.
M. K. Janjua
Lengthy petition; newsclippings
Alice Herz Peace Fund (report)
Obituary of BR

*378 Visa Campaign for the Vietnamese

In the summer of 1965 the Bertrand Russell Peace Foundation attempted to bring representatives of the National Liberation Front to Britain for public and private meetings. Visas were denied them by Her Majesty's Government. A public campaign was mounted to win support for the granting of visas.

Documents .174725–.174921

Nguyen Van Dong
Pham Van Chuong
Draft s.
clippings
Signatories to public l. re visas
Voice of the Unions
Ho Chi Minh
Nguyen Huu Tho
Chou En-lai
South Vietnam National Liberation Front
The Home Secretary
Fenner Brockway
Press s.
James R. Newman
Alternative Perspectives on Vietnam (J. Edgar Edwards, Herbert Kelman)
Martin Hansden
The Times
New Statesman
Archbishop Roberts
Ruth Glass
Lord Silkin
Iris Murdoch
K. W. Wedderburn
Asa Briggs
Lord Thomson
David Glass
The Observer (David Astor)
Ralph Miliband
A. Foster-Carter
John Rankin (encl. signatories to public l.)
Claude Auchinleck
Tom Driberg
Mervyn Stockwood
BR, s. entitled "Message for the Aniversary of Independence of the Democratic Republic of Vietnam"
Frank Soskice
Visa Campaign form l.
BR, press s.
South West Committee for Peace in Vietnam (Pat Dash)
Kingsley Martin
Hugh Jenkins *et al*. (form ls.)
Tribune (Richard Clements)
David Ensor
Harold Walker
Ian Mikardo
Dennis Hobden
Stan Newens
Trevor Park
Malcolm Caldwell
Norman Atkinson
Sydney Silverman
Chinese People's Committee for

World Peace (Li Chu-wen)
Daily Worker
***Punch* (Susan Eserton Jones)**
Eric S. Heffer
H. E. Hinton
Richard Hoggart
Noel Hall
National Union of Mineworkers (Lawrence Daly)
E. R. Dodds
A. J. Ayer
C. H. Dobinson
Lord Boothby (Joyce Foucard)
Michael Redgrave
The Iona Community (G. MacLeod)
Somerset Maugham (Alan Searle)
William Plomer
Hugh Jenkins
Jack Putterill
A. C. Offord
Benn W. Levy
Cu Dinh Ba and Nguyen Van Sao
Alan Sillitoe
Mermaid Theatre (Bernard Miles)
Joseph Needham
Dorothy Needham
Calder and Boyars (John Calder)
Richard Doll
David Holbrook
Vietnam Free Speech Petition (Malcolm Caldwell *et al.*)

*379 Vietnam Solidarity Campaign

The Vietnam Solidarity Campaign was formed about June 1966. The Peace Foundation was a leading sponsor. These files—arranged in chronological order—trace the history of the Campaign's activities and its relationships with similar organizations in Britain (such as the Vietnam Ad Hoc Committee). The files are particularly useful for their copies of minutes, articles, pamphlets, form letters, *Members' Bulletin*, and other forms of propagating the views of the V.S.C.

Documents .174922–.175248

Statements, minutes, articles, pamphlets, form ls. and *Vietnam Solidarity Bulletin*—3 files
David Robinson
Ian Millar
Nguyen Van Hieu
Hands Off Vietnam Committee (Keith Jennings)
Keith Jennings
Campaign for Nuclear Disarmament (Peggy Duff)
London Committee of 100
Tom Nicholls
West Indian Gazette (A. Manchanda)
Bristol Peace Council (George Maidment)
J. B. Gibson
Ernest Tate
Katy R
Fred Twine
Aziz Rattansi
London Welsh Association (Miss Davis)
British-Vietnam Committee (Hilda Vernon)
Bill Ash
Lionel Jeffries
Sunday Telegraph
Press Council
Nicholas Johnson
Socialist Labour League (G. Healy)
Richard Chessum
The Guardian
Committee of Struggle Against U.S. and Henchmen's Persecution of Intellectuals in South Vietnam (Do Xuan Sang)
New Statesman
Britain-Vietnam Solidarity Front (A. Manchanda)
Fenner Brockway
The Militant (Barry Sheppard)
Frank Maguire
The Photo Centre
National Union of Mineworkers (Lawrence Daly)
Felix Greene
Roger Pic
Jill Westby
University of Exeter Socialist Society (Byron Hughes)
Stevenage Youth Peace Action Group (Andrew Morris)
L. P. Chessum
Socialist Society, University of Aston (Mary ?)
The Labour Party (J. Gwyn Morgan)
Anti-Vietnam-Draft Co-ordinating Committee (Dave Axel)

Barbara A. Wilson
Jim Scott
Adrian Lewis
Actiegroep Vietnam (S. Bosgra)
F. Hassan
Richard Daly
Committee of 100 (Janet Viney)
Gordon Norris
Liverpool University Vietnam Committee (Huw Beynon)
BR, form 1.
D. S. Riddell
Marjorie Holt
Guatemalan Committee for Solidarity with Vietnam (E. G. Theilheimer and C. Capuano del Vecchio)
V.S.C., Strathclyde University (R. G. Davis)

*380 British-Vietnam Committee

This Committee's interest in the Vietnam War predated Russell's, and it appears from the first letters that Russell was stimulated into making his first public statement on the question by the Committee's *Bulletin*. The correspondence was regularly with the Committee's Honorary Secretary, Hilda Vernon.

Documents .175249–.175309

The Voice of Vietnam
Hilda Vernon
Essay, leaflets, circulars, *Vietnam Bulletin*
G. H. Burchett

*381 British Council for Peace in Vietnam

The BCPV campaigned more for a negotiated settlement in the Vietnam War than for outright victory on behalf of the National Liberation Front. A chief correspondent for the BCPV was Fenner, Lord Brockway, who, with Russell, had opposed the First World War. He and Russell had some sharp disagreements over policy.

Documents .175310–.175348

Circulars
Amicia M. Young
Fenner Brockway
Dick Nettleton
Barbara Haq

*382 World Vietnam Committee

The World Vietnam Committee was initiated by the Peace Foundation following the first International War Crimes Tribunal. Many invitations to join the Committee were sent out over Russell's signature, but the Committee seems never to have been brought fully into being.

Documents .175349–.175420

RS, notes
"Draft of an International Appeal for the Constitution of the 'World Vietnam Committee'"
Albert B. Cleage, Jr. *et al*. (form l.)
Alex Comfort
Arnold Wesker
E. A. Roberts
E. H. S. Burhop
John Saville *et al*. (form l.)
Dorothy Hodgkin
SVN Peace Committee (Phung Van Cung)

*383 Vietnam: Correspondence with Newspapers

The files, extending from March 1963 to May 1968, contain hundreds of letters written to editors of newspapers and periodicals around the world on the subject of the Vietnam War. Also included, at the end of *383, are articles, clippings and statements on Vietnam. Ralph Schoenman's name appears as the author of several of them.

Documents .175421–.175753

The Times
Washington Post
The New York Times (John B. Oakes)
Reporter Magazine, et al. (form l.)
The Observer (David Astor)
Toronto Star Weekly, et al. (form l.)
New York Herald Tribune
I.F. Stone's Weekly, et al. (form l.)
Peace News (Theodore Roszak)
The Guardian
Sunday Times
Toronto Star Ltd. (Jack Scott)
Bristol Evening Post et al. (form l.)
Dagens Nyheter
Daily Telegraph, et al. (form l.)
New Statesman
Newsweek
San Francisco Sunday Examiner and Chronicle
Delo (Bogdan Pogacnik)
Detroit News
Tribune
Le Monde (Eric Rouleau)
Spokesman-Review
National Guardian
Combat
Manila Times
The Economist
New Leader
New Society
Morning Star
Ramparts
Der Spiegel
Mervyn Millet
The Melbourne Age
Conrad Russell
The Star-Bulletin

2 files of articles, clippings and ss. re Vietnam, including several articles by RS

*384 International War Crimes Tribunal: Essays, Meetings and Reports

These files open with agendas and minutes of the organizing sessions for the International War Crimes Tribunal, held in London, November 1966. They continue with drafts of declarations, transcriptions of Stockholm sessions of the Tribunal held in the spring of 1967, and Russell's messages to the Stockholm sessions held later in 1967. There are many other documents, some of them published in *Against the Crime of Silence* or *Prevent the Crime of Silence*.

Documents .175754–.175907a

Agenda for IWCT, 13-15 Nov. 1966
"The Revised Aims and Purposes of the Tribunal—Draft Declaration"
"Recommendations on Basic Structure, Plan of Work, Declaration of Aims, Time-Table and Procedures"
"The Aims and Purpose of the Tribunal—Draft Declaration"
"Judges and Substitutes"
Günther Anders, "First Draft for Financial Appeal"
"Vlado's [Dedijer's] suggestion about the work of secretariat"
Meeting held 8 Nov. 1966 (minutes)
IWCT Part I, Nov. 1966 (transcription of tape recording)
IWCT Preliminary Conference, Part 2, 13 Nov. 1966
"Draft Declaration of Aims"
"Draft Proposals on Basic Structure, Plan of Work, Declaration of Aims, Time-Table and Procedures"
"Projet de l'Addresse Inaugurale"
"Rules of the International War Crimes Tribunal"
"Proposal by K. Morikaw (Japan) concerning Investigating Team to Vietnam"
"Summary Report of Meetings in Hanoi between President Ho Chi Minh, Prime Minister Pham Van Dong and Personal Representatives of Bertrand Russell, Mr. Ralph Schoenman and Mr. Russell Stetler"
"Proposed Commission to Investigate the Nature of the War in Vietnam and the Role of the United States"
"Addendum au Rapport de Lord Russell"
"Les Buts et Objectifs du Tribunal"
"Genocide: The Copenhagen Judgment of the Russell Tribunal"
"IWCT, Copenhagen session: Results of the Tribunal's deliberations"
"Memorandum on the Stockholm Session of the IWCT"
"America is Guilty" by Geoffrey Sinclair, transcription of article in *Tribune*, 19 May 1967
"Agenda: Copenhagen Session", 20-8 Nov. 1967
"Tape Nine" of Tribunal proceedings
Gustavo Tolentino, "Report to IWCT"
BR, "Address to the Copenhagen Session of the IWCT, 20 Nov. 1967"
BR, "Closing Message to the

Copenhagen Session of the IWCT, 1 Dec. 1967"
Victor Purcell, "The Possibilities for Peace in Southeast Asia"
RS, essay re his trip to Vietnam, Apr. 1966
Notes by Victor Purcell
RS, "The Final Conclusion", 11 Apr. 1966
"When Viewing the War in Vietnam"
"Summary of Facts Concerning the War in Vietnam"
"Vietnam" (Chapter 9)
[Untitled essay]
"Transcription of a Radio Interview Given by Mr. Ralph Schoenman in New York Last Week", 24 Nov. 1967
S. on Czechoslovak conference
"Harold Wilson on Vietnam"
Vladimir Dedijer's s., 28 Apr. 1967
Geoff Coggan's press s., 11 Apr. 1967
J. Axel Hojer, Hugh Mares and John Takman's s., 31 Mar. 1967
Communique, 17 Feb. 1967
Press s., 11 Jan. 1967
Quintin Hoare's s. at Orly Airport, 11 Jan. 1967
War Crimes Press Release, 29 Dec. 1966
Press s. on the appointment of IWCT members
Press s., 9 Aug. 1965
Press s., 19 June 1966
Press s., 14 Dec. 1966
RS? to Vietnam Peace Committee (Do Xuan Oanh), 3 Dec. 1966 (encl: s. on Yugoslavia)
Press s. on "W.C.T. Venue", 7 Oct. 1966
Press ss., some dated 1965 and some 1966
"Draft Paragraphs for Foundation l. to Schwartz"
Laurent Schwartz, "A Statement from Members of the World Scientific Community to their American Colleagues"
Günther Anders, "War and Victory: On the American Aggression in Viet-Nam"
"Address of Welcome to Mian Mahmud Ali Kasuri, Judge, International Tribunal on American War Crimes in Vietnam"
Günther Anders, "Die Inakzeptable Hilfe (Erklärung für die Stockholm Conference on Vietnam)", 16 May 1969
RS, "Private Memorandum to Professor Laurent Schwartz"
Dave Dellinger, "Enroute to Hanoi"
"Lord Russell's 'War Crimes' Trial", transcription of editorial in *Los Angeles Times*, 8 Aug. 1966
Amado v. Hernandez, "Bak Bakan of 'Ka' Amado vs. A Yankee Jingo"
Biographical s. on RS
Günther Anders, "S. on the Occupation of the CSSR"
S. on BR's activities [14 Nov. 1966?]
Günther Anders, "Vietnam—und Kein Ende"
Isaac Deutscher, "Socialist Man", Sept. 1966
Isaac Deutscher, "Message to Japan's Peace for Vietnam Committee", 1966
RS, untitled articles (incl. l. from *Ramparts* [Deborah Sampson] to David Horowitz, 1966)
Leaflets
RSt., "Vietnam Wasteland", 27 Dec. 1967
RS, "S. by Delegate BRPF on Report by American Delegation"
BR, note on Deutscher's death, *The Times*, 30 Aug. 1967
BR, "War and Atrocity in Vietnam", reprinted from *Views*
H. A. DeWeerd, "Lord Russell's War Crimes Tribunal", March 1967

*385 International War Crimes Tribunal: Printed Material

*385 fills fifteen boxes with assorted printed material on Vietnam and the reception of the Tribunal. Some of the documents are unpublished; they include some correspondence.

Documents .160001–.161009

Box 1

Jouffa on criminality of Vietnam war

"The Government of Thailand, Accomplice to USA's War of Aggression in Vietnam"

"Erratum" re M.K. Khan, "Utilisation des gaz de combat au Vietnam"

Solange Bouvier Ajam, "Rapport Juridique sur le Traitement des Prisonniers de Guerre ..."

Alvarez Tabío, "Le Crime de Genocide au Vietnam"

Stanley Faulkner, "International Law and the Military Draft"

Wilfred Burchett, "Report"

Guillermo Frank, "On Vietnam"

Kei Hoashi, *Liberation of Okinawa*

Aims and Objectives of the IWCT

Tariq Ali, "Evidence to the IWCT"

Roger Pic, "Rapport de l'Enquete Effectuée au Sud Vietnam dans le Nambo Central"

Pham Van Dong to Jean-Paul Sartre (mimeo)

"Supplement to the Report of Gisele Halini"

Yves Jouffa, "Report on the Law of War"

Yoshitaro Hirano, "Memorandum of War on the Aggressive Character of the U.S. War in Vietnam"

Carl Oglesby, "Speech"

Henrik Forss, "Report on Examined Patients, Wounded during Bombings in North Vietnam"

Yves Jouffa, "Report on the Question of Arms Forbidden by International Convention"

Peter Limqueco to BR, 1967

RSt. to BR and ER, 1967

[Report on Tokyo Tribunal]

RSt. to BR and ER, 1967

RSt., "Genocide: The Copenhagen Judgement of the Russell Tribunal"

IWCT press releases (ss. by Hiroaki Yoshiza, J.-P. Sartre, BR, Guillermo Frank, Peter Martinson, David Tuck, Yves Lacoste, H. Forss, Shingo Shibata, Nguyen Huu Tho, C. Oglesby, W. Burchett, R. Pic, Jean Michel Krivine and Marcel Francis Kahn and R. Pic)

Behar?, "Report on the Bombing of the Civilian Population of North Vietnam"

L. Matarasso, "Rapport sur le Genocide au Vietnam"

"Crime de Génocide américain au Sud Viet Nam"

Wilfred Burchett, "The United States over Laos"

Box 2

"Interim Report of Natural Science of the Japanese Committee"

"Juridical Viewpoint on the U.S. War of Aggression in Vietnam as War Crime"

"Testimonies on Cooperation with the Participation in the U.S. War of Aggression by the Japanese Government and Monopoly Capitalists"

Lelio Basso, "Summation of the First Two Charges"

Wilfred Burchett, "Testimony on Cambodia"

Shingo Shibata, "Testimony of the Second Japanese Investigation Mission on U.S. Genocide Crimes in Vietnam"

Roger Pic, "Introduction to the Report of the 7th Enquiry Commission ..."

Nguyen Trong Kha, "Up to the Birth of the Strategic Hamlets"

[Interview with soldier]

[Laotian report]

IWCT Agenda, Nov. 25, 1967

Marta Rojas, "Testimony on South Vietnam"

Rena Kahn, "Enquiry at Phnom Penh"

"La Politique Americaine de Concetration de la Population au Sud Vietnam"

Yves Jouffa, "Rapport sur le Droit de la Guerre"

Tsetsure Tsurushima, "Bombing of the Dikes and the Irrigation System in the Democratic Republic of Viet-Nam"

"S. on the Delegation of the Commission of Inquiry of the Democratic Republic of Vietnam on U.S. Crimes in Vietnam"

Lawrence Daly, "Investigation of U.S. War Crimes in North Vietnam"

To Prevent the Crime of Silence: outline of table of contents

"Incendiary Weapons—Poison Gas—Defoliants"

"Technical Report on the Uses of Napalm"

Jean-Paul Sartre, "Opening Speech"

Basso?, speech

Bernard Couret, "Rapport de Cambodge"

Dr. Krivine, "Blesses Examines"

Kykeo Souvannarath, report

"The U.S. Imperialists and Their Agent's Policy of Herding the People into Concentration Camps in South Viet Nam"

"The American Crime of Genocide in South Vietnam"

Pham Thi Yen, report

Medical report

NLF (Nguyen Huu Tho), message

Danish press review

Antonello Trombadori, report

Paik Il Kon, "On the Criminal Troop Dispatch of the South Korean Puppet Clique"

Box 3

Madeleine Riffaud, report

"Comments in the Swedish Press on the Tribunal"

"The Tribunal in Swedish Television"

"Report on Scientific Studies of Weapons Used in Vietnam"

Jean Bertolino, report

Prince Souphanouvong, s.

Gisele Halini, supplement to report

"Les Actes Criminels de Terreur, de Torture, de Deportation et d'Emprisonnement Inhumain Commis par les Imperialistes US et Leurs Agents à l'Encontre de la Population Sud-Vietnamienne"

"Rapports sur les crimes U.S. à l'encontre de [various localities of Vietnam]"

"Temoignage de la 2ème Commission d'Enquête japonaise sur les crimes américains de génocide au Vietnam"

David Tuck, "Testimony"
"Rapport d'Enquete Generale sur les Exactions Commises contre les Populations Civiles"
Jean-Paul Sartre, "Draft s. on genocide"

Box 4

NLF, report
Frank Pestana, "The Law of Land Warfare"
Mr. Rosenwein, "Summary of Report"
Gabriel Kolko, "The Destruction of Dikes: 1944-45, and Korea, 1953"
Charles Cobb and Julius Lester, report on trip to Vietnam
Malcolm Caldwell, report
Jean Chesneaux, "The Trial of Japanese War Crimes in the Far East"

Box 5

"The Text of the S. Which Was Being Read Out by RS during the Regis Debray Trial Last Friday When He Was Arrested"
"Press Rumours on IWCT Dismissed"
RS, "Eichmann and Everyman: The Moral Challenge of Vietnam"
IWCT press s. re membership
"Russell Tribunal/The Accusers", reprinted from *The Economist*, 31 Dec. 1966
Two ss. concerning Cambodia
Vladimir Dedijer, s.
Gordian Troeller and Claude Deffarge, report
BR, ts., "Final Message ... to the Copenhagen Session of the IWCT, December 1, 1967"
Nguyen Hong Phuong, report
Gisèle Halini, "Rapport de la Mission d'Enquete au IWCT"
IWCT, "List of Witnesses from American Army"
"Rapport sur le Crime de Genocide Commis par les Imperialistes Americains au Nord Vietnam"
"Pictures from the Disguised Concentration Camps"
Press Bulletin
"Free Speech" (leaflet)
"Annex No. 1 ... 2 ... 3 ... 4 ... 5 ... 6 ... 7"
Antonello Trombadori, "Rapport d'un Temoin"
NLF, "The Criminal Acts of Terror, Torture, Deportation and Inhuman Imprisonment Committed by the American Imperialists and Their Agents Against the Population of South Vietnam"
Pham Ngoc Thach, report
RS, "Article for the *Vietnam Pictorial Monthly*"
RS, tear sheets of articles in *Africa and the World*
Yves Lacoste, "Report on Bombardements of Dykes and Waterworks"
Nguyen Hong Phuong, "Temoignage"
IWCT press ss. (Dr. Krivine, M. Riffaud, J. Bertolino, M. Rojas, R. Kahn, W. Burchett, B. Couret, A. Trombadori, Cérard Chaliand)
Paik Ilhon, report
Thanh Savanvilay, s.
Edgar Lederer, "Rapport de la Sous-Commission 'Guerre Chimique'"
"Images des Camps de Concentration Deguises"
Wilfred Burchett, "Eyewitness to Second Session"
IWCT, agenda for Nov. 1967
Nguyen Thi Tho, "Testimony"
Polaris leaflet from early 1960s (with note by ER)
Members of the IWCT
"A Proposal concerning a Final Conclusion: an open proposition to each government"

Box 6

L. Matarasso, "Outline of the General Introductory Report"
BR, "Opening Message ... to the Copenhagen Session of the IWCT"

Kim Il Sung, "Let Us Intensify the Anti-Imperialist, Anti-U.S. Struggle", reprinted from *Korea Today*
Shingo Shibata, "We Accuse the American imperialist of genocide crimes in Vietnam"
"Le Gouvernement de la Thailande, Complice des Etats-Uni dans la Guerre d'Aggression contre Le Viet Nam"
Jean-Paul Sartre, "Opening Speech [to Second Session]"
To Prevent the Crime of Silence: outline
L. Matarasso, "Introductory Report to the Second Session"
L. Matarasso, "Report on Genocide in Vietnam"
BR, Roy Jenkins and Harold Wilson, tss. of correspondence
Article on IWCT, ts., pp. 18-27

Box 7

U.S. Air Force ROTC, Air University, "Fundamentals of Aerospace Weapon Systems"
Lelio Basso, "Rapport de Synthese"
Stanley Faulkner, "Violations of International Law by United States in Vietnam War"
Robert Luftig, U.S. court documents
Ms. list of names
"In Bolivia", from *Le Monde*, 12 Oct. 1967
Clippings on Debray
P. 2 of unidentified ts.
Wilfred Burchett, report on Haiphong visit
RSt. to BR and ER, 1967
Untitled mimeo ss.
No More Hiroshimas! (Dec. 1967)
Lelio Basso, "Summation on Genocide"

Box 8

File labelled "Official D.R.V. and N.L.F. Reports"
Ms. notes or memoranda (in different hands)
"Extract of Data Compiled on War in Vietnam", ts. and tscc.
Michael Ross, "Proposals toward the Neutralization and Offensive Disarmament of Indochina"
"Disclosure by an American Pilot" (including photos)
Charles Fourniau, "Les Complicites dans l'Aggression Americaine au Vietnam, Thailande et Philippines"

Box 9

A.K. Schmauss, medical eye-witness report (in German)
"Military-medical expert opinion on the US chemical war-fare in Vietnam"
Horst Rennhack, "Die Mittäterschaft Bonns an den amerikanischen Kriegsverbrechen"
Herbert Landmann, l. on "Zeugenaussage", 1966
Peter Sbrzesny, s.
Ss. in Danish and French press
Untitled s.
Poster honouring BR, 13 March 1970

Box 10

Press bulletins
J. B. Neilands, "Report to the International War Crimes Tribunal"
Supreme Court documents
Jon W. Fuller, "The Application of International Law to Chemical and Biological Warfare"
Gabriel Kolko?, "Research Outline to the Legal Commission of the IWCT: A History of United States Aggression in Vietnam", with a copy of l. from Kolko to RS, 1967
The Partisan, Spring 1967
Tribunal, no. 8

Box 11

IWCT, press ss. (including "Crimes perpetrated by the U.S. imperialists and henchmen against South Vietnam women and children", ss. by Commandant Kouroudeth, Mahmud Ali Kasuri, J.-P. Sartre on Stokely Carmichael and on RS, Mehmet Ali Aybar, NLF)

Box 12

Gérard Chaliand, "Testimony"
Tariq Ali, "Evidence to the IWCT ..."
Mr. Kugai, "Report to the IWCT"
"Comments in the Swedish Press on the Tribunal"
"Johnson is like Hitler!". Interview with BR in *Expressen*, Stockholm, 6 May 1967, p. 14, (re-)translated into English and mimeographed. Datelined Penrhyndeudraeth.
Editorial from *Arbeitet*, 27 April 1967
RSt., ts., "Memorandum on the Stockholm Session of the IWCT", 10 June 1967
"The IWCT"
Gabriel Kolko, "The Historical Background of United States Aggression in Vietnam Since World War II"
IWCT Bulletin, nos. 1–2 (15–22 Dec. 1966)

Box 13

IWCT Bulletin, nos. 3-7 (1 Jan.-14 Apr. 1967)
Bureau of the International Conference for Solidarity with the People of Vietnam (various ss.)
Ma Thi Chu, speech at Women's International Congress for Peace in Moscow
"A Frank Discussion with Mr. Tran-Van-Tung"

Box 14

Bulletin; Front Nasional Pembebasan Vietnam Selatan
"S. on the S.V.N.L.F. on the Situation in S.V. after Saigon Military Putsch"
Nguyen Van Hieu, s.
Vietnam News Agency, press ss.
"S. of the Ministry of Foreign Affairs of the Democratic Republic of Vietnam of 4th January 1966"
"D.R.V. Government S. Condemns Designation of U.S. 'Combat Zone'", 1965
DRV s. on U.S. "peace efforts"
DRV and NLF, ss.
USSR, "TASS S. on South Vietnam"
"Name List of Delegations Participating in the International Conference for Solidarity with the People of Vietnam Against U.S. Imperialist Aggression and for the Defence of Peace"
Various ss. (possibly from above conference), including some by Ho Chi Minh
Cuu Quoc Weekly (various ss.)

Box 15

Typed extract from *Congressional Record*, 5 Aug. 1964
"A Selection of Evidence on the Use of Napalm"
NLF, "U.S. Imperialist's 'Burn All, Destroy All, Kill All' Policy in South Vietnam"
NLF?, "They Are Even More Ruthless Than Hitler!"
RSt., mimeo of "Memorandum on the Stockholm Session of the IWCT", 10 June 1967
"An Open Letter from Vietnamese Mothers to Mothers and Children-Loving People in the World"
BR, *Danger in South-East Asia*
BR, "The Western Press and U.S. War Crimes", Nov. 1966
"Verdict of the Stockholm Session of the IWCT"
BR, *The Labour Party's Foreign Policy*, 1965
[RS], "Speech on Radio Hanoi to Fellow Americans"
Petition from Swedes in support of presence of IWCT
"Statutes of the Tribunal"
"Juridical Viewpoint on the U.S. War of Aggression in Vietnam as War Crime"
Vladimir Dedijer and BR, s.
BR, "Message ... to the IWCT"
Cao Van Nguyen, report
Tribunal, no. 7

Front, nos. 1-3 (1967-8) (including 3 articles by BR)
Kommentar, no. 3 (1968)

*390 International War Crimes Tribunal: Members' Correspondence on Czechoslovakia

In September 1968 Russell organized a declaration regarding the worsening situation in Czechoslovakia. He later organized a conference on the Soviet invasion of Czechoslovakia, involving several of the Tribunal members.

Documents .175908–.176049

Günther Anders
Mehmet Ali Aybar
James Baldwin
Lelio Basso
Lázaro Cárdenas
Student Non-Violent Coordinating Committee (Ethel H. Minor)
Stokely Carmichael
A. Moffat
Lawrence Daly
Simone de Beauvoir
Vladimir Dedijer
David Dellinger
Stevenson P. Clark
Haika Grossmann
Amado v. Hernandez
Melba Hernández
Mahmud Ali Kasuri
Kinju Morikawa
Carl Oglesby
Shoichi Sakata
Jean-Paul Sartre
Laurent Schwartz
Peter Weiss

*400
Publishing Correspondence

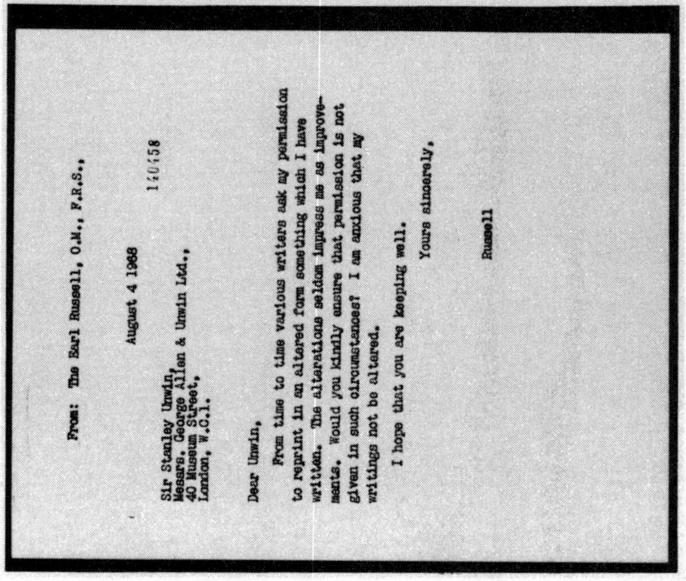

From: The Earl Russell, O.M., F.R.S.,

August 4 1968

140158

Sir Stanley Unwin,
Messrs. George Allen & Unwin Ltd.,
40 Museum Street,
London, W.C.1.

Dear Unwin,

From time to time various writers ask my permission to reprint in an altered form something which I have written. The alterations seldom impress me as improvements. Would you kindly ensure that permission is not given in such circumstances? I am anxious that my writings not be altered.

I hope that you are keeping well.

Yours sincerely,

Russell

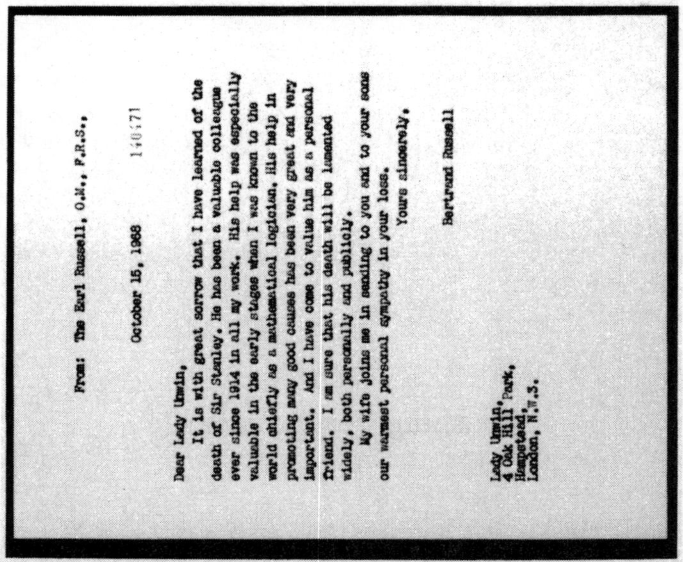

From: The Earl Russell, O.M., F.R.S.,

October 15, 1968

140171

Dear Lady Unwin,

It is with great sorrow that I have learned of the death of Sir Stanley. He has been a valuable colleague ever since 1914 in all my work. His help was especially valuable in the early stages when I was known to the world chiefly as a mathematical logician. His help in promoting many good causes has been very great and very important. And I have come to value him as a personal friend. I am sure that his death will be lamented widely, both personally and publicly.

My wife joins me in sending to you and to your sons our warmest personal sympathy in your loss.

Yours sincerely,

Bertrand Russell

Lady Unwin,
4 Oak Hill Park,
Hampstead,
London, N.W.3.

Plate 4 Letters from Russell to Sir Stanley and Lady Unwin, 4 August and 15 October 1968.

*410 Publishing Correspondence

The fourteen boxes in this class represent the general correspondence of Russell and his staff with publishers of every description. Included is some Vietnam publishing correspondence. There are several files with George Allen & Unwin Ltd., Russell's English publisher since 1916, including one stray letter from 1919. The general correspondence contains much information about translations of Russell's works—e.g., a Russian translation of "Satan in the Suburbs" in *Zvezda*, 1963.

Documents .140001–.147060

A

Anonymous (Colin) 1962
RS to 1963
Abbagnano, Nicola, BR to ... 1968
ABC (Emilio Novoa) 1960
AB CWK Gleerup Bokförlag
(Gunnar Pilesjö) 1967
CF to 1967
Absalom (I. Ramchander) 1969
Academic Press (C. M. Hutt)
to RS 1967
Acta Medica Venezolana (Olga
Adamicska) 1964
RS to 1965
Adam: International Review
(Miron Grindea) 1962
Encl: issue of journal
BR to 1962
*Adamjee Science College
Magazine* (M. Shahid
Yousuf) 1967
CF to 1967
Adamson, Donald 2 1969
CF to 1969
A. D. N. News Agency (Ruth
Kallman) 1958
Aeusrivongse, Nidhi 1968
CF to 1968
Africa and the World (Douglas
G. Rogers, Jeanne
Dunne) 2 1964-8
To RS 3 1964-5
Encl: l. from Patrick R.
Attepoe
BR to 1964
Bill Kaye to 1964
RS to 3 1964-5
PW to 2 1965
Africa Asia (A. E. Gaugat) 1962
Agencia Robotnicza (Jacek
Groszkiewicz) 1967
Encl.
Aguilar to RS 1967
To Macdonald & Co. 1960
Encl: Rathbone Books Ltd.
(W. Foges) to BR, BR to Rathbone Books (W. Foges), Jose
Viñes y Martorell to BR re
Spanish trans. of *Wisdom
of the West*
Aheret (Maxim Ghilan)
to BRPF 1969
CF to 1969
Ahmed, Nasim, CF to 1968
Ahmed, Ziauddin 1968
CF to 1968
Åkerman, Nordal 1963

RS to 1963
Akhbar el yom (Kamal
Raouf) 1966
BR to 1966
Aktiebolaget Svenska Bokförlaget
(B. Socusson) **2** 1962
BR to 1962
Al Ahrâm (Louis Awad,
Muhammed Hasanein
Heikal 1962
NJ to 1962
BR to 1964
Al Gomhouria (R. Habib and
Janine Stacey of the
Embassy of the United
Arab Republic) 1962
To RS 1962
RS to **2** 1962-3
Alam, Pervaiz, CF to 1967
Alberti, Rafael, and Leon,
Maria Theresa 1965
BR to 1965
Aldus Books Ltd. (W. Foges,
Mr. Frame-Smith, Patricia
Quick) **7** 1962-8
BR to **3** 1962-3
CF to 1968
Algemeen Dagblad (J. A.
Redeker), BR to 1963
Ali, Ashraf 1970
PW to 1970
Ali, S. Hamid 1966
BR to 1966
Encl: note to PW
Ali, Tariq, to RSt. 1967
RSt. to 1967
All Jammu & Kashmir Muslim
Conference (S. D. Niez) **2** .. 1966
Encl: clipping and essay
CF to 1966
All Pakistan Women's Association
(Begum Salima Ahmed) 1967
CF to 1967
Allaf, Mowaffak, CF to 1967
The Allahabad Medical Association (S. K. Bhattacharyya) .. 1967
George Allen & Unwin Ltd.
(Stanley Unwin *et
al.*) **53** 1919-68
To NJ 1963
To RS **19** 1963-7
To ER **14** 1963-8
To CF **24** 1963-70
To BRPF 1965
To Anton Felton **2** 1966-8
To RSt. **2** 1967
To Ken Coates 1969
Encl: l. to Robert W. Marks, l. from Aguilar, l. to Z. A. Siddiqui, l. from Laurel Editions (Richard Huett), ls. from Grove Press Inc. (Harry Biraverman), l. from. J. S. Whale, l. from The Gresham Press (J. E. Hughff), l. from *Probe* (F. D. Rabon and F. M. Orkin), ls. from Longanesi & Co. (Maria Gulia Minetti, Carla Tanzi), l. from Broadcasting Stockholm, royalty ss., clippings, reviews, press releases, author's invoices, invitation, publisher's timetable, newsl., office memo
RS to **19** 1962-7
BR to **49** 1962-9
NJ to 1963
ER to **8** 1963-8
CF to **65** 1963-70
R. M. Rehder to 1965
RSt. to **9** 1967
PJ to 1967
PW to **2** 1968-9
Encl: l. from Eugeniuz Chadzicki, notes from CF to BR, BR's preface to *Philosophical Essays*, dust jackets, draft blurb, list of persons to be sent complimentary copies, author's correction lists, note in ER's hand, prospectus for a collection of BR's writings on Vietnam
Allen, Jamie, BR to .... n.d.
Allgemeiner Deutscher
Nachrichtendienst
(Ted Brake) **9** 1966
Alsop, Joseph .... 1947?
American Broadcasting
Company **3** 1962-6
American Dialog (Joseph North,
Anca Vrbrovska) **3** 1964-9
To CF 1969

BR to 1964
RS to 1965
CF to **2** 1969-70
The American Ethical Union (Robert Kopka) **3** 1965-6
RS to **3** 1965-6
American Humanist Association (Edwin H. Wilson) 1953
Encl.
American Peoples Encyclopedia (Bruce Fearing) 1964
RS? to 1964
American Philosophical Quarterly (Nicholas Rescher) 1966
RS to 1966
American Society to Defend Children (Mona Bazaar) 1965
Encl: issues of journal
PW to 1965
American Vegetarian (Symon Gould) 1963
Encl: essay
Ammerman, Robert R. **2** ... 1963
Encl.
BR to 1963
Ananda Bazar Patrika (Tarapada Basu) 1967
Encl: questionnaire
CF to 1967
Anders, Günther **4** 1964-9
To CF 1963
To Mr. Kinsey 1963
Encl: essay
BR to **6** 1962-9
CF to **3** 1963-9
Anderson, Barbara, BR to 1963
Ando, Takatura 1966
CF to 1967
Andrew, Gerda 1963
BR to 1963
Anglica Society (K. Enomoto, Hitoshi Mori of Daigakusha Co. Ltd.) **3** 1962-3
BR to 1963
Animals (Nigel Sitwell) 1969
Anscombe, G. E. M. 1967
BR to 1967
L'Anti-Antitoutiste Pour La Paix (Mr. Henriquez) 1962
BR to 1962
Aomi, Junichi **5** 1962-3
Encl: English summary of his book, *Bertrand Russell*
BR to **4** 1962-4
AY to 1962
Appleton-Century Crofts (Judith Michael) 1962
Encl: l. from Jerry King for Gaines S. Dobbins
BR to 1962
Approach Magazine (Phillip Hodson) 1967
To CF 1967
Encl.
CF to **2** 1967
The Architectural Association (R. D. Underwood) 1968
Encl.
CF to 1968
Arena (Anthony F. Trotman) 1965
To PW 1966
RS to 1965
PW to 1966
Arena (Larry James Sechrest) 1969
CF to 1969
Argentinian Peace Committee (Alberto T. Casella) 1966
Encl.
BR to **2** 1966
Armati, L. F. 1967
Encl.
Arora, R. S. 1965
To RS **3** 1965
Encl.
RS to **3** 1965
Arpelderblad 1966
Arsenescu, Adina 1968
BR to 1968
Asahi Shimbun (Motoo Goto, Y. Senoo) **4** 1965-7
To CF 1966
To RS **2** 1966
CF to 1965
RS to **2** 1966
RSt. to 1967
Askwith, Betty Miller 1969
Askwith, Herbert **2** 1965
Encl.

PW to 1965
Aspecte (Gerhard
Hirschfield) 1969
The Associated Press (Edwin
A. Shenke, Milton Marmor,
Eugene Levin) **2** 1964
To RS **3** 1963-4
To CF 1967
Encl: interview, questionnaire
RS to 1964
CF to (Levin) **3** 1967
PW to 1968
Encl: note in BR's hand re
Milton Marmor interview,
memo from CF
Associated Press Cutting
Services Ltd., AY to 1962
Associated TeleVision Limited
(Bryan Magee, Jack
Gill) **2** 1956-66
(Anthony Firth) to RS 1965
Encl.
RS to 1965
Association of World Federalists
(M. K. Banerjee) 1968
Athenaeum Publishers
(Catherine Hartman) 1967
The Atlantic Monthly Press
(Edward Weeks, Peter
Davison, *et al.*) **44** 1962-70
To CF 1968
To RS **3** 1967
Encl: l. to James A. Scott,
l. to Joannis Kalogiannis,
l. to Philip D. Woodridge,
l. to Karen Popenuck,
reviews, article, royalty
ss., greeting cards, dust
jacket, promotional material
for *Autobiography*
BR to **21** 1962-9
RS to 1967
CF to **11** 1967-8
Encl: corrections to ms.
Atomics & Nuclear Energy
(E. G. Semler) 1958
BR to 1958
Attihe, Ujhelyi 1962
BR to 1963
Audio Fidelity Inc. (Sidney
Frey, Claire Orson) **2** 1962
Encl: clippings
BR to 1962
Aurora Social (Alberto
Lumbreras) **2** 1964-5
BR to **3** 1964-7
Australian Left Review
(Eric Aarons) 1969
Encl.
Authentic Translators (Mohan
Lal Garg) 1962
BR to 1962
Avant Garde (Leslie M.
Pockwell) **2** 1968
Avedon, Richard 1969
BR to 1969
Avenues for Humanised Economics
for the Growth of Mind and
Soul (B. E. Ray) 1964
Encl.
RS to 1964
Aware (Joe Allen) 1969

B

Backwards (J. S. Roe) .... n.d.
Encl: issue of magazine
Bader, Joseph .... 1961?
BR to 1962
Baltimore Sun (Helen F.
Knipp) to RS 1966
RS to 1966
Bambrough, J. R. 1962
Banerjee, A. B. 1969
CF to 1969
Bantam Books, Inc. (Marc
Jaffe) **2** 1962-3
Barber, Peter, RS to 1964
Barbone, Donato, BR to 1964
Arthur Barker Ltd. (Gaye
Poulton) 1963
Barnard, Harry 1962
A. S. Barnes & Co., Inc.
(Thomas Yoseloff) **4** 1963
BR to **4** 1963
Bashir, M. **2** 1963
BR to **2** 1963
Basic Books, Inc. (David
A. McDermott) **2** 1969

Encl.
Baskin, Wade 1966
CF to 1966
"Bastion" Annual Committee
(J. L. Bradley) 1965
RS to 1965
Basu, Nripendra K. 1967
Encl: poems
The Bath Weekly Chronicle & Herald (Raynor D. Chapman) 1965
BR to 1965
Bau (Oswald Oberhuber) 1969
CF to 1969
Der Bayerische Rundfunk
(Gustava Mösler) 1964
RS to 1964
Beacon Press (Frederica Cushman) 1964
Encl: Manutiuspresse to Beacon Press
RS to 1964
Beaver (F. Mansfield, Jr.) 1966
ID to 1966
Bedau, Hugo Adam 1968
Encl.
CF to 1968
Bell, Kenneth 1968
CF to 1968
Bell Telephone Laboratories
(William M. Evan) 1962
Jon Tinker to 1962
Bent (Glyn Holmes) **2** 1964
RS to **2** 1964
Bentley, Nicholas **2** 1966
BR to 1966
Berka, Karel 1966
Encl: biblio. of Czech transs. of BR
BR to 1966
The Pierre Berton Show
(Pierre Berton, Sam Levene) **2** 1964
BR to 1964
RS to **3** 1964
Bertou, Jacques **2** 1967-8
Encl: Jacques Bertou to *Le Monde* 1967
Le Monde (Jacques Fauvet) to Jacques Bertou 1967
CF to 1968
Bertrand, Claude-Jean 1965
BR to 1965
Berveiller, Michel **5** 1962-8
To CF 1967
Encl: questions concerning Vol. I of BR's *Auto.*, curriculum vitae
BR to **4** 1962-8
CF to **2** 1967
Encl: BR's replies to Berveiller's questions
Betes Noires and Straw Men
(William H. Swan) **2** 1964
Encl: issue of newspaper
BR to 1964
RS to 1964
De Bezige Bij (G. Lubberhuizen) **2** 1968
Encl: De Bezige Bij (Marijke Bij) to Insel Verlag (Renate Laux)
BR to 1968
CF to 1968
Bhandari, Veena 1966
BR to 1966
Biquard, P. 1967
Encl: P. Biquard to Joseph Rotblat
BR to 1964
Bird, Mr., BR to 1960
The Bishop's House (L. J. Davey, re *Shire and Spire*) 1962
Bit (Shigeru Shioya) 1969
To CF 1969
A. & C. Black Ltd. (*Who's Who*) 1966
Encl.
The Black Dwarf (D. A. N. Jones and Clive Goodwin) to RS 1968
(Tariq Ali) to BR 1969
Blackie & Son (receipt for permission fee) 1964
Blacksburg Free Press (Thomas J. Saunders), CF to 1968
B. H. Blackwell, Ltd. (P. Hilsdon, G. Crutch) 1962
To BRPF 1966

Encl.
NJ to 1962
RS to **2** 1962
AY to 1962
BR to 1963
PW to 1966
Blackwell, Kenneth **5** 1965-8
To AY 1965
To BRPF 1965
To CF **7** 1966-8
Encl: K. Blackwell to P. A. Schilpp
BR to 1966
CF to **4** 1966-8
RS to **2** 1965
RSt. to 1967
Encl: note by BR re Blackwell
Blackwood, Jr., Andrew W., to *Sunday Times* 1966
BR to 1966
Blaetter fuer Deutsche und Internationale Politik 1958
Bliss, C. K. 1952
Blitz (F. Colaabavala) **2** ... 1964-7
Encl: clippings
BR to **3** 1964-7
RS to **2** 1966
Anthony Blond Ltd. (Anthony Blond *et al.*) **4** 1966-7
BR to **2** 1966
CF to 1966
RSt. to 1967
Blotner, Joseph **2** 1965
BR to 1965
PW to 1965
Blumberg, Herbert H., to BRPF 1968
Board of Trade Advisory Committee, CF to 1967
The Bobbs-Merrill Co., Inc. .. 1968
Encl: article, catalogue
The Bodley Head Ltd. (James Michie, John R. Hews) 1966
To PW 1967
Encl: ER's list of people to be sent a complimentary copy of *Nightmares of Eminent Persons*
Bohemia (Alberto de Los Toyos) 1967
RS to 1967
Bokförlaget Natur och Kultur (Johan Hansson) **4** 1962-8
Encl.
BR to **3** 1962-8
Bolt, Robert **2** 1967-8
To RS 1963
Encl.
RS to **4** 1963-4
BR to **4** 1964-8
Bolton Evening News, CF to 1969
Boni and Liveright (Horace Liveright) 1924
The Bonnier Magazine Group (*Året Runt*) (Stan Möllerström) **2** 1963-4
RS to 1963
Book News 1968
Book of the Month Club, Inc. (Ralph Thompson) 1955
Booth, John Nicholls 1962
Encl: pamphlet, 7 frames from film of BR
BR to 1962
Boston Globe, RS to 1966
Boulton, David, CF to 1964
Bourdet, Claude **2** 1963-5
BR to 1965
Boynton, Robert W. 1962
BR to 1962
Brainwave (V. Desai) 1969
Breakthru: International Poetry Magazine (Ken Geering) **2** 1965-9
Briggs, Michael J. 1967
CF to 1967
British Broadcasting Corporation (Christopher Burnstall, Henry Morgenthau, III, *et al.*) **66** 1960-8
Encl: royalty ss., ls. regarding permission and copyright, transcripts of recordings, clippings, etc.
BR *et al.* to **35** 1961-8
Encl.
British Printing Corporation (Sydney Mayer) 1969

Encl.
CF to 1969
British Soviet Friendship
Society (Pat Sloan) **2** ... 1961-4
To RS 1964
RS to 1964
British Travel (D. R. Stewart)
To CF 1965
CF to 1965
British Weekly Ltd. (Denis
Duncan) 1969
To CF **2** 1969
Encl.
CF to 1969
Bronda, Antonio, RS to 1964
The Brookings Institution
(Mary Lou Van Meers) 1963
BR to 1963
D. B. D. Brothers 1968
Brown, Alec, to Paul ? 1957
Encl: reader's report on
Martin's *L'Heure H– a t'elle sonné?*
Brown, G. Rudstan 1969
Encl.
PW to 1969
Bryn Mawr College Library
(Janet M. Agnew) 1959
Re return of "Forstice"
ms.
Buckman, Peter, to RS 1963
RS to **2** 1963
Buehrer, Edwin T. **2** 1964
RS to **2** 1964
Bugental, J. F. T. **3** 1965-6
Encl.
RS to 1965
Bulgarian Radio and
Television (A. Nevkov) 1967
Bulletin of the Atomic Scientists
(Eugene Rabinowitch *et al.*) **13** 1958-63
Encl.
BR to **8** 1961-9
Encl: Rotblat to BR 1963
ER to 1962
RS to 1963
PW to 1966
Encl: ts. of "The Danger
to Mankind"
Bureau Hongrois pour le
Protection des Droits d'Auteur
(Dr. Boytha), BR to 1963
Burke's Peerage (J. W.
Smallshaw) 1937
Encl.
BR to 1966
J. Viney to 1967
Burleigh, Lionel 1966
BR to 1966
Burnham, C. G., BR to 1964
Burnham, Colin **2** 1966
PW to 1966
Byrne, Kevin 1969

C

Cahiers pour l'Analyse
(Jacques Allain Hiller) 1966
CF to 1966
John Calder Publishers Ltd.
(John Calder) to RS 1962
Encl: John Calder to Jon
Tinker 1962
BR to 1963
California Law Review
(John C. Fossum) 1965
RS to 1965
The California Tech (Leslie
G. Fishbone), RSt. to 1967
Cambrian News, CF to 1970
Cambridge Opinion (Jonathan
Lewis) 1966
CF to 1966
Cambridge Review (Eric
Homberger) .... n.d.
Cambridge University Press
(A. K. Parker *et al.*) **16** 1962-9
Encl: royalty ss.
BR to **2** 1962-4
CF to **3** 1965-9
RSt. to **2** 1967
Cambridge University United
Nations Association (C. J.
Martin) to RS 1965
RS to 1965
Camera Press (T.L. Blau) 1964
To RS 1964

CF to 1964
RS to 1964
Cameron, Ewan **4** 1965-6
Encl.
PW to 1965
BR to 1966
RS to 1966
Campaign in Oxford University for Nuclear Disarmament (Adam Roberts) 1961
BR to 1961
Campus Kaleidoscope (Michael Gross) **2** 1965
PW to **2** 1965
Camus, William 1964
Encl.
Canadian Broadcasting Corporation **2** 1964-7
Encl: royalty s.
To RS 1963
Canadian Dimension (C. W. Gonick) to RS **2** 1966
To Quintin Hoare 1967
RS to 1966
Quintin Hoare to 1966
Deirdre Griswold to 1967
The Canadian Press (Alan Walker, Harold Morrison) **3** 1964-8
RS to **2** 1964
CF to 1968
Cande, Daniel 1963
RS to 1963
Jonathan Cape Ltd. (Tom Maschler, Rina Slater, Anthony Colwell) **6** 1962
To RS **4** 1962-5
Encl: Jonathan Cape Ltd. (Graham C. Green) to Dillon's University Bookshop Ltd.
BR to 1962
Encl: ts. of foreword by BR
RS to **4** 1965-7
CF to 1969
The Caravel Press (M.R. Clarke) **3** 1962
Encl.
NJ to **2** 1962
RS to 1963
Casany, Enrique Iardí 1962
BR to 1962
Catalyst (A. Salvaris and I. J. Richardson) 1958
BR to 1958
Cavalier Magazine (Robert J. Shea) **4** 1965-6
BR to 1965
RS to **3** 1966
ID to 1966
Central Office of Information (F. R. Rea *et al.*) **7** 1962-9
BR to 1962
RS to 1963
CF to 1969
Centre d'Études Nucléaires de Saclay 1969
Centre House (Christopher Hills) .... 1966?
Encl.
The Century Co. (J. L. Morley) 1926
Ceskoslovenský Novinár (L. J. Budiý?) 1968
Chakrabarti, Altulanada, BR to 1964
Chakraborty, Arun Kumar **2** 1969
RS to 1968
Challenge (Alexander McDonald) 1965
Chamarro Turrez, Eduardo .. 1968
BR to 1968
Chambrun, Jacques 1936
Encl: review of *Religion and Science*
Chapman & Hall Ltd. (A. S. W. Winkworth) 1965
PW to 1965
Chatterbox (Evelyn B. Byrne) . . 1966
Encl.
BR to 1966
Chattopadhyay, Santinath **2** 1966-7
BR to 1966
Chicago Sun-Times
Encl: notice
RS to 1966
Chicago Tribune (Alfred C. Ames) 1966
Encl: form l.
RS to **2** 1964-6

Chichester Promoter (Ben Dunk) **2** 1968
BR to 1968
Chirimo (Mrs. O-lan Style) ... 1969
Chisholm, John **2** 1967
CF to 1967
RSt. to 1967
Chorley, Lord 1957
Encl: l. to *The Times*
Christian Life Press (John P.H. Chen) **2** 1962-3
To BR and ER 1962
Encl: clippings, essays
BR to **5** 1962-3
Christian Science Monitor,
RS to 1964
The Chubu Nippon Shimbun (Yutaka Izuta, Ninoru Oda, Yoshito Mano) **3** 1962-4
To AY 1964
Encl: clippings
BR to **2** 1962
RS to 1964
The Churchman (Edna Ruth Johnson) **2** 1963
BR to **2** 1963
Clare (Alastair Dunn) 1966
To RS 1966
RS to 1966
The Clarendon Press (J. H. Price) 1968
Encl: The Clarendon Press (J. K. Cordy) to Allen & Unwin Ltd., Foreign Rights Dept.
CF to **2** 1968
Clemens, Jr., Walter C. 1964
RS to 1964
Cloister Press (J. Charlton) 1959
Encl: page proofs of BR's contribution to Wythenshawe volume
Club de Amigos de la UNESCO de Barcelona (J. Serra Rafols) 1965
RS to 1965
PW to 1965
Coates, K., BR to 1964
Collier-Macmillan Ltd. (Peter L. Boulton) 1967
CF to 1967
Collins Publishers 1962
Combined Universities Campaign for Nuclear Disarmament (Joel Hartt, Dick Clements) **2** 1961
BR to 1961
ER to 1961
Encl: BR's preface to first number of *Our Generation against Nuclear War*
Comitato Italiano per il Disarmo Atomico (G. B. Zorzoli) 1962
BR to 1962
Committee for "Alternatives to Violence" (Larry Ng) 1968
Encl.
CF to 1968
Common Cause Publications Ltd. (Frank Trehern)
Encl: issue of *The Democrat*
RS to 1966
Communicorp Public Relations (Roland Gammon) **3** 1965-8
To RS 1966
To CF **2** 1968
RS to **2** 1965-6
CF to **3** 1968
Compagnia Edizioni Internationali (Giorgio Ribaldi) to Ken Coates 1970
PW to 1970
Compass and Fleet (Peter Barber) **2** 1964
To RS 1964
The Compleat Imbiber (Cyril Ray) 1962
Encl.
BR to 1962
The Concept of Pakistan (M. D. Sofiullah) 1966
RS to 1966
Connections Inc. (David L. Gross) 1967
CF to 1967
Consulta Calabrese per la Pace (Liliana Munzi, Emilio Argiroffi) 1963
CF to 1963

Contemporary Press (P. Watter) 1962
Continuum (J. G. Lawler), BR to 1963
Controversy (Ken Eaton) to RS 1962
To NJ 1962
NJ to **2** 1962
Cope, K. **2** 1964
BR to 1964
CE to 1964
Cornell Daily Sun (Marjorie Holt) 1966
El Corno Emplumado (Margaret Randall and Robert David Cohen) 1968
Corriera della Sera (Renzo Cianfanelli) 1969
CF to 1969
Cosmopolitan Contact (Marion Matarisvan) 1965
Encl: issues of the journal, copy of a 1951 BR l.
RS to 1965
Cotti-Cometti, Giampiero, CF to 1968
Council for Democracy (Marjorie Griesser) 1941
PR to 1941
Council of Scientific and Industrial Research (S. Husain Zaheer) 1964
Encl.
To RS 1964
RS to 1964
Courtenay, R. D. **2** 1963
BR to 1963
RS to 1963
Coward-McCann, Inc., to RS 1967
Crawford, Corine L. 1963
To RS **3** 1964
Encl: ls. to Mr. Eckersley (BBC), l. from Mr. Eckersley, clipping, list of BBC recordings by BR, film outline, sound sequence to film, contract
BR to 1963
RS to **4** 1964
CF to 1969
The Crest (D. M. Greatorex) 1963
BR to 1963
Rupert Crew Ltd. (Shirley Russell) 1967
CF to 1967
BR to Christopher Trent 1967
Cripps, Raymond W. 1962
BR to 1962
Critica Marxista (Emilio Sereni) 1968
Encl.
Cross Currents (Marilyn Rapp) .... n.d.
The Crowell-Collier Educational Corporation (Lance Wallace) 1965
RS to **2** 1965-7
Crown Publishers, Inc. (W. W. Whitman) 1961
BR to 1962
O Cruzeiro Internacional (F. W. Hayman Chaffey) 1963
RS to 1963
CTV Television (David Cook) 1962
Cuadernos para el Diálogo (Emilio Menéndez de Valle) to BRPF 1969
CF to 1969
Cuadernos Universitarios (Carlos Tunnernann Bernheim) 1966
RS to 1966
Current of the World (Fumie Imai) 1958
Y Cymro (Glyn Griffiths) to Tom Kinsey 1963
Encl.
BR to 1963
Il Cyrano (Pasquale Coppola) to BRPF 1968
CF to 1968
Czechoslovak Life (Frantisek Lebenhart) 1967
Encl: article
CF to 1967
Czechoslovak News Agency (Lumomír Fiser, G. Heathcote, D. Rovensky) **3** 1963-70
BR to 1963

CF to 1970
Czechoslovak Radio (Faix Kvetoslav) 1967
Czechoslovak Youth (Lubomír Procházka) **2** 1964-5

D

Daedalus: Journal of the American Academy of Arts and Sciences (Stephen R. Graubard, Geno A. Ballotti, Katharine Strelsky) **5** 1962
BR to **3** 1963
Encl: BR to Joseph Rotblat
Daily Express (R. A. Pugh, D. Hardisty) **2** 1966
CF to 1964
Daily Mail (E. V. Matthewman, James Cameron, Christopher Underwood) **2** 1962
To RS 1966
BR to 1962
Daily Mashriq (Altaf Ahmad Qureshi) to CF 1966
BR to 1966
The Daily Telegraph (Maurice Green, "Peter Simple" [Michael Wharton], *et al.*) **2** 1965-8
To PW **4** 1964-5
To RS **2** 1964-5
Encl: clipping
CF to 1968
PW to **4** 1964-9
Encl.
Daily Worker (George Matthews *et al.*) **5** 1963-5
To BRPF 1965
To CF 1965
To David Horowitz 1966
BR to **2** 1963-6
RS to 1965
PW to **2** 1965
David Horowitz to 1966
Encl.
Dalmaum, Rafael 1963
Dalzell-Ward, A. J. **2** 1968
CF to **2** 1968
Danas (Alexander V. Stafanovic) **2** 1962-3
Encl: questionnaire, clipping
BR to **2** 1962-3
Le Danger Radiologique (Jean Pignero) 1963
Daniel, John 1963
BR to 1964
Das, Prafulla Chandra **4** ... 1965-9
BR to **2** 1963-4
PW to 1965
RS to 1966
CF to 1968
Datta, Nilkanta **3** 1962-3
To NJ 1963
Encl: outline of book, *Bertrand Russell and I*
RS to 1962
NJ to 1963
Davidson, Chandler 1962
BR to **2** 1962-4
Davidson, William C. 1964
To PW 1965
Davies, Mary **2** 1959-60
BR to **2** 1959-60
Encl: paragraph on Margaret McMillan
Davies, Stan Gebler 1967
Encl: article
CF to 1967
Davis, Jerome **5** 1962-3
To BRPF 1966
BR to **3** 1962-3
CF to 1963
RS to 1966
Encl.
Dawe, Alan 1968
Encl.
To CF **2** 1968
CF to **3** 1968
Dawn (Nasim Asmed) 1968
De Benedetti, Andrea 1966
CF to 1966
Debrett's Peerage **3** 1966-9
Encl: proof
December (Curt Johnson) 1963
Encl.
BR to 1963
Decker, Donald G. **2** 1968-9
Encl.

CF to 1968
Decker, Randall E., RS to 1965
De Eguidazu, Fernando 1965
RS to 1965
deLacy, Terence, BR to 1965
De Lavergne, James 1965
To RS **2** 1965-6
RS to **2** 1965-6
Delgado, Rafael Rodriguez,
to ER 1964
Dell Publishing Co. (Richard
Huett, Carole S. Lewis) to
RS **2** 1967
CF to **2** 1967
RS to 1967
Encl: K. T. Fann to RS
Delphic Quarterly (Phoebus
Delphis) 1966
PW to 1966
Demski, Reiner 1969
Denonn, Lester E. **2** 1954-65
To RS **2** 1962
RS to 1962
PW to 1965
BR to **3** 1952-66
J. M. Dent & Sons (Canada)
Ltd. (Jay Allison) 1965
BR to 1966
Deschner, Karlheinz, BR to .. 1964
Destino (Luis Hermanyo) 1962
André Deutsch Ltd. (Piers
Burnett) to RS 1967
RS to 1965
Deutsch-Israelische Studiengruppe
(Heinz Wewer) 1967
RSt. to 1967
Devaux, Philip **2** 1964-5
BR to 1964
RS to 1965
Encl: The Malvern Press
Ltd. (J. C. Fray) to CF
Le Devoir, RS to 1964
de Wespin, M. D., BR to 1964
Dhiman Press of India 1958
The Dial Press Inc. (Donald
Hutter) 1969
Dickens Society of Ceylon
(M. M. Aryaratna) **4** 1967
Encl: Albert Schweitzer to
M. M. Aryaratna
CF to 1967
PW to 1969
Dicker, Harold 1965
BR to 1964
PW to 1966
Dickinson, Thorold 1968
Encl.
CF to 1968
Dionysus (Samaswati
Swaminathan) 1966
Directory of Organisations (Tony
Bunyan) 1968
Encl.
Diskus (Hermann Lohaus) 1967
RSt. to 1968
Disordine (Mark Edward
Kleckner) 1970
*Dod's Parliamentary
Companion* **4** 1962-70
Doern, Russell J. **2** 1967
CF to 1967
Dorchester Advertising Corpor-
ation (Claire Orson) 1962
Doubleday and Co., Inc. (Joan
Kiddy *et al.*) 1969
To AY **2** 1962
To RS 1967
BR to 1962
AY to 1962
RS to 1964
CF to 1969
Douglas, A. 1965
RS to 1965
Dover Publications, Inc.
(Marjory Baucom) 1967
PW to 1967
Dowlite International (Aziz
Ahmed) 1964
BR to 1964
The Draughtsman (J. E.
Mortimer) to Ken Coates ... 1965
Drei Masken Verlag AG 1924
Duffet, John L., CF to 1968
Dummett, Michael, RS to 1963
Dunn, H. B. 1968
To CF 1968
Encl: Oxford University Press
(Ena Sheen) to Dunn, Dunn
to Oxford University
Press (Ena Sheen)

CF to 2 1968
Durband, Alan 1965
Encl.
PW to 1965
Durrant's Press Cuttings
to AY 1962
Encl.
AY to 1962
PW to 1966
E. P. Dutton & Co. Inc.
(Cyril I. Nelson, Walter
Arnold) 2 1965-8
PW to 1968

E

Eastern Horizon, RSt. to 1967
Eastern World (H.C.
Taussig) 1963
BR to 1963
The Economist (Alastair
Burnet) 1966
Encl.
RS to 1966
Edge Magazine (Richard
Glidewell) to BRPF 1965
RS to 1965
Edició de Materials (Ignesi Vidal
i Sanfeliu) to RSt. 1967
RSt. to 1968
Ediciones Hombre Nuevo
(Leonardo César
Schweid) to BRPF 1968
To PW 1968
PW to 2 1968
Encl.
Edition Voltaire (Bernward
Vesper-Triangel) to BRPF .. 1969
Éditions du Burin (Roger
Maria) 4 1965-6
To RS 3 1965-6
To PW 1965
Encl: Roger Maria to Claude
Bourdet
RS to 1965
PW to 2 1965-6
BR to 1966
Éditions du Seuil (Paul
Flamand) 2 1967
BR to 1967
Les Editions John Didier
(John Didier) 5 1963-5
PW to 2 1965
Editôra Civilização Brasileiro
(Enio Silveira) 1969
Editorial Lumen (Maria
Beatriz de Moura)
to BRPF 1964
BR to (Esther Tusquets) ... 1964
RS to 1964
RS to Maria Beatriz de
Moura 1964
Editorial Posada (Guillermo
Mendizabel Lizalde) 1968
Editorial Seix Berral, S.A.
(Rosa Regás) 1968
Encl.
Editoriale Rizzoli (Pautasso)
to BRPF 1967
Education for Teaching (Keith
Thompson) 1969
CF to 1969
Edwards, Paul 2 1962-5
BR to 2 1962-5
Egner, Robert E. 8 1964-8
BR to 6 1964-8
RS to 2 1965-7
Ehly, Jean 1964
To RS 5 1964-5
Encl: questionnaire and essay
RS to 2 1964
Giulio Einaudi Editore
to RS 1967
Ekshan (Nirmalya Acharya) ... 1968
Ekstrabladet (Per Hanghøj) 1966
Elan (Irma Kurtz) 1967
To CF 1967
Encl.
CF to 2 1967
Elan: magazin für junge Leute
(Hans-Jörg Hennecke) 1968
Elbiński, Zygmunt 2 1965
To RS 1965
Encl: Elbiński to Accra
Assembly (Frank E. Boaten),
Elbiński to Higher
Agricultural School
RS to 1965
PW to 1965

Encl: *Direkte Aktion* (Joachim Dunz) to BR, Peace Research Institute-Oslo (Johan Galtung) to BR, issue of *Direkte Aktion*, s. by BR
Eleven Twenty-Seven (J. D. R. Taylor) 1968
Encl: M. P. Priestley to BR
Elfenbein, Hiram 1966
RS to 1966
Elgumhouria (Fathy Ghanem) 1967
RS to 1967
Emley, M. L. B. 1967
CF to 1967
Encounter (Margot Walmsley, Melvin J. Lasky, Bryan Healing) **2** 1962-5
To RS 1965
BR to 1962
PW to 1965
Encyclopaedia Britannica Ltd. (C. H. W. Kent) **2** 1965
PW to 1965
Encyclopaedia Moderna (Ivan Supek) 1966
Encl.
England, Åke 1965
Encl: proofs
Ennis, Robert H. 1967
Encl.
Epoca (Livio Caputo) **2** 1963
BR to **2** 1963
Errington, Lewis 1964
BR to 1964
Escape (Everhard Ottens) 1968
CF to 1968
Espase-Calpe, S. A., to IWCT 1967
Esquire (Harold Hayes *et al.*) **8** 1963-9
To RS 1963
Encl: royalty s.
BR to 1963
RS to 1964
O Estado de S. Paulo (Marco Antonio de Rezende) 1969
et al. (J. Morgan Thomas) 1968
CF to 1968
The Eton Amnesty Group (James Hughes Hallet) 1967
Euratio (Leo H. Secrève) 1965
RS to 1965
Europa Publications Ltd. (P. G. C. Jackson) **7** 1967-9
RS to 1969
Evans Brothers Ltd. (Juliet Crombie) **3** 1967
To CF 1967
Encl.
CF to **2** 1967
Evelyn, Adams & Mackay Ltd. (Anthony Adams) 1968
Encl.
L'Evenement (Emmanuel d'Astier) 1966
BR to **2** 1966
Evening Leningrad (Boris Markov) 1964
The Evening News (R. Dhiman) 1964
BR to 1964
The Exchange Telegraph Co. Ltd. (D. E. Bristow) 1960
ER to 1960
Exit (Edward Johnson) 1965
Encl.
PW to 1965
L'Express, RS to 1964
Expressen (Jussi Anthal) 1967

F

Faber and Faber Ltd. (Richard de la Mare, Jane Morley, T. S. Eliot, Valerie Eliot) 1963
To CF **2** 1966
To NJ **2** 1962
CF to 1966
NJ to 1962
Fact (Ralph Ginzburg *et al.*) **9** 1963-7
To BRPF 1963
To RS **2** 1965-7
Encl: issue of magazine
BR to **4** 1963-4
CF to 1963
Patrick Jordan to 1967

RS to **5** 1965-7
Faim & Soif (Roger
Dauphin) 1962
Fairchild Publications of New
York (Michael Gunton) 1967
CF to 1967
Family (Sheila Sharp) 1962
RS to 1962
Fann, K. T. 1965
To RS 1965
RS to **2** 1965
PW to 1965
CF to 1968
Fanti, G., PW to 1965
Farrell, C. J., to *London
Bulletin* 1968
RSt. to 1968
F.C.I. News Agency Ltd.
(Josef Josten) to CF 1968
Encl.
CF to **2** 1968
Feinberg, Abraham L. **3** ... 1965-8
BR to 1968
RS to 1966
Firth, Glynn **2** 1958
BR to 1958
Fishell, John M., BR to 1964
Flatto, Edwin **2** 1965
BR to **2** 1965
R. B. Fleming & Co. Ltd.
(F. E. Bird) 1965
Flew, A. G. N. (ts. of
review of *Wisdom of the
West*) .... 1959?
Foges, Peter, to CF **2** 1964
To RS .... n.d.
CF to **2** 1964
Encl: note in CF's hand
Folkman, Jerome .... 1968?
Folks-Sztyme (L. Douglas) ... 1963
BR to (L. Douglas and
Y. Korman) **2** 1963
Forecast (Paul Flattery) 1967
RSt. to 1967
Foreign Affairs (Stella
Morel) 1924
Foreign Correspondents Ltd.
(H. C. Taussig, B.M.
Everitt) **3** 1963-5
BR to 1963
PW to 1965
Foreign Publications Service
(Marjorie E. Tobey) **3** 1962
Encl: article, etc.
Forest, Lester, to Appleton,
Century, Crofts, Inc. 1962
BR to 1962
Fortune (Walter Graebner) ... 1951
Forum (R. J. Bromby) 1962
BR to 1962
Forum World Features Ltd.
(John Tusa) 1967
CF to 1967
Four Winds Press (John A.
Pope, Jr.) to BRPF 1968
W. & G. Foyle Ltd. (Christina
Foyle) **2** 1953
Encl: list of guests, Lord
Jowitt's notes as chairman
of *Satan in the Suburbs*
luncheon
Freed, Donald 1967
Freedland, Michael, to
BRPF **2** 1965
To CF **4** 1965
Encl: essay, Christmas card,
Associated Press-Cutting
Services Ltd. to Michael
Freedland, story on BR
HR to 1965
PW to 1965
Encl: note on Michael Freedland
Freedom (Jack Robinson),
RS? to 1963
Freelance Photographers Guild,
Inc. (Arthur Brackman,
Selma Brackman) 1963
To RS 1963
Encl: issue of *Propaganda*
BR to 1963
The Freethinker (Karl Hyde,
David Reynolds) **2** 1968-9
Encl: issues of journal
Freethought Society of America,
Inc. (Madalyn Murray),
BR to 1964
Freifeld, Samuel D., to
RS **3** 1963
RS to **2** 1963
Frenz, Horst 1964

Encl: proofs
RS to 1964
Leslie Frewin (John
Pawsey) 1968
To CF 1968
CF to 1968
Friese Koerier (Laurens ten
Cate) 1962
BR to 1962
Fritz, Jr., Charles A. 1965
Encl: table of contents
RS to 1965
Frontier (Philip
Kerby) **9** 1955-67
To RS **4** 1963-5
Encl: M. S. Arnoni to
Frontier (Philip Kerby),
issue of journal
BR to **7** 1963-6
RS to **6** 1964-6
Frumkin, Robert M. 1964
RS to 1964
Fulcrum (Charles
Bloomstein) **2** 1962-3
Encl.
BR to 1963
Fulton, Leonard V. **3** 1962-3
BR to **3** 1962-3
Richard Fulton Inc. (Richard
Fulton) **2** 1966
BR to 1966
RS to 1966
Funk & Wagnalls, Inc.
(Virginia Carew, Mab
Gray) **2** 1962-3
Encl: tear sheets
BR to 1962

G

Gaberbocchus Press Ltd.
(Stefan Themerson) **4** .. 1963-9
To ER 1969
CF to **2** 1963-9
BR to **3** 1967-9
Gale Research Company
(P. O. Fox) **2** 1968-9
Encl.
CF to 1968
Galileo (Mario H. Otero) 1966
RS to 1966
Gamut Press, Inc.
(Ira Jay Dreyer) 1963
Encl.
BR to 1963
Gandhi Centenary (Om Prakash
Agarwal) 1969
Gardner, Hy 1969
CF to 1969
Gates, George G. 1962
BR to 1962
Gellner, Ernest **6** 1959-62
Encl: Victor Gollancz, Ltd.
(Hilary Rubinstein) to
BR **2** 1959
BR to **4** 1959-64
NJ to 1962
BR to Victor Gollancz, Ltd.
(Hilary Rubinstein) 1959
General Press Cutting Associa-
tion Ltd. (A. P. Phillips) to
AY 1962
AY to 1962
PW to 1966
Genesis (David Giannini) 1968
Gente (Giampiero Rolandi) ... 1964
To RS 1964
RS to 1964
Gerassi, John, to RS 1965
RS to 1965
Ghanian Times, RS to 1966
Ghose, P. K. 1963
Encl: clippings
BR to 1963
Gianni, Ernesto 1967
DN to 1967
Ginsberg, Robert **2** 1967-9
Encl.
CF to 1967
CWK Gleerup .... n.d.
Göktürk, Aksit 1963
BR to 1963
The Golden Horn (Richard
Reid) 1964
To RS 1964
RS to **2** 1964
Goldstein, Cynthia H.,
to BRPF 1965
RS to 1965

Victor Gollancz, Ltd. (Victor Gollancz, Susan Davies, James MacGibbon) 1953
To RS **3** 1964-7
BR to (ms. of l. and blurb) 1966
RS to 1966
Goodwin Press (Hugh Brock) to CF 1967
CF to (Mr. Cooke) **2** ... 1965-6
CF to (Hugh Brock) **3** ... 1967-8
PW to (Cooke) 1966
Encl.
Göpel, Wilfried 1937
Gordon, Jeffrey Sheppard, BR to 1963
Gordon Press Ltd. (Mr. Cook), PW to 1966
Göteborgs-Tidningen (Sven Carlson) 1969
Gottesman, Albert, to RS 1964
Gould, James A. **2** 1966
BR to **3** 1964-6
Granada TV Network Ltd. (Ann E. G. Suudi, Milton Shulman) **3** 1961-2
Encl.
BR to **2** 1961-2
Graves, Stewart 1967
Encl.
CF to 1967
Green River Community College (Louis Wildman) 1967
CF to 1967
Griffin, Jr., C. W. **2** 1966-7
Encl: review of *Auto.*, I
RS to 1966
Gross, Ralph 1969
Grotta, Daniel Taylor 1968
Grove Press (Barney Rosset, Harry Beaverman) to RS **2** 1967
RS to 1967
The Guardian (W. Hartford Tomes *et al.*) **9** 1962-8
To Ken Coates .... n.d.
To Pat Pottle 1963
To CF **6** 1963-70
To G. Coggan 1966
To RS **3** 1964-6
To Quintin Hoare and RS 1966
AY to 1962
BR to **3** 1962-4
CF to **3** 1963-9
RS to **2** 1966
PW to 1969
Guinea Press Ltd. (Kofi Badu) 1965
Gujarat University (K. D. Pundyu) 1963

H

Haagsche Post (S. F. Vanoss) 1924
Haaretz, CF to 1970
Haddow, Alex 1962
Encl: Mary Tibaldi Chiese to BR 1962
Hakumon Herald (Kenji Nakadate, Shigeo Uchida) **2** 1963-6
BR to **2** 1965-6
Paul Hamlyn Publishers to RS 1964
RS to 1964
The Hammersmith Bookshop Ltd. (Ronald Gray) 1964
BR to 1964
The Hand & Flower Press
Encl: royalty s.
The Hansard Society (Stephen King-Hall) 1955
Carl Hanser Verlag (Michael Krüger) to RS 1967
RS to 1967
Haravgi (Tefkros Anthias) **2** 1962-5
Encl: questionnaire
BR to **2** 1962-9
PW to 1966
Harcourt, Brace and Co., Inc. (Jeannette E. Hopkins, Fred Wieck, Mary Walling) **3** ... 1965
Encl: news release
BR to 1962
Harper & Brothers (Cass Canfield) 1924

Harper & Row, Publishers (Jeannette Hopkins, Richard B. McAdoo, Emily T. Ward, M. S. Wyeth, Jr.) **5** 1964-5
(McAdoo's l. removed from Russell's library copy of Anatol Rapoport's *Strategy and Conscience* [New York, 1964])
To RS **3** 1964-7
RS to **4** 1964-5
Harper's Magazine (John Fischer), BR to 1963
George G. Harrap & Co. (C. R. Butterworth) 1967
(Peter M. Sommer) to RSt. **3** 1968
RSt. to **4** 1968
Harrison, Craig R. 1962
BR to 1962
Harrod, Roy **2** 1963-8
Encl: article
BR to 1963
CF to 1968
Harrow Technical College, Students Union (Roger Perry, Alison Ford) 1966
To CF 1967
CF to 1966
Rupert Hart-Davis Ltd. (Suzanne Kinberg) to BRPF 1965
Harvard University Press (Max Hall) to RS 1967
Haslem Hazeh, CF to 1970
Hassan, Riffat 1966
Hearst Magazines (royalty s.) 1961
Heibonsha Ltd. (Jinze Yokoi) to RS 1967
William Heinemann Ltd. Publishers (William Holden) **2** 1962-4
Encl: invitation
BR to 1962
Heinemann Educational Books Ltd. (Alan Hill) 1965
Heipp, Günther **21** 1962-9
Encl: photos of Heipp and A. Schweitzer, booklets, articles, re *Es geht ums Leben!*
BR to **4** 1963-6
CE to **2** 1964
RS to 1967
CF to **3** 1968-9
Help (Richard A. Exley) to BRPF 1968
Hemisphere (R. J. Meguire) **2** 1963
To RS 1963
BR to 1963
RS to 1963
Henderson, Dorothy .... n.d.
To BRPF 1964
BR to **2** 1964
Hepp, Maylon H. 1963
Heppner, Sam, RS to 1964
Heumann, Rainer 1969
Hick, John H. 1968
CF to 1968
Hildrath, Peter 1966
RS to 1966
Hilton, Alice **10** 1962-8
To RS **5** 1964-5
Encl: chap. of a book, invitation, newsl., publisher-author agreement
AY to **2** 1963
RS to **3** 1964-5
BR to 1967
CF to 1968
PW to 1968
Encl: note from PW to CF
The Hindu (S. Suhramin?) to RS? .... n.d.
Hipp, H. Rüdiger, to RS 1963
RS to 1963
Hirschsprung, Herbert, BR to 1966
Hitaka, Ikki 1961
BR to 1961
Hodder and Stoughton Ltd. (Mrs. J. Martin) **2** 1968
BR to 1968
CF to 1968
Hodes, Aubrey **6** 1962-8
To RS **3** 1963-6
Peter Janson-Smith Ltd. (Catherine Perry) to BR (at Hodes's request) 1968

BR to **4** 1952-6
RS to **2** 1963-6
CF to **2** 1968
Encl: CF to Peter Janson-Smith Ltd. (Catherine Perry) 1968
Hofbauer, Imre **2** 1964-5
Encl.
RS to 1964
Hoffman, Randall W. 1958
BR to 1958
Hofheinz, Engelbert, to
RS **2** 1964
To Clara Urquhart 1964
RS to **2** 1964
The Hogarth Press Ltd.
Encl: royalty s., Patricia Spence to The Hogarth Press Ltd. 1965
Holiday (Arnold Ehrlich) 1962
Holt, Rinehart and Winston, Inc. (Linda C. Dickter, Charlotte L. Mayerson) **2** 1964-7
Encl: ts. of BR's "Can We Afford to Keep Open Minds?"
CF to **3** 1965
RS to 1967
Johns Hopkins University (Michael Karnow) 1967
Encl: royalty s.
Horizon Press (Ben Rae-burn) 1967
CF to 1967
Horowitz, David **2** 1964
To ER 1967
To RS **2** 1964
Encl: David Horowitz to Prof. O'Brien .... n.d.
City of Westminster to David Horowitz 1965
David Horowitz to Mr. Deutsch 1965
BR to **3** 1963-7
RS? to 1964
PW to 1965
CF? to **5** 1967
The Hosei Times (Kohei Amano) 1963
BR to 1963
Howard, D.L. 1963
BR to 1963
Hsinhua News Agency to
AY **2** 1962
PW to 1970
Hull Socialist Review (T.W. Fawthrop) 1966
RS to 1966
CF to **2** 1968-9
The Humanist (John McClaughry, Judith Yeldon, *et al.*) **4** 1959-65
Encl: article
BR to 1959
RS to **2** 1964-5
Humanist Broadcasting Council (Kit Mouat) **2** 1963
BR to **2** 1963
Humanistic Judaism (Sherwin T. Wine, Robert Goren and Marilyn Rosenthal) 1967
Encl.
Hungarian Literary Gazette (George Faludy) 1957
The Hutchinson Publishing Group (Harold Harris) to RS 1967
Hynes, Sam L. **2** 1953-4

I

The Illustrated Weekly of India (A. S. Raman) **9** 1964-6
To RS **2** 1965-6
Encl: royalty s.
BR to 1964
RS to **4** 1964-6
PW to **2** 1965-6
Encl: BR's "Answers to Questionnaire Concerning the Future of the United Nations"
L'Illustré (Ch. Abt) 1962
Impact of Science of Society (Bruno Friedman) 1970
CF to 1970
L'Incontro, RS to 1965
India Canada Association (Rao Nanduri) 1969
India International (Ram Aurangebadkar) 1968
The Indian Express (Sitanshu

Das) 1969
PW to 1969
Indian Institute of Technology Mathematics Club (D. S. Tomer) 1968
Indus Times (M. B. Naqvi) 1963
CE to 1963
Information (Preban Dabelsteen) to RS 1965
RS to 1965
The Information Service, CF to 1969
Inheritance (John Larke) to RS 1966
Encl.
RS to 1966
PW to 1966
Insight (Peter L. James) ...... n.d.
Institute for the Unity of Science (Alice Atamian) 1955
The Institute of Radio Engineers Transactions on Electronic Computers (T. C. Bartee) ... 1962
Instituto de Investigaciones de la "Teoria de la Cosmovision" (Estaban Lisa) 1962
Encl: booklet
BR to 1962
Intelligence: The Mensa Journal (Tony Buzań) 1967
Encl: issues of journal
Inter Press Service (Hernán Rodríguez) 1966
To ID 1966
ID to 1966
RS to 1966
Intercom (David H. Jinno) to BRPF 1966
PW to 1966
Intercontinental Press (Joseph Hansen) to CF 1970
CF to 1970
International Centre, 25th Anniversary Committee (B. Abhyankar) **2** 1963
Encl.
BR to **3** 1963-4
International House (Steven Klinger) 1968
International Peace/Disarmament Directory (Lloyd Wilkie) ... 1964
BR to 1964
International P.E.N. (David Carver *et al.*) **9** 1962-9
To CE 1963
Encl: announcements, invitations, booklets (*P.E.N. 1921-1971; The Project for a new English Centre*), membership list, etc.
CE to 1963
BR to 1966
International Press Cutting Bureau (Pauline J. Dunstone) to AY 1962
AY to 1962
PW to **2** 1966-7
International Publishers (James S. Allen), BR to **2** 1963-4
International Publishing Corporation Ltd. (Cecil H. King, Brian Hayes) **2** ... 1964-9
International Socialist Journal (John Halliday), RS? to 1966
International Union of Chemical, Oil & Allied Workers Unions (Pal Forgacs) to BRPF 1968
CF to 1968
International Year Book & Statesmen's Who's Who **2** .. 1963
Internationaler Pressedienst (Gerda Dehnke) 1967
Interpress (George Delf), BR to 1966
Interstate (J. Lynton Jones, Ian G. Hopwood) **2** 1967
To RSt. **5** 1968
Encl: ts. of "Bertrand Russell on Vietnam"
RSt. **6** 1967-8
CF to 1968
Irish Democrat (C. Desmond Greaves) 1955
Encl: draft of l. to *The Manchester Guardian*
The Irish Times (C. R. Mullock) to CF 1969
Encl: clipping
BR to 1964

CF to **3** 1964-9
Encl: "Proposed Correction for Publication in the Irish Times"
Islamia College Magazine (Khwaja Javed Ahmed) 1966
RS to 1966
Israel Imperial News, BR to ... 1968
Issues (Norton Mezvinsky) to CF 1967
Istituto Italiano d'Arti Grafiche to RS 1967
Italian Televisione Corporation 1967
Iwanami Shoten, Publishers (Genzaburo Yoshino, Sumie Mishima) **6** 1961-2
Encl: questionnaires
BR to **3** 1961-4
RS to 1967
Iyengar, B. V. S. 1963
Encl: copy of *I Speak to You Through Letters*
Izvestia (V. Matveev, M. Mikharlov) 1962
To RS 1964
BR to 1962
RS to **2** 1964-6
Jon Tinker to 1962

J

Jaafari, Mohamad Taghi **2** 1963-4
BR to **3** 1963-4
Jaca Book (Laura Geronazzo) to BRPF 1968
RSt. to 1968
Janata, RS to **2** 1966
Japan Broadcasting Corporation (Elizabeth Snowden, Kazuto Yoshida) **2** 1962-6
CF to 1966
Japan Council Against Atomic and Hydrogen Bombs (Kaoru Yasui) 1961
ER to 1961
Japan Information Centre of Bertrand Russell Peace Foundation (Shigetoshi Iwamatsu) **32** 1962-9
To CF **3** 1967
To RSt. 1967
Encl: clippings, pamphlets
BR to **17** 1962-9
RS to 1966
RSt. to **23** 1967
CF to **3** 1968-9
Encl: s. by BR
Jardi, Enric 1963
BR to 1963
Jerusalem Post, CF to 1970
Jeune Afrique (Béchir Ben Yamed) 1966
RS to 1966
Jewish Currents (Morris U. Schappes) 1964
RS to 1964
Jewish Daily Forward (David Liberson) **2** 1964
RS to 1964
CF to 1965
Jewish Youth Organisations Emergency Committee 1967
John O'Gauntlet (Joseph Miller) 1965
To PW 1965
PW to 1965
Johnson, Paul 1968
Jones, Martin, and Wood, Clive 1963
Encl: interview with BR
BR to 1963
Jones, Peter Alan **2** 1962-3
BR to **2** 1962-3
Jornal Santa Cruz (Carlos Alberto Dória) to BRPF ... 1967
Encl.
RS to 1967
Michael Joseph Ltd. (Raleigh Trevelyan, P.H. Hebdon) .. 1966
To RS 1967
The Journal of Human Relations (Don Werkheiser) 1968
Journal of Paraphysics (Benson Herbert) 1968
Journal of Philosophy, RS to 1966
The Jr. Art Gallery (Robert

O. White) 1964
Dr. W. Junk Publishers 1963
BR to 2 1963-4
Juventud Rebelde (Guillermo Cabrera) 2 1967
Encl: questionnaire
CF to 1967
Jyoti (G. Daxina Murthy) 1969

K

Kamel, Michel 1967
Kapluck, Manfred 1966
BR to 1966
Karbø, Lars 1967
CF to 1967
Karia, S.B. 3 1962-7
Encl: clippings, greeting c.
BR to 1962
Kaskeline Film (Wolfgang Kaskeline) 1958
BR to 1958
Katouzian, M.A. 1964
RS to 1964
Kaufmann, George 1919
Encl: l. to Allen & Unwin 1919
Kedzierski, J.Z., BR to 1963
Kegan Paul, Trench, Trubner & Co., Ltd. 1924
Kelly's Handbook (D.H. Springer) 3 1968-9
Encl.
Kendall, Ian 1962
Kerkar, D.S. 1969
Kessler, John J. 1962
BR to 1962
Khan, Ismat Ullah 1968
King (Edward J. Simon) 1966
CF to 1966
King, Mary L. 1966
BR to 1966
Allan King Associates (Richard Leiterman) 2 1962-5
BR to 1962
PW to 1965
RS to 1965
Kingsway (James T. Williams) 1967
RSt. to 1967
Kingswood School (Neal J. Clough) 1962
BR to 1963
Kinsey, Tom, to CF and AY 2 .... [1962]
Encl: H. Christen to Tom Kinsey 1963
clippings, trans.
CF to 1963
Encl: testimonial for Kinsey by BR
Kipanta, N.E. 1963
Encl: ms.
BR to 1963
KLAC Radio Station (Terry Martin) 1966
Klaf, Franklin S., BR to 1963
Kleene, S.C., to RS 1966
RS to 1966
Knape, Wolfgang 1968
Knight, Frida, to CF 1969
Alfred A. Knopf Inc. (Ashbel Green) to RS 1967
PW to 1969
Knorr, Lorenz 1969
Encl: greeting cs.
BR to 1964
CF to 1969
Kobun Sha Ltd. (royalty s.) 1966
Kodansha Ltd. (Kanichi Hayashi) 1970
CF to 1970
The Kojitaetor (David Cowell) 1967
Encl.
Kolokon (R.C. Coward) 1965
To RS 1965
RS to 1965
Konkret (Gitta Goldeer) 2 .. 1963-9
BR's notes re drafting of s. 1963
Korczyn, Amos 1963
BR to 1963
Körner, Stefan, and Shepherdson, ? 1962
BR to 1962
KPFA (A Pacifica Station) (Elsa Knight Thompson,

Michael Korman) **2** 1962-9
KPFK (A Pacifica Station)
(Art Wadsworth) 1962
To RS **6** 1962-3
Encl: KPFK (Art Wadsworth) to Schools for Nonviolence (Committee of 100), radio schedules
RS to **7** 1962-3
BR to (Ben Sweet) 1966
Krüger, Lorenz 1968
Encl.
CF to 1968
Kucera, Vladimir, BR to 1963
The Kukje Shin Bo (Chong Sick Oh) 1963
CF to 1963
Kultur & Gesellschaft (Eugen Weisenseel) to RS 1964
RS to **3** 1964
Kultura (Josef Kodflac) .... n.d.
Kumlehn, Jurgen 1969
BR to 1969
Kurzweil, Z. E. 1969
Encl: article on BR's educational theory
Kyodo News Service
(Takeo Komatsu, Ikuo Kanmuri) **4** 1962-4
BR to 1962
CF to **2** 1966
RS to 1966
The Kyunghyang Shinmoon (Lee Joon-Ku) **2** 1964
Encl.
RS to **2** 1964-5

L

Labour Daily Provisional Founders Council (Ernest Kay) 1965
Encl.
To PW 1965
PW to **2** 1965
Labour Monthly (R. Palme Dutt) 1962
To CF 1970
BR to 1962
RS to 1964
Labour's Voice (Frank Allaun),
BR to 1964
Ladies' Own Weekly (Hidenori Sakurai) 1963
Encl: questionnaire
CF to 1963
The Lady Bessborough Press (Richard Spafford, Bruce Ferguson) 1970
Lake House Bookshop 1969
Lambert, Tom 1965
Langridge, Derek **2** 1966
BR to 1966
Laning, J. S. 1963
Harold Laski Institute of Political Science (P. G. Mavalankar) 1964
BR to 1964
Gius. Laterza & Figli (Enrico Mistretta) 1969
Le Flufy?, F. St. J. 1962
Lehmann, Jerry 1962
Lemkow, Tutte 1966
BR to **2** 1965-6
Lens, Sidney 1963
BR to **3** 1963
Leopardess (Roger W. Higgins) 1965
PW to 1965
Lev, Grigori Mikhailovich ... 1966
BR to 1966
Libby, Gary Russell 1967
BR to 1963
CF to 1967
The Liberal Democrat (Marshall Windmiller) **2** .. 1963
BR to 1963
Liberal Studies Publications Ltd. (G. H. Dickinson) 1963
BR to 1963
Liberation (James Forest, Dave Dellinger, Staughton Lynd) **2** 1963-6
To CF 1964
To RS **6** 1966
To PW 1967
Encl: Richard Gilpin to Gabrielle Edgcomb 1966
CF to 1964
BR to **3** 1965-6

RS to **7** 1966
PW to **3** 1966-7
Liberator (Richard Gibson) ... 1967
BR to 1963
Librairie Larousse (Henriette Dargnies) 1965
RS to 1965
Limbo (Murray Morton) **2** .. 1963-4
To NJ 1963
Encl: questionnaire
NJ to 1963
BR to **2** 1964
Lincolnshire Echo (G. F. Morton) 1964
Lindholm, Arthur W. **2** .. 1964-6
Encl: clipping
BR to 1964
RS to 1964
Lindner, Robert **2** 1952
Lindquist, Hans 1968
BR to 1968
Link (Iqbal Singh) 1962
BR to 1962
Lions Club, Chittagong (B. A. Hawmid) 1963
Literaria (Shuja Nawaz) 1967
RSt. to 1967
Literary Gazette (Leontev) 1962
Encl.
The Literary Guide (Frederick Watts) 1947
Literaturnoe Nasledstvo (G. A. Mendelevich) .... n.d.
Re BR's l. to Gorky
Little, Robert **11** 1962-5
To RS 1962
To CF 1963
Encl: *Reader's Digest* to Robert Little 1962
Little to *Reader's Digest* 1962
poems
BR to **6** 1962-4
CF to **2** 1963
RS to **3** 1962-5
Little, Brown and Company, to BR **5** 1965-9
PW to 1965
RS to **2** 1965
Liveright Publishing Corporation (Arthur Pell, Samuel B. Melner) **8** 1964-70
BR to **2** 1966-8
CF to 1969
Liverpool Daily & Echo (John Pugh) 1969
Living Books Incorporated (invoice) 1966
Locke, Elsie, to Secretary of the Committee of 100 1962
Locken, John 1969
CF to 1969
Lokkalyan (Jeewan Kirloskar) 1968
Lomas, Charles W., to CF **2** 1968
To Barry Feinberg 1968
CF to **2** 1968
Barry Feinberg to 1968
London Weekend Television (Joe Steeples) 1970
Longanesi & C. (Mario Monti) to CF 1968
CF to 1968
Longmans, Green & Co. Ltd. (Michael Hoare) 1967
Look (Leo Rosten, Flora Lewis, Leonard Rubin) **3** 1962-8
To RS 1967
BR to **2** 1962-6
CF to **3** 1966-8
Lorrimer Publishing (Andrew Sinclair) .... 1968?
Encl: poem
Los Angeles Times (Majorie Kirincic, Robert C. Toth) .. 1966
To RS 1964
BR to 1964
RS to **2** 1964-6
Loubeh, Jose Martins Costa, to BRPF 1967
RSt. to 1968
Love Inc. [then *Gandalf's Garden*] (Muz Murray, J. Shelley) **2** 1967-8
To RSt. **2** 1967
Encl.
RSt. to **3** 1967
Lowell-Adams House Printers

(Stephen M. Savage) 1965
PW to 1965
Lud (Juraj Alner and Anton Korman) 1968
Lumea (George Ivascu), RS to 1964
Lyngstad, Sverre 1965
Encl: extracts from BR l. of 1957
PW to 1965
Lyons, Leonard 1962
Encl: clippings
Lyttle, Bradford, to CF 1962
Encl: Lyttle to *Peace News* (Hugh Brock) .... 1963?
CF to **2** 1962-3

M

Maariv (S. Rosenfield, Geula Cohen, J. Finklestone) **2** 1965-6
BR to 1963
RS to **2** 1963-5
PW to 1966
Mace, Alec 1962
BR to 1963
MacGibbon & Kee Ltd. (Susan Herbert) 1967
BR to 1967
Macleod, Joseph 1967
CF to 1967
The Macmillan Company, (Kenneth Heuer, Anne Bailey, John W. Blanpied, *et al.*) **8** 1962-7
To CF **3** 1963-4
To RS **3** 1964-7
Encl: questionnaire
BR to **2** 1962
CF to **3** 1963-9
RS to **2** 1964-5
Encl: BR's foreword and preface to Cook's *The Warfare State* and a list of journals
Madden, Edward H. 1962
Encl.
BR to 1962
Magalhães, Edson 1968
Magee, Bryan 1966
To CF 1967
CF to **3** 1966-7
John Magee Inc. (John Magee) 1962
The Mainichi Newspapers (Masako Saito, Takuo Hayashi) **3** 1961-70
To RS 1965
RS to 1962
CF to 1970
Mainstream (D.R. Goyal, Vimla Shamlal) **4** 1964-5
To RS 1964
RS to **3** 1965
Makashay, Roberta 1962
BR to 1962
Maladinsky, Hans-Peter 1965
PW to 1965
Maltas, D. 1967
CF to 1967
Man (Arthur Brackman) **2** 1962-3
Encl.
BR to **3** 1962-3
RS to 1964
Man and Society (Venetia Newall) **2** 1962
Manabtantri (Anil Banerjee), BR to 1963
Management Science (Martin K. Starr) 1967
Manamperi, C. C., and Fernando, G. M. D. 1967
CF to 1968
Manchester Guardian & Evening News (T. E. Henry *et al.*) **5** 1964-5
RS to **2** 1964-5
Manchete (Fernando Sabino) to RS 1965
To PW 1965
PW to 1965
Manila Chronicle, RS to 1966
Manutiuspresse, RS to 1964
Margolis, Joseph 1967
Encl: contract to reprint
CF to 1967
Mark Twain Journal (Cyril Clemens) **21** 1962-8
To CF 1968

Encl.
BR to **10** 1962-6
RS to 1965
CF to **6** 1966-8
PW to 1968
Marshall, Philip, to RS 1963
Marxism Today (James
Klugmann), CF to 1969
Mashriq (Marion A.
Malik) 1965
To RS 1965
RS to **2** 1965
Maspero, François, to RS 1967
The Massachusetts Review
(John Hicks) 1965
RS to 1965
Mattessich, Richard 1965
PW to 1965
Mavalankar, P. G. 1952
Mayr, Alfred 1965
RS to 1965
McClelland and Stewart Limited
(Marian Tilden) 1963
Encl: Tilden to *Saturday*
Evening Post 1963
Saturday Evening Post to
McClelland 1963
CE to 1963
CF to 1963
McDowell, Richard E. 1966
CF to 1967
McGill Journal of Education
(Margaret Gillett) 1969
McGraw-Hill Book Co.
(Sonia Levinthal) 1962
(Peter Buckman) to RS 1967
BR to 1962
Medlock, Julie **5** .... n.d.
To BR and ER **45** 1962-9
To RS .... [1962]
To PW 1965
Encl: clippings, Medlock to
M. S. Arnoni 1961
To *New York Times* **2** 1967
To President Kennedy 1963
To Dean Rusk 1963
To *The Sun* 1967
To *Sunday Times* 1967
To *New York Herald Tribune*
and *Washington Post* 1966
To Kenneth Lee and Gerry
Hunnius 1967
To *Time* 1967
Accra Assembly (F. E. Boaten)
to Arthur Lall 1963
Accra Assembly (F. E.
Boaten) to BR 1965
BR to **7** 1962-6
ER to .... n.d.
NJ 1962
Encl: Accra Assembly (F.E.
Boaten), BR to 1963
Mehta, Ved, BR to 1961
Meitner-Graf, Lotte 1967
BR to **2** 1967
CF to 1969
Mentor Books, CF to 1969
Mercer, Dilys 1962
The Merlin Press Ltd. (Harry
Braverman and Richard
Seaver) 1967
(M. W. Eve) to Erik
Nyblom **2** 1967
Methuen & Co. Ltd. (Tessa
C. Harrow) 1967
BR to 1967
Miami Times, RS to 1966
Middle East Coexistence
(Shalom ben Benjamin) .... n.d.
Encl.
The Militant (Karolyn
Kerry, Bev Scott, T.
O'Flaherty) **4** 1966-9
(Sam Gordon) to Ken Coates
and CF **2** 1968-9
Mill Newsletter (John M.
Robson) 1965
PW to 1965
Milliyet .... n.d.
Ming Pao Daily News (Louis
Cha) **3** 1965
Encl: clipping
PW to **2** 1965
The Minority of One (M. S.
Arnoni) **7** 1961-3
To CF 1963
To RS **2** 1963
Encl: clippings, ls. between
TMO and Karl E. Korn
BR to **13** 1963-5

CF to **3** 1963
Bill Kaye to **9** 1963-4
RS to 1964
Encl: l. from Korn to BR, l. from RS to Korn
The Mission (M. M. Abdullah) **2** 1965-6
RS to 1965
Misuzu Shobo Publishing Co. (Toshito Obi) **2** 1968
CF to **3** 1968-9
Mitchell, M. 1967
CF to 1967
Mitre (Gwyn Charles Pritchard) 1966
PW to 1966
Moderator (Meredith Ross) 1965
Encl.
RS to 1965
Modern Welsh Publications Ltd. (D. Ben. Rees) 1963
BR to 1963
Arnoldo Monadori Editore (Donatella Ciapessoni) to RS **2** 1967
Le Monde and *Le Monde Diplomatique* (F. Honti *et al.*) **2** 1961-8
To RS .... [1966]
ER to 1961
RS to **2** 1966
PW to **2** 1966
BR to **2** 1968
CF to 1968
The Monist (Eugene Freeman) **6** 1963-5
BR to **6** 1963-5
Encl. offprint (with photo) by P.A. Schilpp
Monocle (Richard Goldberg) 1968
Encl: "Why I Sold Out" questionnaire
Montapert, Alfred A. 1965
BR to 1965
Monthly Review (Leo Huberman *et al.*) **2** 1966-7
To RS **3** 1965-6
To RSt. 1966
To PW 1966
Encl: l. to *Monthly Review* (Paul Sweezy)
PW to 1965
RS to **2** 1965-6
RSt. to 1966
The Montreal Star (Boyce Richardson) 1963
(W. Reinke) to RS 1963
Encl: clippings
RS to **2** 1963-4
Moore, Edward C. 1963
BR to 1963
Morning News (Yehia M. Syed *et al.*) **3** 1962-8
To CF **7** 1962-3
To RS **6** 1963-5
To PW **5** 1966-7
Encl: clippings, *Morning News* to The Muslim Commercial Bank Ltd 1963
CF to **8** 1962-8
RS to **5** 1963-8
PW to **9** 1966-7
Morning Star [see also *Daily Worker*] (George Matthews, W. Brooks) 1967
To RS 1967
PW to 1967
CF to **2** 1967-9
Morrison, David 1905
Re a review for *Mind*
Moser, Roger, to DN 1968
Encl: essay
Muguerza, Javier, BR to 1969
Mukhopadhyay, Santanu 1969
CF to 1969
Munshi, Vijay, CF to 1967
Munzi, Liliana 1963
BR to 1963
CE to 1963
Murfee, J. M. 1969
CF to 1969
Murthi, V. V. Ramana **4** 1962-8
To RS 1963-6
Encl: articles
BR to **5** 1962-8
RS to **4** 1963-6
Musacchio, Enrico 1965
Encl.
RS to 1965

N

El Nacionel (Carlos A. Echanove), ER to 1964
Nar, R. B. 1968
CF to 1968
Narmic (Fay Knopp) to
PW 1969
PW to 1970
Nash, Kevin C., and Lambert, John 1969
CF to 1969
The Nation (C. Massingham), BR to 1921
The Nation (Carey McWilliams, Phil Kerby, *et al.*) **3** 1963-4
To David Horowitz 1966
To RS 1966
Encl: tear sheets
BR to **6** 1963-6
David Horowitz to 1966
RS to **7** 1963-6
National Guardian (Robert Joyce, Cedric Belfrage, Russ Nixon, James Aronson, *et al.*) **4** 1956-66
Encl: Belfrage's interview with BR (1956)
To Karen Wald 1967
BR to **4** 1964-7
RS to **3** 1966
PW to 1966
RSt. to 1967
National Insider (Robert Borzello) to PW 2 1967
PW to 1967
The National Institute of Adult Education (E. M. Hutchinson) 1955
National Lawyers Guild (Benjamin Dreyfus, Barbara Kahn, Phyllis M. Patterson) 2 1963-4
To RS 1964
BR to 2 1963-4
RS to 1964
National Secular Society (William McIlroy *et al.*) **18** 1964-9
BR to 2 1964-8
PW to 1965
RS to **4** 1965-6
CF to **3** 1969
Nationalist, RS to 1966
Nation's Business (William Boyd Craig) 1927
Nature (John Maddox) 1969
Encl.
Nauka i Religia (B. Grigoryan) 1964
BR to 1964
Nava-Kala (S. Bissoondoyal) 1964
BR to 1964
Naya Desh (G. Q. Joarder) 1964
BR to 1964
Naya Payam (Muhammed Akram and Mukhtar Abbas) 1966
RS to 1966
NBC (Romney Wheeler, A. John Graves, Arthur Barron) **3** 1952-62
Encl: NBC (Davidson Taylor) to Wheeler, clippings re interview
NBC News (William R. McAndrews) 1968
NBC Today Show (Hugh Downs) 1969
CF to 1969
N.D.R.A.R.D. West German Television Network (Paul Anderson) 1968
Neelkanth: Kanpur University Magazine (R. S. Tandon) ... 1969
Negelha, Jonas, CF to 1969
Nehru Darshan (V. M. Chatgopakar) 1964
BR to 1964
Jawaharlal Nehru Souvenir Committee (Satish Chander) 1964
Neilson, Robert 1963
Thomas Nelson & Sons (E. M. Milne) 1966
CF to 1966
Nemenzo, Jr., Francisco, CF to **2** 1967
Népszabadság (Imre Patkó) ... 1965
CF to 1965

Neues Deutschland (Franz Krahl) 1964
Neutralität (Paul Ignaz Vogel) 1966
RS to 1966
Die Neuwe Linie (G. van den Boomen) 1963
BR to 1963
New American Library (Oliver Watson), to ER 1965
PW to 1965
New Generation (Glenys Phillips, Anthony P. M. Coxon) 1963
To CF .... n.d.
BR to 1963
The New Leader (Myron Kolatch) 1962
Encl: issue of *Kaigai Hyoron Sha*
CF to 1970
BR to (Daniel James) 1952
New Left Review (Perry Anderson) 1962
NJ to 1962
CF to (David Fernbach) ... 1969
The New Orient (Synd Hossain) 1924
The New Republic (Gilbert Harrison, Christopher Jencks, James Ridgeway) 1958
To RS **2** 1963
BR to **3** 1958-63
RS to **5** 1963-6
New Scientist (Peter Williams, Ian F. H. Low) **4** 1964-9
RS to 1964
PW to 1965
CF to 1967
New Society to PW 1967
RS to 1967
New South Wales Peace Committee for International Co-operation and Disarmament (A. D. Brand) 1963
Encl: press release
New Statesman (John Freeman, Norman MacKenzie, *et al.*) **12** 1958-64
To RS **2** 1962-6
To CF **2** 1963-6
To PW 1964
Encl: questionnaire
BR to **4** 1962-8
RS to **3** 1962-5
CE to 1963
CF to 1963-5
PW to **6** 1964-8
Peter Limqueco to 1967
Janet Viney to 1967
New Statesman and Nation (Kingsley Martin), re BR and preventive war with Russia:
Coward, Chance & Co. (L. P. Tylor) to BR **2** 1951
Coward, Chance & Co. to *New Statesman and Nation* (Martin) 1951
New Statesman and Nation (Martin) to Coward, Chance and Co. 1951
New World Review (Jessica Smith) to BRPF 1965
To RS 1965
RS to 1965
New York Herald Tribune (Dwight E. Sargent) **2** 1963-6
To RS 1963
Encl: tear sheets
BR to 1963
Bill Kaye to 1964
RS to **3** 1964
New York Post (note from Sarah Rollitts, tear sheets) 1961
New York Times (Heather Bradley, Anthony Lewis, *et al.*) **12** 1962-9
To RS **7** 1965-7
To PW **3** 1966
Encl: notifications of ls. not published, royalty ss., questionnaires
CE to **2** 1963
CF to 1965
RS to **5** 1965-7
PW to 1966
BR to **2** 1967-70
New Zealand Listener (M. H. Holcroft) to RS 1964
New Zealand Weekly News (Tony Reid) 1967

Newchapel Observatory (David Howell Trowsdale) 1968
Encl.
Newman, Fred 1968
CF to 1968
Newman, James R. **3** 1962-3
To RS 1963
BR to **6** 1962-3
RS to 1963
Newman, Sol and Edith .... n.d.
Encl: poems
News Chronicle (Brenda A. Ackland) 1956
Encl: E. M. Johnston to *News Chronicle* 1956
Peter Bisset to BR 1956
Elizabeth M. Clark to BR 1956
E. T. Eames to BR 1956
J. Lezarson to BR 1956
Newsman's Gadfly (Walter Gormly) (copies of newsl.) 1963-4
BR to 1964
Newstat, Freeman 1961
Newsweek (Eldon Griffiths, Joan Wharton, Edwin Diamond) **5** 1962-9
Encl: tear sheets
BR to **2** 1962
RS to 1966
Newthink Student Magazine to BRPF **2** 1968
Encl.
Newton-John, Irene **3** 1968-9
Re Born-Einstein ls.
BR to 1968
CF to 1969
Nicolau, Edmund 1966
BR to 1966
NIFA Services (Jeanne Langi) to Ken Coates 1969
CF to 1969
Nivat, Georges 1970
Norddeutscher Rundfunk Hamburg (Thilo Koch, K.-H. Wocker) **2** 1958-67
Encl: clippings re 1958 interview, l. from Karl Stemmer to BR
Norden, Heinz **2** 1967
CF to 1967
The North American Review (Philip R. Marshall) 1963
The Northern Review (Huw Lawrence) 1969
CF to 1969
W.W. Norton & Co. Inc. (Nancy Hagaman, John Benedict, Tanya E. Mairs) 1968
To RS **2** 1964
Encl: W.W. Norton & Co. Inc. (Nancy Hagaman) to Longmans, Green & Co. 1964
W.W. Norton & Co. Inc. (Tanya E. Mairs) to Longmans, Green & Co. 1968
royalty ss.
RS to **2** 1964
CF to 1968
Nott, Kathleen 1963
Nottingham Evening Post (James Brennan) 1964
Encl: clipping
Nouvelle École (Alain de Benoist) to PW 1970
PW to 1970
Nova (Dom Moraes, Peter Crookston) 1967
To ER 1969
To CF 1967
CF to **3** 1967-9
Novaia i Noveishaia Istoria (A. Narochnitski) 1965
BR to 1966
Novosti Press Agency (Natasha Yakovleva, Boris Burkov) **2** 1964
PW to (Iris Smith) 1966
Novy Mir Literary Journal (Alexander Tvardovsky), BR to 1969
Nuclear Tree (Michael Faulkner) 1965
HR to 1965
The Nucleus (M. Jameel) 1966
CF to 1966
La Nuova Italia Editrice 1966

(Mario Casalini) to RS 1968
Encl.
RS to 1966
CF to 1968
Nuqoosh (Mohammad Tufail) 1963
Encl.
CF to 1963
Nymphs International (K. Srihari Rao, Sri Samson Ramakrishniah) **2** 1965-6
PW to 1965

O

Obradovitch, Dusanka 1962
The E.D. O'Brien Organization (Jack Smeaton, E. D. O'Brien) **3** 1966
BR to **2** 1966
The Observer (David Astor, Charles Davy, Terence Kilmartin *et al.*) **14** 1962-8
To RS **7** 1962-4
To BR and ER 1967
To CF **3** 1970
Encl: B. J. Benjamin to *The Observer* 1968
royalty ss., clippings
BR to **7** 1962-8
Encl: s.
PW to 1969
CF to **2** 1970
Bill Kaye to 1964
The Observer Colour Magazine (John Thomson), CF to 1968
The Observer Magazine (Geraldine Wheeler) 1969
CF to 1969
Obunsha Co. Ltd. **4** 1963-9
To CF **2** 1964-5
Encl: royalty s.
BR to 1963
CF to **2** 1963-4
HR to 1965
Odin, Roger **2** 1965
RS to 1965
Ogden, F. K. 1967
BR to 1968
Encl: Barry Feinberg to CF 1968
Oggi (Stefano Archetti) 1967
CF to 1967
Ogoniak (Peter Chumak) **2** 1963-7
BR to 1963
CF to 1967
The Old Bavians' Association (Yaqoob Tawfik) **2** 1967
CF to 1967
Olkar, B. A., RS to 1964
Olshewshy, Thomas A. 1968
CF to 1968
Omroepvereniging Vara (P. W. Goemans) 1969
Oneul (Kim Hyun Shick) 1969
CF to 1969
Ordine Dei Cercatori Di Se'Stessi (P. Conti Tarantino) 1962
Ordoobadi, Ahmad **2** 1966
BR to 1966
Organization for Relief and Development (Michael Fuchs-Carsch) 1965
CF to 1965
The Orion Press, Inc.
Encl: The Orion Press Inc. (Peter Mayer) to *Peace News* (Hugh Brock) **2** .. 1962-3
Peace News (Brock) to The Orion Press, Inc. (Mayer) .. 1963
CF to 1963
Encl: *Peace News* (Brock) to CF 1964
Orr, Akiva, CF to 1969
Otechestven Front (Iliya Kyulyovski) 1964
Encl: Embassy of the People's Republic of Bulgaria (B. Guerassimov) to BR 1964
Otto, Karl, RSt. to 1967
Our Generation Against Nuclear War (Dimitrios Roussopoulos, Elka Cohen) to CF **4** ... 1962-3
Encl.
CF to **5** 1962-3
BR to 1964
Overland (Stephen Murray-

Smith) 1967
RSt. to 1967
Peter Owen Ltd. (Peter Owen, Neil Middleton) **3** 1962
To BRPF **2** 1968-9
To CF
BR to **2** 1962
CF to 1969
Oxford University Press (John Brown, Richard Brain, *et al.*) **41** 1962-8
To RS 1964
To BRPF 1966
To CF **2** 1966-7
To PW 1969
Encl: royalty ss., clippings, Feliks Topolski's drawing of BR
BR to **18** 1962-7
RS to 1964
CF to **10** 1965-9
RSt. to 1967
PW to **2** 1969
Encl: Alvin Deutsch to BR 1962
BR to Deutsch 1962

P

Paci, Enzo 1969
CF to 1969
Pacifica Foundation (Michael E. Tigar) 1962
To RS **2** 1962
Encl: interview, questionnaire
RS to **2** 1962
The Pacifist (Bernard Withers) 1964
RS to 1964
Padhan, Prafulla Kumar 1967
Il Paese (Georgio Fanti) 1961
BR to 1963
Il Paese Oggi (Marino Cavallo) **3** 1964-6
To RS 1964
RS to **3** 1964
PW to 1966
Paese Sera (Georgio Fanti, Fausto Coen) **3** 1961-4
To RS 1961
BR to 1961
RS to **3** 1963-5
Pageant (Howard Cohn) 1963
Pak Scientist (Mohammad Munir) 1967
DN to 1967
Pakistan Features Syndicate (Salahuddin Mohammad) to RS 1967
Deirdre Griswold to 1967
The Pakistan Observer (Abdus Salam) 1967
BR to 1967
The Pakistan Times (Zahid Chaudhuri) **3** ... 1965-6
To RS 1965
RS to **3** 1965-6
Pall Mall Press, RSt. to 1968
Pallas (Victor Houart) 1963
BR to 1963
Palm (Sana-ur-Rehman Ansari) 1966
RS to 1966
Pan Books (C. A. E. Paget) to RS 1967
Pancholi, Manubhai, BR to ... 1963
Panichas, George A. 1967
Encl.
BR to 1967
Pantheon Books (Gail Rentsch) 1968
CF to 1968
Papatheophanous, Helen 1967
CF to 1967
Pappu, V. 1963
To RS 1964
BR to 1964
Parade (Jack Harrison Pollack) 1969
Parallax Publishing Co. Inc. (Peter Workman) to RSt. 1967
Les Parents (Robert Barrat) 1970
Encl: interview with B. Spock
Paris Match (Michel Clerc) **2** 1958
Partisan Review (Caroline Rand Herron) to RS 1967

RS to 1966
Pasado y Presente (José
Aricó) to BRPF 1968
PAX (Tor Bjerkmann) 1964
RS to 1964
Pax Forlag (Einar
Gullord) to Pat Jordan 1967
Peace and Freedom News
(Joan Levenson) 1966
Peace News (Hugh Brock,
Michael Freeman, Michael
Randle, Trevor Hatton, Adam
Roberts, Theodore Roszak
et al.) **7** 1962-4
To BRPF 1966
To CE 1964
To CF **3** 1964-70
To Pat Jordan 1966
To RS **3** 1962-3
Encl: John Richardson to
National Committee of 100
(Peter Cadogan) 1964
National Committee of 100
(Cadogan) to John
Richardson 1964
Michael Cadbury to
Peace News **2** 1964
Peace News to Cadbury 1964
D. Coleman to *Peace News* . 1965
form ls., clippings
BR to **3** 1962-4
RS to **4** 1962-7
CF to **9** 1962-9
CE to 1964
Bill Kaye to 1964
RS to N. J. Griffin 1967
Encl: petition from
Japanese delegation
Peace Research Abstracts
(Alan Newcombe) 1964
Encl.
RS to 1964
Peace Research Newsletter
(David A. Fabri, Ulf
Christensen) 1963
To BRPF 1963
Encl: issue of journal
BR to 1963
CE to 1963
Pears, David F., to CF 1968
CF to 1968
Peckham School Magazine
(Helen d'Ancona) 1966
BR to 1967
Encl: s.
Pecrez?, Lourette,
to DN 1968
Peet, John, RS to 1966
Peking Review (Chou
Pao-li) **2** 1964
BR to 1964
RS to **2** 1964-6
Pelican Books, CF to 1968
Pendas, Francisco **2** 1966-7
Encl: essay
BR to **3** 1963-6
CF to 1967
Penguin Books Ltd. (Dieter
Pevsner, Allen Lane *et
al.*) **22** 1961-7
To RS 1963
Encl: contract, royalty ss.,
Ernst Bader to Penguin
Books Ltd. 1961
BR to **9** 1961-3
RS to 1964
CF to 1968
Encl: BR to Allen &
Unwin 1963
The Pennsylvania Literary Review
(Marc Rosenberg) **2** 1963
Encl.
BR to **2** 1963
RS to 1963
The People, CF to 1969
The People's Korea (Son Jin
Hyung) 1968
Encl: greeting card
Pergamon Press Ltd. (A. J.
Steel) to RS 1967
Periodico Revolucion 1962
BR to 1962
Perseus (S. Fitzgibbon and
L. J. Britton) 1963
BR to 1963
Petersen Engineering Co., Inc.
(Shirley Rohrman) 1963
Encl: Petersen Engineering
Co., Inc. (Rohrman) to
Playboy (Jack J.

Kressie) 1963
Playboy (Pat Pappas) to
Petersen Engineering Co.,
Inc. (Rohrman) 1963
CE to 1963
Petrović, Gajo 1962
BR to 1962
Phaidon Press Ltd. 1963
Philadelphia Inquirer (Eva
Teller) 1964
RS to **2** 1964-6
Philo 1965
PW to 1965
Philosophical Society: Journal
(Sam. Ade. Olaitan) 1963
Philosophy (H. B. Acton) 1960
BR to 1960
PHP Research Institute
(Yutaka Ohbe) 1967
Encl: book and booklet
Phukan, Punya Dar Chetra . . . 1966
To BRPF 1965
PW to 1965
Physics in Medicine and Biology
(Ann V. Watford) 1965
RS to 1965
Pirnia, Hossein 1968
Sir Isaac Pitman and Sons
Limited 1967
Encl.
BR to 1968
Playboy (Hugh M. Hefner,
A. C. Spectorsky, Murray
Fisher *et. al.*) **29** 1963-8
To BRPF 1965
Encl: royalty s., form ls.,
greeting card, tear sheets,
Playboy ts. of "Semantics
and the Cold War"
BR to **9** 1962-6
RS to **5** 1964
Plummer, F. **2** 1966
BR to 1966
RS to 1966
Pointer (Peggy Lang) to RS . . . 1967
Polish Radio and Television . . 1961
Politika (Dusan Pesić) to Mr.
Kinsey 1966
Pollard, Gordon R. **3** 1966
To RS 1966
BR to 1966
RS to 1966
Polvani, G., BR to 1964
Poona Herald (K. P. D.
Rathore) 1964
Encl: clipping
Poorvi Times (Mohd. Zaki) . . . 1965
PW to 1965
Population Review
(S. Chandrasekhar) 1962
BR to 1962
To RS 1965
RS to 1965
Portland Symphony Society
(Jacques Singer) 1963
Encl.
*Portmadoc Urban and District
Guide* (J. M. Watkins) 1966
RS to 1966
Postgirokontoret 1963
Poulton, Gaye, BR to 1964
Prado, C. G. 1968
Encl.
Prafulla Press (Prafulla
Chandra Das) 1964
Prakobsantisukh, Biravan,
BR to 1964
Pratibha (P. K. Agrawal) 1969
Pravda (O. Orestov) 1965
RS to **2** 1965-6
Praxis (Gajo Petrović and
Rudi Supek) **3** 1966-7
BR to 1966
CF to **2** 1967-70
Prensa Latina (Leopoldo
Formoso), RSt. to 1968
Prentice-Hall, Inc. (Holbrook,
Rosemary Greeley, Roger
T. Holloway, Meryl
Riecken) **3** 1964-9
To AY 1964
Encl: royalty s.
BR to 1962
CF to 1964
RS to 1964
Press Council, PW to 1965
Re *Sunday Telegraph*
La Presse (Maurice Dagenais)
to RS 1964
Encl: clipping

RS to 1964
Prest, J. M. 1964
BR to 1964
Private Eye (Jan Erson?) ...... n.d.
CF to 1963
BR to (Paul Foot) 1965
Daniel Coleman to 1965
Priyambada, Sujata 1965
PW to 1965
Probe (F. D. Rabson, F. M. Orkin) **2** 1967
To RS 1966-7
RS to **2** 1966
CF to 1967
Encl: foreword by BR for *Probe*
Psyche (Pervaiz Alam) 1967
RSt. to 1967
Psychical Research Foundation, Inc. (W. G. Roll) 1963
BR to 1963
Psychological Library Publishers 1970
The Public School Leaver (R. N. Windrum) ... 1968
Publishers Association (R. C. Gower), RSt. to 1967
Pulse (H. J. P. Arnold) 1963
BR to 1963
Purabi (Sarbesinar Samal?) ... 1967
Purdy, Bryn 1964
BR to 1964
Pylyshyn, Zenon W. 1968

Q

Q (Jacob Zilber) 1962
Queen (Adrian Bailey, Hugh Johnson) 1967
To CF 1969
RSt. to 1967
La Quinzaine Littéraire (photocopy) 1967

R

Raab, Enrique?, to RS 1967
Rabindra Prasanga (Somendraneth Bose) 1964
RS to 1964
The Racquette (Craig A. Bond) 1966
The Radhakrishnan Number (V. Kalidas) **3** 1962
BR to **2** 1962
The Radical Humanist (S. Bhadra), BR to **2** 1963
RS to 1963
Radio Ariel (Vladimir Alexandrovich and Adolfo Gohardi), RS to 1965
Encl: RS to ID 1965
Radio Free Europe (George Urban) 1963
BR to 1963
Radiodiffusion Télévision Belge (Henri Roanne, Georges Konen) **5** 1961-6
BR to 1961
CF to ER 1966
Radiodiffusion-Télévision Française **2** 1958-61
BR to 1961
Rahman, A. K. M. Siddiqur 1968
CF to 1968
Rai, Rameshwar Nath **2** 1967
RAI-Radiotelevisione Italiano (Sergio Telmon, Roberto Trionfera) **3** 1968
Encl: programme for 1955 discussion
CF to **3** 1967-8
Raines, Halsey 1963
La Raison (Roger Gaudin) 1967
Rajaraman, S. 1968
Rama, K. S. 1968
Ramparts (Warren Hinckle III, Robert Scheer, *et al.*) **2** 1966-7
To BRPF 1966
To CF 1967
To DN 1966
To PJ .... n.d.
To RS **4** 1967
Encl: David Welsh to David Horowitz
BR to 1966
RS to **6** 1966-7

PJ to 1967
PW to 1967
Random House, Inc. (John J. Simon) to RS 1967
Rangappa, K.S. **2** 1962-9
Encl: Macmillan & Co. Ltd. (B. McKenzie) 1969
BR to 1962
CF to 1969
Ranjana Printers 1966
ID to 1966
Rational Review (J.M. Alexander) 1964
The Rationalist Press (C.J.G. Macy) to CF **2** 1969
CF to 1969
Ravji, Valji 1967
The Reader's Digest (Hobart Lewis, Peter Glemser, Marjorie Nicholson) **4** .. 1962-6
To RS **5** 1962-6
Encl.
BR to 1962
RS to **7** 1962-6
Realidade (Paulo Francis) ..... n.d.
To CF 1969
Réalités (Garith Windsor, Muriel Reed, *et al.*) **6** ... 1963-6
To RS 1963
Encl: questionnaire
BR to **3** 1963-6
RS to 1963
ID to 1966
Red Flag (John L. Davis) **3** 1966-8
Redazione (M. Matteatti) 1964
RS to 1964
Redbook Magazine (Jhan Robbins, Norman Hill) **5** 1966
Encl: note, tear sheets of BR interview
RS to 1964
CF to **8** 1963-6
Redmer, Bessie C. 1967
Reedy, Thomas A. 1968
CF to 1968
Reflex (Michael Phillips) 1968
CF to 1968
Reicher-Sgradi, R. 1967
Rejman, A. 1969
Rendi, Aloisio, BR to 1963
Renoir, E.P.A. **2** 1967
To RSt. 1967
RSt. to 1967
Reportér (Adolf Hradecký) ... 1968
The Reporter (Robert Bingham) 1963
BR to 1963
RS to 1964
Republika (Emanuel Micković-Soko) 1967
Resurgence (John Papworth) to RS 1967
RS to 1967
Reuters (R.B. Maclurkin, W.E. Parrott) **3** 1967
CF to **4** 1967
Reveal (Ben Dockter) 1966
Encl: clippings, ls.
Quintin Hoare to 1966
Review of International Affairs (Mil. Mijović) 1961
Revista Ercilla (Erica Vexler P.) 1966
To RS 1966
RS to 1966
Revista Latinamericana de Psicologia (Ruben Ardila) 1968
Revista Universitaria (Alberto Menéndez G.) 1967
BR to 1967
Revolution Africaine (Thomas Blair) 1963
Revolutionary Socialist Students Federation (Regan Scott, *et al.*) 1969
CF to 1969
Revue "Contemporanul" (Georges Cuibus) **2** 1963-6
BR to 1963
Revue Tiers-Monde (G. Tricot, François Perroux) **2** 1964-5
BR to 1964
Rhees, R. 1967
BR to 1967
Rhine, Keith Milton 1964
The Richmond News Leader (Jere Real) to BRPF 1965
RS to 1965

G. Ricordi & C. to RS 1967
Riepe, Dale 1962
BR to 1962
Rischin, Moses 1963
Roberts, F. W. 1963
BR to 1963
Robison, Professor, BR to 1961
Encl: BR to *Encounter*
(Stepen Spender) 1961
Rodker, Joan, RS to 1962
Rogosin, Lionel 1961
BR to 1961
RS? to 1961
Rolandi, Giampiero, to RS ... 1964
Romeike & Curtice (L.
Penn) to PW 1966
The Ronald Press Co.
(E. A. Woodson) 1962
Rorty, Amelie 1965
RS to 1965
Rose, J. **2** 1966
RS to 1966
PW to 1966
Rossi, Mario **2** 1963
BR to 1963
Routledge & Kegan Paul Ltd.
(Terence Lucas) 1970
Deirdre Brooks to 1970
CF to 1970
Rowohlt Verlag GMBH
(R. Sansom) 1965
RS to 1965
Roy, Dilip Kumar 1969
Encl.
CF to 1969
Royal Greek Embassy
(M. Mouzas) 1966
Encl.
RS to 1966
Rubenstein, David **5** 1968-9
Encl.
BR to **2** 1968-9
Ruhman, Walt 1964
To RS **2** 1962
RS to 1962
The Rupam Group of
Newspapers (Gunen
P. Roy-Chaudhuri) 1962
Rushlight (Denis
Knight) **5** 1963-6
To BRPF 1964
To CF 1964
To PW 1965
Encl: l. to *The Catholic Herald*,
l. to *The Times*
BR to **4** 1962-4
CF to 1964
RS to **2** 1964-5
PW to **2** 1965
Russell, John Howard **2** .. 1963-6
To Deborah Rogers 1966
BR to 1963
Deborah Rogers to 1966
RS to **2** 1966
Russell Bibliography Project
(Richard W. Story, Jerrold
L. Patz) **9** 1965-6
To RS **2** 1965
Encl: clipping: "UM
Sophomores Ring Up BR on
his 93rd Birthday"; *New
York Times* interview with
RS
CF to **3** 1965
BR to **2** 1965-6
RS to **3** 1965-6
PW to 1965
Rutgers University Press
(Edna Unkel) 1967
Ryukyu Shimpo (Genichi
Izumi) to RS .... n.d.

S

Sadiq, Anushiravan 1962
BR to 1962
Saga: Senior Citizen's News
(John J. Thompson) 1966
BR to 1966
Sagarin, Edward 1968
CF to 1968
Sahaya, S. 1967
CF to 1967
Salvat Editores, S.A.
(Antonio Comas) 1963
BR to 1963
The San Diego Union
(Joseph E. Brown) 1964
RS to 1964

San Francisco Chronicle,
RS to 1964
Sanehi, Swaran Singh 1967
Sanity (David Boulton) 2 .. 1963-4
To CF 1964
To RS 2 1964
BR to 2 1963-4
CF to 1964
RS to 2 1964
Encl: Society of Friends Peace Committee (Gwen Paine) to BR 1964
RS to Society of Friends Peace Committee (Gwen Paine) 1964
The Sankei Shimbun (Satoru Nakayama, Hiroshi Arakawa) 2 1969
Sanyal, D.C. 1962
Saran, Vishnu 3 1969
Encl.
Sarkar, Hirendra Narayan 1962
BR to 1962
SAS (Aldo Pelazzi)
Encl: receipt from Westminster Bank
Satan in the Suburbs, correspondence re dramatization of:
Edward Albee to 1966
George Allen & Unwin Ltd. (M. Joy Hill) to 1965
John Arden to .... n.d.
Lionel Bart to 2 1965-7
Tutte Lemkov to 2 1965
Joan Littlewood to 1965
Christopher Logue to 2 ... 1965
Harold Pinter to 1965
N.F. Simpson to 1965
Brian Sommerville to 1965
BR to Edward Albee 1966
BR to George Allen & Unwin Ltd. (M. Joy Hill) 2 1965
BR to to Lionel Bart 2 1965-7
BR to Tutte Lemkov 2 1965-6
BR to Christopher Logue 1965
BR to Harold Pinter 1965
CF to David Markham 1969
RS to Brian Sommerville ... 1965
Encl: clipping
The Saturday Evening Post (John Hunt) 2 1967
Encl: sample pages from "Speaking Out" column
BR to 2 1967
Saturday Review (Norman Cousins, Nicholas G. Balint) 1965
To RS 1969
Encl: review of *BR Speaks His Mind* distributed by Sara Rollitts
CF to 2 1965-9
Saur, Heinz, to RS 2 1962-3
RS to 1962
Savelli, Giulio, to RS 1964
DN to 1967
CF to 1967
Scarfe, Gerald, BR to 1968
Schaefer, Philip A. 2 1963
BR to 1963
Schiecke, Ulrich 1963
BR to 1964
Schischkoff, G. 1966
Encl.
BR to 1966
Schneier, Arthur 1963
Encl: clipping
BR to 1963
Schoenbach, Victor J., to CF 1969
Schoenbach, Victor J., and Hoch, Paul K. 1969
Schoenman, Ralph, (list of publishers; form l. sent to various publishers concerning publication of International War Crimes Tribunal) 55 1967
Schoenman, Theodore, ID to 1966
Re BR's introduction to programme on the Webbs
Schrift für Architektur und Stadtebau (Oswald Oberhuber), CF to 1969
Schulburg, Budd, CF to 1968
Schüler? (note concerning possibility of interview) ... 1958?
Schwarzenberger, Georg 1964

BR to 1964
RS to 1964
Scida, Louis 1962
BR to 1962
Science and Humanity (*Znanie*)
(Vladimir R. Keler) 1962
Encl.
BR to **2** 1963
Science & Society (A. Evenitsky)
to PW 1966
PW to 1966
Science & Times (Surendr
Jha) 1966
ID to 1966
PW to 1966
Scînteia (A. Socec, A. Baleanu,
S. Farcasan *et al.*) **2** 1968
To RS **2** 1967
Encl: questionnaire
CF to 1968
Scînteia Tineretului (Carol Roman,
Doina Topor) **2** 1969
Scoop Press Agency Ltd.
(Serge Lemoine) 1969
Scott, James A. 1962
BR to 1962
Scott, Foresman and Co.
(Margaret P. Trexler) 1962
BR to 1962
Search (Anwar Akhter
Ahmed) **2** 1965-6
A Search for an Alternative
to War and Violence (Ted
Dunn) **4** 1963
To [RS] 1963
Encl.
BR to 1963
Sears, John L. 1962
BR to 1962
RS to 1964
Martin Secker & Warburg (Oliver
Stallybrass, Fredric
Warburg) **4** 1962-5
Encl: Martin Secker & Warburg
(Oliver Stallybrass) to
Patricia Spence 1965
Encl: royalty s.
BR to F. Warburg 1962
Segefjord, Bjarne, to RS 1966
RS to 1966
Seikyo Shimbum
(E. Yamazaki) 1969
Selection (Edmund
Marsden) 1962
Sencer, Muammer **2** 1963-7
BR to 1963
CF to 1967
Serra d'Or (Vincente
Navarro) 1965
BR to 1965
Shadan Hojin Correspondents
Club of Japan (Albert
Axelbank) 1964
Shaheen (M.A. Salam Khan,
Syed Neez Ahmad) **4** ... 1965-6
Encl: issue of magazine
RS to **2** 1964-5
PW to 1966
Shami, M.A. 1965
RS to 1965
Sharme, Dhirendra 1968
Encl.
CF to 1968
Sheed and Ward Ltd.,
PW to 1969
Sheffield Telegraph (Martin
L. Green) 1965
RS to 1965
Anthony Sheil Associates Ltd.
(Gillon Aitken) 1968
To CF 1968
CF to 1968
Shell (K.G. Jackson) 1968
Encl: issue of newspaper
The Shenval Press (J. Bowles)
to BRPF 1964
Encl: receipt
Shibata, Shingo, CF to 1969
Shire and Spire (Margaret
Stoneman) **2** 1962-3
Encl: press releases, newspaper
Shui, Chien-tung, CF to 1968
Sibthorp, M.M. 1964
BR to 1964
Siddiqi, Nazeer 1966
RS to 1966
Max Siegel & Associates
(Roy E. Porter) 1966
CF to 1966
El Siglo Illustrado S.A. (Carlos

M. Rama), BR to 1964
Simon and Schuster (M. Lincoln Schuster, Michael V. Korda, *et al.*) **39** 1953-68
To CE 1962
To CF 1968
To RS **4** 1962-7
Encl: Jerome Shoenfield to Simon and Schuster 1953
Oscar Cargell to Simon and Schuster 1953
Simon and Schuster (M. Lincoln Schuster) to Harold Macmillan 1961
Simon and Schuster (M. Lincoln Schuster) to *New York Times* 1962
royalty ss., publisher's advertisements and previews, reviews
BR to **23** 1962-8
RS to **2** 1962-4
CF to **5** 1967-9
Sinha, S.M. 1963
BR to 1963
La Sinistra (Giulio Savelli) 1966
To CF **5** 1967
To RS **2** 1966-7
Encl: George Allen & Unwin (A. Dadlez) to *La Sinistra* (Giulio Savelli) 1967
RS to CF, Ken Coates and RSt. 1967
brochure advertisement
RS to **4** 1966-7
CF to **5** 1967
PW to 1968
Encl: s. by BR
Siriwarnasingha, Wilson 1962
BR to 1962
Sixth Form Opinion (Dyan Wade) **3** 1962
Encl: questionnaire
BR to **2** 1962
NJ to 1962
Sklar, Robert, to RS **2** 1967
To PW 1967
RSt. to **2** 1967
PW to 1967
Slovenski Porocevalec (Sergej Vosnjak) 1958
Smeets Weert (Richard de Grab) **3** 1965-7
Encl.
CF to 1965
BR to 1966
W.H. Smith & Son (Sydney Hyde, E.Q. Savill) **2** .. 1959-68
Smith, William F., and Liedlich, Raymond 1964
To RS 1964
RS to 1964
Snaith, Stanley 1956
Socialist Education Association (R.G. Wallace, Malcolm Peltu) **2** 1965-9
RS to 1965
CF to 1969
The Socialist Leader (Wilfred Wigham) 1963
To RS 1962
Encl: Peter Cadogan to *The Socialist Leader* 1963
CF to **3** 1963
BR to (S. Mukerjee) 1965
Socialist Review (Harry W. Laidler) 1919
Socialisten (Leif Thorsson) **2** 1962
To Committee of 100 1962
BR to 1962
Société Radio-Canada (Gérald Tassé) 1966
CF to 1966
The Society for Indian and Northern Education (Thecla Bradshaw) to George Allen & Unwin 1967
RSt. to 1968
Society for Individual Freedom (Ian McTaggart) 1965
BR to 1965
Society for Pollution and Environmental Control (Nancy Furnes) 1969
Southern Illinois University Press (Vernon Sternberg) .. 1966
BR to 1966
South-West Essex Technical College and School of Art

Students' Union (B. Joyce) 1966
Soviet Russia (G. Rassedin) **2** 1959
BR to (K. Zarodov, G. Rassedin) **2** 1959-63
Mira Vazir to BR re trans. 1960
Sozialistische Hefte (Karl Otto) 1967
To RS 1967
To RSt. **2** 1967
DN to 1967
RS to 1967
RSt. to **2** 1967
Spa, H. 1962
BR to 1962
The Spark (Saurabh Srivastava) 1967
CF to 1967
Spartacus (Alison Finch) to PW 1967
To BRPF 1968
Encl: *Spartacus* (Alison Finch) to Mr. Steckler
The Spectator, PW to 1964
Sphere Books (Richard B. Fisher) to RS 1967
Sphinx (Ian J. A. Stocks) 1958
BR to 1958
Encl: copy of RS's "Bertrand Russell Peace Foundation"
Der Spiegel (H. G. Alexander) to RS **3** 1966
RS to 1964
RSt. to 1966
Axel Springer & Sohn (E. Duncker) 1963
RS to 1963
St. James Press (Josephine Beddoe) 1967
St. Louis Post-Dispatch (Robert Lasch) 1964
To RS 1966
RS to **2** 1964-6
St. Thomas's Hospital Gazette (R. O. Kahan) 1965
RS to 1965
Staatliche Bibliothek Regensburg 1966
RS to 1966
Stander, Philip **3** 1967-8
Encl.
RSt. to 1967
BR to 1968
The Star-Bulletin, BR to 1968
The Statesman, New Delhi (M. Owais) **10** 1962-8
To RS **9** 1964-6
BR to **4** 1962-3
RS to **8** 1962-5
CF to **2** 1965-8
Stephens, Bette 1963
RS to 1963
Stewart, Gloria 1969
Stewart, Iain 1970
Stone, I. F. **3** 1962-3
To NJ .... n.d.
To RS **3** 1963-4
To PW 1965
Encl: *I. F. Stone's Weekly*
BR to **7** 1958-68
CF to 1963
CE to 1963
RS to **2** 1963-7
PW to 1965
Stone, Keith 1969
Encl: poem
CF to 1969
The Stone Wall Press (K. K. Merker) 1965
Strike (Allan Booth) 1964
RS to 1964
The Student (David P. M. Robertson) 1968
Student (Richard Branson) 1968
CF to 1968
Students' Front Against Aggression (M. Amanullah Khan) 1968
CF to 1968
Studie (Ivan Jelinek) 1968
CF to 1968
Studio Radio Bern (Heinrich von Grünigen) 1967
CF to 1967
Subramanian, M. 1962
BR to 1962
Sucesos (Armando Rodriguez) **3** 1967

Suhrkamp Verlag (Marianne Kalow) 1967
CF to 1967
Summers, John 1963
RS to 1963
Sun (Alex X. Snobel, Hugh Cudlipp, T. Field) **4** ... 1964-8
BR to 1968
The Sun: Newspaper of the Guild of Students (Alan Richardson, Brian Yapp, J. K. Stanworth) **2** 1964-5
To BRPF? **2** 1965
To RS **2** 1964
Encl: questionnaire
BR to 1964
RS to **2** 1964-5
PW to 1965
The Sunday Citizen (W. R. Richardson), RS to 1964
The Sunday School Board (Glenda LaFever), CF to 1967
The Sunday Telegraph (Duff Hart-Davis, G. Evans, B. R. Roberts *et al.*) 1968
To RS **3** 1964-6
Encl: clippings, form l.
BR to **2** 1963-5
RS to **2** 1964-6
F. Davis to 1965
PW to **2** 1965-70
The Sunday Times (J. W. Lambert, Priscilla Chapman, B.H. Knightly, Peter Hiley, James Dow *et al.*) **5** 1962-9
To RS **4** 1964-7
RS to **5** 1963-6
CF to 1964
PW to **2** 1968
Encl: 2 anonymous notes
Sunday Times of Ceylon (Sydney Reynolds) **2** 1962
BR to 1962
NJ to 1962
Sura Kavya Samsad (P. N. Mookerjee) 1969
Suyin, Han 1967
BR to **2** 1967
Sveriges Radio (Bertil Forsman, Bo Jarborg, Lars-Eric Örtegren, Jakob von Uexkull) **4** ... 1967-8
To PW **2** 1965
To CF 1967
PW to **2** 1965
BR to 1967
CF to **5** 1967
Sydney Morning Herald (Gavin Souter) 1968
CF to 1968
Sykes, Hugh **2** 1969-70
Syndikalistiska Foreningen (Hans Lindquist), CF to 1968
Synic (Louis Eaks) 1968
Encl: articles
CF to 1968
Szczesny Verlag (Gerhard Szczesny, Willy Hochkeppel) **3** ... 1963-6
Encl: questionnaire
BR to 1963
RS to **2** 1964-6
Szent-Gyorgyi, Albert **2** 1962
Encl: essay
BR to 1962

T

Tabb, Eric, BR to 1962
Tanggaard, E. (Niels Bohr's Secretariat) to RS 1962
RS to 1962
Tanjug (Savo Ratknic) 1964
Tanwir, Ghulam Rasul 1964
BR to 1964
Tappe, Horst 1963
BR to 1963
TASS, RS to 1964
Taylor, Michael 1967
Taylor, Vic, BR to 1963
Tejpal, Nautamlal C. **2** ... 1967-8
Telegraph-Journal (Geoffrey C. Crowe) to CF 1970
Re BR's last s.
CF to 1970
Temple, Robert **4** 1963
BR to **2** 1963
Les Temps Modernes (André Gortz), BR to 1969
Thi Yomiuri (Ninomiya) 1966

RS to 1966
Think (Peter Bristow),
RS to 1964
Think (James B. O'Connell) .. 1966
Thiruvalluvar House
(N. Kannuchamy) 1962
BR to 1962
Thomas, N., BR to 1964
Thompson, Manley 1966
Re comments on Quine's
American Philosophical
Association paper
BR to 1966
Thompson, Jr., H.K. 1963
Encl.
BR to 1963
F. A. Thorpe Publishing (F. A.
Thorpe) 1968
BR to 1968
CF to (B. E. Bassett) 1969
Tidningarnas Telegrambyrå
(Jan-Otto Modig and John-
Bertil Vedin) 1969
Encl: questionnaire
Tidsignal (Bo Hammar)
to RSt. 1966
RSt. to **2** 1966-7
Time Incorporated (Marvin
Zim), RS to 1966
Time Magazine (James A. Linen,
Mrs. Parrish) **2** 1948-64
To RS 1966
The Times (W. J. Haley,
Colin MacLean, Geoffrey
Woolley *et al.*) **18** 1962-9
To RS **7** 1962-6
To G. Coggan 1966
To CF **3** 1968-9
Encl: clipping, advertisement
BR to **2** 1962
AY to **2** 1962
RS to **3** 1962-6
CE to 1964
CF to **7** 1964-7
R. M. Rehder to 1965
PW to **2** 1968
The Times Educational
Supplement (Tyrrell
Burgess) 1959
Encl: clippings
The Times of Karachi,
RS to 1966
Tirnoveanu, M., and
Enescu, G. 1966
RS to 1966
Tobar, Jorge Albarnoz 1966
Tobin, Michael A. 1965
CF to 1965
Today (David Powell) **2** 1962
CF to 1969
Today's Japan (Maurice
Schneps) 1958
BR to 1958
Tofallis, Zannetos 1965
RS to 1965
Topchiev, A. 1961
BR to 1961
Topeka State Journal
(W.G. Clugston) 1951
Encl: clipping of article
by BR
Toronto Daily Star and *Star*
Weekly (Ray Gardner *et*
al.) **9** 1962-6
To RS **5** 1964-6
Encl: E. Bell to *Star*
Weekly 1965
clipping, royalty s.
BR to **9** 1963-6
CF to 1963
RS to **7** 1964-6
Town (Nicholas Tomalin) 1962
Encl.
RS to 1962
Transition (Rajat Neogy) 1965
CF to 1965
Treadgold, Donald W. 1962
BR to 1962
Tremlett, George 1965
To RS 1965
Encl: questionnaire
CF to 1965
RS to 1965
Tribuna (George Cuibus),
RS to 1963
The Tribune (Prem Mohindra)
to RSt. 1968
RSt. to 1968
Tribune (Michael Foot,
Max Madden, Richard

Clements) **3** 1964
To CF **3** 1963-70
To RS 1964
Encl.
RS to **2** 1962-4
CF to **3** 1963-4
BR to 1964
PW to 1964
Peter Limqueco to 1967
Tribune: Ceylon News Service
(Vijaya de Lanerolle) 1958
Trinity Review (A.C.C.
Courtauld) 1966
CF to 1966
Trio International (U.K.) Ltd.
(Michael Green) 1967
Encl.
CF to 1967
The Trumpet, London
(Michael Thornton) 1962
The Trumpet, Long Island,
N.Y. (Allison Freid) 1962
Encl.
Tubman, Marilyn J. 1967
Tucker, John 1968
Encl: article
BR to 1964
CF to 1968
Charles E. Tuttle Co.
(Y. Katahira) 1962
To *Encounter* 1965
PW to 1965
The Twentieth Century
(Richard Findlater, Mary
Turnbull) **2** 1963-4
To RS 1964
BR to 1963
RS to **2** 1964
20th Century and Peace (Nikolai
Pastukhov) 1967
To DN 1967
DN to 1967

U

Új szó 1963
UNESCO (W. Zyss) 1964
Unicrit (Francis Koval
on behalf of Glenn F.
Ireton) .... n.d.
The Union of Mauritian
Students (A.M.
Soormally) **2** 1964
RS to 1964
Union Voice (Ernie Roberts) .. 1963
Encl.
Unione Tipografico-Editrice
Torinese (G. Merlini) 1968
To CF 1969
BR to 1963
CF to 1968
L'Unita (Antonio Bronda) 1969
Encl: questionnaire
United Nations Association
(Nigel Nicolson) 1961
Encl: pamphlet
RSt. to (A.E. Flew) 1967
United News of India (G.G.
Mirchandani) 1968
Encl: questionnaire
United Press International
(John E. Darling) 1967
Encl: clipping
United States Information
Service (William C. Gausmann,
Evelyn Eisenstadt) n.d.-1962
ER to **2** 1960
United States Student Press
Association (Steven d'Arazien),
RSt. to 1967
Universal Knowledge Foundation
(W.W. Farmer) **2** 1963
Encl.
BR to **2** 1963
Universal Pictorial Press
& Agency Ltd. 1967
University College of North
Wales (David Jowett and
D. Chadwick) 1958
BR to 1958
University College of North
Wales Humanist Society
(Gareth B. Evans) **2** 1962
BR to 1962
University of Bombay (B.A.
Olkar) to RS **5** 1964-8
Encl: University of Bombay
(B.A. Olkar) to George
Allen & Unwin

BR to 1964
RS to 1964
CF to 1968
The University of Chicago Law Review (Dallin H. Oaks) 1957
University of Chicago Press (Morris Philipson) to RS ... 1967
RS to 1967
University of Liverpool Guild of Undergraduates (Christopher Hunt) **2** 1966
BR to 1966
RS to 1966
The University of Michigan Press (June Beck, Elisabeth Case) **3** 1962-4
BR to 1962
RS to 1964
Urdu Digest (Altaf Hasan Qureshee) 1966
Encl: questionnaire
BR to 1966
Uris, Norman Burton **2** 1967
Ushio (Katsuya Ikeda) **2** 1967
RSt. to 1967
DN to 1967
Uzzell, Thomas H. 1963
Encl: circular
BR to 1963

V

Valet, Roanne 1967
CF to 1967
Van Ausdell, B. J., to CF 1963
CF to 1963
Vancouver Sun (Donald Cromie, J. O. Bridle, Tom Ardies) **3** 1962-4
To RS **2** 1964
Encl: D. C. Graham to *Vancouver Sun* (Donald Cromie) 1962
clippings
BR to **2** 1963
RS to **3** 1964-6
Van Cutsem, Pierre 1966
BR to 1966
Vande Velde-Schlick, Barbara 1969
Vanguard (Steve Harris) 1968
CF to 1968
van Heijenoort, John 1962
Encl: BR's correspondence with Frege
BR to 1962
Van Kerkhoven, Jan 1967
CF to 1967
D. Van Nostrand Company (D. J. Carpenter) 1962
BR to 1962
Varsity (Julian Mew) 1965
PW to 1965
Vaughan, J., BR to 1965
Encl: message from BR
Vega, J. M., BR to 1964
Vege, Nageswara Rao **4** ... 1964-6
To PW 1966
BR to **3** 1963-6
RS to 1966
PW to **2** 1966
Verlag der Philosophischen Akademie (W. Benary) 1924
Verlag Kurt Desch GMBH (H. J. Mundt, Kurt Desch) **3** 1963
To RS 1967
Verlon, André 1962
BR to 1962
Vie Nuove (Paolo Bracaglia Morante, Antonio Bronda) **2** 1964
RS to **2** 1964
Viet Report, Deirdre Griswold to 1967
Vietnam Day Committee News, PW to 1966
View (Gillian Davies) 1968
To BRPF 1968
RSt. to 1968
Encl: note
Views (Sabby Sagall) **3** 1963-4
To BRPF? **2** .... n.d.
To CF 1965
To RS 1966
Encl: transcript of interview with Pat Pottle and CF, invitation, Christmas cards

CF to **4** 1963-5
BR to 1964
HR to 1965
The Viking Press (Roberta Tyson Rawlings) to RS 1967
Villa, Carlos Escallon 1956
Vinden, Kathleen, to CF **2** ... 1968
Encl: D. Pérez y Pérez to BR 1968
CF to **2** 1968
Visa pour un Enfant (José Linzini) 1967
To RS 1967
RS to 1967
Vogler, Anne 1968
CF to 1968
Vogue (Paul H. Bonner) 1963
Voltaire Verlag (Bernward Vesper-Triangel, Nicholas Neumann)
Encl: Voltaire Verlag (Bernward Vesper-Triangel) to Verlag Kurt Desch GMB? 1967
RSt. to 1967
CF to 1969
von Makal, Paul K. **7** 1966-9
Encl: essays
CF to 1966
von Wright, G.H. **2** 1967
To CF 1967
BR to 1967
CF to 1967
Vyas, R.N. 1963

W

WAIF-International Social Service (Mrs. Jerome Margulis) 1965
RS to 1965
Wainright, Charles Anthony .. 1965
RS to 1965
The Wall Street Journal (William E. Burrows) 1969
CF to 1969
Walrus (Lani Kask) to CF **2** 1967
CF to 1967
War/Peace Report (Richard Hudson) 1962
Encl: text of *Kuboyama, and the Saga of the Lucky Dragon*
BR to **2** 1962-3
Encl: BR's foreword to *Kuboyama, and the Saga of the Lucky Dragon*
Ward, Michael D., to BRPF 1967
RSt. to 1967
Washington Evening Star,
BR to 1963
RS to 1966
Washington Post (James Russell Wiggins, Karl E. Meyer) **3** 1965-9
To CF 1967
To RS **4** 1964-5
Encl: questionnaire
BR to **2** 1963-4
RS to **3** 1964-5
Washington Square Press (Cynthia White) 1964
RS to 1964
Wasson, M.J., BR to 1963
Watan (G.N. Khayal) 1966
BR to 1966
Waters, Timothy J. 1969
Watkins, John M. 1962
BR to 1962
C.A. Watts & Co. (T.M. Schuller, Dorothy Barsby) 1967
To CF 1967
Encl: photocopies of reviews
CF to 1967
Watts, Stephen, BR to 1966
Ways of Peace (Mark Drayoumis) 1962
NJ to 1962
WBAI Radio Station (Hamish Sinclair) 1962
We, The Peoples (S.R. Motwani) 1967
Webb, N. 1965
PW to 1965
The Week (Ken Coates *et al.*) **4** 1963-5
To CF **8** 1965
To RS **3** 1965

To PW 1964
Encl.
PW to 1964
BR to **5** 1964-5
CF to **10** 1965
RS to **2** 1965
Encl: note to CF 1965
Weekend Telegraph (Michael Davison) **3** 1966-8
To CF 1966
To RSt. 1967
Encl.
CF to **2** 1966-8
RSt. to 1967
George Weidenfeld & Nicolson (George Weidenfeld *et al.*) **4** 1961-8
To RS 1967
BR to 1967
Weingarten, Samuel **2** 1966-8
Encl.
BR to 1966
CF to 1968
The West Australian (Griff Richards) 1970
Encl: clipping
CF to 1970
West London Observer
to BRPF 1967
West of England Campaign against Factory Farming (Roger Moody, Reginald Pearce) **2** 1965
To RS 1965
RS to **2** 1965
West Riding Humanist Society (Harry Bales) 1962
Encl: newsl.
Western Australian Medical Students' Society (Beverleigh-Mae Fitch) 1967
CF to 1967
Western Mail (Tony Austin, Diana McConomy, Tom Davies) **2** 1964
BR to **2** 1963-4
Western Review (Cathie Bower) 1964
BR to 1965
Westoby, Frank 1957
Encl: Westoby to Felix Pirani, Pirani to Westoby re *ABC of Relativity*
Who's Who in America (Kenneth N. Anglemire) ... 1967
Encl: form ls., advertisements, tear sheets, correction of BR's *Who's Who* entry
Who's Who in British Science 1956
Der Widerstandskämpfer (Aleksander Cichocki)
to RS 1964
To Tom Kinsey 1963
Wiener, Philip P. 1952
Wiesenthal, Simon 1969
Wilk, Andrzej 1967
CF to 1967
Window on the World (Mary H. Weik) (issue of newsl.) 1963
BR to 1963
CF to 1964
Wisdom (Tufail A. Qureshi) 1966
RS to 1966
Wise, J. Hooper 1951
Wissenschaftliche Buchgesellschaft (Franz Geist) **2** .. 1967-8
To CF 1968
Encl: Appleton-Century-Crofts (Burton C. Frye) to Wissenschaftliche Buchgesellschaft (Franz Geist) 1968
CF to **2** 1968
WNEW-TV (Virginia Woodruff) 1967
CF to 1967
Wolfman, Cyril .... n.d.
Wolman, Benjamin B. 1966
Encl.
CF to 1966
Woman Today (note, issue of magazine containing message from ER) 1958
Woolf, Cecil 1967
Encl: circular, autobiographical sketch corrected by CF
BR to 1967
The Worcester Diocesan

Messenger (Roger Corbet-Milward) 2 1964
Encl: W. Rees-Wright to *The Worcester Diocesan Messenger* 1964
The World (John L. Balderston) 2 1924
World Academy of Art and Science (Stuart Mudd, Hugo Boyko) 3 1963-8
Encl: form ls., biographical sketch of BR, review
BR to 1963
World Outlook (Pierre Frank, Reba Hansen, Joseph Hansen) to BRPF 1966
To RS 2 1965-6
PW to 1965
RS to 2 1965-6
The World Publishing Co. (William Targ, Sarah Rollitts) 1963
To RS 1964
Encl: The World Publishing Co. (Sarah Rollitts) to PAX (Tor Bjerkmann) 1964
BR to 1963
RS to 1964
Encl: PAX (Tor Bjerkmann) to BR 1964
World Union (S. M. Ghose) 1964
BR to 1964
World Union of Jewish Students (Andrew J. Greystoke), BR to 1964
World Youth (Sukhendu Majumder) 1958
Wulfsberg, Fredrik 1967
CF to 1967

Y

Yale Political (Don Gastwirth, Jerome Hamlin) 2 1964
Yearsley, John A. 1962
BR to 1962
Yevonde (Margaret Smythe) 1963
BR to 1963
Yomiuri Shimbun (Toshio Shimizu, Toshiharu Kubo) 2 1962-3
To RS 1963
RS to 1963
York Gazette & Daily (James Higgins) to RS 1964
RS to 2 1964
BR to 2 1964-6
York University Magazine (Richard Carey) 1968
CF to 1968
York Vietnam Group to PW 1965
The Yorkshire Post (Kenneth Young, Tom Greenwell) 2 1962
Young Rationalists' Club (A. S. G. Kassam) 1951
Young Socialist (Elizabeth Barnes, William Reynolds) to RS 2 1966
Encl.
RS to 1966
Young Women's Christian Association of Zambia (Jean Drysdale) 1965
RS to 1965
Yusufzai, Farman 8 1964-6
To RS 2 1964
Encl: poems
BR to 4 1964
RS to 1964
PW to 2 1965-6

Z

Zápisník 63 (Milan Codr) 2 1963
BR to 1963
RS to 1963
Zaustinsky, Julia, BR to 1963
Zeigler, Harley H. 1969
CF to 1969
Zelluk, Graham J. 1963
BR to 1963
Zemedelsko Zname 1958
Zimri (M. J. Engelhard) 1967
CF to 1967
Zo Haderekh (Ruth Lubitz) to BRPF 1970

*500
Political Organizations to 1955

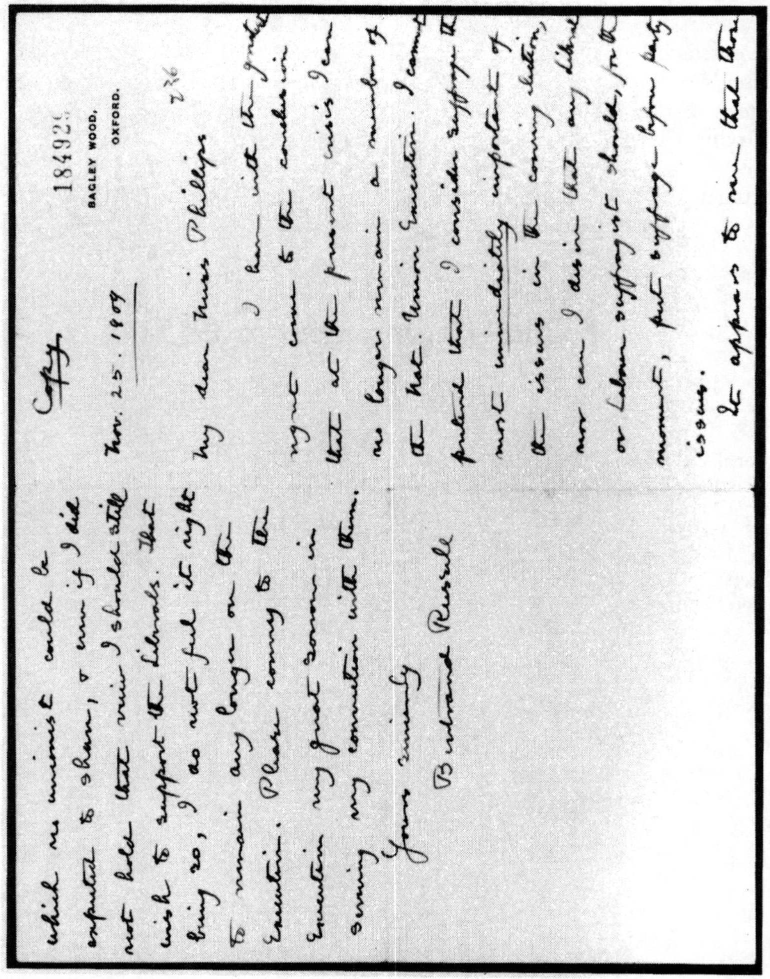

Copy

184929

BAGLEY WOOD,
OXFORD.

Nov. 25. 1909

236

My dear Miss Phillips

I have with the greatest regret come to the conclusion that at the present crisis I can no longer remain a member of the Nat. Union Executive. I cannot pretend that I consider suffrage the most immediately important of the issues in the coming election, nor can I desire that any Liberal or Labour suffragist should, for the moment, put suffrage before party issues.

It appears to me that those which no unionist could be expected to share, & even if I did not hold that view I should still wish to support the Liberals. That being so, I do not feel it right to remain any longer on the Executive. Please convey to the Executive my great sorrow in severing my connection with them.

Yours sincerely
Bertrand Russell

Plate 5 Copy in Alys Russell's hand of Russell's resignation letter of 25 November 1909 to Marion Phillips, Secretary of the National Union of Women's Suffrage Societies.

*510 Women's Suffrage

The outstanding items here are the original copy (in Alys Russell's hand) of Russell's resignation in 1909 from the Executive of the National Union of Women's Suffrage Societies and the reply from the Secretary, Marion Phillips. In Archives I only a later typed copy of Russell's letter was present.

Documents .184901–.184931

National Union of Women's Suffrage Societies (printed notices)
Henry Chaplin
"The Appointment and Duties of Land Tax Commissioners"
Leaflets
Marion Phillips

*600
Nuclear Disarmament

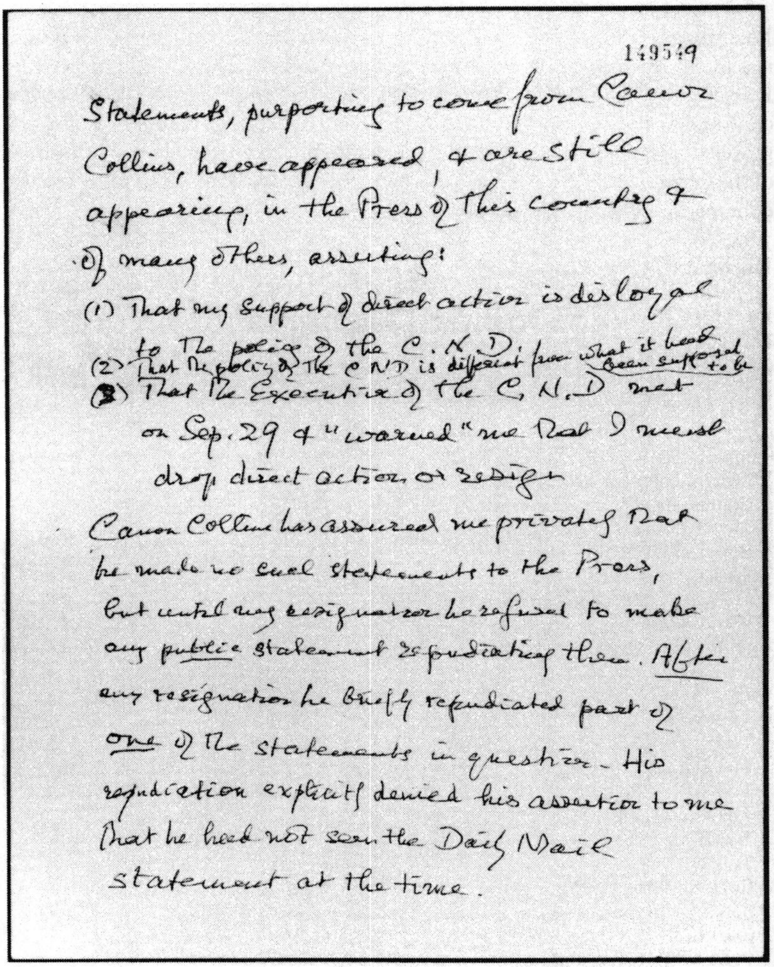

149549

Statements, purporting to come from Canon Collins, have appeared, & are still appearing, in the Press of this country & of many others, asserting:

(1) That my support of direct action is disloyal to the policy of the C.N.D.

(2) That the policy of the CND is different from what it had been supposed to be

(3) That the Executive of the C.N.D met on Sep. 29 & "warned" me that I must drop direct action or resign

Canon Collins has assured me privately that he made no such statements to the Press, but until my resignation he refused to make any *public* statement repudiating them. *After* my resignation he briefly repudiated part of *one* of the statements in question. His repudiation explicitly denied his assertion to me that he had not seen the Daily Mail statement at the time.

Plate 6 Manuscript of statement by Russell on his dispute with Canon L. John Collins over the compatibility of CND and the Committee of 100.

*630 Nuclear Disarmament Campaigns

Beginning in 1962, these files continue the CND files of Archives I. Then there is a file of detailed draft and official statements concerning the split between Russell and Canon Collins. Russell subsequently resigned from CND. The files continue with Committee of 100 documents—letters, statements, mimeographed minutes, etc.—ending shortly after Russell's resignation as President of the Committee early in 1963. A second box is full of leaflets and other printed ephemera. They are not numbered.

Documents .149301–.149717

Campaign for Nuclear Disarmament (L. John Collins, Peter Simmons, J. M. Taylor, Peter Cadogan, Adam Roberts, David Powell, Stuart Hall, Peggy Duff, Margaret Lloyd, K. C. Woodsworth, David E. Spilsbury, David Boulton, Dick Nettleton, *et al.*) **35** 1962-9
To RS **6** 1962-4
To Pat Pottle **2** 1963
To CE **12** 1963-4
To BRPF **18** 1963-6
To CF **8** 1963-9
To HR 1965
To PW 1965
Encl: form ls., press releases, political literature, leaflets, post cs.
1 box of CND literature
RS to **11** 1962-6
BR to **32** 1962-8
CF to **10** 1962-9
AY to 1963
CE to **12** 1963-4
ER to 1964
HR to **6** 1965
PW to **4** 1965-6

Committee of 100 (Peter Cadogan, Ella Morgan, Wendy Butlin, Michael Harwood, David Mathias, Karl Taylor, *et al.*) **35** 1962-5
To BR and ER **2** 1962
To CF **2** 1962
To RS **5** 1962
To Jon Tinker 1962
To ER 1963
To PJ 1963
To BRPF 1965
Encl: Birbeck, Julius, Coburn & Broad to London Committee of 100 (Jon Tinker) 1962
Jon Tinker to Birbeck, Coburn & Broad 1962
Committee of 100 (Cadogan) to Chou En-lai 1962
Committee of 100 (Cadogan) to Jawaharlal Nehru 1962
speeches, political literature, leaflets, minutes etc.
BR to **2** 1962
(not sent)
CF to **9** 1962
BR to **21** 1962-8
ER to 1963

HR to 1965
Encl: "Statement from Bertrand Russell 26 August 1962", "Press Statement" by BR
1 file of notes re clash with Canon Collins in Sept. 1960

1 box of leaflets, pamphlets, and other printed matter relating principally to the Committee of 100

*700
Personal and Family Correspondence

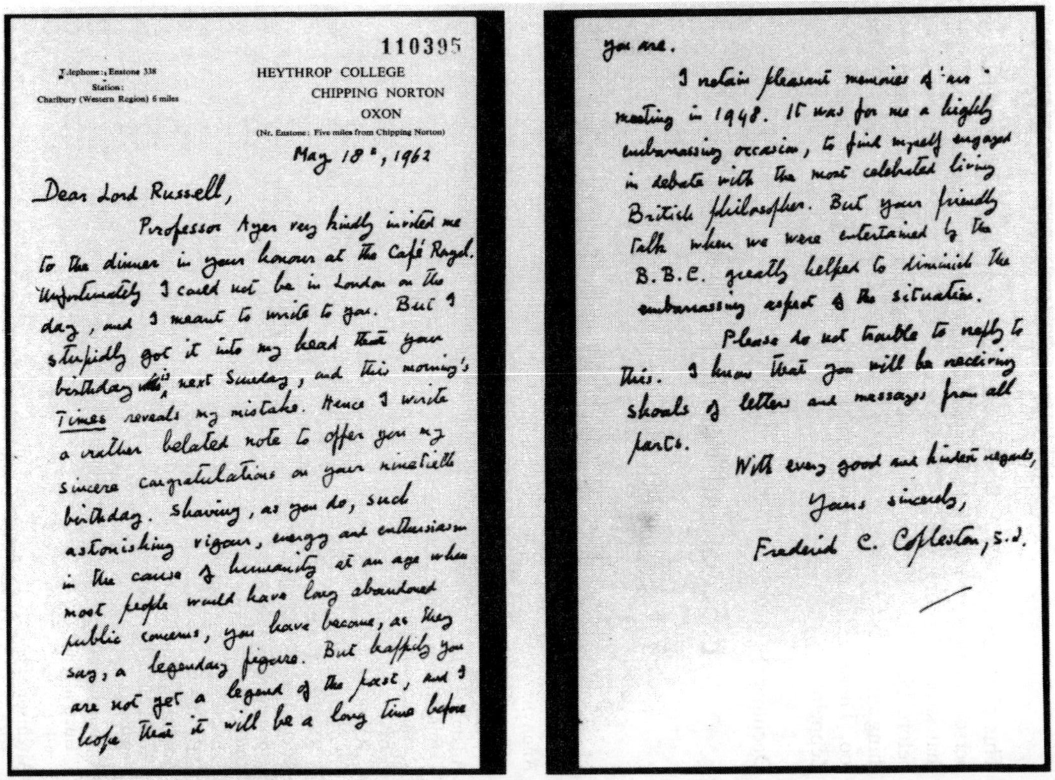

110395

Telephone: Enstone 338
Station:
Charlbury (Western Region) 6 miles

HEYTHROP COLLEGE
CHIPPING NORTON
OXON
(Nr. Enstone: Five miles from Chipping Norton)

May 18th, 1962

Dear Lord Russell,

Professor Ayer very kindly invited me to the dinner in your honour at the Café Royal. Unfortunately I could not be in London on the day, and I meant to write to you. But I stupidly got it into my head that your birthday was next Sunday, and this morning's *Times* reveals my mistake. Hence I write a rather belated note to offer you my sincere congratulations on your ninetieth birthday. Showing, as you do, such astonishing vigour, energy and enthusiasm in the cause of humanity at an age when most people would have long abandoned public concerns, you have become, as they say, a legendary figure. But happily you are not yet a legend of the past, and I hope that it will be a long time before you are.

I retain pleasant memories of our meeting in 1948. It was for me a highly embarrassing occasion, to find myself engaged in debate with the most celebrated living British philosopher. But your friendly talk when we were entertained by the B.B.C. greatly helped to diminish the embarrassing aspect of the situation.

Please do not trouble to reply to this. I know that you will be receiving shoals of letters and messages from all parts.

With every good and kindest regards,

Yours sincerely,

Frederick C. Copleston, S.J.

Plate 7 Father F.C. Copleston to Russell, 18 May 1962.

*710 Personal Correspondence

This class contains correspondence, chiefly non-political, with well-known persons or persons known to Russell, as well as correspondence with others that is of particular interest. In addition, *710 includes any letters written before 1952 (the year Russell married Edith Finch, who kept almost everything since that time). Letters found in books in Russell's library are filed here, too. There are also letters written to Edith Russell (e.g., from Amethe von Zeppelin).

Documents .110001–.112657

A

Anonymous **8** 1905-64
———, Tony **2** 1929
———, V. 1926
Adams, Taylor **6** 1962
Encl: l. to *New York Times*, clippings and newsl.
BR to 1962
AY to 1962
CF to 1962
RS to 1962
Adelaide University Agnostic Society (P. Buny *et al.*) **2** 1963
Encl.
BR to **2** 1963
Administration des Monnaies et Médailles (P. Dehaye) 1966
BR to 1966
Agassi, Joseph 1969
Encl: article
CF to 1969
Aitchison, Peggy **2** 1966-7
BR to 1967
Alexander, John 1955
Encl: photos of personal documents
Allen, George L. **2** 1963
BR to **2** 1963
Almond, Joseph **3** 1967-9
BR to 1968
CF to 1969
American Humanist Association (Bette Chambers *et al.*) **6** 1962-8
To CF 1968
Encl: form ls., clippings
BR to **3** 1963-8
CF to 1964
Amulree, Lord 1966
BR to 1966
Encl: note
Annesley, Priscilla, Lady, BR to 1918
Ansell, Mary, BR to 1966
Encl.
Antony, Jonquil 1965
BR to 1968
Anwar, Saquib 1966
BR to 1966
Armstrong, Eunice B., to BR and ER 1961
To ER **4** 1956-9
Encl: *World Wealth without War*, *et al.*

BR to 1962
Armstrong, William
M. **3** 1967
Encl: 2 tss. "Bertrand Russell Comes to America, 1896"; photocopies of ls. from H. Sidgwick, BR, James Carey Thomas, James Ward, Thomas Craig, S. Newcomb, H. B. Fine, H. M. Butler 1896
BR to **2** 1967
CF to **2** 1967
CF to Barry Feinberg 1967
Arnold, Percy 1966
BR to 1966
Arya, Jitendra 1952
Ashford, Montague B.,
BR to 1964
Asiatic Society 1961
Re Tagore medal
The Athenaeum **8** 1950-69
Encl.
BR to 1968
CF to 1967
Atkinson, Janice 1965
BR to 1965
Avedon Baldwin, Mr.,
BR to 1964
Avery, D. **7** 1955-67
Ayer, A. J. **8** 1962-9
Encl: l. from Corliss Lamont
BR to **5** 1964-9
PW to 1967

B

Baillie, James H. 1965
Encl: clipping
BR to 1965
Baker, Pat, BR to 1964
Bandaranaike, Sirimavo,
to RS 1964
RS to 1964
Bardoe-Darfor, L. L. **3** 1969
BR to **2** 1969
Encl: l. to Master Bertrand Russell Bardoe-Darfor
Barry, Roderick, BR to **2** ... 1964
Bart, Lionel, BR to 1967
Barua, Dilip K. 1964
BR to 1964
Bates, Ken 1966
BR to 1966
Battle, Sol **2** 1968
Encl.
BR to 1968
Bayerl, Leopold 1968
BR to 1968
Beasley, Gertrude 1924
Beaton, Cecil 1968
BR to 1968
Beckman, Viking **6** 1962
To CF 1962
Encl: photo, summary of book
BR to **2** 1962
Bedford, Ian, Duke of **5** .. 1967-9
BR to **4** 1966-9
RS to 1966
Bedford, Nicole, Duchess
of **2** 1967
To ER **2** .... 1963-?
Encl: card
Bedford, Sybille 1965
CF to 1965
Beecroft, Eric 1940
Encl: l. to Robert G. Sproul
Behmann, Heinrich **2** 1923
Encl: offprint, "Die Antinomie der transfiniten Zahl und ihre Auflösung durch die Theorie von Russell und Whitehead". All removed from BR's copy of *Principia*, I (1910)
Bell, Alan S. 1967
Encl: Alys Russell to Lord Haldane 1918
BR to 1967
Berkman, [Alexander],
BR to 1925
Bernays, Paul 1920
Removed from BR's copy of *Principia*, I (1910)
Beveridge, W. H. 1923
Birnberg, Naomi
(Bentwich) 1962
Black?, C. 1921
Blackett, P. M. S., BR to **2** .. 1965
Böll, Heinrich 1964
RS to 1964

Boothby, Lord 1964
BR to **2** 1964-6
Born, Gustav **3** 1969-70
Encl.
BR to **2** 1969-70
Born, Max **7** 1951-68
BR to **10** 1955-69
Encl: Rupert Crawshay-Williams to BR 1951
Boskovitz, Alfred 1923
Removed from BR's copy of *Principia*, I (1910) (now in *210)
Brain, Patricia 1968
ER to 1968
Braithwaite, E. R. 1966
CF to 1966
Brandhurst, Edward F. 1962
BR to 1962
Brandt, Heinz 1967
BR to 1967
Brenan, Gamel .... n.d.
To ER **11** 1958-65
Encl: Phyllis Playter to BR
Brenan, Gerald 1968
BR to 1968
Brill, Klaus **2** 1969
CF to ? 1969
The British Council (A. B. Gerrard, R. J. Parkhouse, Roger Bayes) **5** 1962-9
Encl.
BR to **2** 1962-4
CF to 1967
PW to 1967
British Museum (Ernest Anderson) 1966
BR to **2** 1963-4
RS to 1965
Brittain, Vera **2** 1963-4
Britton, Lionel **2** 1969
BR to 1969
CF to 1969
Broad, C. D. **5** 1947-67
BR to **3** 1959-68
RS to 1966
Brooks, Rachel Gleason 1969
Encl.
BR to **2** 1968-9
Broomhead, Ann 1947
Brown, Frank **2** 1953-4
Removed from BR's copy of *A History of Western Philosophy*
Tom Brown, Tailor (G. W. Brown) **2** 1953-68
Brüden, I., to Elsie? 1916
Brudno, Miriam 1928
Brudno, Mollie R. 2 1928-39
Ms. by PR on verso of 1 l.
Brune, David 1963
BR to **2** 1963
Buber, Martin 1962
Encl: l. from GPO, Returned Letter Branch, re Buber l.
RS to 1962
BR to 1963
Bunge, Mario 1967
Burbank, W. N. L. 1965
Burdett, Maud 1945
Burn, Mary, to ER and BR **2** 1967
To ER **2** 1967
Burn, Michael **10** 1962-9
To ER **2** 1967
BR to **2** .... 196?-8
Burt, Maud K. 1920
Encl: note by BR
Bynum, Terrell Ward 1965

C

Cambridge Union Society (B. H. Pollitt) 1962
BR to 1962
Cambridge University—Magpie and Stump (leaflet) .... 1892?
Cameron ?, Alistair and Peggy 1967
Cameron, Elizabeth and Hamish, to ER .... n.d.
Cant, Catherine B. H. 1962
BR to 1962
Carmiel, Y. 1964
BR to 1964
Carnap, Rudolf, BR to 1965
Encl: envelope addressed by Carnap 1965
Carver Centennial Committee, George Washington (Mallie Robinson, Robert

D. Hobday) **2** 1964
Encl.
BR to **2** 1964
Catlin, George E.
Gordon **5** 1963-4
RS to **3** 1963-4
BR to 1964
Catling & Son **2** 1916
Re auction of BR's goods
to pay fine and court costs
Centenaire de Romain Rolland
(R. A. Francis, Marie
Romain Rolland) **2** 1966
Encl.
BR to **2** 1965-6
The Center Magazine (Harvey
Wheeler) 1969
BR to 1970
Chambers, Bertram M. 1922
Chance, Roger 1969
BR to 1969
Chang, Siang-mei **2** 1962
Chao, Yuen Ren **3** 1965
RS to 1965
BR to **3** 1968
Charles Hamilton Autographs,
Inc., BR to 1966
Chatterji, N. 1967
BR to 1967
Chauncey, Henry, to John
Russell 1940
Chesters, Mary Walsh .... n.d.
BR to 1967
Chevassut, F. G. 1966
BR to **2** 1966
The Chinese (Students)
Association for the Pro-
motion of Education 1924
City of Nottingham Public
Libraries (David E.
Gerard) **3** 1965
RS to **3** 1965
Clark, Kenneth B. 1963
To RS 1963
Clark, Mrs. Kenneth B. 1963
Clark, Ronald W. 1965
Clarke, Francis 1923
Cleaver, Eldridge, BR to 1968
Cockerell, Sydney, to
ER **3** 1960-1
Cohen, Betty **2** 1959
Collins, L. John 1962
BR to 1960
Commission de rédaction des
oeuvres complètes de N. I.
Lobatchevsky (D. Egoroff,
A. Vasiliev, Ben. Kagan) ... 1923
The Committee to Celebrate
the 90th Birthday Anni-
versary of Dr. Harry F.
Ward (Mrs. Royal W.
France) 1963
Encl.
Le Conférence des Sommets
(Pierre Vandendries) .... n.d.
Conseil Suprême de
l'Intellectualité Mondiale
(Anthony Pissanos) 1962
BR to 1962
Cooper-Willis, Irene 1915
Copi, Irving M. 1964
Copleston, Frederick
C. **4** 1948-65
BR to **2** 1962-6
Cousens, Dorothy .... n.d.
Cowell, F. Richard 1968
BR to 1968
Coy, Frederick W. **2** 1921
Crawshay-Williams, Elizabeth,
to BR .... 1953?
To BR and ER 1967
To ER **3** 1967
Crawshay-Williams,
Rupert **5** 1959-66
To ER 1965
Encl: notes on BR's *Auto-
biography*, I
RS to 1967
BR to 1968
Encl: ts. by BR, review
Crone, Winifred **2** 1952
Re S. A. Mellor
Crunden, Alice 1928
Cumming, Richard 1964
BR to 1964
Curwen, Margaret 1964
BR to 1963

D

Dagenais, Ferdinand 1966
BR to 1966
Dakyns, Peggy 1968
BR to 1967
Daniel, Laura 1966
BR to 1966
D'Arcy, M.C. 1967
BR to 1967
Davies, Clive 1962
BR to 1962
de Bono, Edward 1969
CF to 1969
De Chadenedes, Mrs. François (Edith), to ER 1966
Dedijer, Vladimir, BR to 1966
Deighton, Len 1967
Re Ysabele de Ranitz
BR to 1966
RS to 1966
de Selincourt, Paul, BR to 1964
D'Esterre, E. 1923
Deudraeth Rural District Council (J. Ellis) **4** 1968-9
BR to 1968
Dick, Oliver Lawson 1948
Removed from between pp. 200-1 of BR's library copy of *Aubrey's Brief Lives*, ed. Dick (London, 1949)
Dunham, Barrows 1965
Dunn, J.C. 1948

E

Eames, Elizabeth R. **4** 1965-8
Encl: clippings and articles
BR to **6** 1964-9
Eames, Elizabeth R. and Morris 1966
Ede, and Ravenscroft Ltd. **3** 1967-9
Edinburgh City Labour Party (June Hay) 1963
BR to 1963
Edwards, Paul, BR to 1967
Eke, Annie M. 1924
Ellisor, F.L. Page 1965
BR to 1965
Emergency Civil Liberties Committee (Clark Foreman) **7** 1962-3
Encl: ts. by Corliss Lamont
BR to **3** 1962-3
Emery, George L. 1964
BR to 1964
Escuela Preparatoria "Bertrand Russell" (Cristina María Cañedo y Cañedo and Salvador Montes Osèguera) 1968
BR to 1968
Essier, P.W. 1924
The Esterhazy Orchestra Foundation Inc. (David Blum) **2** 1966-7
BR to **3** 1966-7
Estreicjer, Karol 1967
BR to 1967
Evans, John G. 1963
BR to 1963
Everard, [Elizabeth],
BR to 1924
Everett, Horace S. 1969
CF to 1969
Eversley, David 1964
BR to 1964
Exton-Smith, Norman **3** .. 1966-7
BR to **3** 1966
CF to 1967

F

Falk, Avner **2** 1961-2
BR to 1962
Farley, Christopher **3** 1962-3
To BR and ER **6** 1963-5
To ER **6** 1962-4
To RS **22** 1962-5
Encl.
ER to **3** 1962-4
RS to **5** 1963
Fforde, J.S. 1968
Field, Gina **3** 1969
BR to 1969
CF to **2** 1969
Finlay, M.S. 1963
Flexner, Betty 1962
To ER 1969

Foldes, Andor, BR to 1964
Follwell, Joan **2** 1929
Forchhammer, Grethe 1935
Ford, Oliver E. 1964
BR to 1964
Foreign Office (J. H. Sanderson) 1894
Encl: BR's honorary attaché card
Forester, S., to ER .... n.d.
Forster, E. M., BR to 1969
RS to 1966
Forte's, CE to 1962
Foster, Harry 1967
CF to 1967
Foulkes, Paul **8** 1960-9
Encl: reviews of *Wisdom of the West* (l. of 19.7.60 removed from BR's copy of *A History of Western Philosophy*)
Ashbrook, H. F., to BR, and reply 1960
BR to **3** 1964-9
Fox, Barry **3** 1928
Fox-Pitt, Elspeth .... 1934?
Fox-Pitt, Lionel, to Duke of Bedford 1963
CF to **2** 1963-5
Fraenkel, A. 1952
Frankl, Gerald **2** 1961-2
ER to 1961
BR to 1962
Fremantle, Anne **3** 1968-9
BR to **4** 1966-9
Fribourg and Freyer (R. H. Bridgman-Evans) **2** 1967-8
BR to 1968
CF to 1968
Friedlander, Zelda, BR to **2** 1964
RS to 1964
Fromm, Erich **14** 1962-6
To CF 1962
To RS **3** 1963-4
To *Peace News* 1962
Mayer, B. H. (on behalf of Erich Fromm), to RS 1963
Encl: memo, Erich Fromm to Aspen Institute for Humanistic Studies 1964
BR to **8** 1962-6
CF to **2** 1962-3
RS to **3** 1963-4
Fromm, Erich and Anes, BR to 1967
Fry, G., to Alys Russell 1921

G

Gannon, Patricio **3** 1964
RS to 1964
Garnsey, D. A., BR to 1968
Re Jon and David Wood
Gault, David **2** 1968
BR to 1968
Gibbins, John R. 1969
CF to 1969
Giblin, L. F. 1950
Encl: "The Crisis in Democracy"
Gilbert, Martin .... n.d.
BR to 1963
Giles, Lionel **2** 1922-3
Removed from BR's copy of *The Problem of China*
Goffe, Elisabeth 1964
Encl.
BR to 1964
Goldman, Emma 1924
Gonin, Michael S. 1965
BR to 1965
Gooch, George P. 1967
Encl: ts. review of BR's *Auto.*, I
BR to 1967
Gould, Nicholas 1969
CF to 1969
Grant, David 1967
CF to 1967
Grattan-Guinness, Ivor **2** .. 1967-9
CF to 1969
Green, Paul **2** 1965
To BRPF 1966
BR to 1965
PW to **2** 1965
RS to 1966
Green, Paul and Elizabeth **2** .... ?-1969
Grew, Richard L. **2** .... n.d.

BR to 1962
CF to 1967
Griffin, Nicholas J. **3** 1964-8
[To RS] **3** .... n.d.
BR to **2** 1964-7
RS to **3** 1965-6
CF to **2** 1966-8
Griffin, Stuart H., BR to 1963
Griffith, Gwilym O. **2** 1962
BR to 1962
Griffiths, H., ER to 1967
Griffiths, Lillian, to
ER **2** 1954
To BR and ER **2** 1954-5
Griffiths, Leslie M. S. 1967
Encl.
BR to **2** 1963-7
Griffiths, Ruby .... n.d.
Groom, Robert, BR to 1963
Gropius, Walter, RS to 1962
Gross, Fine & Krieger,
Chalfen (C. Krieger) 1969
Gueron, Maurice 1952
Gurwala, Shiv Narain 1962
BR to 1962

H

Haldane, Helen Spurway 1969
Encl: l. from McMaster University (K. Blackwell)
BR to 1969
Haldane, J. B. S. **2** 1932-61
Encl: proof of article
Halsbury, Earl of 1968
Hambleton, Ronald 1968
Theodore Hamblin Ltd.
(G. W. D. McLaren) **2** .. 1966-8
To CF **2** 1968
Encl.
CF to **2** 1968
Hanarth, Rachel 1967
BR to 1967
Hand, Fanny 8 to ER ... 1959-61
Hand, Judge Learned 1952
To BR and ER 1957
Harburg, E. Y. 1965
To BRPF 1963
Encl.
CF to 1963
RS to 1965
Harding, Stan (a page concerning whom torn from *Institute Journal* published by Institute of Journalists) 1925
Harrison, Royden **3** 1966
BR to **2** 1966
CF to 1966
Hartley, Leslie, to ER 1957
Harvey, Dorothy (née
Dudley) **4** 1927-8
Havighurst, Alfred F. **3** 1965
BR to **2** 1965
Haymon, Mark **2** 1969
BR to 1969
CF to 1969
Hearnshaw, J. B. 1967
CF to 1967
Heinemann, F. H. **2** 1967
BR to **2** 1967
Hell, Michael 1956
Encl: translations of Soviet articles on BR
Heller, Joseph 1962
To RS 1962
Encl.
BR to 1962
RS to 1962
Hemstreet, Robert 1968
BR to 1968
Henkin, Leon **2** 1963
Encl: article
BR to 1963
Hervey, Helen 1965
Heyerdahl, Thor 1962
Encl: article
Hill, Leslie 1963
BR to 1963
Hill, L. Rowland 1963
Encl.
Hocking, William Ernest 1963
Encl: essay
BR to 1963
Hodin, J. P. 1964
BR to 1964
Hogben, Lancelot 1969
To CF 1968
ER to 1961
CF to **2** 1968

BR to 1969
Holland, Kevin **3** 1964-8
To BR and ER **2** 1969-70
BR to **3** 1968-70
Holmes, A. W. **2** 1954
Holroyd, Michael **5** 1966-8
BR to **4** 1966-8
Holter, Norman J. 1969
BR to 1969
Honig, Camille R. .... n.d.
PW to 1966
Hook, Sidney 1964
Hooper, S. E. **2** 1924
Encl: Report of Organising Committee of British Institute of Philosophical Studies
Hotel Portmeirion (M. Trevor-Williams) to ER **3** 1967
ER to 1967
Howard, John N. 1964
BR to 1964
Howland, Blanche Winifred .. 1962
Huang Sung Kang **3** 1956
BR to 1956
Hughes, E. 1908
Hughes, Valerie 1964
BR to 1964
Huntingdon, ? 1967
Huntingdon, Margaret **2** ... 1967
To ER 1967
Huxley, Julian, to BR and ER **2** 1965-9
To BR 1967
BR to 1964
Huxley, Juliette, **3** ...... 1963?-7
To BR and ER 1969
To ER **4** 1967
Encl: re Huxleys' golden wedding anniversary

I

The Institute of Mathematics and Its Applications (P. G. Wakely) 1969
To CF **2** 1969
CF to **2** 1969
The International Faculty of Mental Sciences at Haarlem (J. L. van Essen-de Savornin Lohman) **3** .. 1967
Encl: essay
BR to **2** 1967
CF to 1968
International Grotius Foundation for the Propagation of the Laws of Nations (Hans Keller) **8** 1962-8
Encl: pamphlets
RS to **2** 1962-3
BR to **3** 1962-4
CF to **3** 1963-9
Irshad, Hakim Syed, BR to ... 1963

J

Jackson, Annabel ("Tiny") Huth .. 1942
Jacobsohn, Samuel 1919
Removed from BR's copy of *Principia*, I (1910)
Jacobson, Roy, BR to 1963
Jacoby, E. G. 1969
Jarett, Arthur William 1967
BR to 1967
Jencks, Richard W. 1969
Joachim, Harold H. .... 1892?
Joad, Doreen **4** 1929
Joesten, Joachim, BR to 1966
Jones, Mr., ER to 1961
Jones, Judith, BR to 1963
Jordan, Mr., BR to 1966
Joseph, Linda 1962
BR to 1962
Judge, Anthony **3** .... n.d.
Encl: essays
BR to **3** 1962

K

Kallen, H. M. **2** 1915-24
Kaneko, Mitsuo **2** 1968-9
BR to 1968
Kang, Sugwon, BR to 1968
Kar, Ida, to ER 1968
Encl: pamphlets
ER to **2** 1968

(note from CF about Ida Kar, n.d.)
Karl, Frederick R. **2** 1965-6
Encl: H. S. Thayer to BR 1966
RS to 1966
Karolyi, Catherine **2** 1967
Encl.
BR to 1967
Karolyi, Michael ..... n.d.
Kassman, Alec 1969
Encl.
Kastner, Harold **5** 1952-65
BR to **2** 1963-4
PW to 1965
Kaufmann, George V. 1919
Keene, Donald 1952
Kemelman, Arthur F. 1962
BR to 1962
Kern, Joseph 1962
BR to 1962
Keynes, Margaret **2** 1967-8
BR to 1968
Kielland, Nalle **5** 1965
Encl: 2 ls. from Phylis Urch, l. from Constance Malleson
BR to 1965
Kimbrell, Markete, BR to 1962
King-Hele, Desmond **4** 1964-8
Encl: essay
BR to **3** 1964
RS to **2** 1964
Kirwood, Mary, to BR and ER 1962
Kiskadden, Peggy 1969
BR to 1969
Klein, Alexander 1949
Encl: l. from A. Einstein 1949
Kneeland Frantz, Virginia, to ER 1960
Knestrick, Ray E. 1924
Knight, Frida **3** 1969
Encl.
BR to 1969
CF to 1969
Koch, Chris, BR to 1966
Koestler, Arthur **3** 1946
Encl: l. and draft petition
Koestler, Mamaine 1946
Kon, T. S. **2** 1965-6
BR to 1965
Konkokyo Church of Izuo (Toshio Miyake) 1962
BR to **2** 1962-4
Koo, Joo Ok 1962
BR to 1962
Koslow, Julian **4** 1962-6
Encl.
BR to **4** 1962-4
Kreisel, Georg 1966
Encl: s. for Gödel as Foreign Member of Royal Society
BR to 1966
Kubersky, C. 1966
CF to 1967
Kunkel, Dudley S. 1963
BR to 1963
Kunstler, William M. **2** 1968-9
CF to 1968
BR to **2** 1969
Encl: re Honeywell Corporation advert of BR
Kuntz, Paul G. 1969
CF to 1969
Kutzko, Philip 1962
BR to 1962

L

Lackides, George 1962
BR to 1962
Lacombe, Pierre 1965
BR to 1965
Lagercrantz, Marika 1963
CF to 1963
Lago, Mary M. 1969
BR to 1969
Lagriffaul, Henri **3** 1966-7
BR to **2** 1966
Laidlaw, S. Graham 1962
Encl.
BR to 1962
Lall, R. B. 1963
BR to 1963
Lamont, Corliss **7** 1924-69
To RS 1964
Encl.
BR to **13** 1962-9
RS to **2** 1962-4

CF to 1967
Lane, Mark, BR to 1968
Larson, Cedric A. 1963
BR to **2** 1963-4
Lasch, Zora 1964
BR to 1964
Laski, Marghanita 1964
BR to 1964
Lawson, Arthur **2** 1962-7
Encl: ls. to *Sunday Times* and BBC
BR to **2** 1962
Leakey, R. D. 1967
CF to 1967
Leite, J. J. 1963
BR to 1963
Lennon, John, BR to 1969
Lennon, John, and Ono, Yoko .... n.d.
BR to 1970
Lessing, Doris, BR to (not sent) 1967
Leu, Lucy 1964
BR to 1964
Lever, H. .... n.d.
BR to 1962
Levine, Mrs. G., BR to 1963
Levine, Isaac Don 1962
BR to 1962
Levy, Paul **2** 1967-8
To CF **2** 1968-9
Encl: Dorothy Moore to BR
CF to **3** 1967-9
BR to 1968
Lewis, Andrew 1963
BR to 1963
Lieberman, Myron 1963
BR to 1963
Lindop, Patricia (Mrs. G. P. R. Esdale) 1963
BR to 1963
Lindquist, Ligne 1935
Littlewood, D. E. **2** 1965
BR to **3** 1965
Loewe, Raphael **2** 1969
BR to 1969
London, Fritz 1923
Removed from BR's copy of *Principia*, I (1910)
London Library 1968
Encl.
BR to 1967
CF to 1968
Longville, Timothy, BR to ... 1963
The Louise Pettibone Smith 75th Birthday Tribute (Mrs. Royal W. France) **4** 1962-6
Encl.
BR to **4** 1962-6
Lowe, Victor **11** 1963-7
BR to **9** 1963-7
Luard, G. D. 1952
Lucas, Bill J. **2** 1968-9
BR to 1968
CF to **3** 1969
Lucas, Mrs. Bill J. (Diana) 1968
Lucas, F. L. 1929
Luehrs, Jr., Fred U. 1952
BR to 1952
Lunggren, Mollie 1967
BR to 1967
Lurie, Meyer 1963
BR to 1963
Lye, Brenda 1965
BR to 1965

M

Maas, Henry **2** 1963-6
BR to **2** 1963-6
Maass, Otto 1958
MacDiarmid, Hugh 1962
BR to **2** 1962
MacIntyre, Alasdair, BR to ... 1964
MacMurray, Paul C., BR to .. 1963
Magee, Bryan **2** 1969
CF to 1969
Malleson, Bridget 1969
Malleson, Joan .... n.d.
Malleson, Lady Constance **6** 1928
Encl: 1937(?) l. from Elizabeth Russell to Priscilla Countess Annesley, photos, clipping
Malleson, Miles **2** 1924-66
CF to 1968

Mandel, George 1968
BR to 1968
Mann, Katia (Mrs. Thomas),
to Mrs. Tedesco 1955
Mannin, Ethel **4** 1930-62
BR to **2** 1930-62
Encl: cable, l. to Rickey Austin
Manning, Helen Taft,
to ER .... n.d.
Marcel, Gabriel, RS to 1962
Marcus, Raymond J.,
BR to 1963
Marcuse, Herbert .... n.d.
Markham, David **4** 1963-9
Encl.
CE to 1963
BR to 1969
Marshall, Rachel E. .... n.d.
CF to 1969
Martin, B. Kingsley 1921
Maxwell, Grover 1968
McCreery, Nigel 1962
BR to 1962
McCullough, Peter J.,
BR to 1963
McHaigh, H. 1951
McKenney, John L. 1958
McLendon, Hiram J. 1965
BR to 1965
McNally, Josette 1962
Meinong, Alexius, BR
to **3** 1904-7
Typed copies sent to BR for correcting
Meitner-Graf, Lotte 1964
BR to 1964
Mellor, Stanley A. (Hope Street Church,
Liverpool) **2** 1924
Melton, Barry **2** 1963
BR to **3** 1963-4
Menszer, John and Barbara ... 1968
Encl.
CF to .... n.d.
Menuhin, Yehudi 1967
BR to **2** 1967
Meyerhoff, Mary, BR to 1966
Migeon, Jean-Pierre,
BR to 1963
Miller, Mrs. W. 1966
Milligan, Spike **2** n.d.-1969
BR to **2** 1966
Mitchell, David, BR to 1964
Mitford, Nancy 1962
Mitton, Alexander W. D. 1968
Moore, Brenda 1966
BR to 1966
Moore, Dickin 1962
BR to 1962
Moore, G. E. 1924
Moore, John G. **2** 1968
CF to **2** 1968
Moorthy, E. P., BR to 1963
Moran, John H. **2** 1968
CF to **2** 1968
Morgan, D. E. 1962
BR to 1962
Morgan, L. O., BR to 1965
Morrell, Lady Ottoline 21
(filed in RA1) 1920-35
Morris, Reginald 1967
CF to 1967
Morris, Steven 1968
BR to 1968
Mortimer, John 1967
Morton, G. F., BR to 1964
Moscovitz, Shaler 1962
BR to 1962
Mosley, Gordon 1968
CF to 1968
Moss, Jacques 1965
PW to 1965
The Mountaineering Association (J. E. B. Wright) 1966
Encl.
BR to 1966
Muggeridge, Malcolm 1963
BR to 1963
Mumfor, Lewis 1965
BR to 1965
Encl: BR to *Daily Worker*
Mumford, Philip S. .... n.d.
BR to 1962
Mundle, C. W. K. **8** 1967-8
Encl: essays
BR to **5** 1967-9
Murdoch, Iris .... n.d.
BR to **2** 1967
Murphey, Allene 1966

BR to 1966
Murray-Brown, Jeremy,
to CF 1963
Myers, Ruth H. 1969

N

Nachbar, Ann .... n.d.
Nader, Ralph, BR to 1966
Naess, Arne 1956
Nahm, Milton, to ER 1969
ER to 1969
Nathan, Otto, BR to 2 1963-4
National Council of Labour
Colleges (J. P. M. Millar) ... 1924
Neilands, J. B.,
BR to 4 1967-9
Neill, A. S. 1968
BR to 1968
Nemetz, Peter N. 1965
Re their BR shirt
BR to 1965
Newman, Lyn 1968
BR to 1968
"Nicola, Dr." (Thomas William
Stewart), printed extract
re 1913
Encl: note by BR
Noel-Baker, Philip 1962
(Angela Killick) 1967
(Helen Armstrong),
to RS 2 1962
To ER 1963
Encl: recorded interview
between H. C. Kicer
and Philip Noel-Baker
ER to 1963
Noferl, Dorothy G. 1964
BR to 1964
Norman, C. H. 1964
Norton, Lucy 1967
BR to 1967
Noufflard, Henriette 1963
BR to 1963

O

O'Connor, D. J., BR to 1964
Encl: article on BR
Offord and Meynell Ltd.
(James Shiel) 1967
re prayer book of Lady
John Russell
BR to 1967
Onassis, Aristotle Socrates,
BR to 1963
Oppenheim, Frank M. 1969
Origo, Marquesa, BR to 1966
O'Rourke, D. T. 1964
BR to 1964
Orwell, Sonia 2 1967-8
Encl.
CF to 1967
Ouang, Tien Ki 1924
Owen, I., BR to 1964
Ozmon, Howard 2 1965-8
Encl: copies of 4 ls. from
BR, clippings
RS to 1965
CF to 1968

P

Pach, L., BR to 1964
Pachter, H. 1958
Encl: clipping of A. Kohlberg's
l. quoting BR
Pamplin, Brian 1962
BR to 1962
Panikar, I. A. 1962
BR to 1962
Pankhurst, Sylvia, BR to
(copy) 1932
Paradine, C. G. 1962
Removed from BR's copy
of *Human Knowledge*
Parkash, Om, BR to 1963
Parkhurst, Eleanor 1952
Partridge, Frances, to
ER 2 1961
Re D. MacCarthy's ls.
Paterson, Toni, BR to 1962
Paulos, John 2 1966-8
BR to 1966
Pavlichenko, Korneev 1962
BR to 1963
Pavlov, I. P. 1935

Pavlowitch, K. St. 1955
Pawlowski, Gareth L. **2** 1968
CF to 1968
Peano, Augusto 1963
BR to 1963
Peirce, David N. 1963
BR to 1963
Peretz, Martin, BR to 1966
Perez y Perez, D., BR to 1968
Perman, George **2** 1962
BR to 1962
Pessagno, George, BR to 1966
Pharis, Katharine C. **2** 1963
BR to **2** 1963
Philipp, June **2** 1963
BR to 1963
Philips Price, M. 1968
BR to 1968
Philpot, Terry G. **3** 1967-70
PW to **2** 1967-70
CF to 1969
Piatkiewicz, Wladyslaw 1962
BR to 1962
Pitout, Trevor Rex .... n.d.
BR to 1968
Plummer, ?, BR to 1953
Popper, Karl R. 1965
Encl.
BR to 1965
Portnow, Julius 1967
Encl.
BR to 1967
RSt. to 1967
Pozzo, Mario Del 1963
Prasad, P. A. Soorya **5** 1963-9
BR to **3** 1963-6
Prasad, V. V. 1947
Re Gandhi's reply on lying
"Premio Mantegna" 1964
RS to 1964
Price, M. 1969
Prichard, Dr. O. M. Tristan,
BR to 1966
Principal Probate Registry,
PW to 1969
Printing and the Mind of
Man (P. H. Muir) 1962
Encl: manifesto signed by
Frank Francis, Stanley
Morrison, John Carter
BR to 1962
Purcell, H. D. 1965
Purcell, Victor 1952
To RS **4** 1962-4
To CF **2** 1964
RS to **2** 1962-4
BR to **2** 1963
CF to **3** 1964
Pym, Christopher 1969
Encl: copy of l. from BR
to Pym's father, 1922
CF to 1969

Q

Quaranta, Mario .... n.d.
Quine, W. V., BR to 1967
Quirk, William E. **2** 1962
Encl.
BR to 1962

R

Raaflaub, David H. 1968
BR to 1968
Radhakrishna, Mr., BR to ... 1963
Radhakrishnan, S. 1967
Rae, John 1966
Raf, S. Nathaniel 1962
BR to 1962
Rammgal, Yanetz, BR to 1964
Ramsey, Frank P. **2** ...... [1924]
Encl: re *Principia* (including
5 pp. removed from between
pp. 14-15 and 64-5 of BR's
library copy of *Principia*,
I [1910])
Randall, Jr., J. H. 1957
BR to 1957
Randolph, Gertrude 1962
RS to **2** 1962
Ratliff, William F. 1966
BR to 1966
Read, Charles 1923
Encl: medical report on
Read by A. P. Brown?
Read, Herbert **2** 1962
BR to **2** 1962-7
Redgrave, Vanessa **3** ... n.d.-1968

RS to 1962
CF to **3** 1962-3
BR to **3** 1963-8
Rees, Joan **3** 1954
Encl: on verso of l.
BR to 1954
BR to **2** 1954
Reich, Ebbe, BR to 1966
Reichenbach, Hans **2** .. 1923-n.d.
Undated l. removed from
BR's copy of *Principia*,
I (1910)
Reichenbach, Maria **3** 1963-9
To RS **3** 1962-3
RS to **3** 1963
CF to 1963
BR to 1969
Reichl, Miriam **3** 1962
BR to 1962
Rendell, Kenneth W.,
BR to 1966
Richardson, Heather E.,
to BR and ER 1965
Encl: memo from CF
Richardson, Lewis F. 1951
BR to 1951
Robbins, Ruth 1968
Robert, Gustave 1921
Robinson, David J. 1967
Robinson, T. M., BR to 1963
Rodgers, Mrs. Gordon 1969
Rosenbaum, S. P. **4** 1968-9
Encl.
BR to **2** 1966
CF to **2** 1968
Rosenzweig, Saul **2** 1965
CF to **2** 1965
Roshwald, Mordecai **2** 1962-4
Encl: articles
BR to 1964
CE to 1964
Rothrock, Addison M. 1967
BR to 1967
Rothschild, Lord **2** 1962-6
RS to **2** 1962-6
Roy, Dilip Kumar 1969
Ruja, Harry 1966
Encl: l. to Allen & Unwin
(M. Joy Hill)
BR to 1966
CF to 1969
Rumashevskaia, Mrs.,
BR to 1963
Bertrand Russell Society of
Japan (Ikki [or
Kazuteru] Hitaka) **6** ... 1966-9
BR to **6** 1961-8
Encl.
Russell, Alys **2** 1917
BR to **68** .... 1907-[10?]
Russell, Mauri **4** 1964-9
To PW 1965
Encl.
BR to 1963
RS to **2** 1965
PW to 1965
CF to **3** 1964-9
Russell, William 1964
BR to 1964
Ryan, William F. 1969
To CF 1969
CF to 1969

S

Sagan, Carl, BR to 1962
Encl: card
Sahay, S. N. **2** 1963-5
BR to **2** 1963
PW to 1965
Salisbury, Donald 1964
BR to 1964
Sanger, Charles P. 1920
Sanger, Dora,
BR to **6** 1930-54
(photocopies)
Sanger, Margaret 1923
Sarbey, Mrs. M. D. 1969
CF to 1969
Savalle, Victor 1968
Encl.
BR to 1968
Saxena, D. C. 1970
Schapsmeier, Frederick H.,
BR to 1963
Schaumann, H. 1963
Encl.
BR to 1963
Schieber, Tilman, BR to ... 1964

Schiessel, R. 1963
BR to 1963
Schilpp, Paul A. **4** 1963-8
Encl: M. S. Finlay to BR
BR to **4** 1963-8
Encl.: l. to M. S. Finlay
Schireson, Peter L.,
BR to 1964
Schneider, Sally Russell 1963
BR to 1963
Schoelm, Raymond E. 1963
BR to 1963
Schoenman, Helen, to
ER **2** 1962
Schoenman, Ralph **2** . . 1964-n.d.
To ER . . . . n.d.
To HR 1965
To HR and Keith
Richardson(?) 1965
To AY, NJ and CF **3** 1962
ER to 1964
HR to **2** 1965
Schoenman, Theodore **4** . . 1965-8
Encl: l. to Tze-Koong
Wang, l. from Tze-Koong
Wang, Mrs. Carol Rees
(Louis M. Rabinowitz
Foundation Inc.) to BR
BR to **5** 1965-8
Encl: l. to Mrs. Carol Rees
Schreyer, Lester 1964
BR to 1964
Schutzberger, Faye 1963
BR to **2** 1963-4
Schwabach, Deborah 1965
PW to 1965
Schwartz, J. **4** 1959-63
BR to **4** 1959-63
Schweitzer, Albert **7** 1962-5
(Ali Silver) 1965
Encl: ts., record, etc.
BR to **9** 1962-5
CF to 1963
RS to 1965
RS to Ali Silver 1965
Scott, Margaret 1968
Seale, John R. **7** 1956
Encl.
Seeger, Peter . . . . n.d.
Encl.
BR to **2** 1966-7
Seldes, Gilbert **3** 1969
Encl: copies of ls. from BR,
1922-57
BR to 1963
RS to **2** 1963-9
CF to **2** 1969
Sellers, Peter, BR to **2** 1964
Encl.
Sen, Krishna 1951
Encl: including ms. (1 leaf)
of corrections by BR to
History of Western
Philosophy. Removed from BR's
copy of *A History of*
Western Philosophy
Sencourt, Robert **3** 1967-8
To ER **2** 1967
BR to **3** 1965
ER to 1968
Sheffer, Henry M. 1923
Sherwin, Larry 1964
BR to 1964
Shew, Ernest **4** 1967-8
CF to **2** 1967-8
BR to 1968
Shubart, Robert Franz 1963
Silcox, Lucy **2** . . . . 1924?-32?
Silverman, Sidney,
CF to 1964
Lady Simon of Wythen-
shawe 1969
BR to 1964
Simons, Enid 1963
RS to 1963
Simons, G. L. **10** 1962-9
Encl.
BR to **7** 1963-70
RS to **2** 1965
CF to 1970
Simons, Sheila 1962
BR to 1962
Simpson, F. A. 1962
BR to 1962
Simpson, Roger A. 1966
BR to 1966
Simson, George 1965
RS to 1965
Sinclair, Donald 1962
BR to 1962

Singh, G. 1965
BR to 1965
Singh, Surya Nath 1964
BR to 1964
Singh, Yuvaraj Karan 1952
Sitnam, E. 1967
BR to 1967
Slater, John G. **2** 1965-7
To DN 1968
To CF **3** 1968-9
BR to 1965
CF to **4** 1967-8
Slobinsky, Emilio, to RS 1962
RS to 1962
Smiley, T. J. 1963
BR to 1963
Smit, H., BR to 1963
Smith, Charles (Mr. & Mrs.),
BR to 1963
Smith, David M. 1962
BR to 1962
Smith, Grover 1964
RS to 1964
Smith, H., BR to 1963
Smith, Lewis 1964
BR to 1963
Smith, R. S. 1969
Snow, C. P., to RS **2** 1962
RS to **2** 1962
Snyder, Alice D. 1926
Removed from BR's copy
of *The Analysis of Mind*
Society of Separationists, Inc.
(Madalyn Murray O'Hair) .. 1969
Encl.
CF to 1969
Soldo, John J. 1969
Speart-Binns, John 1969
Spencer, E. M. 1926
Spencer Brown, G.
("David") **5** 1966-7
To BR and ER 1967
Encl: ts., "The Independence
of Sheffer's Postulates for
Boolean Algebras"
BR to **5** 1966-7
ER to 1967
CF to 1967
Spender, Stephen, CF to 1969
Stanbury, B., BR to 1963
Starostin, E. V. 1969
BR to 1969
Stein, Gordon 1968
Stephenson, P., BR to 1963
Stetler, Russell, to ER 1967
ER to 1967
Stevens, Jr., Herbert H. 1968
Encl: copies of BR to
Stevens (1951), Albert
Einstein to Stevens, essay
BR to 1968
Stewart, Mary 1968
BR to **2** 1968
Stewart, Ralph 1965
PW to 1966
Stickland, Nicholas and
Stefan **3** n.d.-1962
Stickland, Irina **6** 1962-8
To RS 1962
BR to **5** 1960-9
BR to to Dr. and Mrs.
Stickland 1962
Stickland, Ursula **4** n.d.-1965
Stokowski, Leopold **2** 1967-8
BR to 1969
Strickland, Kathleen 1963
BR to 1963
Stuart, John (former
tutor) 1922
Stucki, Alice **9** 1928-9
Sumbuddhananda, Swami,
BR to 1963
Summers, Orville E. 1963
Susskind, David (Talent
Associates—Paramount
Ltd.) **2** 1963-4
(Jean Kennedy) to RS 1962
RS to **2** 1962
BR to 1964
Suttles, Wayne, BR to 1963
Svadost, Ermar 1963
BR to 1963
Svensson, Gustav, BR to 1964
Swartz, William 1967
Swindon Public Libraries
Philosophical Society (Thomas
M. Anderson) **2** 1963-7

T

Tabibi, A. 1967
Re *Leo Tolstoy's Message to Sir Bertrand Russell*
Tabibi, Sharahm **3** 1967
RSt. to 1967
Tacer, Yavuz 1962
BR to 1962
Täckmark, Sven Erik 1969
BR to 1964
CF to 1969
Tanikawa, Tetsuzo, BR to ... 1963
Tanner, Cicely (née Young) 1968
Re Grace Chisholm
CF to 1968
Tate, Allen B., BR to 1963
Tatlock, J.D. 1926
Removed from BR's copy of *The Analysis of Mind*
Taylor, George and Dorinda **2** 1968
Encl: photos of Ravenscroft
CF to 1968
BR to 1968
Taylor, George R., BR to 1964
Taylor, Margaret R. **2** 1969
CF to 1969
Tedesco, Melanie 1956
Telsey, S. W. 1964
BR to 1964
RS to 1964
Thatcher, David S. 1968
BR to 1969
Themerson, Franciszka **2** ... 1967
ER to 1967
Themerson, Stefan .... n.d.
BR to 1969
Encl.
To CF **2** 1963-9
CF to **5** 1963-9
Thero, U. Saranankara **2** ... 1962
BR to **2** 1962
Thirkell, Angela, to ER **2** 1957
Thompson, Joan Lee (alias Gogi Braby, Joan Standage, "Joan Henry") **7** 1952-68
To ER **5** 1960-7
ER to 1967
Thompson, Michael 1966
RS to 1966
Thomson, Gladys 1962
BR to 1962
Thomson, Peter 1969
CF to 1969
Thorndike, Sybil **3** 1964-8
Encl: clipping
BR to **5** 1964-8
Thorndike, Sybil, and Casson, Lewis 1968
Tomkinson, Anne .... 1970?
BR to 1970
Tomkinson, C. M. H. **2** 1963
BR to 1963
Topham, Tony 1968
Toynbee, Arnold 1969
To BR and ER 1969
(Hermine Rocke) to ER 1969
BR and ER to 1969
Toynbee, Philip 1969
BR to 1969
Trelleck Parochial Appeal Committee (F.C. Coy) 1952
Treuhaft, Robert, and Mitford, Jessica, BR to 1967
Trevelyan, Charles 1922
Re Union of Democratic Control
Trevelyan, Elizabeth .... 1916?
Trevelyan, Julian .... n.d.
To CF 1966
To ER **2** .... n.d.
BR to **2** 1964-7
CF to **3** 1966-7
Trevelyan, Mary **2** .... n.d.
To ER **8** .... n.d.
ER to 1968
Trevelyan, Mary and Julian, to ER **4** .... n.d.
To BR and ER **4** .... n.d.
Trevor-Roper, Hugh, BR to **2** 1964
(one not sent)
Trost, A. H. .... 1926?
Questions re BR's course, "The Problems of Philosophy". Removed from BR's copy of *The Analysis of Mind*,

with 1 typed sheet asking two more questions dated 6 Dec. 1926
Tucci, Niccolo, to AY 1963
To RSt. 1963
RS to 1963
Tucci, Vieni, AY to 1962
Tuck, Gene **2** 1962-3
BR to 1962
Tudor-Hart, Beatrix **2** 1929
Encl: photo
Tuli, Kailash **3** 1963-7
BR to 1964
Turner, H. H. 1904
Turner, Martin 1964
BR to 1964
Tynan, Kenneth, CF to 1965
Tzakov, Boris, BR to 1963

U

Underwood, Austin to BR and ER 1962
Encl: clipping
BR to 1962
University College Library, London (I. Angus), BR to 1963
University College of Wales Humanist Society (David Holmes) 1965
The University of Aston in Birmingham (G. J. Shute, E. H. Stubbes) **2** 1966-8
Encl.
BR to 1968
University of Toronto Library (Robert H. Blackburn) 1963
BR to 1963
Unwin, A. H. 1961
Encl.
Upton, J. Duane 1969
Urquhart, Clara **5** 1961-9
To ER 1961
To RS **10** 1962-5
To CF **3** 1962
To CE **5** 1964
To PW **2** 1969
Encl: ls. to Mr. Ferentinos and Chaim, s.
CF to **5** 1962-3
BR to **4** 1963-4
RS to **2** 1964
CE to 1964
PW to **5** 1965-9
Encl: s. signed by BR
Usmani, M. A. 1965
BR to 1964
RS to 1965

V

Valente, Philip 1964
Encl.
BR to 1964
RS to 1964
Van Olphen, H., CF to 1969
Velikovsky, Immanuel 1964
Vicic, J. 1963
BR to 1963
Encl: note by ER
Viney, Janet to ER 1967
von Glahn, Jeffrey 1962
BR to 1962
von Ossietzky, Maud, and Leonard, Hans 1963
Encl: Prof. Friedrich to BR, journal
von Schwarze, Klause E. R. **3** 1962
Encl.
BR to **4** 1962
von Zeppelin, Amethe **7** .. 1959-68
To BR and ER **5** .... 1962-n.d.
To ER **21** 1958-67
Encl: Michelangelo Mühe to ER; Chinese prints; Catherine Vukovic to BR
BR to 1966
ER to **2** 1959
Vosseler, Marion 1968
BR to 1968
Vowles, Joy 1962
BR to 1962

W

Wagner, John 1964
BR to 1964
Walczer, Theodore, BR to ... 1963

Waley, Arthur, to PW 1965
PW to 1965
RS to 1966
Walker, Harold 1924
Walker, Ian 1966
BR to 1966
Walker, Scot 1962
BR to 1963
Wallace, Irving 2 1964-9
BR to 1964
Walsh, Maurice N. 2 1968
BR to 1968
Walter, Nicolas 1962
Encl: issue of *Anarchy*
Wang, Hao 3 1957
Ward, Helen 1962
BR to 1962
Wardell, Gareth 1969
CF to 1969
Wasserman, Ben 1962
BR to 2 1962
RSt. to 1967
Waterlow, Mrs. Rupert 2 1968
BR to 1968
Waterworth, Hanson 1965
BR to 1964
PW to 1965
Watney, Annette H. 1962
BR to 1962
Watson, Barbara 1963
BR to 1963
Watson, H. 1962
BR to 1962
Webb, Beatrice 1921
Webster, S. E. 1959
Encl.
BR to 1959
Weiner, T. 1952
Encl: l. from A. Einstein
Weinman, Maryann 1967
Weintraub, Stanley 1967
CF to 1967
Weir, H. A. 1969
CF to 1969
Weirstein, Jacob J. 1966
RS to 1966
Wells, Dee 2 1967
Wells, Gip 1968
BR to 1968
Wells, H. G. 1924
Welsh Office (Alan Greedy) .. 1965
PW to 1965
Wenger, Elisabeth, BR to 1969
Werbos, Paul J. 1962
BR to 1962
Werres, Johannes P. 1964
Encl.
BR to 1964
Werskey, Gary 1968
BR to 1968
Wertheimer, Robert G. 1963
BR to 2 1963
West, G. A., BR to 1963
West, Rebecca 1967
To RS 1964
RS to 1964
BR to 1967
Encl: Rebecca West to BR, 1929
Weston, Grainger 3 1964-5
BR to 3 1964
Weyditch, Ivan Walter V. 2 1963-4
Encl: American Embassy in U.S.S.R. (Terrence F. Catherman) to Ivan Walter V. Weyditch; Nicolas Slonimsky to Weyditch
BR to 3 1963-4
Weyl, Richard, BR to 1963
Wheaton, Donald 3 1963-6
Encl: poems
BR to 2 1963-6
Whettam, Graham 3 1962-9
Encl: Graham Whettam to *The Guardian*
BR to 3 1962-9
Whincop, Katherine E. .... n.d.
Whitaker, Ben, M.P. 2 ... 1968-9
BR to 1968
CF to 1969
White, Alan R. 1963
BR to 1963
White, W. Alan 2 1967
CF to 1967
Whitechapel Bell Foundry (Mears & Steinbank) 1966
Mrs. A. Khan to 1967
Whiteman, John B., to ER ... 1967
Whitman, Samuel 1964

RS to 1964
Whitten, Phillip, BR to 1969
Whyte, L. L. **7** 1965-8
Encl.
BR to **4** 1967
(one l. not sent)
Wieluch, Doman **4** 1963-4
BR to **3** 1963-4
Wienand, W. G. 1962
BR to 1962
Wiener, Martin J. 1967
Encl: May Wallas to Martin J. Wiener
CF to 1967
Wiener, S. **2** 1963
BR to 1963
Wight, R. 1962
BR to 1962
Wightman, G. 1962
BR to **2** 1962-3
Wilder, Isabel 1964
Willi, Ernst **8** 1962-7
To RS 1962-7
Encl: photos and essay
BR to **5** 1963-6
PW to 1967
CF to 1967
Williams, Sir Osmond ("Michael") **8** 1956-68
To ER **3** 1964-8
Encl.
ER to **2** 1967-8
BR to **2** 1968
Williams-Ellis, Amabel **2** 1956-67
To ER **2** 1958-67
Williams-Ellis, Amabel and Clough, BR to 1968
Williams-Ellis, Cicely, to ER . . . . n.d.
Williams-Ellis, Clough **6** 1957-68
To ER **2** 1956-68
Encl: G. Morina to Clough Williams-Ellis, Lewis Mumford to C. Williams-Ellis
Wilson, David Q. **2** 1967
BR to 1967
Wilson, Edmund, BR to 1963
Wilson, F. W., BR to 1963
Winser, Pearl 1952
Encl.
Winsten, C., BR to 1964
Winter, Mike, and Brecher, Howard 1967
BR to 1967
Wisdom, J. O. 1962
BR to 1963
Wittgenstein, Ludwig, BR to 1915
(photocopy)
Wittrock, John W. 1966
BR to 1966
Wohlgemuth, A. 1922
Removed from BR's copy of *The Analysis of Mind*
Wood, Alan, to ER **7** 1956-7
Wood, David **6** 1963-8
To BR and ER **2** 1969
BR to **4** 1968-70
Wood, Jonathan **5** 1963-70
BR to 1969
Encl: BR to R. W. G. Mackay, BR to the Secretary of the Alan Wood Trust Fund, David Garnsey to BR, BR to David Garnsey, Allfields Chartered Accountants to BR, photos
Wood, Mary, to ER **3** 1956-7
Wood, Pamela 1969
To ER **4** 1967-9
To BRPF . . . . n.d.
To BR and ER **8** 1965-9
Wood, Pamela *et al.*, to BR and ER . . . . n.d.
Woods, James H. 1923
Woods, P. A. 1962
BR to 1962
Woolf, Sheila **2** 1967
CF to 1967
Worden III, Edward Chauncey **2** 1963
Encl.
BR to **2** 1963-4
World in Action, Granada TV (Bill Grundy) 1963
BR to 1963
World Union of Freethinkers (Charles Bradlaugh Bonner) **4** 1962-6

Encl.
BR to 2 1962-6
RS to 1966
Encl: s. from BR
Wright, Gregory 2 1965-7
Encl: essays
PW to 1965
Wyatt, Ena .... n.d.
BR to 1963

Y

Yamamoto, Sanehiko 1951
Yogi, Alfred Schmielewski ... 1968
Encl: l. from S. Radhakrishnan
Young, A. Morgan 1923
Young, Anthony, RS[?] to ... 1963
Yourgrau, Bertrand 1964
End: poem
Yourgrau, Wolfgang 3 1964-8
Encl: articles, resume
To CF 1968
BR to 2 1964
Encl: BR to Prof. Firth 1959
BR to Peter Diamandopoulos 1968
RS to 1965
CF to 2 1968
Yule, Alastair, to RS 5 1962-3
To RS and NJ 3 1962
ER to 2 1963
RS to .... n.d.
Encl: telegram from BR to Miss Morgan re arrival of Yules at Plas Penrhyn ...... n.d.

Z

Zahn, Franklin 1969
CF to 1969
Zaki, Khalid, to BRPF 1965
Zatloukal-Williams, Richard,
BR to 2 1963
Zhang, Xienf 3 1962
BR to 2 1962
Zienau, Sigurd 1969
BR to 1969

*710 Personal Correspondence (Embargoed)

In the agreement between Lord Russell and McMaster University for Archives I, his correspondence with living members of his family was embargoed until the survivor of Russell and the person concerned had been dead five years. The embargo applied also to correspondence with Lady Ottoline Morrell and Lady Constance Malleson. This clause was made applicable to Archives II as well. Thus the correspondence listed below has been separated from *710. Since the original listing, the correspondence with Lady Constance Malleson has been removed from the embargo. That with Lady Ottoline Morrell was removed from the embargo in 1975, that with Lucy Russell in 1980, and that with Dora Winifred Grace (Dora Russell, née Black) in 1991. The asterisks denote files that have been removed from the embargo; exceptions are in parentheses. More documents will be removed from the embargo as time goes on.

Documents .103001–.107260

Alaoui, Ahmed 1965
Barry, Griffin **2** 1933
To DR 1927
Encl: clipping
DR to 1933
Barry, Roderick **3** 1955-61
Encl: s. re conscientious objection
Bath Academy of Art (Clifford Ellis) 1963
To Mrs. S. Cooper-Willis 1961
Encl: exam paper, calendar of courses
BR to **3** 1963-5
Encl: draft of l.
Beacon Hill School (DR) (re John and Kate Russell) **5** 1933-4
Anonymous ls. from pupils to **5** .... n.d.
(Olive Harrington) to 1929
Encl: archival s. of number of report cs., report cs. for John and Kate 1933-4, health reports for John and Kate 1933-4, list of pupils' I.Q., review of *Thinking in Front of Yourself and Other Plays*, garter
* Beaman, Joanna, to BR and ER 1961
Blach, Peter, to BR and PR .... 1940?
To PR **3** n.d.-1949
* Boyd, J. Lister (fee receipt) 1955
Albert Bridge School (E. M. Spencer) 1926
Encl: report cs. for John Russell, 1925-6
British Embassy (Reginald? Williams) 1942
Burke's Peerage, BR to 1969
The Cadogan Hotel, ER to ... 1962
Encl: note
Cooper-Willis, Susan, to BR and ER .... n.d.
To ER **3** n.d.-1962
Encl: prospectus
Dartington Hall School (William Burnlee Curry, H. A. T. and Lois Child *et al.*) **81** 1930-65
To PR **7** 1935-48
Encl: l. to Crompton Llewelyn Davies, l. from Crompton Llewelyn Davies,

l. to Coward, Chance & Co.,
l. from Coward, Chance & Co.,
l. to Dr. Oberman, l. to the
Superintendent of Police,
growth records of John and
Kate Russell 1934-8,
doctor's report re Kate's
vision, health certificates,
notices, school calendar,
invitations, reports, article
BR to **85** (in Rec. Acq. 263) 1932-65
PR to **3** 1934-47
* Davies, Mansel **2** 1965
BR to **3** 1965
Dryden, Anne (daughter of
John Conrad and Susan
Russell) **6** n.d.-1965
To BR and ER **226** 1954-69
To ER **7** 1958-69
To BR, ER, Sarah
and Lucy 1964
To Katharine Tait
et al. .... 1960?
Encl: l. to RS from Anne,
Sarah and Lucy Russell,
birthday cs., drawing, notes,
receipt, national health
service cs., identity c.,
drawing album for BR
entitled "All Heart"
BR to **2** 1958-63
BR and ER to **12** 1960-7
BR and ER to Anne,
Sarah and Lucy **5** 1960-1
ER to Anne, Sarah and
Lucy 1961
Encl: BR to Crickhowell
Riding Club (Mrs. Pragnell),
extract of l. from Julian
Trevelyan, schedule
Dryden, Anne and Ian 1968
To BR and ER **18** 1966-70
To ER 1967-9
To CF 1968-9
Encl: address, changes of
address, note from ID,
birthday cs.
BR and ER to **2** 1968
CF to **2** 1969
Encl: ER to the Glaslyn Hotel
Dryden, Ian (né Pyle) **3** 1966
To BR and ER **2** 1966
ER to **2** 1966-7
BR to **3** 1966
BR and ER to 1969
CF to 1969
Encl: BR to H. E. Madams,
H. E. Madams to BR, Midland
Bank Ltd. (J. O. Williams)
to BR, reference l. by BR re
Ian Dryden
Eton College (Richard
Martineau *et al.*) **6** 1952-5
To PR **14** 1952-4
Encl: fee receipts, Conrad
Russell's course reports, two
essays by Conrad, tutor's
remarks, notices
BR to 1952
PR to 1952
Encl: notes by PR
Gardiner, C. F. 1965
Encl: bill for Lucy Russell's
instruction
BR to **2** 1965
Grace, Dora Winifred
* (formerly Russell, née
Black) **498** 1918-69
Encl: l. from Margaret Durdy,
l. to *The Observer*, l. from
Hugh Brock, ss., brochures,
clippings
BR to **16** 1928-68
Encl: l. from Vandercom,
Stanton & Co. (R. W. B.
Stanton), l. from Midhurst
Rating Authority (C. E. H.
Parham), calling c.
Grace, Dora Winifred,
to ER 1954
To John Russell **2** 1935
To John and Kate
Russell **16** 1935
To Katharine Tait (née
Russell) **35** 1935-8
To Anne Dryden 1961
To Metropolitan Borough
of Chelsea (John T.
Jefferys) 1924
To Mr. Reed 1920

To Betty Ross .... 1933?
To Jack Tanner .... n.d.
Olive Harrington (on behalf of DR) to H. L. Williams ... n.d.
Encl: advertisement to rent Carn Voel for holidays, Cambridge Pocket Diary 1918-1919, envelope, clippings, sheet
John Russell to .... n.d.
Amy Malken Field to ...... n.d.
Metropolitan Borough of Chelsea (John T. Jefferys) to 1924
* Grace, Dora Winifred, re China
Y. R. Chao to **2** 1924
Daily Herald (Hamilton Fyfe) to **2** 1924
Arthur Ponsonby to 1924
Société des Nations Service de la République de Chine to 1924
R. P. Scott to 1924
Y. T. Toni? to 1924
Charles Trevelyan to 1924
Sydney Waterlow to 1924
Griffith, Miss, ER to 1960
* Harrods Ltd. (G. Hutchings) **3** 1956
Encl: estimate, note
BR to **3** 1956
Holloway Sanatorium 1955
Encl: receipt
Jones, A., to ER 1961
Kingsmuir School (Lucy Francis, G. Pilkington) **2** 1954-6
Miss Griffith to 1953
Encl: course reports for Anne, Lucy and Sarah
Lindsay, Susan. *See* Russell, Susan, below.
Lycée Français de Londres (A. Gaudin) 1967
Encl: list of students, prospectus of courses
BR to **2** 1962
Malleson, Lady Constance
* (Colette O'Niel) **130** .. 1916-67
To BR and PR 1941
To John Russell 1927
Encl: ts. of *Letters to Bertrand Russell from Constance Malleson 1916-69* [acquired directly from Lady Constance Malleson by McMaster], reviews of *In The North* and *Fear in the Heart*, form l. to *The Times*, section of Mabel B. Annesley's *As the Sight is Bent, An Unfinished Autobiography*, sheets entitled "Prison Letters", typist's note re "Prison Ls.", title page, schedule of theatre tour, clippings, calender, plots, essay, book summary, p.c., birthday greeting, note on envelope
* BR to **76** 1917-68
Encl: 2 ls. from Lady Priscilla Annesley, l. from Nalle Kielland, l. from Bridget Malleson, Miles Malleson to CF, l. from Jonathan Cape Ltd. (Veronica Wedgwood), l. to Underwood Business Machines, l. from British Olivetti Ltd. (J. B. Nichol), excerpt from Colette's *Letters from BR*, photo
* Malleson, Lady Constance (Colette O'Niel), to
Alf Ahlberg 1947
To T. Cash 1943
To Hampden Jackson 1946
To H. W. Leggett 1950
To Mummerley? .... n.d.
Encl: note re Nalle Kielland's ls., agreement s. re *Philosopher of the Century*
Alf Ahlberg to 1947
George Allen & Unwin to .. 1960
H. Hed Back? (the Lapp Warden) to 1947
Liebet Butterworth to **2** .. 1967
Faber and Faber Ltd. (T. S. Eliot) to 1961
Professor Gryffyold to ..... n.d.
Imperial War Museum

(H. Foster) to 1947
Sir Coleridge Kennard to ... n.d.
Nalle Kielland to **117** ... 1949-71
Hie Konning? to 1947
H. W. Leggett to 1950
Lavinia Mallows to 1958
Nick Malleson to 1958
Miles Malleson to **5** ... 1921-57
Thérèse Nicod to **2** 1957
Gertrude Parry to .... n.d.
Milde Plunket to .... n.d.
The Queen (C. M.
Kegan) to 1956
RS to **4** 1964-6
Benjamin Snellman and
Marja Järvinen to 1944
Trinity College Library
Cambridge (A. Hakron)
to 1958
Karl Gustav von Mannerheim
to 1946
Anne Winter to 1944
Dorothy Wrinch to 1962
Encl: reviews of Kennard's
books, clippings
*Malleson, Miles **2** 1966-7
To ER **5** 1967
Encl: l. from Constance Malleson
to Miles Malleson
BR to **2** 1967
ER to 1967
Markham, Olive, to ER **2** ... n.d.
Millar-Danks, S., to ER 1960
Milward, Kristin .... n.d.
BR to 1962
Moreton Hall School
(Bronwen Lloyd-Williams
et al.) **30** 1956-67
Encl: l. to Susan Lindsay, l.
from Susan Lindsay, pamphlets,
form ls., invoices, report c.
To BR and ER 1962
To ER **21** 1956-65
Encl: l. from Coward, Chance
& Co. (L. P. Tylor) to ER,
l. from DR to Moreton Hall
School (Bronwen Lloyd-
Williams), form ls.
BR to **33** 1956-64
Encl: entrance form
ER to **12** 1956-65
Encl: l. to Harrods Book
Dept.
Morrell, Lady Ottoline,
to PR 11 (in RAI) 1934-5
Murray-Davis, B. **5** 1955-61
BR to 1957
National Museum of Wales
(W. F. Grimes) 1934
O'Neill, Dr. Desmond **21** .. 1955-7
Encl: l. from R. J. Abbott,
l. from R. Macdonald
BR to **2** 1957
Palmer, R. W., to ER .... n.d.
Pearce, Dr. J. W. D.
(bill) 1955
Portmeiron Hotel (Michael
Trevor-Williams) 1967
To ER 1961
BR to 1967
ER to 1961
*Putney High School
(prospectus) .... n.d.
Randell, Dr. John B.
(bills) 1955
Rattenbury, Simonette, to
BR and ER 1962
To ER **2** 1962
ER to **2** 1962
Reed, Norah 1957
BR to 1957
Reed, Sonia, to BR
and ER 1958
Regents Park Nursing
Homes & Co-operation Ltd.
(bills and receipts) 1955
Russell, Conrad **43** ..... 1946?-69
To BR and ER **15** 1967-70
To ER **15** 1967-9
To CF **2** 1968
To Constance Malleson 1949
Encl: transcription of l.
in British Museum (Sir
Edward Burton to Sir Henry
Layard), photos, essay,
articles, pamphlet, colouring
notebook, French notebook,
writing notebook, drawing
BR to **14** 1958-68
ER to **4** 1967-9

CF to **2** 1968-9
Encl: addresses of Conrad and Elizabeth (née Franklin) Russell in ER's hand

Russell, Conrad and Elizabeth (née Franklin), to BR and ER **2** 1968-9
Encl: notes

* Russell, Edith (née Finch) **26** 1948-69
Encl: notes, valentine, birthday and Christmas cs., ms. entitled "What was Bertrand Russell really like?" [given by ER in Oct. 1972], ms. entitled "Synopsis of 'Work in Progress'"
BR to (photocopies) **40** 1948-61
Encl: poem, schedule of tour appointments

* Russell, Edith (née Finch) to Andrea Andreen 1959
To Constance Malleson **10** 1970-2
To Peggy A. Middleton ... 1961
To Herbert Read 1961
To Anna Westergaard 1959
Andrea Andreen to 1959
Encl: appeal
Sir Sydney Cockerell to 1960
Committee of 100 (Michael Randle) to 1961
Edith de Chadenedes to **6** 1965-70
Encl: clipping
Constance Drake to BR and ER 1961
Encl: poem
Edith Draper to 1957
Jacob Epstein to 1959
Fanny Hand? to 1961
Folly? to 1965
Virginia K. Frantz to **3** 1961-4
B. Hazleton to **4** 1967-8
Rita Kipling to **2** .... n.d.
Hugh J.C. Mackarness to .. 1960
Pessy? A. Middleton to 1961
Herbert Read to 1961
Julian and Mary Trevelyan to 1961
UNESCO Secretariat to .... n.d.
Anne Westergaard and Esther March to 1959
Amethe von Zeppelin to **2** 1968-9
Encl: note

Russell, Elizabeth (née Franklin) 1968
To BR and ER 1968
To ER **3** 1967-9

Russell, John Conrad **58** .. 1928-69
To BR and PR **113** 1933-45
To Conrad Russell 1945
To PR **4** 1939-45
Encl: l. to BR and PR from Katharine Tait (née Russell), poem, drawings, teeth, chart, plays, issues of *Ours, A Nature Magazine*, note
BR to **18** 1938-69
BR to John and Kate Russell **24** 1934-9
PR to John and Kate Russell 1935

Russell, John Conrad, re Navy to Local Draft Board Number 5 (Mr. Pitts) 1942
Encl: notes, note from Lieutenant Pole, naval message, form ls., pamphlet, memoranda, address list, s. of accounts, leave ticket, membership c., income tax return, permit to depart US

Russell, John Conrad, to Mrs. Dixon 1942
To Pat Grace 1944
To R. Griffiths 1954
To Constance Malleson **8** 1931-2
To Lucy Russell .... n.d.
To [Alan] Skelly 1944
To Robert Trevelyan 1940
Encl: l. from Childs-Fleet (Glyn Mills) to BR, note on envelope in Colette's hand school documents, essays and exercises, mss., Harvard thesis ("An Analysis of

the Principal Occasions
and Causes of Democracy"),
theatre programme, ticket,
medical c., newsl., note from
"Granny", invitation,
sheet, drawings, hospital
c., certificate, p.c.,
British Museum rules,
notice, c.
DR to **2** .... n.d.
Anonymous to .... n.d.
Harriet Barry to **6** 1944
Encl: birthday cards, booklet
Harriet Barry to John
and Kate Russell **3** 1936
Rod[erick Barry?] to .... n.d.
Mary Berenson to 1936
Cindy? to
Encl: Christmas c.
Coward, Chance & Co.
(Louis Tylor) to **3** 1944-50
Encl: bill, receipt
Douglas C. K. Dix to
Encl: Christmas c.
Mary Elsie to 1944
Mary Elsie to John and
Kate Russell 1934
Jackie [Gordon?] to **3** 1944
Encl: Christmas c.
Pat Grace to 1935
Pat Grace to John and
Kate Russell **5** 1935-6
J. Graves to
Encl: envelope
Harvard University (David
W. Bailey) to 1939
Encl: table c., affidavit of
University, dental appointment
c., leaflet, brochures
Sommerville Hastings to ... 1944
Encl: bills, sheet
E. P. Hawkshaw to
Encl: receipt
A. K. Hay to **7** 1944-5
Sir Thomas Hemming to
DR? .... n.d.
Greg Henderson to 1944
Jack [Pritchard?] to **3** 1945
Jean? to 1943
Katharine Lambton to 1945
Lewis W. Lewis to 1943
Maurice? to 1944
Hans Meyerhoff to .... n.d.
Dan Neylan to 1944
Nuit? to 1944
Pam? to .... n.d.
H. A. Hollond to .... n.d.
David Pule to 1944
Alex Reid & Lefevre
Ltd. (Alex Reid) to 1944
[Alan] Skelly to 1944
Maud Stanley to 1944
Steve? to 1944
Richon Tek? to **4** 1945
U.C.L.A. to
Encl: c., page from
directory
Arthur Waley to .... n.d.
J. N. Ward? to **2** 1945
* Russell, Lucy **10** n.d.-1967
To ER **12** n.d.-1967
To BR and ER **165** 1954-70
ER to 1962
Encl: picture, cs., play
programme, train time
table in ER's hand, ms. "A
Fantasy of Sorts", lists,
medical c., note, photo
To RS 1962
(*) To Kate and Charlie Tait ... 1960
BR to **2** 1966-9
ER to 1962
BR and ER to **9** 1962-9
CF to **2** 1968
NJ to 1962
CF to to G.P.O. **3** 1968
G.P.O. to CF 1968
Russell, Sarah **10** 1954-64
Encl: c.
To ER **5** 1960-6
To BR and ER **232** 1954-69
Encl: c., play programme,
form for family allowance, l.
from Lycée de Londres
BR and ER to **16** 1959-69
BR and ER to Sarah and
Lucy Russell 1962
BR to **2** 1963-6
BR to Child and Co. 1966
Child and Co. to BR 1966

BR to Mr. Lock 1967
Russell, Sarah, to CF .... n.d.
CF to 1969
Anne, Sarah and Lucy Russell to RS .... n.d.
To Griff? .... n.d.
To Kate and Charlie Tait ... 1960
* Russell, Susan (née Lindsay) **9** **1950-60**
To BR and ER **3** 1959-60
To ER 1955
Encl: Anne Russell to Mr. Williams, national health service medical c., identity c., poems
ER to 1955
Encl: l. from Dilip Kumar Roy to BR, l. from BR to Dilip Kumar Roy, note in ER's hand
Sadler's Wells School (Arnold L. Haskell, E. Leith) **2** 1954-5
Encl: brochures
BR to 1964
Salop County Council (vaccination cards, form l.) 1960-1
Salt, Patrick, to ER **2** 1967
ER to 1967
Spence, Patricia (formerly Russell, née Spence) **291** 1931-62
Encl: l. from Ministry of Education, Awards Branch (W. G. Easeman), cs., notes
To John Russell **13** ... 1935-44
Encl: clipping, list
To Kate Russell **46** 1934-8
Encl: clipping
To John and Kate Russell **37** 1934-9
Encl: photo
To DR 1933
Encl: "Comments on Dora's letter of April 4th 1933"
BR to **74** 1930-49
Encl: ms. ["BR's account of break-up with Peter"]

Spence, Patricia, to Crompton Llewelyn Davies 1933
To Anna Juriskoni 1946
To San Diego League for the Defense of Democracy (Harry C. Steinmetz) 1940
To George Sturgis **2** 1939
To R. H. Ward 1939
Encl: clipping
R.D. Gillespie to 1945
Pat Grace to 1935
Encl: clipping
Anna Juriskoni to 1945
Celeste MacFadden to ..... n.d.
San Diego League for the Defense of Democracy (Harry C. Steinmetz) to 1940
Joan Sangree to .... n.d.
Harry P. Schenck to 1941
Encl: l. from Philip A. Marden to Emily P. Bacon
Sheffield City Libraries (J. P. Lamb) to 1937
George Sturgis to 1939
Theta Upsilon Sorority (Grace Levey) to .... n.d.
Alice Crunden to BR and PR **2** 1934
Edwina Crunden to BR and PR 1934
Stackler, Susan to BR and PR .. n.d.
Spence, Patricia: mss. *Portmeirion Gazette & Deudraeth News* (3 issues); "Birth of Conrad, 1937", "[On Kate]", "On Mending Old Shoes", "The International Significance of the Indian Problem" (by BR and PR), poem. 2 boxes of ls. from friends, family and acquaintances [see *713 .134101-.134385] **253** 1932-5
Encl: pianoforte agreement, photos, calling c.
St. Andrew's Hospital 1955
Encl: medical case history form, invoice
Tait, Anne **2** .... n.d.
To BR and ER **2** .... n.d.

Tait, David **7** 1959-69
To BR and ER **17** 1960-9
Encl: note
BR to **3** 1963-8
BR to Tait children 1957
BR to Lucy Russell 1968
BR to Sarah Russell 1968
BR and ER to **3** 1969
Tait, Katharine (née
Russell) **208** 1931-67
To BR and ER **32** 1955-70
To BR and PR **167** 1933-48
To PR **33** 1935-43
To Conrad Russell 1941
To CF 1966
To Alice Stück .... n.d.
To Sherry .... n.d.
To Witten .... n.d.
Encl: l. to BR from David,
Anne and Jonathan Tait, l.
to BR from David Tait,
l. to BR from John Tait, l.
to BR and ER from David Tait,
clippings, greeting cs., gift
tags, poems, short stories,
various childhood drawings
and paintings, examination
papers, grades, notebooks,
photos, photo album, birth
announcements
BR to **70** 1934-68
BR to Charles Tait 1965
DR to John and Kate Russell 1940
ER to 1961
PR to 1935
CF to **2** 1966
Encl: poems by children at
Beacon Hill School in BR's
hand, sheet by BR entitled
"Answers to questions *re*
scholarship"
Tait, Katharine, to John Conrad
Russell **7** 1943-4
Anonymous to **12** 1935
Granny [Black] to .... n.d.
Alice and Edwina Crunden
to (c.) .... n.d.
Pat Grace to **21** 1935-7
Theodore Hamblin Ltd.
to .... n.d.
Encl: prescription for glasses
Harriet Ward to **4** 1940
Townsend, Tessa, to ER 1963
Trevelyan, G. M. 1942
Encl: l. from Cambridge
University (E. Harrison)
to J. Burnaby
* **Urch, Phyllis 2** **1965**
BR to **1965**
Van Teslaar, Amiel,
to BR and PR 1943
BR and PR to 1943
Vinogradoff, Julian **2** ... 1911?-67
BR to 1967
* Wallace, Delight S.,
to BR and ER 1967
Ward, Harriet (daughter of
Griffin Barry and
DR) 1947
To ER .... n.d.
Encl: doctor's certificate
L. E. Waterman Co. (s. re BR's
handwriting), notes in PR's
hand .... n.d.
Williams-Ellis, Amabel ...... n.d.
Wordsworth, Christopher,
to ER **2** 1958
ER to 1958
York Clinic (T. A. Munro) ... 1955
Encl: l. to DR, bills, receipts

*712 Miscellaneous Personal Documents

From Russell's passports to his death certificate, this box contains a variety of documents that have no other likely classification.

Documents .107261–.107276

1 box consisting of: a black wallet containing BR's birth certificate, 3 photos of Alys Russell, and a list of books in Alys's hand; a black wallet inscribed "Aktiebolaget Svenska Handelsbanken"; a brown wallet containing 4 photos of John and Kate Russell; World War I Permit Book, l. and pass from the Garrison Commander; notebook, 1960-5; visa to Soviet Russia, 1920; address book, 1956; membership cs. for the National Trust, 1966; BR's passports, 1931-6, 1941-6; family tree (January 1937); and printed cs. and pencils, cs. printed "Earl Russell", membership c. for Communita Europea degli Scrittori, international certificate of vaccination against smallpox (1950) and leaflets, London Library c., 1969-70, keys, sheet of photos of children at Beacon Hill School, death certificate (with ls. from CF to the undertakers, the crematorium, and the town clerk of Colwyn Bay). Also gross earnings and royalty ss. for a few years; schedule of public lectures in America, 1927; biographies of BR (with l. from Central Office of Information [C. Mackintosh]).

***713 Patricia Spence (Embargoed**
See Addenda.

*720 Miscellaneous Correspondence

This category of correspondence is formed from those letters that belong neither to the Personal Correspondence nor to the political, family or publishing classifications. There are 28 boxes, many of the letters accompanied by short replies from Russell. Since most of these letters are repetitive in content (e.g., requesting Russell's autograph) and did not elicit significant replies, the correspondents are not individually listed.

Documents .120001–.132656

28 boxes, or 12,656 documents.

*721 "Cranks"

Every well-known figure must receive crank mail, but Russell seems to have received more than his share. Possibly it was his reputation as a sage that attracted the letters. His staff regularly annotated such mail "crank". (See also Russell's "Cranks", in his *Collected Stories* [London: Allen & Unwin, 1972].) While there may be nothing so dismal as an anonymous crank letter, pseudonymous crank letters can be very entertaining. See, for example, the letters and enclosed "cheques" (ranging from $5000 to $2,000,000,000) from the "Virgin Express Alexandra I". *721 is arranged alphabetically. The correspondents are not individually recorded.

Documents .135001–.136195

5 boxes, or 1,194 documents, classified under a heading favoured by Russell's secretariat.

*724 90th Birthday Tribute

Archives I has a collection of letters received on Russell's 90th birthday (1962). This box supplements it in an important way. The letters here were written chiefly in response to Ralph Schoenman's requests for tributes to be printed in the tribute booklet, *Into the Tenth Decade* (1962). There is also a signed scroll presented by British Members of Parliament.

Documents .117001–.117498

Anonymous
Lord Adrian
Lady Clare Annesley
A. J. Ayer
David Ben-Gurion (Michael Gir)
Norman Bentwich
Hilda Bernard
Leonard Bernstein (Helen Coates)
Niels Bohr (E. Tanggaard)
Robert Bolt
Max Born
Charles W. Bonner
Lord Boyd Orr
Vera Brittain
Benjamin Britten (J. W. Cullen)
Fenner Brockway
Jacob Bronowski
Martin Buber
Pablo Casals
Lewis Casson and Sybil Thorndike
George E. Gordon Catlin
Charlie Chaplin
Czechoslovak Pugwash Committee (Theodor Nemec)
Moshe Dayan
Cecil Day-Lewis
Salvador de Madariaga
Die Deutschen Atomwaffengegner
Isaac Deutscher
Gerald Durrell (Leslie Naton)
A. E. Dusorp
Mischa Elman
William Empson
Edith Evans
B. M. Evers
Festival Panamericano de Musica Pablo Casals (José García Borrás)
Foreign Press Association (E. Von Holzer)
Mrs. Forester
E. M. Forster
Elspeth Fox Pitt
Ernest Gellner
P. J. Giblin
John Gielgud (I. E. Sucker)
M. Gluckman
Victor Gollancz
E. H. Greaves
Graham Greene (Josephine Reid)
R. P. Greenish
Walter Gropius
Robin Guthrie
Shinzo Hami
Lancelot Hogben
Harold Holt Ltd.
Aldous Huxley
Julian Huxley
Institute of Physics and Mathematics,

University of Chile
Gunnar John
Kenneth Kaunda
Amrit Kaur
Martin Luther King, Jr.
Paul Kletzki
Lily Krauss
Fos. Küllheim
Barbara Laine
Corliss Lamont
A. Lasareau (Rumanian People's Republic)
Marghanita Laski
Patricia J. Lindop
Kurt Litschauer
J. E. Littlewood
Edith Livingstone
Margaret Lloyd
London Symphony Orchestra Ltd. (Ernest Fleischmann)
Wilson MacDonald
Archibald MacLeish (Ardis Jubson)
Constance Malleson
Miles Malleson
Malvern Press Ltd.
Wolf Mankowitz (Jacqueline John)
Somerset Maugham (Alan Searle)
I. R. Maxwell & Co.
Dannel McCollum
Julie Medlock (encl: summary of her 1950-1 work with BR)
Pierre Mendès France
Hans Meyerhoff
Darius Milhaud
Arthur Miller (Elizabeth Hannum)
Henry Moore
D. M. Morandini
Tatsuo Morito
Charles Munch (Leonard Burkat)
Musicians' Union (Harry Francis)
Otto Nathan
National Federation of Building Trades Operatives (H. G. Taylor)
Jawaharlal Nehru
M. H. A. Newman
Kwame Nkrumah
Sean O'Faolain
Robert Oppenheimer
Wendy Parker
Linus Pauling
Lester B. Pearson (Mary E. Macdonald)
Margery Pelham (Stephanie Grant)
Roger Peyrefitte
Pablo Picasso
R. P. Dominique Pire (A. Beaudry)
William Plomer
Michael Polanyi
Rajendra Prasad (R. K. Ramabhyani)
Victor Purcell
Salvatore Quasimodo
W. V. Quine
Michael Redgrave
Marcus W. Richardson
Eleanor Roosevelt
John Rothenstein
Lord Rothschild
Royal Festival Hall (T. E. Bean, S. L. Bacon)
Edmund Rubbra
Miss Russell
Alberto Saldarriaga V.
Rudolf Schwarz
Morris Shalit
Grazia Denig Shaw
Peter and Jeanne Sheridan
William L. Shirer
Alan Sillitoe
Edith Sitwell (Elizabeth Salter)
C. P. Snow
Dr. Soekarno (Burhanudin Mohamad Diah)
George Solti (Enid M. Blech)
Léonie Somming
Sacha Soprano
Southern California Council for a Sane Nuclear Policy (Mark Doran)
Dennis Gray Stoll
S. H. J. Sugunasiri
Georges Tanesse
U Thant
Stefan Themerson
J. Christian Thiel
Hans Thirring
Norman Thomas
Joan Lee Thompson
R. Thorpe
Arnold Toynbee (Norah Williams)
G. M. Trevelyan (E. A. Thomas)
Hugh Trevor-Roper

Uomini e Idee (Corrado Piancastelli)
Wilfrid Van Wyck Ltd.
Vittorio Vèdele
Verband der Kriegsdienstverweigerer (Hermann Kofrudafl)
Ellen Waller
Carina Carington-Walters
Philip P. Wiener
Ernst Willi
Robin Wilson
Leonard Woolf
D. Woolfenden
World Parliament Association (Gilbert McAllister)
J. Worthy
F. P. Wyer
Ernest B. Zeisler

1 file of miscellaneous material re birthday tribute, including MPs' tribute and a poster

*725 95th Birthday Letters

Russell's 95th birthday was on 18 May 1967. There was no public celebration, but some members of the public and friends sent their congratulations to him. See also Archives I, *725.

Documents .117501–.117635

American Philosophical Association, Western Division (Arnold Levison)
Günther Anders
Surya Kumar Banerjee
George L. Barnard
Richard G. Bechaud
Surinder Bedi
William Betts
Murad Bey
Margareta Björklund
Jack Black
I. D. Bond
Boy Scouts of Bengal (A. K. Sil)
David P. Boyd
Lord Boyd Orr
Fenner Brockway
Clarence F. Browne
Martha Browne
E. H. S. Burhop
Donald R. Burleson
Dale Carney
Raiharan Chakrabarti
Christlich-Demokratische Union Deutschlands (Gerald Götting)
E. Clar
Albert L. Colloms
Alex Comfort
Committee to Free Morton Sobell (Helen Sobell)
Conference Committee for the Public Interest (Julie Medlock)
Continuum 1 Ltd. (Anton Felton)
Czechoslovak Committee of the Defenders of Peace (Josef Macek)
Harvey N. Davies
Alvarez del Vayo
Jürgen Eidam
Fred M. Eisenberg
Samuel A. Eisenstein
The Encyclopedia of Philosophy (Paul Edwards)
Richard Fallin
Kuang Tih Fann
Mollie Fletcher
Grace Forester
Friedensrat der Deutschen Demokratischen Republik (Walter Friedrich)
Erich and Anis Fromm
James E. Grice
Robin Guthrie
Sybil Habermel
Werner Hachenberger
Irving Heller
Marian Holland
Hungarian Peace Council (Endne Sik)
Jack Huntingdon
Margaret Huntingdon

Yukiko Iinuma
Leopold Infeld
Nicholas Johnson
Hans Keller
M. P. Khan
? Kuratowski
Zora Lasch
London Workers Committee (A. T. Hart)
Victor Lowe
Mary Lynch
Muriel F. MacSwiney
E. C. Marsden
J. M. Marsden
Stefano Martini, Guilliemo Guillieri, Giorgio Laceroloti
Hugh D. McKell
Ralph Miliband
Michael E. Miller
Mervyn Millett
Spike Milligan
Academician Millionscikov
Rosemary Morris
Khodr Nabbouh
Carol Ochs and Mickey Kempner
D. N. Pathak
Walter Pearson
Kari Peven, Susan Messer, Susan Trowell
Dennis Podden
Poona Herald (David Rathore)
P. A. S. Prasad
Mohan Lal Rajput
Lauritz H. Ramussen
John Rector
Maria Reichenbach
Barbara Rickards
Frances Ronald
Bertrand Russell Peace Foundation, Philippine Branch (Ramon Suzara)
Louis Rybka
Tsuruko Saito
Michael A. Schenkelberg
Lewis Barnard Scholnick
Gabriela Senchea
Marian Shelford
Kalu I. Singh
Soviet Peace Committee (Nikolai Tikhonov, Michael Kotov)
Antonio Spreafico
S. K. Sreshta
Ray Stanich
Warren E. Steinkraus
Students of University of California (William Stuart Radley *et al.*)
Ramon Suzara
Tony Topham
Arnold Toynbee
United Nations Association, Hemel Hempstead Branch (J. G. Gaddes)
Vietnam Solidarity Campaign, Hull Branch (Alan I. Rooney)
Kastich Vlada
Volkszeitung (the editor)
Karl Graf von Westphalen and Lorenz Knorr
Heinz Wachter
Nannie Welker
Ernst Willi?
Richard Williams
David Wood
World Council of Peace (Romesh Chandra)
Winifred Wyatt
Youth Against War and Fascism (Martin Key)

*726 Condolences on Russell's Death: Answered by Lady Russell

Russell died on 2 February 1970. Edith Russell received many condolences. She personally replied to the following.

Documents .118001–.118108

Nell ?
Puggy and Hamish (encl: obituary)
Edith ?
Norah ?
Liz ?
Dinah ?
George Allen & Unwin (Rayner Unwin)
A. J. Ayer
Ian and Nicole [Duke and Duchess of Bedford]
Eileen and J. D. Bernal
Jack Black
Peter Blackett
Lister Boyd
Gogi Braby
Elias Bredsdorff
Fenner Brockway
Mary Burn
Michael Burn (encl: unpublished obituary)
R. A. B. Butler
? Byrd
Yuen Ren and Buwei Chao
Dorothy Cousens
Rupert Crawshay-Williams
Louise Crenshaw
T. Deutscher
Anne and Ian Dryden
Elizabeth Ramsden Eames
Mrs. Edwards
Elizabeth R.
Patricia Esdale and Joseph Rotblat
Elwyn and Nici Evans
Elsie A. Fairbairn
Jo Farley
Betty Flexner
Mag Flexner
William Welch Flexner
Grace Forester
Augusta K. Gardner
Dorothy Hawksley
Ralph Hawtrey
Kevin Holland
? Huntingdon
Margaret Huntingdon
Julian Huxley
Juliette Huxley
Yukiko Iinuma
D. Jones, K. Lloyd, T. Mullock
Catherine Karolyi
E. S. Wells Kerr
Peggy Kiskadden
Corliss Lamont
Zora Lasch
Ed Lewis
John Lloyd
Margaret Lloyd

Bronwen Lloyd-Williams
Mildred and Russell Lynes
Julie Medlock
Lotte Meitner-Graf
Rosemary Morris
Michelangelo Mühe
V. ("Folly") Orffa
D. Owen
Marjorie Tyler Paul
Katherine M. Peek
Daphne Phelps
Maria Reichenbach
D. H. Richards
Jeannette Riegler
Anthony Russell
Athenaïs Russell
Dora Russell
Guy Russell
John Conrad Russell
John and Aliki Russell
Martin Russell
Edie Schoenman
Theodore and Helen Schoenman
Violet Stephens
Caro Stillwell
Franciszka and Stefan Themerson
Dorothy Thompson
Arnold Toynbee
Julian Trevelyan
Mary Trevelyan
Mary Unwin
Louise Watson
Anne Whiteman
Osmond ("Michael") Williams
Vivienne Williams?
Amabel Williams-Ellis
Harold Wilson
David Wood
Pamela Wood

Notes by ER

*727 Condolences on Russell's Death: General

The many condolences, coming from all over the world and itemized here, were answered by Russell's staff.

Documents .119001–.119732

Anonymous
A & M Hearing Aids Ltd (M.C. Bruce)
William Abbott, *et al.* (Department of Philosophy, University of Waterloo)
Anouar Abdel-Malek
Mahmoud El Abeidi
José Luís Abellán, J. Cañero, M. Tejeda
Accademia Lincei (Beniamino Sere)
Accademia Nazionale dei Lincei (Enrico Cerulli)
Adams, Thomas F.
African National Congress of South Africa (Reg September)
Derek Allen
Alppilan Sosialistiseura Helsinki
Tony and Betty Ambatielos
Amnesty International (Bella Marshall) (Encl: BR Peace Committee [Nikos Kiaos *et al.*])
Amnesty International, Stockholm
Günther Anders
Frank J. Angeloff
Erich Annisfrom
Th. M. Ariaans
Murray Aronson
Wendy Arrowsmith and Pat Butlin
Association Internationale des Juristes Democrates (Joe Nordmann)
Association of Scientific Workers of India (P.C. Sen)
Australian Seamen's Union Members
Mehmet Ali Aybar
Pham Van Bach (Chairman, CECAV)
David L. Ball
F. Ballesteros
Kali Krishna Banerjee
L. L. Bardoe-Darfor
Eileen, Michael and Eleanor Barratt-Brown
Marcia Beckett
Mr. and Mrs. F. D. Berman
Donatella Bernstein
Ulanco Bert
Michel Berveiller
Zulfikar Ali Bhutto
Rowena Bingham
Nguyen Thi Binh (Paris Conference)
Black Power Movement Racial Adjustment Action Society (Herman Edwards)
Ken Blackwell and William Ready
R.T. Blackwood
Hugo Blanco
Erika Blatter
Robert Blum
Stephen Bodington

John Boler
Allan R. Bomhard
P. S. Borday
Ada v. Böselager
Philip Bowles
Philip Braithwaite *et al.*
Sonia Breeze
Brighton College of Education Students' Union (Stewart Reed)
The Britain-Tricontinental Organisation (Eric Desmond)
The British Council (R. M. Auty, G. L. H. Hitchcock, Ljeposava Rakonic Okucani)
British Humanist Society (Michael Lines)
The British Peace Committee (Joan Gabriel) (encl: cables from Czechoslovak Peace Committee, Prague, Hungarian Peace Council [R. Endre Sik])
Mario Elisa de S. e Brito
BRPF, Nottingham
BRPF, Queensland Branch
Orio Buccellato
Evelyn C. Buch
E. M. Buhaire
Jain Burgess
E. H. S. Burhop
Margaret Butcher
Geoffrey Butterworth
D. Morris Calhoun
The Cambridge Society of Bombay (L. K. Jha)
Campaign for Nuclear Disarmament (John Cox *et al.*)
Dawn and Bob Capland
Lazaro Cardenas
José Carreras
Catalana Castellui
Lillian Dorothy Cates
Arthur Charles
John H. Charles
Helen Chester
Dr. Christofinis
Harold Citrynell
City Law College, Dacca (Aleem Al-Razee)
George Clark
Irene Clark
Denis Cobell (encl: obituary notice)
Comite Cubano de Solidaridad con el Pueblo de Viet Nam (Melba Hernández)
Comite de Defensa de los Derechos Humanos (Rosa Alarco)
Comite Intellectuels Vietnam (Nguyen Xien)
Comite Mexicano de Solidaridad con Vietnam (Pablo Sandoval Cruz and Raquel Tibol)
Committee Moratoire du Vietnam (Edward Martin Sloan)
Confederation of Iranian Students
Congreso Republica, Venezuela (J. A. Perez Diaz)
Edithe Dunham Couey
Mrs. M. J. Llewellyn Crilson
Paul Crosser
Cuban Embassy
Jim and Audrey Curtis
Czytelnik
Dalbard
Jessie Dally
Lawrence Daly
Mohammad Lateef Dar
Shashikant J. Dave
W. Austin Davies
Tino Davini
Carlo Demarchi
Harry de Metrópolis
Alan Denson (encl: his *Intimate Voices*)
Juan Aguilar Derpich
Mario Elisa de S. e Brito
Eunice Michel Díaz
Pham Van Dong
Lize Dorfman
Joâo A. Da Costa Doria
Columbo Dorinto (?)
Michael Duff
Jürgen Eidam
Lee Eisler
Juan Elua
Ian M. Emberson
English Centre of International P. E. N. (David Carver)
English Literary Circle (Baher Nasir Aryum *et al.*)
Henry A. Epstein
Escuela Preparatoria Bertrand Russell

(Salvador Montes Oseguera)
F. H. Aroca Fabregat
M. Fairweather
Domenico Falco
Giudo Fanti
Mian Gulmohn Nagi Fazilpur
Federation of Iranian Students in Italy
Abraham L. Feinberg (encl: obituary)
Gina Field
Sheila Fisher
Edwin Flatto
Wolfgang Foges
Iris Folkman
Mr. and Mrs. Yvon Fortin
Armando Fortun Valdes
Paul Foulkes
Fourah Bay College, Sierra Leone (Harry Sawyer)
Angus and Andrew Franpz
Andrew Gibson Frantz
W. R. Fraser
Hinda Fremet
Friedensrat der Deutschen Demokratischen Republik (Guenter Drefahl, Werner Ruempl)
Ricardo A. Frondizi
F. Frons
C. Gangadharan
Adwaita P. Ganguly
Marco Ganzini
Roy Garner *et al.* (Friends of BRPF, Sydney)
Antonio Gasperin
Mary Gawthorpe
Junino Gemma
General Council of Trade Unions of Japan (Toshikatsu Horii)
Eduardo Genovés
GI Civil Liberties Defense Committee (Stacey Seigle) [BR was Honorary Chairman]
John A. Giguére
S. Glen
Velibor Gligoric
Glyn, Mills & Co. (Child & Co.)
Madeline Goddard
J. and P. Godfrey
Vladimir Golubooj?
Luciano García González
Alec Gordon
Richard Graydon
Paul Green
Roger Green
Randall A. Greene
Greenfield Recorder-Gazette (Wayne A. Smith)
R. P. Greenish
Arnie Greenstein
Mr. and Mrs. Dick Gregory
Alois Grohs
Allano Guatti
Gilberto Guevara and Raul Alvarez
Carlos Gutierrez Reynares
Hampstead and Camden
Hanoi Université (Nguyn Hu Lontum, Director)
Harlech Branch Labour Party (A. Hughes)
Stephen R. Harrison
Trevor Hatton
Michael Heaton
Wyldbore Heisler
Hemel Hempstead CND (I. Berkovitch)
Mrs. Thomas M. Higgins
L. A. Hill
Evelyn Hillman
Hiroshima House
Ikki Hitaka
Albert Ho
Hoangh Ming Hiam
Douglas Holdchock?
Marjorie and Harold Holt
Robert Hoogenboom and Jenny Keys
Humanist Society of New Zealand, Christchurch
Ian R. Hunt
Hyde Park University, Florida
Judith Hyland
Yukiko Iinuma
Nyor Ikhoivhe
Shigetoshi Iwamatsu
M. K. Janjua
Japan Committee (Kinju Morikawa)
Japan Council Against Atomic and Hydrogen Bombs (Gensuikyo)
Japan Information Centre of BRPF (Shigetoshi Iwamatsu)
James A. Jennings
Jerusalem Liberation Committee

(Saulieman Nabulsy)
J.B. Johnson
Peter Johnson
Mr. and Mrs. Albert Jones (sweep)
M. Jones Morris (post woman)
Alexandrino Pedro Duarte Jorge
K.M. Joseph
Tukaram Yashneantrao Kakade
Sushil Kumar Kalia
Linda and Bill Kaye
Pat Kelley
A.J. Khanji
Enno Kind
Tom Kinsey, Pat Pottle, Alastair Yule
Karl Kleiner
Gloria M. Klekar
Steven H. Klitzman
Kodansh Encyclopaedia, Tokyo
Komeito Party (Yoshikatsu Takeiri)
V.K. Krishna Menon
M.A. Labon
Corliss Lamont (encl: obituary)
J. Ludlow Landero
Giorgio La Pira
Fran Lawers
Leeds C.N.D. Committee (Michael Dalton)
Leeds University Unions
Legislative Assembly of Assam (P.D. Barua)
Keith C. Lehsana
John and Yoko Lennon
Leonard P. Liggio
Peter Limqueco
Alexander Lindsay, Samuel Smyth, Dowall Corvin
London Region Campaign for Nuclear Disarmament (Kenneth D. Cowan)
The London School of Economics (Walter Adams)
Nicolos Lopez *et al.*
Anna Marie Lowry
Blanche Lucas
L.H. Luscombe
Macalli
P.D. Magariños D.
Mir Ijaz Mahmood
Basil Dale Malan-De Mèrindols
David Maler
Fati Marjani
Mark Twain Journal (Cyril Clemens)
James W. Marquis, Norman G.O. Pereira
Margory Marshall
Stephanie M. May
Douglas McGarvey
Tessie McGough
William McIlroy
Margaret Meeus
G.L. Mehta
Peter Meier
Jonathan Mendham
Rafael Tirado Mendoza, Felipe Tirado Segura, Ricardo Tirado Segura
V.B.G. Menon
Charles Middleton
Mervyn Millett
Minffordd Post Office
Ricardo Molgosa
Pierre Moraviah Morpeau and Claude Badin
Kit Mouat
Movement for Colonial Freedom (Barbara Haq)
Movimento Paz Soberania Pueblos Cuba (Cuban Movement for Peace and Sovereignty)
Mr. and Mrs. Ralph Muscatell
P.C. Nanavaty
Pha Nanh
C.S. Nanjundaiah
National Committee, British Society for Social Responsibility in Science (Robert Smith)
National Council for Civil Liberties (Tony Smythe)
National Council of Women in India (M.R. Parakh)
National Union of Australian University Students
National Union of Finnish Students
Stan Newens
Patrick Newman
New Zealand Peace Council (F.G. Clements)
Nguyel? *et al.*
Brian G. Nicholson
Dorothy G. Nifer?
The Noken Daur (Abdul Karim Shorish Baloch)

David Nolan
Nottingham University, Dept. of Philosophy
Nouvelle Ecole (Alain de Benoist)
Mahn J. Paw Aye Nyein
Hui Chong Ong
Operai Italiani (Gianni Forlano *et al.*)
Paul Oppenheimer
Organizacion Mexicana por la Libertad de los Presos Politicos (Mexican Organization for the Release of Political Prisoners)
Leo Pach
Pakistan Philosophical Congress (Ahmed and Dev)
Pakistan Writer's Guild
Suryadeo Pande
Lloyd Cicd Peacanz
Jon D. Pearce
D. W. Peetz
Maurice A. and Elizabeth Pelter
Michael Peristerakis
Beatrice Perkins
J. H. Perry
Mrs. John N. Peterson
Philosophical Society of Edinburgh (Richard Cumming)
Philosophy Society, Reading University
Harold Plumstead
Polish Peace Committee (Tikhonov Kotov)
Seymour Porter-Bryant
Portuguese Democrat Movement (Guilherme Godinho *et al.*)
Portuguese Students Committee (Jose Laranjo)
Jagdish Prasad
P. A. S. Prasad
Mariotti Prenzo
Michel Priem
John Privitera
Pugwash Committee of the American Academy of Arts and Sciences [and?] of the U. S. Pugwash Group (Bernard T. Feld)
Quatrième Internationale (Pierre Frank)
Philip Rabbidge
Eugene Rabinowitz
Dr. Raghunandan
Inez Randall
Aswini Kumar Rath
Rationalist Federation Australasia Pacific Countries
Rationalist Press Association Limited (Constance Dowman)
Diana Readhead
Reading Co-ordinating Committee for International Understanding (Frida Knight)
William Ready
Kelly Scott Reed
Julius Reichbach
Religious Society of Friends (Elfrida Vipont Foulds, Elizabeth Dearden)
W. Renardo?
Mariotti Renzo
Vernon Reyman
Godfrey Richardson
W. N. B. Richardson
Tom Riglar
B. D. Roberts
Maria Josefa López Roldan
Christopher Ronald
Hilary Rose
Seth Rosner
Robert H. Ross
The Royal Society of Literature (Mrs. J. M. Patterson)
David Rubenstein *et al.*
Rumanian Ambassador (Vasile Pungan)
Agnes Russell
Ellen Russell
Mauri and Pam Russell
Sharon Russell
Ray Ryan
Tsuruko Saito (CSBRPF)
Mian G. N. Salazillpur
Hal Salisbury
Esther Sanders
University of Saskatchewan (J. W. T. Spinks)
University of Saskatchewan, Regina (Erich M. Peter)
Giulio Savelli
Jean Schellinck
Sheldon Schorer
Laurent Schwartz

Rudolf Schwarz-Otava
Francisco Sforsa
Arthur O. Shachman
Sheth H.P. Arts & S.M. Panchal Science College, India
Yasuharu Shima
Bluma Shinar
Mukesh Shukla
John R. Sievers
Lady Simon of Wythenshawe
Mary Sirhan
Mme. Paul Sisc?
Slough College Students Union (N. M. Fares)
Peggy Smith
Socialist Party, Tokyo (Narita)
Société Etudes Philosophiques
South Vietnam Peace Commitee (Phung Van Cung)
Spanish Workers' Defence Committee
T. Roy Sparkes
The Spokesman (Robin Murray, Mike Rustin, Raymond Williams, Sigurd Zienau)
Doris and Eddie Steckler
Stefan
Russell Stetler
Louis B. Stettner
Bill Stetznmeyer
Bala Subramanian
Sudbury Mine, Mill & Smelter Workers' Union (J. Astgen)
Ignacio Sved
Jirina and I. Lubor Svobodova
Swedish Peace and Arbitration Society
Hugh Sykes
Dora Taylor
Hazhir Teimourian
U Thant
Nguyen Huu Tho and Huynh Tan Phat
A.V. Thomas
Xuan Thuy
Josip Broz Tito
Torre Tøndel
Syed Mohammad Tonki
Tony Topham
City Council of Toronto
Awna Troga
M. Trussler
Patrick and Pauline Tuft
Tont Hat Tung
Austin Underwood
Unión Nacional de Mujeres Mexicanas (Martha L. de Tamayo and Dolores Soleto Vazquez)
Union of Australian Women (Betty Mawdsley)
United Malaysian and Singaporean Students Action Front (Stephen Chang)
Universidad Autonoma de Chihuahua, Mexico (Gaspar Orozco)
Catherine Vardin
Ardeleanu Vatra
Victims of Repression in Peru (John Edmunds)
Vietnam Peace Committee
Voice of Women/La Voix des Femmes, Québec (Claire Culhane)
Michael von der Goltz
Geoffrey Wadsworth
Phyllis Helen Walker
War Resisters' International (Helga Weber, Devi Prasad)
Julio Alvarez del Vayo
Ian G. Weir
Welwyn Garden City & District Trades Council (Horace Ball)
W. Duncan Wemyss-Smith
A.W. Wenting
Mary and John Wheeldon
Graham Whettam
John Whitehead
Charles Williams
Richard and Barbara Wilson *et al*.
Women's International Democratic Federation
World Congress for World Federation (Sanjib Chaudhuri)
World Welfare Association (G.S. Abdul Hameed)
Erika Worthington
Helen Rosita Wright
Setsuo Yamada (Mayor of Hiroshima)
Law Wai Yan
Youth Campaign for Nuclear Disarmament
Yugoslav League for Peace, Independence and Equality of Peoples

Hideki Yukawa
Jerel Zoltick

Carbons of virtually identical replies signed variously by CF, PW and Ken Coates

South Asian (and other) Departments of the Foreign Office
Encl: 73 ls. from nationals of various countries forwarded to ER

*728 97th Birthday

A small file of letters has accumulated here. The Christmas cards for Russell's last years have been shelved with those belonging to Archives I. They have more than an autograph interest: sometimes there are interesting messages from old friends or distinguished admirers.

Documents .119733–.119781

Birthday

1968 and 1969

The 1969 box includes ls. from the following:

Günther Anders
Fanny Barkai
Ernest M. Belzagny
John M. Bender
C.?B. Bows?
Judy Brook
Ken Browne
Michael and Mary Burn
Encl: transcript of "J.S. Mill" to BR, 18 May 1969, and of appended signatories to the document referred to in Clark's *Life of Bertrand Russell* (1975), p. 633.
August E. Cook
Helen Cromwell Curtis
Austin Davies
O. Delmos
G.S. Elborn
Anton Felton
Peter Fenton
Paul Foulkes
Jill Geach
Helen Gilstos?
Ann Gold
Ian Graham
S. Liaqat Hussain
Andrew Jarvis
Vikramajit Kumar
Jacques Le Bohec
P. Bruce B. Leeming
Hesta Lovejoy
Donald and Priscilla Lowne
David Maddock
Meharchand
Ardeleanu Misu
Mohammed Ebrahim Moazzini
Mihailo Momcilovic
Mohammad Munir
P.R.K. Narayanan
Ed and Ila Norman
M. O'Brien
D. Owen
Terry Philpot
Leon Rosenbloom
Sarah Russell
Tsuruko Saito
Jean Marie Savanyu
David Smith
Wm. F. Stanton
Mohan Sud
Paulette Sultan
Darian Trussler
Simon Walker

Dennis M. Warren
Melvin B. Yoken

Christmas
1967, 1968 and 1969

**730–737 Frank Russell, Russell Relatives, and Stanley Relatives

John Francis Stanley Russell (1865–1931), the 2nd Earl Russell, and his younger brother, Bertrand, exchanged much correspondence. Most of their correspondence is in Archives I, but a few letters are located here. In *735 there is correspondence between Russell and Frank's friend Miss Otter, and the script of a radio programme on his trial for bigamy. *736 contains correspondence with Russell's relatives on the Russell side, and *737 correspondence with Stanley relatives.

Documents *730.108101–.108105; *735.108106–.108119; *736.108120–.108219m; *737.108220–.108339

*730 Frank Russell and BR

Russell, Frank **3** 1924-9
  BR to 1918

*735 Frank Russell

CF to Barry Feinberg 1970
  Encl: BR, s. on Frank Russell's death
Otter, Amy E. **6** 1931
  Encl: valuation list of Amberley pictures, silver, furniture and various books
  BR to **4** 1931
Thomas, Donald: "Tried by Their Peers, 2. The Trial of Lord Russell (who died in 1931) for Bigamy—1901" (1970)

*736 Russell Relatives

Forester, Grace **5** . . . . n.d.
  To ER **11** . . . . n.d.
  BR to 1969
Lloyd, John Russell **9** 1967-9
  BR to **5** 1967-9
  CF to Barry Feinberg 1969
Lloyd, Margaret **4** 1967-8
  To ER **4** 1962-7
  To BR and ER 1967
  BR to **5** 1968
  ER to 1967
Russell, Agatha, Lady (typed extracts of l.) **2** . . . . n.d.
Russell, Athenaïs 1967
  BR to 1967
Russell, Flora **22** 1957-65
  To BR and ER **3** 1963-5
  To ER **73** 1957-65
  Encl: BR to Anthony Russell **2** 1967
  Anthony Russell to BR 1967
  NJ to Flora Russell 1962
  Molly Eldon to BR 1967
  BR to **3** 1964-5
Russell, Mrs. Gilbert (receipt) 1944
Russell, Harold, to Mrs. McEwen 1925
Russell, John 1967
  Aliki Russell to BR **2** 1954-67
Russell, Martin **2** 1968
  BR to 1968
Russell, Maud **2** 1963

To ER **3** 1956-7
Encl: l. to *The Times* from Woodrow Wyatt; handwritten note by ER
BR to **3** 1963
ER to 1957

Russell, Rollo, BR to (copies) **17** 1885-98
Agatha Russell to (copy) ... 1864
V.H. Stanton to (copy) ..... n.d.

Strong, Rupert **5** 1967
To ER 1967
Eithne Strong to BR 1967
Encl.
BR to **2** 1967-8
ER to 1967

***737 Stanley Relatives**

Henley, Lady Dorothy **5** .. 1966-7
Encl: Carol Eden to
ER **2** 1966
Morton Eden 1966
BR to **2** 1966-7
ER to Carol Eden 1966

Fox Pitt, Elspeth **6** 1956-65
BR to **2** 1965
CF to 1965

*740 Invitations

The invitations filed here are public invitations—mainly to make speeches and attend ceremonies. Some of the invitations came from organizations with which Russell had been associated long ago, such as the Cambridge Heretics. To some he sent messages to be read and possibly published. These files supplement the publishing and political correspondences, which also contain many invitations. The Trinity College, Cambridge, entry contains the business correspondence (mainly form letters) resulting from Russell's life fellowship.

Documents .115001–.116435

The 1,435 documents range alphabetically from the Aberystwyth Socialist Society to the Yugoslav Philosophical Association.

*750 Russell's Dictation

Russell customarily dictated his correspondence and articles to his wife Edith. Virtually all of this class is devoted to dictated replies to correspondence. Because of the magnitude of the task it is not indexed or available in typescript. It is however a very useful source of information, not least for being arranged chronologically. Shelved with the Archives II portion of this class is the very much larger portion which came with Archives I.

Documents .132701–.132740

1955, 1956, 1959, 1960, 1961, 1967-69

Some were held together by a clipped note by ER: "Some Letters dictated to ER in 1967-69".

*751–752, 754 Embargoed Financial Correspondence

***751 contains Russell's correspondence with his accountant, Percy A. Popkin & Co. In the mid-1960s, Anton Felton became his accountant. *752 also contains Russell's bank passbooks. One side itemizes deposits, and the other withdrawals. *754 contains miscellaneous financial correspondence.**

Documents *751.100001–.100187; *752.100188–.100476; *754.100501–.100566

Bank of America (s. of account, cancelled cheques, miscellaneous debit) 1940
Barclays Bank Ltd. (D. Wynn Jones *et al.*) **35** 1959-69
To BR and ER **15** 1968-70
Encl: receipts, ss. of account, cancelled cheques
BR to **21** 1953-68
ER to **7** 1964-8
Brown, Shipley & Co. Ltd. (income tax certificates) 1960-2
Browns of Chester Ltd.
to ER **11** 1956-60
Encl: bills, ss. of account, slip re goods for approbation
ER to **6** 1956-7
Encl: l. to Burnets & Co., ls. from Dorothy Mackay, l. to Dorothy Mackay, lists of children's sizes, list of clothes needed, list of clothes returned
Dr. to Dicks (bill) to ER 1961
Ellis Davies & Co. 1959
Glyn, Mills & Co. (Child & Co.) **55** 1922-70
To ER 1969
Encl: form ls., deposit s., list of standing instructions, bank guarantee, passbooks, cancelled cheques, income tax certificates
BR to **30** 1950-69
ER to **3** 1959-69
CF to **3** 1967-9
Encl: l. from BR to Coward, Chance & Co. (L. P. Tylor), l. from BR to R. W. G. Mackay, l. from BR to Chesterton & Sons, l. from BR to Mr. Stubbs, l. to BR from Langlois Harding & Co.
Guardian Assurance Co. Ltd. 1954
Encl: insurance policies
Imperial Chemical Industries Ltd. (stockholder s.) 1946
"Income" (list of income in BR's hand) .... 1900?
Inland Revenue **2** 1953-4
Encl: form ls., leaflets
Lee Abbey Hotel (bills) 1925
Lotus & Delta Ltd., to
ER **2** 1956
Encl: bills, invoices
ER to **2** 1956
Encl: sheet of items to

purchase
Midland Bank Ltd. (J. O. Williams *et al.*) 5 1956-66
Encl: s. of account, bank wallet
BR to 2 1961-3
Percy A. Popkin & Co. (later H. E. Madams, A.F.A.) **114** 1949-66
To ER **24** 1955-65
To BR and ER 1949
Encl: investment income lists, receipts, withholding s., note as to financial affairs, l. from J. E. Glesson, ls. from Barker Preston & Co. (B. P. H. Preston)
BR to **39** 1950-9
ER to **6** 1956-7
Encl: l. from ER to Brown, Shipley & Co., gross earning lists, ss. entitled "Answers to Questionnaire" and "Replies to Questionnaire"
R. W. Pressprich & Co. (stockholder ss.) 1960
Ryman, Ltd., Stationers, ER to 1961
F. H. Salter & Son (bill) 1960
W. H. Smith & Son Ltd. (bill) 1960
The Young Idea (Mrs. Sheldon Price) (bills) 1954

*753 Financial and Legal Correspondence (Embargoed)

*753 contains Russell's bank deposit books and cheque-book stubs. The former record individual deposits, with the date, beneficiary and amount, but seldom with any note on the source. The latter provide date, payee and amount. Sometimes they are filled out in other hands.

Documents .102501–.102678

Bank deposit books:
1950, 1952-60, 1962, 1968

Cheque book stubs:
1935-37, 1947-56, 1958-69

*760 Legal Correspondence (Embargoed)

The first major dispute dealt with in the embargoed legal correspondence concerns Russell's letting of Telegraph House from his brother. The second concerns Russell's divorce from his second wife. This part of the correspondence is sometimes annotated by Russell in ball-point pen. Russell's legal firm throughout is Coward, Chance & Co., of whom Crompton Llewelyn Davies was Russell's chief contact until his death in 1935; L. E. P. Tylor succeeded him.

Documents .101001–.102160; .133001–.133924

Coward, Chance & Co. (Crompton Llewelyn Davies, L. E. P. Tylor *et al.*) **899** 1927-69
To BR and ER **2** 1961-2
To BR and PR **5** 1934
To DR **49** 1928-59
To ER **113** 1954-69
To PR **17** 1933-53
To CF **2** 1968-70
To Miss Griffith 1956
To Olive Harrington 1932
Encl: ls. to and from Withers & Co. (John J. Withers), ls. to and from Rowe & Maw (F. Graham Maw), l. from Ottoline Morrell, ls. to and from E. M. H. Lloyd, ls. to and from F. M. Meynell, ls. to and from Vandercom, Stanton & Co. (Richard Buckland), ls. from Frank Russell, l. to Withers & Co. (John J. Withers) from Frank Russell, ls. to Olive Harrington, ls. to and from Wontner & Renwick, l. to and from A. J. Johnston, l. from Burn & Berridge, l. from Constable & Maude, l. from Constable & Maude to Withers & Co. (John J. Withers), l. to G. M. Hilbery, l. from Farebrother Ellis & Co. to Withers & Co. (John J. Withers), ls. to and from Passport Office (Herbert Martin), ls. to and from Lewis & Lewis and Gisborne (H. P. Gisborne), l. from Passport Office (J. W. Stafford) to DR, l. to Collins & Collins, ls. to Lewis & Lewis and Gisborne from PR, l. to Percy A. Popkin, l. from Langlois, Harding & Co., l. to Percy A. Popkin from H. M. Inspector of Taxes, l. from Conrad Russell, l. from Gibbon & Rogers, ls. from Francis Walshe, l. from Conrad Russell to G. J. McWatters, l. from T. A. Munro, ls. from Wilmer & Broun (Hugh R. H. Smith), l. from Glyn Mills & Co. to PR, l. from Desmond O'Neill, l. to the Commissioners of Inland Revenue, l. to and from Ministry of Pensions and National Insurance (R. Shipley), ls. to and from Lewis W. Taylor (Peter Proudall), l. from L. J. Collins, l. from William Charles Crocker, ls. from G. D. Morgan, l. to Merioneth Education Committee, l. from H. E. Madams, l. from Plenty & Son Ltd. (G. T. Shoosmith), ls. to and from

McMaster University (Kenneth Blackwell), ts. of correspondence re disputation over Telegraph House 1927-30, omnibus correspondence prepared by Coward, Chance & Co., s. as to apportionments, memorandum, affidavits of John J. Withers, Alfred William Anger, Ernest Puller, ss. of accounts, schedule of fixtures and fittings, particulars of the trust fund, electrical installation at Telegraph House, statutory declarations, proposed agreements between BR and Amy E. Otter, instructions to settle deed of separation, clippings, draft, extract of Judicature (Consolidation Act 1925), list of furnishings at Telegraph House, 1932 school account, objections to draft agreement received, will of Amy Elizabeth Otter, 2 sheets entitled "Earl Russell and Miss Otter", 3 copies of draft agreement of Amy E. Otter, document re BR's settlement trust, alternative draft of application, message to BR by telephone, schedule of deeds and documents, bills, receipts, note re Russell v. Russell, extract from deed securing annuity, copy of appointment of guardian, petition for decrease of maintenance, memorandum by DR, reply to memorandum, summonses, summons and minutes of order, "L.E.P.T. 1, 2, 3", capital account, note in PR's hand, deed of covenant, BR's 1951 will, BR's divorce decree from PR, opinion of Mr. Young, list of securities, trustees' accounts, BR's 1955 will, school reports on Conrad Russell, essays by Conrad Russell, report from G. B. M. Lansdown, certificate of posting, court welfare report, affidavits of DR re John Russell's divorce, comments on DR's affidavit by ER, order for custody of BR's grandchildren, trustee ss. signed by ER, draft order from DR's solicitor, opinion re Committee of 100, instructions for execution of codicil, affidavits of interveners (BR and ER), invitation, page from *Debrett's Illustrated Peerage*, explanatory note re 1963 wills of BR and ER, affidavits of BR and ER, affidavit of G. D. Morgan, Sarah Russell's application for scholarship

BR to **228** 1928-69
DR to **22** 1928-55
ER to **37** 1954-69
PR to **3** 1933-53
CF to **5** 1967-9
Olive Harrington to
5 1931-2

Encl: ls. between BR and ER, ls. between BR and Francis Meynell, l. from Amy E. Otter, ls. to DR re Beacon Hill (E. H. Russell, Colin Hill, Dorothy Garner, Richard Garner, Henry F. Forbes, M. Savan, David Garnett, Mabel Colenberg, E. Samuel, J. E. Ainsworth Johnstone, Phyllis Bernard, Guy and Cicely Ramsey, E. Mary Bennett, Ralph W. Wood, G. E. Haywood), l. to DR from Ottoline Morrell, l. from DR to Ottoline Morrell, l. from BR to W. H. Norton, l. to DR from Kingsley Martin, ls. from Anne, Lucy and Sarah Russell to DR, l. from BR to Vandercom, Stanton & Co., l. from BR to Mr. Lummus, l. from BR to Mr. Ettlinger, l. from DR to BR and Crompton Llewelyn Davies, l. to BR from Ted Lloyd, l. from BR to Ted Lloyd, l. from BR to Mr. Rogers, l. from BR to Percy A. Popkin, l. to BR and ER from Delight Wallace, deed of separation, reference l. for Elizabeth Cross by BR and DR, reference l. for Rosemary Natt by BR, instructions concerning BR's *Autobiography*, ss. by Lucy Silcox and Rhoda Brenan, s. in BR's hand, page of points in ER's hand, form l. and meeting minutes from Committee of 100, recorded telephone conversation, note in ER's hand re

Ahmed Abdi (Alaoui), note in CF's hand

*761 1935 Divorce Documents (Embargoed)

These miscellaneous documents relating to Russell's divorce from his second wife, Dora, include "An Inventory of the Furniture and Household Effects at 'Telegraph House', Harting, Petersfield." This document is interesting for its listing of the books in Telegraph House, among other things.

Documents .133925–.134005

1 box, including Heads of Agreement, s. of the petitioner (BR), settlements re John and Kate Russell, affidavits by Elsie Carter, Lily Howell, Mary Lyle Gilchrist, Harris Russell, Margaret Wilson, Florence Elizabeth Pearl Freeman, Alan Maberly, William Riggs, Rosemary Pritchard, Donald Paterson, Catherine Jane Ormerod, Tom Helm, John Owen Edwards, John Craven Pritchard, L.P. Tylor, instructions to Constable & Maude, List X (school furniture), List Y (articles to be specially noticed), affidavit of Petitioner in Reply to the Answer to Petition for Maintenance, deed of gift, petition (DR), memorandum, s. of Mary Farrell (née Bailey), s. of BR, inventory of furnishings (and library) at Telegraph House, s., one file of correspondence, note, marriage certificate of BR and DR, degree, bill, affidavit of BR, deed poll, schedule of documents, "D.W.R. 2", draft of BR's will (1936), earnings record, l. from Rowe & Maw to Coward, Chance & Co.

*762 Later Legal and Business Correspondence

On the legal side various lawsuits dominate the correspondence. Russell felt obliged to check journalistic scurrility when it blackened his name. The *Penthouse* file contains, in addition to the first issue of the British edition (March 1965), two copies of a pre-publication brochure falsely listing Russell among the future contributors.

Documents .113001–.113252

T. J. Arnode 1916
Birkbeck, Julius, Coburn & Broad 1962
Editor of *The Daily Sketch*
Jon Tinker
Mr. Murrell
Swepstone, Walsh & Son
Cannon Brookes & Odgers (T. Cannon Brookes) 1958
Chesterton & Sons, Surveyors 1958
John Mowlem and Co. Ltd.
City & West End Properties Ltd. (M.P. Hoare) 1916-21
Consolidated Stock (s. of interest) 1947
J. Davis Builder & Decorator 1926
L. Frumkin & Co., Wines, Spirits, Cigars .... 1962?
Dr. Bulkeley Gavin 1921
General Post Office, Accountant General's Department, W. Hawks 1947
Gibbon & Rogers, Chartered Surveyors 1956
Guardian, Daily Mirror, B. M. Birnberg & Co. 1964-6
Encl: B. M. Birnberg & Co., Solicitors
Benedict Birnberg
Lovell, White & King
Editor of Economist Newspapers Ltd.
Editor of *The Daily Mirror*
Editor of *The Beaver*, London School of Economics
L. A. Lee Howard
Oswald Hickson, Collier & Co.
International Union of Socialist Youth (Sture Ericson)
The British Traders' Association (R. H. Hunter)
James Evans
Various legal documents
Scandinavian Airlines System Ltd.
Hampton & Sons Auctioneers & Valuers 1956
Peter Jones Ltd. (S. F. Hayward) 1921
Langlois, Harding & Co. 1953
Lywood & Sons 1945
Hugh R. Manes (re Honeywell) 1968
Ministry of Pensions and National Insurance 1966
National Cooperative Quarries (share certificates) 1906-7

De Pinna & John Venn
Pennington's Auctioneers and Estate Agents (M. Hester) 1958
Penthouse suit 1964-5
Encl: Editor of *The Times*
Benedict Birnberg
John Braine
B. Lloyd-Davies
J. B. Poznansky
Various legal documents; *Penthouse*, vol. 1, no. 1 (Mar. 1965); pre-publication brochure (illustrated)
Plenty & Sons, Ltd., Engineers 1954
Price, Waterhouse & Co. (L. E. Halsey) 1908-9
Fabia, Lady Stanley of Alderley (s. of receipts and payments re estate)
Rabinowitz & Boudin (Leonard B. Boudin) 1966-9
Katharine Tait
RS, s. re passport
Scorer & Harris, Notaries Public 1967
Spett Rai Radio Televione Italiana 1955
Various Legal Suits 1965-9
Edward J. Ennis
Coward, Chance & Co. (B. D. S. Loch)
Metropolitan Police, Rochester Row Police Station
Michael Barratt-Brown
Kenneth Fleet
Union Transport Finance Ltd. 1966
Venezuelan Oil Concessions stock certificate 1947
War Stock (s. of interest) 1947

*800
Legal Correspondence

Directors 113192

the Earl Russell, OM, FRS
the Countess Russell
Christopher Farley
Ralph Schoenman

3 & 4 Shavers Place
Haymarket
London SW1, England

telephone
Whitehall 4209 & 4200
cables
Russfound London SW1

Bertrand Russell Peace Foundation

3 December, 1964.

To the Editor of The Times

Sir:

A matter has been brought to my notice which demands immediate attention. The new magazine to be called Penthouse is about to begin publication. I had never heard of this magazine until yesterday. I now learn that in its advertising material it suggests that I am to be a contributor to the first number. There is no truth in this. I have had no communication whatsoever with this magazine.

The advertising material at the same time shows that the magazine is to be devoted mainly or entirely to pornography. This is not the sort of magazine with which I care to be connected and I am not surprised to have received a number of indignant protests at the use of my name in this connection.

Yours faithfully,

Bertrand Russell

Plate 8 Unpublished letter to *The Times*, 3 December 1964, re *Penthouse*'s use of Russell's name.

*811 Legal Actions: City College of New York

Russell retained little of his correspondence from 1938–44, a period he spent in the U.S., but he did keep apparently full files on the CCNY case (see Archives I). This letter belongs in those files as an example of the sort of correspondence generated by the case. There is no indication Russell answered the letter.

Documents .113253

Harriet M. Lovell to BR 1940
Re her ms. on sex, religion and war
Encl: photo

*900
Works by Others, Films, Tapes, Photographs, Clippings, Etc.

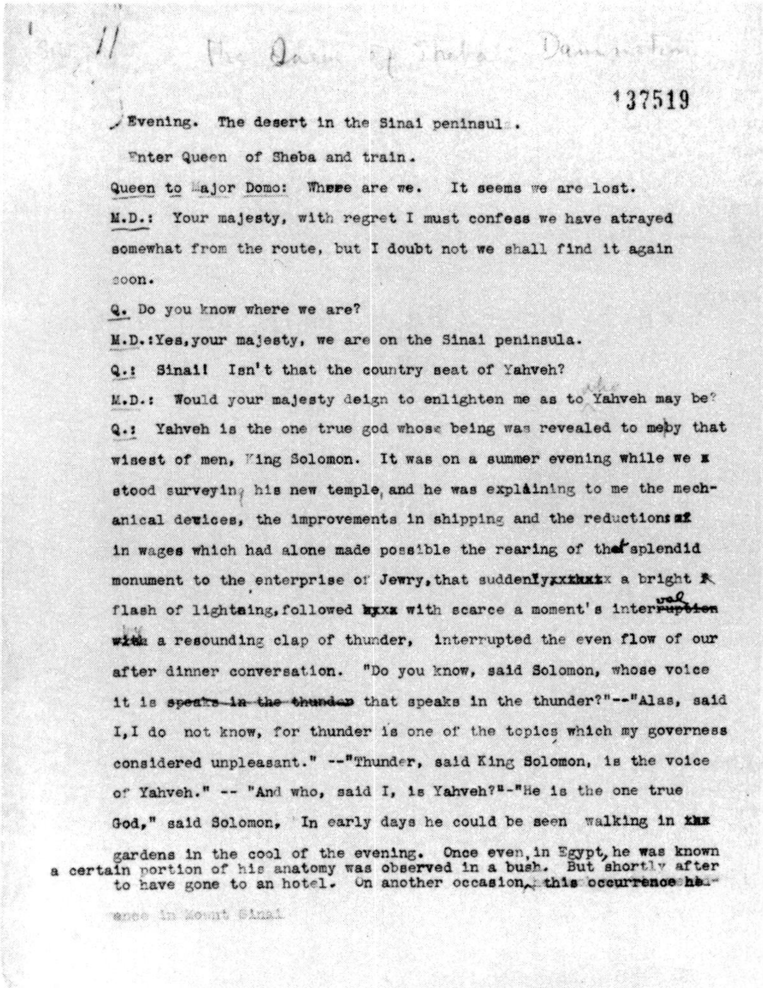
The Queen of Sheba Damnation

137519

Evening. The desert in the Sinai peninsula.

Enter Queen of Sheba and train.

Queen to Major Domo: Where are we. It seems we are lost.

M.D.: Your majesty, with regret I must confess we have strayed somewhat from the route, but I doubt not we shall find it again soon.

Q. Do you know where we are?

M.D.: Yes, your majesty, we are on the Sinai peninsula.

Q.: Sinai! Isn't that the country seat of Yahveh?

M.D.: Would your majesty deign to enlighten me as to who Yahveh may be?

Q.: Yahveh is the one true god whose being was revealed to me by that wisest of men, King Solomon. It was on a summer evening while we stood surveying his new temple, and he was explaining to me the mechanical devices, the improvements in shipping and the reductions in wages which had alone made possible the rearing of that splendid monument to the enterprise of Jewry, that suddenly a bright flash of lightning, followed with scarce a moment's interval by a resounding clap of thunder, interrupted the even flow of our after dinner conversation. "Do you know, said Solomon, whose voice it is ~~speaks in the thunder~~ that speaks in the thunder?"--"Alas, said I, I do not know, for thunder is one of the topics which my governess considered unpleasant." --"Thunder, said King Solomon, is the voice of Yahveh." -- "And who, said I, is Yahveh?"-"He is the one true God," said Solomon, In early days he could be seen walking in gardens in the cool of the evening. Once even, in Egypt, he was known a certain portion of his anatomy was observed in a bush. But shortly after to have gone to an hotel. On another occasion, ~~this occurrence~~ ...

...ance in Mount Sinai

Plate 9 Russell's revisions on an anonymous typescript, "The Queen of Sheba's Damnation" (1930).

*910 Works by Others

Authors sent their works in progress on every conceivable topic to Russell. So did publishers with their prospective books. The self-published did the same. The result is that Russell had to develop a standard response to such requests for advice: that if he read all their works, he would have no time to write his own. Sometimes correspondence is attached to the item concerned. This class does not include a large number of political works listed in other classes. It does include the original typescripts of the contributions to *Bertrand Russell: Philosopher of the Century*, edited by Ralph Schoenman.

Documents .137001–.137836

A

Abian, S. "Co-ordinate Representation of the Functions of a Complex Variable". 1951. Mimeo ts. L. from Abian to BR.

Adayr, Frederic. "The Only Alternative". 1955. Xerox of ts. L. from Adayr to BR.

Aitken, Sir Max. *A Speech delivered by ... to the Anglo-Rhodesian Society*. Nov. 1969.

Ali, Medi. "The Raging Pandemic". 1958. Ms. L. from Ali to BR.

Alley, Rewi. *Greetings for 1969*. (A booklet of Chinese photos.)

Altamirano, Horacio Espinosa. *Oda Iracunda*. Mexico City: Ediciones Bellesta, 1966. 2 copies.

Amerikanerne I Junglen. n.d.

Ancel, Marc. *The Death Penalty in European Countries*. Council of Europe: 1962.

Applied Optics, 3 (Oct. 1964): 1090-1162.

Aspden, H. "The Physics of Space-Time". Privately printed, 1969.

"Are All Empirical Statements Merely Hypotheses?" Ts. (No author.)

Aron, Raymond, ed. *World Technology and Human Destiny*. Ann Arbor: The University of Michigan Press, 1963. Bound galley proofs.

Ashford, A.E. "Thus Have I Learned". Ms.

Athens Daily Post, 19 May 1963.

Athens News, 29 May 1963.

Attlee Memorial Appeal.

Auriol, Vincent. "Allocution au Congrès des Anciens Combattants de Yugoslavie". 1955. Ts. L. from Auriol to BR. L. from Pierre Schneits to BR.

——. "Discours de Chicago". 1955. Ts.

Avellaneda, Juan de Dios. "Carta que Mexico Manda". 1955. Printed s. L. from Avellaneda to BR.

B

I Bambini dell'Asilo. (Phonograph record.)

Bartley, III, William Warren. "Religion at Harvard: The Philosopher, The Pundit, The Priest, and the President". *The Harvard Crimson*, 28 Mar. 1958: 3-6. L. from Bartley

to BR.

Basri, Saul A. "A Deductive Theory of Space and Time". 1961. Mimeo ts.

Basu, Jitendra Nath. "Press and Peace". 1955. Ts. L. from Basu to BR.

Bay, Christian. "Academic Government and Academic Citizenship in a Time of Revolt". Ts.

Beckman, Viking. "Gesellschaft von Morgen". Ts.

——. *Morgondagens Samhälle*. Booklet.

——. *Morgondagens Verklighet*. Booklet.

Behman, Heinrich. "Deskription und limitierte Variable". 1952. Ts. L. from Behman to BR.

——. "Das Russellsche Paradoxon und die formale Logik". Mimeo ts.

Belet, Robert. "Regard sur l'Europe et la Paix". 1955. Ts. L. from Belet to BR.

Belilos, Leon. "A Neutral's Scheme for World Disarmament". Tscc.

"Bertrand Russell Peace Foundation". Mimeo ts. Outlines its aims, areas of concern, etc.

Berveiller, Michel. "L'homme doit'il survivre?" *Le Revue de Paris*, 69 (1962).

Bevington, Helen. *When Found, Make a Verse of*. New York: Simon and Schuster, 1961. Bound galley proofs. L. from Simon and Schuster (Henry W. Simon) to BR; BR's reply.

"Beweis der Formel:". Ms. 2 leaves. (No author.) Removed from inside front cover of BR's library copy of *Principia*, I (1910).

Bierich, Marcus. "Die Definition der Zahl". 1947. Ts.

——. "Freges Lehre von dem Sinn und der Bedeutung der Urteile und Russells Kritik an dieser Lehre". Hamburg: 1951. Thesis.

Binet, F.E. "Notes on a Remark by Lord Russell". *The British Journal for the Philosophy of Science*, 7 (1954): 67-70.

——, and Szekeres, G. "On Borel Fields over Finite Sets". *The Annals of Mathematical Statistics*, 28 (June 1957): 494-8. L. from Binet to BR.

——, and Watson, G.S. "Algebraic Theory of the Computing Routine for Tests of Significance on the Dimensionality of Normal Multivariate Systems". *The Journal of the Royal Statistical Society*, **B**, 18 (1956): 70-8.

Birnberg, Naomi. "The Opening of a New Heaven on a New Earth or the Gospel of the Emancipation of Womanhood". 1950. Ts. L. from Birnberg to BR.

Bisgyer, Maurice, ed. *B'nai B'rith*. 12th ed. Washington: Supreme Lodge of B'nai B'rith, 1955?

Bishop, Peter H.H. "Models and These Times". 1955. Mimeo ts. L. from Bishop to BR.

Bivona, Francesco. *Running Mouse*. New York: 1964. Mimeo ts.

Black Dwarf. Pre-issue, May Day 1968.

Blackett, P.M.S. "Nuclear Weapons and Defence: Comments on Kissinger, Kennan and King-Hall". Mimeo ts. 1956.

Bonyun, David A. "Credo". Ts. L. from Bonyun to BR.

Boole, George. "Of Propositions Numerically Definite". Reprinted from *Transactions of the Cambridge Philosophical Society*, 11 (1868): 1-16. Signed by BR.

Border Impact, no. 2 (1962?).

Borgese, Elisabeth Mann. *Ascent of Woman*. New York: George Braziller, 1963. Bound galley proofs.

Boschi, Gaetano. "Psychological Investigation on the Ways to Follow in Order to Avoid the Danger of an Atomic Destruction of the World". 1955. Ts.

Bouda. "Abrüstung tut not". Ts.

Boulding, Kenneth E. "The Peace Research Movement". 1962. Mimeo

ts.

Bowden, L. D. "The Theory of Logical Types". Keble College: n.d. Thesis.

Boyle, Sir Dermot. *The Nuclear Deterrent*. London: The Air League, 1963.

Braatöv, Tryvge. "Experimental Neurasthenia and Intellectual Overstrain". *The Journal of Nervous and Mental Disease*, 105 (May 1947): 477-92. Quotes BR's *In Praise of Idleness and Other Essays*.

Bradley, B.F. *Trade Unionism in India*. London: Modern Books Ltd., [1932].

Brandenburg, Nelly Louise. *Zwischen Staub und Sternen*. Regensburg: Druck Joseph Habbel, 1950.

Brandy, Carlos. "El rostro de la muerte". *Marcha*, 6 Oct. 1962. A poem dedicated to BR.

Braverman, Harry. *The Future of Russia*. New York: Macmillan, 1963. Uncorrected galley proofs.

Bredsdorff, Elias. "Moralists *versus* Immoralists: the Great Battle in Scandinavian Literature in the 1880's". *Scandinavica*. N.d.

——. "Nonsense in the Nursery". Reprinted from *Orbis Litterarum*, 19 (1955): 335-64.

Bridel, Gaston. "Bonne chance!". *Tribune de Genève*, 21 June 1955. Filed with Scheurer material.

Briggs, Richard I. "Reflections on Vietnam" and "Average Briton Backs Viet, Ambassador Says". 1967. 2 clippings.

British Society for Social Responsibility in Science. *BRSRS*, nos. 1-2 (1969).

Brook Advisory Centres. *Annual Report*. 1967.

Brother's Face: A Bulletin of Council for Promotion of Communal Harmony, no. 1 (1965?).

Bruns, Günter Von, and Schmidt, Jürgen. "Eine Filtertheoretische Formulierung der Kontinuumhypothese". *Zeitschrift für Mathematik*, 1 (1955): 91-2.

Bryant, John. "Cybernetics and Scientific Philosophy". 1969. Mimeo ts.

Bryn Mawr Alumnae Bulletin, Winter 1966.

Buckley, Marjorie. "To Keep The Trust". Play. Mimeo ts.

Buffard, Henri. "La Democratie Nouvelle Salut de L'Humanité". Mimeo ts.

Bulletin of the Atomic Scientists, 17 (Nov. 1961).

Bulletin of the Workers' Control Conference, no. 4: 25 Mar. 1968.

Burger, Henry G. "Agonemmetry: Adaptability through Rivalry; An Institution Evolving Genetics and Culture". Reprinted from *Systematics*, 5 (June 1967).

Burton, H. "Cephalosporins". 1966. Mimeo ts.

Burton, John W. "From Areas of Agreement". 1966. Mimeo ts. L. from Burton to BR; reply from BR.

C

Caesar, Irving. "A Plan to Eliminate the Surprise Attack and Create an Atmosphere in which Progressive Steps towards Disarmament can be Undertaken". Mimeo ts. L. from Caesar to BRPF. L. to Caesar from BR.

The Campaign for the Limitation of Secret Police Powers. *The Secret Police and You*. 1956? Pamphlet.

Canada-Vietnam Newsletter, 1966-7. Selected issues.

Capps, Arthur W. "Solving the World's Food Problem with Heat Husbandry Techniques". 1955. Mimeo ts. L. from Capps to BR.

Carter, Norwood. "Proposal: To Establish in Canada a University of Quality". 1967. Xerox of ts.

Cassirer, Eva. "On Logical Structure". *Aristotelian Society Proceed-*

ings, 1964: 177-98.

Celebrity Register, pp. 653-4 ("Russell, Bertrand").

Ceniza, Claro R. "The Rational Basis of the Problems of Philosophy with their Probable Solutions". 1956. Ts.

Chakrabarti, Raiharan. *New India*. Calcutta: Hindusthan Library, 1964.

——. *For His Love*. Calcutta: Sree Ranjan Kumar Das, 1974.

Chappelow, Alan. Untitled mss., ls., pamphlets and notes.

Chevreuse, Jacques. *Défense de la Paix*. Monte Carlo: Editions Regain, 1961.

Chomsky, Noam. *American Power and the New Mandarins*. New York: Pantheon, 1969. Bound galley proofs.

Christian, Gerald. "O England, Lovely England!". 1955. Ts. L. from Christian to BR.

Christians, Rudolf. "Die Welt-Einheitsschrift als Subtraktions-Rest der Lateinischen und Gotischen Schrift". Pamphlet. L. from Christians to BR.

Cifarelli, Antonio Pippo. *Bianco e Nero*. Milan: 1955.

Clarke, Tom. "Sassoon". Play. Mimeo ts.

Clement, William C. "Seeing and Hearing". 1953. L. from Clement to BR.

Clemmer, Robert E. "Stray Thoughts of an Inquisitive Mind". 1958. Ts. L. from Clemmer to BR.

"Comments on the Article by Teller and Latter in *Life*". Xerox of ts. (No author.)

"The Conflict between Science and State in the U.S.S.R." 1949. Mimeo ts. (No author.)

"Contributions to the Logical Theory of Intuition". Ts. (No author.)

Creasey, John. *They Didn't Mean to Kill*. London: Hodder and Stoughton, 1960.

Creedy, F. "A Berkeleyan Dialogue". Ts. L. from Creedy to BR.

Crosser, Paul. "The Cult of the Philosophy of Whitehead in the United States of America". 1968. Mimeo ts.

Crossword, 4 (Nov. 1969).

Cruel Sports, n.s., 10 (1968).

D

Dailey, Edward D. "Tentative Solution to the Problem of Knowledge". Mimeo ts. L. from Dailey to BR.

The Daily Tribune. N.d. Headline: "COMMITTEE OF 100 HAS H-BOMB/ RUSSELL DECLARES WAR".

Dank Fredskonferences Forretningsudvalag. *Danmark og Krigen i Vietnam*. Nov. 1965. Pamphlet. Includes clippings.

Darlaine, Manon. "The Atomic Crucifixion of Mankind". 1955. Ts. L. from Darlaine to BR.

Dass, Benarsi. "Mind's Physical Reactions: Parity Laws". 1955. Ts. L. from Dass to BR.

de Abreu, Joselito. *Um Dia, Amanhã*. Salvador, Brazil: Artes Gráficas Editora, 1968.

Degen, Charles. "Age Need Not Wither You". 1955. Mimeo ts. L. from Degen to BR.

Delt, Lydia, and Martin, Paul, transs. *L'Histoire d'une vie* by Constantin Paoustovski. Paris: Gallimard, 1963.

de Mayolo, Santiago Antunez. "La Cause de la Gravitation Universelle d'apres la Physique Nucleaire". Reprinted from *Actas de la Academia Nacional de Ciencias Exactas, Fisicas y Naturales de Lima*, 18 (1955).

De Menezes, Adolpho Justo Bezerra. "Brazil and the Afro-Asiatic World". Mimeo ts.

Devon Committee of 100. *Thought and Action*, Sept. and Oct. 1964. Mimeo ts.

DeVries, Peter Hugh. "Pierre de Fermat's Truly Marvelous

Proof—An Imaginary Reconstruction for the Even Powers". *Journal of Recreational Mathematics*, 2 (Apr. 1969): 85-94.

Dhandhania, Jugal Kishore. *Solutions of All Our Problems by Humanism.* Calcutta: Dhandhania & Sons, 1964.

Diary. Jan.-June 1969. (No author.)

Direct Action, 9 (Apr. 1968).

Direct Action for a Nonviolent World, no. 103 (12 Dec. 1969).

Disordine, 1, no. 1 (Sept. 1969).

Dodwell, P. M. C. "Forgotten Men". 1952. Ts. L. from Dodwell to BR.

Duhring, Nathan. "Immortality: Physically, Scientifically, Now". 1962. Mimeo ts.

Dunn, Halbert L. *Creative Destiny in Action.* Nov. 1953. Leaflet. L. from Dunn to BR.

——. "Man's Search for Truth". Mimeo ts.

E

Echanove T., Carlos A. "Una voz que Enaltece y que Consuela". *El Nacional*, 3 Nov. 1962.

Eddington, Arthur S. "The Combination of Relativity Theory and Quantum theory". *Communications of the Dublin Institute for Advanced Studies*, **A**, no. 2 (1943).

Eddy, Amos. "Freedom". 1958. Ts. L. from Eddy to BR.

Edelberg, Victor. "Extreme Precision of Observation of √ Binomial Variance σ of Universe. New Theorem". Ms. L. from Edelberg to BR.

Education Advisory Committee, Parliamentary Group for World Government. *World Wise.* 1968.

Edwards, David V. "The Movement for Unilateral Nuclear Disarmament in Britain". Swarthmore College: March 1962. Thesis.

Effendi, Aslam. "'The Race between Folly and Wisdom' and Other Essays". Tscc. L. from BR to Effendi, 1965.

"Epistemology and Communication Theory". Ts. (No author.)

"Escape from Atom Suicide". *Sunday Pictorial*, 10 July 1955. Filed with Marett material.

F

Facci, Joseph. *A Plan for a Democratic Public Opinion.* Washington: 1947.

Factual News Information, 1, no. 1: Sept. 1969.

Faustinelli, C. "The Way of Peace and Wealth". Ts.

Federal Union 21. (Anniversary brochure.) With photo of BR.

Ferrari, León. "Palabras Ajenas". Mimeo ts.

Final Report of the Press Commission. Sessional Paper XI. Columbo, Ceylon: 1964.

Fischer, Hans. "I Urschrift". Mimeo ts.

Fischhof, Georg, and Oerley, W. A. "1×1 des erfolgreichen Lebens". Mimeo ts. Includes printed material from *Forum-Verlag*.

Fisher, John J. "Santayana on James: A Conflict of Views on Philosophy". Reprinted from *American Philosophical Quarterly*, 2 (Jan. 1965): 1-7.

Fishman, Jerry. "Bock in a Wineglass: Three Cents". Ts.

Flex, Konrad. *Was bedeutet Zarathustras Untergang und warum unterblieb er?* Erlangen: 1955.

Ford, Donald. "General Purposes Committee Report (No. 1)". 8 March 1960. Article on civil defence in London.

Ford, Thomas N. "Feasibility Study for a Cattle Development Enterprise in Bolivia, South America". Xerox of ts.

Foreign Office. [Translations from the Soviet press on scientific and related subjects]. 1947-55. Mimeo tss. 14 ls.

to BR from Foreign Office (C. R. A. Rae, J. H. A. Watson, T. S. Tull, J. H. Peck, J. O. Rennie).

Forster, J. A. V. "Thoughts". 1955. Ms. L. from Forster to BR.

Foster-Jakob, R. "General Principles of Size Relation". 1956. Ts. L. from Foster-Jakob to BR.

Foudery, Ernest. "Klein Borschlag". 1955. Ms. L. from Foudery to BR.

Friedrich, C. J. "The Deification of the State". *Review of Politics*, 1 (Jan. 1939): 18-30.

Fromm, Eric. "To President John F. Kennedy and Chairman Nikita Khrushchev". 1962? Mimeo ts.

Fukumoto, Matsuo. *Prevention of a Final War and Cooperationism*. 1968. Pamphlet.

Fulbright, J. W. "Statement on Department of Defense Research in Foreign Policy Matters". *Congressional Record*, 25 Aug. 1965: 20905. L. from Fulbright to BR.

G

Gabor, D. "Light and Information". 1951. Mimeo ts.

Gabriel, Ralph Henry. "The Doctrines of the American Democratic Faith". In *The Course of American Democratic Thought*. New York: Roland Press, 1940.

Gabrilovitch, L. E. "Bertrand Russell". 1950. Ts. Trans. of article in *Novoye Russkoye Slovo*, 14 Nov. 1950. Ls. from Gabrilovitch to BR.

"Gal Uno Successful Services". Mimeo ts. (No author.)

Gandhi Marg, 9 (Jan. 1965). Includes BR's contribution to "India and the Chinese Bomb".

Mahatma Gandhi on Nuclear Arms. (Anti-Nuclear Arms Convention, Pamphlet 1.) New Delhi: Gandhi Peace Foundation, 1962.

Ganesamoorthy, S. "A Critical Study of Scepticism". Madras: 1956. Thesis.

Garbauskas, A. "The Theory of the Spirit and the Foundations of Psychology". 1957. Mimeo ts. L. from Garbauskas to BR.

Geasland, Elizabeth Gordon. "The Miquon School". Mimeo ts.

Gellner, E. "Am Anfang war das Wort". Galley proofs.

——. "Ethics and Logic". *Aristotelian Society Proceedings*, 1955: 157-78.

——. "Is Belief Really Necessary?". *Hibbert Journal*.

——. *Words and Things*. London: Victor Gollancz, 1959. Galley proofs.

General Council of Trade Unions of Japan. "Minutes of the Meeting of Delegates from South East Asian Countries for Exchanging Views and Information". July 1967. Mimeo ts.

"Gilgamesh". Mimeo ts. (No author.)

Gittings, John, and Gott, Richard. *NATO's final Decade*. London: London Region CND, 1964.

Goddard, Leonard. *Philosophical Thinking*. Inaugural Public Lecture at Armidale, New South Wales. 17 Oct. 1962. Pamphlet. L. from Goddard to BR.

Goldewski, Joseph de Gozdawa-. "Is Russia to be Accepted?". June 1965. Mimeo ts.

Goodenough, Erwin R. *Toward a Mature Faith*. New York: Prentice-Hall, 1955. Bound galley proofs.

Gottstein, K. "Über die Wissenschaft von der Politik". Mimeo ts.

Goussinsky, Boris. "On the Concepts of the Continuous and the Infinite in Mathematics". 1969. Mimeo ts.

Grant Brown, R. "A New Theory of Money". 1952. Pamphlet. L. from Grant Brown to BR.

——. "To Prevent a Slump". 1952. Ts. L. from Grant Brown to BR.

Grelling, Kurt. "Identitas indiscernibilium". Reprinted from *Erkenntnis*, 6 (1937).

Grew, Frederick J. "Some Random Thoughts on Euclid, Zeno and Cantor". Aug. 1966. Xerox of ts.

Gupta, Hari Kishan. *A Brief Introduction of Vriddha Jan Samman Samiti*. Agra: 1963. Pamphlet. L. from Gupta to BR. L. to Gupta from BR; BR's reply.

H

Haldar, S. "Russell and his Fallacies". 1955. Ts. L. from Haldar to BR.

Haldimann, Herman Gottfried. *Die Notwende*. N.p.: n. publisher, n.d. Also untitled ts. and l. dated 1956.

Halding, John. "Blick Zurück Bertrand Russell". Newsclipping (source unknown). 21 May 1967.

Hancock, Alan. *Logical Philosophy*. 1945. Pamphlet.

——. *A Philosophic Outline*. 1944. Pamphlet.

Harding, D.E. "Visible Gods: A Modern Socratic Dialogue". Mimeo ts.

Harrison, James M. "The Construction of Economics". Mimeo ts.

Harrisson, T.H. "Living with the People of Malekula". Reprinted from *The Geographical Journal*, 88 (Aug.-Oct. 1936).

Hawkins, Jr., Eugene H. Untitled ts. 1968. L. from Hawkins to BR.

Hemp, W.J., and Gresham, C.A. "Hut-circles in North-west Wales". Reprinted from *Antiquity*, 18 (Dec. 1944), 183-96.

Hills, Christopher B. *The Power of the Doctrine*. N.p.: New Era Press, 1959?

Holt, Geo. H. "The Blackest Chapter in the History of Mankind". 1956. Xerox of ts.

Holz, Walter B. *Das Euklidsche Dreieck und seine engere Kreisbogenverwandtschaft*. Hagan: Otto Grabow Verlag, 1955.

Hopkins, Peter. "Law against War: A Plea for Law & Enforcement against Governmental Mass Homicide". Ts. 1966. L. from Hopkins to BR.

Horton, Syd. "Fireweed". Ts.

Hubbard, L.R. "Plan for World Peace". 1964. Mimeo ts. Form l. from Philip W. Warren.

Hubbard, Omar. "A Semantic Comment on Frege's Solution of Russell's Paradox". 1958. Ts. L. from Hubbard to BR.

Hudgens, Mary Jane. "A Beatnik Speaks Up". 1960. Mimeo ts. L. from Hudgens to BR.

——. "Nonconformity in the U.S.: A Criticism of the Social Class System in America". 1960. Mimeo ts. L. from Hudgens to BR.

The Humanist, May 1962. With a cover photo of BR.

The Humanist Gazette, 1, no. 1: Oct. 1968.

Humanist News, Jan. 1969.

Humes, H.L. "Some Reflections on the Epitaph of Daniel Bernoulli". Xerox of ms.

Hutten, Ernest Hirschlaff. "On Existence and Complementarity in Physics". *American Journal of Physics*, 11 (Dec. 1943): 328-34.

Huxley, Julian. "A Discussion on Ritualization of Behaviour in Animals and Man". 1966. Ts.

——. "Cultural Process and Evolution". Reprinted from *Behavior and Evolution*, ed. Anne Roe and G.G. Simpson. 1958.

Huxley, Juliette. "Wild Lives of Africa: Part 1: Fishes and Rhinos". *Animals*, 3 (10 Mar. 1964): 365-71.

I

"Institute". Ts. (No author.)

"Integration in Operation". Mimeo ts. (No author.)

International English Language Association. *Information Circular No. 2*. 1955. L. from Bernard Scott to BR.

The International War Crimes Tri-

bunal. *Verdict of the Stockholm Session of the International War Crimes Tribunal*. London: The International War Crimes Tribunal, 1967.
——. Pamphlet published by The Canadian Committee for the International War Crimes Tribunal.
Involve, 1 (n.d.).
Isis Film Productions Ltd. "To Reason Why". 1964. Ts.
Izvestia. 1962. Contains a message from BR.

J

Jaaj, S. S. *Vice and Virtue*. Delhi: Atma Ram & Sons, 1964.
Jacobus, Abraham. "Means of Resolving International Tension". July 1955. Mimeo ts. L. from Jacobus to BR.
Jamaiker, Stanley. "A Logical Approach to Grammar". 1966. Mimeo ts. L. from Jamaiker to BR.
James, William. *The Moral Equivalent of War*. London: Housmans, n.d.
Jaspers, K. "Die Aufgaben der Philosophie in der Gegenwart". Ts.
Jermakow, W. "About the property of the sector of the circle to increase infinitely". 1957. Xerox of ms. L. from Jermakow to BR.
——. "About the similitude of the circles". 1957. Xerox of ms.
Johnson, Phoebe Wynn. "A New Realism: The Shaping by Life of a Credo". 1957? Essay privately printed, accompanied with psychic notes re Rollo Russell. L. from Johnson to BR.
"Joint Conference of Those Engaged in the Work of Peace and Constructive Action". 15-16 Dec. 1962. Mimeo ts. No author.
Jolly, Stephen, trans. *Nine Gates*, by Jirí Langer. London: James Clarke, 1961.
Jones, Hugo T. Untitled ms. 1955. L. from Jones to BR.
Jones, Victor. "The High Jinks of Canon Saull". Ts.
Jørgensen, Carl. "The Relation Is/Ought: Hume's Problem". Reprinted from *Theoria*, 28 (1962): 53-69.
The Journal of Symbolic Logic, 3 (Dec. 1938).

K

Kapitza, P. L. "Recollections of Lord Rutherford". Reprinted from *Proceedings of the Royal Society*, **A**, 294 (1966), 123-37.
Karlin, Kenneth G. "The Empirical Significance of Tillich and Maritain". Mimeo ts.
Kellogg, Rhoda. "How Sex Myths Destroy Us". 1954. Mimeo ts.
Kendall, D. G. "Norbert Wiener". *Journal of the London Mathematical Society*, 43 (1968): 763-4.
——. "Branching Processes Since 1873". *Journal of the London Mathematical Society*, 41 (1966): 385-406.
——. "A Statistical Approach to Flinders Petrie's Sequence-Dating". Pp. 657-80.
—— and Daley, D. J. "Stochastic Rumours". *Journal Institute Maths Applics*, 1 (1965?): 42-55.
Khwaja, Saluddin Ahmed. *One-Man-Show of Photographs*. Sahiwal: District Social Welfare Society, 1967.
Kimpson, Prudence A. "A Psycho-Philosophical Examination of the Theory of Evolution". 1957. Ms.
King, Heath. "Value Considerations in Psychology". Xerox of ts.
King, Preston T. "Notes on the Displacement of Ideologies by Problem-Solving". 1965. Mimeo ts.
King-Hall News-Letter, 19 Apr. 1959.
Klemke, E. D., ed. *Essays on Bertrand Russell*. Urbana, Ill.: University of Illinois Press, 1970. Unbound galley proofs.
Knight, Margaret. *Christianity: The*

Debit Account. London: National Secular Society, 1965.
Kobylinski, Stanislaw K. "Chopin—10 Scenes". 1950. Ts. L. from Kobylinski to BR.
——. "Truth, Error, Lies". 1950. Ts.
Kohli, G. *Famous Puzzles*. Bombay: Humanitarian Mission, 1969?
——. *Right & Wrong*. Bombay: Humanitarian Mission, 1969?
——. *Social Evils*. Bombay: Humanitarian Mission, 1969?
Komaki, Sanehide. "Revised English Summary of 'The Respect of Life', Part 2". 1959. Mimeo ts.
Kounoupis, Georgios N. *Delphiki Idea: Aggelos kai Eua Sikelianou* .... Athens: 1960.
Kouznetsov, B. "Complementarity and Relativity". *Philosophy and Science*, 33 (Sept. 1966): 199-209.
KPFA Folio, 24 Aug.-6 Sept. 1964.
[Krassner, Paul]. "Diabolic Dialogues: John Foster Dulles & Bertrand Russell". *The Realist*, no. 1 (June-July 1958): 23.
Krausser, Peter. "Humes Problem in kybernetischer Perspecktive". Reprinted from *Philosophia Naturalis*, 7 (1962): 451-74.
Krimm, Martin C. "A Mood of Contemplation". Mimeo ts.
——. "To Teach or to Not-Teach in the Tangle of the Mind". Oct. 1967. Mimeo ts.
Kührer, Alfons. "Betrachtungenen zu zwei Versuchen von Michelson".

L

Labon, M.A. "A Reevaluation of Atomic Structure; and as Compared with Solar System Structure". 1968. Ts.
Lacombe, Pierre. "Why War?". Mimeo ts.
Lamont, Corliss. *Freedom of Choice Affirmed*. 1967. Galley proofs.
Lankenau, D.J. Untitled ts. of ls. Re air pollution. 1965.
Lapp, Adolph. Untitled ts. L. from Lapp to BR, 1957.
Larsen, Egon. *You'll See: Report from the Future*. London: Rider and Co., 1957. Bound galley proofs.
Laski, Harold. "The Early History of the Corporation in England". Reprinted from *Harvard Law Review*, 30 (1917): 561-88.
——. "The Political Ideas of James I". Reprinted from *Political Science Quarterly*, 34 (June 1919): 290-304.
——. "The Responsibility of the State in England". Reprinted from *Harvard Law Review*, 32 (1919): 447-73.
LaVerne, Albert A. "The Anatomy of Violence". 1967. Ts. L. from LaVerne to BR.
La Via, Luigi. "Apunti sulla Verità". *Teoresi*, 23 (1968): 219-62.
——. "Quid Est Veritas". *Teoresi*, 24 (1969): 29-82.
Lawyers Committee on American Policy Towards Vietnam. "American Policy vis-a-vis Vietnam". New York: Congressional Record, n.d. Form l. from Studies in the Third World (RS), 1971.
Lebzeltern, Gustav. "Syllogism Considered from a Psychologist's Standpoint". Ts.
Leclerq, René. "Introduction to a Mathematical Logic of Discovery". Xerox of ts.
Léonard. *Demain: La Vie Quotidienne en 1970*. Neuchatel: Editions de la Baconnière, 1963.
Leonhard, Susanne. "Bertrand Arthur William Russell—ein großer Mathematiker". *Deutsche Rundschau*, 83 (May 1957): 500-4.
"Letter Re Space-Time". Mimeo ts. (No author.)
LID News Bulletin, 7 (Summer-Fall 1967). (League for Industrial Democracy.)
Lienau, C. C. "Quantitative Aspects of Organization". From *Human Biology*, 19 (Dec. 1947): 163-216.

Liljenberg, Bengt. "Tre Dikter". *Lyrikvännen*, 12 (1965): 13. L. to BR from Liljenberg.

Lister, R. P. *The Rhyme and the Reason*. 1962. Bound galley proofs. L. from Harcourt, Brace & World, Inc., to BR.

Little, Robert P. "In Praise of the Invisible". Pamphlet.

Littlewood, D. E. "Space Time Distribution of Spinors". June 1964. Mimeo ts. L. from Littlewood to BR.

Llewellyn, Alun. "Immortal Ragman". Poem. 1954. Ts. L. from Llewellyn to BR.

Lubischew, Alexander A. "Philosophical Aspects of Taxonomy". Reprinted from *Annual Review of Entomology*, 14 (1969): 19-38.

Lukacs, George. Article re Marx. *The New International*, Summer 1957: 180-97.

Lutaud, Olivier. "L'Accord du peuple, Londres, ler Mai 1649". Photocopy.

Luther, Edward A. "The Completed History of the Battle of Upminster Common, Hornchurch, Essex". 1951. Mimeo ts. L. from Luther to BR.

Luther, Otto. "The Dynamic Field". 1960. Mimeo ts. L. from Luther to BR.

M

MacColl, Hugh. "Corrections for MacColl's *Symbolic Logic*". Ms.; 1 leaf. Removed from BR's library copy.

Magill, Lincoln C. "P. S. (Epistle V)". 1958. Ts. L. from Magill to BR.

Magnissalis, Kostas G. "The Established Patterns of Thought: A Basic Antinomy in the Age of Nuclearation". Abstract from *Productivity*, 1966.

——. [Greek text as well].

Makal, P. "Exact and Descriptive Determinism". Xerox of ts.

Mantius, H. K. "Reality in Fundamental Physics". 1955. Mimeo ts.

Marett, R. R. "When is it Genius?". 1941. Ms. L. from Nora Marett to M. Taylor. L. from Taylor to BR.

"Mark Lane's Inquiry of the President's Assassination". Mimeo ts. (No author.)

Martin, C. B. "A Religious Way of Knowing". 1952. Ts. L. from Martin to BR.

Marvin, F. S., ed. *Progress and History*. London: Oxford University Press, 1920. Filed with notes and extensive annotation by B. N. Seal.

Mass-Massacre of the Muslims in India. London: Human Rights Committee, n.d.

Matarisvan, Marion. "The Future of Mankind: Communism, Capitalism Or?". 1955. Ts. Ls. from Matarisvan to BR. L. to Matarisvan from BR. Cards with BR quote on "The Secret of Happiness".

——. "Planetary Legion for Peace". 1957. Mimeo ts. Ls. from Matarisvan to BR.

Matthias, L. L. "The Other Side of the USA". 1965? Ts.

Matthysse, Steven W. "Utopia". Yale University: 1960. Thesis.

McKenney, John L. "Concerning Russell's Analysis of Value Judgments". Reprinted from *Journal of Philosophy*, 55 (24 Apr. 1958): 382-9.

"The Meaning of the Iron Curtain". 1955. Mimeo ts. (No author.)

Mehta, Vishwanath. *Towards Truer Democracy*. Simla: Visvakala, 1965.

"Melanges 'Anchoina'". 1966-7. Mimeo ts.

Melman, Seymour, ed. *A Strategy for American Security–An Alternative to the 1964 Military Budget*. New York: Group of Independent Specialists, 1963.

Mercer, David. "Climate of Fear". Mimeo ts.

Merican, Haji K. Sultan. "The Worlds". Ts. outline.

Merriam, Eva. "The Double Bed".

Mimeo ts.
——. "The Enquiry". Mimeo ts.
——. "The Nest". Mimeo ts.
——. "The Wedded Lovers". Mimeo ts.

Midula, Beniamino. *Conformismo, Convenzionalismo e Realtà nella Scienza*. Palermo: Industria Graficâ Nazionale, 1966.

Millard, Alfred. *The Long Story Summarized in Verse*. Santa Barbara, California: Alfred Millard, 1960. L. from Millard to BR.

Miller, Hershel S. "In Behalf of Benevolence". 1962. Mimeo ts. L. from Miller to BR. L. to Miller from ER.

Millett, Mervyn R.O. "Proposal for the Establishment of an Institute of Eucalyptus Information and Research". 1969. Mimeo ts.

"The Misguided Obstructionists". 21 Sept. 1961. Ts. No author.

Mitchell, Adrian. "Adrian Mitchell's Guide to the Underground". *The Guardian*, 12 Oct. 1967, p. 9. Below an unsigned article, "Priests and Prophets of Permissiveness".

Mitrovich, Paul. "Un Esay de Inter-Lingvistiqe". Ts.

Morehouse, Russel A. "Wanted, at once—the Need is Urgent". 1955. Ts. L. from Morehouse to BR.

Morris, John. "The Recall of Parliament". 1961. Ts.

Motamed, Amir Ferydoun. *De la Métrique*. Tehran: 1962.

Mukherjee, Provas Chandra. "Universal Theology and Metaphysics". Ts.

Mundle, C.W.K. "Anglo-Linguistic Philosophy". N.d. Article.
——. "Linguistic Philosophy: Its Nature, Causes and Cure". 1967. Mimeo ts.

Murmann, Hans. "Nachschlagworte von A ... bis Z". Mimeo ts.

N

The Nation, 187 (18 Oct. 1958). L. from Carey McWilliams to BR. L. to McWilliams from BR.
——. 187 (1 Nov. 1958): 302-4.

National Committee of 100. *Mankind Against War*. 1962. Multilingual pamphlet.

National Guardian. 30 July 1966. Includes "Bertrand Russell's Appeal to the American Conscience on Vietnam".

"Natural Solids". Ts. (No author.)

"Nemesis". 1969. Ts. (No author.)

"The New Life". Mimeo ts. (No author.)

New Statesman, 62 (22 Sept. 1961). Includes Adam Roberts's "The Police at Midnight".

Nicod, J.G.P. "A Reduction in the Number of Primitive Propositions of Logic". Reprinted from *Proceedings of the Cambridge Philosophical Society*, 19 (Jan. 1917): 32-41. Removed from inside front cover of BR's library copy of *Principia*, I (1910).

Nimeh, William. "Save Our Society". Ts. L. from Nimeh to BR.

Nirenstein, David. "Selected Poems". 1957. Ts. L. from Nirenstein to BR.

Nitto, Sotaro. "On the Theory of Continuity and the Principle of Differential Calculus". 1951. Ts.

Nizer, Louis. "A Chapter from My Life in Court". Mimeo ts.

Nkrumah, Kwame. *Axioms*. Unbound galley proofs.

Nørlund, Ib. *Møde med Vietnam*. Udgiver: Forlaget Tiden, 1966.

O

Ofstad, Harold. "The Ethics of Resistance to Tyranny: An Attempt to Formulate some of the Dilemmas Involved". 1960. Mimeo ts.

Okinawa–Island of Tragedy. Pamphlet. N.d.

Oliphant, M.L.E., *et al.* S. from Pugwash. 1957. Mimeo ts.

L'Opinion Européenne, 5 (15 Apr. 1963): 353-60.

O'Reilly, Edward. 1953. Untitled ts. Re Fermat's last theorem. L. from O'Reilly to BR.

El Oriente de Asturias. 1958. Includes BR's "La Guerra por la Paz".

Orloff, Constantin. *The Fundamentals of Practical Spectral Arithmetic and Algebra*. Vrsac, Yugoslavia: Libertatea, 1955.

——. "Methode Spectrale Practique d'Évaluation Numérique des Déterminants et de Résolution du Système d'Equations Linéaires". *Bulletin de la Société des Mathématiciens et Physicians de la R. P. de Serbie*, 1-2 (1953): 17-30.

Orr, Sydney Sparkes. "Some Reflections on the Cambridge Approach to Philosophy (I)". *Australasian Journal of Psychology*, Sept. 1946: 32-3.

Osborn, Reuben. "A Rational Basis for Ethics". 1967? Ts.

Ostermarsch 63. With a photo of BR on the back cover.

The Other Side, no. 2 (Mar. 1963).

"Outline: Petition to the United Nations". Ts. (No author.)

Ozmon, Howard. "Bertrand Russell: Socrates of Our Age (1872-1970)". *Kappan*, 52 (Nov. 1970): 146, 152-3.

P

Packe, Michael St. John. *The Life of John Stuart Mill*. London: Secker and Warburg, 1954. Bound page proofs. A few annotations by BR.

Pakistan Spotlight International. Aug. 1966.

Pa'Lante, 1962.

Palmer, Harold. "Psychiatric Prolegomena: A Plea for the Help of Philosophy". *Philosophy*, 1952?: 39-50, 311-32. L. from Palmer to BR. L. to Palmer from BR.

Parisen, Jr., Robert James. Diary. 1967.

——. "The Novum". 1964. Ms.

——. "Speculari". 1964. Ms.

Parker, Andrew. "Disarmers Issue a 'Black Paper'". Ts. 1962.

The Partisan, 2 (Winter 1966).

Passports. 1 sheet of 1920 regulations.

Patel, Essop Moosajee ("Aesop"). "Burning Aloe Arises". Ts. L. from Patel to BR, 1968.

Pauling, Linus. "Modern Structural Chemistry". Reprinted from *Les Prix Nobel en 1954*, 1955: pp. 91-9.

Pavlov, V.S. "Philosophy Categorically Rejects Force [original in Russian]". 1955. Ts. L. from Pavlov to BR. L. from E.H.S. Burhop to BR.

Peace News, supplement, 16 Nov. 1962.

Pedetztun, David. "Credo of a Sceptic". Ts. of trans. from *Lamerhav*, 18 May 1962. On BR.

Perren, John C. *Peace or War?* Pamphlet.

Perseus, Mar. 1964. Includes BR's "A Will to Resist".

P.H.H.B. "Models, Independent Localities, and Communities". Mimeo ts.

Phillips, Ludwig. "Hitler: World's Most Fantastic Criminal". *Liberty*, 15 (July 1959): 46-7.

"A Philosophy of Living". Ts. (No author.)

Piel, Gerard. "The Fork in the Road". June 1962. Mimeo ts.

Poesia Toda, no. 2 (1968?).

[Poetry]. Some of it with revisions in BR's hand in answer to an author's queries; 1 leaf dated ?1919 by BR.

Polish Weekly, 24 (20 June 1962). Includes A. Tokarczyk's "Bertrand Russell's Works in Poland".

Poole, H.W. Long l. (ts.) re philosophy of physics. 1958. L. to Poole from BR.

Popper, Karl R. "The Demarcation between Science and Metaphysics". 1955. Mimeo ts.

——. "On the Sources of Knowledge and of Ignorance". 1955. Mimeo ts.
——. "Three Views Concerning Human Knowledge". Reprinted from *Contemporary British Philosophy*.
"Population Problems". Ts. Found in Russell's library copy of A. M. Carr-Saunders' *Population* (1925). (No author.)
Prabhu, S. S. "What is Wrong with this World?". 1955. Ts. L. from Prabhu to BR.
Pravda, 1962. Contains a message from BR.
Pritt, D. N. "The Wethersfield Case". *Labour Monthly*, Sept. 1962: 425-9.
——. *Liberty in Chains: An Examination of the New McCarthyism*. London: Committee for Democratic Rights in the U.S.A., n.d.

Q

Quan, Stanislaus. "The Solution of the Achilles Paradox". Reprinted from *Review of Metaphysics*, 16 (Mar. 1963): 473-85. L. from Quan to BR.
"The Queen of Sheba's Damnation". Ts. revised by BR. Faintly pencilled date: Sept. 9, 1930. (No author.)

R

Raman, K. V. Untitled ms. 1956. L. from Raman to BR.
Rand, Rose, trans. "Prolegomena to Three-Valued Logic". *Polish Review*, Summer 1968: 3-61.
Rangappa, K. S. "Gandhiji's Sadhana". 1963. Ts.
Reddaway, G. F. N., comp. [Mimeo ts. of science articles published in Soviet journals.] Dec. 1956.
Reichbach, Juliusz. "About Derivative and Definite Integrals". 1968. Mimeo ts.
——. "Statistical Densities in the Decidability Problem of the First-Order Functional Calculus". 1968. Mimeo ts. Circular l. from Reichbach.
Reichenbach, Hans. "Die Kausalstruktur der Welt und der Unterschied von Vergangenheit und Zukunft". Reprinted from *Sitzungsberichte der Bayerischen Akademie der Wissenschaften Mathematisch-naturwissenschaftliche Abteilung*, 1925: pp. 133-75.
——. "Letter on the Justification of Induction". July 1939. Ts. L. from Reichenbach to BR.
Richards, C. "Meet Truth: A Reply to Bertrand Russell's Essay, *Why I am Not a Christian* and his Preface to his Whole Collection of that Title". Ts.
Rigg, John. "1066-2066". 1952. Ts. L. from Rigg to BR.
Rights, 1 (Mar. 1954). Prints l. from BR's secretary on Einstein.
Ringer, Gerald J. "The Bomb as a Living Symbol: An Interpretation". Florida State University: 1966. Thesis.
Roberts, Adam, *et al. Civilian Defence*. London: *Peace News*, n.d.
——. "Bertrand Russell and the Vietnam Tribunal". *New Society*, 2 Feb. 1967: 156-9.
Rogers, Donald Clyde. "Satori". Xerox of ms. L. from Rogers to BR.
Ross, Lawrence F. J. *World War III and the Southern Hemisphere*. Pamphlet.
Rossi, Mario. *The Third World: The Unaligned Countries and the World Revolution*. New York: Funk & Wagnalls, 1962. Galley proofs.
Roszack, Theodore. "Looking for the Marchers". 1965. Article.
Rudiak, M. "Hungarian Situation". 1960. Ms. L. from Rudiak to BR. Includes clippings and ls. to others.
The Rushlight, no. 7 (Autumn 1965).
Russell, Edward Thomas. "The Key to Paradise". 1943. Ts. L. from Russell to BR, 1950s?
Russell, Virginia. "An Explanation of Gravity". 1959. Mimeo ts. L. from

Russell to BR.
——. "Relative Velocities as a Source of Cosmic Power". 1959. Mimeo ts.
——. "The Universal Field". 1959. Mimeo ts.
"Russell Letters Sold to Canada". *The Observer*, 31 Mar. 1968: 3.

S

Sargent, Vernon Rhodes. "[Notes on] *A History of Western Philosophy*". 1961. Ms. Includes clippings.
Sawhny, Bhim. "The Pope Replies to His Critics". 1969. Ts. L. from Sawhny to *The Times*. L. from Sawhny to *The Daily Telegraph*.
Scheurer, Paul. "Appel aux Hommes Responsables". *Tribune de Genève*, 28 June 1955. L. from Scheurer to BR. L. from René Bovard to BR.
——. "Comment Abolir la Guerre?". *Tribune de Genève*, 21 June 1955.
Schmidt, Jürgen. "Konfinalität". *Zeitschrift für math. Logik und Grundlagen d. Math.*, 1 (1955): 271-303. L. to Schmidt from BR. Re lexicography and *Principia Mathematica*.
Schmielewski, Yogi Alfred, trans. and ed. *The Gospel of the Twentieth Century*. Toronto: Yoga Forum of Canada, 1968? Bound galley proofs.
Schoenman, Ralph, ed. *Bertrand Russell: Philosopher of the Century*. London: George Allen & Unwin, 1967. Original tss., galley proofs, page proofs.
Schonfield, Hugh J. *The Birth of a World People*. London: Dennis Dobson, 1956. Bound page proofs. L. to BR from Putnam & Co., 1956.
Schott, Günter S. "Wir Wollen Nicht Aussterben". Ts.
Schutz, Robert R. "Every Man a Prince". Mimeo ts.
Science Reporter (Nehru Commemoration Number), 1 (July-Aug. 1964).
Seal, B.N. "Conversation: A Decaying Art?" *The Indian Listener*, n.d.
——. "The Fundamental Concepts of Mathematical Logic". Notebook.
——. "Progress". Ts.
——. "Signs and Symbols". Ts.
——. "Some Aspects of Astronomy". Ms.
——. "The Theory of Induction (The Logical Doctrine of Induction)". Notebook.
——. Three untitled notebooks.
——. "Western Influence on India". Ts.
——. [See also F.S. Marvin, above.]
Seal, Brajendranath. *The Quest Eternal*. London: Oxford U.P., 1936.
The Second International Congress of Classical Studies. 1954. Papers individually published or mimeographed as part of the Congress proceedings.
Sharland, B.W. "To a Fine Summer". 1955. Ms. L. from Sharland to BR.
Sherman, Paddy. "The Sad, Shadowy December of a Great Mind". *The Province* (Vancouver), 6 May 1967: p. 4.
Shneidman, Edwin S. "Children of the Bomb". 1969. Mimeo ts. L. from Shneidman to BR.
Shwayder, D.S. "Wittgenstein's *Tractatus*: A Historical and Critical Commentary (Abstract)". Mimeo ts. Abstract of Oxford thesis.
Sibley, Mulford. *Unilateral Initiatives and Disarmament*. Philadelphia: American Friends Service Committee, 1962.
Sie+er, 16 May 1967. Includes Robert Lucas's "Frauen und Frieden".
Siegel, Gerald M. "The Pied Piper of Death? The Theological Basis of the Life and Work of Henry R. Luce: A Documentary". Xerox of ts.
Sil, Arun Kumar. *If Winter Comes: A Book on Human Emergency*. Calcutta: The St. John Ambulance Brigade (India), 1965?
Simon, Sidney. "The Art of Losing". Mimeo ts.
——. "In Splendid Isolation". Mimeo

ts.
"The Sky, the Earth". Film script. Ts. and tscc. (No author.)
Smith, N. A. "The Road to Mass Poverty". Mimeo ts.
"Social Imperialism?". (No author.) Ts. of article in *Manchester Guardian*, 10 Aug. 1953. Evidently regarded (erroneously) as written by BR.
"Social Influences". 1955. Ts. (No author.)
Socialist Attack, 2, no. 2 (n.d.). With an opinion poll favouring BR.
Socialist Leader, 55 (6 July 1963).
Société Britannique de Philosophie de Langue Française. *Actes: Résumés des communications*. 1962. Signed by the participants. L. to BR from Axel Stern, 1962.
Sokolinski, Joseph D. "We All Come from the Earth". Mimeo ts.
Sommerville, John. "Are Historicist Hypotheses Scientifically Possible? A Critique of Popperism". Mimeo ts.
——. "The East-West Ideological Drift". *Co-Existence*, 1 (May 1964): 7-14.
——. "World Authority: Realities and Illusions". *Ethics*, 76 (Oct. 1965): 33-46.
Soviet Peace Fund. "Charter of Soviet Peace Fund". Ts. 2 copies.
Spencer Brown, G. ("David"). "Design with the NOR". 1961. Mimeo ts.
——. *Laws of Form*. Xerox of ts. Ms. additions.
Spivack, Morris Redman. "Revision of Newton's Law of Gravitation". 1967. Mimeo ts.
SSRS Newsletter, 62 (June 1957).
Stafford, Richard. "Cain's Corner". Mimeo ts.
——. *Lash-Tide*. Copenhagen: C. A. Reitzel, 1957.
Stebbing, A. Francis. "In Pursuit of Happiness". Ts.
Steichen, Edward. *The Family of Man*. New York: Macco Magazine Corporation for the Museum of Modern Art, 1955.
Stevenson, David. "The Meditations of William Shakespeare". Mimeo ts.
I. F. Stone's Weekly, 9 (31 July 1961). Contains s. by BR on Berlin.
——, 10 (8 Oct. 1962).
Stuber, Ernst. "Stürme, Sonnenflecke, Erdengesetze". Mimeo ts.
Sullivan, Dan. "The Experience Universe". 1960. Ts.
Sunday Citizen, 30 Sept. 1962.
Svantesson, Sven. "Memento regarding Connections between Atomic Bomb-Tests, Solar Activity and Explosions, Weather and Earthquakes". 30 June 1962. Mimeo ts.
Swarajya, 6 (2 June 1962). Includes C. Rajagopalachari's "Bertrand Russell".
Swift, Basil. "Essays". Ts.
Szabó, Miklós. "Fighting the Viet-Cong". Ts.
Szaulski, Florian. "Metamorphosis". 1961. Ts.
Szent-Györgyi, Albert. "Psalmus Humanus and Six Prayers". 1964. Mimeo ts. L. from Szent-Györgyi to BR. L. to Szent-Györgyi from BR.
Szilard, Leo. "The Voice of the Dolphins". 1960. Mimeo ts.

T

Tarski, Alfred. "On Undecidable Statements in Enlarged Systems of Logic and the Concept of Truth". Reprinted from *Journal of Symbolic Logic*, 4 (Sept. 1939), 105-12.
——. "Sur les *truth-functions* au sens de MM. Russell et Whitehead". Reprinted from *Fundamenta Mathematicae*, 5. Removed from inside front cover of BR's library copy of *Principia*, I (1910).
——. "Sur quelques théorèmes qui équivalent à l'axiome du choix".

Reprinted from *Fundamenta Mathematicae*, 5. Removed from inside front cover of BR's library copy of *Principia*, I (1910).

Tendulkar, D. G., ed. *Jawaharlal Nehru in Pictures*. Bombay, India: The Times of India Press, 1964.

Terkel, Studs. "Born to Live". 1962? Mimeo ts.

Thomas, A. J. "Art in the Atomic Age". Mimeo ts.

"The Time Has Come to Hold Another Magna Charter" [*sic*]. Mimeo ts. (No author.)

Tinbergen, N. "On War and Peace in Animals and Men". *Science*, 160 (20 June 1968): 1411-18. Xerox.

Tokyo Tribunal. "Mr. President and Members of the Tribunal, Ladies and Gentlemen!" Mimeo ts.

Topchiev, Alexander. "Predotvratit' opasnost' atomnoi voiny" ["Preventing Atomic War"]. *Vestnik Akademii nauk SSSR*, 9 (1957): 3-12. Includes mention of Pugwash conference.

Trepra, Jauun Nekamota?. Untitled ts. 1956.

Triad. "The Time Has Come". Mimeo ts.

Tribune, 12 July 1963. Includes column by Francis Flavius on BR.

True World Order. Various pamphlets, newspapers and brochures on Swami Vishnu-devananda.

Truth Quest, 4 (July 1955). Includes "Bertrand Russell Protests Against Nuclear Warfare".

Tsuruoka, Misao. "Extinction or Survival?". 1959. Mimeo ts.

——. "How is the World Turning?—The Finality of International Politics and Economy". Printed in Japanese characters. N.d.

——. "Outlines of Philosophy of Co-Existence and Co-Growth". Mimeo ts.

Tucker, John. "Gödel and Epimenides". *Aristotelian Society Proceedings*, 1958: 25-48.

U

Uenaka, Sōtarō. "New Atomic Construction Theory". 1955. Mimeo ms.

Ulrich, E. "Moral und Glaube". 1959. Ts. L. from Ulrich to BR.

United States Air Force ROTC Air University. "Fundamentals of Aerospace Weapon Systems". Mimeo ts.

United States Information Service. *Towards a World without War*. 1962?

Untitled ms. addressed to Robert M. Hutchins. 1950. (No author.)

Untitled notebooks. (No author.)

Untitled ts. (German). With mathematical formulas. (No author.)

Untitled ts. Re metaphysics of Emmet and Collingwood. (No author.)

Untitled Xerox of ts. Re Julius Hartnack's "Movement, Moments and Beginning". (No author.)

Usborne, Henry. "Is 'Minifed' the Price of Peace?". 1968. L. from Usborne to BR.

Ushenko, Andrew. "Hume's Theory of General Ideas". Reprinted from *The Review of Metaphysics*, 9 (Dec. 1955): 236-51.

V

Van Dooren, L. A. T. *The Adequate Answer*. Carnforth, Eng.: Latimer Pub. Co., 1966.

Van Essen, Jac. "Bertrand Russell—ein Kämpfer für die Menschheit". 1967. Mimeo ts. 9 copies.

van Heerden, P. J. "The Foundation of Mathematics". Mimeo ts.

——. "The Philosophical Implications of the Double Slit Diffraction Experiment". Mimeo ts.

——. "Predicting Intelligently". 1969. Xerox of ts. L. to *The British Journal for the Philosophy of Science* from van Heerden. L. from *The British Journal for the Philosophy of Science* to van Heerden. Form l. to

BR.
——. "Proposal for a Fundamental Theory of Physics". Mimeo ts.
——. "Proposal for a Fundamental Theory of Physics: The finished Formulation". Mimeo ts.
van Rossum, Roger. "Les Bombes Nucléaires et Leurs Effets sur le Corps Humain". Reprinted from *Scalpel*, 1963-4.
Venis, Martin A. "Pros and Cons of H-Bomb Shelters". 1958. Mimeo ts.
Vierra, Robert S. "The Exact Science of Economics". 1961. Mimeo ts.
"Vinoba on the Sino-Indian Conflict". Mimeo ts. (No author.)
Voice of Women, no. 21 (1 July 1962).
Von Ardenne, Manfred. *Die Verwendung der für militärische Zwecke angehäuften Weltvorräte an Spaltmaterial zum Wohle der Menschheit.* 1956. Pamphlet.
von Schoen, Rolf. "Zusammenfassung und kurze Erläuterungen zum Inhalt des beiliegenden Manuskripts 'Zum Kampf um Freiheit' Weidervereinigung und Weltfrieden". Mimeo ts.
von Wright, G.H. "On the Idea of Logical Truth (I)". Reprinted from *Societas Scientiarum Fennica, Commentationes Physico-Mathematicae*, 14 (1948): 1-20.

W

W. "Occasional Verse". Xerox of ts.
Wallace, Frank. "If There Be Time". 1958. Ts. L. from Wallace to BR.
Walter, Nicolas. *Nonviolent Resistance.* London: Nonviolence 63, 1963?
——. "The RSGs 1919-1963". Solidarity Pamphlet no. 15, n.d.
Warburg, James P. "Disarmament and Atomic Energy Control. A Working Paper". 1955. Mimeo ts.
——. "Introduction to Working Papers on a New Approach to United States Foreign Policy". 1955. Mimeo ts. L. from Warburg to BR.
——. "United States Foreign Economics Policy. A Working Paper". 1955. Mimeo ts.
——. "United States Policy on Asia. A Working Paper". 1955. Mimeo ts.
——. "United States Policy in Europe. A Working Paper". 1955. Mimeo ts.
——. "United States Policy in Latin America. A Working Paper". 1955. Mimeo ts.
——. "United States Policy in the Near East. A Working Paper". 1955. Mimeo ts.
Ward, A.J.B. "An Application of a Philosophical Theory and a Mathematical Notation to the Problem of Perception (Particularly Visual)". 1969. Xerox of ts. L. from Ward to BR.
Webb, Sidney and Beatrice. *The Truth about Soviet Russia.* Preface by Bernard Shaw. London: Longmans, Green, 1942.
Weight, Ellen Comfort. "The Ultimate Weapon". 1963. Ts. L. from Weight to BR. L. to Weight from BR.
Weinschenk, Jacob H. *Ratiocinationes Maesti Poetae.* Fresno, California: Senior Citizens' Village, 1966.
Weiss, Adnard. "Administration". 1955. Ts. L. from Weiss to BR.
——. "Peace—Means: Peace and Love for One's Neighbour". 1955. Ts.
Weiss, John. "What Every Schoolboy Knows". *New University Thought*, 2 (Spring 1962): 19-24.
Weiss, Paul. "Two-Valued Logic—Another Approach". Reprinted from *Erkenntnis*, 2 (1931): 242-58.
——. "The Metaphysics and Logic of Classes". Reprinted from *The Monist*, Jan. 1932: 112-54.
Wells, D.G. "A Model for Thought, Language and Problem-Solving". 1969. Mimeo ts.
Wellwood, R.E. "The Social Organism: An Essay on Sociobiology".

1960. Mimeo ts.
Wemyss-Smith, W. Duncan. "Who is Holding Humanity to Ransom?". 1969. Ts. L. from Wemyss-Smith to BR.
Wheeler, J.G. 1960. Untitled ts. re BR's *Why I am Not a Christian*. L. from Wheeler to BR.
Whymant, Neville. *Chinese Ministry of Information Pamphlets*, no. 7: *Classics*; no. 9: *Education*; no. 10: *Philosophy*. London: Chinese Ministry of Information, 1946.
Wicks, John. 1963-4. Miscellaneous ls., clippings etc.
Wiesenthal, Simon. "The Sunflower". Xerox of ts.
Wilhelm, Wolfgang. "Uberlassen Sie das Dag!". Ts.
Williams, Donald C. "The Realistic Interpretation of Scientific Sentences". Reprinted from *Erkenntnis*, 7 (1939?): 169-78.
——. "On the Derivation of Probabilities from Frequencies". Reprinted from *Philosophy and Phenomenological Research*, 5 (June 1945): 449-84.
Williams, Roger J. "Biochemical Individuality—An Inescapable Basic Factor in the Alcoholism Problem". 1956. Mimeo ts. L. from Williams to BR.
Williamson, H.A. "The Strategy of Mankind". 1953. Mimeo ts. L. from Williamson to BR.
Wills-Johnson, Alistair. "The Financial Basis of Free Enterprise". 1958. Ts. L. from Wills-Johnson to BR.
Winbolt, S.E. "A Late Celtic Settlement on Nore Hill, Eartham". Reprinted from *Sussex Archaeological Collections*, 72: 265-74.
Witchell, John B. Untitled mimeo ts. re Linus Pauling.
Wittmer, Sylvia? Untitled ms. 1958. L. from Wittmer to BR.
Wood, Alex. *Atomic Energy: Notes on the Course of Negotiations for Its Control*. London: National Peace Council, 1949?
Wood, Marshall K. "The National Security Dilemma: Challenge to Management Scientists". 1960. Mimeo ts. L. from Ernest Dale to BR. L. to Ernest Dale from BR.
World Constitution Coordinating Committee. Broadsheet, 1962?
World Federation, 38 (Apr. 1965): 1-4.
Wright, Miriam L. "An Education Plan: Joy in Love". Mimeo ts.
Wrinch, Pamela N. "Science and Politics in the U.S.S.R.: The Genetics Debate". Reprinted from *World Politics*, 3 (July 1951): 486-519.

Y

Yourgrau, Wolfgang. "Collegium Naturalis Philosophiae". *Archives Internationales d'Histoire des Sciences*, 15 (1951): 374-82.
——. "General System Theory and the Vitalism-Mechanism Controversy". *Scientia*, 46 (Nov. 1952): 1-5. L. from Yourgrau to BR, 1955.
——. "A History of Western Philosophy by Bertrand Russell". 1946. Ts. Includes Yourgrau's curriculum vitae.
——. "On Recent Trends in Natural Philosophy". *South African Journal of Science*, 47 (Jan. 1951): 169-75.
——. "Reflections on the Natural Philosophy of Goethe". *Philosophy*, 26 (Jan. 1951): 1-16.
——, and Livingstone, Donald. "On the Nature of Mathematical Constants". *Revista Methodos*, 1957: 1-27.
Youth Against the Bomb, 5 (Jan. 1963).

Z

Zabara, Jacob. "Reflex and Autorhythmicity: A Formal Model". Xerox of ts.
Zarogikas, G. "The Anti-Atomic Shelter". Play dedicated to BR. Mimeo ts.

Zeleznik, Carter. Mimeo tss. Re teaching of mathematics. Ls. from Zeleznik to BR. L. to Zeleznik from BR. 1960.

Ziferstein, Isidore. "Psychological Habituation to War: A Socio-psychological Case Study". *American Journal of Orthopsychiatry*, 37 (Apr. 1967): 457-68.

*930 Films

Two films received with Archives II concern Vietnam. The others comprise a very valuable extended interview with Russell by Ralph Miliband of the London School of Economics. The interview was conducted in 1965. It is valuable not least because Miliband, on occasion, presses Russell to argue further for his positions.

"South Vietnam"
  Toxic chemical warfare in Vietnam
[Bertrand Russell interviewed by Ralph Miliband]
  "Man in the 20th Century"
  "War and Peace"
  "Wealth and Poverty"
"Medical Organisation in N. Vietnam at War"

*940 Tape Recordings

Almost all the audio tapes are related to the work of the International War Crimes Tribunal. The first one has Russell's welcoming speech to the preliminary conference in London, 13 November 1966.

War Crimes Tribunal, 1966. Tape 1. Record of Initial Days Proceedings of Preliminary Conference. Part 1. Sunday, 13 Nov., 3-5:15.

War Crimes Tribunal, 1966. [Tape 2.] Part 2. Side 1. Sunday, 13 Nov., 5:15-7. Side 2. Beginning morning session, 10-1. (Continued to lunch break.) Beginning 4 o'clock session, 4:30-5.

War Crimes Tribunal, 1966. Tape 3. Side 1. Monday, 14 Nov. (continuation of 4 o'clock session). Side 2 (continuation of 4 o'clock session).

War Crimes Tribunal, 1966. Tape 4. Side 1. Monday, 14 Nov., 9:30 session continued.

War Crimes Tribunal, 1966. Tape 5. Side 1. Tuesday, 15 Nov., afternoon session continued. Side 2. Continued [from] last 20 minutes [to] end session 8:10.

"US War Crimes in Vietnam". Compiled by Prof. Shingo Shibata and presented by the Alice Herz Peace Fund. Side 1 (in English). Foreword by the Alice Herz Peace Fund. Comment by Prof. Shibata. "Alice Was Her Name" (Words & Music: Ruth Jacobs; lst and 2nd verses). "Lotus Flower to the Memory of Alice Herz" (words: S. Fukao; music: M. Hayashi; in Japanese). Sung by Mrs. Sadato Shibata. Side 2 (in Japanese). Comment by Prof. Shibata. "Alice Was Her Name" (all 5 verses). Sung by Mrs. Shibata.

"Hanoi Faces the Escalade". 1 reel.

"The Pragmatic Warriors". A documentary tape recording about the war in Vietnam—its effects on Americans who take part in it, and on the Vietnamese people; produced for Radical Education Project by Jeremy Lustig. 1 reel.

"Stockholm Tribunal Session". Folkchs Hus. 3 reels.

"News Roundup". CBC. 9 Aug. 1963. Interview with Bertrand Russell. 1 reel.

"Sunday Morning Magazine". CBC-CBL FM (Toronto). 28 July 1963. Special Interview with Bertrand Russell. 1 reel.

"Mark Lane Press Conference, Kingsley Hotel". 29 June 1964.

"The Nuclear Arms Race". Talk by Dr. Jerome Frank of the Johns Hop-

kins University, Baltimore, Maryland, U.S.A. 1 reel. From Arthur J. Wadsworth.

"Latin America Meeting, 1968". Ken Coates—Olas; Robin Blackburn—Debray. 1 reel.

"Stockholm Session War Crimes Tribunal". 9 reels.

John Conrad Russell. First part of (2 reel sides) Sombrero Bongo. Second part of Sombrero Bongo (1 reel side). First part of Contradictions. First reel on second reel side. 3 reels. **Embargoed**.

Untitled tape. 1 reel. (Emitape label.)

*950 Photographs

The photographs that came with Archives II have been interfiled with those of Archives I. The great majority are unpublished.

Amberleys
  Approx. 50 unframed photos, 6 framed
Pre-World War I
  Approx. 10 assorted snapshots
1914-45
  65 snapshots, mostly of children
Beacon Hill School
  7 snapshots, 4 large photos
John, Kate and Dora
  2 framed photos, 22 studio portraits, 12 snapshots
Peter and Conrad
  2 x-rays of Peter's skull, 17 studio photos of Conrad, 22 studio photos of Peter (some with Conrad), about 20 snapshots
Ottoline Morrell
  6 photos
Constance Malleson
  7 photos
Lucy and Sarah Russell
  photos, proofs of studies and of Anne
Miscellaneous
  about 70—subjects unrecognisable, etc.
BR
  Assorted paintings, drawings, etc. (about 6)

**970–975 Obituaries of Bertrand Russell, etc.

This large collection of published obituaries is based on the clippings supplied to Lady Russell or Christopher Farley by the International Press Cutting Bureau. (A large collection elsewhere in the Russell Archives supplements this class.) Russell's Middle East statement of 30 January 1970 was the subject of press comment at the same time, and a number of clippings on it have been preserved. *971 contains newsclippings on other subjects, 1960–65, particularly nuclear warfare. The title of *972, "Odds and Ends", appropriately describes the miscellaneous nature of the contents. *973 has valuable early inventories of the Archives. *974 contains photocopied correspondence relating to heads of state correspondence in Archives I and to Russell's *Autobiography*. *975 contains dozens of spare copies of Russell's statements, and a possibly complete run of *Vietnam Solidarity Bulletin*.

***970 Obituaries**

(1) Newspapers:
3 Feb. 1970 through March 1971
(2) Magazines
(3) Clippings re Middle East Statement (BR's last s.)

***971 Newsclippings**

1960-1965 (particularly 1964-5)

***972 Odds and Ends**

2 boxes of fragments, advertisements, circular ls., etc., almost all printed

***973 Archival Lists**

Proof copy of Barry Feinberg, ed., *A Detailed Catalogue of the Archives of Bertrand Russell* (London: Continuum 1 Ltd., 1967)
Xerox copy of ts. of above
Earlier tss. and mss. listing BR's papers (including some by ER)

***974 Photocopies**

Photocopies of correspondence: heads of states (some for the purpose of embargo)
Photocopies of correspondence: used in *Autobiography*?

***975 Mimeographed Statements**

Box 1

"*Peace News* Discussion on IWCT"
"Proposals for Improving the Situation of Jews in the Soviet Union"
RS, untitled s. on Dr. Goodlet

Box 2

RS, "... Speech at Meeting on Fifth Anniversary of the NLF of SV, 20 Dec. 1966"
RS, "Speech ... at International Conference for the Liquidation of

Foreign Bases, Dajakarta October, 1965"
"'Briefing' Policy Paper—Vietnam Peace Missions"

Boxes 3-5

Vietnam Solidarity Bulletin, vol. 1, nos. 4–5 (July–Sept. 1966)

Addenda

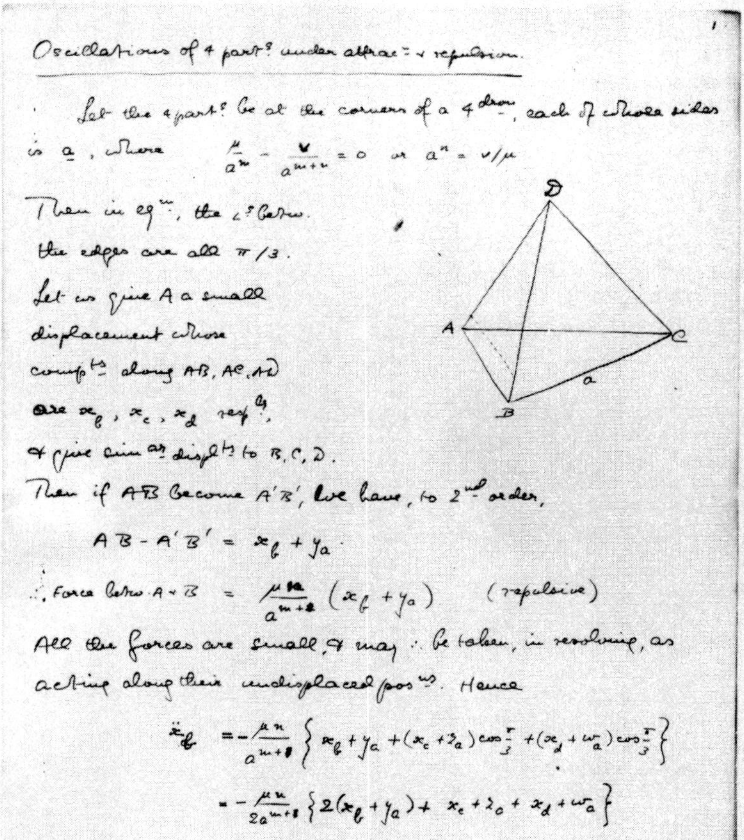

1

Oscillations of 4 part^s under attrac^n & repulsion.

Let the 4 part^s be at the corners of a 4^dron, each of whose sides is a, where $\frac{\mu}{a^m} - \frac{\nu}{a^{m+n}} = 0$ or $a^n = \nu/\mu$

Then in eq^m, the ∠s betw. the edges are all $\pi/3$.

Let us give A a small displacement whose comp^ts along AB, AC, AD are x_b, x_c, x_d resp^y, & give sim^ar displ^ts to B, C, D.

Then if AB become A′B′, we have, to 2nd order,

$$AB - A'B' = x_b + y_a .$$

∴ Force betw. A & B $= \frac{\mu n}{a^{m+1}}(x_b + y_a)$ (repulsive)

All the forces are small, & may ∴ be taken, in resolving, as acting along their undisplaced pos^ns. Hence

$$\ddot{x}_b = -\frac{\mu n}{a^{m+1}}\left\{x_b + y_a + (x_c + z_a)\cos\frac{\pi}{3} + (x_d + w_a)\cos\frac{\pi}{3}\right\}$$

$$= -\frac{\mu n}{2a^{m+1}}\left\{2(x_b + y_a) + x_c + z_a + x_d + w_a\right\}$$

& twelve similar eq^ns.

Put $1/k^2 = \frac{\mu n}{2a^{m+1}}$. ~~Then eq^ns become~~

Plate 10 First leaf of notes on "Oscillations of Four Particles under Attraction & Repulsion" (*c.* 1897). Found in Russell's copy of J. L. Lagrange's *Mécanique analytique*.

*210 Book Manuscripts

1948

Corrections and Emendations for "The Practice and Theory of Bolshevism". Tscc. 1 leaf.

Prefatory Note to Second Edition [of *The Practice and Theory of Bolshevism*]. June 1948. Ms.; tscc. 2 leaves.

1956

[*Logic and Knowledge*]. Signature from page proofs (pp. 5–20). Corrections in pencil in Robert C. Marsh's hand.

[Preface to *Logic and Knowledge*]. Tscc. 1 leaf.

c.1959

Postscript (to My Autobiography). Ts. corrected in Russell's hand. 3 leaves.

[*Wisdom of the West*]. Galley proof of Russell's foreword and 2 signatures of the book (pp. 145–160, 161–176).

1962–3

The Queen of Sheba's Nightmare. Two separate page proofs of the proposed delux folio edition consisting of title-page, facsimile of the first page of Russell's ms., and lithograph illustration by Hans Erni. The 2 proofs are identical except for having different illustrations. However, the edition, which was proposed by Aldus Books, was never published.

Unarmed Victory. Ts.; tscc. and ms. (mainly in ER's hand). In Russell's hand are a table of contents, a leaf entitled "Documents for Cuban 'Settlement'", and a leaf entitled "Points to be made in Chap IV". Other material includes an abstract of Chapter I, the first part of Chapter II, parts of Chapters III and IV, a mimeo ts. of some of Russell's correspondence with heads of state, and 2 newsclippings.

*220 Article Manuscripts

1893

Notes on Land and Lotze. Nov. 1893. Ms. 4 leaves. Removed from Russell's copy of H. Helmholtz's *Wissenschaftliche Abhandlungen*, Vol. II (Leipzig, 1883).

1894

[Notes on geometry]. Ms. 4 leaves. Removed from Russell's copy of W. Killing's *Die Nicht-Euklidischen Raumformen in analytischer Behandlung* (Leipzig, 1885).

1895

Bosanquet pp. 125–132. Ms. 1 leaf. Removed from Russell's copy of B. Bosanquet's *Logic, or the Morphology of Knowledge*, Vol. II (Oxford, 1888).

1897?

Oscillations of Four Particles under Attraction & Repulsion. Ms. 5 leaves. Removed from Russell's copy of J. L. Lagrange's *Mécanique analytique*, Vol. I (Paris, 1811).

1897

Wundt. Ms. 1 leaf. Removed from Russell's copy of W. Wundt's *Die physikalischen Axiome and ihre Beziehung zum Causalprincip* (Erlangen, 1866).

1898

Hertz. Ms. 1 leaf. Removed from Russell's copy of H. Hertz's *Die Prinzipien der Mechanik in neuem Zusammenhange dargestellt* (Leipzig, 1894).

1901

Borel's Proof of Schröder–Bernstein Theorem. April 1901. Ms. 1 leaf. Removed from Russell's copy of E. Borel's *Leçons sur la théorie des fonctions* (Paris, 1898).

1912

Bergson Laughter. Ms. 1 leaf. Removed from Russell's copy of H. Bergson's *Laughter* (London, 1911).

1919

Plotinus. Ms. 7 leaves. Removed from Russell's copy of W. R. Inge's *Philosophy of Plotinus*, Vol. I (London, 1918).

1933?

Cobden's Writings. Ms. 1 leaf. Removed from Russell's copy of *The Political Writings of Richard Cobden*, Vol. II (London, 1868).

c.1935–40

["Western civilization has changed ..."]. Tscc. 3 leaves. The first leaf is unfoliated, and the other leaves are foliated 15 and 16.

1937?

Ure. Ms. 1 leaf. Removed from Russell's copy of P. N. Ure's *The Origin of Tyranny* (Cambridge, 1922).

1942?

Spain, 1939 [trans. of Sahl's poem, "Spanien"]. Ms. 1 leaf. Removed from Russell's copy of H. Sahl's *Die hellen Nachte, Gedichte aus Frankreich* (New York, 1942).

1956

[Notes on Lowenthal]. Ms. 1 leaf. Removed from Russell's copy of M. Lowenthal's *The Federal Bureau of Investigation* (New York, 1950). L. from Margaret Lloyd to Russell, 1956, is on the verso of the leaf.

c.1957–8

Against [Nuclear] Tests. Ms. 1 leaf.

1958

[Statement] Sent at Request of U.S. Nobel Prize Winners as Address at their N.Y.C. Dinner, to Mezerik, Unovirs, New York. 7 Jan. 1958. Ts. corrected.

1960

Philip Noel-Baker's Work. 27 Jan. 1960. Ts. corrected in ER's hand. 2 leaves. Published as "Philip Noel-Baker", *International Relations* (Journal of the David Davies Memorial Institute of International Studies), 2 (April 1960): 1–2.

1962

Speech for the Tenth Pugwash Conference. 3 Sept. 1962. Tscc. 4 leaves.

Notes for Speech in Field—"Thank you celebration". 10 Nov. 1962. Ms. 1 leaf.

The Menace to Human Survival. 1 Oct. 1963. Tscc. 3 leaves. First published in *Frontier*, 15 (Nov. 1963): 9–10.

1965

Notes for Mtg in London [title on separate piece of paper in CF's hand]. Ms. 1 leaf.

1966

Press Statement [re the bombing of Hanoi]. 16 Dec. 1966. Ts. corrected. 1 leaf.

Undated

Alastor. Ms. 1 leaf. Removed from Russell's copy of *The Complete Works of Percy Bysshe Shelley*, Vol. III (London, 1885).

["Most of us agree in having thought the Labour Party Manifesto good ..."]. Ts. 1 leaf.

*315 General Political Correspondence

Anonymous 2 1916–27
Encl: tscc. of speech given to the House of Commons

Rana, Kiranjit Singh, BR to .. 1962

*320 World Affairs

India 1962
V. V. Ramana Murti

United Kingdom 1955
Harold Macmillan (encl: "Geneva—A Message to the Foreign Ministers", 21 Oct. 1955, mimeo ts. signed by BR, Lord Boyd Orr, Sir Richard Coppock, and C. F. Powell)

U.S.S.R. 1962
Nikita S. Khrushchev

*376 IWCT: General Correspondence on Vietnam

Resist (Noam Chomsky)

*410 Publishing Correspondence

Bowes, Stuart **3** 1964–5
Encl: flyer re Bowes' book
BR to 1964
PW to 1965
Cassirer, Eva **2** 1959
Encl: German trans. of part of *My Philosophical Development*
BR to 1959
Crucible (George Gordon) 1965
Encl: issue of journal containing a condensed version of BR's "The Cold War and World Poverty"
News Limited of Australia, card .... n.d.
Penguin Books Ltd. (Dieter Pevsner), BR to 1963
RS to 1963
Encl: blurb by ER for *Unarmed Victory*
Politiken (Ander Kirkeby?, Elias Bredsdorff) **2** 1921–59
BR to 1959
School and College, card ...... n.d.
The Times, BR to 1963
Encl: clipping of the l.

*430 Radio and Televison

British Broadcasting Corporation (Peter Duncan) 1954
Encl: transcript of radio interview of BR and John Ellison; abstract of 6 talks by BR on "Then and Now" series
Columbia Broadcasting Corporation, cheque stub 1942

*625 The Pugwash Movement—Correspondence 1953–67

Hideki Yukawa
Chou Pei-Yuan
photograph of BR and others
["Statement by 8 eminent scientists & self ..."]. Ms. notes by BR
? Leghait
Pugwash Continuing Committee (Joseph Rotblat)
Rotblat's "Bertrand Russell's Work for Peace". Tscc.
Cyrus Eaton
Czechoslovak Pugwash Committee (Theodor Nemec)
Anne Eaton
A. V. Topchiev
The New York Times
Linus Pauling
Betty Royon
Continuing Committee of the Pugwash Conferences on Science and World Affairs
Yugoslav Pugwash Group (Ivan Supek)

*625 The Pugwash Movement—Printed Material 1957–64

Betty Royon

The Cleveland Press, clippings re Cyrus Eaton
Questions and Answers about Pugwash, leaflet
New York Herald Tribune, "Pugwash Conference Not 'Mr. Eaton's'"
Joseph Rotblat, *The History of the Pugwash Conferences*
Soviet News, no. 4947
Pugwash Coswa Continuing Committee, minutes of the 18th meeting
Akron Beacon Journal, clipping
The Washington Post, clipping

*710 Personal Correspondence

Anonymous 3 1917–33
——, Antonia .... n.d.
——, C. G.? 1895
——, E. W. H. 1919
——, Grethe .... n.d.
Encl. drawing
BR to anon. 1927
Andrews, Norah, to ER 1967
Argyl?, Michael .... n.d.
Barnes, E. W. c.1918
Berenson, Bernard?, photo ... n.d.
Born, Max 1963
de Capsevich, Heronim 1948
Delteil, Caroline .... n.d.
Ducasse, ? 1925
Elvey, Maurice 2 1919
Flexner, Betty, to ER 1967
Frantz, Virginia Knowland, to ER 1966
Hartley, Norah, to ER 1966
A History of Western Philosophy.
BR's file of ls. on:
Boulton, John 1945
Chessman, A. 1947
Dunten, M. T. 1946
Gianased, Al .... n.d.
Lewis, Bernard D. K. 1946
Merrill, John P. 1946
Pipes, Richard E. 1946
Pratt, R. S. 1947
Robertson, Donald 1946
Encl: notes
Rothbarth, Otto 1946
Taylor, Jr., Greer M. 1946
Van den Hooff, Arnold ... 1947
Jones, H. E. 1963
Jones, J. Elwyn 1963
Landow, Florence 1961
Owen, Mably 1963
Russell, Alys, poem. Removed from BR's copy of Oliver Goldsmith's *The Vicar of Wakefield* (London, 1890) .... n.d.
Russell, Rollo 1902
Annotated by BR with references to Frege and Kerry. Removed from BR's copy of Thomas Carlyle's *Critical and Miscellaneous Essays*, Vol. VII (London, 1888).
Underwood, Austin 1961
Wohlgemuth, A. 1919

*713 Patricia Spence (Embargoed)

Most of the letters in this class are addressed to Patricia Helen Spence, who became Russell's third wife. Some letters are addressed to BR and a few others to both. All date from 1932–5.

Documents .134101–.134385

Anonymous (incl: personality traits rating game, with BR's scores on himself and others)
Barclays Bank Limited (W. A. Wall)
Nelto Beazley
Clive Bell
Bob
John Boxall
C. M. Bowra
Jill Bray

Gamel Brenan
Gerald Brenan
Rhode Brenan
British Red Cross Society (form l.)
Dorothy Cater
Christine (an aunt)
Cicely (a cousin)
Clifford
Clare Crighton?
Alice Crunden
Dartington Hall (W. B. Curry)
Crompton Llewelyn Davies
Moya Llewelyn Davies
Margaret Davison
Beryl de Zoete
Jack Dunman
Emilia
C. J. Evans
R. Flaherty to Miss Hounsfield
Elspeth Fox Pitt
Minna Gundersen
Grace E. Hadow
Frank Hardie
Olive Harrington
Harrods Limited
D. A. Hawkin
C. M. Haycraft
I. Emilie Hutton
Ira
Isabel
Jennifer
John
Frida Laski
Margaret L. Lee
Lorenzo
David Low (removed from BR's copy of *Social and Political Ideas of the Victorian Age*)
Joan Malleson
Miles Malleson
Margaret
Francis Meynell
Vera Meynell
Naomi Mitchison
Lady Ottoline Morrell
Myfanny
The National Adoption Society (Helen A. Blackburne?)
Polly Hester Norton
W. W. Norton
C. J. Orwood
Rosalinde Ossie
Amy E. Otter
Frieda Pathler
Edna Pearce
Eric Phillips
Eileen Power
Roy Randall
Richard [Llewelyn Davies?]
A. L. Rowse
Rowe and Maw Solicitors (F. Graham Maw)
Dora Russell (secretary)
Katharine Russell
Sarah
Lucy Silcox
Frank Penn Smith
Mrs. Spence (Patricia's mother)
Judith Stephen
Karin Stephen
Raymond Streatfield
Josephine Sykes
Toni
Adam von Trott
Freda Utley
Anna Valentino
Arthur Waley
Eleanor Watterson
Amber Blanco White
Amabel Williams-Ellis
Ruth Wills
Zita

*723 Birthday Letters 1961

Prue ?
Battersea Campaign for Nuclear Disarmament
Eleanor Ferris and Billie Kiger
Corliss Lamont
Lady Constance Malleson
Anne Russell
Lucy Russell

*724 90th Birthday Tribute

Huang Van Noi *et al.*

*725 95th Birthday Letters

Field Marshal Sir Claude Auchinleck
Joan Baez
Ian and Nicole [Duke and Duchess of Bedford]
Gamel and Gerald Brenan
British Council for Peace in Vietnam
Tamara and Isaac Deutscher
Cyrus Eaton
Alec Heddow
Juliette Huxley
London Mathematical Society
B. J. Lucas
Spike Milligan
Thérèse Nicod
Gabrielle and Paul Oppenheim
Royal Institute of Philosophy (Godfrey Vesey)
Esther and I. F. Stone
Trinity College, Cambridge (Master and Fellows)

*736 Russell Relatives

Forester, Grace .... 196?
Lloyd, Margaret 1952

*910 Works by Others

["As a teacher I came to the conclusion ..."]. Ms. (No author).

Berry G. G. ["A 'classical' series is any well-ordered series ..."]. Ms.

["The Fund in question ..."] Ms. (No author).

Głos Wolnych. 1948 (contains M. Horoszewicz, "Bertrand Russell—szczęśliwy pesymista").

Lavenham Suffolk. Lavenham: L. & K. Ransom, n.d. Leaflet.

["Let us first consider the well-ordering by classes ..."]. Ms. (No author).

McLendon, Hiram J. "Has Russell Answered Hume?" *The Journal of Philosophy*, 49 (28 Feb. 1952): 145–60.

——. "Uses of Similarity of Structure in Contemporary Philosophy." *Mind*, 64 (Jan. 1955): 79–95.

——. "Has Russell Proved Naive Realism Self-Contradictory?" *The Journal of Philosophy*, 53 (26 April 1956): 289–302.

Ministry of Reconstruction. *Report of Committee on Trusts*. London: His Majesty's Staionery Office, 1919.

New Cuba: Bulletin of the Britain–Cuba Committee. Summer 1964.

New Successes of the Doctrine of the Work of "The Road to Peace and to Moral Democracy" by Boris Gourevitch. Robert M. MacIver, ed. New York: Union for the Protection of the Human Person by International Social and Economic Co-operation, Inc., 1959.

New Zealand Soil News, no. 3 (Dec. 1953). Re molybdenum research. Also many other articles and journal issues related to this topic.

Problem ["Let M & N stand for ..."]. 1917? Ms. (No author).

The Significance of the Book, "The Road to Moral Democracy", by Boris Gourevitch. New York: Union for the Protection of the Human Person by International Social and Economic Co-operation, Inc., 1957.

——. *Appendix*. [Same publishing information].

"Soviet Foreign Policy, Calendar of Events 1959". Supplement to *New Times*, no. 1 (Jan. 1960).

Index of Names

Index of Names

The following items are recorded in the Index: all names of persons and organizations, periodicals and newspapers, Russell's books, and the bold sub-headings in classes such as *330 World Affairs. Generally not recorded are the names of individuals in Russell's secretariat, the staff of the BRPF, titles of books, articles and Russell's manuscripts, and cities and countries (except when the country's name occurs as a sub-heading). The Introduction and the introductory notes to the classes are not indexed. Bold type in the Index indicates that the item occurs as a sub-heading.

Because of the number of names on a page, index references include a column indicator. The left-hand column is denoted by "a" after the page number and the right-hand by "b".

A

A & M Hearing Aids Ltd 294a
A la Consciencia de la humanidad 96a
Aall, Cato 23a
Aarons, Eric 198b
AB CWK Gleerup Bokförlag 195a
Abaya, Hernando J. 148a
Abayavardena, Hector 23a, 172b
Abbagnano, Nicola 195a
Abbas, Mukhtar 222b
Abbawy, L. M. 103b
Abbott, Angela 87a
Abbott, R. J. 279b
Abbott, William 294a
Abboud, Ferik Ibrahim 113a
ABC 195a
ABC of Relativity 241b
Abdel-Malek, Anouar 23a, 106b, 107a, 294a
Abdel-Rahman, I. H. 47b
Abdi, Ahmed (Alaoui) 311a
Abdul, S. 25b, 129b
Abdullah, M. M. 153b, 221a
Abdullah, Tariq 124b
Abdulle, Mohommed 23a
Abeidi, Mahmoud El 294a
Abellán, José Luís 294a
Abelman, Jane 37a
Abend Zeitung 174b
Abendroth, Wolfgang 121b, 122a, 157a
Aber, Joel 167a
Aberdeen CND 152b
Aberdeen Students Campaign for Nuclear Disarmament 23a
Aberman, Sidney 23a
Abhoy Ashram 23b
Abhyankar, B. 146b, 214a
Abian, S. 321a
Abraham, Rudy 23b
Abrahams, Sue 124a
Abrams, G. W. 170a
Abrams, Susan Stanich 164a
Absalom 195a
Abt, Ch. 213b
Academic Press 195a
Accademia Lincei 294a
Accademia Nazionale dei Lincei 294a
Accidental War 114a
The Accra Assembly for the World Without the Bomb 80a, 100a, 115b, 151b, 154b, 207b, 220b
Acharya, Nirmalya 207b
Ackland, Brenda A. 224a
Act or Perish 114a
Acta Medica Venezolana 195a
Actas de la Academia Nacional de Ciencias Exactas, Fisicas y Naturales de Lima 324b
Actiegroep Vietnam 179a
Action Civique Non-Violente 23b
Action for Human Rights in Iran 103a
Action pour Une Assemblée Constituante Mondiale 164a
Acton, H. B. 228a
Acton Society Trust 87a
Acuña, Raúl I. 149b
Ad Hoc Committee for an Anti-Wallace/Le May Demonstration 23b
Ad Hoc Middle East Non-Intervention Committee 107a-b
Adam International Review 195a
Adamicka, Olga 195a
Adamjee Science College Magazine 195a
Adams, Anthony 208b
Adams, G. Howard 23b
Adams, Marion 87a
Adams, Michael 107a
Adams, Pam 87a
Adams, Ruth 142a
Adams, Taylor 85b, 136b, 255a
Adams, Thomas F. 294a
Adams, Walter 154a, 297a
Adamson, Donald 195a
Adayr, Frederic 321a
Addington, J. W. 3a
Addis, Laird 87a
Adeane, Michael 123b
Adelaide University Agnostics Society 255a
Adelaide University ALP Club 170a
Adelakum, D. G. 23b
Aden **93a**
Aden Trades Union Congress 23b, 93a
Ades, Bernard 87a
Adhi, S. Ahmad 153b
Adjei, Peter A. 151b
Adkins, Edward R. 23b
Adkins, Warren D. 23b
Adlam, Edith M. 148b
Adler, Esther H. 87a
Adler, Marvin 23b, 79a, 135b
Administration des Monnaies et Médailles 255a
Adrian, Lord 287a
Advocate General, American Army 139a
Ady, D. Howard 24a, 164a
Aero Institute 142a
Aeusrivongse, Nidhi 195a
Afful, Samuel 131a
Afghanistan **93a**

Africa and the World 14a, 75b, 95a, 130a, 188b, 195a
Africa Asia 195b
Africa, Asia, Latin America 148a
African National Congress of South Africa 294a
Afro-American Students in Cuba 135b
Afro-Asian Peoples' Solidarity Organization 107b, 164a
Afro-Asian Solidarity Association of Ceylon 172b
Afro-Asian Solidarity Committee of Burma 24a, 171b
Afroasian Youth Organization 24a
Aftonbladet 17b, 113a
Agarwal, Chandra Prakash 24a
Agarwal, Om Prakash 210b
Agassi, Joseph 255a
Agencia Robotnicza 195b
Agirnasli, Niyazi 106b
Agnew, Janet M. 201a
Agrawal, P. K. 228b
Agudas Israel World Organisation 24a, 111b, 134a
Aguiar, Valmir Gentil 171a
Aguilar, Juan 96a, 195b, 196b
Aharonovicz, David 110a
Aheret 195b
Aherne, Sheelagh 169b
Ahidjo, Ahmadou 94b
Ahimsa Shodh-Peeth 24a
Ahlberg, Alf 278b
Ahmad, Asrar 108b
Ahmad, H. K. 103b, 125b, 126b
Ahmad, Mansur 108b
Ahmad, Syed Neez 233b
Ahmed, ? 298a
Ahmed, Anwar Akhter 233a
Ahmed, Aziz 206b
Ahmed, Begum Salima 196a
Ahmed, Mrs. J. E. 24a
Ahmed, Khwaja Joved 215a
Ahmed, M. Samir 107b
Ahmed, Mohammed Sid 107b
Ahmed, Nasim 195b
Ahmed, S. 108b
Ahmed, Tasadduq 108b
Ahmed, Ziauddin 195b
Ahron, Jonis Israel 134b
Ahson, Akmal 153b
Aiken, Ian D. 74a, 127a, 129b
Ainslie, Rosalynde 129b
Air-India 102b
Aitch, K. 24a
Aitchison, Keitch 24a
Aitchison, Peggy 255a
Aitken, Sir Max 321a
Aitkin, Gillon 233b
Ajam, Solange Bouvier 186a
Ajiboye, Emmanuel Ola 24a
Ajina, Rahim 103b
Aké Siméon 104b
Akerman, Nordal 195b
Akerrén, Bo Y. 158a
Akhbar el Yom 196a
Akhbar El Yom Organization 156b
Akhurst, M. G. 87a
Akiyama, Minoru 142a
Akram, Muhammed 222b
Akron Beacon Journal 352a
Aktiebolaget Svenska Bokförlaget 196a
Aktionsgemeinschaft gegen die atomare Aufrüstung der Bundesrepublik 24a
Aktiv 17a
Akumu, Denis 127a
Al Ahram 106b, 107b, 111a, 114a, 149b, 156b, 196a
Al Alaoui, Mustapha 108a
Al Fatah 107a
Al Gomhouria 196a
Al Hamishmar 104a, 107a
Al Haj, Aziz 154a
Al Hila Central Prison 126b
Al Jawahiri, Mohamad Mahdi 126a, 154a
al Kadhafi Moamer 105b
Al Kholi, Lotfi 107b, 149b
Al Sabah, Abdullah Al Salim 105b
Al Talia Review 107b
Alaez, Amadeo 113a
Alam, Pervaiz 196a, 229a
Alaoui, Ahmed 276a
Alarco, Rosa 109a, 128a, 295b
Al-Ard Co. Ltd. 104a
Alarman 137b
al-Asil, Naji 103a
Al-Attar, Mohamed Said 47a, 119a, 131a
Al-Bahrani, Nouri 107a
Albania **93a**
Albanian Delegation 151a
Albanian Peace Committee 93a
Al-Barzani, Moustafa 125b
Al-Bazzaz, Abdul Rahman 103a
Albee, Edward 232a
Alber, Jens 175a
Albert, Fajersztajn 39a, 170b
Alberti, Leon 196a
Alberti, Maria Theresa 196a
Alberti, Nicholas 24a
Alberti, Rafael 196a
Albrecht, Herbert O. 24a
Alcan Jamaica Ltd. 131b
Alcobendas, Miguel 164a
Alcock, N. Z. 32b
Aldea, Melanie 129a
Aldermaston March Committee 164a
Aldouby, Z. H. 24b
Aldred, Guy 24b
Aldus Books Ltd. 196a, 349a
Alemayehu, Haddis 97a
Alexander, ? 33b
Alexander, Mrs. ? 94a
Alexander, Cynthia 24b
Alexander, H. G. 16a, 174b, 235a
Alexander, J. M. 230a
Alexander, John 255a
Alexander, K. J. W. 24b
Alexander, Prof. Y. 107a
Alexander Defence Committee 129b, 130a
Alexanderian, M. 112b, 120a
Alexandrovich, Vladimir 229b
Algeneen Dagblad 196a
Algeria **93a, 120a**
Algerian Ambassador 120a
Algerian Delegation 151a
Algerian Peace Committee 120a
Algiers Appeal 93a, 151b
Algiers Conference on Denuclearization of the Mediterranean Basin **151a**
Alhadeff, Boaz I. 24b
Al-Hafidh, Amin 130b
Ali, Ashraf 196a
Ali, Baquer 108b
Ali, F. 24b
Ali, Medi 321a
Ali, Mohammed 17b, 136a, 139b
Ali, S. B. 24b
Ali, S. Hamid 196a
Ali, Syed Ashraf 24b
Ali, Tariq 24b, 160a, 162b, 164a, 186a, 190a, 196a, 199b
Al-Joundi 174a
Alkahammar, Gunnar 122b
al-Khawaja, Falah 126a
Alkilic, Nikmet 131a
All India Peace Council 102b, 154a
All Jammu & Kashmir Muslim Conference 196a
All Japan Federation of Student Autonomies 144a
All Pakistan Women's Association 196a
Allaf, Mowaffak 113b, 196a
The Allahabad Medical Association 196a
Allard, A. 170b
Allaun, Frank 52a, 115b, 121a, 217b
Allegranza, Helen 114a
Allen, A. W. 79a
Allen, Jr., Charles R. 24b, 100a, 142a
Allen, David G. 39a
Allen, Derek 294a
Allen, Donna 24b, 138b, 164a
Allen, Duane 166b
Allen, Emily A. 24b
Allen, George, L. 255a
Allen, Jaimie 168a, 196b
Allen, James S. 214b
Allen, Joe 198b
Allen, Lloyd M. 24b
Allen, Seawillow 24b
Allen, Steve 24b
George Allen & Unwin Ltd. 64a, 84a, 117b, 142b, 174b, 196a, 203a, 216a, 227b, 232a, 234a, 234b, 238b, 268a, 278b
Allende, Salvador 95a
Aller, S. 130a
Alley, Rewi 321a

Alleyne, Sydney Burnett 82b
Allfields Chartered Accountants 274b
Allgemeiner Deutscher Nachrichtendienst 99a, 100a, 196b
Alliance for Jobs or Income Now 24b
Alliance in Action for the Federal Elections of 1969 24b
Allison, James L. 87a
Allison, Jay 206a
Allison, Michael H.G. 24b
Alloy, Evelyn 24b
Alloy, Jack 24b
Alma Mater Society of the University of Victoria 94b, 172a
al-Mirza, Ahmed al-Haj Ali 126a
al-Mirza, Hadi 126a
Almogy, Saul 24b
Almond, Joseph 255b
Alner, Juraj 219a
Alonso, Luis Ricardo 95b, 152b
Alonso Rivera, Luis 24b
Alppilan Sosialistiseura Helsinki 294a
Al-Rawi, Fouad 103a
Al-Razee, Aleem 295a
Al-Sammar'e, Abdulla Saloom 103a
Al-Shamy, Assayed Abdul Wahab 119a
Alsop, Joseph 196b
al-Sulh, Kadhim 24b, 105b
Altamirano, Horacio Espinosa 321a
Alternative Perspectives on Vietnam 176a
Alterovici, E. 112b
Altman, Jehezkiel 112b
Altbach, Philip 76a
Alvarado, Juan Velasco 109a
Alvarez, Osvaldo Paredes 24b, 96a, 173a
Alvarez, Raul 296b
Al-Washi, Yehya G. Roomi 126a
Alway, R. 152a
Al-Zoubaidi, Tarik 148b
Amancio, Luis Ricardo Barata 24b
Amano, Kohei 213a
Ambassade de Belgique 87a
Ambassador of Afghanistan 93a
Ambassador of the Republic of Cuba 143a
Ambatielos, Anthony 123a, 124a, 294a
Ambatielos, Betty 25a, 123a, 294a
Amberley 303a
Amberley, Kate **3b**
Ambrose, David D. 25a
Amby, Christen 97a, 165b
Amdur, Irving 25a
Amer, A. 161a, 174a
American Academy of Chinese Culture, Inc. 150a
American Ambassador to Britain 140a
American Broadcasting Company 196b
American Civil Liberties Union 135b
American Committee for Cultural Freedom 135a
American Committee for the Protection of the Foreign Born 135b
American Committee on Africa 25a
The American Council for Judaism 25a, 107a
American Deserters Committee 164a
American Dialog 196b
American Dialogue 127a
American Embassy 25a
American Embassy in U.S.S.R. 273b
The American Ethical Union 197a
American Federation of World Citizens 135b, 155b
American Friends Service Committee 164a, 334b
American Friends Service Committee on Ending the War 25a
American Humanist Association 13a, 150a, 197a, 255b
American Humanist Association, Minnesota Chapter 149b
American Humanist Association, New York Chapter 150a
American Humanist Organization 118a
American Journal of Orthopsychiatry 339a
American Journal of Physics 327b
American Liberation League 150b
American People's Encyclopedia 197a
American Philosophical Association, Eastern Division 237a
American Philosophical Association, Western Division 290a
American Philosophical Quarterly 197a, 325b
American Servicemen's Union 25a
American Society to Defend Children 197a
American Vegetarian 197a
Americans Want to Know 25a, 171b
Amerikanerne I Junglen 321a
Ames, Alfred C. 202b
Amikan, Herzl 135a
Amin, Shahid M. 108b
"Les Amis de la Fondation Russell" 174a
Ammann, W. 122a
Ammar, Taieb 114a
Ammer, Stefan 98b
Ammerman, Robert R. 197a
Amnesty for Greek Political Prisoners 122b, 123b
Amnesty for Iraqi Political Prisoners (International Committee) 126b
Amnesty International 25a, 98b, 101a, 101b, 106a, 109a, 110a, 114b, 117a, 120b, 121a, 123a, 125b, 126b, 127a, 127b, 128a, 128b, 129a, 129b, 130a, 131a, 131b, 133a, 134b, 138b, 142a, 153a, 156a, 164a, 294a
Amnesty International, Stockholm 294a
Amnesty International, Swedish section 130a
Amneus, Thomas 87a
Amsterdam-Rotterdam Bank 87a
Amswych, M.H. 82b
Amulree, Lord 255b
An, Phan Thi 45a
The Analysis of Mind 7a
Anand, C.L. 89b
Anand, J.K. 25a
Ananda Bazar Patrika 197a
Anarchy 273a
Ancel, Marc 321a
Anders, Günther 93b, 136a, 142a, 153a, 157a, 184a, 185a-b, 192a, 197a, 290a, 294a, 301a
Andersen, H. 25a
Anderson, Barbara 197a
Anderson, Bo 25b
Anderson, Bruce 25b, 169a
Anderson, Ernest 257a
Anderson, Francis 90b
Anderson, G. 169b
Anderson, G.R. 26a
Anderson, L.S. 25b
Anderson, Martha 25b
Anderson, Paul 222b
Anderson, Perry 25b, 103a, 223a
Anderson, Richard 170a
Anderson, Thomas M. 270b
Ando, Takatura 197a
Andreasen, Werner B. 173a
Andreen, Andrea 280a
Andrew, Gerda 197a
Andrews, D.H. 114b
Andrews, Nora 352a
Andrews, Mrs. P. 12a-b
Andrews, Richard M. 164a
Ang, Crispina L. 109b, 128a
Angeloff, Frank J. 149b, 294a
Angeloff-Hoefsmit, Mevrouw G. 87a
Anger, Alfred William 310a
Anglemire, Kenneth N. 241b
Anglica Society 197a
Anglo-Cypriot Friendship Council 96a
Anglo-French Vietnam Weekend 164a
The Anglo-Greek Luncheon 123a
Anglo-Rumanian Refugee Committee 129b
Angus, I. 272a
Animals 197a
Ann Arbor Defence Fund 139a
The Annals of Mathematical Statistics 322b

Annerl, Walter 93b
Annesley, Lady Clare 287a
Annesley, Mabel B. 278b
Annesley, Lady Priscilla 255b, 264b, 278b
Annisfrom, Erich 294a
Annuaire Internationale des Prisonniers Politiques 97b
Annual Report 323a
Another Mother for Peace 25b
Ansari, Sana-ur-Rehman 226b
Anscombe, G.E.M. 197a
Ansell, Mary 255b
Anstey, J.H. 25b
Anthal, Jussi 208b
Anthias, Tefkros 211b
L'Anti-Antitoutiste Pour La Paix 197a
The Anti-Apartheid Movement 25b, 110a, 111a, 129b
Anti-Franco Appeal Fund 130a
Antiquity 327a
Anti-Vietnam-Draft Coordinating Committee 164a, 178b
Anti-Vietnam War Demonstration 164a
Antonis, Basil 108a
Antonis, Paulette 25b, 108a
Anvar, Françoise 103a, 125a
Anwar, Saquib 255b
Aomi, Junichi 144b, 197b
Aoyama World Federation Society 25b
Apcarian, S.H. 25b, 153b
Apeco Ltd. 87a
Apithy, Migan 97a
Apostolesco, Helen 129a
Appeal for Amnesty in Spain 25b, 130a
Appeal for Release of Albert Luthuli 130a
Apple, Jr., R.W. 158a
Applebaum, H. 67a
Appleton-Century-Crofts 197b, 209b, 241b
Applied Optics 321a
Approach Magazine 197b
Aquilar, Roberto Monsivais 127a
Arab Lawyer Union 25b, 107a, 107b
Arab Socialist Union 106b, 111a, 114b
Arab Students Union in U.K. and Ireland 125b
Arab Tourist Union 105a
Arai, Yoshio 145a
Arain, Shafiq 114a
Arakawa, Hiroshi 232a
Aranda, Gustavo Silva 109a
Arbeitet 190a
Arbenz Guzman, Jacabo 158a
Archangel Agency 87a
Archetti, Stefano 225b
The Architectural Association 197b
Archiv-Dienst 175a
Archives Internationales d'Histoire des Sciences 338b
Archiv für universelle Entwicklungspolitik 174b
Ardeleanu, N. 25b
Elizabeth Arden Ltd. 151a
Arden, John 232a
Ardies, Tom 239a
Ardila, Ruben 230b
Aref, Abdul Salem 103a-b, 126a 154a
Aren, Sadun 106b, 157b
Arena 197b
Arena, University of Texas at Arlington 197b
Arendt, Hannah 91a
Arendt, Niels Henrik 173b
Aret Runt 200b
Argentina **120a, 141a, 169a**
Argentinian Peace Committee 197b
Argiroffi, Emilio 203b
Argyl?, Michael 352a
Argyle, Sylvia 30b, 164a
Ariaans, Th. M. 294a
Aricó, José 227a
Arik, Sara 116a
Aristotelian Society 9b
Aristotelian Society Proceedings 323b-324a, 326b, 336a
Arley, Niels 25b
Arlott, John 116a
Armah, Kwest 100a
Armando Carello, Luis 169a
Armati, L.F. 197b
Armendáriz, Antonio 106a, 127a
Armenians **120a**
Arms Control and Disarmament 155a
Armstrong, David 26a
Armstrong, Eunice 255b
Armstrong, Helen 266a
Armstrong, Noel 26a
Armstrong, P. 62b
Armstrong, Patrick 48a
Armstrong, R. 26a
Armstrong, William M. 256a
Army Apprentices School 131b
Arnode, T.J. 313a
Arnold, Herr 99b
Arnold, Cheryl 118a, 167b
Arnold, David 85a
Arnold, H.J.P. 229a
Arnold, Percy 256a
Arnold, Walter 207a
Arnoni, M.S. 14a, 115b, 117a, 123b, 134a, 135b, 137b, 139a, 142a, 147a, 155b, 210a, 220a-b
Aroma, Martin F. 114a
Aron, Raymond 321a
Aronson, James 222a
Aronson, Murray 294a
Aronstein, Georges 94a, 135a
Arora, R.S. 197b
Arpelderblad 197b
Arrau, Claudia 26a
Arrowsmith, Wendy 294a
Arsenescu, Adina 197b
Arshidat, Shafik 25b, 107a, 107b
Artioli, Mauro 54b
The Artists Civil Right Assistance Fund 150b
Artists' Protest 164a
The Arts and Professions Committee for the Defense of Bill Epton 26a
Arts et Progrès 116b
Arts Festival 164a
Arya, Jitendra 256a
Aryaratna, M.M. 206a
Aryum, Baher Nasir 295b
Asad Aid Committee 127b
Asadullah, M. 26a
Asahi Evening News 69a
Asahi Shimbun 197b
Asahigaoka Senior High School 26a
Asambla Nacional por la Libertad de los Presos Politicos y la Derogacion del Delito de Disolucion Social 26a
Asamblea Unica Mundial 26a
Asano, Tadashi 145a
Ash, Bill 178a
Ash, David 26a
Ash, Michael 26a
Ash, Ranjana 124b
Ashbrook, H.F. 260a
Ashby, Graham 26a
Ashford, A.E. 321b
Ashford, Montague B. 256a
Ashfords & Sons 87a
Ashton, C.J. 26a
Ashton, David 26a
Ashton, Robert W. 26a
Ashworth, Brian 26a
Asia 148a
Asian Socialist Conference 62b
Asiatic Society 256a
Askwith, Betty Miller 197b
Askwith, Herbert 197b
Asmed, Nasim 205b
Asociacion por la Responsabilidad Social del Investigator Cientifico 136b
Aspden, H. 321a
Aspecte 198a
Aspen Institute for Humanistic Studies 260a-b
Aspinwall, David 143a
As-Safa 105b, 126a
Assembly of Captive European Nations 26a
Assis, Maria de Lourdes 26a
Associacao de Estudantes de Instituto Superior Tecnico 128b
Associated Insurers (British Electricity) Management Committee 87a
The Associated Press 189a
Associated Press Cutting Services Ltd. 198a, 209b

Associated-Rediffusion Ltd. 36b
Associated TeleVision Limited 198a
Association contre le Danger Radiologique 26a
Association d'Athens des Familles des Exiles et Prisonniers Politiques 124a
Association de Parents des Expatriotes Politiques Grecs à Angleterre 100b
Association des Combattants pour la Liberte et Demokratie 26a, 98b
Association des Juristes Vietnamiens 163a, 164b
Association for International Cooperation and Disarmament 26a, 169b
Association Internationale des Juristes Democrates 126a, 294a-b
Association of Greek Democratic Lawyers 123a
Association of Scientfic Workers of India 294b
Association of Victims of Nazi Persecution 26b
Association of World Federalists 198a
Association por la Responsabilidad Social 141a
Association pour le Désarmament Général et le Progrès Social 173b
Association pour le Développement du Droit Mondial 26b
Associazione Italiana Giuristi Democratici 121b
Astgen, J. 299a
Astor, David 152b, 176b, 183a, 225a
Atamian, Alice 214a
Atassi, Nureddin 113b
The Athenaeum 256a
Athenaeum Publishers 198a
Athens Association of Families of Political Exiles and Prisoners 122b
Athens Association of Political Exiles and Prisoners 101a
Athens Daily Post 321b
Athens News 321b
Athinaki 101a, 123b
Atkinson, Mrs. 147a
Atkinson, Janice 256a
Atkinson, Norman 176b
Atkinson, Ralph B. 26b, 29b, 137a
Atlantic Monthly 11b
Atlantic Monthly Press 198a
Atlantic Peace Foundation 13a, 26b
Atlas Photography Ltd. 87a
Atomics & Nuclear Energy 198a
At-Tarik Review 13b, 106b
Attepoe, Patrick R. 195b
Attile, Ujhelyi 198a
Attlee, Earl 114a, 116a, 121b
Attlee Memorial Appeal 321b
Attorney-General of the German Democratic Republic 99a
Atwood, Thomas 26b
Auchinleck, Field Marshall Sir Claude 26b, 176b, 354a
Auckland Hiroshima Day Committee 26b
Auden, W.H. 128a
Audio Fidelity Inc. 198a-b
Audits and Accounts Office, Office of the High Commissioner for Pakistan 108b
Aumack, Lisa 164b
Aurangebadkar, Ram 213b
Auriol, Vincent 121b, 321b
Auropa Public Relations Agency 105a, 143a
Aurora Social 198b
Auslaender, Gizella 111a
Aust, Ernst 122a
Austin, George 26b
Austin, Jonathan 26b
Austin, Rickey 265a
Austin, Warren 24a
Australasian Journal of Psychology 332a
Australia **93b, 169a-170b**
Australia and New Zealand Congress for International Cooperation and Disarmament 26b, 93b
The Australian 51a, 147a
Australian Branch of BRPF **141a**
Australian Left Review 198b
Australian Seamen's Union 294b
Australian Women's Project Against French Tests in the Pacific 93b
Australians and New Zealanders against the Vietnam War 26b, 27a
Austria **93b, 170b**
Austrian Fascist Organization 55b
Authentic Translators 198b
The Autobiography of Bertrand Russell 8a, 198a, 199b, 211a, 258b, 260b, 310b, 349a
Auty, R.M. 295a
Avant Garde 198b
Avanzada Nacionalista de Venezuela 27a
Ave, Tomoji 145a
Avedon, Baldwin 256a
Avedon, Barbara 25b
Avedon, Richard 198b
Avellaneda, Juan de Dios 321b
Avenues for Humanised Economics for the Growth of Mind and Soul 198b
Avery, D. 256a
Avila, Horacio 27a
Avon, Mme. 174a
Avon, The Earl of 158a
Avorn, Jerry L. 27a
Avram, Miriam 134b
Avyaktananda, Swami **80a**
Awad, Louis 196a
Aware 198b
Axel, Dave 178b
Axelbank, Albert 27a, 105a, 144b, 162b, 164b, 233a
Axioms 331b
Axon, Gordon V. 27a
Ayarian, Mary 117a
Aybar, Mehmet Ali 106b, 157a, 189b, 192a, 294b
Ayer, A.J. 30b, 46a, 116b, 124b, 131b, 177a, 256a, 287a, 292a
Ayusawa, Iwao 144a
Aziz, A. 172b
Azmeh, Youssef 62a
Azurdia, Enrique Peralta 101b

B

Ba, Mr. 164b
Ba, Cu Dinh 162b, 177a
Ba'ath Party 125b
Babu 142b
Bacaleinick, Maria Lucia 171a
Bach, Pham Van 163a, 164b, 294b
Back, E.W. 27a
Back?, H. Hed 278b
"Background to Czechoslovakia" 121a
"Background to Tashkent" 109a
Backhaus, Carl 144a
Backwards 198b
Bacon, Emily P. 282b
Bacon, S.L. 288b
Bader, Ernst 227b
Bader, Godric E.S. 71a
Bader, Joseph 198b
Bader, Scott 71a
Scott Bader Commonwealth 71a
Badin, Claude 297b
Badu, Kofi 211b
Baer, Hans J. 98b
Baer, Walter 27a
Baertling, Olle 27a
Baez, Joan 354a
Bagai, Kaj Pal 153b
Bageac, Nicolae 110b
Baggen, J. 45b
The Baghdad Hotel 148b
Baharis, Mr. 96a
Bahrain **93b**
Bahraini Students 93b
Bahraini Students in Beirut 93b
Baier, Anton 170b
Bailey, Adrian 229a
Bailey, Anne 219a
Bailey, David 281a
Bailey, J.E. 87a
Bailey, Maisie 27a
Bailey, Shirley 27a
Baillie, James H. 256a
Baines, Peter 70b
Baja, Tiburcio 128a
Bajpai, U.S. 102a
Baker, Pat 256a

Baker, Peter Shaw 27a, 102b
Balcombe, R. 164b
Balcombe, Rosalyn 27a
Baldelli, G. 130a
Balderston, John L. 242a
Baldwin, C. 27a
Baldwin, James 146b, 148b, 157b, 192a
Baldwin, Roger 125a
Bales, Eric 69b
Bales, Harry 241a
Balewa, Abubakar Tafewa 108a, 127b
Balint, Nicholas 232b
Ball, Adrian 27a
Ball, David L. 294b
Ball, Horace 299b
Ballantyne, Ian 146b
Ballesteros, F. 294b
Ballin, Ruth 27a
Ballotti, Geno A. 205a
Baloch, Abdul Karim Shorish 297b
Baltimore Sun 198b
Baltra-Cortés, Alberto 115b
Balzer, Friedrich-Martin 174b
I Bambini dell'Asilo 321b
Banajsová, Maria 173a
Band, Lee Jung 105a
Banda, Hastings 105b
Bandaranaike, Sirimavo 95a, 256a
Bandhu, Bhadra 27a
Banerjee, A.B. 198b
Banerjee, Anil 219b
Banerjee, Kali Krishna 294b
Banerjee, M.K. 198a
Banerjee, Surya Kumar 290a
Banfield, Alan 27a
Bangsvej, Peter 173a
Bank of America 307a
The Bank of Japan 145a
Bank of London and South America Ltd. 87a
Banks, R.V. 36b
Banks, Stan 27a
Bannister, Derek D. 79a
Banque Nationale de Belgique 87a
Bantam Books, Inc. 198b
Bao, Luyi 27b
Bao, Nguyen Ba 164b
Bao-Dai, H.M. 158a
Baquero, Luis Gomez 164b
Barash, Feiga 135a
Barbajosa, Gil 27b
Barbasevich, Vyacheslav Yanovich 27b, 152b
Barbeitos, Jarbas 171a
Barber, Peter 198b, 203b
Barbey, Anne 33b, 111a
Barbone, Donato 198b
Barclay, Gary M. 27b
Barclays Bank 87a, 307a, 352a
Bard, Dick 174a
Bardoe-Darfor, Bertrand Russell 256a
Bardoe-Darfor, L.L. 256a, 294b
B'ari, Shmuel 103b
Barkai, Fanny 301a
Arthur Barker Ltd. 198b
Barleze, Carlos Rogério 171a
Barlovatz, A. 27b, 152a
Bärlund, Raimo 105a
Barna, Minhaj 108b
Barnard, George L. 290a
Barnard, Harry 198b
Barnes, E.W. 352a
Barnes, Elizabeth 242b
Barnes, Emily 170a
Barnes, Jack 73b, 115b
A.S. Barnes & Co., Inc. 198b
Barnett, Donald L. 48b, 164b
Barnett, Nat 135b, 138b
Barnitt, Bruce 147a
Barr, B. 87a
Barrat, Robert 226b
Barratt-Brown, Eileen 294b
Barratt-Brown, Eleanor 294b
Barratt-Brown, Michael 27b, 294b, 314a
Barreiros, Luis 164b, 171a
Barreto, António 128b
Barreto e Costa, Fernando 137a
Barrett, J.F. 27b
Barrett, Lynda 27b
Barron, Arthur 222b
Barron, D.L. 134a
Barron, Zelda 27b
Barry, Griffin 276a, 283b
Barry, Harriet 281a
Barry, Roderick 256a, 276a, 281a
Barsby, Dorothy 240b
Bart, Lionel 232a, 256a
Bartee, T.C. 214a
Barthe, José Miguel 164b
Bartley, III, William Warren 321b
Barton, Anthony 61a
Barton, Hugo R. 27b
Barton, William E. 40b
Barua, Dilip K. 256b
Barua, P.D. 297a
Baruk, H. 73b
Barzani, Mostafa 125b
Barzegar, Ali 125a
Barzman, John 44a
Başaran, Ayhan 27b, 158a
Basch, Beti 110b
Basham, W.R. 27b
Bashan, Raphael 103b
Bashir, M. 198b
Basic Books, Inc. 198b
Baskeyfield, C.P. 143b
Baskin, Wade 199a
Basques 120a
Basquin, T. 116b
Basri, Saul A. 322a
Bassett, B.E. 237a
Bassi, J.J. 27b
Basso, Lelio 109b, 128b, 157a, 187a-b, 189a, 192a
Bastable, Helen 34a, 96a, 135a
"Bastion" Annual Committee 199a
Bastion, Charlton 27b
Basu, Jitendra Nath 322a
Basu, Nripendra K. 199a
Basu, Rabindranath 102b
Basu, Tarapada 197a
Bates, Ken 256b
Bates, Margaret 146a
Bath Academy of Art 276a
The Bath Weekly Chronicle & Herald 199a
Battersea Campaign for Nuclear Disarmament 353b
Battle, Hellen 98b, 99a
Battle, Sol 256b
Bau 199a
Baucom, Marjory 206b
Bauer, F. 91a
Baxter, Rosemarie 27b
Bay, Christian 27b, 172a, 322a
Bay, John G. 27b
Bayati, N.K. 103b
Bayer, Martin 87a
Der Bayerische Rundfunk 174b, 199a
Bayerische Staatszeitung 100a
Bayerl, Leopold 175a, 256b
Bayes, Roger 257a
Baykurt, Fakir 114a
Baylis, N. 27b
Bayoomi, Hussain Ali 119a
Bazaar, Mona 27b, 197a
Bazaars, O.K. 87a
Beach & Beach 87a
Beacon Hill School 276a, 283a, 284a
Beacon Press 199a
Beadle, Jasmine M. 164b, 168b
Beaman, Joanna 276b
Bean, T.E. 288b
Bearman, Ronald 28a
Beart, J. 102b
Beas World Travel Agency Ltd. 143a
Beasley, Alec C. 28a, 94b, 146b, 152b
Beasley, Gertrude 256b
Beasley, Michael 143a
Beaton, Cecil 256b
Beaton, Leonard 28a, 47b, 142a
Beaudry, A. 288b
Beaujard, E. 116b
Beauregard, Laurent A. 28a
The Beaver 19a, 313b
Beaver, Hugh 142b
Beaverman, Harry 211a
Beazley, Nelto 352a
Bechaud, Richard G. 290a
Beck, June 239a
Beck, Michael 84a
Becker, Moshe 28a
Beckett, Marcia 294b
Beckley, Michael 117a
Beckman, E. 87a
Beckman, Viking 256b, 322a
Bedau, Hugo Adam 199a
Beddoe, Josephine 235a
Bedford, Ian, Duke of 149a, 256b, 260a, 292a, 354b
Bedford, Nicole, Duchess of 256b, 292a, 354b

Bedford, Sybille 256b
Bedggood, L.R. 147a
Bedi, Surinder 290a
Beecroft, Eric 256b
Beelzebub 135a
Beeton, Nick 96a
Beeton, P.D. 28a
Beghetti, John 169b
Behar, Dr. 160a
Beheiren-"Japan Peace for Vietnam!" Committee 145b, 164b
Behman, Heinrich 256b, 322a
Behrisch, Arno 121b
Behrman, S.N. 42a
Bei Veroffentlichung in Ihrem Pressedienst 98a
Beilis, Jacov 112b
Belcher, C. 28a
Belet, Robert 322a
Belfast Young Socialists of the North Ireland Labour Party 28a
Belfrage, Cedric 222a
Belfrage, Sally 150a
Belgium **94a, 120a-b, 170b-171a**
Belilos, Leon 28a, 322a
Bell, Alan 164b
Bell, Alan S. 256b
Bell, Clive 352b
Bell, E. 237b
Bell, Herbert 148b
Bell, Kenneth 199a
Bell, Ralph P. 87a
John Bell and Croyden 87b
Bell Telephone Laboratories 199a
Belland, Christopher C. 28a
Bellavista, Luciano 28a
Beloch?, Henry 87b
Belous, Charles 28a
Belton, Henry 28a
Belton, Howard 28a
Belzagny, Ernest M. 301a
Ben Barka, Mehdi 97b
Ben Bella, Ahmed 93a, 106b, 120a
Benary, W. 239b
Bench, P.G.H. 28a
Ben-David, Joseph 150a
Bender, John M. 301a
Bendick, D. 147a
Benedict, John 224b
Benediktsson, Bjarni 102a
Benenson, Peter 25a, 98b, 117a, 120b, 121a-b, 127b, 128a, 129b, 131a, 133a, 138b, 142a
Ben-Gurion, David 28a, 103b, 287a
Benitez, Thomas C. 109a
Benjamin, B.J. 225a
Benjamin, D.J. 28a
Benjamin, Hilda 99a
Benjamin, Jack 28a, 28b
Benjamin, Shalom ben 220b
Ben-Moshe, Yehuda 34a, 104a, 107a
Benn, Anthony Wedgwood 87b
Benn, S. Edwin 28b
Bennett, E., Mary 310b
Bennett, W.C. 28b
James Bennett Pty. Ltd. 169a
Benney, Robyn 28b, 170b
Benowicz, Paul Wechselblatt 133a
Bensen, Bert 131b
Bensen, S.B. 148b
Bent, John A. 28b, 199a
Bentacourt, Romulo 132a
Bentele, Hilde 174b
Bentinck, Baron Adolph 149a
Bentley, Jerry H. 28b
Bentley, Nicholas 199a
Bentsion, Aleksandrovitch 133b
Bentwich, Norman 287a
Ben Yamed, Béchir 215b
Berck, Roger 170b
Berei, Andor 175b
Berenson, Bernard? 352a
Berenson, Mary 281a
Berger, D. 161a
Berger, Denis 130b, 157b, 161a
Bergman, June 116b
Bergman, Lowell 168b
Bergman, Walter 135b
Bergol, Alexander 28b
Bergson, H. 350a
Bergström, Curt 116b
Bergstrom, David Lawrence 28b
Berka, Karel 199a
Berkeley, Leonard 116a
Berkman, [Alexander] 256b
Berkovitch, I. 296b
Berl, Bernard 110a
Berlin, Isaiah 28b, 111a
Berliner Arbeitsausschuss "Gegen den Atomted" 99b
Berman, Mr. and Mrs. F.D. 294b
Bernadotte, Berlil 142b
Bernadotte, Count Sigvard 28b, 142b
Bernal, Eileen 83b, 138b, 142b, 292a
Bernal, J.D. 19a, 28b, 84b, 95a, 151a, 153a, 156a, 164b, 168b, 292a
Bernal, Margaret 28b
Bernard, Hilda 287a
Bernard, Phyllis 310b
Bernard, Vilem 121a
Bernardino, José 17b, 128b
Bernardino, Luis 28b, 128b
Bernays, Paul 256b
Bernhardt, H. William 108a
Bernheim, Carlos Tunnernann 204b
Bernoulli, Daniel 327b
Bernstein 349b
Bernstein, Donatella 294b
Bernstein, L. 134a
Bernstein, Leonard 287a
Berry, William A. 28b
Berryman, John 87b
Bert, Ulanco 294b
Bertolini, Renato 97b, 98a, 143a
Bertolino, Jean 187b, 188b
Berton, Pierre 199a
Bertou, Jacques 199a
Bertrand, Claude-Jean 199b
Berveiller, Michel 199b, 294b, 322a
Bery, Esther 134b
Betancur, Belisario 112a
Betes Noires and Straw Men 199b
Bethwite-Thomson, Isabel 116a
Bettelheim, Charles 107a, 161a
Betts, William 290a
Bevan, Yolande 28b
Beveridge, W.H. 256b
Bevington, Helen 322a
Bevis, B. Cecil 28b
Bewley, Jean R. 124b
Bey, K. Murad 58a, 107a, 290a
Beynon, Huw 179a
Bezerra, Raimundo 58a
Bhadra, S. 229b
Bhandari, Veena 199b
Bhat, A.N. 28b
Bhatnager, V.M. 29a
Bhatt, Govind 29a
Bhattacharyya, Nrisinha Prasad 153b
Bhattacharyya, S.K. 196a
Bhutto, Zulfiquar Ali 29a, 108b, 158a, 294b
Biafra **151b**
Bidwell, Sydney 148a
Bierdrager, E.A. 76a
Bierich, Marcus 29a, 144a, 322a
Bigart, Homer 158a
Bigg, Emma M. 87b
Bigg, Lester 87b
Bij, Marijke 199b
Billis, D. 73b, 111a
Binch, Paul 29a
Binding, D.C. 29a
Binet, F.E. 322a-b
Bing, Harold F. 121b
Bingham, Jim 137b
Bingham, Robert 230b
Bingham, Rowena 294b
Binh, Nguyen Thi 118b, 294b
Binh, V.H. 94b
Biolly, M. 58a
"Biological and Chemical Warfare" 154b
Biquard, P. 199b
Biraverman, Harry 196b
Birbeck, Julius, Coburn & Broad 251b, 313a
Bird, Mr. 199b
Bird, Eugene H. 135a
Bird, F.E. 209a
Birkett, Grania 107a
Birla, B.M. 87b
Birmingham Indian Association 29a
Birnbaum, Jacob 111b
Birnberg, Benedict 123b, 148b, 313b, 314a
Birnberg, Naomi 256b, 322b
Birnberg, Srul 113a
B.M. Birnberg & Co. 313a-b
Birnstingl, Martin 160a
Bischoff, Peter 164b
Bisgyer, Maurice 322b

Bishop, Daphne E. 29a
Bishop, Peter H.H. 322b
Bishop of Durham 3a
Bishop of Hongkong 120b
The Bishop of Llandaff 116a
The Bishop's House 199b
Bisset, Peter 224a
Bissoondoyal, S. 222b
Biswas, Chitta 154a
Bit 199b
Bitar, Salah 113b
Bittrich, Dr. 83b, 175a
Bivona, Francesco 322b
Bjerkmann, Tor 227a, 242a
Björklund, Margareta 290a
Blach, Peter 276b
Black, Mr. and Mrs. 133a
Black?, C. 256b
Black, Dora Winifred 277b (See also Dora Grace)
[Black], Granny 283a
Black, J. 131b
Black, Jack 290a, 292a
Black, Paul 29a
The Black Dwarf 199b, 322b
A. & C. Black Ltd. 199b
Black Panther Party 139b
Black Power Movement Racial Adjustment Action Society 294b
Blackburn, Osmon 47b
Blackburn, Robert H. 272a
Blackburn, Robin 152a, 173a, 342a
Blackburne?, Helen A. 353a
Blackett, Peter 292a
Blackett, P.M.S. 29a, 142b, 158a, 256b, 322b
Blackham, H.J. 30b, 98b
Blackie & Son 199b
Blacksburg Free Press 199b
Blackwell, Kenneth 200a, 261a, 294b, 310a
Blackwell, Rob 170a
B.H. Blackwell, Ltd. 199b
Blackwood, R.T. 294b
Blackwood, Jr., Andrew W. 200a
Bladimiros, B. 101a
Blaetter fuer Deutsche und Internationale Politik 99a, 200a
Blair, Thomas 230b
Blake, F. 131b
Blake, Robert 29a
Blanco, Castelo 94a
Blanco, Hugo 109a, 128a, 294b
Blanco, Mireya 27a
Bland, Phillip S. 87b, 166b
Blankenship, Ben F. 29a, 166b
Blanpied, John W. 219a
Blatter, Erika 294b
Blau, T.L. 201b
Blazeković, Milan 157b
Blech, Enid M. 288b
Blecher, Israel-Maushovits 113a
Bleiberg, Germán 128a, 130a
Bleisch, Günter 121b
Bligh, P.D. 143a
Blindell, Walter R. 29a
Bliss, C.K. 200a
Blitz 200a
Bloch, Walter 174b
Block, Joanna 134b
Block, Mollie 134b
Block, Morris 134b
Blond, Anthony 200a
Blond, Neville 29a
Blood, A. 29a
Bloom, David Lee 139a
Bloom, John 29a
Bloomstein, Charles 210a
Blotner, Joseph 200a
The Blue Rag 29a, 125b
Bluhm, Walter 29a
Blum, David 150b, 259b
Blum, Fred H. 47b
Blum, Robert 173b, 294b
Blum, William 29a, 164b
Blumberg, Herbert H. 200a
Blumberg, Irving Samuel 29a
Blumenson, Eric 148b
Bo, Mai Van 162b
Board of Deputies of British Jews 103b, 111b, 134a
Board of Trade Advisory Committee 200a
Boardman, Donnell W. 158a
Boaten, Frank E. 100a, 154b, 207b, 220b
Boatswain, E. 126b
The Bobbs-Merrill Co., Inc. 200a
Bober, A.S. 104a-b
Bobrishchev-Pushkin, V. 134a
Bockelmann, Oberbürgermeister 99a
Bocu Music Ltd. 29a
Bodington, Stephen 294b
The Bodley Head Ltd. 200a
Bofman, Robert 29a
Bog, Charles M. 120b, 122b
Boggs, Grace Lee 136a
Boggs, James 135b, 137b, 150a
Bögholm, K. 29b
Bohemia 200a
Böhm, Gerhard 122a
Böhme, Anita 98b
Böhme, Gotthard 98b
Bohr, Niels 287a
Niels Bohr's Secretariat 236b
Boiley, Michel 110a
Boissenot, M. 29b
Boissier-Palun, Leon 110b
Bokförlaget Natur och Kultur 200b
Boksenbaum, Martin 136a
Bolanos, Jorge 95b
Boler, John K. 82a, 295a
Bolivia **94a**
Bolkan, W. 122b
Böll, Heinrich 256b
Bolle, Maurice 97b, 98a-b
Bolshoi Ballet **141b**
Bolt, Robert 146b, 152a, 200b, 287a
Bolte, Paul 135b
Bolton Evening News 200b
Bomb-test suits 29b, 136b, 137a, 142a
Bomhard, Allan R. 295a
Bond, Craig A. 229b
Bond, I.D. 290a
Bond, James Arnold 150a
Bonetti, Alberto 29b
Boni and Liveright 200b
Bonner, C. Bradlaugh 85a, 274b
Bonner, Charles W. 287a
Bonner, Paul H. 240a
Bonnett, F.M. 29b
Bonnevie, Carl 29b
The Bonnier Magazine Group 200b
Bonny, R. 171a
Bonvoisin, Baron P. 87b
Bonyun, David A. 322b
Book News 200b
Book of the Month Club, Inc. 200b
Boole, George 322b
Booth, Albert 148b
Booth, Allan 235b
Booth, John Nicholls 200b
Boothby, Lord 177a, 257a
Boothman, Derek 53b
Boots the Chemists 164b
Bopin, Pho 94b
Boran-Hatko, Behice 106b
Borday, P.S. 295a
Border Impact 322b
Borel, E. 249b
Borell, Marta 117b
Borges, Roberto William 164b
Borgese, Elisabeth Mann 322b
Born, Gustav 149b, 257a
Born, Max 100a, 115a, 129b, 136a, 149a, 152b, 156b, 158a, 257a, 287a, 352a
Bornschein, Earl J. 29b
Bornstein, Steven A. 29b, 138b
Borra, Yvon 29b
Borrás, José García 287b
Borshchevsky, Shevach 113a
Borshchevsky, Zinaida 113a
Borsook, Eve 29b
Borzello, Robert 222a
Bos, José Martin-Chico 29b
Bos, Marianne 29b
Bosanquet, B. 349b
Bosch, José 175a
Boschi, Gaetano 322b
Bose, Nripendra Nath 23b
Bose, Somendraneth 229a
Bosgra, S. 179a
Boskovitz, Alfred 257a
Bossin, André 26b
Boston Globe 200b
Botril, Norbet 175a
Bottomly, Mr. 37a
Bouda 322b
Boudali, Nouri 113b
Boudin, Joseph 148b
Boudin, Leonard B. 133a, 136a, 138b-139b, 142b, 148b, 158a, 314a

Boudouresque, M. 151a
Boujasson, M. 31b
Boukema, H. J. 29b
Boulding, Kenneth E. 322b
Boulding for Congress 29b
Boulton, David 31a, 155a, 200b, 232a, 251a
Boulton, John 352b
Boulton, Peter L. 203a
Boumedienne, Houari 93a, 120a
Bourdet, Claude 29b, 58a, 142a, 200b, 207a
Bourne, H.E. 29b
Bouteflika, Abdelaziz 93a, 120a
Bouvier-Ajam, Solange 126a
Bovard, René 29b, 41a-b, 334a
Bowden, John 143a
Bowden, L.D. 323a
Bowen-Gotham, A. 146b
Bower, Cathie 241a
Bowes, Stuart 131b, 351a
Bowes, Wesley J. 148a
Bowles, J. 233b
Bowles, Philip 295a
Bowra, C.M. 352b
Bows?, C? B. 301a
Boxall, John 352b
Boxer Indemnity Advisory Committee 29b
Boy Scouts of Bengal 290a
Boyd, Andrew 95a
Boyd, David P. 290a
Boyd, Frances 29b
Boyd, J. Lister 276b, 292a
Boyd-Orr, Lord 27b, 30a, 133b, 149a, 287a, 290a, 351a
boyFrank, Manuel 30a
Boyko, Hugo 84b, 242a
Boyle, Sir Dermot 323a
Boynton, Robert W. 200b
Boytha, Dr. 201b
Bozic, Sreten N. 30a
Bozkus, C. 106b
Bozorgmehr, M. 103a
Braatov, Tryvge 323a
Braby, Joan 'Gogi' (later Mrs. Joan Lee Thompson) 271a, 288b, 292a
Brackman, Arthur 209b, 219b
Brackman, Selma 209b
Bradley, B.F. 323a
Bradley, Heather 137a, 223b
Bradley, J.L. 199a
Bradshaw, Thecla 234b
Brahms, Flemming 30a, 173b
Brain, Patricia 257a
Brain, Richard 226a
Brain, Russell 142a
Braine, John 152a, 314a
Brainwave 200b
Braithwaite, A. 65a
Braithwaite, E.R. 257a
Braithwaite, Philip B. 146a, 295a
Brakarenko, Maksim 134a
Brake, Ted 196b
Bramel, Mr. 156b
Brand, A.D. 223a
Brandenburg, Nelly Louise 323a
Brandhurst, Edward F. 257a
Brandi, Ida Maria Moretzsohn 171a
Brandon, J.W. 89b
Brandt, Annelie 121b
Brandt, Heinz 99a, 121b, 257a
Brandtzaeg, Brita 108a
Brandy, Carlos 323a
Branko, Rudolf 30a
Branner, H.C. 141b
Branson, Richard 235b
Brás, Juan Mari 158a
Brassloff, F.L. 99a-b
Bratby, John 30a
"Bratislava Conference" 126a
Braud, Jas. 116a
Brauer, Daniel 169a
Braund, D.G. 131b
Brauner, Clara 110b
Braverman, Harry 220b, 323a
Bray, Barbara 30a
Bray, J.M. 170a
Bray, Jill 352b
Brazil **94a, 120b, 171a**
Brazil, M.G. 126b
Brazzaville **95a-b**
Break the Nuclear Monopoly, Eliminate Nuclear Weapons 155b
Break-Through to Disarmament 30a
Breakthru: International Poetry Magazine 200b
Brecher, Howard 274b
Bredsdorff, Elias 141b, 292a, 323a, 351a
Breeze, Sonia 295a
Breit, Dr. 55b
Brem, Maxwell 175b
Brenan, Gamel 257a, 353a, 354a
Brenan, Gerald 257a, 353a, 354a
Brenan, Rhoda 310b, 353a
Brennan, Mr. 135a
Brennan, James 30a, 77a, 121b, 146b, 224b
Brenner, Otto 121b
Brereton, J.L. 80b
Breslau, Musia 135a
Brewer, Colin 30a
Brewer, Tom 33a, 118a, 165a, 166b
Brewin, Andrew 151b
Brezhnev, L. 116b
Bridel, Gaston 323a
Bridgman-Evans, R.H. 151a, 260a
Bridle, J.O. 239a
Briemberg, Mordecai 119a, 171b
Brier, Bob 30a
Brigade der Deutsch-Sowjetischen Freundschaft 30a
Briggs, Asa 176a
Briggs, Michael J. 200b
Briggs, Richard I. 323a
Brightman, C. 160a
Brighton College of Education Students' Union 295a
Brighton Defence Fund 30a
Brighton Kemp Town Labour Party 87b
Brighton Peace Action Group 30a
Brill, Klaus 257a
Brindley, Terry 30a, 164b
"Bring the Boys Home" Newsletter 170a
Bring the Troops Home Now Newsletter 30a
Briot, L.N. 170a
Briottet, M. 121a
Briottet, Roger 61b
Brisbane Friends of the United Nations 170a
The Brisbane Professionals for Peace 30a
Bristol Evening Post 183a
Bristol Peace Council 178a
Bristol Vietnam Concert Committee 30a-b
Bristow, D.E. 208b
Bristow, Peter 237a
Britain-Cuba Association 96a
The Britain-Tricontinental Organisation 295a
Britain-Vietnam Solidarity Front 178b
British Aid to Algeria Committee 87b, 127b
The British Alexander Defence Committee 130a
British Artists' Protest 164b
The British Association for World Government 30b
British Broadcasting Corporation 20a, 30b, 79a, 117a, 131b, 200b, 204a, 351b
British Campaign for Peace in Vietnam 30b, 164b
British Committee for Portuguese Amnesty 30b, 128a
British Committee for the Defence of Freedom in Iraq 126a
British Committee for the Defence of Human Rights in Iraq 126a, 154a
The British Council 257a, 295a
British Council for Peace in Vietnam 30b, 164b, **181a**, 354a
British Council for World Government 30b
British-Cuba Committee 30b, 152b
British Delegation 151a
British Delegation to Paris Conference 124a
British Eagle International Airlines 87b
British Embassy 121a, 276b
British Embassy in Athens 122b
British European Airways 87b
British Humanist Association 30b, 98b
British Humanist Society 295a
British Insurance Association 87b
The British Journal for the Philosophy of Science 322a, 336a
British Medical Journal 28b

British Motor Corporation 87b
British Movement for Freedom in Russia 30b
British Museum 257a, 279b
British Olivetti Ltd. 87b, 278b
The British Peace Committee 30b, 122b, 164b, 295a
British Poster Advertising Association 31a
British Printing Corporation 200b
British Red Cross Society 353a
British Secretary of State 70b
British Society for Social Responsiblity in Science 323a
British-Soviet Friendship 14a
British Soviet Friendship Committee 31a
The British Soviet Friendship Society 201a
The British Traders' Association 313b
British Travel 201a
British Universities' Ad Hoc Committee on Vietnam 165a
British-Vietnam Committee 118a, 153a, 178a, **180a**
British Weekly Ltd. 201a
British Who Killed Kennedy? Committee 50b
Brito, Mario Elisa de S. e 295a
Brittain, Vera 152a, 257a, 287a
Britten, Benjamin 31a, 152a, 287a
Britton, L. J. 227b
Britton, Lionel 257a
Brno District Manifestation for Peace 173a
Broad, C. D. 257a
Broadcasting Stockholm 196b
Broadhead, Geoff 147a
Brock, ? 31a
Brock, Hugh 88b, 211a, 219a, 225b, 227a, 277b
Brockway, Lord Fenner 31a, 107b, 108a, 114b, 118b, 121b, 131b, 142b, 151b, 154a, 166b, 176a, 178b, 181a, 287a, 290a, 292a
Broda, Christian 93b
Brody, L. B. 31a, 123a
Broide, Rachel 113a
Bromby, R. J. 209b
Bromley Technical College Students' Association 31a
Bronda, Antonio 201a, 238b, 239b
Bronfen, George B. 158a
Bronowski, Jacob 287a
Bronshteim, Elka 116a, 133b
Brook, Judy 31a, 123a, 301a
Brook, W. J. 87b
Brook Advisory Centres 323a
Brooke, Henry 123b
Brooke, Nancy 129b
Brookes, T. Cannon 313a
The Brookings Institution 201a
Brooks, Deirdre 231a
Brooks, Gordon 165a
Brooks, Jeremy 31a, 114a
Brooks, Olga 87b
Brooks, Rachel Gleason 257a
E. H. Brooks & Son 87b
Broomhead, Ann 257a
Brophy, Brigid 128a
Brothers, D. B. D. 201a
Brother's Face: A Bulletin of Council for Promotion of Communal Harmony 323a
Brothers to All Men 31a
Brotke, Rosemarie 175a
Brotman, A. G. 111b
Broughton, Viv 33a
Browder, Clara 87b
Brown, Mrs. 31a
Brown, A. J. 155b
Brown?, A. P. 267b
Brown, Alec 201a
Brown, Bill 167b
Brown, Freda 79a
Brown, Frank 257a
Brown, G. W. 257b
Brown, G. Rudstan 201a
Brown, George 17b, 154b
Brown, Harrison 31a
Brown, J. J. 126b
Brown, John 226a
Brown, Joseph E. 231b
Brown, Leonard 17b
Brown, Noel 126b
Brown, Tom 257b
Brown, Warwick D. 31a
Brown, Shipley & Co. Ltd. 307a, 308b
Brownbill, Eric J. 31b
Browne, Clarence F. 290a
Browne, Ken 301a
Browne, Martha 290a
Brownbill, Eric J. 31b
Brownlow, Donald G. 31b
Browns of Chester Ltd. 307a
BRSRS 323a
Bruce, David K. E. 25a, 118b, 133a, 134b, 135b, 138b
Bruce, M. C. 294a
Bruce, Richard H. 170a
Bruck, Carlheinz 122b
Bruck, Elsbeth 31b, 174b, 175a
Brüden, I. 257b
Brudno, Mollie R. 257b
Brun, Ellen 173a-b
Brune, David 257b
Brunner, Sir Felix 31b
Brunsdon, Jean 165a
Bruwer, André J. 165a
Bryan, Derek 95a
Bryant, B. 171b
Bryant, John 323b
Bryn Mawr Alumnae Bulletin 323b
Bryn Mawr College Library 201a
Buber, Martin 103b, 133b, 134a, 257b, 287a
Buccellato, Orio 295a
Buch, Evelyn C. 295a
Buch, T. 136b
Buchanan, Thomas G. 155a
Buchbinder, Heinrich 31b, 113b, 115b
Bucher, Ewald 99b, 122a
Buchrer, Edwin T. 201a
Buck, Pearl 42a
Buckland, Richard 309a
Buckley, Marjorie 323b
Buckman, Peter 201a, 220a
Budai, Leslie 124b
Budiý, L. J. 202b
Buffard, Henri 323b
Bugentel, J. F. T. 201a
Buhaire, E. M. 295a
Building Workers' Industrial Union of Australia 126b, 169b, 170a
Bulgaria **94a-b, 171b**
Bulgarian Embassy 33b
Bulgarian Peace Committee 171b
Bulgarian Radio and Television 201a
Bulkeley, G. 87b
Bulkeley, J. 56a
Bullard, ? 29a
Bulletin 141a
Bulletin; Front Nasional Pembebasan Vietnam Selatan 190a
Bulletin of the Atomic Scientists 142a, 155a-b, 201a, 323b
Bulletin of the People's Socialist Party 130a
Bulletin of the Workers' Control Conference 323b
Bulletin of the World Council of Peace 153a
Bullock, Lawrence F. 170b
Bunche, Ralph J. 147b
Bundesjustizministerium 100a
Der Bundesminister des Auswärtigen 99b
Bundespräsidialamt 99b
Bunge, Mario 257b
Bunnell, Fred 62b
Bunri Shoin, International Division 104b
Buny, P. 255a
Bunyan, Tony 148a, 206b
Burbank, W. N. L. 257b
Burchett, G. H. 180a
Burchett, Wilfred 16a, 31b, 158a, 165a, 171b, 186a-187a, 188b, 189a
Burdett, Maud 257b
Burdon, K. 65b
Bureau Africain d'Information 31b
Bureau Hongrois pour la Protection des Droits d'Auteur 201b
Bureau of the International Conference for Solidarity with the People of Vietnam 162b
Bureau of the International Conference for Solidarity with the People of Vietnam against US Imperialist Aggression and for the Defence of Peace 105b, 190a
Burger, Henry G. 323b
Burgess, Jain 295a

Burgess, Tyrrell 237a
Burgin, Ida 135a-b
Burhop, E.H.S. 31b, 126a, 182a, 290a, 295a, 332b
Burkat, Leonard 288a
Burke, Kenneth 31b
Burke's Peerage 201b, 276b
Burkov, Boris 224b
Burleigh, Lionel 201b
Burleson, Donald R. 290a
Burma **94b, 120b, 171b**
Burn, Mary 257b, 292a, 301a
Burn, Michael 257b, 292a, 301a
Burn & Berridge 309a
Burnaby, J. 283b
Burnet, Alastair 207a
Burnets & Co. 307a
Burnett, Ed 31b
Burnett, I.B. 36b
Burnett, Piers 117b, 206a
Ed Burnett, Inc. 31b
Burnham, Colin 201b
Burns, John O'Malley 139a
Burns, Peter 142b
Burns, Ray D. 79b, 171b
Burnstall, Christopher 200b
Buro, Andreas 31b, 50a, 61b, 100a
Burris, Barbara 31b
Burroughs Corporation 87b
Burrows, William E. 240a
Burt, Maud K. 257b
Burton, Mr. 135a
Burton, Sir Edward 279b
Burton, H. 323b
Burton, John W. 323b
Burton, Steven J. 133a
Busby, H. Duane 31b
Bush, T.N.W. 32b
Bushkoff, Mrs. E. 117a
Butcher, Margaret 295a
Butler, H.M. 256a
Butler, Joyce 31b, 117b
Butler, Nevile 29b
Butler, R.A. 130b
Butler, R.A.B. 292a
Butler, Sidney G. 57b
Butlin, Pat 294a
Butlin, Wendy 251b
Butt, Joyce R. 31b
Butter, Sam 53b
Butters, John H. 31b
Butterworth, C.R. 212a
Butterworth, Geoffrey 295a
Butterworth, Liebet 278b
Buxton, Jane 31b, 87b
Buxton, Ronald 116b
Byng, Robert 114b
Bynner, Bill 31b
Bynum, Terrell Ward 257b
Byrd, ? 292a
Byrne, Evelyn B. 202b
Byrne, Kevin 201b
Buzań, Tony 214a

C

C. Jefe del Departamento de Prevencion 106a
Caamano, Francisco 97a
Cable, J.E. 114a, 118b
Cabral, Amilcar 158a
Cabrera, Guillermo 216a
Cadart, Claude 161a
Cadbury, Michael 227a
Cadogan, Peter 102b, 155b, 227a, 234b, 251a-b
The Cadogan Hotel 276b
Caesar, Irving 323b
Cahane, Elisabeth 110a
Cahiers pour l'Analyse 201b
Cahill, Rowan John 170b
Cahn, Regina 113a
Caine, Sidney 154a
Calder, Alexander 31b
Calder, Ritchie 31b, 93a, 142b
Calder and Boyars 177a
John Calder (Publishers) 117b, 177a, 201b
Caldorin, Adilcio 165a
Caldwell, Julius A. 32a
Caldwell, Malcolm 32a, 148a, 160a, 165a, 176b, 177a, 188a
The Calgary Herald 26a
Calhoun, D. Morris 295a
California Law Review 201b
California State College Teach-In 165a
The California Tech 201b
Callado, Antonio 32a
Callinan, Michael 95b, 121a
Calverd, Alan 32a
Calwell, Arthur A. 147a
Çambel, Perihan 131a
Cambodia **94b, 171b**
Cambodia, Chef du Cabinet 94b
Cambrian News 201b
Cambridge Free Front 32a
Cambridge Magazine 9b
Cambridge Opinion 112a, 201b
Cambridge Review 201b
The Cambridge Society of Bombay 295a
Cambridge Union Society 257b
Cambridge University 283b
Cambridge University Campaign for Nuclear Disarmament 32a
Cambridge University—Magpie and Stump 257b
Cambridge University Press 201b
Cambridge University United Nations Association 201b
Camera Press 201b
Cameron?, Alistair 257b
Cameron, Clyde R. 147b
Cameron, Elizabeth 257b
Cameron, Ewan 202a
Cameron, Hamish 257b
Cameron, James 139b, 158a, 165a, 205a
Cameron, Louis-Jacques 32a
Cameron?, Peggy 257b
Cameroons **94b, 120b**
Camey, Elizabeth Ann 32a
Cammack, Edward 87b
Camon, Dr. 138a
Campagna per Disarmo Nucleare 32a
Campaign against Imperialism 152a
Campaign Caravan Workshops 131b
Campaign for a World Constituent Assembly 32a
Campaign for Nuclear Disarmament 10b, 18a, 114b, 165a, 178a, 251a, 295a
CND North-West Regional Committee 154b
Campaign for Peace in Vietnam 32a, 165a
The Campaign for the Liberation of the Trotskyists Jailed in Mexico 127b
Campaign in Oxford University for Nuclear Disarmament 202a
Campbell, Craig, S. 32a
Campbell, Douglas K. 32a
Campbell, Janice 173a
Campbell, Jock 32a, 142a
Campbell-Purdie, Wendy 32a
Campus Kaleidoscope 202a
Camus, William 202a
Canada **94b, 171b-172b**
Canada-Vietnam Newsletter 171b, 323b
Canadian Broadcasting Corporation 202a, 341b
Canadian Campaign for Nuclear Disarmament 32b, 94b
Canadian Committee for the International War Crimes Tribunal 17a, 172a
Canadian Dimension 171b, 202a
Canadian Institute of International Affairs 94b
Canadian Peace Research Institute 32b
The Canadian Press 202a
Cañaveral, M. Parra 32b
Çandar, Cengiz 84b
Cande, Daniel 202a
Cañedo y Cañedo, Cristina María 259b
Cañero, J. 294a
Cang, Joel 40a, 112a
Cannon Brookes & Odgers 313a
Cant, Catherine B.H. 257b
Cantor, ? 327a
Canvia, Alfredo Ovando 94a
Caparros, Antonio 141a
Jonathan Cape Limited 117b, 140a, 202a, 278b
Capella, Basil 70b
Capitini, Aldo 104b
Capland, Bob 295a
Capland, Dawn 295a
Capps, Arthur W. 323b
Caputo, Livio 208a
The Caravel Press 143a, 202a
Carballo, Fernanda 130b
Carbe, André H. 174b
Cardenas, ? 173a

Cárdenas, Lázaro 32b, 136a, 157a, 192a, 295a
Cardiff Peace Committee 32b
Cardinale, H. E. 109a
Cardinas, ? 95b
Care Marcel 174a
Careswell, John 33a
Carew, Virginia 210a
Carey, Richard 242b
Cariboni, Raúl 149b
Cargell, Oscar 234a
Carlin, R. H. 172a
Carlson, Chris 32b
Carlson, John Roy 143a
Carlson, Sven 211a
Carlyle, Thomas 352b
Carmichael, Neil 148a
Carmichael, Stokely 15b, 17a, 139b, 157a, 189b, 192a
Carmiel, Y. 257b
Carnap, Rudolf 139b, 257b
Carney, Dale 290a
Carol, Becker 134b
Caron, Herbert S. 112a, 134a
Carpenter, D. J. 239b
Carr, E. H. 148a
Carreras, José 295a
Carrington, J. F. C. 175b
Carritt, Joan 84b, 166b, 168b
Carroll, Jane 32b
Carroquino, J. 32b
Carr-Saunders, A. M. 333a
Carter, Elsie 312a
Carter, John 267a
Carter, Michael J. 32b
Carter, Norwood 323b
Carver Centennial Committee, George Washington 257b
Carver, David 214b, 295b
Cary, Alexis 174a
Casa de las Americas 95b
Casa della Culture e della Ricreazione 32b
Casad, R. H. 130a
Casalini, Mario 225a
Casals, Pablo 32b, 149a, 174a, 287a-b
Casany, Enrique Iardí 202a
Casartelli, Victorio 95b
Case, Elisabeth 239a
Case, James 150a
Casella, Alberto T. 197b
Cash, T. 278b
Cashman, Margaret J. 167b
Caspar, John 142a
Cassirer, Eva 323b, 351a
Casson, Lewis 271b, 287a
Castellui, Catalana 295a
Castle, Barbara 129b
Castro, C. O. Corrêa de 171a
Castro, Fidel 95b, 152b, 163a, 172b
Castro, José Luna 109a
Catalyst 202b
Cator, Dorothy 353a
Cates, Lillian Dorothy 295a
Catherman, Terence F. 273b
The Catholic Herald 231a
Catholic Peace Fellowship 165a
Catlin, George E. Gordon 142b, 258a, 287a
Catling & Son 258a
Catroux, René 127b
Caulkett, Roger 143a
Caullet, Jean 61b
Caussin, Ricardo Zabala 172b
Cavalier Magazine 202b
Cavallo, Marino 226a
Cavara, Paolo 87b
Cavell, G. 73a
Cavendish, A. P. 87b
Caxton Hall 156a
CBA International 145a, 154a
CBL FM (Toronto) 341b
Ceausescu, Nicolae 110a
Ceauşu, Leiba 110a
Ceccatto, G. N. 121a
Celebration of "October 28th, 1940" 123b
Celebrity Bulletin 143a
Celebrity Register 324a
Ceniza, Claro R. 324a
Centenaire de Romain Rolland 258a
Center for the Study of Armament and Disarmament 32b
Center for the Study of Democratic Institutions 32b, 40a, 147b
The Center Magazine 258a
Central Commission for the Prosecution of War Crimes in Poland 98a
The Central Committee of the Repatriation of the Greek Refugees 124a
Central Office of Information 202b, 284b
Central Police Headquarters, Manchester 144b
Central Standing Committee of General Association of Korean Residents in Japan 127a
Centre d'Études Nucléares de Saclay 202b
The Centre for Group Studies 106b
Centre House 202b
Centre International pour le Développement 142b
Centre Liegeois d'Action pour la Non-Violence 32b
Centro di Studio e Documentazione sul Vietnam e Il Terzo Mondo 165a
Centro Studie Iniziative per la Piena Occupazione 32b, 127b, 149a
The Century Co. 202b
Celli, Anne 28b
Cercle Laique d'Etudiants de Grenoble 174a
CERGE 32b, 135b, 138b
Cerid, Munir 168a
Cerulli, Enrico 294a
Cerveny, F. M. 32b
Ceskoslovenský Novinár 202b
Ceylon **94b-95a, 120b, 172b**
Ceylon Rationalist Association 172b
Cha, Louis 220b
Chaabi, M. 131a
Chadha, P. C. 102b
Chadwick, D. 238b
Chadzicki, Eugeniuz 196b
Chaffey, F. W. Hayman 204b
Chagall, Marc 33a
Chaim, Mr. 272a
Chakeri, K. 48b, 125a
Chakotin, Serge 33a
Chakrabarti, Atulanada 110b, 202b
Chakrabarti, Raiharan 290a, 324a
Chakraborty, Arun Kumar 202b
Chakraborty, S. 168b
Chaliand, Gérard 188b, 190a
Challenge 202b
Chalmers, Mrs. N. 65b
Chamarro, Eduardo 202b
Chamberlaine Brothers & Edwards 154b
Chamberlin, Mark A. 137a
Chambers 122b
Chambers, Bertram M. 258a
Chambers, Bette 149b, 165a, 255b
Chambers, John 143a
Chambers, Judy 143a
Chambrun, Jacques 202b
Champney, Horace 150a
Chamungwana, G. M. 33a
Chance, Roger 258a
Chand, Bool 24a
Chander, Satish 222b
Chandler, Lloyd 87b, 116a
Chandra, Romesh 291b
Chandrasekhar, S. 228b
Chandvadkar, Neela 153b
Chang, Francis W. 97b
Chang, Siang-mei 258a
Chang, Stephen 299b
Chan-Lieu, Dang 157a
Chao, Buwei 292a
Chao, Yuen Ren 258a, 278a, 292a
Chaplin, Charlie 287a
Chaplin, Henry 247a
Chaplin, Susan 112a
Chapman, Mrs. (Elizabeth Goucher) B. Burgoyne 87b-88a, 169a-b
Chapman, D. R. 147a
Chapman, Dan 142a
Chapman, Meg 33a
Chapman, Priscilla 236a
Chapman, Raynor D. 199a
Chapman & Hall Ltd. 202b
Chappelow, Alan 324a
Charge d'Affaires of the People's Republic of China in the United Kingdom 95a
Charles, Arthur 295a
Charles, D. 147b
Charles, John H. 295a

The Charlotte Observer 123a
Charlton, J. 203a
Charochandra College Teachers' Council 102b
Chase, G.R.H. 143a
Chatgopakar, V.M. 222b
Chatroussat, Jet S. 33a
Chatterji, N. 258a
Chattillon, Jean 171b
Chattopadhyay, Santinath 33a, 202b
Chaudhuri, Asim Kumar 102b
Chaudhuri, Sanjib 299b
Chaudhuri, Zahid 109a, 226b
Chauncey, Henry 258a
Chauvel, Jean 97b
Chauvin, Jean René 33a
Chebila, Mohammed 120a
Chef Adjoint de la Représentation Permanente du Front National de Libération du Sud Vietnam en URSS 162a
Chef des Bundeskanzleramtes 99b
Chemical and Biological Warfare Group 165a
Chemins de Fer Britanniques 143a
Chen, John P.H. 203a
Chen, Yu-hsi 97a
Cheney, Howard 33a
Cheng, Jane 161a
Cheng, Lily 174a
Chernenkoff, John J. 37a
Cherry, Hugh 146a
The Chesapeake and Ohio Railway Co. 115b, 142b
Chesneaux, Jean 165a, 173b, 188a
Chessman, A. 352b
Chessum, L.P. 178b
Chessum, Richard 178b
Chester, Helen 295a
Chester Council for Peace in Vietnam 165a
Chester Telephone Area 88a, 148b
Chesters, Mary Walsh 258a
Chesterton & Sons 307b, 313a
Chevassut, F.G. 258a
Chevreuse, Jacques 324a
Chevrier, D. 88a
Chiari, Roberto 109a
Chiba, Hideo 33a, 115b
Chicago Sun-Times 202b
Chicago Tribune 118b, 138a, 202b
Chichester Promoter 203a
Chief Justice of the American Judiciary 85b
Chief Rabbi of Israel 112a
Chilba, Yoshio 25b
Chilcot, J.A. 114b
Child & Co. 281b, 296a, 307a
Childs-Fleet 280b
Chile **95a, 172b**
China **95a, 120b, 172b**
Chinese Ministry of Information 338a
Chinese People's Committee for World Peace 176a-b
The Chinese (Students) Association for the Promotion of Education 258a
Chingford Nuclear Disarmament Committee 33a
Chiolkosz, Adam 109b
Chiriboga, Jose Cherrez 146a
Chirimo 203a
Chirinos, Edmundo 132a
Chirinos, Jorge 165a
Chisholm, Grace 271a
Chisholm, John 203a
Chislehurst Constituency Labour Party 33a
Chitty, Christopher 33a
Cholewa, Kazimierz 33a
Chomsky, Noam 140a, 324a, 351a
Chorley, Lord 33a, 115a, 126a, 203a
Choroszewski, Jan 109b
Chou En-lai 95a, 110b, 120b, 176a, 251b
Chou Pao-li 227b
Choublarian, Rouben 112b
Chowdhury, Ambikagiri Roy 33a
Christchurch Press 146b
Christchurch Star 146b
Christen, H. 216b
Christensen, Ulf 227a
Christian, Gerald 324a
Christian Action 129b
Christian Life Press 203a
Christian Science Monitor 119a, 203a
Christian Service Association 153b
Christianity and Crisis 53b
Christians, Rudolph 324a
Christiansen, Elspeth 14a, 33a, 169a
Christie, Jean 88a
Christie, Stuart 130b
Christis, Phoebus S. 96a
Christlich-Demokratische Union Deutschlands 290a
Christofinis, Dr. 295a
Chu, Ma Thi 165a, 190a
The Chubu Nippon Shimbun 203a
Chumak, Peter 225a
Chuong, Pham Van 162b, 176a
Chuong, Tham Van 163a
CHURCH 33a
The Churchman 203a
Ciafanelli, Renzo 204a
Ciapessoni, Donatella 221a
Cichoski, Aleksander 98a, 241b
Cifarelli, Antonio Pippo 324a
Cini, Marcelo 160a
Cioffi, Frank 154b
Ciotori, D.N. 133a
Citizens' Committee for Disarmament 33a
Citizens Committee of Inquiry 133a, 136a
Citizens' Committee for Nuclear Disarmament, San Francisco 118a
Citizens for Governmental Restraint, Inc. 33b, 165a
Citizens Protest 165a
Citrynell, Harold 295a
City & West End Properties Ltd. 313a
City Law College Dacca 295a
City of Manchester Conservative Association 146b
City of Nottingham Public Libraries 258a
Civilian Establishment and Pay Office, U.K. 131b
Claesseno, J. 60b
Clar, E. 290a
Clare 203a
The Clarendon Press 203a
Clark, Ann 126b
Clark, Elizabeth M. 224a
Clark, George 33b, 156a, 295a
Clark, Grenville 33b, 137b
Clark, Irene 295a
Clark, K.B. 44a
Clark, Kenneth B. 14a, 137b, 138b, 258a
Clark, Mrs. Kenneth B. 258a
Clark, Len 33b
Clark, Robert K.F. 172a
Clark, Ronald W. 258a, 301a
Clark, Stevenson P. 192a
Clark, Thomas Lawson 137a
Clark, Webber D. 88a
Clark, William 61b
Grenville Clark Institute for World Law 33b
Clarke, C.R.A. 88a
Clarke, Francis 258a
Clarke, James 328a
Clarke, M.R. 202a
Clarke, Mary 115b
Clarke, Pat 164b
Clarke, Richard 31a
Clarke, Tom 324a
Classic 37b
Claude, Lily 161a
Clauet, Jean Pierre 174a
Clausen, Christa 48b
Cleage, Jr., Albert B. 182a
Cleanthous, A. 96a
Cleaver, Eldridge 258a
Clegg, R. 147a
Clemens, Cyril 219b, 297b
Clemens, Jr., Walter C. 203a
Clement, William C. 324a
Clements, Dick 203b
Clements, F.G. 297b
Clements, Richard 176b, 237b-238a
Clemmer, Robert E. 324a
Clerc, Michel 226b
Clerical and Administrative Workers' Union 115b
Cleveland Committee on Soviet Anti-Semitism 112a, 134a
The Cleveland Press 352a
Clifford, Harry W. 33b, 150a
The Cloister Press Limited 203a
Clough, Neal J. 216a

Club de Amigos de la UNESCO de Barcelona 203a
Clugston, W.G. 237b
Clyne Radio Ltd. 88a
Coates, Helen 287a
Coates, Ken 14b, 33b, 80b, 95b, 113a, 114b, 118b, 128b, 196b, 203a-b, 206b, 211a, 220b, 224a, 234a, 240b, 300a, 342a
Coates, R.A. 81a
Cobb, Charles 188a
Cobden, Richard 350a
Cobell, Denis 295b
Cockburn, Alex 33b
Cockerell, Sir Sidney 258a, 280a
Codr, Milan 242b
Coen, Fausto 226a
Coggan, Geoffrey 28a, 33b, 172a, 185a, 211a, 237a
Cohen, Betty 258b
Cohen, David 112a
Cohen, Elka 225b
Cohen, Geula 219a
Cohen, Robert David 204a
Cohen, Robert S. 165a
Cohen, Sam 87a
Cohn, Howard 226b
Cohn-Michel, Moritz 110a
Cohn, Regina 133b
Colaabavala, F. 33b, 200a
Colasante, Peter 60a-b, 108a
Cole, K.D. 88a
Coleman, Daniel 33b, 227a, 229a
Colenberg, Mabel 310b
Collectif Intersyndical pour la Paix au Vietnam 165a
College of Cardinals 62a
Collet's Holdings Ltd. 88a
Collette-Kahn, S. 128b
Collick, Percy 116a
Collier, William L. 88a
Collier-Macmillan Ltd. 203a
Collins, Ellen E.H. 122b
Collins, L.J. 309b
Collins, L. John 59a, 93a, 251a, 252a, 258b
Collins, Marjory 33b, 150a
Collins, Jr., F. Warren 33b
Collins & Collins 309b
Collins Publishers 203b
Colloms, Albert Lionel 88a, 98b, 99b, 290a
Colne, Judith 33b, 127a
Colonial Office 37a
Columbia **172b**
Columbia Broadcasting Corporation 351b
Colwell, Anthony 202a
Comas, Antonio 231b
Combat 183a
Combined Universities Campaign for Nuclear Disarmament 33b, 203a
Comfort, Alex 115b, 152a, 182a, 290a
Comiskey, N.R. 37b, 142b
Il Comitato della Pace di Pesaro e Urbino 33b
Comitato Italiano per il Disarmo Atomico 203b
Comitato per la Settimana di Agitazione per il Vietnam 17a, 165a
Comité Algérien de la Paix 151a, 156b
Comite Asopes 122b
Comité Belge Contre la Préscription des Crimes Nazis 98a
Comité Central des Réfugiés Politiques de Grèce 101a, 124a
Comite Cubano de Solidaridad con el Pueblo de Viet Nam 295b
Comité Cubano de Solidaridad con Viet-Nam del Sur 95b, 157b
Comité d'Action des Intellectuels pour les Etudiants 165a
Comité d'Action Intellectuals Vietnamiens 162a
Comité d'Action pour l'Exposition 33b, 110b
Comite de Defensa de los Derechos Humanos 295b
Comite de Defensa do los Presos Politicos en Mexico 127b
Comité de Solidarité à la Révolution Kurde 173b-174a
Comité de Solidarité à la Révolution Yéménite 119a
Comité de Solidarité Belgique-Vietnam 170b
Comité d'Organisation du Colloque International 11b
Comité Haitien Dominicain de Solidarité 101b
Comité Hellenique pour la Détente Internationale et la Paix 100b, 124a
Comité Intellectuels Vietnam 295b
Comité International de la Croix-Rouge 134b
Comité International pour la Défense des Droits de l'Homme 116b
Comité International pour l'Amnistie aux Detenus Politiques et le Respect des Droits de l'Homme en Irak 126b
Le Comite Iranien de Defense à Bucharest 125b
Comite Mexicano de Solidaridad con Vietnam 295b
Comité National Coordinador del Apoyo a la Revolución Cubana 115a
Le Comité National des Artistes du Japon 144b
Comité Organizador de la Organizacion Latinoaméricana de Solidaridad 95b
Comité Portugal Libre 109b
Comité pour la Défense d'Ahmed Ben Bella 120a
Comité Senegalais de Soutien au Vietnam 33b-34a
Comité Viet Nam National 161a
Comité Vietnam de Toulon 174a
Commercial Bank of Australia 169b
Commission de rédaction des oeuvres complètes de N.I. Lobatchevsky 258b
Commission D'Histoire de la Fédération Internationale des Resistants 97b
Commission for Investigation of the U.S. Imperialist War Crimes in Vietnam 163a
Commission on US War Crimes 163a
Commissioners of Inland Revenue 309b
Committee Against the Blockade of Cuba 34a
Committee for Afro-Asian People's Solidarity of Thailand 113b
Committee for "Alternatives to Violence" 203b
Committee for April 17 March Against the War in Vietnam 165a
Committee for Biafran Artists 34a
Committee for Cultural Relations with Foreign Countries, Information Department, Hanoi 165a
Committee for Democratic Rights in the U.S.A. 34a, 135a, 333a
Committee for Freedom in Mozambique 110a
Committee "For Freedom of Heinz Brandt" 121b
Committee for G.I. Rights 34a, 139b
Committee for Human Rights 122a
Committee for May 10th Demonstration 34a
Committee for Nonviolent Action 34a, 136b
Committee for Nuclear Disarmament London Region 326b
Committee for Nuclear Disarmament of the Arab-Israeli Region 34a, 104a, 107a
Committee for Solidarity with the Victims of Repression in Peru 34a, 128a
Committee for the Defence of Obi B. Egbuna 131b
The Committee for the Defence of the Iraqi People 126a
Committee for the Defence of the Iraqi People, Leipzig 126a
Committee for the Defence of the Kurdish People's Rights 125b, 126b
Committee for the English Publication of *Vietnam–A Voice from the Villages* 165a
Committee for the Freedom of

William Worthy 137a
Committee for the Protection of Human Rights 122a
Committee for the Release of the Detainees in British Guyana 101b
Committee for the Release of Greek Political Prisoners 122b
Committee for the Release of Political Prisoners in Venezuela 132a
Committee for Vietnam Protest 170a
Committee Moratoire du Vietnam 295b
Committee of Afro-Asian and Caribbean Organizations 129b
Committee of Americans Abroad for an Honorable Foreign Policy 34a, 165a-b
Committee of Families of Political Detainees in Muar and Batu Gajah Detention Camps 127a
Committee of Fifth Marathon March for Peace 100b
Committee of Indian Parliamentarians for Peace 102b
Committee of 100 11a-b, 12a, 69a, 131a, 152a, 154b, 155b, 179a, 218b, 234b, 251b, 252a, 310a-b, 324b
Committee of 100 in Greece 100b
Committee of 100, London 165b, 251b, 280a
Committee of Seven to Appeal for World Peace 105a
Committee of Struggle Against U.S. and Henchmen's Persecution of Intellectuals in South Vietnam 162a, 178a
Committee of Struggle Against U.S. Imperialists 118a
Committee of the Iranian National Front in West Berlin 124b
Committee on Vietnam 147b, 165b
Committee to Aid the Bloomington Students 88a, 137b
Committee to Aid the Monroe Defendants 34a
The Committee to Celebrate the 90th Birthday Anniversary of Dr. Harry F. Ward 258b
Committee to Defend the French Students 34a, 97b
Committee to Defend the Rights of P.F.C. Howard Petrick 139b
Committee to Explore Trade Possibilities with the People's Republic of China 155a-b
Committee to Fight U.S. Imperialism 68b
Committee to Free Morton Sobell 290a
Committee to Honor Dr. Willard Uphaus 137b
Committee to Uphold the Right to Travel 137b
Common Cause Publications Ltd. 203b
Commonwealth Trading Bank of Australia 170a
Communications of the Dublin Institute for Advanced Studies 325a
Communicorp Public Relations 203b
Communist Party of Germany 99a
Communist Party of Great Britain 34a, 115b, 152b
The Communists (Stockholm) 34b
"Communists, Democrats & Trade Unionists, UAR" 131a
Communita Europea degli Scrittori 284a
Community Television of Southern California 150a
Compagnia Edizioni Internationali 203b
Companhia Carris de Ferro de Lisboa 128b
Compass and Fleet 19a, 203b
The Compleat Imbiber 203b
The Concept of Pakistan 203b
Concerned Citizens 34b
Concerned Citizens of Palo Alto 165b
Concord Films Council 34b
Confederation of Iranian Students 103a, 106b, 125a, 295b
Confederation of Iranian Students, Hamburg 125b
Conference Against Repression in Spain 14b, 130b
Conference Committee for the Public Interest 290b
Le Conférence des Sommets 94a, 258b
Conference for a General Amnesty for the Detainees and Political Exiles and for the Rights of Man in Greece 122b
Conference for the Denuclearisation of the Mediterranean 13b
Conference in Opposition to the War in Vietnam 14a
Conference Internationale de Solidarité avec le Peuple Vietnamien 165b, 170b
Conference of Study of the Situation of the Jewish Minority in the USSR 112a
Conference of the International Confederation for Disarmament and Peace 13a
Conference of the Japan Council Against Atomic and Hydrogen Bombs 104b
Conference of Uncommitted Nations 11a
Conference of World Freethinkers 19a
Conference on Human Rights in the Middle East 105b
Conference on "World Government" 12a
Conference on the Situation of Jews in the Soviet Union 112b
Conference pour la Denuclearisation du Bassin Méditerraneen sur Mer et sur Terre 106b
Conferenza Europea per L'Amnistia dei Detenuti Politica e per le Liberta Democratiche in Venzuela 132a
Congo **95a-b, 121a, 152a**
Congres des Droits de l'Homme 107a
Congreso Republica, Venezuela 295b
Congress for Cultural Freedom 34b
Congress for Disarmament and International Cooperation 34b
Congress for International Cooperation and Disarmament 170a
Congress of Canadian Women 126a, 172a
The Congress of Scientists on Survival 34b
Congress of the Confederation of Iranian Students 125a
Congressional Record 190b, 326a
Conklin, Geoffrey Reed 136a
Conn, Goldberg & Co. 88a
Connections Inc. 203b
Conseil Central des Comités Antidictatoriaux Grecs 101a
Conseil Federal Espagnol 34b
Conseil National des Victimes Spoliés d'Allemagne 98a
Conseil National du Mouvement de la Paix 173b
Conseil Suprême de l'Intellectualité Mondiale 258b
Consolidated Stock 313a
Constable & Maude 309a, 312a
Constandopoulos, Nicos 100b
Constantina, Vlasceanu 129a
Constantinou, Constantinos D. 122b
Constantopoulos, N. 123b
Consulat Général de France 97b
Consulta Calalrese per la Pace 203b
Contemporary British Philosophy 333a
Contemporary Films Ltd. 130b
Contemporary Issues 140a
Contemporary Press 34b, 204a
Continental Congress of Solidarity with Cuba 12a, 94a, 95b, 152b
Continuing Committee of the Pugwash Conferences on Science and World Affairs 351b
Continuum 204a
Continuum 1 Ltd. 290b
Controversy 204a
Conway, John 143a, 166b
Cook, ? 219a
Cook, August E. 301a

Cook, Clifford 89b
Cook, David 204b
Cook, E.O. 34b
Cook, Fred J. 34b, 125a, 135b, 138a, 142b
Cook, John William 141a
Cook, Judith 80b
Cooke, Mr. 211a
Cooke, Alistair 51b
Cooke, L. 88b
Cookson, Sybil 34b, 93b
Cooper, Chester L. 118b, 138b
Cooper, Sheila 146a
Cooper-Willis, Irene 258b
Cooper-Willis, Mrs. Susan 276a-b
Co-operative Bookshop Ltd. 34b
Cooperative Retail Services 88a
Coordinating Committee for International Service 34b
Cope, K. 204a
Copi, Irving M. 258b
Copleston, Frederick C. 258b
Coppock, Sir Richard 351a
Coppola, Pasquale 204b
Corbet-Milward, Commander 34b, 242a
Cordy, J.K. 203a
Corneliani, Gaetana E. 34b
Cornelius, A.R. 158a
Cornell, Tom 165a
Cornell Daily Sun 204a
Cornil, Maurice 158a
El Corno Emplumado 204a
Coronet 10b
Correa, L.Y. 171a
Corridon, Juliana M. 34b
Corriere della Sera 104b, 204a
Corvin, Dowall 297a
Cosmopolitan Contact 204a
Cosmopolitan Institute of Public Affairs 34b
Cossio, Carlos 141a
Costantopoulas, N. 123b
Costello, Christopher 35a
Cosyn, Maurice R. 32a, 164a
Cotlar, Mischa 47b, 136b, 141a
Cotti-Cometti, Giampiero 165a, 204a
Cottino, Amedeo 127a
Cottman, Kenneth 114a, 131a
Cotton, Eugenie 151b, 173b
Couey, Edithe Durham 295b
Couland, Jacques 126b
Coulson, C.A. 115b
Council for Democracy 204a
Council for the Advancement of Arab-British Understanding 107a
Council of African Organizations 119a, 165b
Council of Scientific and Industrial Research 204a
Country Beautiful 137b
Coupal, Roy 88a
Couret, Bernard 187b, 188b
Couroucis, Evangelos 35a, 122b
Courquin, Jean-François 174a
Coursault, P. 121a
Courtauld, A.C.C. 238a
Courtenay, R.D. 204a
Court of Governors, LSE 154a
Coury, Henri 156a
Cousens, Dorothy 258b, 292a
Cousins, Frank 35a, 78a, 129b
Cousins, Norman 70a, 232b
Couteau, Pierre 126a
Coventry Cathedral 88a
Coventry Centre for Socialist Education 114b
Covietnamex 165b
Cowan, Kenneth D. 297a
Coward, R.C. 216b
Coward, Chance & Co. 88a, 223b, 277a, 279a, 281a, 307b, 309a, 310a, 312a, 314a
Coward-McCann, Inc. 204a
Cowell, David 216b
Cowell, F. Richard 258b
Cowlishaw, David 156b
Cox, Barry 59a
Cox, Courtland 158a
Cox, Edwin H. 91b
Cox, John 295a
Coxon, Anthony P.M. 223a
Coy, F.C. 271b
Coy, Frederick W. 258b
Coyle, Paddy M. 98b
Coyne, Charles 30b
Craft, Michael 33b, 47a, 65b
Craig, David B. 13a, 118a
Craig, Thomas 256a
Craig, William Boyd 222b
Cramb, B.W. 169b
Crane-Robinson, C. 133a, 134b
Crankshaw, Edward 35a
Crautzfeldt, O. 98a, 122a
Craver, W.T. 35a, 175a
Crawford, Corine L. 204a
Crawshay-Williams, Elizabeth 258b
Crawshay-Williams, Rupert 165a, 257a, 258b, 292a
Creasy, John 324a
Creedy, F. 324a-b
Creighton, H. Campbell 111b
Cremona, L. 7a
Crenshaw, Louise 292a
The Crest 204b
Creutzfeldt, O. 122a
Rupert Crew Ltd. 204b
Crichton, Dorothy 35a
Crickhowell Riding Club 277a
Crighton?, Clare 353a
Crilson, Mrs. M.J. Llewellyn 295b
Cripps, Raymond W. 204b
Critica Marxista 204b
Crnobrnja, Bogdan 132a
Crocker, Ruth 35a
Crocker, William Charles 309b
Crombie, Juliet 208b
Cromie, Donald 239a
Crone, Winifred 258b
Cronk, G.F. 137b
Crookston, Peter 224b
Cropper, Frank 35a, 52b
Crosbie, Philip 3a
Cross, Elizabeth 310b
Cross, Ephraim 88a
Cross Currents 204b
Crosser, Paul 35a, 295b, 324b
Crossword 324b
Crowe, Geoffrey C. 236b
The Crowell-Collier Educational Corporation 204b
Crown, Joseph H. 52b, 166b
Crown Publishers, Inc. 204b
Crucible 351a, 353a
Cruel Sports 324a
Crunden, Alice 258b, 282b, 283a
Crunden?, Edwina 282b, 283a
Crutch, G. 199b
Cruz, J.V. 148a
O Cruzeiro Internacional 204b
Csaba, Michael 124b
Csendes, Francis E. 35a
CTV Television 204b
Cuadernos para el Diálogo 204b
Cuadernos Universitarios 204b
Cuallinor, Raymond 148b
Cuarto, C. Allen-Ocho 142b
Cuba **95b-96a, 121a, 172b-173a**
Cuba: Alegre Como Su Sol 96a
Cuba Hurricane Relief Fund 152b
Cuba Sixtyeight 96a
Cuban Crisis 110b, 136b, 152b
The Cuban Embassy 35a, 152b, 295b
Cuban Embassy in Great Britain 95b
Cuban Movement for Peace and Sovereignty of Peoples 152b, 297b
Cuc, Thu 165a
Cudlipp, Hugh 236a
Cuesmes, Noel 170b
Cuibus, Georges 230b, 237b
Cukurs, Andris 35a
Culhane, Claire 299b
Cullen, J.W. 287a
Victor Cullen & Sons 148b
Cultural Congress of Havana 96a
Cumming, Richard 258b, 298a
Cuneo, Gertrude B. 88a
Cung, Phung Van 132a, 167b, 182a, 299a
Current of the World 204b
Curry, W.B. 353a
Curtis, A.L. 142b
Curtis, Audrey 295b
Curtis, Helen Cromwell 301a
Curtis, Jim 295b
Curwen, Margaret 258b
Cushman, Frederica 199a
Cuthbert, J.H. 54b
Cuu Quoc Weekly 35a, 118a, 162a, 190b
Cwietkowicz, Joseph 134b
Y Cymro 204b
Cymro, Plaid 82a
Cyprus **96a**

Cyprus Conciliation Committee 96a
Cyprus High Commission 96a
Cyrankiewicz, Josef 109b, 156a
Il Cyrano 204b
Czech Embassy 96b
Czech P.M. 67a
Czechoslovak Committee of the Defenders of Peace 290b
Czechoslovak Life 204b
Czechoslovak News Agency 12b, 204b
Czechoslovak, Peace Committee, Prague 295a
Czechoslovak Pugwash Committee 287a, 351b
Czechoslovak Radio 17b, 98a, 205a
Czechoslovak Youth 205a
Czechoslovakia **96b-97a, 121a, 173a**
Czechoslovakian Ambassador to the United Kingdom 96b
Czerny, Mr. 96b
Czytelnik 295b

D

D.R.V. 189a
Dabbagh, Hassan Ali 105b
Dabelsteen, Preban 214a
da Costa Doria, João A. 35a, 94a, 295b
da Curba, Miguel Luis C. 35a
Dada, Mohammed B. 172b
Dadlez, A. 174b, 234a
Dadoo, Jusuf M. 151b
Dadvar, J. 35a
Daedalus: Journal of the American Academy of Arts and Sciences 205a
J.W. Dafoe Foundation, University of Manitoba 88a
Dagenais, Ferdinand 259a
Dagenais, Maurice 228b
Dagenham Motors Ltd. 143a
Dagens Nyheter 96a, 119a, 130b, 183a
Dahleh, Hani 107a
Dahne, Eberhard 121b
Dahomey **97a**
Daigakusha Co. 144a
Dailey, Edward D. 324b
Daili, A. 153b
Daily Express 143a, 205a
Daily Herald 278a
Daily Mail 11a, 205a
Daily Mashriq 205a
The Daily Mirror 313a, 313b
The Daily Sketch 313a
Daily Telegraph 95b, 98b, 111a, 115b, 118a, 122a, 124a, 129b, 135b, 141b, 150b, 183a, 205a, 334a
The Daily Tribune 324a
Daily Worker 15a, 99a, 121b, 123b, 177a, 205a, 221b, 265b
Daimler-Benz Aktiengesellschaft 88a
Daimler Hire Ltd. 88a
Dairett, Marie 28b
Daković, Predrag 35a
Dakyns, Peggy 259a
Dalbard 295b
Dale, Ernest 338b
Dale, Martin A. 107b
Dale, Rowland 35a
Dales, Elizabeth 26b, 35b, 97b, 98a, 99b, 100a, 122a
Daley, D.J. 328b
Dallalien, Lance 115b
Dally, Jessie 295b
Dalmaum, Rafael 205a
Dalton, Michael 297a
Daly, Lawrence 35a, 94b, 148a, 157b, 177a, 178b, 187a, 192a, 295b
Daly, Richard 85a, 179a
Dalzell-Ward, A.J. 205a
Dambassis, Andréas 122b
Damdin, M.P. 158a
Damon, Frances 149b
Danas 205b
d'Ancona, Helen 227b
Danek, Cyril 35a, 173a
Danger in South East Asia 190b
Le Danger Radiologique 205b
Dangerfield, Philip 167b
Daniel, John 205b
Daniel, Laura 259a
Daniels, John C. 148a
Danish Branch **141b**
Danish Whitsuntide March 165b
Dank Fredskonferences Forretningsudvalag 324b
Dankové, Olga 35a
Dannenberg, Linda 15b, 139a
Danning, Peter A. 122a
Dansey, Michael 79a
Dansk Bertrand Russell Rad 173a
Den danske Forberedelseskomité 173a
Danziger, Victoria 110a
Dar, Mohammad Lateef 102b, 295b
d'Arazien, Steven 238b
D'Arcy, Martin C. 142a, 259a
Dargnies, Henriette 218a
Dark Ghetto 14a, 138b
Darlaine, Manon 324b
Darling, Brian 94a
Darling, E.W. 35a
Darling, John E. 238b
Darr, John 149b
Darr, Jr., John W. 35b
Dartington Hall School 276b, 353a
Dartmouth Street Trust 88a
Darwent, Brian 88a
Das, Praffulla Chandra 205b, 228b
Das, Sitanshu 213b-214a
Das, Sree Ranjan Kumar 324a
Dash, Pat 176b
da Silva, F.H. Lopes 35b
da Silva, M.C.H. 110a
Daskalopoulos, Nikos G. 122b
Dass, Banarsi 324b
d'Astier, Emmanuel 173b, 208b
Datta, Nilkanta 205b
Daud, Dato Nik 127a
Dauphin, Roger 209a
Dave, Shashikant J. 295b
Davey, L.J. 199b
Davidon, William C. 205b
Davidson, Angus 35b
Davidson, Ann 143a
Davidson, Chandler 205b
Davidson, Donald 35b
Davidson, William C. 165b
Davies, Clive 259a
Davies, Crompton Llewelyn 276b, 282b, 309a, 310b, 353a
Davies, D.M. 91b
Davies, Gillian 239b
Davies, Harvey N. 290b
Davies, Jeffrey 35b
Davies, John 35b
Davies, Mansel 35b, 89a, 277a
Davies, Mary 205b
Davies, Moya Llewelyn 353a
Davies?, Richard Llewelyn 353b
Davies, Stan Gebler 205b
Davies, Susan 211a
Davies, Tom 241a
Davies, W. Austin 295b, 301a
David Davies Memorial Institute of International Studies 350b
Ellis Davies & Co. 307a
Davini, Tino 295b
Davis, Miss 178a
Davis, Mr. & Mrs. ? 88a
Davis, Mrs. 147b
Davis, Don 150a
Davis, F. 236a
Davis, Fieling 150a
Davis, Herman 121a
Davis, J. 313a
Davis, Jerome 19a, 35b, 205b
Davis, John L. 67a, 127b, 130b, 132a, 230a
Davis, Mary L. 25a
Davis, R.G. 179a
Davis, Robin 143a, 155b
Davison, Margaret 353a
Davison, Michael 241a
Davison, Peter 198a
Davy, Charles 225a
Dawe, Alan 205b
Dawley, Robert P. 35b
Dawn 205b
Peter Dawnay Publishers 88a
Dawson, G.M. 170a
Day, Ron 172a
Dayan, Moshe 287a
Day-Lewis, Cecil 287a
de Abreu, Joselito 324b
de Almeide, Pedro Bieira 35b
De Algemene Cenrale 116a
de Arrocha, Angela Delli

Sante 35b
Dear Bertrand Russell 8a
Dearden, Elizabeth 298b
Deason, Derek A. 112a, 116b
"Death and Pillage in the Congo" 152a
de Ávila, José Wanderley Quevedo 171a
Debbaut, Pierre 35b, 120b
de Beauvoir, Simone 136a, 139b, 157a, 192
De Benedetti, Andrea 205b
de Benoist, Alain 224b, 298a
De Bezige Bij 199b
de Bock, G.A. 75b
De Bock, Walter 105b
de Bono, Edward 259a
de Braulaycourt, L. 97b
Debray, Regis 189a
Debrett's Illustrated Peerage 205b, 310b
de Brunhoff, S. 165a
de Bustamente, Jorge Sanchez 169a
de Capsevich, Heronim 352a
de Castro, Josue 85a, 136a, 142b, 158a
December 205b
De Chadenedes, Mrs. François (Edith) 259a, 280a
Decker, Donald G. 205b
Decker, Randall E. 206a
Declaration of Members of the International War Crimes Tribunal 96b
Declarations of the Russell Conference on Czechoslovakia 96b, 97a
de Còrdova Castro, Federico 35a, 95b, 152b
Decornoy, Jacques 158a
Decrez, Laurette 35b, 131b
Decter, M. 134a
Dedijer, Vladimir 119a, 136a, 141b, 142b, 156b, 157a, 161a, 184a, 185a, 188a, 190b, 192a, 259a
Dedijer Conference **141b**
De Eguidazu, Fernando 206a
Deer, John 57a, 166b, 169b
De Félice, Jean-Jacques 120a
Defence and Aid Fund 88a
Defence Committee for Victims of Nazi Persecution 35b, 97b, 98a, 99b, 100a, 122a
Defence Market Digest 155b
Defenders of 3 against HUAC 36a, 138b, 139a
Defensor, Benjamin 128a
Deffarge, Claude 188a
de Gámez, Tana 95b
de Gaulle, Charles 84a, 97b, 121a, 156a
Degen, Charles 324b
de Gortari, Eli 127b
Dehaye, P. 255a
de Hevesy, George 130a
Dehnke, Gerda 214b
Deighton, Len 148a, 259a
Dejean, Georges 53a
de Jager, E. 36a
de Keyser, Ethel 110a, 111a, 130a
deLacy, Terence 206a
de la Mare, Richard 208b
De la Métrique 331a
de Lanerolle, Vijaya 238a
Delaney, Shelagh 152a
de la Torre, Haye 36a
De Lavergne, James 206a
Delegation of Aden 151a
Delegation of the Peace Movement of South Vietnam of the Helsinki Congress 153a
Delf, George 59b, 214b
Delhi Gandhi Smarak Nidhi 102b
de Lippe, Jürgen 36a
Dell Publishing Co. 206a
Dellinger, Dave 39b, 143b, 157a, 185a, 192a, 217b
Delmos, O. 301a
Delo 183a
de Lobaton, Guillermo 128a
de Lobaton, Jacqueline 109a, 128a
De Los Toyos, Alberto 36a, 172b, 200a-b
Delphic Quarterly 206a
Delphis, Phoebus 206a
Delt, Lydia 324b
Delt, Martin 324b
Delt, Paul 324b
Delteil, Caroline 352a
del Vayo, Julio Averez 142a, 290b 299b
del Vecchio, C. Capuano 179a
de Madariaga, Salvador 34b, 287a
Demarchi, Carlo 295b
De Marco, Clara Hermann 36a
Demars, J. 174a
de Mayolo, Santiago Antunez 324b
de Meeûs, Anthony 117a
De Menezes, Adolpho Justo Bezerra 324b
de Metrópolis, Harry 295b
de Miranda, Alvaro 128b
The Democrat 203b
Democratic Committees of Resistance 101a
Democratic German Report 165b
Democratic Republic of Vietnam 189a
Democratic Workers' Congress 172b
Democratic Youth 'Gregory Lambrakis' 123a
Démocratique Palestinien 107a
de Molinero, Mme. Libertad Piconnell 174a
de Moraes Barros, Ademir 164b
Demos, Kathleen 36a
de Moura, Maria Beatriz 207b
Demski, Reiner 206a
Den Bok, Irene 88a
Deneke, Berhane 97a
Denmark **97a, 173a-b**
Denonn, Lester E. 206a
Denson, Alan 295b
J.M. Dent & Sons (Canada) Ltd. 206a
Deodhekar, Govind N. 102b
de Oriol, Antonio Ma 113a
Department of State, Washington 142b
De Pinna 314a
Deppenwiese, Manfred 36a
De Rango, E. 88a
de Ranitz, Ysabele 259a
de Rezende, Marco Antonio 208a
de Robillard, Edwin 74a
de Rodriguez, Magdalena 152b
Derpich, Juan Aguilar 295b
Derrick, Jonathan M. 36a
Derricourt, Robin M. 36a
Dershowitz, Leah 111b
Desai, Barney 130a
Desai, Chaudrakaut J. 110b
Desai, Sharad N. 129b
Desai, V. 200b
Desch, Kurt 239b
Deschner, Karlheinz 206a
de S. e Brito 295b
de Selincourt, Paul 259a
Deshmukh, C.D. 153b
de Silva, F.H. Lopes 128a
De Silva, G.R. 153b, 172b
Desmond, Barry 130a
Desmond, Eric 295a
Desmond, Thomas C. 88a
Desnoyers, C. 57b-58a
de Souza, Arno Francisco 171a
Desson, Guy 173b
Dessouki, Salah 106b, 107b, 111a
D'Esterre, E. 259a
Destino 206a
de Tamayo, Martha L. 299b
Detoman, O. 88a, 172a
Detroit News 183a
Detter, Karl 120b
Detzner, Hubert 174b
Deudraeth Rural District Council 259a
Deutsch, Mr. 213a
Deutsch, Alex T. 36a
Deutsch, Alvin 226a
André Deutsch Ltd. 117b, 206a
Deutsch-Israelische Studiengruppe 206a
Deutsche Friedensgesellschaft 36a, 99b
Deutche Friedens-Union 99b, 121b
Deutsche Rundschau 329b
Deutsche Volkszeitung 100a, 174b
Die Deutschen Atomwaffengegner 287a
Deutscher, Isaac 36a, 40a, 114a, 136a, 153a, 157a, 185b, 287a, 354a
Deutscher, Tamara 36a, 148a, 157b, 292a, 354a
Dev, ? 298a

Dev, Vasu 36a
de Valle, Emilio Menéndez 240b
Devaux, Philip 206a
Devcich, P.E. 147a
de Villiers, K.M. 91b
Le Devoir 206a
Devon Committee of 100 324b
De Vries, Peter Hugh 324b
DeWeerd, H.A. 185b
de Wespin, M.D. 206a
Dewhurst, V. 126a
de Zoete Beryl 353a
de Zulueta, P.F. 114a, 152b, 155a
Dhadda, Siddharaj 102b
Dhalla, Kamrudin 165b
Dhandhania, Jugal Kishore 325a
Dhandhania & Sons 325a
Dhiman, R. 208b
Dhiman Press of India 206a
Diablo Press Ltd. 88a
Diah, Burhanudin
  Mohamad 102b, 288b
The Dial Press Inc. 206a
Diamond, Edwin 224a
Diamond, Frieda 149b
Diamandopoulos, Peter 275a
Diaz, Eunice Michel 295b
Diaz, Marisa Olive 36a
Dick, Oliver Lawson 259a
Dickel, Friedrich 99a
Dickens, James 148a
Dickens Society of Ceylon 206a
Dicker, Harold 206b
Dickie, James 36a
Dickinson, G.H. 217b
Dickinson, G. Lowes 29b
Dickinson, Thorold 206b
Dicks 307a
Dickter, Linda C. 213a
Didier, John 207b
Diedisheim, J. 173b
Diego 128a
Digges, Alec 130a
Dillon's University Bookshop 202a
Dimos, Tasopoulos 124a
Din, Khawayah, Ahmad 37b
The Diner's Club 88a
Dinh, Nguyen Huu 168b
Diniz, Jaime 171a
Dino, Abidine 14a, 36b, 106b, 114a, 130b, 146a, 161a
Dins, John L. 17a
Dionysus 206b
Diori, Hamani 108a
Diouf, Aldou 110b
Direct Action 325a
Direct Action Committee 36b
Direct Action for a Nonviolent World 325a
Le Directeur, Palais de Justice 94a
Diretory of Organizations 206a
Direkte Aktion 208a
Dirrecion General de Gobierno 106a
Diskus 206b
Disordine 206b, 325a
Dissent 36b
Divine Light Mission 36b
The Divorce Law Reform Association 36b
The Divorce Law Reform Union 36b
Diwakar, R.R. 102b
Diwaker, S.C. 153b
Dix, Douglas C.K. 281a
Dixon, Mrs. 280b
Dixon, George H. 36b
Dixon, H.L. 88a
Dixon, Ian 36b, 88a
Dixon, Mary W. 36b
Dixon, Nita 88a
Dixon, Robin 36b
Djaffr, Djennrdi 151b
Djahansuz, Mr. 125a
Djanab, Dr. K. 106b
Djilas, Milovan 49b
Dmitrievna, Gorgier Ivan 134a
Do, Xuan Van 79b
Dobbins, Gaines S. 197b
Dobinson, C.H. 177a
Dobson, Dennis 334a
Dockter, Ben 230b
Dodds, E.R. 177a
Dodds, Elizabeth 103b
Dod's Parliamentary Companion 206b
Dodwell, P.M.C. 325a
Doern, Russell J. 206b
Doeune, Hong Hoeung 94b
Doganis, T. 100b, 124a
Dolan, Joe 36b
Dolci, Danilo 36b, 127a, 133b, 136a, 144a, 149a, 157a, 158a
Doll, Richard 177a
Doller, E. 98a
Dominican Committee of Wives and Families of Political Prisoners 36b
Dominican Republic **97a, 121a**
Dominican Republic Organization of Afro-American Unity 138b
Donat, Ilon 37a
Dong, Nguyen Van 162a, 176a
Dong, Pham Van 162b, 184b, 186a, 176a, 295b
Donnbassis, George 123a
Dopsin, N. 88a
Doran, E.C. 37a, 146a
Doran, Mark 288b
Dorchester Advertising Corporation 206b
Dorfman, Lize 111a, 117a, 295b
Dorheim, Becky 135b
Dória, Carlos Alberto 171a, 215b
Dorinto?, Columbo 295b
Dörner, Renate 174b
Dorrance, D.R. 173b
dos Anjos, Marçal Oliveira 171a
dos Anjos, Mario Negreiros 171a
Doubleday and Co., Inc. 206b
Douglas, A. 206b
Douglas, L. 98a, 209a
Douglas, Paul 46a
Doukhobor Society of Canada 37a
Dover Publications, Inc. 206b
Dovis, José 168b
Dow, James 236a
Dower, John W. 165b
Dowlite International 206b
Dowman, Constance 298b
Downes, Mr. 131b
Downie, Bruce G. 170a
Downing, John 166a
Downs, Hugh 222b
Dowson, Claire 172a
Dowson, Ernest 143a
Dowson, Ross 171b
Doyle, Louise Jackson 88a
Drachman, A. 88a
Dragoumis, John N. 122b, 145b
Dragoli, A. 111b
Drake, Constance 280a
Draper, Edith 280a
The Draughtsman 206b
Draughtsmen's and Allied Technicians Association 129b
Drayoumis, Mark 240b
Drefahl, Guenter 296a
Drei Masken Verlag AG 206b
Drexel, Helen Carter 37a
Dreyer, Ira Jay 210b
Dreyfus, Benjamin 222a
Driberg, Tom 176b
Drubetzky, Eidea 111a
Dryden, Anne (formerly Russell) 277a, 277b, 292a
Dryden, Ian (formerly Pyle) 277a, 277b, 292a
Drysdale, Jean 242b
Dsaulniers, Louise 11b
Duarte Jorge, Alexandrino Pedro 297a
Dubcek, A. 51a
Dube, K. 111a
Dubinsky, Melvin 42a
W.E.B. Dubois Clubs of America 165b
Ducasse, ? 352a
Dudderdge, H.J. 127b
Dudley, Martha W. 36a, 138b, 139a
Duff, Michael 295b
Duff, Peggy 165b, 178a, 251a
Duffet, John L. 206b
Duggan, John A. 88a
Dugger, Ronnie 136a, 137b
Duhring, Nathan 325a
Dulles, John Foster 329a
Dummett, Michael 206b
Duncairn Divisional Labour Party 88a
Duncan, Denis 201a
Duncan, Donald 158a, 160a
Duncan, Peter 351b
Duncker, E. 235a
Dundas, Malcolm 37a
Dundee, Lord 116b, 133a
Dundee Humanist Group 37a
Dunham, Barrows 259a
Dunham, W.R. 37a

Dunk, Ben 203a
Dunlop Rubber Co. Ltd. 88a
Dunman, Jack 353a
Dunn, Alastair 203a
Dunn, H.B. 206b
Dunn, Halbert L. 325a
Dunn, J.C. 259a
Dunn, Ted 233a
Dunne, Jeanne 195b
Dunne, R. 37a
Dunstone, Pauline J. 214b
Dunten, M.T. 352b
Dunz, Joachim 208a
Durán, Luis 117b
Durante, Jimmy 42a
Durband, Alan 207a
Durdy, Margaret 277b
Durham Colleges Labour Club 37a
Duriaud, François 37a
During, Z. 147b
Durrant's Press Cuttings 207a
Durrell, Gerald 287b
Duschinsky, Greta 88a
Dusorp, A.E. 287b
Dutt, R. Palme 217a
E.P. Dutton & Co. Inc. 207a
Duve, Arne 37a
Dwyer, Robert 117a
Dyas, W. Martin 34b
Dyball, Jane 128a
Dyer-Bennett, Miriam 37a

E

Eaby, Christian 37b
Eady, M. 88a
Eagan, E. 157b
Eaks, Louis 236b
Eames, E.T. 224a
Eames, Elizabeth Ramsden 138b, 259a, 292b
Eames, Morris 259a
Easeman, W.G. 282a
East Pakistan Students Union 108b
Eastern Horizon 207a
Eastern Horizon Monthly Review 101b
Eastern World 207a
Eastman, E. Philip 48a
Eaton, Anne 37b, 351b
Eaton, Cyrus 37b, 124b, 165b, 351b, 352a, 354a
Eaton, Ken 204a
Eban, Abba 104a
Ebbert, George C. 37b, 146a
Eber, John 58a, 96a, 118a, 126b, 166b
Eberhart, Roland F. 37b
Ebiri, Kutlay 63a
Ecclestone, John 172a
Echanove T., Carlos A. 222a, 325a
Echevarria, Ramon 78a
Eckersley, Mr. 204a
Eckhoff, Douglas N. 147a
Eco Contemporaneo 37b, 141a
The Economic Consequences of Disarmament 155b
The Economist 108b, 183a. 188a, 207a
Economist Newspaper Ltd. 313b
Eddington, Arthur S. 325a
Eddy, Amos 325a
Ede, J. Chuter 115b
Ede, and Ravenscroft Ltd. 259a
Edelberg, Victor 325a
Edelman, Elka 113a
Eden, Carol 304a
Eden, Morton 304a
Edenborough, Alan 37b
Edgcomb, Gabrielle 217b
Edge Magazine 207a
Edginton, J.D. 37b
Edició de Materials 207a
Ediciones Hombre Nuevo 207a
Edilman, Mosche 113a
Edinburgh City Labour Party 259a
Edinton, J. 167a
Édition du Burin 207a
Edition Voltaire 207a
Éditions du Seuil 207a
Les Editions John Didier 207b
Editōra Civilização Brasiliero 207b
Editorial Lumen 207b
Editorial Posada 207b
Editorial Seix Berral 207b
Editoriale Rizzoli 207b
Edmonds, John 165b
Edmonds, Laurie 37b
The Edmonton Journal 172a
Edmunds, David W. 137a
Edmunds, John 34a, 109a, 128a, 299b
Education Advisory Committee, Parliamentary Group for World Government 325a
The Education Journal 135b
Education for Teaching 207b
Edwards, ? 37b
Edwards, Mrs. 292b
Edwards, Bob 37b, 101b
Edwards, David V. 325a
Edwards, George 37b
Edwards, George D. 88a
Edwards, Herman 294b
Edwards, Hugh 37b, 88b
Edwards, J. Edgar 176a
Edwards, John Owen 312a
Edwards, Owen 56a
Edwards, Paul 207b, 259a, 290b
Edwards, Robert 130b
Effendi, Aslam 37b, 108a, 325a-b
Egall, Peter 37b
Egbimike, Ken A. 37b
Eglash, Rodney S. 112a
Egner, Robert E. 207b
Egoroff, D. 258b
Egorov, E. 13b
Egwu, Igbo N. 37b
Ehly, Jean 207b
Ehrem, Prince Mohmed 38a
Ehrlich, Arnold 213a
Ehrlich, Irma 96b
Eichmann, ? 188a
Eidam, Jürgen 174b, 290b, 295b
Eilam, Aviva 38a
Giulio Einaudi Editore 207b
Einstein, Albert 100a, 114b, 115a, 142a, 149a, 263a, 270b, 273a, 333b
Eisenberg, Fred M. 290a
Eisenstadt, Evelyn 238b
Eisenstein, Anatol 38a
Eisenstein, Samuel A. 290a
Eisler, Lee 295b
Eke, Annie M. 259a
Ekstrabladet 207b
Elamin, H. 84b
El-Amir, N.K. 126b
Elan 100a, 174b, 207b
Elan: magazin für junge Leute 207b
ElBarky, S.B. 105b, 107a
Elbiński, Zygmunt 207b
Elbogen, Milton 135b
Elborn, G.S. 301a
El Din, Khaled Mohey 107b, 149b, 156b, 159a
Eldon, Molly 303b
Eleven Twenty-Seven 208a
Eleventh Congress World Association of World Federalists 144a
El-Feki, Ahmed Hassan 107b
Elfenbein, Hiram 208a
El-Gayar, Mahmoud 107b
Elgumhouria 208a
El-Hannaoui, Kamal Eddine 107b
Eliot, T.S. 208b, 278b
Eliot, Valerie 208b
Elisabeth, Queen of the Belgians 38a, 94a, 149a
Elizabeth II, Queen of England 114a, 292b
Elizonde, José Rodriguez 172b
El Kadi, Ali Hussein 151a
El Katib 149b
El Khalifa, El Khatim 113a
el-Kony, Mohamed 107b, 131a
Elliot, A. 158a
Elliot, Elsie 38a, 101b
Elliot, J. 38a
Elliot, Jeff M. 38a
Elliot, Rodney S. 146b
Ellis, Charles R. 38a
Ellis, J. 259a
Ellis, Nathalie 38a
Ellis, R.A. 38a
Ellison, John 351b
Ellisor, F.L. Page 259a
Ellman, Michael 38a, 117a
Ellscheid, Robert 38a
Elman, Mischa 287b
El Mokri, Abbas 122b
El Naggar, Said 107b
Elorrio, Juan García 169a
El-Samir, Faisel 154a
Elsebai, Youssef 107b, 164a
El-Shibib, Talib 105b, 107a
Elsie, Mary 281a

Elua, Juan 295b
Elvey, Maurice 352a
Embajada de México en Inglaterra 127a
Embassy of Israel 127a, 154b
Embassy of Soviet Union 153a
Embassy of the Federal Republic of Germany, Press Department 99b
Embassy of the People's Republic of Bulgaria 94a, 225b
Embassy of the Republic of the Congo in the United Kingdom 95a-b
Embassy of the Republic of Liberia, London 105b
Embassy of the United Arab Republic 156b, 196a
Embassy of the United States 133a
Emberson, Jan M. 295b
Emergency Action Conference, Stockholm Conference on Vietnam 165b
Emergency Civil Liberties Committee 135b, 137a, 139a, 259b
Emeruwa, John N. 38a
Emery, George L. 259b
Emley, M.L.B. 208a
Emmanueli, Antonio 38a
Empson, Jake 167b
Empson, William 287b
Encounter 177a, 208a, 231a, 238a
Encyclopaedia Britannica Ltd. 208a
Encyclopaedia Moderna 208a
The Encylopedia of Philosophy 290b
End the Draft Committee 38a, 136a
End the Draft's Downdraft 136a
Enescu, G. 237b
Eng, Aw Say 38a
Engel, E. 75a
Engelhard, M.J. 242b
Engbrincke?, Ken A. 108a
Engelskirchen, Howard 79a, 140a
England, Åke 208a
England, Gordon 131b
English Centre of International P.E.N. 295b
English Electric Company 88b
English Literary Circle 295b
Enlightened Citizens Committee 136a
Ennals, Martin 59a, 115a, 131a
Ennis, Edward J. 314a
Ennis, Robert H. 208a
Enomoto, K. 197a
Enright, T. 165b
Ensor, David 176b
Enthoven, Martin 101b, 110a, 128b, 133a
Epoca 208a
Epstein, Henry A. 295b
Epstein, Jacob 280a
Epton, Bill 138b, 139b
Erder, Necat 106b
Erenberg, Adele 138b
Erhard, Ludwig 99b
Erhel, Jean-Yves 173b
Erickson, Arthur W. 38a
Ericson, Sture 313b
Erixson, Sven 88b
Erkenntnis 337b, 338a
Erlander, Tage 113a
Erler, Frank 175a
Erlich, Reese W. 38a
Ernest, Gisela 172b
Ernest, Rosalie 88b
Erni, Hans 349a
Eroglu, Hayri 79b
Errboe, Mogens 173b
Errington, Lewis 208a
Erson?, Jan 229a
Erwin, Pastor 170b
Es geht ums Leben! 212b
Escape 208a
Eschefeld, Rita 98b
Escuela Preparatoria Bertrand Russell 259b, 295b
Esdale, Mrs. G.P.R. 264a
Esdale, Patricia 292b
Esenin-Volpin, Alexander Sergeevich 117a
Eshkol, Levi 104a
Espase-Calpe, S.A. 208a
Esquire 137b, 208a
An Essay on the Foundations of Geometry 7a
Essex, M. 90a
Essex University 114b
Essier, P.?W. 259b
Esslin, Gundrun 91a
O Estado de S. Paulo 208a
The Esterhazy Orchestra Foundation Inc. 259b
Estonian Aid, Inc.—Eesti Abi 111b
Estreicjer, Karol 259b
Etcheverry, G. 110b
Ethiopia **97a, 121a**
Ethiopian Delegation 151a
Ethiopian People's Movement Council 97a
The Eton Amnesty Group 208b
Eton College 277b
Ette La'al 125a
Ettlinger, Mr. 310b
Euclid 327a
Euratio 208b
Europa Publications Ltd. 208b
European Commission of the Rights of Man 86b
European Committee for the Freedom of Mexican Political Prisoners 127b
European Jewish Publications Ltd. 156a
European Organizations of the National Front of Iran 106b, 174b
Evan, William M. 199a
Evang, Karl 158a
Evans, Avril M. 38a
Evans, C.J. 353a
Evans, Charles 88b
Evans, David L. 138a
Evans, Edith 287b
Evans, Elwyn 292b
Evans, Miss G. 88b
Evans, Gareth B. 238b
Evans, George 236a
Evans, Gwynfor 38a, 114b
Evans, James 38b, 313b
Evans, John G. 259b
Evans, Myfanny 92a
Evans, Nici 292b
Evans, Rik 123a
Evans, W. Houghton 38b
Evans Brothers Ltd. 208b
Evan-Thomas, Katharine 38a
Evelyn, Adams & Mackay Ltd. 208b
L'Evenement 173b, 208b
Evening Leningrad 208b
The Evening News 208b
Evening News of India 153b
Evening Standard 88b
Evenitsky, A. 233a
Evensen, Lars 38b
Everard, [Elizabeth] 259b
Everett, Horace S. 259b
Everett, Jr., Robert W. 152b
Everingham, Douglas N. 88b, 147a, 169b
Everitt, B.M. 209a
Evers, B.M. 287b
Eversley, David 259b
Everybody's 10b
Everyman III 34a, 38b
Evron, E. 103b
Ewén, Stud. Görta 38b
The Exchange Telegraph Co. Ltd. 208b
Executive Committee of Iranian National Front Organization in Great Britain 124b
Exit 208b
Exley, Richard A. 212b
L'Express 153a, 208b
Expressen 17a, 190a, 208b
Ex-Service Movement for Peace 38b, 165b
Exton-Smith, Norman 259b
Eyres, Anthea 170a
Eyuboglu, Sabahattin 106b
Ezzell, F. 38b

F

Faber and Faber Ltd. 208b, 278b
Fabregat, Faustino Aroca 165b, 296a
Fabri, David A. 227a
Fabsic, Jiri 38b
Facci, Joseph 325b
Fackler, Ernest 38b
Fact 208b
Factory for Peace 38b, 152b
Factory Scheme **153a**
Facts on Iran 125a

Fählender, Inger 109a, 128b
Fahy, Julian 38b
Faim & Soif 209a
Fairbairn, Elsie A. 292b
Fairbrass, F.C. 38b
Fairchild Publications of New York 209a
Fairweather, M. 296a
Faisal ibn Abdul Aziz, King 110b
The Faith of a Rationalist 154b
Faix, Kvetoslav 98a
Fakhrutdinova, Sugda Berkhanova 38b, 134a
Fakih, O.A. 105a
Falber, Reuben 34a
Falco, Domenico 296a
Falk, Avner 104a, 259b
Fallgatter, Marvin 88b
Fallin, Richard 38b, 290b
Faludy, George 213b
Family 209a
Family Trustee Company Ltd. 88b
Famous Puzzles 329a
Fang, Isidor, Rosa & Leo 113a
Fann, Kuang Tih 206a, 209a, 290b
Fanti, Giorgio 146a, 174a, 209a, 226a
Fanti, Giudo 296a
Farcasan, S. 233a
Fardoonii, M.S. 38b
Farebrother Ellis & Co. 309a-b
Faredoon, Mahmood 38b
Fares, N.M. 299a
Farley, Christopher **143a**, 148b, 259b
Farley, Jo 292b
Farley, P. 88b
Farmer, W.W. 238b
Farqui, Jacko 104a
Farr, A.F. 38b
Farrell, C.J. 209a
Farrell, Mary (née Bailey) 312a
Farrington, B. 38b
Farstad, Norah 108a
Fast, Howard 39a
Faulkner, Michael 224b
Faulkner, Stanley 160a, 186a, 189a
Faure, Edgar 121b
Faustinelli, C. 325b
Fauvet, Jacques 199a
Fawcett, H. 114b
Fawcett, John T. 39a
Fawthrop, T.W. 213b
Fay, Samuel P. 175b
Fazilpur, Mian Gulmohd Nagi 296a
F.C.I. News Agency Ltd. 39a, 209a
"F.D." 82a
Fearing, Bruce 197a
Fearing, Mrs. Bruce 39b
Feder, Paul J. 88b
Federacion de Mujeres Dominicanos Comision Familias Prisoneros Constitucionalistas 121a
Federacion Estudiantes Universidad Tecnica Estado Chile 172b
Federacion Iberica de Juventudes Libertarias 130a
The Federal Council for the Advancement of Aborigines and Torres Strait Islanders 39a, 93b
Federal Parole Board 136b
Federal Union 10b, 39a, 325b
The Federated Gas Employees' Industrial Union 39a, 170b
Fédération Générale du Travail de Belgique 171a
Fédération Internationale des Droits de l'Homme 123a, 128b
Fédération Internationale des Résistants 39a, 97b
Fédération Internationale Terre des Hommes 108a, 174a
Fédération Nationale des Jeunes Gardes Socialistes 39a, 170b
Federation of Iranian Students in Italy 296a
Federation of Students Islamic Societies in U.K. and Eire 131a
Federation of United Kingdom and Eire Malaysian and Singapore Student Organizations 106a
Fédération pour le Respect de l'Homme et de l'Humanité 97b
Fei, G. 87b
Feied, Frederick 39a
Feigenbaum, Stan A. 39a
Feigin, T. 113a
Fein, Louis 39a
Feinberg, Abraham L. 94b, 158a, 171b, 209a, 296a
Feinberg, Barry 218b, 225b, 256a, 303a, 303b, 344a
Feingold, Gene 148b
Fekete, Paul 39a
Felber, Jean Dameron 135b
Feld, Bernard 298a
Feldinger, Frank 148b
Feldman, Edwin 39a
Feldman, Ernestina 110a
Feldman, Gloria 83b, 118b
Feldman, Sergiu 88b
Feldman, Victor 39b
Feldmar, Andrew 137a
Fellman, Christer 63a
Fellowship of Reconciliation 39b, 118b
The Fellowship Party 39b
Felton, Anton 143a, 196b, 290b, 301a
Feltrinelli, Giangiacomo 88b, 142a
Feltz, N. 47a
Fembul, David 154b
Fenton, Peter 301a
Ferentinos, Mr. 123a, 272a
Ferguson, Alan 39b
Ferguson, Bruce 217b
Fernandez, Maria Cecilia Vidigel 130b
Fernández, Roberto Sosa 117b, 132a
Fernando, G.M.D. 219b
Fernbach, David 94a, 223a
Ferneyhough, Beatrice 94b
Ferrand, James F. 61a
Ferrari, Leon 169a, 325b
Ferreira, Alfredo Guí 171a
Ferreira, R. 109b, 128b
Ferris, A. 39b
Ferris, Eleanor 353b
Ferry, W.H. 40a, 147b
Ferzan, Abdul Karim 39b
Festenstein, Hilliard 129b
Festenstein, Iris 129a
Festival Panamericano de Musica Pablo Casals 287b
Fforde, J.S. 259b
Fialho, José Carlos T. 165b
Fiat Societa per Azioni 88b
Field, Amy Malken 278a
Field, Elsie 39b
Field, Gina 259b, 296a
Field, S.S. 39b
Field, T. 236a
Fields, F. Herbert 39b
Fiesta Cultural Association 39b
Fife, Michael 148b
Fifth Ave. Vietnam Peace Parade Committee 39b
Filho, Antonio de Deus Teles 39b
Filho, Noronha Rodrigues 39b
Filinis, Kostas 124a
Filippov, Ivan 39b
Filton, Anthony 88b
Finberg, J. 39b, 131b
Final Report of the Press Commission 325b
Finch, Alison 235a
Finch, P.W. 39b
Finchley Central Ward, Labour Party 165b
Findlater, Richard 238a
Fine, H.B. 256a
Finerly, L.S. 46a
Fink, Robert 148b
Finkelstein, Y. 104a
Finklestone, J. 129a, 219a
Finland **97a, 173b**
Finlay, M.S. 259b, 269a
Finn, Robert 148b
Finucan, Michael 45a
F.I.R. Geschichtskommission 143a
Firshman, A.B. Nathan 104b
Firth, Prof. 275a
Firth, Anthony 198a
Firth, Glynn 209a
Firth, Hugh 39b
Fischberg, Perl 111a
Fischer, Georges 158a
Fischer, Hans 325b
Fischer, John 137a, 212a
Fischhof, Georg 325b

Fischof, Oerley 325b
Fiser, Lumomír 204b
Fiser, Zbynek 165b
Fishberg, Phyllis Sara 116b
Fishbone, Leslie G. 201b
Fishell, John M. 39b, 209a
Fisher, Brian 40a, 175b
Fisher, Carol 40a, 152a
Fisher, Carolyn 138a
Fisher, David 122a
Fisher, John J. 325b
Fisher, Murray 228a
Fisher, Ralph 40a
Fisher, Richard B. 235a
Fisher, Robert 148b
Fisher, Sheila 296a
Stella Fisher Bureau 88b
Fishman, Jerry 325b
Fishwick, Colin 40a
Fitch, Ana Norma Bazúa 40a
Fitch, Beverleigh-Mae 170a, 240a
Fitch, Robert 166b
Fitzgerald, Brian 143a
Fitzgibbon, S. 227b
Fladung, Hans 122a
Fladung Defence Committee 98a, 122a
Flaherty, R. 353a
Flamand, Paul 207a
Flamm, Irving H. 40a
Flapan, Simha 104a
Flatow, A. 169b
Flattery, Paul 209a
Flatto, Edwin 209a, 296a
Flavius, Francis 336a
Flechtheim, Ossip. K. 48b, 121b, 122a
Fleet, Kenneth 314a
Fleischmann, Ernest 288a
Fleischmann, Miriam 40a
R.B. Fleming & Co. Ltd. 209a
Flemish Action Committee for Eastern Europe 112b
Fletcher, J.B. 168a
Fletcher, John E. 170b
Fletcher, Mollie 290b
Fletcher, Richard 80b, 165b
C. & I.K. Fletcher Ltd. 3a
Flew, A.E. 238b
Flew, A.G.N. 209a
Flex, Konrad 325b
Flexner, Betty 259b, 292b, 352b
Flexner, Mag 292b
Flexner, William Welch 292b
Florakis, Lambros 124a
Flowers, Farouk 53a
Flug, Ewald 40a
Flying Magazine 143a
Focus on Soviet Jewry 40a, 112a
Foden, B. 170a
Fogelman, Aron 111b
Fogelman, Baruch 111b, 133b
Foges, Peter 98a, 155b, 209a
Foges, Wolfgang 195b, 196a, 296a
Foldes, Andor 260a
Foley, B.M. 88b
Foley, James 88b
Foley, Maurice 128b
Folk, Philip 170b
Folkman, Iris 296a
Folkman, Jerome 209a
Folks-Sztyme 209a
Follwell, Joan 260a
Folly, ? 280a
Food and Agricultural Organization 115a
Foot, Hugh 114a, 142b
Foot, Michael 40a, 114a, 141b, 142a, 237b
Foot, Paul 229a
Forbes, David 40a
Forbes, Henry F. 310b
Forchhammer, Grethe 260a
Ford, Alison 212a
Ford, Donald 325b
Ford, Oliver E. 260a
Ford, Thomas N. 325b
Ford & Son 88b
The Ford Film Library 143a
Foreberger, Mr. 122a
Forecast 209a
Foreign Affairs 129b, 209a
Foreign Affairs Bulletin 97b
Foreign Correspondents Ltd. 209a
Foreign Minister of Afghanistan 84b
Foreign Minister of Burma 84b
Foreign Minister of Cambodia 84b
Foreign Minister of Ceylon 84b
Foreign Minister of Japan 84b
Foreign Minister of Nepal 84b
Foreign Minister of Thailand 84b
The Foreign Office 29b, 40a, 123b, 130b, 133a, 141b, 260a, 325b-326a
Foreign Press Association 287b
Foreign Publications Service 209a
Foreman, Clark 135b, 137a, 259b
Forest, James 40a, 217b
Forest, Lester 209b
Forester, Mrs. 287b
Forester, Grace 290b, 292b, 303a, 354a
Forester, S. 260a
Forgacs, Pal 214b
Forlano, Gianni 298a
Forman, Hilda S. 40b
Forman, James 139b, 140a, 150a, 158b
Formosa **97a-b**
Formosan Committee for Liu's Human Rights 127a
Formoso, Leopoldo 228b
"Forms of Protest" 118b
Forrer, Paul T. 88b
Forrest, H. 79a
Forsman, Bertil 236a
Forss, Henrik 186b
Forst, G.N. 172a
Forsten, Aarne 173b
Forster, E.M. 260a, 287b
Forster, J.A.V. 326a
Forte, Charles 131b
Forte's 260a
Fort Hood Three Defense Committee 15b, 139a
Fortin, Mr. and Mrs. Yvon 296a
Fortoul, Frédéric 61b
Fortun Valdes, Armando 296a
Fortune 209b
Forum 209b
Forum-Verlag 325b
Forum World Features Ltd. 209b
Fosdick, Harry Emerson 42a
Fossum, John C. 201b
Foster, Harry 260a, 279a
Foster-Carter, A. 176b
Foster-Jakob, R. 326a
Foucard, Joyce 177a
Foudery, Ernest 326a
Foulds, Elfrida Vipont 298b
Foulkes, Paul 260a, 296a, 301a
Foundation Bulletin 141b
Four Lights 155b
Four Winds Press 209b
Fourah Bay College, Sierra Leone 296a
Fourniau, Charles 189b
Fournier, K. 110b
Fourth International 156a
Fourth Marathon March Committee 101a, 123a
The Fourth World Conference Against A & H Bombs and for Disarmament 144a
Fowler, Hugh 165a
Fowler, Nadia 108a
Fox, Barry 260a
Fox, P.O. 210a
Fox, Phil 40b
Fox, Philip 40b
Fox Pitt, Elspeth 260a, 287b, 304a, 353a
Foyer, Jean 97b
Foyle, Christina 209b
W. & G. Foyle Ltd. 209b
Foyle's Literary Luncheon 11a
Fraenkel, A. 260a
Fraidenraich, N. 40b
Frampton, Geoffrey 40b
Frame-Smith, Mr. 196a
France **97b, 121a-b, 173b-174a**
France, Mrs. Royal W. 258b, 264b
France, Ruth C. 156b
France-Observateur 97b
Francia, Henry 165b
Francis, Frank 267a
Francis, Harry 288a
Francis, Lucy 278a
Francis, Paulo 230a
Francis, R.A. 258a
Franck, H.G. 130a
Franco, Francisco 130b
Frank, Guillermo 186a-b
Frank, Jerome D. 40b, 53b, 341b
Frank, Pierre 242a, 298a
Frankel, Charles 40b
Frankl, Gerald 260a
Franpz, Andrew 296a
Franpz, Angus 296a

Frantz, Andrew Gibson 296a
Frantz, Virginia Knowland 352b
Fraser, W.R. 296a
Fraternelle des Amicales de Camps Verbroedering van de Vriendenkringen der Kampen 98a-b
Fray, J.C. 206a
Frederick, Harry 40b
Frederiksen, Richard 173a
Free Greece Campaign 101a
Free Speech Campaign 117b
Free Speech Petition on Behalf of the South Vietnamese National Liberation Front 165b
Free Trade Hall 146b
Freed, Donald 209b
Freedland, Michael 209b
Freedom 209b
Freedom and Organization 7b
Freedom Press 77b
Freedomways 136a
Freelance Photographers Guild, Inc. 209b
Freeley?, Alexandra 170a
Freeman, Eugene 221a
Freeman, Florence Elizabeth Pearl 312a
Freeman, John 116a, 223a
Freeman, Michael 227a
The Freethinker 209b
Freethought Society of America, Inc. 209b
Frege, G. 9a, 239b, 352b
Frehhammer, Grethe 260a
Frei, Eduardo 95a
Freid, Allison 238a
Freifeld, Samuel D. 209b
Frelimo 109b
Fremantle, Anne 260a
Fremet, Hinda 296a
Frémont, Jean 40b
French, E. 88b
French Delegation 151a
French Radio 97b
Freney, Denis W. 40b, 165b, 173b
Frenk, Chaim 111b
Frenk, Ester 111b
Frente de Libertaçao de Mocambique (Frelimo) 109b
Frente de Libertação Nacional e Colonial 58a, 110a, 128b
Frente Internacional de Derechos Humanos 106a, 127b
Frente Patriotica de Libertaçáo Nacional 130b
Frenz, Horst 209b
Freud, Arthur 40b
Freund, Hugo 174b
Frewin, Leslie 210a
Frey, Roger 97b
Frey, Sidney 198a-b
Fribourg and Freyer 151a, 260a
Friedensrat 175a
Friedensrat der Deutschen Demokratischen Republik 40b, 290b, 296a
Friedenthal, Sara 111a
Friedlander, Zelda 40b, 129b, 260a
Friedman, Bruno 213b
Friedman, Thomas B. 40b
Friedrich, C.J. 326a
Friedrich, Walter 40b, 99a, 149b, 151b, 175b, 290b
Friel, Patrick 40b
Friends Service Council, Quakers 40b
Friendship Centre 144b
Friendship Universal 40b
Friese Koerier 210a
Fritchey, Clayton 138a
Fritchman, Stephen H. 160a
Fritz, Jr., Charles A. 210a
Fromer, Robert 145b
Fromm, Anis 260b, 290b
Fromm, Erich 121b, 260a, 260b, 290b, 326a
Fromm, Joseph 79b
Frondizi, Ricardo A. 169a, 296a
Frons, F. 296a
Front 130b, 191a
Front Patriotique de Liberation Nationale de Portugal 128b
Frontier/the Voice of the New West 18b, 109a, 135b, 137a, 138a-b, 210a, 350b
Frost, Everett C. 76a
Frumkin, Robert M. 210a
L. Frumkin & Co. 313a
Fry, G. 260b
Frye, Burton C. 241b
Fuchs-Carsch, Michael 225b
Fucs, Ronald 171a
Fujimaki, Shimpei 144b
Fukao, S. 341b
Fukumoto, Matsuo 326a
Fukushima, Yoichi 160a, 175b
Fulbright, J. William 85b, 119a, 147a, 155b, 326a
Fulcrum 210a
Fuller, Jon W. 189b
Fullerton, Hamish 40b
Fulljames, R. 41a
Fulton, James G. 136b, 137a, 138a-b
Fulton, Leonard V. 210a
Richard Fulton Inc. 210a
Funai, Yukiko 145a
Fundamenta Mathematicae 335b-336a
Furnes, Nancy 234b
Furtado, Celso 158b
Fuse, T. 41a
Fussell, Diana 127a
Futerman, Elka 134b
Fyfe, Hamilton 278a

G

Gaberbocchus Press Ltd. 210a
Gabor, D. 326a
Gabriel, Joan 295a
Gabriel, Ralph Henry 326a
Gabriel, Sebyeza 113b
Gabrilovitch, L.E. 326a
Gacetilla Austral 141a
Gaddes, J.G. 291b
Gadea, Hilda 128a, 132a, 158b
Gaess, Roger 41a
Gago, Estevão 128b
Gaida, Werner 98b
Gaitskell, Hugh 152b
Gaitskell, Julie 148b
Gakken Co. 144b
Gale, John E. 49b
Gale Research Company 210a
Galeshan, Dave 54b
Galileo 210a
Galitzine, Theo 41a
Gallet, Jean-Pierre 171a
Gallois, André 41a
Galtung, Johan 208a
Gama, Admario 171a
Gambert, Stephen R. 41a
Gamble, Frederick Herbert 114b
Gamble, Maria 41a
Gamester, Phil 171b
Gammon, Roland 203b
Gamut Press, Inc. 210b
Gan, William N. 148a
Gandalf's Garden 218b
Gandhi, Indira 102a, 124b
Gandhi and Man in Evolution 165b
Gandhi Centenary 210b
Gandhi Marg 326a
Mahatma Gandhi on Nuclear Arms 326a
Gandhi National Memorial Fund 102b
Gandhi Peace Foundation 102b, 326a
Gandhi Smarak Nidhi 102b
Gandy, J.K. 41a
Ganesamoorthy, S. 326a
Gäng, Peter 174b
Ganguly, Adwaita P. 296a
Gannon, Patricio 260b
Ganzini, Marco 296a
Garaudet, Madeleine 161a
Garbaukas, A. 326b
García, Juan Pablo 127a
García González, Luciano 296a
Gardiner, A.D. 52b
Gardiner, C.F. 277b
Gardiner, Gerald 116a
Gardiner, Lord 142b
Gardner, Mr. and Mrs. 142b
Gardner, Augusta K. 292b
Gardner, Hy 210b
Gardner, N.H. 45b
Gardner, Ray 12a, 118a, 237b
Garfield, Allan 41a
Garg, Mohan Lal 198b
Garner, Dorothy 310b
Garner, Richard 310b
Garner, Roy 41a, 141b, 147b, 170a, 296a
Garnett, David 310b
Garnett, Tony 41a
Garnsey, D.A. 260b, 274b

Garot, Jean-Claude 96a
Garrison, Jim 139b, 155a, 156b
Garst, Jim 41a
Garvard, Timothy F. 41a
Garwood, Darrell N. 88b
Garza, Richard 105b, 127b
Gasperin, Antonio 296a
Gastón, Nilita Vientós 41a
Gastwirth, Don 242a
Gates, George G. 210b
Gaudin, A. 278a
Gaudin, Roger 229b
Gaugat, A.E. 195b
Gaughey, Andrew D. 41a
Gault, David 260b
Gausmann, William C. 238b
Gaven, Christian 174a
Gavin, Dr. Bulkeley 313a
Gawthorpe, Mary 296a
Gawthrop, Frank 32a
Geach, Jill 301a
Gebliast, Paul 175a
Geccato, C.N. 25b
Geering, Ken 41a, 200b
Geesland, Elizabeth Gordon 326b
Geffner, Edward 29b
Geisendorfer, James V. 41a, 138a, 150a
Geist, Franz 241b
Geller, Israel 129a
Gellner, Ernest 210b, 287b
Gemma, Junino 296a
General Assembly of International Permanent Committee for Amnesty for Political Prisoners and the Respect of Human Rights in Iraq 126b
General Assembly of the United Nations (Greece) 123b
The General Association of Korean Residents in Japan 145a
The General Confederation of Greek Labour 123a-b
General Council of Trade Unions of Japan 144b, 296a, 326b
General Guarantee Corporation Ltd. 88b
General Post Office 313a
General Press Cutting Association Ltd. 210b
The General Representation Abroad of the Kurdish Revolution 125b
General Representation of the Kurdish Revolution 126b
General Strike for Peace 41a
The General Union of Arab Students 107a-b
Generalbundesanwalt 99b
Genesis 210b
Geneva Reception and Information Centre for Deputations to Conferences Concerned with Disarmament 41a
Genovés, Eduardo 296a
Genschel, Rudolph 41b
Gensuikyo 296b
Gente 210b
Genteman, Paul 41b, 172a
Genthner, James 41b
Geoffrey, M. 174a
The Geographical Journal 327a
George, K. 101a
Gerard, David L. 41b, 258a
Gerassi, John (Tito) 150a, 160a, 210b
Gerhardsen, Einar 108a
German and International Youth Information Service 121b
German Branch, BRPF **143b-144a**
German Democratic Republic: Chancellory of the Council of State, Protocol and Organisation Department 99a, **175a-b**
German Democratic Republic Delegation 151b
German International 98a
German Metal Workers' Union 99a
German Peace Union 100a
German Socialist Student's Union 121b
Germany **97b-98b, 121a-b**
Germany (East) **98b-99a, 121b**
Germany (West) **99a-100a, 121b-122a**
Geronazzo, Laura 215a
Gerrard, A.B. 257a
Gerrosi, S. 143a
Gerst, Karl 41b
Gertung, Niels-Henrik 173b
Gerz, Mira 111b
Gessner, Peter 88b
Getz, Andrew 41b
Ghana **100a-b, 122b**
Ghana Peace Council 100b
Ghanacom 41b
Ghanaian Times 210b
Ghanem, Fathy 208a
Gharahbeiglu, B. 51b, 124b
Gheorghiu-Dej, Gheorghe 110a, 129a
Ghibernae, M. 110a
Ghilan, Maxim 104a, 195b
Ghosal, Sundar 102b
Ghose, P.K. 210b
Ghose, S.M. 242a
Ghosh, S.C. 14b, 145b
GI Civil Liberties Defense Committee 296a
Gianased, Al 352b
Giannatasio, Luis 115a
Gianni, Ernesto 210b
Giannini, David 210b
Giao, Nguyen Ngoc 165b
Giard, Philippe 174a
Gibbins, John R. 260b
Gibbon & Rogers, Chartered Surveyors 309b, 313a
Giblin, L.F. 260b
Giblin, P.J. 287b
Gibor, Aharon 41b
Gibson, Homer 172a
Gibson, J.B. 178a
Gibson, Richard 218a
Gidwani, M.M. 41b
Gielgud, John 287b
Gietzelt, D. 26a
Giguére, John A. 296a
Giladi, Gita 135a
Gilbert, C.M.J. 153b
Gilbert, Martin 260b
Gilbert, Mary 41b
Gilchrist, Mary Lyle 312a
Giles, Lionel 260b
Gill, J.S. 41b
Gill, Jack 198a
Gillard, Frank 131b
Gillespie, R.D. 278a
Gillett, Margaret 220a
Gillon, Rebecca 129a
Gilly, Adolpho 127a
Gilpin, Richard 217b
Gilroy, W.J. 33a
Gilstos?, Helen 301a
Gimignani, Gastone 32b
Ginsberg, Robert 210b
Ginzburg, Ralph 208b
Gir, Michael 287a
Gira, I.H. 174b
Girodias, Maurice 121a
Gisborne, H.P. 309b
Gisela 128a
Gispert, Eduardo H. 96a
Gittings, John 33b, 145b, 165b, 326b
Gittings, Richard Gilbert 47a
Gjerløv-Knudsen, C.O. 97a, 141b
Gladwyn, Lord 41b
Glasgow Vietnam Solidarity Campaign 41b
Glaslyn Hotel 277a
Glass, Bentley 41b
Glass, David V. 152b, 176a
Glass, Ruth 176a
Glazer, Robert 143a
Glazer, T.I. 112b
CWK Gleerup 210b
Glemser, Peter 230a
Glen, S. 296a
Glenfield, William R. 41b
Glenn, John R. 41b, 94b
Glesson, J.E. 308a
Glezer, Ber 113a
Glezer, Paulina 113a
Glezou, Tassia 122b
Glick, Ira 41b
Glidewell, Richard 207a
Gligoric, Velibor 296a
Global Books 41b
Glockman, J. 90a
Głos Wolnych 354a
Glover, Jake 42a, 135b
Glozar, M. 96b
Glozman, Maya 134a
Glubb, Faris 52a, 143a, 145b
Gluckman, M. 287b
Glyn, Mills & Co. 88b, 154b, 296a, 307a, 309b
Gobel, José Llanusa 96a

Goberman, Elie 135a
Goddard, Don 42a, 150a
Goddard, Leonard 326b
Goddard, Madeline 296a
Theodore Goddard & Co. 148b
Gödel, Kurt 263b
Godfrey, J. 296a
Godfrey, P. 296a
Godinho, Guilherme 298a
Godwin, George 42a, 42b
Godwin, Mack 70a
Goemans, P.W. 225b
Goffe, Elisabeth 260b
Gohardi, Adolfo 229b
Göktürk, Aksit 210b
Gold, Alan 112a
Gold, Ann 301a
Gold, Eva 167a
Goldberg, Arthur J. 42a, 107a
Goldberg, Richard 221a
Goldblatt, Hava 134b
Goldbloom, Sam 26b, 170a
Goldeer, Gitta 216b
The Golden Horn 114a, 210b
Goldenberg, Eva 113a
Goldewski, Joseph de Gozdawa 326b
Goldfarb, Samuel 42a
Goldhammer, Joachim 42a, 110b, 129a
Goldman, David 42a
Goldman, Emma 260b
Goldreich, Abraham Jacob 42a
Goldschlaeger, Ignatz 110b, 129a
Goldschläger, Alda Ilana 129a
Goldschläger, Rosa 110a
Goldschmidt, John 86a
Goldsmith, Oliver 352b
Goldstein, Cynthia H. 210b
Goldstone, Julian S. 42a
Goldwater, Barry 13b, 18b, 70b, 115b
Gollan, John 34b, 115b, 152b
Gollancz, Victor 111b, 210b, 211a, 287b, 326b
Golubooj?, Valdimir 296a
Gomes, Rui Galapez 130b
Gomez, Emileo Abreu 26a
Gomez, Ruy Luiz 78b, 128b
Gomulka, Wladyslaw 109b, 156a
Gonick, C.W. 202a
Gonin, Michael S. 260b
Gooch, George 260b
Good Neighbor Publications, Inc. 42a
Goodenough, Erwin R. 326b
Goodlet, Dr. 344b
Goodman, Anthony 131b
Goodman, Peter 42a
Goodwin, Clive 136a, 199b
Goodwin Press Ltd. 88b, 211a
Goonewardene, Leslie 148b
Göpel, Wilfried 211a
Gorbach, Alfons 93b
Gordin, I. 113a
Gordina, Risa 111a
Gordon, Alec 296a
Gordon, Anita 95a
Gordon, Eric 148b
Gordon, George 351a
Gordon, Haim 42a
Gordon, J.C. 129a
Gordon?, Jackie 281a
Gordon, Jeffrey Sheppard 42b, 95a, 118b, 137b, 211a
Gordon, Joseph 42b
Gordon, Michael 42b
Gordon, Mitchell 42b
Gordon, Ronald W. 42b
Gordon, Sam 42b, 220b
Gordon Press Ltd. 211a
Goren, Robert 213b
Goring, Marius 115a
Gorkin, A.F. 133b
Gorky 218a
Gormly, Walter 224a
Görög, I. 42b
Gortz, André 236b
Gosse, Keith 42b
Goswamuy, Shyam 42b
Göteborgs-Tidningen 211a
Goto, Motoo 197b
Gotsche, Mr. 99a, 121b
Gott, Richard 65b-66a, 326b
Gottesman, Albert 211a
Gottesman, Dvora 111b
Gottfried, Mrs. Alex 71b
Götting, Gerald 29a, 99a
Gottlieb, Bill 25a, 107a
Gottstein, K. 326b
Gough, W.M. 172a
Goulart, Joao Belchior Marques 94a
Gould, Bob 169a
Gould, James A. 211a
Gould, Nicholas 260b
Gould, Symon 197a
Gourevitch, Robert 354b
Goussinsky, Boris 326b
The Governor of Cairo 106b
Gower, R.C. 229a
Gowon, Yukubu 108a
Goyal, D.R. 219b
Goyal, Narenda 42b
GPO, Returned Letter Branch 257b
Grace, Dora Winifred (*See* Russell, Dora)
Grace, Pat 280b, 281a, 282b, 283a
Graebner, Walter 209b
Graeff, Thomas L. 42b
Graham, Alistair 47a
Graham, D.C. 239a
Graham, Donald V. 88b, 172a
Graham, Ian 301a
Gralmann, ? 122a
Grammatikakis, V. 123b
Granada TV Network Ltd. 211a
Grand National Convention on Vietnam 16a
Granelle, Mr. 174a
Granelle, Mrs. 174a
Grani 116b
Granik, Atara Stern 111a
Granirer, Fany Yakovlevna 111a
Granma 17b
Grant, Allen Frederick 42b
Grant, David 260b
Grant, Edmund 42b
Grant, Stephanie 288b
Grant Brown, R. 326b
Granten, Marilyn 172a
Gräßner, Sigrid 98b
Grattan-Guinness, Ivor 260b
Graubard, Stephen R. 205a
Graves, J. 281a
Graves, John 42b, 222b
Graves, Stewart 211a
Gray, Camilla 42b, 116b
Gray, Guy W.S. 42b
Gray, J.O.D.G. 42b, 171b
Gray, Mab 210a
Gray, Ronald 211b
Graydon, Richard 296b
Gray's Point–Sutherland Communist Party 170a
Grayson, Jeffrey 42b
Greatorex, D.M. 204b
Greaves, C. Desmond 48b, 214b
Greaves, E.H. 287b
Greece **100b-101b, 122b-124a, 175b**
Greedy, Alan 273b
Greek Alumni Associations of Cyprus 96a
Greek Ambassador 100b, 122b, 123b
Greek Committee Against Dictatorship 101a
Greek Committee for Nuclear Disarmament 101a-b
Greek Delegation 151b
Greek National Resistance 123a
The Greek Relief Fund 101a
Greek Society for Nuclear Disarmament, Bertrand Russell 42b, 123a
Greek Youth Association for Nuclear Disarmament 124a
Greek Youth "Bertrand Russell" Committee for Nuclear Disarmament 100b
Green, Anthony 42b
Green, Ashbel 216b
Green, Elizabeth 260b
Green, Graham C. 202a
Green, L.C. 171b
Green, Martin L. 233b
Green, Maurice 205a
Green, Michael 238a
Green, Paul 260b, 296b
Green, Roger 296b
Green, S.W. 43a
Green River Community College 211a
Greenbaum, Benjamin 115b
Greenberg, Jacob 61b
Greene, Felix 43a, 156b, 165b, 178b
Greene, Graham 43a, 118b, 158b, 165b, 287b
Greene, Randall A. 296b

Greenfield Recorder-Gazette 296b
Greenish, R.P. 287b, 296b
Greensand, Blaine 146a
Greenstein, Arnie 296b
Greenwell, Tom 242b
Greet, Dr. 43a
Gregor, Norman 43a
Gregory, Anne 70b
Gregory, C.C.L. 43a
Gregory, Dick 138a, 139b, 165b, 296b
Gregory, Mrs. Dick 296b
Gregory, Frank 43a, 90b
Gregory, M. 43a
Grelling, Kurt 326b
Gresham, C.A. 327a
The Gresham Press 196b
Greve, Marie 174a
Grew, Frederick J. 327a
Grew, Richard L. 260b
Greystoke, Andrew J. 242a
Grice, James E. 290b
Griesser, Marjorie 204a
Griffen, William L. 43a
Griffin, Jr., C.W. 155b, 211a
Griffin, Evan D. 88b
Griffin, Merv 138b
Griffin, Nicholas J. 227a, 261a
Griffin, Stuart H. 261a
Griffith, Miss 278a, 309a
Griffith, David 43a
Griffith, Gwilym O. 261a
Griffith, Raymond 170a
Griffiths, Eldon 224a
Griffiths, Glyn 204b
Griffiths, H. 261a
Griffiths, Leslie M.S. 261a
Griffiths, Lillian 261a
Griffiths, R. 280b
Griffiths, Ruby 261a
Griffiths, Will 126a
Grigoletto, Getulio G. 43a
Griicrush 43a
Grigoryan, B. 222b
Grimau, Julian 130a
Grimberg, Eugenia 111a
Grimes, W.F. 279b
Grimsell, C.P. 90b
Grinberg, Eva 112a, 135a
Grinberg, Michal 112a, 135a
Grinberg, Miguel 37b, 120a, 141a
Grindal, Morten 113a, 147b
Grindae, Miron 195a
Grippa, Jacques 170b
Griswold, Deirdre 16b, 17a, 56b, 86a, 103a, 139a, 226b, 239b
Groen, H. 45b
Grohs, Alois 96a, 172b, 296b
Gromyko, Andrei A. 108b, 116b
Groom, Robert 261a
Grooms, John 43a
Gropius, Walter 261a, 287b
Gros, André 97b
Gross, David L. 203b
Gross, Michael 202a
Gross, Ralph 211a
Gross, William F. 43a
Gross, Fine and Krieger, Chalfen 261a
Grosseman, Jerome 46b
Grosser, Willi 43a
Grossmann, Haika 192a
Groszkiewicz, Jacek 195b
Grotta, Daniel Taylor 211a
Group of (Anonymous) Polish Intellectuals 109b
Groupe de Recherche et d'Action pour le Règlement du Problème Palestinien 32b
Groupe d'Etudes et d'Action Socialiste Tunisien 131a
"Groups for Three" Amnesty International 98b
Grove, Mr. 147b
Grove Press Inc. 196b, 211a
Gruber, Gerd 175a
Grunbaum, M. 43a
Grunberg, Simon 129a
Grundy, Bill 274b
Grundy, Peter 29a, 125b
Grunitsky, Nicholas 113b
Grupo Cultural Melchor Ocampo 43a
Gryffyold, Professor 278b
Guanche, Daniel Camejo 127b
The Guardian 10a-b, 11a, 12b, 13b, 25a, 30a, 37a, 40b, 41a, 42a, 42b, 64b, 75b, 77b, 83b, 96a, 96b, 99b, 100a, 100b, 101a, 103a, 103b, 110a, 111a, 113a, 114a, 115b, 118a, 120b, 122b, 123a, 138a, 141a-b, 146b, 155a-b, 156a-b, 178a, 183a, 211a, 214b, 273b, 313a, 331a, 335a
Guardian Assurance Co. Ltd. 307b
Guast?, G. Ronald 123a
Guatemala **101b**
Guatemalan Committee for Solidarity with Vietnam 179a
Guatti, Allano 296b
Guerassimov, B. 225b
Guerin, ? 161a
Guérin, Daniel 130b, 131a, 173b
Guerin, M. 43a
Gueron, Maurice 261a
Guerra Theilheimer, Edmundo 165b
Guevara, Che 96a, 148b, 156a
Guevara, Ernesto 158b
Guevara, Gilberto 296b
Guha, A.K. 43a
Guild Gazette 114b
Guillaume, A. 43a
Guillet, Bernard 174a
Guillieri, Guilliemo 291a
Guimarães, Murilo Humberto de Barros 43a
Guinea **101b**
Guinea Press Ltd. 211b
Gujarat University 88b
Gujarat University, India 211b
Gulbekain, Yedvard 53b
Gulbenkian, P. 112b, 120a
Calouste Gulbenkian Foundation, Lisbon 88b
Gullord, Einar 227a
Gumucio, Mariano Baptista 94a, 117b
Gunderson, Minne 353a
Gunnar, John 288a
Günther, Dietrich 122a
Günther, Hans 170b
Gunton, Michael 209a
Günyol, Vedat 106b
Guon, Pak Il 159a
Guppy, Nicholas 43a
Gupta, Anirudha 43a
Gupta, Hari Kishan 327a
Gupta, K.L. 90a, 102a
Gupta, Prem Dayel 153b
Gupta, Shri Prakash 43a
Gurgel, Idelberto F. 171a
Guriel, R.M. 135a
Gurwala, Shiv Narain 261a
Gurwitz, Benzion 111a
Guthrie, Paul J. 101a
Guthrie, Robin 287b, 290b
Gutierrez Raynares, Carlos 296b
Gutiérrez G., V. Manuel 126a
Gutman, Jeremiah S. 43a
Guttman, Simon 43a, 108a
Guyana **101b**
Guzman, Martin Luis 112b
Gwynn, Arthur ap 88b
Gyaw, U. Hla 24a, 171b
Gypsy Council Liaison Committee 88b

H

H.A.T. 276b
H.M. Stationery Office 89a
H.M. Inspector of Taxes 309b
Haag, Anna 174b
Haagsche Post 211b
Haaretz 104b, 127a, 211b
Habaybeh, Anwar 105b
Habbel, Druck Joseph 323a
Habermel, Sybil 290b
Habiba, Retig 196a
Hablitschek, Wolfgang W. 171a
Hachenburger, Werner 43b, 175a, 290a
Hacker, M. 88b
Hacopian, Roland 43b
Haddad, Phelippe Nagi 120b
Haddow, Alex 211b
Hadha, ? 43b
Hadjiandreou, Maria 100b
Hadow, Grace E. 353a
Hagaman, Nancy 224b
Hagerty, Jr., H.R. 43b
Hagerty, Jr., Mrs. H.R. 43b
Hague, T.E. 43b
Hahn, Mrs. Joseph 43b
Hahn, Kurt 43b, 98b
Hahn, Otto 165b
Haigh, James 39b
Haile, Menassie 97a

Hailsham, Lord 43b
Hainsworth, Malcolm 43b
Haiti **101b**
Haitin, Genia 133b
Hajda, Joseph 43b, 98a, 173a
Hájek, Jirí 96b
Haksar, P.N. 102a
Hakumon Herald 144a, 145a, 211b
Haldane, Helen Spurway 261a
Haldane, J.B.S. 261a
Haldane, Lord 256b
Haldar, S. 327a
Halding, John 327a
Haldimann, Herman Gottfried 327a
Halevy, Benjamin 158b
Haley, W.J. 237a
Halfhill, Robert Wakefield 43b
Halford, Henry, Montefiore & Co. 88b
Halifax, Lord 43b
Halifax Vietnam Council 165b
Halini, Gisèle 109a, 160a, 186a, 187b, 188a
Hälker, Kurt 63a, 98a, 99a, 100a, 175a
Hall, Conway 123b
Hall, Max 212a
Hall, Noel 177a
Hall, R.O. 120b
Hall, Stuart 148a, 251a
Hall, Theodore 88b
Hall, William James 43b, 147a
A.E. Hall Dairy 143a
The Hall Syndicate, Inc. 134a
Hallet, James Hughes 208b
Hallett, Molly 88b
Hallgren, Carl 43b
Halliday, Fred 167a
Halliday, John 214b
Halliday, Jon 143a
Hällstrom, Björn 146a
Hallström, Olle 113a
Halsall, J.C. 89b
Halsbury, Earl of 261a
Halsey, L.E. 314a
Halsted, G.B. 9a
Halter, Aubrey J. 94b
Hamai, Shinzo 43b, 144b
Hambleton, Ronald 261a
Theodore Hamblin Ltd. 261a, 283a
Hambro, Eduard 80b, 147b
Hambros Bank Ltd. 88b
Hamburger, Bella 110a
Hamburger, L. 110a
Hamburger Komitee zur Wahrung Demokratischer 100a
Hameed, G.S. Abdul 299b
Hameed, S.A. 43b
Hamers, Arno 32b
Hami, Shinzo 287b
Hamilton, A. 101a
Hamilton, Reina 135b
Charles Hamilton Autographs, Inc. 258a
Hamlin, Jerome 43b, 242a
Hamly, Edna 116a
Paul Hamlyn Publishers 211b
Hamm, Michael 175a
Hammar, Bo 143b, 237a
Hammer, Mrs. Anselm 44a
Hammer Film Productions 44a
Hammerschmidt, Hans 146b
The Hammersmith Bookshop Ltd. 211b
Hammond, Janette 33a
Hammond and Champres Ltd. 88b
Hampstead and Camden 296b
Hampstead Borough Council 143a
Hampstead Group, Committee of 100 131a
Hampton & Sons 313b
Hamwi, M. Radwan 113b
Hanafi, A.M. 103a
Hanarth, Rachel 261a
Hancock, Alan 327a
Hancock, Bertram 44a
Hand, Fanny 261a, 280a
Hand, Judge Learned 261a
The Hand & Flower Press 211b
Handley, Ellenor 148a
Hands Off Vietnam 178a
Hanghøj, Per 207b
Hankinson, Wendy 44a, 145b
Hannum, Elizabeth 288a
Hanoi Université 296b
Hansard Parliamentary Debates 38a, 46a
Hansard Society 211b
Hansden, Martin 44a, 176a
Hansen, Arne Bjerring 148b
Hansen, Aslak 44a
Hansen, Clarence 147a
Hansen, Henrik Holm 173a
Hansen, Joseph 214a, 242a
Hansen, Reba 242a
Carl Hanser Verlag 211b
Hansler, W.D. 44a
Hansson, Johan 200b
Haolam Hazeh 104b, 127a
Haouari, Souiah 93a, 156b
Haq, Barbara 58a, 96a, 108a, 113b, 130a-b, 156a, 166b, 181a, 297b
Harada, Tomin 145a
Haravgi 211b
Harburg, E.Y. 261a
Harcourt, J.T. 44a, 211b
Hardcastle, William 11a
Hardie, Frank 353a
Harding, Christopher 170a
Harding, D.E. 327a
Harding, Neville 44a
Harding, Stan 261b
Hardisty, D. 205a
Harewood, Earl of 91a
Harlech Branch Labour Party 296b
Harlem Youth Opportunities Unlimited, Inc. 44a
Harlowe, Marie 44a
Harman, Avraham 104a
Harman, C.L. 44a
Harman, W.R. 44a
Harman Healy & Co. 143a
Harod, H. 44a
Haroon, Mahmoud A. 108b
Harper, Malcolm 167a
Harper & Brothers 211b
Harper & Row, Publishers 212a
Harper's Magazine 137a, 212a
George G. Harrap & Co. 212a
Harries, Morfudd 44a
Harrington, Olive 276a, 278a, 309a, 310b, 353a
Harris, Audrey 143a
Harris, Connie W. 131b, 143a, 172b
Harris, Gavin 30b
Harris, H. 44a
Harris, Harold 213b
Harris, Isabelle 172a
Harris, John 16b, 139a
Harris, John 172a
Harris, John Robert 44a
Harris, Judith 44a
Harris, Morgan 44a
Harris, Steve 239b
Harris, W.J.H. 54a, 69a, 141a, 147b
Harrison III, Bradford 44a
Harrison, Craig R. 212a
Harrison, E. 283b
Harrison, Gilbert 223a
Harrison, James M. 327a
Harrison, Linda 173b
Harrison, Reg 170a
Harrison, Royden 148a, 261a
Harrison, Sonia 88b
Harrison, Stephen R. 296b
Harrisson, T.H. 327a
Harrod, Sir Roy 212a
Harrods Book Dept. 279b
Harrods Ltd. 278a, 353a
Harrow, Tessa C. 220b
Harrow Technical College, Students Union 212a
Hart, A.T. 291a
Hart, Alex 44a
Hart-Davis, Duff 236a
Rupert Hart-Davis Ltd. 212a
Hartley, Leslie 261b
Hartley, Norah 352a
Hartman, Catherine 198a
Hartnack, Julius 336b
Hartt, Joel 203b
Hartwell, Eric 132a
The Harvard Crimson 321b
Harvard Law Review 329a
Harvard University 157a, 281a
Harvard University Press 212a
Harvard-Radcliffe Committee to End the War in Vietnam 44a
Harvey, Audrey 148b
Harvey, Dorothy (née Dudley) 261b
Harvey, Philip 158b
Harvey, Ronald F. 143a, 148b
Harwood, Michael 251b
Has, Jiri 96b

Has Man a Future? 11b, 19a
Hashimi, M. 126a
Hashmi, Amis 108b
Hashtroodi, M. 106b
Haskell, Arnold L. 282a
Haslem Hazeh 212a
Hassan, F. 179a
Hassan, Riffat 212a
Hassan II, King 108a
Hassouna, Abdelhalek 107a
Hastings, Summerville 281a
The Hatfield Press Ltd. 88b
Hatjistephanidis, Gregory 122b
Hatsuoka, Shoichiro 89a
Hatton, Trevor 227a, 296b
Hauber, W.J.R. 44a
Haughey, Charles J. 126b
Haunaer, Karen 69a
Hauser, Richard 106b
Hausler, Gunnel 117a, 132a
Hausmann, Gordon 112a, 156a
Havana Cultural Conference 95b
Havighurst, Alfred F. 261b
Hawkes, Anthony 44b
Hawkes, Ken 95b
Hawkeswell, Marjory L. 44b, 172a
Hawkin, D.A. 353a
Hawkins, Dora 44b
Hawkins, Jr., Eugene H. 327a
Hawks, W. 313a
Hawkshaw, E.P. 281a
Hawksley, Dorothy 292b
Hawly, Jan 143a
Hawmid, B.A. 218a
Hawtrey, Ralph 292b
Hay, A.K. 281a
Hay, June 259a
Hayashi, Kanichi 216b
Hayashi, M. 341b
Hayashi, Takuo 219b
Hayashi, Yujiro 145a
Haycraft, C.M. 353a
Haydon, B.W. 66a
Hayes, Brian 44b, 214b
Hayes, Harold 208a
Haymon, Mark 261b
Haynes, Jim 148b
Hayward, S.F. 313b
Haywood, G.E. 310b
Hazeldine, Nigel 174a
Hazleton, B. 280a
Head, Viscountess Dorothea 44b
Heald, Johnson, Garton & Co. 131b, 142b
Healey, Albert 44b
Healey, D.T. 32a, 165a
Healing, Bryan 208a
Healy, G. 178b
Hearnshaw, J.B. 261b
Heathcote, G. 204b
Heaton, Michael 296b
Hebdon, P.H. 215b
Heckstall-Smith, Hugh W. 44b
Haddow, Alec 354a
Heelas, Terence 44b
Heffer, Eric S. 108a, 148a, 177a
Hefner, Hugh M. 228a
Heibonsha Ltd. 212a
Heidelberger, Michael 44b
Heikal, Muhammed Hasanein 42a, 106b, 107b, 111a, 114a, 149b, 156b, 196a
Heilmann, Albert 44b
Heimann, M. 58a
Heimann, Jean-Pierre 110a
Heimbach, Roy 88b
Heinemann, F.H. 261b
Heinemann, Jean 173b
William Heinemann Ltd. Publishers 212a
Heinemann Educational Books Ltd. 212a
Heiner, Gianni A. 44b
Heipp, Günther 69a, 99b, 144a 175a, 212a
Heiser, Bryan M. 44b
Heisig, Georg 174b
Heisler, Francis 44b, 137a, 142a
Heisler, Wyldbore 296b
Heisler & Stewart 62b, 137a, 142a, 156b
Heistek, L.J. 88b
Heitmann, Erna 99b
Hélier, Odile 174a
Hell, Michael 261b
Hellenic Committee for International Détente and Peace 122b
The Hellenic Postman of Canada 171b
Heller, Howard 44b
Heller, Irving 290b
Heller, Joseph 261b
Helling, Fritz 99b
Helm, Tom 312a
Helmholtz, H. 349b
Help 212b
Helsinki Conference 153a
Hemel Hempstead CND 296b
Hemisphere 212b
Hemispheric Council to End the Vietnam War 166a
Hemming, Sir Thomas 281a
Hempl?, Frank 88b
Hemp, W.J. 327a
Hemstreet, Robert 261b
Henderson, Arthur 116a
Henderson, Dorothy 212b
Henderson, Greg 281a
Henderson, Hamish 148a
Hendricks, Henry W. 44b
Hendrickson, John 89a
Hendrix, P. 44b
Heney, John 44b, 170a
Henkin, Leon 261b
Hennecke, Hans-Jörg 207b
Henriod, Gerard 110a
Henriquez, Mr. 197a
Henry, Claudine 143a
Henry, Maurice 45a
Henry, Norman 89a
Henry, Rondel D. 45a
Henry, T.E. 219b
Henschel, Liesbeth 98b
Henshaw, Paul 149b
Henson, Barbara 45a
Hepburn & Ross Ltd. 89a, 151a
Hepp, Maylon H. 212b
Heppner, Sam 212b
Hepworth, Barbara 116a
Herald (India) 153b
Herald Tribune 137a
Herbath, J.V. 45a
Herbert, Benson 215b
Herbert, Susan 219a
Herce, Alberto López 113a
Herd, Eric 147a
Herles, J.A. 121b
Herman, Mary 89a
Hermanson, Mr. 113b
Hermenau, Herman P. 45a
Hermes, Helene 34a, 97b
Hernandez, Amado V. 157a, 185b, 192a
Hernández, Melba 157b, 192a, 295b
Herneck, Friederich 45a
Herrington, Richard A. 45a
Herron, Caroline Rand 226b
Herterich, Elmar 122a
Hertling, Helmut 99b
Hertz, H. 349b
Hertz Drive Yourself Stations of Ontario Ltd. 89a
Hertz Rent a Car 89a
Hervey, Helen 261b
Hervia, Miguel Gomez 166a
Herz, Alice 341b
Herz, Hermann 45a
The Alice Herz Peace Fund 45a, 145b, 175b, 341a
Herzog, Roland 174b
Herzog, Yaakov 104a
Hess, Anita 168b
Hess, Rudolf 43b, 45a
Hess, Wolf Rudiger 45a, 122b
Hester, Hugh B. 45a
Hester, M. 314a
Hetherington, A. 120b, 123b, 141b
Heumann, Rainer 212b
Hewgill, John 45a
Hewitt, David 45a
Hews, John R. 200a
Heyerdahl, Thor 261b
Heym, Stefan 174b
Heyn, Herman M. 45a
Hibbert Journal 326b
Hick, John H. 212b
Hickerson, George H. 45a
Hickey, Helen 45a
Hickey, O.M. 146a
Hicks, Calvin 45a
Hicks, Elsa 47b
Hicks, John 220a
Hicks, N. 45a
Oswald Hickson, Collier & Co. 313b
Hickson, Lakeman & Holcombe 89a
Hidaka, Rokuro 144b

Hidden, R.L. 174b
Hieblinger, Leo B. 96b
Hierest?, Heinz 116a
Hieu, Nguyen Van 118a, 132a, 156a, 162a, 178a, 190a
Higgins, James 242b
Higgins, Roger W. 217b
Higgins, Mrs. Thomas M. 296b
Higgs, G. 45a
High Commissioner for Ghana 100a
High Committee for the Defense of the Iraq People 103b, 126a
Highams, S. 45a
Higher Agricultural School 207b
Highsmith, D.J. 45b
Hijner, C. 45b
Hilaly, Agha 108b
Hilbery, G.M. 309a
Hilborn, K.H.W. 12b
Hilburn, John E. 45b
Hildrath, Peter 212b
Hildred, W. 62b
Hiley, Peter 118b, 236a
Hilgart, Arthur 45b
Hill, Alan 212a
Hill, C.F.L. 89a
Hill, Colin 310b
Hill, E. 146a
Hill, Frank 122b
Hill, J. 170a
Hill, L. 45b
Hill, L.A. 296b
Hill, L. Rowland 261b
Hill, Leslie 261b
Hill, M. 114b
Hill, M. Joy 232a, 268a
Hill, Margo Strange 89a
Hill, Marion S. 45b
Hill, Maurice 45b
Hill, Norman 230a
Hill, W.W. 45b
Hiller, Jacques Allain 201b
Hillman, Evelyn 296b
Hills, Christopher B. 202b, 327a
Walter Hill's Poster Advertising Co. Ltd. 45b
Hilsdon, P. 199b
Hilton, Alice Mary 149b, 212b
Hilton, Rodney H. 148a
Hinckle III, Warren 229b
Hindemith, Joachim 99a
Hindu 153b, 212b
Hindustan Times 153b
Hindusthan Library 324a
Hing-Ear 94b
Hinton, Eleanor 146a
Hinton, H.E. 177a
Hinton, Jennifer 80a
Hintze, Mrs. Edward 45b
Hipp, H. Rüdiger 212b
Hirano, Yoshitaro 186a
Hirfan, S. 45b
Hiroo Ochiai Executive Committee 78a
Hiroshima, City of 144b, 145b
Hiroshima Day Committee 45b
Hiroshima Day Demonstrators in Athens 101a, 123b
Hiroshima House 296b
Hiroshima House Foundation 45b, 145a
Hiroshima Peace Declarations 1967-8 85b
Hiroshima-Nagasaki 145a
Hirotsu, Kazuo 144b
Hirsch, Carl 158b
Hirsch, Roland A. 45b
Hirsch, Sigismondo 45b
Hirschfield, Gerhard 198a
Hirschsprung, Herbert 212b
A History of Western Philosophy 257b, 260a, 352b
Hitaka, Ikki 11b, 12a, 104b, 145b, 212b, 268b, 296b
Hitaka, Kazuteru 145a, 268b
Hitchcock, G.L.H. 295a
Hitchens, Christopher 45b
Hitler 190a, 332b
Hloch, Miroslav 121a
Ho, Albert 296b
Ho, Ro Jai 127a
Ho Chi Minh 18b, 62b, 80a, 132a, 142b, 162a-b, 163a, 176a, 184b, 190b
Hoa, Nguyen Van 163a
Hoang, Michel 125a
Hoangh Ming Hiam 296b
Hoang-Linh 79a
Hoare, M.P. 313a
Hoare, Michael 218b
Hoare, Quintin 90a, 185a, 211b, 230b
Hoashi, Kei 45b, 175b, 186a
Hobday, Robert D. 257b-258a
Hobden, Dennis 176b
Hobin, Richard 143a
Hoch, Paul K. 115a, 172a, 232b
Hochkeppel, Willy 236b
Hochleitner, E. 93b
Hock, Horst 98b
Hocking, William Ernest 261b
Hodder and Stoughton Ltd. 212b, 324a
Hodes, Aubrey 103b, 104a, 145b, 212b
Hodge Unit Trust Managers Ltd. 89a
Hodgetts, R. 128b
Hodgkin, D.M.C. 158b
Hodgkin, David K.R. 147a
Hodgkin, Dorothy 45b, 163a, 182a
Hodgkin, Thomas 45b
Hodgson, Rica 88a
Hodin, J.P. 261b
Hodjiendreou, Maria 124a
Hoegler, Michael 45b
Hoekstra, H. 112a
Hoey, Elizabeth 117a
Hofbauer, Imra 213a
Hoffman, Hallock 32b
Hoffman, Paul G. 46a, 115a, 142b
Hoffman, Randall W. 213a
Hoffman, Richard C. 46a
Hoffmeyer, Henrik 158b
Hofheinz, Engelbert 213a
Hofmann, Warner 24b
Hofstatter, Moritz 46a
Hogan, Juan Luis 141a
The Hogarth Press Ltd. 213a
Hogben, Lancelot 261b, 287b
Hoggart, David 46a
Hoggart, Richard 177a
Hogget, David 143a
Hogstedt, Christer 73b
Hojer, J. Axel 160a, 185a
Hokanson, Tore 152b
Holbrook, David 177a
Holbrook, Rosemary Greeley 228b
Holcroft, M.H. 223b
Holdchock?, Douglas 296b
Holden, William 212a
Holder, Mrs. 143a
Holdershaw, G. 46a
Holiday 213a
Holland, Kevin 262a, 292b
Holland, Marian 290b
Holland, S.L. 53b
Hollis, F.R. 46a
Hollond, H.A. 281b
Holloway, Roger T. 228b
Holloway Sanatorium 278a
Hollstein, Fritz 100a
Holmes, A.W. 262a
Holmes, D.R. 101b
Holmes, David 272a
Holmes, Glyn 199a
Holmes, Margaret 89a, 147b
Holmes, Rexford 89a
Holroyd, Michael 262a
Holt, Geo. H. 33b, 327a
Holt, Harold 147b, 179a, 296b
Holt, Julian 46a
Holt, Marjorie 179a, 204a, 296b
Harold Holt Ltd. 287b
Holt, Rinehart and Winston, Inc. 213a
Holter, Norman J. 262a
Holyoake, Keith 70b, 108a, 146b
Holz, Walter B. 327a
Homberger, Eric 201b
Home, Lord 123b
Home Office 46a, 114b, 117b, 123b, 128b
Home Secretary 131a, 176a
Homero, Humberto 64b
The Homosexual Law Reform Society 46a, 131b
Honchar, Cornelia Wallis 173b
Hone, Basil 46a
Honourable Society of the Middle Temple 131a
Hönel, Herbert 170b
Honey, P.J. 46a, 132a, **153a**
Honeywell Corporation 263b, 313b
Honfield, J.M. 80b
Hong Kong **101b, 175b**
Honig, Camille R. 262a

Honti, F. 221a
Hood, B.E. 87a
Hood, Talbot 111b
Hoogenboom, Robert 296b
Hook, Sidney 10b, 136b, 139a, 262a
Hooper, Denis E. 46a
Hooper, R.G. 46a
Hooper, S.E. 262a
Hope, Karen 46a
Hope Street Church, Liverpool 265a
Hopf, H.J. 144a
Hopkins, Jeannette E. 211b, 212a
Hopkins, Peter 46a, 327a-b
Hopper, C.R. 141b
Hopwood, Ian G. 214b
Horak, Jan 46a
Horbatiuk, Peter 46a
Horig, Donald F. 35b
Horii, Toshikatsu 145b, 296a
Horizon Press 213a
Horlemann, Jürgen 175a
Horman, Charles 148b
Horn, Rae P. 46a
Horne, Geoffrey M. 46a
Horne, John G. 46a
Hornstein, D. 46a
Horoszewicz, M. 354a
Horowitz, A.B. 146a
Horowitz, David 118b, 142a, 148a, 150b, **153a**, 185b, 205a, 213a, 222a, 229b
Horowitz, Gus 170a
Horsley, A.S. 89a, 146b
Horton, Syd 327b
Hosegood, J. Edmund 46a
The Hosei Times 213a
Hoshins, J.F. 143a
Hospodka, Jaroslav 96b
Hossain, Synd 223a
Hotel Portmeirion 262a
Hotel Le Royal, Phnom Penh 171b
Houart, Victor 226b
Hoult, Thomas Ford 46a, 166a
Hounsfield, Miss 353a
Houphouet-Boigny, Felix 104b
House Committee on Un-American Activities 139a
House of Commons 46a, 130a, 350b
The House of Free Speech 46a
House of Lords 46b
Houses of Parliament Sports and Social Club 89a
Housing Ad Hoc Committee 46b
Houston, W. Clyde 172a
Hovell, Harry 46b
Howard, D.L. 213a
Howard, John N. 262a
Howard, L.A. Lee 313b
Howe, Irving 36b
Howell, Lily 312a
Howes, Kenneth 46b
Howland, Blanche Winifred 262a
Howland, Larry 46b
Howlett, Muriel 39a
Howson, Joan 46b
Hoxa, Enver 93a
Hradecký, Adolf 230b
Hruza, Frantisek 96b
Hsieh Chi-mei 95a
Hsing, Lu 145a
Hsinhua News Agency 95a, 213b
Hsiung Hsiang-hui 95a
Hua, Kim Min 127a
Huang Sung, Kang 262a
Huang, Wen-Shan 46b, 150a
Hubbard, John H. 46b
Hubbard, L.R. 329b
Hubbard, Omar 327b
Huberman, Leo 127a, 137a, 221a
Hubrig, Kurt 99b
Huddleston, Jr., James L. 46b
Huddy, Elmina 89a
Hudgens, Mary Jane 327b
Hudson, James H. 29b
Hudson, Richard 240a-b
Huett, Richard 196b, 206a
Huff, Jane 89a
Hugh-Jones, Phillip 89a
Hughes, A. 296b
Hughes, A.M. 79a
Hughes, Mrs. Bill 89a
Hughes, Byron 178b
Hughes, Cyril 46b
Hughes, E. 262a
Hughes, Emrys 52a, 116a, 146b
Hughes, John 46b
Hughes, Valerie 262a
Hughes for Senate 46b
Hughff, J.E. 196b
Hui, Henry 171b
Hull Socialist Review 213b
Hulton, Mr. 58b
Human Biology 329b
Human Knowledge 266b
Human Relations and Communications Today 46b
Human Rights Commission of the U.N. 125a
Human Society in Ethics and Politics 154b
The Humanist 213b, 327b
Humanist Broadcasting Council 213b
Humanist Fellowship of Victoria 172a
The Humanist Gazette 327b
Humanist Group Action 131a
Humanist News 327b
Humanist Society of New Zealand, Christchurch 296b
Humanistic Judaism 213b
Hume 354b
Hume, Noel 169b
Humes, H.L. 327b
Humphrey, Clifford 62b
Humphrey, Hubert H. 62b, 115b, 138a
Humphrey, J.H. 46b
Humphrey, John P. 125a
Humphrey, Terence J. 46b
Humphreys, W.F. 91b
Humphry, Derek 37a
Hund, Friedrich 100a, 115a
Hungarian Ambassador 102a, 124b
Hungarian Chargé d'Affaires 124b
Hungarian Literary Gazette 213b
Hungarian Peace Council 290b, 295a
Hungarian Sports News 89a
Hungarian Writers' Association Abroad 124b
Hungary **101b-102a, 124b, 175b**
Hunn, J.K. 146b
Hunnius, F.C. ("Gerry") 32b, 46b, 47b, 220b
Hunt, Christopher 239a
Hunt, Helen 46b
Hunt, Ian R. 296b
Hunt, J.M. 90a
Hunt, Jane 89a
Hunt, John 232b
Hunt, R.A. 46b
Hunt, William G. 3a
Hunter, Anne 47a
Hunter, Charlotte 78b
Hunter, Coll M. 47a
Hunter, Michael 112a
Hunter, Paul 42a
Hunter, R.H. 313b
Huntingdon, ? 262a, 292b
Huntingdon, Jack 290b
Huntingdon, Margaret 262a, 290b, 292b
Huq, Fazlun 108b
Hurford, Jeffrey 38b
Hurlbut, Stewart W. 156b
Hurst, Fanny 42a
Hurtado, Jose Arata 47a
Hurvitz, Joseph 134b
Hurwitz, Leo 47a
Husein, Ahmed 47a
Hussain, S. Liaqat 301b
Hussain, Zakir 102a
Hussein I, King 105a
Husseini, M. 84b
Hussen, Abdirazak Hagi 110b
Hussey, M. 89a
Husslein, H. 133a
Huston, Ervin L. 47a
Hutchings, G. 278a
Hutchings, J.F. 47a
Hutchins, Robert M. 336b
Hutchinson, E.M. 222a
Hutchinson, John 67a
Hutchinson, Royal D. 47a
The Hutchinson Publishing Group 213b
Hutchison, Jean 47a
Hutt, Avis 30a
Hutt, C.M. 195a
Hutten, Ernest Hirschlaff 327b
Hutter, Donald 206a
Hutton, I. Emilie 353a
Huxley, Aldous 287b
Huxley, Christopher V. 47a
Huxley, Julian 262a, 287b, 292b,

327b
Huxley, Juliette 262a, 292b, 327b, 354a
Huybrechts, Paul 47a
Hyde, Karl 209b
Hyde, Sydney 234b
Hyde Park University, Florida 296b
Hyland, Judith 296b
Hyland, Matthew P. 47a
Hyman, Martin 152a
Hynes, Sam L. 213b
Hyung, Son Jin 104b, 227b

I

Iacomuzzi, Eduardo 169a
Ibrahim, M.V. 143a
Ibrahimi, Akhdar 120a
Icardi, Ruben Angel 166a
Iceland **102a**
Ideologie 94a
Ignotus, Paul 124b
Iimima, Kooko 144b
Iimura, Haruo 144b
Iinuma, Yukiko 144a, 291a, 292b, 296b
Ikeda, Katsuya 239a
Ikhoivhe, Nyor 296b
Ilhon, Paik 188a
Iliescu, E. 129b
The Illustrated Weekly of India 14a, 213b
L'Illustré 213b
Illustrierte Zeit im Bild 175a
Illyas, H.M. 47a
Imai, Fumie 204b
Immer, T. 98a
An Imminent Danger to Peace 155b
Impact of Science on Society 213b
Imperial Chemical Industries Ltd. 307b
Imperial Iranian Embassy 125a
Imperial War Museum 278b
Impraim, T.K. 100b
In Praise of Idleness and Other Essays 323a
"Income" 307b
L'Incontro 213b
Incze, Jenö 102a, 124b
Les Indépendants Republicains Yéménites 47a
Independent Labour Party 47a, 154b, 166a
Independent Negro Committee to End Racism and Ban the Bomb 135b
The Independent Nuclear Disarmament Election Committee 47a
India **102a-b, 124b, 351a**
India Canada Association 213b
India Council of Cultural Relations 147b
India International 213b
Indian Branch, BRPF **144a**
Indian Correspondence **153b**
The Indian Express 213b
Indian Institute of Technology Mathematics Club 214a
The Indian Listener 334a
Indian Press **153b**
Indian Students Hostel 89a
Indian Workers Association, Great Britain 124b
Indonesia **102b-103a, 124b**
Indonesia-Djakarta Conference For the Liquidation of Foreign Military Bases **154a**
The Indonesian Organization for Afro-Asian Peoples Solidarity 47b
Indus Times 214a
Industral Aids Limited 122b
INF Information 125a
Infeld, Leopold 47b, 142a, 291a
Information 214a
Information Bulletin 144a
The Information Bureau of the P.R.G. of the Republic of South Vietnam in Paris 163a
The Information Service 214a
Information Service of the Peace Council of the German Democratic Republic 98a
Informations-Dienst zur Notstandsgesetzgebung 175a
Inge, W.R. 350a
Ingénieur Oboudyat 124b
Inghe, Gunnar 158b
Inheritance 214a
Inland Revenue 89a, 307b
Inner London Telephone Centre 89a
Inönü, Ismet 96a, 131a
Inquiry 138a
Insel Verlag 199b
Insight 214a
Inspector of Taxes 89a
Institut für Weltwirtschaft an der Universität Kiel 48a
Institute for Research and Development of Vocational Rehabilitation of Disabled 123b
The Institute for Strategic Studies 47b, 142a, 155a
Institute for the Unity of Science 214a
Institute for Training in Non-Violence 47b
Institute for Workers Control 113a
Institute Journal 261b
Institute of Commonwealth Studies, Oxford University 166a
Institute of Jewish Affairs 109b
Institute of Journalists 261b
The Institute of Mathematics and Its Applications 262a
The Institute of National Planning 47b
Institute of Physics and Mathematics 287b
The Institute of Radio Engineers Transactions on Electronic Computers 214a
Instituto Croata Latinoamericano de Cultura 157b
Instituto de Investigaciones de la "Teoria de la Cosmovision" 214a
Instituto del Libro 96a
Intelligence: The Mensa Journal 214a
The Intelligentsia Committee of Karachi 47b
Inter Press Service 214a
Intercom 214a
Intercontinental Press 214a
International Amnesty Meeting for Iraqi Political Prisoners 125b, 126a-b
International Association of Democratic Lawyers 160b, 170b
International Balzan Foundation 47b
International Brigade Association & Friends of Republican Spain 130a
International Centre, 25th Anniversary Committee 214a
The International Children's World Peace Crusade 47b
The International Club 47b
International Committee to Defend Eldridge Cleaver 136a, 140a
International Confederation for Disarmament and Peace 47b, 104b
International Conference 142a
International Conference against Foreign Military Bases 154a
International Conference against War Danger 102b
International Conference for Solidarity with the People of Vietnam against U.S. Imperialist Aggression for the Defence of Peace 190b
International Conference for the Liquidation of Foreign Bases 344b-345a
International Conference of Parliamentarians in Cairo 18b, 107b
International Conference of Parliamentarians on the Middle-East Crisis 107b
International Conference of Youth and Students for Disarmament, Peace, and National Independence 89a
International Conference on Economic Sanctions against South Africa 129b
International Conference on General Amnesty for Iraqi Political Prisoners 125b

International Congress of Mathematicians 47b
International Control Commission 171b
The International Faculty of Mental Sciences at Haarlem 262a-b
International Fellowship of Reconciliation 48a
International Grotius Foundation for the Propagation of the Laws of Nations 262b
International House 214a
International Institute for Peace 48a, 113b, 153a, 166a, 170b
International League Against Conscription 48a
International League for Peace and Universal Brotherhood 48a
International League for the Rights of Man 50b, 52b, 125a
International Learning Systems Corporation Limited 48a
International Liaison Committee of Organisations for Peace 48a
International Literary Agents 48a
International Literary Management 157b
International P.E.N. 214b
International Peace/Disarmament Directory 214a-b
International Peace March 48a
International Politics Society, University College of Wales, Aberystwyth 166a
International Press Cutting Bureau 214b
International Publishers 214b
International Publishing Corporation Ltd. 214b
International Red Cross, Geneva 104a
International Registry of World Citizens 48a
International Relations 350b
International Review Service 48a
International Socialist Journal 109b, 128b, 148b, 157a, 161a, 214b
International Society Kurdistan 125b
International Students Committee 103a
International Union of Chemical, Oil & Allied Workers Unions 214b
International Union of Socialist Youth 313b
International Union of Students 12b, 48a, 166a
International War Crimes Tribunal 15b, 16a-b, 17a-b, 18a, 19a, 96b, 97a, 140a, 162b, 184a, 185a-b, 186a-b, 187a, 188a-b, 189a-b, 190a-b, 327b-327a, 344b
The International Whitsun March 150b
International Year Book & Statesmen's Who's Who 214b
International Youth Camp 96a
Internationale der Kriegsdienstgegner 48b, 166a, 174b
Internationale Föderation der Widerstandskämpfer 98a
Det Internationale Krigsforbrydelses-Tribunal 166a, 173b
Internationaler Pressedienst 214b
Internationales Treffen der Vertreter der Jugend und Studenten 98b
Interpress 214b
Interstate 18a, 214b
Inter-University Jewish Federation of Great Britain and Ireland 112a
Intourist 116b
Investwar 175b
Involve 328a
The Iona Community 48b, 177a
Ionnidou, Elli 124a
Iowa Socialists League 48b
Ipekçi, Cetin Altan Abdi 106b
Iqbal, Afzal 108b
Iran **103a, 124b**
Iran Report 125b
Iranian Committee for the Defence of Imprisoned Graduates 125a
Iranian Committee for the Defence of Political Prisoners in Iran 103a, 125b
Iranian Committee in London for the Defence of Political Prisoners in Iran 125b
Iranian National Front 89a
Iranian National Front Organisation in England 103a
Iranian National Front Organizations in Europe 125a
Iranian National Front Organization in Great Britain 124b
Iranian Students Association in the USA 125a
Iranian Students Defence Committee 125a
Iranian Students in Moscow 125a
Iranian Students Scholarship Fund 48b, 125a
Iranian Students' Society 125a
Iranian Students Society in Great Britain 103a, 125a
Iranian Students Union of Freiberg 125a
Iranische Studentvereinigung 124b
Iranishe Studentvereinigung Stuttgart 125a
Iranischer Studentenverein 125a
Iraq **103a-b, 125b-126b**
Iraqi Airlines 148b
Iraqi High Committee 103b, 125b
Iraqi News 125b
Iraqi Society, Leeds University 143a
Iraqi Statements **154a**
Iraqi Students' Annual Conference and Spring Festival 103b
Iraqi Students' Society 103b, 153b
Iraqi Students' Society in the U.K. 103b, 125b, 126a, 129b
Ireland **103b, 126b**
Ireton, Glenn F. 238a-b
Irie, Yoshihiko 145b
Irish Ambassador 126b
Irish Democrat 48b, 214b
The Irish Times 96b, 214b
Irshad, Hakim Syed 262b
Isa, Ibrahim 103a
Isaksson, Hans 148b
Isely, Philip 84b, 147b
Isenberg, Howard 48b
Ishida, Reiko 165a
Ishido, Kaoru 145b
Ishido, Seirin 144a
The Isis 131a
Isis Film Productions Ltd. 328a
Islam, James N. 48b
Islam, Kamrul 108a
Islam, M. S. 48b
Islam, Tajul 48b, 108b
Islamia College Magazine 215a
Isle of Thanet Constituency Labour Party 143a
Ismail, Dr. 106a
Ismail, Mohomed Hafez 107b, 149b
Isono, Fujiko 145a
Ispahani, M. A. H. 48b, 108b
Israel **103b-104b, 127a**
Israel Imperial News 104b, 215a
Israel Palestine Committee 107a
Israel Peace Committee 104a
Israeli Ambassador to the U.K. 106b
Israeli Consul General 106b
Israeli Socialist Organization 166a
Israeli Socialist Organization, Students' Committee 104a, 104b
Israelit, Esther 111a
Israelitische Kultus-Gemeinde Innsbruck 134a
Israilovici, Willy 129a
Issel, Karl-Heinz 48b
Issues 215a
Istituto Italiano d'Arti Grafiche 215a
Istiwani, Ambassador 113b
Italian Branch BRPF **144a**
Italian Communist Party 48b
Italian Conference on Portuguese Political Prisoners 128b
Italian Council of the BRPF 144a
Italian Delegation 151b
Italian Peace Committee 48b
Italian Televisione Corporation 215a
Italy **104b, 127a**
Itinerant Action International 126b, 131b

Ivascu, George 219a
Iverson, Carl 116a
Ivory, Paul 48b
Ivory Coast **104b**
Iwamatsu, Shigetoshi 104b, 144a, 145b, 147a, 215b, 296b
Iwanami Shoten, Publishers 144b, 215a
IWCT Bulletin 190a
Iyengar, B.V.S. 215a
Iyengar, V.K.S. 102a
Izumi, Genichi 231b
Izuta, Yutaka 203a
Izvestia 111b, 134a, 153a, 215a, 328a

J

Jaafari, M.T. 215a
Jaaj, S.S. 328a
Jaber, Mustafa 105a, 143a
Jaca Book 215a
Jack, Homer 70a, 71b
Jackson, ? 166a
Jackson, A.C. 169b
Jackson, D.E. 49a
Jackson, Esther 136a
Jackson, Hampden 278b
Jackson, K.G. 166a, 233b
Jackson, Kay 146b
Jackson, Monica 127b
Jackson, P.G.C. 208b
Jackson, Annabel ("Tiny") Huth 262b
William Jackson Books Ltd. 89a
Jacob, Nicolas 128b
Jacobi, ? 127b
Jacobs, Nicholas 111b, 134a
Jacobs, Ruth 341b
Jacobsen, Steen 173a
Jacobsohn, Samuel 262b
Jacobson, Roy 262b
Jacobson, S. 49a, 129b
Jacobus, Abraham 328a
Jacoby, E.G. 262b
Jacoby, Sheldon 38a
Jaeger, Friedrich 49a
Jaeger, R. 99a, 100a
Jaffe, Marc 198b
Jaffer, Ahmed E.H. 49a, 108a, 124b
Jaffar, Khalid M. 105b
The Jaffna Thirukkural Cultural Society 49a
Jagan, Cheddi 101b
Jaghbir, Mahmud 120b
Jagoda, Ilsnen ? 49a
Jahn, Gunnar 147b
Jahnke, Peter 49a
Jaikervi, Altaf H. 49a
Jaime, Gabriel Ruiz 48a
Jakobi, Georg 122a
Jakobi, Irene 122a
Jakobs, Stephen Dean 148b
Jaluat, Ricardo 148b
Jamaiker, Stanley 328a
Jameel, M. 224b
James, Bert 49a, 147b
James, Daniel 223a
James, N. 49a
James, Peter L. 214a
James, William 328a
Jamieson, G.L. 49a
Jammu & Kasmir Plebiscite Front 108b
Janata 215a
Janjua, M.K. 49a, 108b, 175b, 296b
Janner, Sir Barnett 103b
Jannor, G. 36b
Janos, Peter 102a
Peter Janson-Smith Ltd. 212b, 213a
Janvrin, Fred W. 139a
Japan **104b-105a, 127b, 144a, 154a, 175b**
Japan Broadcasting Corporation 215a
Japan Civil Liberties Union 105a, 145b
Japan Committee 296b
Japan Committee for the Investigation of U.S. War Crimes in Vietnam 160a, 161a, 166a, 175b
Japan Congress against A- and H-Bombs 145a
Japan Council Against Atomic and Hydrogen Bombs 12a, 17b 49a, 104b, 131a, 144a, 215a, 296b
Japan Council of Organizations of Atomic Bomb Victims 104b
Japan Information Centre of BRPF 145b, 215a-b, 296b
Japan Lawyers International Liaison Association 145a
Japan 'Peace for Vietnam' Committee 49b, 104b, 145b, 164b, 185b
Japan Postal Workers' Union 142a
Japan Revolutionary Communist League 144b
Japan Socialist Party 144b
Japanese Civil Liberties Union 145b, 166a
Japanese Scientists' Mission for the Investigation of U.S. War Crimes in Viet Nam 166a
Japanese Section of the British Broadcasting Corporation 144b
Jarborg, Bo 236b
Jardi, Enric 215b
Jardot, Maurice 120a
Jarett, Arthur William 262b
Jaroschek, Alfred 109b, 156a
Järvinen, Marja 279a
Järvinen, Pentti 16b
Jarvis, Andrew 301b
Jason, Alfred 112a
Jasovich-Pantaleon, Rosa 174b
Jaspers, K. 328a
Javsicas, Gabriel 49b
Javed, Fareed 108b
Jay, John 117a
Jayaratne, Osmund 172b
Jayavidya, C. 49b
Jefferys, John T. 277b, 278a
Jeffries, Lionel 178a
Jehali, Hussain 49b
Jelinck, Ivan 235b
Jemmett, J. 49b
Jencks, Christopher 223a
Jencks, Richard W. 262b
Jenkins, Alice 89a
Jenkins, C. 49b
Jenkins, G.D. 89a, 169b
Jenkins, Hugh 176b, 177a
Jenkins, Roy 114b, 189a
Jennings, E. 76a
Jennings, James A. 296b
Jennings, Keith 178a
Jennisen, I. 89a
Jensen, Erik Vagn 49b, 173a
Jensen, Gunnar 173a
Jensen, Marjorie 32b
Jensen, Marlene 147a
Jensen, Nadine 166a
Jensen, Victor 89a
Jepsen, Hans Lyngby 173a
Jepson, Charles A. 49b
Jermakow, W. 328a
Jerome, A. 49b
Jersey Association for Nuclear Disarmament 49b
Jerusalem Liberation Committee 104a, 105a, 107a, 143b, 296b
Jerusalem Post 104b, 127a, 215b
Jerusalem Prize 103b
Jervis, John 143b
Jespersen, Knud 97a, 112a
Jessup, Philip 73a
Jeune Afrique 215b
Jewish Book Centre 112a
The Jewish Chronicle 89a, 122a, 129a
Jewish Community Centre of Milwaukee 112a
Jewish Currents 215b
Jewish Daily Forward 112a-b, 215b
Jewish Minorities Research 134a
Jewish Newsletter 154b
Jewish Observer & Middle East Review 89a
Jewish Youth Organisations Emergency Committee 215b
Jews in Eastern Europe 112b, 117a, 133b, 134a
Jha, L.K. 295a
Jha, Surendr 233a
Jiffy Packing Company 89a
Jiménez, Humberto Miguel 106a
Jinno, David H. 214a
Jiráska, M. 96b
Jitrik, Noe 141a
Joachim, Harold H. 262b
Joad, Doreen 262b
Joader, G.Q. 222b
Job Vacancies **145b-146a**
Jodai, Tano 145a
Joe, Calypso 49b

Joesten, Joachim 174b, 262b
Johansen, Ivar 49b
John, Brian 49b
John, Jacqueline 288a
John O'Gauntlet 215b
Johns Hopkins University 213a
Johnson, Albert P. 49b
Johnson, Arnold 89a
Johnson, Curt 205b
Johnson, Mr. and Mrs. David 89a
Johnson, Edna Ruth 203a
Johnson, Edward 208b
Johnson, Hewlett 133b
Johnson, Hugh 229a
Johnson, J. 148b
Johnson, J.B. 297a
Johnson, Jerome R. 135b
Johnson, Lyndon B. 13a, 14b, 15b, 16b, 19a, 39a, 55a, 62b, 63b, 70b, 66b, 72a, 75a, 78b, 83a, 110b, 118b, 132a, 137b, 138b, 139b, 147a, 154a, 173a, 190a
Johnson, Mike 146b
Johnson, Nicholas 143b, 166a, 178b, 291a
Johnson, Paul 96b, 215b
Johnson, Peter 297a
Johnson, Phoebe Wynn 328a
Johnson, Russell 143b, 158b
Johnson, Stella 148b
Johnson, Warren Russell 89a
Johnston, A.J. 309a
Johnston, Brian E. 94b
Johnston, D.A. 89a
Johnston, E.M. 224a
Johnston, Ken R. 148b
Johnstone, J.E. Ainsworth 310b
Johnstone, V.E. 132a
Johnstone, William A. 172a
Jolls, Shirley 34a, 139b
Jolly, Stephen 328a
Jonas, Mary 148b
Jonassen, Niels 143b
Jones, Mr. 262b
Jones, Mrs. 43a
Jones, A. 278a
Jones, Mr. and Mrs. Albert 297a
Jones, Ashton 137a-b
Jones, D. 292b
Jones, D.A.N. 199b
Jones, D. Wynn 307a
Jones, Emrys 89a
Jones, Erica Lloyd 169b
Jones, H.A. 89a
Jones, H.E. 352b
Jones, Hugo T. 328a
Jones, J. Elwyn 352b
Jones, J. Lynton 166a, 214a
Jones, Judith 262b
Jones, Martin 215b
Jones, Paul 166a
Jones, Peter Alan 215b
Jones, Susan Eserton 177a
Jones, Thomas A. 49b
Jones, V. Duncan 48a
Jones, Victor 328a
Jones, W.M. 89a
Jones, Walter Benton 49b
Jones-Hughes, F. 90b
Peter Jones Ltd. 313b
Jones Morris, M. 297a
Joon-Ku, Lee 217a
Jopling, L.A. 49b
Jordan 105a
Jordan, Mr. 262b
Jordan, Clive 91b
Jordan, E.E. 101a
Jordan, Joseph 49b
Jordan, Patrick 49b, 80b, 107a, 208b, 227a
Jorge, P. 96a
Jørgensen, Carl 328b
Jørgensen, Jørg. 97a
Jornal Santa Cruz 215b
Joseph, Dinda 65b
Joseph, K.M. 153b, 297a
Joseph, Linda 262b
Michael Joseph Ltd. 215b
Josephson, Eric 49b
Joshi, J. 124b
Joshi, S.M. 86a
Josten, Josef 39a, 209a
Jouffa, Yves 160a, 186a-b, 187a
Journal 14a
Journal Institute Maths. Applics. 328b
The Journal of Human Relations 215b
The Journal of Nervous and Mental Disease 323a
Journal of Paraphysics 215b
Journal of Philosophy 215b, 330b, 354b
Journal of Recreational Mathematics 325a
The Journal of Symbolic Logic 328b, 335b
Journal of the London Mathematical Society 328b
The Journal of the Royal Statistical Society 322b
Joven, Grupo 141a
Jowett, David 238b
Jowett, Harold Uttley 49b
Jowitt, Lord 209b
Joy, George 89a
Joyce, B. 235a
Joyce, Robert 222a
Joyce, Stella 127a
Jubson, Ardis 288a
Judge, Anthony 262b
Jugend, Gilberto 171a
Jumabhoy, Ameer 49b
Júnior, Nino Gariglio 171a
The Jr. Art Gallery 215b
Dr. W. Junk Publishers 216a
Juriskoni, Anna 282b
Juventud Rebelde 95b, 216a
Juzwiak, C. 49b
Jyoti 216a

K

K.K.L. Executors and Trustees Co. 89b
KLAC Radio Station 21b
K.L.M. Royal Dutch Airlines 154a
Kabemba, J.A. 95b
Kadar, Janos 101b, 102a, 124b
Kader, Emile Abdul 151a
Kagan, Alfred 166a
Kagan, Ben 258b
Kagan, Rosa 117a
Kaganowicz, Joel 134b
Kahan, R.O. 235a
Kahane, Wilhelm 50a, 129a, 166a
Kahler, Gerda 122a
Kahn, Barbara 222a
Kahn, Francis 160a
Kahn, H. 73b
Kahn, J.M. 50a
Kahn, Marcel-Francis 156a, 186b
Kahn, Rena 187a, 188b
Kahn, Robert 89b
Kahol, Om Prakasha 102b
Kaigai Hyoron Sha 223a
Kaiser, Edmond 108a, 174a
Kaiser Bauxite Company 131b
Kakade, Tukaram Yashneantrao 297a
Kalia, Sushil Kumar 297a
Kalidas, V. 229b
Kalinin, V.I. 74b, 116b
Kaliska, Lea 113a
Kallai, Gyula 102a
Källberg, Sture 50a
Kallen, H.M. 262b
Kallman, Ruth 195a
Kalogiannis, Joannis 198a
Kalogiannis, John 123b
Kalow, Marianne 236a
Kamasaki, Fumitaka 145a
Kambites, John 171b
Kambona, Oscar S. 113b
Kamel, Michel 216a
Kampagne für Abrustung 175a
Kampagne für Abrüstung Ostermarsch der Atomwaffengegner 50a, 100a, 142b
Kampagnen mod Atomvåben 50a
Kampanjen Mot Atomvapen 113a
Kane, John F. 50a
Kane, Randall P. 89b
Kaneko, Mitsuo 262b
Kang, Sugwon 262b
Kanmuri, Ikuo 16b, 217a
Kannuchamy, N. 237a
Kansas City Area Committee to End the War in Vietnan 166a
Kapitza, P.L. 328b
Kaplan, Albert 50a
Kaplan, Howard S. 50a
Kaplan, Musya 111b
Kapluck, Manfred 50a, 216a
Kar, Ida 262b, 263a
Karachi Leader 16b
Karalasingham, V. 50a

Karame, Rashid 105b
Karbi, S. 111a
Karbø, Lars 216a
Karia, S.B. 216b
Karim, A.R. 166b
Karin, A.A. 126a
Karl, Frederick R. 263a
Karlin, Amalie Z. 134b
Karlin, Kenneth G. 328b
Karni, Habiba 113a
Karnow, Michael 213a
Karolyi, Catherine 263a, 292b
Karolyi, Michael 263a
Karstadt, Elieser 135a-b
Kartawinata, Arudji 154a
Kashmir 105a
Kashmir Committees for Afro-Asian Peoples Solidarity 50a
Kasiouras, Christos 124a
Kask, Lani 240a
Kaskeline, Wolfgang 216a
Kaskeline Film 216a
Kassam, A.S.G. 242b
Kassebaum, Robert G. 50a
Kassem, Abdul 108b
Kassem, Abdul Karim 103a
Kassman, Alec 263a
Kastler, A. 50a
Kästner, Erik 116a
Kastner, Harold 263a
Kaston, Maryna 50a
Kasuri, Mahmud Ali 157a, 185b, 189b, 192a
Katahira, Y. 145a, 238a
Katayama, Kazuo 50a
Katayama, Y. 145a
Katilungu, Simon 119a
Katjavivi, P. 111a
Katkov, George 116b
Kato, Nobuyuki 144b
Kato, Yoshio 145a
Katouzian, M.A. 216a
Katsantonis, Giannis 123a
Katz, Aaron 133a
Katz, Mina 134b
Katzman, Eleanor 50a
Katzman, Sam 50a
Kaufman, E. 103b
Kaufman, E. 104a
Kaufmann, George V. 216a, 263a
Kaunda, Kenneth 84b, 119a, 288a
Kaur, Rajkumari Amrit 102a, 102b, 288a
Kautz, Elfriede 121b
Kautz, Johannes 121b
Kawabata, Yasunari 145a
Kawakami, Jotaro 11b, 144b
Kawan, ? 175a
Kay, Eileen 121a
Kay, Ernest 217a
Kay Laboratories 89b
Kaya, Seiji 144b
Kaye, Bill 25a, 36a, 122a, 143b, 166a, 195b, 221a, 223b, 225a, 227a, 297a
Kaye, David 148b
Kaye, Linda 297a
Kayibanda, Gregoire 110b
Kaylon, Charles 50a
Kazi, Mazhar S. 108b
Kazmi, Hasnain 82b
Keats, Mark 50b
Keble College 323a
Keck, Alan J. 50b
Kedari, Elka 111a, 129b
Kedzierski, J.Z. 145b, 216a
Keeler, W.S. 50b
Keene, Donald 263a
Keenleyside, Hugh 59a
Keesings Publications Ltd. 143b
Keet, D.L. 50b
Kefford, Kenneth D. 146a
Kegan, C.M. 279a
Kegan Paul Trench, Trubner & Co., Ltd. 216a
Keister, John R. 50b
Keita, Modibo 106a
Keith Jr., Carl 50b
Kekkonen, Urho Kaleva 97a
Keler, Vladimir R. 233a
Keller, Hans 50b, 131b, 262b, 291a
Keller, Wilhelm 99b
Kelley, Pat 297a
Kellogg, Rhoda 328b
Kelly's Handbook 216a
Kelman, Herbert 176a
Kemal, Y. 131a
Kemelman, Arthur F. 263a
Kemp, Ian 90b
Kempner, Mickey 291a
William Kempner Ltd. 143b
Kendall, Dan 150b
Kendall, D.G. 328b
Kendall, Ian 216a
Kendall, Walter 148b
Kennan, George 153a
Kennard, Sir Coleridge 279a
Kennedy, Edward M. 55a
Kennedy, Flo 23b
Kennedy, Jean 270b
Kennedy, John F. 39a, 41b, 45b, 59a, 75a, 76b, 80b, 83a, 136b, 137b, 138a, 152b, 220a, 326a
The John F. Kennedy Foundation 50b
Kennedy, Robert 70b
Kent, C.H.W. 208a
Kenya, **105a, 127a**
Kenyatta, Jomo 105a
Kepesis, Nikandros 123a
Kepper, Douglas 50b, 104a, 130b, 165b
Kerby, Philip 135b, 210a, 222a
Kerkar, D.S. 216a
Kern, Coralee 50b
Kern, Joseph 263a
Kerr, E.S. Wells 292b
Kerr, Lorin E. 89b
Kerr, Russell 115a
Kerr, Seamus 126b
Kerry 352b
Kerry, Karolyn 220b
Kertesz, D. 50b
Kessel, Lipmann 158b
Kessler, John J. 216a
Ketzalkoatl 50b
Kevenk, Genziz 106b
Key, Martin 14a, 291b
Key, Theo 50b
Keynes, Margaret, Lady 263a
Keys, Donald F. 118b, 167b
Keys, Jenny 296b
Kha, Nguyen Trong 187a
Khaibawi, H. 126b
Khalaf, Khadim M. 103a
Khan, Mrs. A. 273b
Khan, Abdul G. 174a
Khan, Amanullah 50a, 108b
Khan, Audrey 106a, 148b
Khan, Inamullah 85a
Khan, Ismet Ullah 216a
Khan, M.A. Salam 233b
Khan, M.K. 186a
Khan, M. Amanullah 235b
Khan, Mohammed Ayub 84b, 108b, 127b
Khan, M.P. 291a
Khan, Nguyen 132a
Khan, Rashid 153b
Khan, General 162a
Khani, H. 125a
Khanji, A.J. 50b, 297a
Khayal, G.N. 240b
Khindaria, B. 50b
Khrushchev, Nikita 39a, 59a, 62b, 76b, 111b, 112b, 116b, 117a, 121b, 133a-134b, 151b, 154b, 155a, 326a, 351a
Khwaja, Saluddin Ahmed 328b
Khyber Express Ltd. 37b
Kiaos, Nikos 123a, 124a, 294a
Kiapma Consolidation Bureau 103a
Kicer, H.C. 265a
Kidd, H. 154a
Kiddy, Joan 206b
Kidrica, Aleja B. 76a
Kiefer, Alexander 56a
Kiefer, Christie W. 50b
Kielland, Nalle 263a, 278b, 279a
Kiem, Tran Buu 158b, 163a
Kier, Christian 80b
Kiger, Billie 353b
Killick, Angela 266a
Killing, W. 349b
Killu, H. 148b
Kilmartin, Terence 225a
Kilpatrick, H.G. 147b
Kimball, G.V. 128b
Kimbrell, Markete 263a
Kimpson, Prudence A. 328b
Kinberg, Suzanne 212a
Kind, Enno 297a
King 216a
King, Cecil 50b, 214b
King, Fergus 50b
King, Heath 328b
King, J. 51a
King, Jerry 197b
King, Jr., Martin Luther 18a,

25a, 133b, 138b, 139b, 140a, 288a
King, Mary L. 216a
King, Preston T. 328b
King, R.W. 89b
King, Sam 165b
King, Slater H. 148b
Allan King Associates 216a
King Screen Production 148b
King, Wood & Company, Auctioneers, Surveyors & Valuers 89b
King-Hall, Stephen 60b, 211b
King-Hall News Letter 328b
King-Hele, Desmond 263a
Kingshill, Peter 148b
Kingsmuir School 278a
Kingsway 216a
Kingswood School 216b
Kinsey, Mr. 197a, 228a
Kinsey, Richard 51a
Kinsey, Tom 204b, 216a, 241b, 297a
Kipanta, N.E. 216b
Kipling, Rita 280a
Kiragosian, Karapet Boghos 117a
Kirby, Pat 143b
Kirincic, Majorie 218b
Kirk, G.A. 52b
Kirk, N.E. 147b
Kirkby, Connie W. 129a, 130a
Kirkeby?, Ander 351a
Kirkley, Leslie 142a
Kirkshaw-Grigg, D. 146b
Kirloskar, Jeewan 218b
Kirsch, Ida 51a, 166a
Kirsch, Irving 51a, 76a
Kirschenbaum, Walter L. 51a
Kirwood, Mary 263a
Kiskadden, Peggy 263a, 292b
Kishore, R. 85a
Kissin, S.F. 121b
Kissinger, Jr., William G. 51a
Kitamura, Tokutaro 84b
Kitazawa, Yoko 47b
Kitching, Jean 117a
Kitezawa, Masao 47b
Kjøbenhavns Telefon Aktieselskab 89b
Klaf, Franklin S. 216b
Klare, Michael 105b
Kleckner, Mark Edward 206b
Kleene, S.C. 216b
Klein, Alexander 263a
Klein, James 51a, 112a
Klein, Lena M. 98a
Kleiner, Karl 297a
Klekar, Gloria M. 297a
Klemens, Frantisek 121a
Klemke, E.D. 328b
Kletzki, Paul 288a
Klinger, Steven 214a
Klitzman, Steven H. 297a
Kloos, Peter 129a
Klotsch, Gerd 174a
Klüber, Theodor 51a
Kluge, Werner 175a
Klugmann, James 220a
Knape, Wolfgang 216b1a
Knapp, Gertrude M. 51a
Kneeland-Frantz, Virginia 263a
Kneller, Glenn S. 51a
Knepler, Florence 100a
Knestrick, Ray E. 263a
Knight, Denis 69a, 231a,
Knight, Frida 66b, 216b, 263a, 298b
Knight, Frances 142b, 165a
Knight, Harry G. 74a-b
Knight, Jack 114b, 143b
Knight, Margaret 328b
Knight, S. 165b
Knightly, B.H. 236a
Knipp, Helen F. 198b
Knobel, Jakob 51b
Knoper, Wolfgang 98b
Alfred A. Knopf Inc. 216b
Knopp, Fay 222a
Knorr, Lorenz 99b, 121a-b, 122a, 216b, 291b
Knottenbelt, Martin J. 51a, 104b, 169b
Knoxshire, & Mountain District Free Press 56b
Koach, K.H. 51a
Kobun Sha Ltd. 145a, 216b
Kobylinski, Stanislaw K. 329a
Koch, Christopher 166a, 263a
Koch, Harold M. 173a, 174a
Koch, Otto 51a
Koch, Thilo 224a
Kockenbier, J. 51a
Kodak Ltd. 149a
Kodansh Encyclopaedia, Tokyo 297a
Kodansha Ltd. 216b
Kodflac, Josef 217a
Koelling, Sidney 51a
Koestler, Arthur 263a
Koestler, Mamaine 263a
Koffler, Eleonora 110a, 129a
Koffman, Josephine 51a
Kofrudafl, Hermann 289a
Kohlberg, Alfred 51b, 266b
Kohli, G. 329a
Kohls, Stanley 51b
Kohn, Phil 51b
Koilman, Chana 135a
The Kojitaetor 216b
Kolacek, Lubos 97a
Kolankowska, Elzbieth 109b
Kolatch, Myron 223a
Kolhatkar, D.M. 124b
Kolko, Gabriel 51b, 160a, 166a, 188a, 189b, 190a
Kolko, Joyce 160a
Kolokon 216b
Komakí, Sanelude 329a
Komatsu, Takeo 217a
Komeito Party 297a
Komitet do Spraw Radia I Telewizji 51b
Komittee der Antifaschistischen Widerstandskämpfer 99a
Komittee der Hundert 51b
Komittee der Iranischen National-Front 51b
Komittee gegen den Krieg in Vietnam 16b
Komittee zum Schutze der Menschenrechte 98a, 99a, 122a
Kommentar 191a
Kon, Paik Il 187b
Kon, T.S. 263a
Kondor, Judith 51b
Konen, Georges 229b
Koningberger, Hans 145b
Konkokyo Church of Izuo 144a, 263b
Konkret 216b
Konning?, Hie 279a
Kontum, Nguy-Nhu 166a
Koo, Joo Ok 263b
Koochin, W.J. 171b
Kopka, Robert 197a
Korbin, Kenneth 51b
Korbonski, Stefan 26a
Korczyn, Amos 216b
Korda, Michael V. 234a
Korea **105a, 127a**
Korea Today 189a
Korm, Mihaly 102a
Korman, Anton 219a
Korman, Michael 217a
Korman, Y. 209a
Korn, Karl E. 220b, 221a
Körner, Stefan 216b
Koslow, Julian 263b
Kossuth 175b
Kostenko, Leo 116b, 153a
Kostodoros, N. 123b
Kostopoulis, Mr. ? 124a
Kostov, Dimitar 171b
Kosygin, Alexei N. 15b, 97a, 108b, 111a, 112b, 116b, 117a, 132a, 134a, 135a
Kotov, Michael 74b, 117b, 291a
Kotov, Tikhonov 298a
Kotsaki, [Thetis] 100b, 101a, 122b, 124a
Kounoupis, Georgios N. 329a
Kouroudeth, Commandant 189b
Koutroukis, George 124a
Kouznetsov, B. 329a
Koval, Francis 238a
Kovanda, Karel 97a
Kovoor, Abraham T. 172b
KPFA (A Pacifica Station) 216b
KPFA Folio 329a
KPFK 150a, 217a
Kraan, H.A.C.v.d. 65a
Krag, Jens Otto 97a
Krahl, Franz 223a
Kramer, Helmut 17a
Kramer, Robert 88b
Kransdorf, Jean 42a
Krasova, Eva 173a
Krassner, Paul 329a
Kraus, Jon 89b
Krausener, Gilbert 173b
Krauss, Lily 288a
Krausser, Peter 329a
Kravetz, Marc 166a
Krebs, Allen M. 139a
Kreisel, Georg 263b
Kressie, Jack J. 227b-228a

Kretchmer, M. 135a
Kreuzschule Dresden 51b, 175a
Kreves, Eugene 51b
Krieger, C. 261a
Krimm, Martin C. 329a
Krinski, Beth 51b
Krishna Menon, V.K. 102b, 156a, 158b, 166a, 297a
Krishnan, O.N. 51b
Krivine, Jean-Michel 160a, 186b, 187b, 188b
Kröger, Alice 117a, 132a
Krone, Gunnar 175a
Krooth, Dick 166a
Kropp, Werner 51b
Krüger, Lorenz 217a
Krüger, Michael 211b
Kry, Nguon Chhay 94b
Kubersky, C. 263b
Kubo, Toshihanu 242a-b
Kuboyama, and the Saga of the Lucky Dragon 240b
Kuby, Clemens 143b
Kucera, Vladimir 217a
Kuchuk, F. 96a
Kuehl, Gertrude A. 146a
Kufa University Founding Organization 103b
Kugai, Saburo 166a, 175b, 190a
Kuhling, Lulu 142a
Kührer, Alfons 329a
Kuhrt, David 166a
The Kukje Shin Bo 217a
Kulczynski, Stanislaw 156b
Küllheim, Fos 288a
Kultur & Gesellschaft (Eugen Weisenseel) 217a
Kultura 217a
Kumar, Vikramajit 301b
Kumlehn, Jurgen 217a
Kunelius C.E. 172b
Kunene, Raymond 111a
Kurihiro, Masao 144b
Kunkel, Dudley S. 263b
Kuno, Osamu 145a
Kunstler, William M. 263b
Kuntz, Paul G. 263b
Kuo Mo-jo 95a
Kuppeschmidt, S. 134b
Kuratowski, ? 291a
"Kurdish and Arab Students of Iraq" 125b
"Kurdish and Arab Students on Hunger Strike" 126a
Kurdish Facts West-Asia 125b
Kurdish Students in Europe 125b
The Kurdish Students Society in Europe and the Iraqi Students Society in U.K. 125b
Kurokawa, Toru 144a-b
Kurth, D.I. 149b
Kurtha, A.N. 174a
Kurtz, Irma 207b
Kurz, Eugene 171b
Kurz, J.J. 91a
Kurzweil, Z.E. 217a
Kusin, Mr. 52a
Kutzko, Philip 263b
Kuwait **105b**
Kvetoslav, Faix 173a, 205a
Kyncl, Karel 173a
Kyodo News Service 16b, 217a
Kyoto Buddhist Association 52a
Kypraioy, Maria 123b
Kyriakidou, Marie 122b, 123a
Kyulyovski, Iliya 225b
The Kyunghyang Shinmoon 217a

L

Labadie Collection of Social Protest Literature 52a
Labanovsky, Esther 116a
Labon, M.A. 297a, 329a
Labour Daily Provisional Founders-Council 217a
Labour Government 146a
Labour Monthly 217a, 333a
The Labour Party 52a, 178b, 350b
Labour Party, East Midlands Regional Council 166a
"The Labour Party's Foreign Policy" 114a, 118a, 143b, 146a, 190b
The Labour Peace Fellowship 52a, 114a, 166b
Labour Union Associations of Jordan 107a
Labour's Call 121a
"Labour's Goldwater" 115a
Labour's Voice 217b
Labra, Paco Pendas 130a
Lacasa, B. 52a
Laceroloti, Giorgio 291a
Lacey, Terry 148a
Lackides, George 263b
LaCombe, Pierre 263b, 329a
Lacoste, Yves 186b, 188b
Ladies' Own Weekly 217b
The Lady Bessborough Press 217b
LaFever, Glenda 236a
Laffers, Eva 124b
Laffers, Zoltan 101b
Lafferty, Jerome A. 171a
Lafue-Véron, Madeleine 120a
Lagercrantz, Marika 263b
Lago, Mary M. 263b
Lagrange, J.L. 349b
Lagriffaul, Henri 263b
Laguna, Jair R. Peixoto 52a
Laidlaw, S. Graham 263b
Laidler, Harry W. 234b
Laiho, Janko 173b
Laine, Barbara 288a
Laird, Bruce 98b, 121a
Lake House Bookshop 217b
Lall, Arthur 220b
Lall, Diwan Chaman 102b
Lall, R.B. 263b
Lâm, Mai 163a
Lamb, J.P. 282b
Lamb, Maila E. 142a
Lambert, Mr. 87b
Lambert, Eric 52a
Lambert, J.W. 236a
Lambert, John 222a
Lambert, R.F. 121b
Lambert, Tom 217b
Lambert, Tony 167a
Lambrakis, Gregory 101a, 122b, 123b
Lambton, Katharine 281b
Lamont, Corliss 10b, 115b, 135a, 136b, 138a, 139b, 140a, 147a, 149b, 154a, 166b, 256a, 259b, 263b, 288a, 292b, 297a, 329a, 353b
Land 349b
Landau, Moshe 158b
Landau, Stephen 25b, 134b
Landero, J. Ludlow 297a
Landes Nordrhein-Westfalen 122a
Landmann, Herbert 189b
Landow, Florence 352a
Lane, Allen 227b
Lane, Mark 115b, 136a, 156b, 264a, 330b, 341b
Lang, Peggy 149a, 228a
Lange, Dr. 100a
Lange, Morton 122a
Langer, Harvey 90b
Langer, Jirí 328a
Langford, M. 48a
Langford, Norman 116a
Langguth, Jack 158b
Langi, Jeanne 224a
Langignon, Michel 173b
Langley, Philip 34a
Langlois, Harding & Co. 307b, 309b, 313b
Langridge, Derek 217b
Langstone, G.A. 52a
Laning, J.S. 217b
Lankenau, D.J. 329a
Lansang, Jose 158b
Lansang, Teodoro 148a
Lansdown, G.B.M. 310a
Lanvin, Jean-Pierre 23b
Laos **105b**
The Laotian Embassy 105b
La Pira, Giorgio 104, 106b, 142a, 297a
Lapp, Adolph 329a
Lapp, Ralph E. 155b
Laquer, Walter 112a
Laranjo, Jose 64a, 298a
Larbuck, Ken 103a
Larke, John 214a
Larnach, John 52a, 147b
Larsen, Egon 329b
Larsen, Elma C. 172a
Larsen, P. 166b
Larsen, Reidar 133b
Larsen, Steffen 50a
Larson, Cedric A. 264a
Lasch, Robert 138a. 235a
Lasch, Zora 264a, 291a, 292b
Laski, Frida 353a
Laski, Harold 329a

Harold Laski Institute of Political Science 217b
Laski, Marghanita 264a, 288a
Lasky, Melvin J. 208a
Latendorf, Abel Alexis 166b
Guis. Laterza and Figli 217b
Latey, M.B. 117a
Latin America 148a
Latin America **105b**
Latin American Congress of Solidarity with Cuba and the Right of the Peoples to Self-determination 95b
Latin American News Agency 16b
Latter 324a
Lau, Ha Van 163a
Lau, Philip 52a
Laucks, Irving F. 89b
Laukvik, Unn 78a
Launags, Freds 52a
Laurel Editions 196b
Laurent, Pierre-Marie 173b
Laurin, Jean Mac. 52a
Laux, Renate 199b
Lavan, George 56b
Laver, Margaret 86a
La Verne, Albert A. 329b
La Via, Luigi 329b
Lavrides, George 124a
Lawaha, Mr. 110b
Lawers, Fran 297a
Lawford, Evelyn L. 52a
Lawler, J.G. 204a
Lawrence, Denise G. 167a
Lawrence, Huw 224b
Lawrence, J.D. 105b
Lawson, Arthur 264a
Lawyers Committee on American Policy Towards Vietnam 52b, 166b, 329b
Lawyers Vietnam Committee 147a
Layard, Sir Henry 279b
Layfield, John 169b
Lazareanu, A. 110a, 129a, 288a
Lazarescu, F. 129a
Lazaro, A. 130b
League for Democracy in Greece 52b, 101a, 123a
League for Democracy in Greece Relief Committee 123a
League of Arab States 107a
League of Arab States, London Office 105b
League of Iranian Socialists in Europe 125a
Leakey, R.D. 264a
Leamass, Sean F. 103b
Leary, Frank 52b
Leavitt, Frank J. 52b
Lebanon **105b, 127a**
Lebenhart, Frantisek 204b
Le Bohec, Jacques 301b
Lebzeltern, Gustav 329b
Leckie, Robert 137b
Leclerq, René 329b
Lecoin, Louis 121a
Lederer, Edgar 188b
Lee, Eileen 143b
Lee, Jennie 114b, 116b, 141b
Lee, Kenneth 47b, 220b
Lee, Margaret L. 353a
Lee, Ronald 126b
Lee, W. 172b
Lee Abbey Hotel 307b
Lee Tsung-ying 101b
Leeds C.N.D. Committee 297a
Leeds University Union Conservative Association 125b
Leeds University Unions 297a
Leeming, David A. 157b
Leeming, P. Bruce B. 301b
Lees, Thomas 52b
Leet, Don 52b
Le Flufy, F. St. J. 217b
Le Gal, Francis 102a
Leggett, H.W. 278b, 279a
Leggett, T. 144b
Leghait, ? 351b
Legislative Assembly of Assam 297a
Le Grève, Pierre 120b
Legum, Colin 142b
Lehmann, Jerry 217b
Lehsana, Keith C. 297a
Leibler, J.J. 56b
Leicester Secular Society 52b
Leicester University Students' Union 166b
Leier, Herbert 170b
Leite, J.J. 264a
Leite, Ruiz Gonzaga de Oliviera 152b
Leiterman, Richard 216a
Leith, E. 282a
Leizer, Mr. & Mrs. Gordon 112b
Lemilchama Wetipul Behazalet Rechush Yehudy 52b
Lemkow, Tutte 217b, 232a
Lemoine, Serge 233a
Le Mouton, R. 52b
Lenart, Joseph 96b
Lennon, John 264a, 297a
Lennon, M. 126b
Lennon, Yoko 297a
Lens, Sidney 217b
Lentakis, Andreas 124a
Lenton Ward Labour Party 52b
Lenzini, José 173b, 174a
Leo, Grigoria Mikhailovich 243a
León, Argeliers 78b
Léon, Juan Martinez de 131b
Léonard 329b
Leonard, Hans 272b
Leonhard, Susanne 329b
Leoni, Raul 117b, 132a
Leontev 218a
Leopardess 217b
Lerman, I.M. 135a
Leroy, Andre 122b, 124a
Leslie, M. 89b
Lessing, Doris 264a
Lester, Julius 139b, 188a
Lester, Michael 3a
Lettesge?, R.O. 172b
Leu, Lucy 264a
Lev, Grigori Mikhailovich 217b
Levene, Sam 199a
Levenson, Joan 227a
Lever, H. 264a
Levey, Grace 282b
Levi, Moise Victor 52b
Levick, R.B.M. 52b
Levin, Eugene 198a
Levin, Mrs. Miriam 98a, 138b
Levine, Mrs. G. 264a
Levine, Isaac Don 264a
Levinthal, Sonia 220a
Levinson, Arnold 290a
Levy, Benn W. 89b, 93a, 177a
Levy, G. 122b
Levy, Howard 17b, 139b
Levy, L. 152b
Levy, Paul 264a
Lewin, S. 111a
Lewis, Adrian 179a
Lewis, Andrew 264a
Lewis, Anthony 117a, 223b
Lewis, Bernard D.K. 352b
Lewis, Carole S. 206a
Lewis, Ed. 52b, 292b
Lewis, Flora 139b, 218b
Lewis, Florence 52b
Lewis, Hobert 230a
Lewis, John 150b
Lewis, Jonathan 112a-b, 201b
Lewis, Joseph 135b
Lewis, Lewis W. 281b
Lewis, Malcolm 112a
Lewis, Oscar 158b
Lewis, R.D. 125b
Lewis, Stephen 151b
Lewis & Lewis and Gisborne 309b
Lewisham Council for Community Relations 131b
Leyden, Peter 52b
Lezarson, J. 224a
Li Chu-wen 95a, 120b, 177a
Li Shon-pao 95a
Libby, Gary Russell 217b
The Liberal Democrat 217b
Liberal Studies Publications Ltd. 217b
Liberation 143b, 217b
Liberator 218a
Liberi e Svizzeri 52b
Liberia **105b**
Liberson, David 112a-b, 215b
Liberty 332b
Librairie Larousse 218a
Libreria Editorial Jorge Alvarez S.R.L. 169a
Libya **105b**
Libyan Delegation 151b
Lichauco, Benjamin 128a
Lichtig, Maurice 97b, 98a, 99b
Lichtman, Susan 172b
LID News Bulletin 329b
Liebe, John P. 171b
Lieber, R. 66a
Lieberman, Myron 264a

Leibowitz, H. 137b
Liebowitz, H. 137b
Lienau, G.C. 329b
Life 324a
Life of Bertrand Russell 301a
Lifshutz, Bernard Lee 89b
Liggio, Leonard P. 140a, 150b, 297a
Light, Peter 52b
Lighten, Harold C. 146b
Ligue Belge pour la Défense des Droits de l'Homme 53a, 94a, 117a, 130b, 135a, 152a
Ligue des Etats Arabes Bureau de Paris 174a
Ligue Francaise pour la Défense des Droits de l'Homme et du Citoyen 126a
Ligue les Etats Arabes 161a
Ligue Mondial pour la Paix 53a
Likan, Barbara 53a, 137b, 138a
Liljenberg, Bengh 330a
Lilley, E. 168a
Lim, Leng Soon 53a
Lima, Osorio 53a
Limbo 218a
Limqueco, Peter 18a, 82a, 109b, 148a, 157b, 186b, 223b, 238a, 297a
Lincolnshire Echo 218a
Lincona, Alejandro G. 127b
Lindeman, David B. 53a
Linden, F.C. 53a
Lindenhof, Mannheim 174b
Linder, Leslie 26b
Lindholm, Arthur W. 218a
Lindop, Patricia J. 264a, 288a
Lindner, Robert 218a
Lindquist, Hans 218a, 236b
Lindquist, Ligne 264a
Lindsay, Alexander 297a
Lindsay, Susan (*see* Russell, Susan)
Linen, James A. 237a
Lines, Michael 295a
Link Magazine 218a
Linke, K. 98a
Linsell, L.A.C. 53a
Linzini, José 240a
Lions Club 218a
Lipman, Carol 167b
Lippold, Kay 53a
Lipshitz, Devorah 111a, 135a
Lipschutz, Isidore 154b
Lipsig, Harry H. 67b, 121a
Lipski, S.K. 147a
Lipton, Marcus 122b, 123b
Lis, G. 124a
Lisa, Estaban 214a
Liskovsky, Rebecca 111b
The Listener 57b
Lister, Enrique 151b
Lister, R.P. 330a
Listowel 96a
Literaria 218a
Literary Gazette 218a
The Literary Guide 218a
Literaturnoe Nasledstvo 218a
Literaturnaia Gazeta 111b, 112b
Kurt Litschauer 288a
Little, R.P. 53a
Little, Robert 218a
Little, Robert P. 330a
Little, Brown and Company 218a
Little River High School 53a
Littlewood, D.E. 264a, 330a
Littlewood, J.E. 288a
Littlewood, Joan 232a
Littman, Marianne 174a
Litvinoff, Emanuel 53a, 99b, 109b, 110b, 111a-b, 117a, 129a, 132a, 133a, 133b, 156a
Litvinov, Pavel 116b
Liveright, Horace 200b
Liveright Publishing Corporation 218b
Liverpool Daily & Echo Ltd. 218b
Liverpool Road Pottery Ltd. 143b
Liverpool School of Tropical Medicine 89b
Liverpool University Vietnam Committee 179a
Living Book Incorporated 218b
The Living Word Islamic Propagation Centre 53a
Livingstone, Edith 288a
Livshitz, Isaak 116a
Livshitz, Sophia 116a
Liwag, Juan R. 109b
Liwschitz, I. 134b
Llacar, Perfecto E. 148a
Llewelyn, Alun 330a
Lloyd, E.M.H. 309a
Lloyd, John Russell 166b, 292b, 303a
Lloyd, K. 292b
Lloyd, Margaret 100a, 122a, 251a, 288a, 292b, 303b, 350a, 354a
Lloyd, Ted 310b
Lloyd-Davies, B. 314a
Lloyds Bank Ltd 89b
Lloyd's Bookshop 89b
Lloyd-Williams, Bronwen 279a, 293a
Lobatchewsky, N. 9a, 258b
Lobb, Warwick 53a, 170b
Lobo, I. 102b
Local Forum 53a
Loch, B.D.S. 314a
Lock, Mr. 282a
Lock, Desmond 53a
Locke, Elsie 218b
Locken, John 218b
Lockheed Missiles and Space Company 89b
Lodge, Albert 123a, 131a-b
Lodge, Henry Cabot 147a, 149b
Loeber, R.M. 53a
Loeff, Israel 103b
Loewe, Raphael 264a
Lofstedt, Rey 41a, 60a
Logan, Jimmy 53a, 166b
Logan, Judy 53a, 166b
Logic and Knowledge 349a
Logodi, L. 101b
Logue, Christopher 94a, 232a
Lohani, Q. 108b
Lohaus, Hermann 175a, 206b
Lohman, J.L. van Essen-de Savornin 262b
Lohse-Link, Rosel 99b
Loka Shikshana Trust 102b
Lokkalyan 218b
Lolan, N.R. 53a, 127a
Lomas, Charles W. 218b
Lomax, Sir John 53a
Lombardi, Riccardo 133b, 166b
The London Association for the Protection of Trade 53a
The London Book Co. 37b
London Bulletin 17b, 51b, 78a, 96a, 209a
The London Committee for the Armenian Cause 53b, 112b, 120a
London Committee of 100 11b, 104a, 114a, 124a, 130b, 178a
London Electricity Board 89b
London Forum 39a
London, Fritz 264a
London Library 154b, 264b, 284a
London Mathematical Society 354a
London Region CND 145b, 297a
The London School of Economics 114b, 115a, 297a, 313b
L.S.E. Labour Club 146a
London School of Economics Fight **154a**
London School of Economics Meeting **146a-b**
London Students' "Peace in Viet-nam" Committee 53b
London Symphony Orchestra Ltd. 288a
London Trade Union Peace Committee 53b
London University Socialist Society 146a
London Weekend Television 218b
London Welsh Association 178a
London Workers Committee 291a
Long, Gerald 59a, 150b
Long, Rodney 53b
Longanesi & Co. 196b, 218b
Longier, Henri 11b
Longmans, Green & Co. Ltd. 218b, 224b
Longo, Luigi 104b, 112a
Longstaff, D. 53b
Longton, Denzil 53b
Longville, Timothy 264b
Lonsdale, Kathleen 158b
Lontum, Nguyn Hu 296b
Look Magazine 28b, 142a, 218b
Loomis, Mildred J. 71a
Loots, W. 53b
Lopez, Ann 53b
López, Antonio Daríe 158b

Lopez, Nicolos 297a
Lord, David 53b
Lord, F.M. 53b
Lorda Alaiz, F.M. 53b
Lorentzon, Peter 113a
Loring, James 91a
Lorrimer Publishing 218b
Los Angeles Times 79b, 138a, 185b, 218b
Losey, Dorothy 145b
Lossin, Yigal 116a
Lotus & Delta Ltd. 307b
Lotze 349b
Loubeh, Jose Martins Costa 218b
Loubeh, Silvio 53b
Lourie, Arthur 103b, 154b
Love Inc. 218b
Lovejoy, Hesta 301b
Lovell, Bernard 73a
Lovell, Harriet M. 317a
Lovell, White & King 313b
Loveman, Lenore 53b
Loving Peoples of World Sohyo 145b
Low, David 353a
Low, Ian F.H. 223a
Lowe, Daniel 133a
Lowe, Victor 264b, 291a
Lowell-Adams House Printers 218b
Lowenfels, Walter 127a
Lowenthal, M. 350a
Lowne, Donald 301b
Lowne, Priscilla 301b
Lowny, Anna Marie 297a
Lowrie, Arthur 106b
Lozano, Julio Toro 171a
Luard, G.D. 264b
Lub, Gleb 173a
Lubberhuizen, G. 199b
Lubbock, Eric 149a
Lubelska, Anna 53b
Lubischew, Alexander A. 330a
Lubitz, Ruth 242b
Lübke, Heinrich 99b, 122a
Lucan, Lord 46b
The Lucanian Fellowship Ltd. 53b
Lucas, Bernard 174a
Lucas, Bill J. 264b, 354a
Lucas, Mrs. Bill J. (Diana) 264b
Lucas, Blanche 148b, 297a
Lucas, F.L. 264b
Lucas, Robert 334b
Lucas, Terence 231a
Luce, Henry R. 334b
Luce, Phillip Abbot 135b, 166b
Luchins, Daniel 53b
Lud 219a
Luehrs, Jr., Fred U. 264b
Luftig, Robert 189a
Lunggren, Mollie 264b
Luisi, Hector 115a
Lukacs, George 330a
Lukesh, Eva 96b
Lumbreras, Alberto 106a, 127a, 198b
Lumea 219a
Lumley, A.B.H. 134b
Lummus, Mr. 310b
Lumsden, Malvern M. 53b
Luna, Benjamín Laureano 106a, 127b
Lund, Caroline 139b
Lupul, Johann 110a
Lurb, C. ? 106a
Lurcy, Reine 54a
Lurie, Meyer 264b
Luscombe, Leslie H. 54a, 297a
Lussu, Joyce 144a
Lustig, Jeremy 54a, 139a, 341b
Lutaud, Olivier 330a
Luther, Edward A. 330a
Luther, Otto 330a
Lutuli, Albert J. 25a, 130a
The Albert Lutuli Rectorial Campaign 54a
Lutzeier, Dan P. 87b
Lutzenberger, Jose 54a
Luzzato, Lucio 151b
Lycée Français de Londres 278a
Lye, Brenda 264b
Lynch, Mary 291a
Lynch, Patrick 126b
Lynch, William 3a
Lynd, Staughton 139a, 150a, 158b, 166b, 217b
Lynes, Russell 293a
Lynes, Winifred 293a
Lyngstad, Sverre 219a
Lyons, Leonard 219a
Lyons, Paul J. 101a
Lyrikvännen 330a
Lyttle, Bradford 219a
Lywood & Sons 154b, 313b

M

M.J. 3a
Maariv 103b, 219a
Maas, Elton R. 54a
Maas, Henry 264b
Maas, Otto 264b
Maasing, Ulo 54a
Maastleugen, P. 89b
Maberly, Alan 312a
Mabey, Richard 143b
Mabon, Dickson 116a
Macalli 297a
Macapagal, Diosdado 109a, 128a
MacCarthy, D. 266b
Macco Magazine Corporation 335b
MacColl, S. 9a
MacDiarmid, Hugh 152a, 264b
Macdonald, Dwight 89b
MacDonald, J. Ramsay 54a
Macdonald, Mary E. 288b
Macdonald, R. 279b
MacDonald, W. 143b
MacDonald, Wilson 288a
Macdonald & Co. 195b
Mace, Alec 219a
Macek, Josef 290b
MacFadden, Celeste 282b
Macfarlane, E.C. 37a
MacGibbon, James 211a
MacGibbon & Kee Ltd. 219a
Machover, M. 104a, 107a
MacInnes, Stewart 170a
MacIntyre, Alasdair 264b
MacIver, Robert M. 354b
Mackarness, Hugh J.C. 280a
Mackay, Dorothy 307a
MacKay, Hamish 137a
MacKay, R.W.G. 274b, 307b
MacKenzie, Compton 54a, 123b, 152a
MacKenzie, Norman 223a
Mackie, William 137a
Mackintosh, C. 284a
MacLachlan, T.R. 54a
MacLean, Colin 123b, 129b, 237a
MacLeish, Archibald 288a
Maclennan, Marion H. 23a
Macleod, Joseph 219a
Lord MacLeod of Fuinary 48b
Maclurkin, R.B. 230b
Macmillan, Harold 152b, 234a, 351a
Macmillan, Neil 149a
MacMillan & Co. Ltd. 219a, 230a
MacMurray, Paul C. 264b
Macpherson, Kathleen 91b
Macrae, J.E.C. 115a
MacSwiney, Muriel F. 173b, 291a
Macy, C.J.G. 230a
Maczioch, Günter 109b, 156a
Madams, H.E. 89b, 277b, 308a, 309b
Madden, Edward H. 219a
Madden, Max 237b
Maddock, David 301b
Maddox, John 222b
Madeira, Maria Bernardo Ramos 171a
Mafufnik, Abercrombie 61a
Magalhães, Edson 219a
Magalhães, Manuel Barbedo de 54a
Magariños D., P.D. 297a
Magariños, Sophie 54a
Magee, Bryan 198a, 219a, 264b
Magee, John 219b
John Magee Inc. 219b
Maggi, Mike 167b
Magill, Lincoln C. 330a
Maglione, Michael C. 54a
Magnissalis, Kostas G. 330a
Magpie and Stump 257b
Maguire, Frank 89b, 178b
Mahadevan, T.K. 165b
Mahapatra, Debaprasad 153b
Mahboub, A.F.M. 107b
Mahdi, Molvi Ghazanfar 54a
Mahida, Ebrahim Mahomed 54a
Mahmood, Mir Ijaz 297a
Mahnaoui, Michel 120b
Mahncke, Horst 174b
Maidment, George 178a
Mail 153b
Main, G.H. 146a

Mainichi Daily News 144b
The Mainichi Newspapers 219b
Mainstream 14a, 219b
Mairs, Tanya E. 224b
Maison de la Mutualité 174a
Majdalany, Marguerite G. 113b, 130b
Majithia, Sardar Surjit Singh 108b
Majlis, K. 108b
Majumdar, Mukunda Bihar 54a
Majumder, Sukhendu 242a
Makal, P. 330a
Archbishop Makarios 96a
Makashay, Roberta 219b
Makino, Tsutomu 144b
Mäkitalo, Arto 54a, 173b
Makiya, Mohammed 103b
Makoto, Ada 164b
Makous, Ibrahim 113b
Maladinsky, Hans-Peter 219b
Malan-De Mèrindols, Basil Dale 297a
Malawi **105b-106a**
Malay, Ricardo 148a, 166b
Malay, Steve 54a
Malayian National Liberation League 106a
Malaysia **106a, 127a**
Maler, David 297a
Malhas, Lufti 54a
Malhotra, A.K. 54a
Malhotra, B. 153b
Malhotra, D.N. 54a
Mali **106a**
Malik, Abdullah 108b
Malik, Jacob 82b
Malik, Marion A. 220a
Maliki, Alahji Abdul 127b
Mall, Mahmood 54a
Mallalieu, E.L. 54b
Mallatrat, H.H. 31a
Malleson, Bridget 264b, 278b
Malleson, Lady Constance 8a, 263a, 264b, 278a-b, 279a-b, 280a-b, 288a, 353b
Malleson, Joan 264b, 353a
Malleson, Miles 264b, 278b, 279a, 288a, 353a
Malleson, Nick 279a
Mallett, Gwendolyn 135b
Mallows, Lavinia 279a
Maloff, Sr., Peter 54b, 171b
Maloff's Research Library 171b
Malta **106a**
Maltas, D. 219b
Maltby, Brian 54b
Maltby, Veronica 54b
Malter, Friedel 98a, 99a
Malvern Press Ltd. 206a, 288a
Mamouri, Mahmoud 151b
Man 219b
Man and Society 219b
Manabtantri 219b
Manacorda, Eduardo 54b
Management Science 219b
Manampari, C.C. 219b
Manas Publishing Company 54b
Manchanda, A. 178a-b
Manchester & District Young Fabian Group 166b
Manchester Guardian & Evening News Ltd. 219b
Manchester Meeting 146b
Manchester Poster Services Ltd. 146b
Manchete 219b
Mandel, Ernest 54b, 120b, 170b
Mandel, George 265a
Mandela, Nelson 25b, 129b
Manes, Hugh R. 54b, 160a, 313b
Manessis, Nicola 91b
Mani, Rahman 37b
Manila Banking Corporation 89b, 148a
Manila Chronicle 109a, 128a, 219b
The Manila Times 109a, 128a, 183a
Mankewitz, Wolf 288a
Mankind Against War 331b
Manley, Roy 87a
Manly and Pittwater Newspapers Ltd. 170a
Mann, Andre 120b
Mann, Erika 54b
Mann, Golo 54b
Mann, Katia (Mrs. Thomas) 265a
Mannin, Ethel 126a, 154a, 265a
Mannine, Alice 54b
Manning, Charles A.W. 129b
Manning, Jr., Charles R. 48a
Manning, Helen Taft 265a
Mano, Yoshito 203a
Manolakas, G. 123b
Manolo, Señor 96a
Mansfield, Senator Michael J. 47a
Mansfield, Peter 168a
Mansfield, Jr., F. 199a
Mantius, H.K. 330a
The Manufacturers Hanover Trust Co. 145a
Manuilow, T. 146a
Manuscript Exhibition Appeal Committee 111a
Manutiuspresse 199a, 219b
Manwell, Clyde 54b
Mao Tse-tung 95a
Mapam 103b
Maraghee, Mrs. Farangees 54b
Maragides, Steve 54b
Marák, V. 54b
Marathon Peace March 101a
Marcel, Gabriel 265a
March, Esther 280b
March for the Maimed 166b
March on Washington for Jobs and Freedom 54b
March 16th Mobilization Committee 54b
Marcha 132a, 149b, 323a
Marchant, Kelly 54b
Marchesi, Claudio 54b
Marchok, Michele 54b
Marcos, Ferdinand E. 109b, 128a
Marcucci, C. 153a
Marculescu, Lidia 129a
Marcus, Raymond J. 265a
Marcus do Amaral, Acelo 141a
Marcusa, Herbert 158b, 265a
Marcy, Sam 168b
Marden, Philip A. 282b
Mares, Hugh 185a
Marett, Nora 330b
Marett, R.R. 330b
Margai, Albert 110b
Margai, Milton 110b
Margain, ? 94b
Margolis, Joseph 219b
Margulis, Mrs. Jerome 240a
Maria, Roger 207a
Mariam, Yohannes Kidane 97a
Marica, John 54b
Marin, John 54b
Marinello, Juan 58a, 152b
Maritain, Jacques 328b
Marjani, Fati 297a
Markanys?, Peter 101b
Markham, David 232a, 265a
Markham, Olive 279a
Markov, Boris 208b
Markovitch, Micheal 55a
Markpress, Biafran Overseas Press Division 108a
Marks, Abraham J. 103b
Marks, Robert W. 196b
Markus-Verlag GHMB 55a
Marlowe, Patrick 122b
Marmor, Judd 89b
Marmor, Milton 198a
Maroney, Jr., James N. 55a
Marques, Cândido 55a
Marquis, James W. 297b
Marrus, Michael R. 173b
Marsden, E.C. 291a
Marsden, Edmund 233b
Marsden, J.M. 291a
Marsh, Bess 84b, 168b
Marsh, Cristel 98b
Marsh, Richard W. 116a
Marsh, Robert C. 349a
Marshall, Bella 294a
Marshall, Margory 297b
Marshall, Mildred H. 55a
Marshall, Philip 220a, 224b
Marshall, Rachel E. 265a
Marston, Howard E. 55a
Martalogawa, E.A. 154a
Marti, José 121a
Martin, ? 201a
Martin, Barnaby 38b, 55a
Martin, Betty Jean 55a
Martin, C.B. 330b
Martin, C.J. 166b, 201b
Martin, Denny 55a, 93b
Martin, Eddie 166b
Martin, F.M. 89b
Martin, George William 55a
Martin, Gladys 130a
Martin, Gordon E. 172a
Martin, H.A.J. 65a
Martin, H.B. 16b-17a
Martin, Henry A. 55a
Martin, Herbert 309b

Martin, I.C. 55a
Martin, Ian 170a
Martin, Mrs. J. 212b
Martin, Key 168b
Martin, Kingsley 116a, 176b, 223b, 265a, 310b
Martin, L. 171b
Martin, Monty 166b
Martin, O. 171b
Martin, Terry 216b
Martin, William J. 166b
Martineau, Richard 277b
Martinet, Renée (Mme. Marcel) 55a, 173b
Martinez, Alberto 166b
Martinez, J.M. 55a
Martinez, Sebastian Murcia 55a
Martini, Stefano 291a
Martins, Venerando C. 171a
Martinson, Peter 186b
Martionetti, Thomas 55a
Martorell, Jose Viñes y 195b
Maruki Gallery for the Hiroshima Panels 105a
Maruyama, Ihio 104b, 145b
Maruyama, Masao 145a
Marvin, F.S. 330b, 334b
Marxism Today 220a
Marxist Society 127b
Marzani, Carl 98a, 153a
Marzani & Munzell Publishers 153a
Mascarenhas, Ubiratan R. 89b, 171a
Maschler, Tom 117b, 202a
Mashiach, Lea 55a, 113b, 130b
Mashriq 220a
Mason, John J. 55a
Mason, Margery 89b
Maspero, François 97b, 174a, 220a
The Massachusetts Review 220a
Massali, Hassan 125a, 174b
Massamba-Debat, Alphonse 95b
Masseron, Julien 89b
Massingham, C. 222b
Mass-Massacre of the Muslims in India 330b
Masson, Hervé 174b
Matarasso, Léon 160a, 186b, 188b, 189a
Matarisvan, Marion 204a, 330b
Matatu, G. 66a
Mateos, Adolfo Lopez 106a
Matheopoulos, Alekos 124a
Matheson, P.C. 55a
Mathews, Denis 95a
Mathey, Barbara 174a
Mathias, David 152a, 251b
Mathiesen, Niels 48a
Mathu, E.W. 105a
Matkovskiy, Nikolai 117b
Matos, Sebastiao 171a
Matspen 166a
Matsuda, Michio 158b, 166b
Matsumoto, Takuo 145a
Matsumura, Yusuke J. 145a
Matteatti, M. 230a
Mattern, Douglas 34b, 165b
Mattessich, Richard 220a
Matthewman, E.V. 205a
Matthews, Florence 55a
Matthews, George 99a, 122b, 123b, 205a, 221b
Matthews, John 55a, 109b
Matthews, Mervyn 116b
Matthews, R.D. 55a
Matthews, Richard 55a
Matthews, Thomas M. 55a
Matthias, L.L. 330b
Matthysse, Steven W. 330b
Mattila, Asko 173b
Matveev, V. 215a
Matysiak, Henryk 26b, 98b
Mau, Ngo Duc 168b
Maugham, Somerset 177a, 288a
Maung, U. Hla 94b
Maurer, E.N.G. 110a
Maurer, Ion Gheorghe 110a, 129a
Mauriac, François 55a, 97b, 135a, 157a, 158b
Mavalankar, P.G. 217b, 220a
Maw, F. Graham 309a
Mawdsley, Betty 299b
Maxwell, A. 140a
Maxwell, Grover 265a
Maxwell, Max 85a
Maxwell, Robert 146b
I.R. Maxwell & Co. 288a
May, Andrew 55b
May, M. Stephanie 55b, 115b, 137a, 140a, 297b
May 2nd Committee 166b
The May Second Movement 118b
Mayer, B.H. 260a
Mayer, Daniel 112b, 126a
Mayer, Peter 225b
Mayer, Sydney 200b
Mayerson, Charlotte M. 213a
Mayfield, Martin 55b
Mayne, Stanley 152b
Mayo, Edna 96b, 121a
de Mayolo, Santiago Antunez 324b
Mayor of Cavala and the Chairman of the Municipal Council 96a
Mayr, Alfred 220a
Mazzawi, Musa 55b
Mazzolini, Ulisse 47b
M'Ba, Leon 97b
McAdoo, Richard B. 212a
McAdoo, William 32b, 138b
McAfee, Margaret 149a
McAllister, Gilbert 289a
McAlpine, T. 153a
McAndrews, William R. 222b
McCabe, Michael 55b
McCarthy, Tony 155b
McClaughry, John 213b
McClellan, Christina 146b
McClellan, Hugh D. 55b
McClelland and Stewart Limited 220a
McColl, Charles P. 55b
McCollum, Dannel 166b, 288a
McCollum, Vashti 166b
McConomy, Diana 241a
McCormick, Carson 55b
McCormick, Thomas W. 55b
McCreery, Nigel 265a
McCullough, Jeannette 172b
McCullough, Peter J. 265a
McCullough, Stewart J. 166b
McDermott, David A. 198b
McDonald, Alexander 202b
McDonald, D. 151b
McDowell, Richard E. 220a
McEwen, Mrs. 303b
McFarland, Lilian Cook 55b, 123a
McFarlane, Ruth 85a
McGahey, Michael 151a
McGarvey, Douglas 297b
McGill Debating Union 133a, 134b
McGill Journal of Education 220a
McGlynn, T.R. 55b
McGough, Tessie 297b
McGovern, Jr., James C. 166b
William McGovern & Co. Ltd. 89b
McGraw-Hill Book Company 220a
McGregor, Eduardo Ferrer 127b
McGuinness, Sonia 152a
McHaigh, H. 265a
McIlroy, William 114b, 131b, 222a, 297b
McIntosh, E.C. 55b
McIntyre, Lindsay 55b
McKeldin, Theodore R. 42a
McKell, Hugh D. 291a
McKelvey, Donald 167a
McKenna, B. 131b
McKenney, John L. 265a, 330b
McKenzie, B. 230a
McKenzie, Patricia Anne 55b
McKissick, Floyd 158b
McLaren, G.W.D. 261a
McLaughlin, John J. 55b
McLendon, Hiram J. 265a, 354b
McManus, M.J. 55b
McMaster University 261a, 278b, 310a
McMichael, Joan K. 166b
McMillan, Carole 152b
McMillan, Margaret 205b
McNally, C.V. 55b
McNalley, Josette 265a
McReynolds, David 34a, 81b
McShane, Philip 56a
McTaggart, Ian 234b
McTaggart-Cowan, P.D. 172a
McWatters, G.J. 309b
McWilliams, Carey 53b, 123a, 135b, 222a, 331b
McWhirter, Norris 56a
Mealia, Dick 167a
Meally, Victor 56a
Mears & Steinbank 273b
Mechoulam, Alberto 56a

Medawar, Charles 125b, 126b
Medgyesi, G. 101b
Medical Aid Committee for South Vietnamese Peoples 166b
Medical Aid Committee for Vietnam 56a, 160a, 166b
Medical Aid for Biafra Committee 56a, 108a
Medlock, Julie 100a, 220a, 288a, 290b, 293a
Medwedyk, P. 117a
Meeting in Madison Square Garden 115a-b
Meetings of Portuguese Students Abroad 130b
Meeus?, Margaret 297b
Meguire, R.J. 212b
Meharchand 301b
Mehra, M.N. 102b
Susheela Mehra Memorial Hospital 89b
Mehryar, A.H. 106b, 125a
Mehta, Apurva J. 153b
Mehta, G.L. 153b, 297b
Mehta, Jivraj N. 102a
Mehta, Ved 220b
Mehta, Vishwanath 330b
Meier, Peter 297b
Meinicke, Fritz 51b, 122a
Meinong, Alexius 265a
Meir, Golda 104a
Meister, Zinovet Filipovich 56a
Meitner-Graf, Lotte 220b, 265a, 293a
Melas, Michel 100b, 124a
The Melbourne Age 183b
Mellor, Rev. Stanley A. 258b, 265a
Melly, George 152a
Melman, Seymour 56a, 142a-b, 330b
Melner, Samuel B. 218b
Melton, Barry 265a
Members of the Collective of the Metal Workers Industry in the Institute for Data Processing, Dresden 175b
The Memorial Commitee 98a
The Menard Time 135b
Mendelevich, G.A. 218a
Mendelson, John J. 117b
Mendès France, Pierre 112b, 121b, 133b, 158b, 288a
Mendham, Jonathan 297b
Mendizabel Lizalde, Guillermo 207b
Mendoza, Raphael Tirado 297b
Menendez, Antonio 106a
Menéndez G., Alberto 230b
Meng, Heinrich 89b
Menne, Lothar 100a
Menon, C.A. 102b, 149a
Menon, E.P. 48a, 56a
Menon, N.B. 102a
Menon, V.B. Gopinatha 153b, 297b
Menon, V. Krishna (see Krishna Menon, V.)
Mensah, Johnnie J. 100b, 149a
Menszer, Barbara 265a
Menszer, John 265a
Mentor Books 220b
Menuhin, Yehudi 265a
Menzies, Robert G. 147a-b
Mercantile Bank Ltd. 89b
Mercer, David 330b
Mercer, Dilys 220b
Mergs, Mary 34a
Merican, Haji K. Sultan 330b
Merioneth Education Committee 309b
Merioneth Labour Party 56a
Merker, K.K. 235b
Merki, E. 56a
Merle, Robert 56a, 120a
The Merlin Press Ltd. 220b
Merlini, G. 238b
Mermaid Theatre 177a
Merrett, Alicia 156a
Merrett, Stephen 166b
Merriam, Eva 330b
Merrill, John P. 352b
Merriton, Peter 149a
The Mershon Report 114a
Mertens, André 56a
Mertens, M.S. 56a
Merton, Thomas 12b
Merton Council for Peace in Vietnam 166b
Merton Friends of China 166b
Meshgin-Poosh, Mansoor 103a
Messer, Susan 291a
I.G. Metall 99a, 121b
Metcalfe, M.J. 89b
Methodist Federation for Social Action 137a
Methodist International House 89b
Methuen & Co. Ltd. 220b
Metraux, Daniel 56a
Metrgar, Sara Frida 116b
Metropolitan Borough of Chelsea 277b, 278a
Metropolitan Police Central Ticket Office 143b
Metropolitan Police Rochester Row Police Station 314a
Mettas, Jean 128b
Mew, Julian 239b
Mexican Ambassador to the United Kingdom 106a
Mexican Committee for Soviet Jews 112b
Mexican Organization for the Release of Political Prisoners 298a
Mexico **106a, 127a**
Meyer, Charles 94b
Meyer, Dr. 99b
Meyer, I. 56a
Meyer, Joseph 75a, 89b, 146a, 149a, 150a
Meyer, Karl E. 240b
Meyer, Sarah 56a
Meyer, Stefan 122a
Mever-Heine, Ilse 173b
Meyerhoff, Hans 281b, 288a
Meyerhoff, Mary 265a
Meyers, Franz 99b
Meyerson, Mike 165b
Meynell, Francis 309a, 310b, 353a
Meynell, Vera 353a
Mezerik, A.G. 48a, 56a, 350a
Mezvinsky, Norton 25a, 215a
Mı Articulo 67b
Miami Times, 220b
Miasf, Hilda 141a
Michael, Judith 197b
Michaels, Cyrus 56a
Michie, James 200a
Michigan Free Speech Defence Committee 139a
Mickovic-Soko, Emanuel 230b
Middle East **106b-107b**
Middle East Coexistence 220b
Middle East Conference (Proposed) 106b
Middle East Non-Intervention Committee 56a
Middle East Nuclear Appeal **154b**
Middle East—United Arab Republic **107b**
Middlebro', Tom 172a
Middleton, Charles 297b
Middleton, Neil 226a
Middleton, Peggy A. 280a
Midhurst Rating Authority 277b
Midland Bank Ltd. 174b, 277b, 308a
Midorikawa, Toru 56b, 144b
Midulla, Beniamino 331a
Mielke, Lloyd L. 56b
Migeon, Jean-Pierre 265a
Migneau, L. 134b
Mihajlov, Mihajlo 133b
Mihali, Berthold 110a
Mijović, Mil. 230b
Mikardo, Ian 176b
Mikhailov, M. 153a, 215a
Mikhailusenko, Igor 56b
Miklos, Szabo 56b
Mikoyan, Anastas I. 117a
Miles, Bernard 177a
Miley, Ray L. 173b
Milhaud, Darius 288a
Miliband, Ralph 56b, 176a, 291a, 340a
The Militant 56b, 150a, 178b, 220b
Militant Labour Forum 109a, 128a
Mill, John Stuart 301a, 332a
Mill News Letter 220a
Millar, Haldis 56b
Millar, Ian 178a
Millar, J.P.M. 266a
Millar-Danks, S. 279a
Millard, Alfred 331a
Miller, Arthur 158b, 288a
Miller, B. 126b
Miller, Cecil 147b
Miller, David H. 54a, 89b
Miller, F. Eugene 89b

Miller, Frederick J. 56b
Miller, Hershel S. 331a
Miller, Ian 89b, 166b
Miller, Joseph 215b
Miller, Michael E. 291a
Miller, Mike 34a
Miller, Mrs. W. 265b
Miller, Warren 150a
Millett, Mervyn R.O. 56b, 116a, 146b, 183b, 291a, 297b, 331a
Milligan, Spike 265b, 291a, 354a
Millionscikov, Academician 291a
Millis, Walter 147b
Milliyet 106b, 220b
Mills, Glyn 280b
Mills, Stan 148a
Millspaugh, Frank 82a
Milne, E.M. 222b
Milne, John E. 56b
Miltke, Renata 175a
Milton, Barry 56b
Milton, Naw 148b
Milward, Kristin 279a
Minces, Juliette 161a
Mind 221b, 354b
Mindaki, Stella 175b
Mindel, Jacob 136b
Minello, Nelson 149b
Minetti, Maria Gulia 196b
Minffordd Post Office 297b
Ming Pao Daily News 220b
Minh, Vo-Than- 149b
Minister of Justice for Lower Saxony 99b
Minister of Justice of the Federal Republic of Germany 99b
Minister of the Interior, German Democratic Republic 99a
Der Ministerpräsidenten des Landes 99b
Le Ministre de la Cour (?) 124b
Ministre des Affaires Etrangères du Gouvernement Royal du Cambodge 94b
Ministry of Education, Awards Branch 282a
Ministry of Information, Cambodia 171b
Ministry of Justice, German Democratic Republic 99a
Ministry of Pensions and National Insurance 309b, 313b
Ministry of Reconstruction 354b
Minke, Fritz 56b
Minojetti, Luigi 56b
Minor, Ethel H. 107a, 139b, 157b, 192a
Minor, Robert W. 150a
The Minority of One 13a, 14a-b, 15a, 40a, 63a, 115b, 117a, 118a, 123b, 134a, 135b, 137a-b, 138a, 139a-b, 142a, 147a, 155a, 220b
Minorsky, V. 56b
Minskers, Advokats J. 56b
Mintoff, Dom 106a
Miranda, Alvaro 56b, 148b
Miranda, Shakuntala 109b
Mirchandani, G.G. 238b
Mirelman, José 57a
Miro, Juan 57a
Miroslav, Subrt 57a
Mirza, Akhtar 57a
"Miscellaneous" **154b, 155a**
Misha, Kristaq 93a
Mishima, Sumie 215a
Mishler, Elliot G. 149a
Misroch, Rafael 116b
The Mission 221a
Mission of the Malayan National Liberation League 57a
Mission of the Malayan National Liberation League in the People's Republic of China 106a, 124b, 127a
Missirliu, Alexandre 110a, 129a
Missirliu, Sandu 173b
Mister, Harry 143b
Mistretta, Enrico 217b
Misu, Ardeleanu 301b
Misuzu Shobo Publishing Co. 104b, 221a
Mitcalfe, Barry 147a
Mitchell, Adrian 331a
Mitchell, Charles 92a
Mitchell, D.J. 117b
Mitchell, David Henry, III 36b, 57a, 136a, 139b, 265b
Mitchell, M. 146a, 221a
Mitchell, Peter 172b
Mitchison, Naomi 353a
Mitford, Jessica 271b
Mitford, Nancy 265b
Mitre 221a
Mitrovitch, Paul 331a
Mitton, Alexander W.D. 265b
Miutzer, H. 110a
Miyake, Toshio 144a-b, 263b
Miyake, Yasuo 145a
Miyari, Mesanori 144a
Miyata, Matakatsu 57a
Mkparu, F C. 57a, 108a
Moazzini, Mohammed Ebrahim 301b
Mobilisation Committee, Sydney 57a, 166b, 169b
Mobutu, President 95b
Møde med Vietnam 331b
Modemann, Richard 57a
Moderator 221a
Modern Welsh Publications Ltd. 221a
Modig, Jan-Otto 237a
Moffat, A. 192a
Mohammad, Salahuddin 226b
Mohamed, Audrey 57a
Mohammed, Noor 108b
Mohan, Brij 57a
Mohieddin, Khaled 107b, 156b
Mohile, S.D. 57a
Mohindra, Prem 237b
Mo-jo, Kuo 156b
Molgosa, Ricardo 297b
Möllerström, Stan 200b
Molnár, István 124b
Molodtsov, S.W. 48a, 75a
Molony, Dan 89b
Molotov, V.M. 159a
Moltke, Kai 173a
Momcilovic, Mihailo 301b
Momigliano, A. 80b
Arnoldo Monadori Editore 221a
Monaghan, L.W. 57a
Monash University Anti Conscription Society 166b
Le Monde 16a, 93a, 94a, 119a, 183a, 189a, 199a, 220a
Le Monde Diplomatique 221a
Mondejar, Felix 121a
Mongar, J.L. 57a
Mongar, Jack 74a
The Monist 221a, 337b
Monjardino, João 57a, 128b
Monaco **107b**
Mongolian People's Republic 108a
Monkman, Kenneth 91a
Monocle 221a
Monod, Michel 57a
Monro, Jack 57a
Montapert, Alfred A. 221a
Monteiro, Jairo Messias 171a
Montenegro, Ilson Falcone 57a
Montgomery, Field Marshall 70b
Montgomery, Lawrence 57a
Montgomery, of Alamein, Viscount 121b
Monthly Review 89b, 137a, 156b, 221a
Monthly Review Press 94a
Monti, Mario 57a, 218b
Monti, Raffaello 57a
Monti, Silvio 57a
The Montreal Star 33a, 221b
Moody, Roger 57b, 241a
Mookerjee, P.N. 236a
Moon, Loyn 102b
Mooney, Thomas J. 168a
Moore, Mr. 147a
Moore, Brenda 265b
Moore, Dickin 265b
Moore, Dorothy 264a
Moore, Edward C. 221b
Moore, Emily C. 101a, 124a
Moore, G.E. 9b, 265b
Moore, Henry 57b, 288a
Moore, J.T. 57b
Moore, John G. 265b
Moore, Jr., Kenyon 147b
Moore, Lillian 57b
Moorthy, A.T. 95a
Moorthy, E.P. 265b
Moraes, Dom 224b
Morais, V.L. 57b
Moran, John H. 265b
Morandini, D.M. 82b, 288a
Morante, Paolo Bracaglia 239b
Moravia, Alberto 132a, 136a, 159a
Morawski, Jerzy 109b, 112a
Morehouse, Russel A. 331a
Morel, Stella 209a
E.D. Morel Memorial Fund 79a

Morelli, Anna Tanasescu 110a
Moreno, Carlos Rogelio 169a
Moreno, Juvenal González 172b
Moreton Hall School 279a
Morgan, Miss 275a
Morgan, Ada M. 57b
Morgan, D.E. 265b
Morgan, Dorothy P. 57b
Morgan, Ella 251b
Morgan, G.D. 309b, 310b
Morgan, J. Gwyn 178b
Morgan, Jr., John McC. 174b-175a
Morgan, L.O. 265b
Morgan, Patricia 57b
Morgan Guaranty Trust Company 57b
Morgan Freiheit 132a
Morgenthau, Hans J. 147a
Morgenthau, III, Henry 200b
Hitoshi Mori of Daigakusha Co. Ltd. 197a
Mori, Koji 144b
Morikawa, Kinju 157a, 166a, 175b, 184a, 192a, 296b
Morina, G. 274a
Morita, Ichi 84b
Morita, N. 144b
Morita, Sadao 144b
Moritaki, Ichiro 11b, 49a, 57b, 104b, 144b, 145a
Morito, Tatsuo 288a
Morland, Simon 57b
Morley, J.L. 202b
Morley, Jane 208b
Morning News 221b
Morning Star 114a, 124a, 183b, 221b
Morocco **108a, 127b**
Morpeau?, Pierre Moraviah 297b
Morrell, Lady Ottoline 265b, 279b, 309a, 310b, 353a
Morrell, Roy 57b
Morris, ? 98a
Morris, Andrew 178b
Morris, Edita 57b, 145a
Morris, Ira 45b, 116b, 145a
Morris, John 149a, 331a
Morris, Reginald 265b
Morris, R.M. 117b
Morris, Rosmary 291a, 293a
Morris, Steven 265b
Morrison, Mr. 147a
Morrison, David 221b
Morrison, Harold 202a
Morrison, Stanley 267a
Morrow, Elizabeth 89b
Morrow, Geoffrey 89b
Morse, Elsa Peters 153a
Morse, Wayne 138a, 146b, 155b
Morse Economic Consultant Service 153a
Mortada, Mary S. 57a
Morten, M. 75b, 130a
Mortensen, Arne Thing 97a
Mortimer, J.E. 206b
Mortimer, John 265b
Mortimer, Rex 170a
Morton, Andrew R. 89b
Morton, B.S. 57b
Morton, G.F. 218a, 265b
Morton, Murray 218a
Moscovici, Clara 110a, 129a
Moscovitz, Shaler 265b
Moscow Conference on Disarmament 121b
Moscow Radio 19a
Moseley, Lorraine 57b, 169a
Moser, Roger 221b
Moshowitz, Israel 117a
Moskoff, Costis 123a
Mösler, Gustava 199a
Mosley, Gordon 265b
Mosrafa, Barzani 103b
Moss, David 57b
Moss, Jacques 265b
Moss, Norman 57b
Mossadegh, Mohammed 103a, 159a
Moszczeński, Jan 109b
Motamed, Amir Ferydoun 331a
"Mothers" 166b
Mouat, Kit 213b, 297b
Moulik, Ranapriya 167b
Mount Roskill Citizens for Peace 57b
The Mountaineering Association 265b
Moura, Manuel 109b, 128b
Mouvement contre l'Armement Atomique (Paris) 57b
Mouvement de Jeunesse, Nice 58a
Mouvement de Soutien aux Peuples de L'Angola et des Autres Colonies Portugaises 109b-110a
Mouvement Révolutionnaire Basque de Libération Nationale E.T.A. 120a
Mouzas, M. 231a
Movement for Colonial Freedom 58a, 96a, 108a, 113b, 118a, 121a, 126b, 130a-b, 154a, 156a, 166b, 297b
Movement for Human Rights 58a, 107a
Movement for the Liberation of Portugal (Frente de Libertação Nacional e Colonial) 58a
Movement for the Preservation of Pakistan 108b
The Movement of Defending Iraqi People 125b, 126a, 154a
Movement of Support for the Peoples of Angola and Other Portuguese Colonies 58a
Movimento Cristão Brasileiro pela Paz 58a
Movimento Democratico de Liberation de Portugal y Sus Colonias 128b
Movimento Paz Soberania Pueblos Cuba (Cuban Movement for Peace and Sovereignty) 297b
Movimento por la Paz y la Soberania de los Pueblos 58a, 152b
Mowinckel, Johan 173a
John Mowlem and Co. Ltd. 313a
Mowshowitz, Israel 58a
Moxon, Oliver 58a
Moyer, Edward P. 58a
Mozambique Liberation Front 110a
Msika, Jean-Ange 114a, 121a
Mtingwa, Mr. 113b
Muflis, Shiv Prasad 34b
Mufti, N. 126a
Muggeridge, Malcolm 265b
Muguerza, Javier 221b
Mühe, Michelangelo 272b, 293a
Muir, P.H. 267a
Muirden, Geoff 166b, 170b
Mukerjee, S. 234b
Mukherjee, Harry 47a
Mukherjee, Hira 166a
Mukherjee, Provas Chandra 331a
Mukherjee, S.K. 58a
Mukhopadhyay, Santanu 221b
Muladore, R.W. 89b
Mulla, A.S.A. 37b
Muller, Dr. 122a
Muller, H.J. 58a
Müller, Jiri 97a
Mullock, C.R. 214b
Mullock, T. 292b
Mumford, Lewis 159a, 265b, 274a
Mumford, Philip S. 265b
Mummerley ? 278b
Munch, Charles 288a
Mundle, C.W.K. 265b, 331a
Mundstock, James 79a
Mundt, H.J. 157b, 239b
Mung, Ung 94b
Munir, Mohammad 226b, 301b
Munk, Arthur W. 58a
Munnich, Ferenc 124b
Muñoz, Lorenzo Garcia 58a-b
Munro, Kenneth 58b
Munro, T.A. 283b, 309b
Munshi, Vijay 221b
Munzi, Liliana 145b, 203b, 221b
Murakami, Rokuzo 144a
Murdoch, Iris 116a, 152a, 176a, 265b
Muret, André 58b
Murfee, J.M. 221b
Murmann, Hans 331a
Murphey, Allene 265b
Murphy, T.M. 58b
Murray, Alan 58b
Murray, Christine 169a
Murray, F. 58b
Murray, Hilda 172a
Murray, Madalyn 15a, 138a, 209b
Murray, Muz 218b
Murray, Robin 299a
Murray, S.M. 58b
Murray Newsletter 138a
Murray-Brown, Jeremy 266a
Murray-Davis, B. 279b

Murray-Smith, Stephen 225b-226a
Murrell, Mr. 313a
Murti, V.V. Ramana 102b, 221b, 351a
Murthy, G. Daxina 216a
Musacchio, Enrico 221b
Muscatell, Mr. & Mrs. Ralph 297b
Museum of Modern Art 58b, 335b
Musgrave, James L. 58b
Musicians' Union 288a
The Muslim Commercial Bank Ltd. 221b
Musri, G.N. 58b
Muste, A.J. 34a, 58b, 76a, 85a, 136b, 138a, 139a, 152b, 166b
Muta, Sueo 58b
Mutiti, Aaron 149a
Muto, Ichiyo 145b
Muziol, Dr. 48a
My Philosophical Development 351a
Myall, R. 89b
Myers, Alvin 58b
Myers, G. 58b
Myers, Ruth H. 266a
Myerson, Michael 105b
Myrdal, Gunnar 58b

N

NAACP (National Association for the Advancement of Colored People) 58b
N.L.F. 188b, 189a
Nabbouh, Khodr 291a
Nabulsi, Suleiman 105a, 297a
Nachbar, Ann 266a
El Nacional, 222a, 325a
Nader, Ralph 150b, 266a
Nadic, Nadir 106b
Nadkarmi, Mahendra 102b
Naess, Arne 147b, 266a
Naeve, Virginia 58b
Naga National Council 102a
Nagai, Yohio 144b
Nagar, D.S. 58b
The Nagasaki Council Against A- and H-Bombs 58b
The Nagasaki-Hiroshima Pilgrimage for Peace 144a
Nagel, Julian 59a
Naggar, A.M. 161a, 174a
Nagy, Imre 102a
Naheem, Abbas 59a
Nahm, Milton 266a
Nahum, Hector 59a
Naird?, D.D. 98b
Nakadate, Kenji 144a, 211b
Nakamura, Kenji 145a
Nakano, Yoshio 144b
Nakashima, Wendy 26a, 138b
Nakayama, Satoru 232a
Nambara, Shigeru 144b
Nanavaty, P.C. 59a, 102b, 297b
Nanduri, Rao 213b
Nandy, Margaret 127b
Nanh, Pha 164b, 297b
Nanjundaiah, C.S. 297b
Nano, Thanas 93a
Naqui, M.B. 214a
Nar, R.B. 222a
Narayan, Jayaprakash 59a
Narayanan, P.R.K. 301b
Narita ? 161a, 299a
Narmic 222a
Narochnitski, A. 224b
Naserallah, Mohammed 93b
Nash, Edward F. 59a
Nash, Kevin C. 222a
Nasrullah, Mir 102b
Nassar, Salim 105b, 126a
Nasser, Gamal Abdel 11b, 70b, 86a, 107b, 131a, 149b, 156b
Nassis, J. 59a
Nathan, Abe 59a, 104a
Nathan, Otto 133b, 142a, 149b, 266a, 288a
The Nation 53b, 115b, 123a, 137a, 135b, 138b, 222a, 331b
The National Adoption Society 353a
National American Party 59a
National Association of Black Students 140a
National Awami Party of Pakistan 127b
National Campaign for the Abolition of Capital Punishment 59a
National Committee British Society for Social Responsibility in Science 297b
National Committee for a Sane Nuclear Policy 53b
National Committee for the Control of Radiation Hazards 59a
National Committee of 100 227a, 331b
National Confederation of Labour of Spain in Exile 130b
National Cooperative Quarries 313b
National Coordinating Committee to End the War in Vietnam 59a, 166b
National Council for Civil Liberties 59a, 114b, 131a, 297b
National Council for Peace U.A.R. 149b
National Council for the Abolition of Nuclear Weapons Tests 43a
National Council of Churches of New Zealand 147a
National Council of Labour Colleges 266a
National Council of Women in India 297b
National Cypriot Committee 96a
National Educational Television 150a
National Farmers Union 59a, 150a
National Federation of Building Trades Operatives 288a
National Federation of Labour Unions 148a
National Federation of Pakistani Associations 131a
National Guardian 59a, 136a, 139a, 147b, 183a, 222a, 331b
National Herald 153b
National Hotel, Bedford Way 90a
National Insider 222a
National Institute for Social Work Training 90a
The National Institute of Adult Education 222a
National Iraqi Defence Committee, Budapest 125b, 126a
National Joint Action Campaign for Women's Equal Rights 131b
National Kurdish Movement in Europe 125b
National Lawyers Guild 222a
National Liaison Committee for New Zealand Committee on Vietnam 147a
National Liberation Front Central Committee 15a, 118a, 162a-b, 163a
National Liberation Front in Bahrain 126a
National Liberation Front Venezuela (London Committee) 132a
National Mobilization Committee to End the War in Vietnam 59b
National Museum of Wales 279b
National Peace Council 59b
National Representation of the National Liberation Front of South Vietnam in the Social Republic of Czechoslovakia 162a
National Secular Society 114b, 131b, 222a, 329a
National Strike Committee of Mexico 106a
National Tunisian Opposition 59b
National Union of Australian University Students 297b
National Union of Finnish Students 297b
National Union of Mineworkers 128b, 148a, 166b, 177a, 178b
National Union of Popular Forces 127b
National Union of Public Employees 116a
National Union of Women's Suffrage Societies 247a
National Youth Campaign for Nuclear Disarmament 117b, 155a, 167a
National Youth Conference 59b
National Youth Conference for Solidarity with Vietnam 17a
Nationalist 222b
Nation's Business 222b
NATO 32b
Naton, Leslie 287b
Natt, Rosemary 310b

Nature 222b
Naturfreundejugend Deutschlands 121b
Nauka i Religia 222b
Nava-Kala 222b
Navaratnam, C. 49a
Manuel Navarre Luna Literary Workshop 54b
Navarro, Vincente 233b
Navon, I. 103b
Nawaz, Shuja 218a
Naya Desh 222b
Naya Payam 222b
Nazis **97b, 98a, 100a**
NBC 222b
NBC News 222b
NBC Today Show 222b
N'Dao, N'Dene 151b
N.D.R.–A.R.D. West German Television Network 222b
Neal, Charles E. 59b, 167a
Nebauer, Anneliese 98b
Nebez, J.T. 125b
Nedelcovic, Bosco 59b
Needham, Dorothy 177a
Needham, Joseph 73b-74a, 177a
Neelkanth: Kanpur University Magazine 222b
Neergaard, Kasper 173a
Nefa Services: J.L. Printing and Stationery Supplies 90a
Negalha, Jonas 128b, 222b
Negrete, Ladislao Lopez 106a
Negro Advancement Council 59b
Nehru Darshan 222b
Nehru, Jawaharlal 14a, 102a, 110b, 124b, 251b, 288a, 334a
Jawaharlal Nehru in Pictures 336a
Nehru Peace Prize **147b**
Jawaharlal Nehru Souvenir Committee 222b
Nehryar, Mr. 125a
Neighbors, E. Laverne 59b
Neilands, J.B. 160a, 167b, 189b, 266a
Neild, R.R. 75b
Neill, A.S. 266a
Neilson, Robert 222b
Neitzke, Colleen 167a
Nelson, Cyril I. 207a
Nelson, Floyd B. 59b
Thomas Nelson & Sons Ltd. 222b
Nem, M. So 94b
Nemec, Theodor 287a, 351b
Nemenzo, Jr., Francisco 148a, 222b
Nemoto, Chie 59b, 144a
Nenni, Pietro 90a, 104b, 142a
Neo Marxist Movement 59b
Neogy, Rajat 237b
Népszabadsúg 222b
NER 103b
Neruda, Pablo 59b, 136a, 172b
Nettleton, Dick 30b, 59b, 146b, 165a, 181a, 251a
Netzer, Joseph 104a
Neues Deutschland 223a
Neumann, B.H. 90a
Neumann, Clive 94b
Neumann, Nicolas 240a
Neutralität 223a
Die Neuwe Linie 223a
Nevers, R.A. 59b
Nevins, George 59b
Nevkov, A. 201a
Nevo, Eviatar 59b, 104a, 154b
New America 136b
The New American Library Inc. 150a, 223a
New Cuba: Bulletin of the Britain-Cuba Committee 354b
New Fraternal Jewish Association 111b
New Generation 223a
The New Leader 10b, 135a, 136b, 139a, 183a, 223a
New Left Review 90a, 94a, 103a, 152a, 154b, 223a
New Morality for the Atomic Age 57b
The New Orient 223a
New Outlook 103b, 104a, 154b
The New Republic 11a, 138a, 223a
New Scientist 82b, 223a
New Society 167a, 183b, 223a, 333b
New South Wales Humanist Society 59b, 170a
New South Wales Peace Committee for International Co-operation and Disarmament 223a
New Statesman 12a-b, 13b, 51b, 86a, 96b, 115a, 116a, 135b, 138a, 140a, 146a-b, 147a, 156a, 176a, 178b, 183a, 223a, 331b
New Statesman and Nation 223b
New Times 354b
New University Thought 337b
New Women's and Mother's Pilgrimage to Rome for Peace 97b-98a
New World Review 223b
New York Committee for the General Strike for Peace 60a
New York Federation of Anarchists 60a
New York Herald Tribune 90a, 94a, 118a-b, 135b, 137a-b, 138a, 183a, 220a, 223b, 352a
New York Post 83a, 223b
New York Review of Books 155a
The New York Times 13a, 28b, 55b, 58b, 68b, 73a, 75b, 76b, 81b, 115a, 117a, 135b, 136b, 137a-b, 150a, 152b, 183a, 220a, 223b, 231b, 234a, 255a, 351b
New York Times London Bureau 117a
New York Times Magazine 27b, 136b, 172b
New Zealand **108a**
New Zealand Assistance to the Republic of Vietnam 147a
New Zealand Branch, BRPF **146b-147b**
New Zealand Broadcasting Corporation 147a
New Zealand Campaign for Nuclear Disarmament 60a
New Zealand Peace Council 297b
New Zealand Listener 146b, 223b
New Zealand Press Association Ltd. 147a
The New Zealand Rationalist and Humanist 147a
New Zealand Soil News 354b
New Zealand Social Credit League 147a
New Zealand Weekly News 223b
Newall, Venetia 219b
Newchapel Observatory 224a
Newcomb, S. 256a
Newcombe, Alan 227a
Newell, Frances 170a
Newens, S.C. 148a
Newens, Stanley 60a, 115a, 176b, 297b
Newman, Edith 224a
Newman, Fred 224a
Newman, James R. 142b, 176a, 224a
Newman, Lyn 266a
Newman, M.H.A. 288a
Newman, Patrick 297b
Newman, Sol 60a, 224a
A.D.N. News Agency 195a
News Chronicle 224a
News Limited of Australia 17b, 351a
News from Cuba 152b
Newsman's Gadfly 224a
Newstat, Freeman 224a
Newsweek 146b, 183a, 224a
Newthink Student Magazine 224a
Newton, B.L. 29b
Newton Park College Socialist Society 167a
Newton-John, Irene 224a
Nexö-Andersen, Johanna 121b
Neyens, D. 170b
Neylan, Dan 281b
Ng, Larry 203b
Ngeth-Sophy 94b
Nguyel ? 297b
Nguyen, Cao Van 190b
Nho, U. 60a
Nhu, Ngo Dinh 159a
Niaz, S.D. 60a
Niazi, M.A.K. 60a
Niblock, Tim 60a
Nice, Lester A. 60a
Nichol, J.B. 278b
Nicholas, Harry 78a, 115a
Nicholas, Len 114a, 115a
Nicholls, Tom 178a
Nicholson, Brian G. 297b
Nicholson, David 167a
Nicholson, Marjorie 230a
Nicod, J.G.P. 331b
Nicod, Thérèse 279a, 354a

"Nicola, Dr." 266a
Nicolaides, Melis 123b
Nicolau, Edmund 224a
Nicolescu, Miron 151b
Nicolson, Nigel 238b
Nielsen, Karsten Hald 173b
Nielsen, Niels Erik 173a
Nielsen, Wayne H. 90a, 167b
Niemöller, D. Martin 142b, 156a, 159a, 167a
Niez, S. D. 196a
NIFA Services 224a
Nifer?, Dorothy G. 297b
Niger **108a**
Nigeria **108a, 127b**
Nigeria High Commission 127b
Nightmares of Eminent Persons 7b, 200a
Nii, Masashi 60a
Nike, W. G. 60a
Nikkah, Parviz 125a
Nikolá, J. 104a
Nikolaides, Melis 101a, 123a
Nimeh, William 331b
Nimitz, Mildred 60a
The 1919 Independence Revolutionary Elders' Club 105a
Ninomiya 236b
Nipankal, V. S. 153b
Nir, Michael 147b
Nirenstein, David 331b
Nirvan, N. 126b, 174a
Nishida, Koichi 105a
Nishikawa, Soshyu 145a
Nishimura, Kanichi 144b
Nitto, Sotaro 331b
Nivat, Georges 116b, 224a
Nixon, M. 93b
Nixon, Moya 151a
Nixon, Russell 138b, 144b, 222a
Nizer, Louis 331b
Nkrumah, Kwame 84b, 101b, 288a, 331b
No Arms for Nigeria Campaign 60a
Noad, Gwen Lloyd 90a, 170b
Nobel Institute 147b
Nobel Peace Prize **147b**
Noble, Francis 149a
Noble, G. 172b
Noble, Sheila 95b
Nocolopoulos, Jannis 124a
Noel, D. E. 167a
Noel-Baker, Philip 80b, 155b, 266a, 350b
Nofer, Dorothy G. 266a
The Noken Daur 297b
Nol, Lon 94b
Nolan, David 298a
Non Violent Action in Vietnam 60a
Nonesuch Records Limited 11a
Nordahl, Bjorn 60a
Norddeutscher Rundfunk–Hamburg 224a
Norden, Eric 40a
Norden, Heinz 224b
Nordess, Nedville E. 75a
Nordmann, Joë 160b, 170b, 173b, 294b
Norihiro, Maéhata 145a
Noris, F. 107b
Nørlund, Ib 331b
Norman, C. H. 266a
Norman, Ed 301b
Norman, Ila 301b
Noronha-Rodrigues, A. A. 58a, 128b
Norrie, Mavis 165b
Norris, Gordon 60a, 179a
Norris, R. M. 60a
Det Norske Studentersamfund 108a
Norstad, Lauris 155a
Norteamericanos Amigos de Cuba 152b
North, Joseph 196b
North American Coalition for Biafran Relief 60a, 61a, 108a
North American Congress on Latin America 105b
The North American Review 224b
North Herts Youth for Peace 167a
Northcott, Cecil 116a
Northern Branch Itinerant Action 126b
The Northern Review 224b
Northfield and Mount Hermon Schools 90a
Norton, Lucy 266a
Norton, Polly Hester 353a
Norton, W. H. 310b
W. W. Norton & Co. Inc. 224b, 353a
Norvell, Daniel R. 60b
Norway **108a**
Norwegian Campaign for Nuclear Disarmament 108a
Norwegian Embassy 108a
Norwood, Woody 60b
Notario, Luis Arranz 60b
Nott, Kathleen 224b
Nottingham Evening Post 146b, 224b
Nottingham Test Campaign 30a
Nottingham University, Dept. of Philosophy 298a
Noufflard, Henriette 266a
Nouvelle École 224b, 298a
Nova 224b
Novaia i Noveishaia Istoria 224b
Novak, Betty Jones 60b
Novoa, Emilio 195a
Novosti Press Agency 13b, 224b
Novotny, Antonin 96b
Novoye Russkoye Slovo 326a
Novy Mir Literary Journal 224b
Nowak, Hannelore 122a
Ntihinyurwa, Theodore 110b
Nuasami, A. Rahman 93b
Nuclear and Conventional War **155a-b**
Nuclear Disarmament **155b, 156a**
Nuclear Information 155b
Nuclear Tree 224b
Nuclear War Information Centre 60b
The Nucleus 224b
Nunes, Amaro Coelho 128a
Núñez, Alba Antonia Griñán 95b
Nunn, A. C. 60b
La Nuova Italia Editrice 224b
Nuqoosh 225a
Nuremberg Trials 139b
Nuresh, Fuman 146a
Nußbaum, Hans-Georg 117a
Nussen, Josef 129a
Nu-Swift International Ltd. 90a
Nutley, Jack K. 60b
Nuttall, Jeff 143b
Nyblom, Erik 220b
Nye, L. J. J. 54a, 169b
Nyein, Mahn J. Paw Aye 298a
Nyerere, Julius K. 61b, 113b, 131a, 147b
Nyman, I. 116a
Nymphs International 225a

O

Oakes, John B. 28b, 183a
Oakeshott, Walter Fraser 90a
Oaks, Dallin H. 239a
Oanh, Xuan 163a, 185a
Oba, E. N. 127b
Oberhuber, Oswald 199a, 232b
Oberman, Dr. 277a
Obi, Toshito 104b, 221a
Obote, Milton 114a
Obradovitch, Dusanka 225a
Obrenavic, Milan 60b
O'Brien, Prof. 213a
O'Brien, Conor Cruise 60b, 100a-b, 142a, 150a
O'Brien, H. A. 143b
O'Brien, Kathleen Cruise 150a
O'Brien, M. 60b, 301b
O'Brien, Mike 168a
The E. D. O'Brien Organisation 225a
The Observer 13b, 65a, 65b, 99b, 100a, 101a, 118b, 122a, 123b, 131b, 142b, 152b, 176b, 183a, 225a, 277b, 334a
The Observer Colour Magazine 225a
The Observer Magazine 225a
Obunsha Co. Ltd. 144b, 225a
Ochs, Carol 291a
Ockels, John 60b
Ockels, Kay 60b
O'Connell, James B. 237a
O'Connell, Pat 60b
O'Connor, D. J. 266a
O'Connor, Donald M. 60b
O'Connor, Harvey 60b
O'Connor, Jessie Lloyd 60b
Oda 145b
Oda, Makoto 104b
Oda, Ninoru 203a
Odin, Roger 225a
Odinga, Ajuma Oginga 105a

Oesterr Gewerkschaftsbund Niederösterreichischer Badminton-Verband 93b
O'Faolain, Sean 288a
Ofer, Ludwig 60b
Office of the Representative Abroad of the Patriotic Front of Thailand 113b
Offord, A.C. 177a
Offord and Meynell Ltd. 266b
O'Flaherty, T. 220b
Ofstad, Harold 60b, 331b
Ogbourne, John 60b
Ogden, F.K. 225a
Oggi 225b
Oglesby, Carl 157b, 186b, 192a
Oglesby, Leslie E. 61a
Ogoniak 225b
Oh, Chong Sick 217a
O'Hair, Madalyn Murray 138a, 270a
O'Halloran, M.V. 61a
O'Hanlon, F. 61a
O'Hara, Coral 61a
Ohbe, Yutaka 228a
Ohkawa, Mr. 144b
Ohno, Masao 166a
Ohta, Kaoru 144b
Ohye, Mrs. Saburo 61a
Oji, Ihejika Sam 61a, 108a
Okada, Masahiro 144a
Okamoto, Tatsuo 61a
Okaya, Sojiro 144b
Okinawa-Island of Tragedy 331b
Okinawa Prefecture Council Against Atomic and Hydrogen Bombs 145b
Okishio, Nobuo 61a
Okucani, Ljeposava Rakonic 295a
Olaitan, Sam. Ade. 228a
Olalia, Rolando M. 148a
Old, John W. 169b, 170b
The Old Bavians' Association 225b
Oldhage, Hans 61a
Oldman, Susan 140a
Oleniuk, Carole 172a
Oliano, Forlio Ulo 167a
Olinky, Oded 61a
Oliphant, M.L.E. 142b, 167a, 332a
Olivart, José Maria Albaigés 167a
de Oliveira Leite, Luiz Gonzaga 73b
de Oliveira, Raimundo Bezerra 36a
Oliver, Maria Rosa 141a
Olkar, B.A. 225b, 238b
Olshewsky, Thomas M. 225b
Olson, G. 113a
Olson, Vernel 137a
The Olympia Press 121a
O'Malley Burns, John 139a
O'Mara, E. 143b
Omroepvereniging Vara 225b
Onassis, Aristotle Socrates 266b
One World Council 61a
Oneill, Mr. 147a
O'Neill, Dr. Desmond 279b, 309b
O'Neill, James P. 61a
O'Neill, William Michael 61a
Oneul 225b
Ong, Hui Chong 298a
Ong, T.S. 61a
O'Niel, Colette (*see* Malleson, Lady Constance)
Ono, Yoko 264a
Ontario Institute for Studies in Education 61a
Ooms, Laurette 169a, 170b
Operai Italiani 298a
Operation Outrage (The North American Coalition for Biafran Relief) 61a
Operation Truth 61a
L'Opinion Européenne 332a
Oppenheim, Frank M. 61a, 266b
Oppenheim, Gabrielle 354a
Oppenheim, Paul 354a
Oppenheimer, Ernest Kant 61a
Oppenheimer, Paul 61a, 298a
Oppenheimer, Robert 288a
"Oppression in South Arabia" 111a
Oquendo, Eddie 34a, 139b
Orbis Litterarum 323a
Ordaz, Diaz 106a, 127b
Ordine Dei Cercatori Di Se' Stessi 225b
Ordoobadi, Ahmad 225b
Oregon Mobilization to End War in Vietnam 167a
O'Reilly, Edward 332a
Orestov, O. 228b
Orffa, V. ("Folly") 293a
Organisasi Indonesia Untuk Setiakawan Rakjat Asia-Afrika 103b
L'Organisation de Solidarité des Peuples d'Afrique, d'Asie et L'Amérique Latine 96a
Organisation des Nations Neutres 61b
Organisation of African Unity 121a
Organisations Européenes du Front National Iranien 103a
Organisationsburo des Internationalen Jugendtreffens 98b
Organising Committee of British Institute of Philosophical Studies 262a
Organizacion Mexicana por la Libertad de los Presos Politicos 298a
Organization for Relief and Development 225b
Organization of Afro-American Unity 136a
Organization of Families of Greek Political Prisoners 123b
Organization of Iranian Students 125b
Organization of Solidarity of the Peoples of Asia, Africa and Latin America 95b
El Oriente de Asturias 332a
Origo, Marquese 266b
The Orion Press, Inc. 225b
Orizuru-kai 144b
Orkin, F.M. 196b, 229a
Orloff, Constantin 332a
O'Rourke, D.T. 266b
Orozco, Gaspar 229b
Orozco, J.A. Boutista de 50b, 61b
Orpington C.N.D. 167a
Orr, A. 61b, 107a
Orr, Akiva 225b
Orr, Hugh Robert 28a
Orr, Sydney Sparkes 332a
Orson, Claire 198b, 206b
Örtegren, Lars-Eric 236b
Orton, Jean 79a
Ortuno, Rene Barrientos, President of Bolivia 94a
Orwell, Sonia 165a, 266b
Orwood, C.J. 353a
Osborn, Mrs. 135a
Osborn, J.H. 116a
Osborn, Reuben 332a
Osborne, John 152a, 167a
Osborne, John R. 118b, 167a
Osborne, Keith 90a, 166b
Osborne, King & Megran 90a
Osèguera, Salvador Montes 259b, 296a
Oser, Chancellor 71a, 113b
Osman, M.A. 61b
Ossie, Rosalinde 353a
Osterheld, Dr. 99b, 125b
Ostermarsch der Atomwaffengegner 61b
Ostermarsch 63 332a
Osterreiche Botschaftinder UdSSR 133a
Ostfeld, William 77b
Ostroumoff, Mrs. I. 111b
Otechestven Front 225b
Otero, Mario H. 210b
The Other Side 332a
Othman, Nabil 107b
Otsuka, Kinnosuke 145a
Ottens, Everhard 208a
Otter, Amy E. 303a, 310a, 310b, 353a
Otter, Lawrens 61b, 152a
Otto, Karl 122a, 225b, 235a
Otton, G.G. 123b
Ouang, Tien Ki 266b
Ouchi, Hyoe 145a
"Our Dogs" Publishing Co. Ltd. 90a
Our Generation 203b
Our Generation Against Nuclear War 225b
Ours, A Nature Magazine 280b
Maitre Oussedik 61b, 121a
Outhred, M.E. 170a
Outlook 147a
Overland 225b
Overseas Development Institute Ltd. 61b

Overseas Press Club 104a
Overy, Bob 167a
Overy, Christine 90a
Owais, M. 109a, 235b
Owen, Bob 61b
Owen, D. 293a, 301b
Owen, David 79a, 115a
Owen, I. 266b
Owen, Mably 352b
Owen, O.W. 61b
Owen, Peter 226a
Peter Owen Ltd. 226a
Owens, Chris 170a
OXFAM 142a, 162b, 167a
Oxford Committee for Famine Relief 61b
Oxford University Humanist Group 167a
Oxford University Press 206b, 226a
Oxford Vietnam Committee 167a
Oxford Vietnam Peace Movement 167a
Oxon, Jennifer 61b
Oyler, Percy W. 90a
Ozan, Evnur 61b
Özek, Dr. Cetin 106b
Ozmon, Howard 13b, 168a, 266b, 332a

P

P.E.N. 1921-1971; The Project for a New English Centre 214a
P.H.H.B. 332b
PHP Research Institute 228a
W. Pace 90a
Pacem in Terris 61b
Pach, Leo 266b, 298a
Pachter, H. 266b
Paci, Enzo 226a
Pacifica Foundation 216b-217a, 226a
The Pacifist 226a
Packe, Michael St. John 332a
Paco 62a
Paddington, J.R. 131b
Padhan, Prafulla Kumar 226a
Il Paese 226a
Il Paese Oggi 16b, 226a
Paese Sera 13a, 174a, 226a
Page, Benjamin B. 173a
Page, Robert R. 61a
Pageant 226b
Paget, C.A.E. 226b
Pahlevi, Mohammed Reza 103a, 124b, 125a
Pahor, Boris 62a
Paine, Gwen 232a
Paine, Thomas 10a, 135b
Painter, Colin 62a, 155a
Pair, Gordon A. 149b
Pak Scientist 226b
Pak-China Friendship 62a
Pakhtoon, Ganesha Singh 62a
Pakistan **108a-109a, 127b**
The Pakistan Association of World Federalists 108b, 124b
Pakistan/China Friendship 128a
Pakistan Council for World Government 108b
Pakistan Features Syndicate 226b
The Pakistan Islamic Council for International Affairs 108b
Pakistan *Morning News* 109a
Pakistan National Oils Limited 62a
The Pakistan Observer 226b
The Pakistan Parliamentary Group for World Government 108b
Pakistan Philosophical Congress 298a
Pakistan Spotlight International 332a
Pakistan Times 109a, 226b
Pakistan's Writer's Guild 298a
Pal, Yash. 62a
Pa'Lante 332a
Palestine Democratic Front 107a
Palestine Liberation Movement 107a
Palestine Liberation Organization 62a
The Palestine Problem 107a
Palestine Solidarity Campaign 107b
Palfreyman, M.J. 62a
Palkovitch, I. 111a
Pall Mall Press 226b
Pallas 226b
Palm 226b
Palme, Olaf 113b
Palmer, Mrs. 147a
Palmer, Harold 332a
Palmer, Helen G. 147a
Palmer, Jeremy M. 90a
Palmer, R.W. 279b
Palmstierna, Hans 159a
Palmstierna-Weiss, Gunila 155a
Pálosi, Catherine 62a
Pamm 29a
Pamplin, Brian 266b
Pan American World Airways 90a
Pan Books 226b
Panakal, Thomas 62a
Panama **109a**
Panaveli, Vargis 146a
Panayides, T. 70b
Pancholi, Manubhai 226b
Pande, Suryadeo 298a
Panichas, George A. 226b
Panikar, I.A. 266b
Pankhurst, Sylvia 266b
Pantheon Books 226b
Panvini, Rosa Bianca 104b
Paoustovski, Constantin 324b
Papademetriou, D. 124a
Papademetriou, K. 96a
Papadimitrou, Irene 124a
Papadopoulis, George 100b
Papadopoulos, Raphael 101a
Papandreou, George A. 100b, 124a
Papanek, Jan 125a
Papatheophanous, Helen 226b
Papayianis, Stefanos 124a
The Paper 139a
Pappas, Pat 228a
Pappu, V. 226b
Papworth, Andrew 13a, 131a, 164a
Papworth, John 62a, 230b
Parade 226b
Paradine, C.G. 266b
Pärakh, M.R. 297b
Parallax Publishing Co. Inc. 226b
Paramount Ltd.—Talent Associates 270b
Paranagama, D.M. 62a
Pare, Mrs. Eugene 62a
Les Parents 226b
Parent's Defense Committee for Berkeley Students 138b
Parera, Francisco Abad 62a-b
Parham, C.E.H. 277b
Paris Conference 294b
Paris Conference on Spain 113a
Parisen, Jr., Robert James 332b
Parish, David 62b
Paris-Match 97b, 226b
Parivar, Ali 62a
Park, Erich 111b
Park, Trevor 176b
Parkash, Om 266b
Parker, A.K. 201b
Parker, Andrew 332b
Parker, Dave ? 62b
Parker, Elsie 62b
Parker, Howard M. 62b
Parker, Wendy 288a
Parkhouse, R.J. 257a
Parkhurst, Eleanor 266b
Parliamentary Group for World Government 62b
Parliamentary Library, Canberra 169b
Parmar, S.S. 62b
Parmenter, Enid 62b
Parmer, Devore 62b
La Parole de Popolo 62b
Parrett, R.C. 88b
Parrish, Mrs. 237a
Parrott, W.E. 230b
Parry, Gertrude 279a
Parry, Hilda M. 57b
Parry, Thomas 90a
Tom Parry & Co. 90a
Parsons, P.J. 88a
Parti Communiste Français 112a-b
The Partisan 189b, 332b
Partisan Review 226b
Partito Communista Italiano 104b
Partito Socialista Italiano Unita Proletaria 167a
Partridge, Frances 266b
Parviz, Edelat-Manech 124b
Pasado y Presente 227a
Passalides, Jean 100b
Passport Office 309b
Passports 332b
Pasternak, Aleksander 62b

Pastukhov, Nikolai 238a
Patel, "Aesop" 332b
Patel, B.V. 62b
Paterson, E.F. 167a
Paterson, J. Craig 62b
Paterson, Toni 266b
The Paterson State College Beacon 137b
Pathak, D.N. 291a
Pathler, Frieda 353b
Patiño, Julio 127b
Patkó, Imre 222b
Patmore, R.H. 172a
Paton, Florence 115b
Paton, John 115b
Patterson, E.F. 122b
Patterson, Mrs. J.M. 298b
Patterson, Mark 62b
Patterson, Phyllis M. 222a
Pattinson, R.C. 62b
Patton, James G. 59a, 150a
Patz, Jerrold L. 231b
Paul, B. 146a
Paul, E.H. 137a
Paul, Geoffrey D. 122a
Paul, Marjorie Tyler 293a
Paul, Maurice 137a
Paul II 128a
Pauling, Ava Helen 25a, 152a
Pauling, Linus 62b, 115b, 133b, 136b, 142a, 147b, 149a, 152b, 155a, 156a, 159a, 288a, 332b, 338a, 351b
Paull, Thomas Egginton 62b
Paulos, John 266b
Pautasso 207b
Pavilion Hotel, Scarborough 90a
Pavillon, Olivier 128b
Pavlichenko, Korniev 266b
Pavlov, I.P. 266b
Pavlov, V.S. 332b
Pavlowitch, K. St. 267a
Pawlowski, Gareth L. 267a
Pawsey, John 210a
PAX 12b, 227a, 242a
Pax Forlag 227a
Payne, Harry H. 90a
Payne, P.J. 90a
Paynter, W. 62b, 128b
Pazourek, Vlad. 145b
Pe, Tin 94b
Peacanz, Lloyd Cicd 298a
Peace Action in Australia 147a
Peace and Freedom News 227a
Peace and Freedom Party of California 62b
Peace Association 63a
Peace Committee USSR 75a
Peace Council 107b
Peace Council of the German Democratic Republic 63a, 98a, 99a, 100a, 175a
Peace in Vietnam Committee (Socialist Society) 63a
The Peace Lodge of the Theosophical Society 63a
The Peace Movement in Linköping 63a
Peace Movement of South Vietnam 152b
Peace News 12a, 28a, 50b, 82b, 110b, 123b, 131a, 156a, 167a, 183a, 219a, 225b, 227a, 260a, 332b, 333b, 344b
Peace or War? 332b
Peace Pledge Union 63a
Peace, Power and Politics in Asia Conference 141b
Peace Publications Limited 63a
Peace Research Abstracts 227a
Peace Research Institute (Oslo) 63a, 208a
Peace Research Newsletter 227a
Peace Research Project 35b
Peace Seals 90a
The Peacemaker 150a
Peacemakers 131b
Peake, Lady Catherine 100b, 123a
Peano, Augusto 267a
Pearce, Edna 353b
Pearce, Dr. J.W.D. 279b
Pearce, Jon D. 146b, 147a, 298a
Pearce, Reginald 241a
Pears, David F. 227a
Pears Trophy 154b
Pearson, C.J. 63a
Pearson, Frances 63a
Pearson, Lester B. 94b, 147b, 288b
Pearson, Walter 291a
Peat, Sidney H. 63a
Pecht, J. 111a
Peck, J.H. 326a
Peckham School Magazine 227b
Pecrez ?, Laurette 227b
Pedetztun, David 332b
Peek, Katherine M. 293a
Peet, John 83a, 165b, 227b
Peetz, D.W. 298a
Pei-Yuan, Chou 351b
Penkonen, Elis 63a
Peirce, David N. 267a
Peking Review 227b
Pelazzi, Aldo 232a
Peled, Benyamin 104a, 106b, 127a
Pelegri, Antoni 63a
Pelham, Margery 288b
Pelican Books 227b
Pell, Arthur 218b
Pellegrini, Anne 63a
Pellegrini, Gesualdo 63a
Pellenin, Jean-Pierre 172b
Pellerin, Michel 172b
Pelleya, Rene 121a
Pellizzari, A.A. 48a
Pelter, Elizabeth 298a
Pelter, Maurice A. 298a
Peltu, Malcolm 234b
Peltz, Frances 112a
Penberthy, Tom 63a, 172a
Pence, Joseph A. 63a
Pendas, Francisco 227b
"Pendennis" 81a
Pendzey, Luba 117a
Pene, Walter 63a
Penetz, Martin 157a
Penguin Books Ltd. 227b, 351a
Peniche Fortress 128a
The Peninsula Committee for the Abolition of Nuclear Tests 156b
Penkaitis, Anton 134b
Penn, L. 231a
Pennington's Auctioneers and Estate Agents 314a
The Pennsylvania Literary Review 227b
Penrhyndeudraeth 152b
Penthouse 314a
Pentreath, M. 98b
Peonides, P. 96a
The People 227b
People's Co-operative Bookstore Association 63a, 90a
People's Daily, Peking 95a
The People's Korea 67b, 104b, 127a, 227b
Percikow, Henri 63b
Pereira, Norman G.O. 297b
Perelmutter, Fania 111a
Perera, N.M. 148b
Peretz, Martin 12b, 14b, 167a, 267a
Perez, Faustina 159a
Peréz, José 78a, 130b
Perez Diaz, J.A. 295b
Pérez y Pérez, D. 240a, 267a
Pergamon Press Ltd. 227b
Periodico Revolucion 227b
Peristerakis, Michael 42b, 100b, 122b, 123a-b, 298a
Perkins, Beatrice 298a
Perlman, Nathan D. 63b
Perlongo, Robert 63b
Perman, George 267a
Permanent Representative of the Czechoslovak Socialist Republic to the United Nations 96b
"The Perplexities of John Forstice" 7a, 201b
Perren, John C. 332b
Perroux, François 230b
Perry, Catherine 212b, 213a
Perry, J.H. 298a
Perry, Roger 212a
Perseus 227b, 332b
Persson, Yngve 113a, 157b
Peru **109a, 128a**
Peruvian Committee for Human Rights, Havana 128a
"Pervert", Ronald L. 123a
Pesa, Lazar 110a
Pesić, Dusan 228a
Pessagno, George 267a
Pestana, Frank 188a
Peter, Erich M. 298b
Peters, Charles R. 63b
Peters, Wilhelm 80a
Petersen, Lyman L. 90a
Peterson, Mrs. John N. 298a
Peterson, Wilfred A. 42a
Peterson Engineering Co., Inc. 227b-228a

Petrakis, Emmanuel 40b, 131b
Petran, Tabitha 103b
Petrick, Howard 139b
Petrović, Gajo 228a-b
Petruzzellis, Joseph 63b
Pettyjohn, Bob 63b
Peven, Kari 291a
Pevsner, Dieter 227b, 351a
Peyrefitte, Roger 288b
Pezzagno, Bramante 63b
Pfeiffer, E.B. 167b
Pflug, Raymond J. 63b
Phaidon Press Ltd. 228a
Pharis, Katharine C. 267a
Phat, Huynh Tan 299a
Phelps, Daphne 293a
Phelps, Jon 63b
Philadelphia Daily News 118a
Philadelphia Evening Bulletin 118a
Philadelphia Inquirer 137b, 228a
Philadelphia Resistance 167a
Philadelphia University Committee to End the War in Vietnam 167a
Philipovich, William 63a
Philipp, June 267a
Philipp, R. 175b
Philippine Committee for Freedom in South Vietnam 148a
Philippines **109a, 128a, 147b**
Philippines Free Press 109b, 113a
Philips-Price, M. 267a
Philipson, Morris 239a
Phillips, A.P. 210b
Phillips, Eric 353b
Phillips, Glenys 223a
Phillips, Glyn O. 63b, 142b, 155b
Phillips, Ludwig 332b
Phillips, Marion 247a
Phillips, Michael 230a
Phillips, Pauline 84a
Phillips, Rex 149a, 167a
Bernard Phillips & Co. 90a
Philo 228a
Philosopher of the Century 278b
Philosophia Naturalis 329a
Philosophical Essays 196b
Philosophical Society: Journal 228a
Philosophical Society of Edinburgh 298a
Philosophy 228a, 332a, 338b
Philosophy and Phenomenological Research 338a
Philosophy and Science 329a
Philosophy Society, Reading University 298a
Philpot, Terry G. 267a, 301b
Phinney, W.P. 63b
Phizo, A.Z. 102a
The Photo Centre 178b
Phu, Nguyen 167a
Phukan, Punya Dar Chetia 228a
Phuong, Nguyen Hong 188a-b
Phurissard, Norodom 94b
Physics in Medicine and Biology 228a
Piancastelli, Corrado 289a
Piatkiewicz, Wladyslaw 267a
Pic, Roger 63b, 160b, 178b, 186a-b, 187a
Picasso, Pablo Ruiz 159a, 288b
Pickett, Michael 31a
Picot, Suzanne 90a
Piel, Gerard 90a, 142a, 332b
Pierce, C.S. 63b
Pierce, David 63b
Pierce, S.H. 63b
Piggott, Reginald 167a
Pignero, Jean 26a, 205b
Pilau, Liton Lanes 171a
Pilegaard, Asger 173a
Pilesjö, Gunnar 195a
Pilichowski, Czeslow 98a
Pilkington, G. 278a
Pillai, K. Govinda 175b
Pillai, Santosh Kumar 153b
Piller, Mina 134b
Pillokat, A. 135a
Pillow, Woll 63b
Pincus, Harry 79a, 140a
Ping, Shen 95a
Ping-po 95a
Pinkerton, William M. 157a
Pinter, Harold 232a
Pipenelis, Papayotis 100b, 123b
Pipes, Richard E. 352b
Pipon, Captain H.C.P. 63b
Pirani, Felix 241b
Pire, R.P. Dominique 288b
Pirelli, Leopoldo 90a
Pirinsky, George 171b
Pirnia, Hossein 228a
Pissanos, Anthony 258b
Sir Isaac Pitman and Sons Limited 228a
Pitmans College 143b
Pitout, Trevor Rex 267a
Pitt, John Gare 145b
Pitts, Mr. 280b
Pixner, Vivien 152b
Plá, Manuel 63b
Plant, E.N. 63b
Plate, Annaluise 175a
Platts-Mills, John 126a, 154a
Playboy 13a, 18b, 137b, 156b, 227b-228a
Playford, John 63b
Playhill?, Joe 142a
Playter, Phyllis 257a
Pleas, David R. 63b
Plenty & Sons Ltd. 309b, 314a
Pliskina, E.T. 63b
Plochmann, Carolyn G. 63b
Plogstedt, Sibylle 64a
Plomer, William 177a, 288b
Ploog, Jürgen 64a
Plotinus 350a
Plum, Niels Munk 64a, 141b
Plummer, ? 267a
Plummer, F. 228a
Plummer, Howard 64a
Plumstead, Harold 298a
Plunket, Milde 279a
Pockwell, Leslie M. 198b
Podden, Dennis 291a
Poeschel, Renate 144a
Poesia Toda 332b
Pogacnik, Bogdan 183a
Poger, Ruth 64a
Poggioli, Yves 64a
Pointer 107a, 149a, 228a
Pojani, Petraq 93a
Poland **109b, 156a**
Polanyi, Michael 130b, 288b
Poldy, Franzi 64a
Pole, Lieutenant 280b
Pole, Phoebe 165b
Polevoi, Boris 117b
Poli, P. 97b
Polish Cultural Fund 64a
Polish Peace Committee 109b, 156b, 298a
Polish Radio and Television 228a
Polish Review 333a
Polish Western Press Agency 109b
Polish Weekly 332b
Political Detainees of Chalkida Prison 123a
Political Ideals 13a
Political Prisoners' and Exiles' Families' Association 123a
Political Prisoners in the Aegina Prison 123a, 124a
Political Prisoners of AMFISSA 123b
Political Prisoners of Trikala Prisons 124a
Political Science Quarterly 329b
Political Union Board of Stanford University 15a
Politika 228a
Politiken 351a
Politisk Revy 173b
Polk, David C. 64a
Pollack, Jack Harrison 226b
Pollard, Gordon R. 94b, 172a, 228a
Pollio, Armando 64a
Pollitt, B.H. 257b
Polonkey, C. James 64a
Polvani, G. 228b
Pomeroy, Celia 64a
Pomeroy, William J. 64a, 128a, 148a
Pompidou, Georges 97b
Ponsonby, Arthur 79a, 278a
Il Ponte 104b
Ponte, Lowell 64a
Pool, Joe 139a
Poole, H.W. 332b
Poole, Susan 117a
Poona Herald 228b, 291a
Poorman, Roy T. 64a
Poorvi Times 228b
Pope, Jr., John A. 209b
Pope Paul II 128a
Popenuck, Karen 198a
Popkin, Percy A. & Co. 308a, 309b, 310b
Popp, F.C. 64a
Popper, Karl R. 267a, 332a

Popular Union of the Cameroons 120b
Population 333a
Population Review 228b
Poremsky, V. 64a
Portantiero, Carlos 141a
Portele, Gerhard 64a
Porter, Charles O. 156b
Porter, Richard 32a
Porter, Roy E. 233b
Porter-Bryant, Seymour 298a
The Portland Finance Company 90a
Portland Symphony Society 228b
Portmadoc Urban and District Guide 228b
Portmadoc Waterworks Co. 90a
"Portmeirion Gazette & Deudraeth News" 282b
Portmeirion Hotel 262a, 279b
Portnow, Julius 267a
Portnoy, Dina 167a
Portugal **109b-110a, 128a**
Portuguese Amnesty Conference 128b
Portuguese and Colonial Bulletin 109b, 128b
Portuguese Canadian Democratic Association 128b
Portuguese Democrat Movement 298a
Portuguese Students Association Committee in Great Britain 64a, 128b
Portugese Students Committee 298a
Postgirokentoret 228b
The Postmaster General 116b
Postnikoff, John N. 37a
Post Office Corporation 115a
Potiris, Giannis 123b, 124a
Potter, D.F. 64a
Pottle, Pat 36b, 64b, 86a, 100b, 131a, 211a, 239b, 251a, 297a
Potts, A. 122b
Poulsen, Hans Hansted 173a
Poulton, Gaye 198b, 228b
Pour les Indépendants Républicains Yéménites 131a
Powell, C.F. 64b, 91a, 142a, 167b, 168b, 351a
Powell, David 237b, 251a
Powell, Joan 64b
Powell-Evans, John 64b
Power, Eileen 353b
Powers, C.A. 64a
Powers, F. 64b
Powles, John 90a, 170a
Pownall, A. 64b
Poznansky, J.B. 314a
Pozniak, Richard A. 64b
Pozo, Agapito 127a
Pozo, Juan Luis 167a
Pozzo, Mario Del 267a
Prabhu, S.S. 333a
The Practice and Theory of Bolshevism 7a, 349a
Prado, C.G. 228b
Prafulla Press 228b
Pragnell, Mrs. 277a
Prain, Ronald L. 64b
Prakash, Marcia 64b
Prakash, Om 171b
Prakobsantisukh, Biravan 228b
Prasad, C.S. 64b
Prasad, Devi 81a, 102b, 132a, 150a, 168a, 299a
Prasad, Jagdish 298a
Prasad, P.A. Soorya 267a, 291a, 298a
Prasad, Rajendra 288b
Prasad, Rajeshwar 102a
Prasad, V.V. 64b, 267a
Der Präsident des Schleswig-Holsteinischen Landtages 99b
Prassah, David 48b
Pratap, Raja Mahendra 64b
Pratibha 228b
Pratt, Enrico 28a
Pratt, R.S. 352b
Pravda 74b, 76b, 152b, 228b, 333a
Praxis 228b
Premananda, M. 64b
"Premio Mantegna" 267a
Prendergast, Dennis S.W. 172a
Prensa Latina 228b
Prentice-Hall, Inc. 228b
Prenzo, Mariotti 298a
Preparatory Committee for Khartoum Conference on Southern Africa 111a
Prescott, Cornelia 64b
Presidencia de la Republica, México, el Secretario Privado 64b
M. le Président de la Cour d'Appel Spéciale 124b
President of India 50b
Presmont, John 64b
The Press 147a
Press Council 178a, 228b
Press Council of India, Union Finance Minister, New Delhi 67a
La Presse 228b
Pressman, Gillian 64b
P.W. Pressprich & Co. 308b
Prest, J.M. 229a
Preston, B.P.H. 308a
Preston, Stephen 172a
Barker Preston & Co. 308a
Prewett, J. Neill 64b
Prica, Srdja 119a, 132a
Price, Anthony 64b
Price, J.H. 203a
Price, M. 267a
Price, Mrs. Sheldon 308b
Price, T.C. 146a
Price, Waterhouse & Co. 314a
Prichard, Dr. O.M. Tristan 267a
Priem, Michel 298a
Priemer, Rolf J. 174b
Priestley, Jaquetta 65a
Priestley, M.P. 208a
Prime Minister of Greece 96a
Prime Minister of Malaysia-Indonesia 84b
Prime Minister of Singapore 84b
Prime Minister's Office, Athens, Greece 124a
Primeklles, Leon 65a
Prince, Renate 30a
The Prince of Monaco 107b
Principal Probate Registry 267a
Principia Mathematica 7b, 256b, 257a, 262b, 264a, 267b, 268a, 322a, 331b, 334a, 335b-336a
Pringle, Frank E. 65a
Printing and the Mind of Man 267a
Prior-Palmer, Diane M. 69b
Prismon, Donald 65a
Prison Reform Council 65a, 131b
Prisoner of Conscience Library 65a
Prisoners in the Hilla Prison 121a
Pritchard, Gwyn Charles 221a
Pritchard?, Jack 281a
Pritchard, John Craven 312a
Pritchard, W.D.N. 65a
Pritchard Jones, Hugh 65a
Pritt, D.N. 333a
Private Eye 229a
Private Secretary to the Hungarian Embassy 102a
Private Secretary to the Postmaster General 114a
The Private Secretary to the Prime Minister (Greece) 123a
Private Secretary to the Prime Minister of Hungary 101b
Private Secretary to Queen Elizabeth II 123b
Prividera, Hector 167b
Privitera, John 298a
Priyambada, Sujata 229a
Probe 196b, 229a
The Problem of China 260b
Probyn, Brian 65a
Proceedings of the Cambridge Philosophical Society 331b
Proceedings of the Royal Society 328b
Procházka, Lubomír 205a
Pro-Contra 174a
M. le Procureur Général 124b
Productivity 330a
The Progressive 64a, 149b
Progressive Labor Party 138b
Progressive World 28a
Project Unilat 65a
Pronina, N.I. 65a
Propaganda 290b
Propaganda Voor Federale Wereldregering 65a
"Protest and Proposition for 1970" 35b
Protest Movement Against the Plan for Nuclear Missile Sites in South Eastern France 65a

Proudall, Peter 309b
The Province 334b
Provinzano, Annette 135b
Provisional Committee of the Association of Released Political Prisoners 124a
Provo, Lea 90a
Prunair, Jacques 65a
Prust, A. J. (Jean) 90a, 147a
Psyche 229a
Psychical Research Foundation, Inc. 229a
Psychological Library Publishers 229a
Ptacek, Paul 65a, 98b
Public Meetings 156a
The Public School Leaver 229a
Publishers Association 229a
Puggy & Hamish 292a
Pugh, John 218b
Pugh, R.A. 205a
Pugwash Coswa Continuing Committee 352a
Pugwash Committee of the American Academy of Arts and Sciences [and?] the U.S. Pugwash Group 298a
Pugwash Conference 11b, 35b, 336a, 350b
Pugwash Continuing Committee 65a, 351b
Puig, André 157a
Pule, David 281b
Puller, Ernest 310a
Pullium, Jr., Ray 65b
Pullrick, G.F. 65b
Pulse 229a
Punch 177a
Pundyu, K.D. 211b
Pungan, Vasile 110a, 129a, 298b
Purabi 229a
Purcell, H.D. 267b
Purcell, Victor 27a, 142a, 185a, 267b, 288b
Purdue & Greenhill 90a
Purdy, Bryn 229a
Purice, Uta 110a
Putnam and Co. 334a
Putney High School 279b
Putterill, Jack 177a
Puxon, Grattan 88b, 126b, 131b
Pylyshyn, Zenon W. 229a
Pym, Christopher 267b
Pym, Diana 52b, 100b, 101a, 123a-b
Pyromaglou, K. 100b
Pytoravuth, Nguon 94b

Q

Q 229a
Quadir, Qazi Abdul 62a
Quail, Bernard 65a
Quaker Action Group 65b, 167a
Quaker Group, Wellingborough 65b
Quan, Stanislaus 333a
Quaranta, Mario 267b
Quasimodo, Salvatore 90a, 288b
Quat, Trantrong 162a
Quatrième Internationale 298a
Quebec-Washington-Guantamo Walk for Peace 65b
Queen 229a
The Queen 279a
The Queen of Sheba's Nightmare 349a
Queensland Peace Committee for International Co-operation and Disarmament 65b
The Quest Eternal 334b
Qui, Nguyen Linh 35a
Quick, Patricia 196a
Quigly, E.P. 124b
Quilter, Eileen 156a
Quine, W.V.O. 267b, 288b
Quintanilla, Luis 65b, 159a
Quintero, A. 121a, 132a
La Quinzaine Littéraire 229a
Quirk, William E. 267b
Qureshee, A.H. 79b
Qureshee, Altaf Hasan 239a
Qureshi, Altaf Ahmad 205a
Qureshi, Muhammad Siddique 65b
Qureshi, Tufail A. 241b

R

R., Katy 178a
Raab, Enrique 90a, 229a
Raaflaub, David H. 267b
Rabbidge, Philip 298a
Rabelo, Genival 65b
Rabindra Prasanya 229a
Rabinovitz, Jacob 104a
Rabinowitz, Eugene 201a, 298a
Rabinowitz, Victor 90a, 135b, 149b, 161a
Rabinowitz & Boudin 133a, 136a, 138b, 142b, 314a
Louis M. Rabinowitz Foundation Inc. 90a, 149b, 269a
Rabon, F.D. 196b
Rabson, F.D. 229a
Racherbäumer, Jürgen H. 65b
The Racquette 229b
Racy, R.F. 65b
Rada, Jiri 65b
Radcliffe, J.M. 65b
Radford, Jim 65b, 131b, 167a
Radhakrisha 70a
Radhakrishna, Mr. 267b
Radhakrishnan, Sarvepalli 67a, 102a, 149a, 267b, 275a
The Radhakrishnan Number 229b
Radical Alliance 65b
Radical Education Project 66a, 167a
The Radical Humanist 229b
Radice, Francis W. 66a
Radio Ariel 229b
Radio Cologne, Germany 130b
Radio Frankfurt 41b
Radio Free Europe 111b, 229b
Radio Free Zimbabwe Committee 66a
Radio Hanoi 190b
Radio WMCA Editorial 152b
Radiodiffusion Télévision Belge 229b
Radiodiffusion-Télévision Française 229b
Radley, William Stuart 291
Rae, C.R.A. 326a
Rae, John 267b
Raeburn, Ben 213a
Raess, Mr. 102a
Raf, S. Nathaniel 267b
Raffles, G. 66a
Rafols, J. Serra 203a
Raghunandan, Dr. 298b
Rahim, J.A. 108b
Rahman, A.K.M. Siddiqur 229b
Rahman, Tunku Abdul 106a, 127a
Rai, Rameshwar Nath 153b, 229b
RAI-Radiotelevisione Italiana 229b
Raines, Halsey 229b
La Raison 229b
Raj, D.F. Sundra 106a
Raj, V.S. Durai 66a
Raja, S. 66a
Rajagopal, A. 66a
Rajagopalachari, C. 66a, 335b
Rajan?, Harma 153b
Rajaraman, S. 229b
Rajput, Mohan Lal 291a
Ram, M. Jaya 172b
Ram, Suresh 85a, 102b
Rama, Carlos M. 233b-234a
Rama, K.S. 229b
Ramabhyani, R.K. 288b
Ramadan, H. 126a
Ramakrishniah, Sri Samson 225a
Raman, A.S. 213b
Raman, K.V. 333a
Ramaswamy, K. 66a
Ramat Gan Students Council 66a
Ramchander, I. 195a
Ramello, Catone 66a
Ramírez, Jorge A. 66a
Rammgal, Yanetz 267b
Rampla, Mr. 66a
Ramparts 115a, 136a, 183b, 185b, 229b
Ramsey, Frank P. 267b
Ramsey, Ronald B. 15b, 66a, 167a, 173b
Ramussen, Lauritz 291a
Rana, Kiranjit Singh 350b
Rand, Rose 333a
Rand Corporation 66a
Randall, Edward 90b
Randall, Inez 298b
Randall, J. 66a
Randall, Jr., J.H. 267b
Randall, Roy 353b
Randell, Dr. John B. 279b
Randle, Michael 44a, 50a, 66a,

110b, 227a, 280a
Randolf, Gertrude 267b
Random House, Inc. 230a
Rangappa, K.S. 102b, 230a, 333a
Ranjana Printers 230a
Rankin, John 176b
Rann of Kutch 109a
L. & K. Ransom 354a
Rao, D. Kishan 153b
Rao, K. Venkata 66a
Rao, Nageswara 66a
Rao, K. Srihari 66a, 225a
Rao, Suresh 66b
Raouf, Kamal 196a
Rapacki Campaign 155a
Rapi, Eugene S. 66b, 150a
Rapoport, Anatol 159a, 212a
Rapp, Marilyn 204b
Rappaport, C.D. 111b
Raquiza, Llacar & Associates 148a
Rasker, Albert J. 66b
Rasmussen, Hans Kaalund 66b
Rasmussen, Lauritz H. 66b
Rasmussen, Viggo J. 91b
Rassedin, G. 235a
Rassekh, M. 103a
Rastogi, A.K. 66b
Rastrong, Hans Petter 66b
Ratcliff, A.R.N. 66b
Rath, Aswini Kumar 298b
Rathbone Books Ltd. 195b
Rathgeber, Walter 174a
Rathore, David 291a
Rathore, K.P.D. 66b, 228b
Rational Review 230a
The Rationalist Association of N.S.W. 170a
Rationalist Federation Australasia Pacific Countries 298b
Rationalist Press Association Limited 230a, 298b
Ratknic, Savo 236b
Ratliff, William F. 267b
Rattansey, Salima 66b
Rattansi, Aziz 178a
Rattenbury, Simonette 279b
Rauchwerger-Wechselblatt, Anna 133a
Rausse, Dr. 175a
Rautenstrauch, Mrs. Walter 66b
Raveh, Yitzhak 159a
Raven, Mr. 66b
Raven, Mrs. C.E. 171a
Ravji, Valji 230a
Rawlings, Roberta Tyson 240a
Rawlins, David B. 66b
Ray, B.E. 198b
Ray, Cyril 203b
Raymaekers, L. 94a
Rea, F.R. 202b
Read, Bert 66b
Read, Charles 267b
Read, Herbert 95b, 110b, 142b, 152a, 267b, 280a
Read, R.M. 66b
The Reader's Digest 53a, 218a, 230a
Readhead, Diana 298b
Reading and District Co-ordinating Committee for Disarmament 66b
Reading Co-ordinating Committee for International Understanding 298b
Ready, William 294b, 298b
Real, Jere 230b
Realidade 230a
The Realist 329a
Réalités 230a
Rebelo, Jorge 109b
Receiver of the Metropolitan Police 38b
Recht, J. 97b
Rector, John 291a
Red Flag 127b, 230a
Redazione 230a
Redbook Magazine 230a
Reddaway, G.F.N. 333a
Redeker, J.A. 196a
Redfern, H. 63a
Redgrave, Michael 177a, 288b
Redgrave, Vanessa 13b, 149a, 267b
Redman, Jean 90b
Redman, L. 66b
Redmer, Bessie C. 230a
Redston, F.S. 66b
Reed, Mr. 277b
Reed, Adolph L. 66b
Reed, Gordon 66b
Reed, Jr., Mrs. Henry Hope 67a
Reed, Kelly Scott 298b
Reed, Muriel 230a
Reed, Norah 279a
Reed, Richard L. 67a
Reed, Rufus H. 90b
Reed, Sonia 279b
Reed, Stewart 295a
Reedy, Thomas A. 230a
Rees, Mrs. Carol 269a
Rees, D. Ben 221a
Rees, Joan 268a
Rees, Tom 67a
Rees-Wright, W. 242a
Reflex 170a, 230a
Regás, Rosa 207b
Regelson, Leon 67a
Regener, Leo 175b
Regents Park Nursing Homes & Co-operation Ltd. 279b
Registani, B.P.N. 67a
Registre International des Citoyens du Monde 67a
Regmarad 167a
Rehder, R.M. 149a, 196b, 237a
Reich, Ebbe 173a, 268a
Reichbach, Juliusz 298b, 333a
Reichenbach, Hans 10a, 268a, 333a
Reichenbach, Maria 268a, 291a, 293a
Reicher-Sgradi, R. 230a
Reichl, Miriam 268a
Reid, Alex 281b
Reid, John V. 67a, 171b
Reid, Joseph 67a
Reid, Josephine 287b
Reid, L. 26b
Reid, Ralph 67a
Reid, Richard 114a, 210b
Reid, Tony 223b
Reid, W.M. 90a
Reid, W.R. Rodger 90b
Alex Reid & Lefevre Ltd. 281b
Reif, Arnold E. 90b
Reik, Miriam 34a
Reilly, Beatrice 90b, 172a
Reimann, Max 67a, 99a
Reimbold, William 90b
Reinecke, Aiko 97a
Reinecke, John 97a
Reinfarth, Heinz 98a
Reinke, W. 221b
Reiss, A. 134a
Reitman, Mr. 135a
Reitzel, C.A. 335a
Reizin, S. 90b
Rejman, A. 230a
Relecom, Xavier 170b
Religion and Science 18b, 202b
Religious Society of Friends 298b
Relvani, K.N. 67a, 153b
Remez, Aharon 104a
Renard, Marcel 90b
Renardo?, W. 298b
Rendell, Kenneth W. 268a
Rendi, Aloisio 230b
Rennhack, Horst 189b
Rennie, J.O. 326a
Renoir, E.P.A. 230b
Renow, Lilly 67a
Rentsch, Gail 226b
Renwick, M. 67a
Renzo, Mariotti 298b
Report 143b
Report of the Commission on Itinerancy 126b
Reportér 230b
The Reporter 230b
Reporter Magazine 183a
Représentation Commerciale de la République Démocratique du Viêt-Nam en France 162b
Réprésentation du Front National de Liberation du Sud Vietnam en Tchécoslovaquie 132a
Republic of the Philippines, Department of Justice, Board of Pardons and Parole 109a-b
Republic of the Philippines Senate 109b
Republika 230b
Rerabek, Jaroslav 67a, 121a
Rescher, Nicholas 197a
Reserve Bank of India 90b
Reserve Bank of New Zealand 90b
Resist 351a
Resistance 67a
Reston, Jr., James 67a
Resurgence 230b
Retig, Habiba 113a

Reto, Roberto 67a
Rety, John 67a
Reuters 18a, 139b, 230b
Reveal 230b
Review of International Affairs 230b
Review of Metaphysics 333a, 336b
Review of Politics 326a
Revista Ercilla 230b
Revista Latinamericana de Psicologia 230b
Revista Methodos 338b
Revista Universitaria 230b
Revolución 11b, 152b
Revolution Africaine 230b
The Revolution of Iraki Kurdistan 126b
Revolutionary Socialist Students Federation 230b
Revolutionary Workers' Party (Trotskyist) 67a, 127b, 130b, 132a
Revue "Contemporanul" 230b
Le Revue de Paris 322a
Revue Tiers-Monde 230b
Reyman, Vernon 298b
Reynolds, Barbara 67a, 144b, 145a
Reynolds, David 209b
Reynolds, Sydney 236a
Reynolds, William 242b
Reynolds News 114a
Reznik-Fishman, Esther 113a
Rhee, Syngman 52b
Rhees, R. 230b
Rhine, Keith Milton 230b
Rhodesia **110a**
Riadh, Hussain 159a
Riazuddin, Akhtar 67a
Ribaldi, Giorgio 203b
Ricci, Cesare 67a
Rice, C. Edward 67b
Rice, Charles E. 67b
Rice, Donald 67b
Rice, Mervyn 117b, 168b
Richards, C. 333b
Richards, Colin 67b
Richards, D.H. 67b, 293a
Richards, Gordon 67b
Richards, Griff 241a
Richardson, Alan 236a
Richardson, Boyce 33a, 221b
Richardson, E.H. 147a
Richardson, Godfrey 298b
Richardson, Heather E. 268a
Richardson, I.J. 202b
Richardson, John 227a
Richardson?, Keith 269a
Richardson, Lewis F. 268a
Richardson, M. 67b
Richardson, Marcus W. 288b
Richardson, P.B. 122b
Richardson, Tony 94a
Richardson, W.N.B. 298b
Richardson, W.R. 236a
Richardson Institute News 155a
Richmond Council for Peace Education 67b
The Richmond News Leader 230b
Richter, Sviatoslav 67b
Rickards, ? 67b
Rickards, Barbara 291a
Rickards, David A. 67b
G. Ricordi & C. 231a
Riddell, D.S. 41b, 179a
Riddell, John 172a
Ridder, Helmut 100a, 116a
Ridgeway, James 223a
Ridley, Walter 67b
Rieber, Gretel 113a, 130b
Riecken, Meryl 228b
Riedel, Alfred 144a
Riegler, Jeannette 293a
Riemeck, Renate 155a
Riepe, Dale 231a
Ries, A.F. 172a
Riesel, Victor 134a
Riexinger, Theodor 174b
Rifa, Zaid 105a
Rifaat, Kamal 106b, 107b, 111a, 114a, 149b, 156b
Riffaud, Madeleine 187b, 188b
Rigg, John 333b
Riggs, William 312a
Right & Wrong 329a
Rights 333b
Riglar, Tom 298b
Rijni, Hasan 47b
Riley, A. 67b
Riley, Nathan 149a
Ring, Priscilla 73b, 109a, 128a
Ringer, Gerald J. 67b, 333b
Rink, K. 146a
Riochet, Margaret 67b
Ríos, José 67b
Rios?, W. 109b
Riposanu, Pamfil 67b, 121a
Risch, ? 67b
Rischia, Moses 231a
Risholm, Olle 67b
Ritey, Hector J. 34b
Ritsumeikan University Caravan Club 144a
Rix, Leo 67b
Rixwani, Shakir 67b
Ro, Jai Ho 67b
Roa, A. 130b
The Road to Peace? 79b
Roanne, Henri 229b
Roback, A.A. 67b, 111b, 134a
Robbins, George 172b
Robbins, Jhan 230a
Robbins, Lord 115a
Robbins, Ruth 268a
Robert, Geneviève 174a
Robert, Gustave 268a
Roberts, Adam 202a, 227a, 251a, 331b, 333b
Roberts, Archbishop 176a
Roberts, B.D. 298b
Roberts, B.R. 126b, 236a
Roberts, Carol 67b
Roberts, Emrys P. 74b
Roberts, Ernie A. 182a, 238b
Roberts, F.W. 231a
Roberts, G.R. 68a
Roberts, Glyn 68a
Roberts, John 27a
Roberts, John C.H. 68a
Roberts, K.M. 89a
Robertshaw, P.? 126b
Robertson, David P.M. 235b
Robertson, Donald 352b
Robertson, Grady F. 68a, 167a
Robertson, Margaret 68a
Robertson-Justice, James 146b
Robin, D. 143b
Robinson, Aiken 68a
Robinson, Desmond A. 131b
Robinson, David J. 40a, 90b, 114b, 178a, 268a
Robinson, Dorothy 129a
Robinson, F. 90b
Robinson, Jack 209b
Robinson, Joan 148a, 159a
Robinson, Mallie 257b
Robinson, T.M. 268a
Robison, Professor 231a
Robson, John M. 220b
Rocca file **156a**
Rocca, Sr., Bernard T. 68a, 156a
Roche, Stephen R. 68a
Rocheta, Manuel Ferrajota 128b
Rocke, Hermine 271b
Rockefeller, David 90b
The Rockefeller Foundation 90b
Rode, Margarethe 68a
Rodenberg, Ludwig 68a
Röder, Rosemarie 90b
Rodger, R. 68a
Rodgers, (Mrs.) Gordon 268a
Rodinov, I.M. 133a
Rodinov, Jona 112b
Rodinson, Maxime 106b, 107a
Rodker, E. 90b
Rodker, Joan 231a
Rodney Youth Centre, Liverpool 90b
Rodrigues, Alberto Antonio de Noronha 128b
Rodriguez, Armando 235b
Rodriguez, Daniel 68a
Rodriguez, Eddie 68a
Rodriguez, Enrique I. 68a
Rodriguez, F.J. 62a
Rodríguez, Hernán 68a, 214a
Rodriguez, José 159a
Roe, Anne 327b
Roe, J.S. 198b
Roger, Deborah 231b
Roger, Hedebouw 68a
Rogers, Mr. 310b
Rogers, Donald Clyde 333b
Rogers, Douglas G. 195a-b
Rogers, James C. 67b, 73b
Rogers, Norma 136a
Rogers, R.S. 143b
Rogosin, Lionel 68a, 231a
Rogow, Arnold A. 149a
Rohloff, Dr. 99b
Rohrman, Shirley 227b-228a

Rojas, Marta 17b, 187a, 188b
Rojo, Ricardo 141a
Rolandi, Giampiero 210b, 231a
Roldan, Maria Josefa López 298b
Rolfs, William C. 68a
Rolin, Henri 159a
Roll, Klara 111a
Roll, W.G. 229a
Rolland, Marie Romain 258a
Rollitts, Sarah 223b, 232b, 242a
Rolls Prestcold Appliances Ltd. 90b
Roman, Carol 233a
Rome Conference on Soviet Jews 12b, 134a
Rome Daily American 68b
Romulo, Carlos P. 148a
Ronald, Christopher 298b
Ronald, Frances 291a
The Ronald Press Co. 230a
Roome, K.H. 131b
Rooney, Alan I. 167b, 291b
Rooney, Vicky 167b
Roosevelt, Eleanor 288b
Rooum, Donald 68a
Roper, John 146b
Roper, Raymond H. 68a
Rorty, Amelie 231a
Rose, Hilary 298b
Rose, J. 231a
Rose, John 146a
Rose, Klaus 122a
Rose, Steven 167b
Rose, Sue 84a
Rosen, Dennis 90b
Rosen, Martin 90b
Rosenbaum, S.P. 268a
Rosenberg, Ethel 10b
Rosenberg, Julius 10b
Rosenberg, Marc 227b
Rosenberg, Mordechai 116a
Rosenberg, Naomi 68b
Rosenberg, Wolfgang 147b
Rosenbloom, Leon 301b
Rosenfeld, Herbert T. 68b, 142a, 147b, 167b
Rosenfield, S. 219a
Rosenthal, Marilyn 213b
Rosenthal, Stanley 68b
Rosenwald, Peter J. 68b, 142b
Rosenwald, Ruth F. 68b, 122a
Rosenwein, Mr. 188a
Rosenzweig, Mania 111a
Rosenzweig, Saul 268a
Rosewall, Peter 149a
Roshchin, S. 134b
Roshwald, Mordecai 268a
Rosner, Seth 298b
Ross, Alan 149a
Ross, Betty 278a
Ross, Emory 149a
Ross, Jerry 68b
Ross, John A. 68b
Ross, Lawrence F.J. 68b, 141a, 146b, 333b
Ross, Meredith 221a
Ross, Michael 189b
Ross, Robert H. 298b
Rosset, Barney 211
Rossi, Mario 12a, 231a, 333b
Rossi, Roberto 68b
Rossi-Landi, Ferruccio 94a
Rosten, Leo 218b
Roston, Michael 68b, 150b
Roszack, Theodore 167a, 183a, 227a, 333b
Rotblat, Joseph 27a, 31b, 65a, 68b, 81b, 142b, 155b, 199b, 201a, 205a, 292b, 351b, 352a
Roth, Edith P. 68b
Roth, S.J. 109b
Roth, Saul 90b
Rothbarth, Otto 352b
Rothenstein, John 288b
Rothman, Jerry 53a
Rothrock, Addison M. 268a
Rothschild, Lord 268a, 288b
Rothstein, Andrew 90b
Roth-Warren Pharmacists 90b
Rouleau, Eric 107a, 183a
Roussopoulos, Dimitrios 225b
Routledge & Kegan Paul Ltd. 231a
Rovensky, D. 204b
Rowe & Maw 309a, 312a, 353b
Rowen Onllwyn Ltd. 90b
Rowlson, Tom 68b
Rowohlt Verlag GMBH 231a
Rowse, A.L. 353b
Roy, Asok Kumar 153b
Roy, Claude 174a
Roy, Dilip Kumar 231a, 268a, 282a
Roy, Jitendra Kumar 153b
Roy, Manojit 68b
Roy, Sukhen 68b
Royal Albert Hall 141b
Royal Federation of Malaya Police 106a
Royal Festival Hall 288b
Royal Greek Embassy 231a
The Royal Institute of International Affairs 95a
Royal Institute of Philosophy 354a
Royal Moroccan Embassy 122b
Royal National Institute for the Deaf 90b
Royal Naval Association 90b
Royal Netherlands Embassy 149a
The Royal Society 142b
The Royal Society of Literature 298b
Royal Sportsman Hotel 90b
Royall, Mrs. J. 33a
Roy-Chaudhuri, P. 231a
Royon, Betty 37b, 115b, 142b, 351b
Roza, O. 110b
Rozen, Ana 111a
Rozsypal, Hanu 68b
Rozsypal, Ing Joseph 68b
Ruark, Robert 68b
Rubbra, Edmund 288b
Rubbra, F. 68b
Rubenstein, Charles 68b
Rubenstein, Christopher 68b
Rubenstein, David 231a, 298b
Rubenstein, Simon 134b
Rubin, Jerry 168a
Rubin, Leonard 218b
Rubinstein, Hilary 210b
Ruda, Harris 69a
Rudenko, ? 159a
Rudge, Alzira 120b
Rudiak, M. 333b
Ruempel, Werner 175a, 296a
Ruf, Hannes 69a
Ruffulo, Virginia 39b
Rugiles ?, O.R. 69a
Ruglio, Elena 95b
Ruhman, Walter 231a
Ruiz, Marino 69a
Ruiz, Vincenzo Arangio 134a
Ruja, Harry 107a, 268a
Rulf, Werner 122b
Rumania **110a-b**
Rumania—Civil Liberties (Jews) **110b**
Rumanian Ambassador 298b
Rumanian Delegation 151b
Rumanian Jews **128b-129b**
Rumanian People's Republic Legation 128b
Rumashevskaia, Mrs. 134a, 268b
The Rupam Group of Newspapers 231a
Rupoz, J. 167b
Rush, C. 90a
Rush, Catherine 69a
The Rushlight 69a, 231a, 333b
Rusin, Michele 69a
Rusk, Dean 220a
Russell, Miss 288b
Russell, Lady Agatha, 303b, 304a
Russell, Agnes 298b
Russell, Aliki 293a, 303b
Russell, Alys 256b, 260b, 268b, 284a, 352b
Russell, Anne (later Dryden) 277a, 278a, 282a, 310b, 353b
Russell, Anthony 293a, 303b
Russell, Athenaïs 293a, 303b
Russell, Bill 172a
Russell, Conrad 183b, 277b, 279b, 280a-b, 283a, 309b, 310a
Russell, Jr., David 69a
Russell, Dora 277b, 278a, 282a, 293a, 353b
Russell, E.H. 310b
Russell, Edith 186b, 280a
Russell, Edward Thomas 333b
Russell, Elizabeth (née Franklin) 280a-b
Russell, Elizabeth (formerly von Arnim) 264b
Russell, Ellen 298b
Russell, F.B. 73b
Russell, Flora 303b
Russell, Frank **303a**, 309a
Russell, Mrs. Gilbert 303b
Russell, Gustavo Cabrera 69a
Russell, Guy 293a

Russell, Harold 303b
Russell, Harris 312a
Russell, John 97a, 293a, 303b
Russell, John Conrad 258a, 276a-b, 277a-b, 278a, 280b, 281a, 282a, 283a, 284a, 293a, 310a, 342a
Russell, John Howard 231b
Russell, Lady John 3a, **3b**, 266b
Russell, Lord John **3a**
Russell, John and Kate 312a
Russell, Kate (*see* Tait, Katharine)
Russell, Lucy 277a-b, 278a, 280b, 281b, 282a, 283a, 353b
Russell, Margaret 90b
Russell, Martin 293a, 303b
Russell, Maud 303b
Russell, Mauri 135b, 268b, 298b
Russell, Pam 298b
Russell, Patricia (*see* Spence, Patricia)
Russell, Rachel 3b
Russell, Richard 15b
Russell, Robert W. 69a
Russell, Rollo 3b, 304a, 328a, 352b
Russell, Sarah 277a, 278a, 281b, 282a, 283a, 301b, 310b
Russell, Sharon 298b
Russell, Shirley 204b
Russell, Susan (née Lindsay) 277a, 278a, 279a, 282a
Russell, Virginia 333b, 334a
Russell, William 268b
Bertrand Russell and I 205b
Russell Bibliography Project 231b
Bertrand Russell Committee of 100 in Greece 101a, 101b, 123b
Russell Conference on Czechoslovakia 96b, 97a
Russell Foundation **148a**
Bertrand Russell Humanist Club 150a
Bertrand Russell Institute for Advanced Political Studies 149b
Bertrand Russell Journal for India 144a
BR Peace Committee 294a
Bertrand Russell Peace Foundation 16a, 17a, 32a, 69a, 97a, 106a, 117b, 124b, 125a, 149a, 164a, 185b, 205a, 235a, 322a
BRPF, Nottingham 295a
BRPF of Australia 124a
Bertrand Russell Peace Foundation, Philippine Branch 291a
BRPF Queensland Branch 295a
Bertrand Russell: Philosopher of the Century 334a
Bertrand Russell Society of Japan 268b
Russell Relatives **303a**
BRPF, Sydney 296a
Russell Tribunal 186b, 188a
Russian Revolution—50th Anniversary 148a
Russineks, Raissa O. 111a
Russo, Serofino 69a
Rustin, Bayard 54b
Rustin, Mike 299a
Rutecki, John F. 69a
Rutgers University Press 231b
Rutherford, Jan 69a
Růzek, M. 96b
Rwanda-Urundi 110b
Ryan, A.P. 153a
Ryan, N.F.M. 69a
Ryan, Ray 298b
Ryan, Robert 90b
Ryan, William F. 268b
Rybka, Louis 291a
Ryman Ltd., Stationers 308b
Ryukyu Shimpo 231a

S

S., M. 69a
Sa-ab Salem 105b
Saar-Freundeskreis des Albert Schweitzer-Spitals in Lambarene-e.V. 69a, 99b
Sabbeth, Joseph C. 90b
Sabino, Fernando 219b
Sablad, Balbino G. 148a
Sachs, Luiz Carlos 171a
Sachs, Mendel 69b
Sackey, Augustus D. 100b
Sackheim, Ben 90b
Sacks, Lawrence R. 69b
Sacks, William M. 69b
Sadighi, Ghulam-Hossein 106b
Sadiq, Anushiravan 231b
Sadler, Mark David 69b
Sadler's Wells School 282a
Sadosky, Manuel 69b
Sady, Jodo José 171a
Saenz, Maria C. 169a
Saga: Senior Citizen's News 231b
Sagall, Joseph and Mrs. 69b
Sagall, Sabby 239b
Sagan, Carl 268b
Sagarin, Edward 231b
Sahabi, F. 125a
Sahay, S.N. 268b
Sahaye, S. 231b
Sahl, H. 350a
St. Andrews, Arthur 69b
St. Andrew's Hospital 282b
St. George, George 69b
St. James Press 235a
St. John Ambulance Brigade (India) 334b
St. John, M. Gregory 69b
St. John, Ortega 69b
St. Kilda-Brighton Peace Action Group 169b
St. Kitts Prisoners' Defence Fund 69b
St. Louis Post-Dispatch 40a, 138a, 235a
St. Pancras Building Society 69b
St. Saviours Church 90b
St. Thomas's Hospital Gazette 235a
Saito, Kiyoshi 144b, 145a
Saito, Masako 145b, 219b
Saito, Tsuruko 69b, 144a, 291a, 298b, 301b
Sakata, Shoichi 145a, 157a, 159a, 192a
Sakharov, A. 64a
Sakurai, K. 69b, 217b
Salam, Abdus 142b, 226b
Salam, M.A. 233b
Salazar, Antonio de O. 128a
Salazillpur, Mian G.N. 298b
Saldana, F. 69b
Saldarriaga V., Alberto 288b
Salinas, Siles 94a
Salisbury, Donald 268b
Salisbury, E. 166b
Salisbury, Hal 298b
Salisbury, Harrison E. 117a, 159a
Saller, K. 99b
Salomon, Arnold 130a, 143b
Salomon, Sarah 69b, 104a, 111a
Salonge, Jobita 159a
Salop County Council 282a
Salt, Liz 69b
Salt, Patrick 282a
Salter, Elizabeth 288b
F.H. Salter & Son 308b
Salthouse, Ella 65a
Saltman, David B. 69b
Salton, Harold G. 69b
Saltzman, Arnold 90b
Salvadori, Max 69b
Salvaris, A. 202b
Salvat Editores 231b
Salveson, Christopher 78b
Salzburger Nachrichten 170b
Samal ?, Sarbesinar 229a
Sampson, Deborah 185b
Sampson, Ronald V. 69b
San Diego League for the Defense of Democracy 282b
The San Diego Union 231b
San Francisco Chronicle 138a, 232a
San Francisco Sunday Examiner and Chronicle 183a
San Jacinto High School 70a
Sancha, Justo Silvestre 167b
Sanchez Porras, Julian Antonio 70a
Sanctuary, the 70a
Sandén, Bertil 70a, 116a
Sanders, Esther 298b
Sanderson, J.H. 260a
Sandoval, Cruz Pablo 295b
Sandperl, Ira 70a
Sandy, Clive 70a
SANE 70a, 71b, 118b, 167b
SANE-U.S.A. 156b
Sanechi, Swaran Singh 232a
Sang, Do Xuan 178b
Sanger, Charles P. 268b
Sanger, Dora 268b
Sanger, F. 116a
Sanger, Margaret 268b
Sangree, Joan 282b
Sanity 146b, 155a, 232a
The Sankei Shimbun 232a

Sankey, R. 143a
Sano, B. 144b
Santamaria, Haydée 95b
Santamarina, Sergio Rojos 95b
Santiago, Dominique 126b
Sanjabi, Karim 106b
Sansom, R. 231a
Santayana, George 325b
Santhanam, K. 70a
Santhi, S. 70a
Santillan, Juan Alberto Camilo 70a
Sanyal, D.C. 232a
Sao, Mr. 164b
Sao, Nguyen Van 35a, 70a, 146b, 162a, 177a
Sapin, R. 70a
Sapriza, H. Almada 141a
Saprykin, I. 116b
Sarajcic, Ivo 119a
Saran, Helen G. 90b
Saran, Vishnu 232a
Sarbey, Mrs. M.D. 268b
Sardin, Eva 116b
Sarferaz, R.M. 70a
Sarfrazahmad, Mian 70a
Sargent, Dwight E. 137a, 223b
Sargent, Vernon Rhodes 334a
Sarja, Mamie 70a
Sarjit ? 70a, 105a
Sarkar, Chittaranjan 153b
Sarkar, Hirendra Narayan 232a
Sarley, Lois M. 70a
Sarley, W.N. 70a
Sarma, P.V. 57a, 106a, 124b, 127a
Sartre, Jean-Paul 70a, 93a, 94a, 104b, 106a, 109a, 112b, 118a, 119a, 136a, 157a, 161a, 167b, 186a-b, 187b, 188a, 189a, 189b, 192a
Sarva Seva Sangh 70a
SAS 232a
Sashin, Donald 155b
Saskatchewan, University of 298b
Saskatchewan, University of, Regina 298b
Sasella, Leo 70a
Satan in the Suburbs 209b, 232a
Satter, Herbert 98b
Sattler, James 70a, 175a
The Saturday Evening Post 29a, 220a, 232b
Saturday Review 232b
Saudi Arabia 110b
Saull, Canon 328b
Saunders, David 70b
Saunders, Peggy 58a
Saunders, Thomas J. 199b
Saur, Heinz 232b
Saur 100a
Savage, Stephen M. 219a
Savalle, Victor 268b
Savanvilay, Thanh 188b
Savanyu, Jean Marie 301b
Save Biafra Committee 108a
Save Greece Now 123b
Save Our Sons 70b
Savelli, Georges 173b
Savelli, Giulio 95a, 107a, 232b, 234a, 298b
Savill, E.Q. 234b
Saville, John 148a, 182a
Sawbridge, Fred 85b
Sawhory, Bhim 334a
Sawyer, H. 70b
Sawyer, Harry 296a
Saxena, D.C. 268b
Saxena, Mathura Prasad 70b
Saxton, R.S. 168a
Saydan, Can 84b
Sbrzesny, Peter 189b
Scallan, Oliver 90b
Scalpel 337a
Scamell, E.D. 70b
Scandinavian Airlines System Ltd. 313b
Scandinavian Conference on the Situation of Jews in the Soviet Union 112b
Scandinavica 323a
Scanlon, Hugh 70b
Scarborough New Left Club 70b
Scarfe, Gerald 232b
Scarlett, Joseph K. 90b
Scaron, Pedro 132a, 149b
Scarpbrook, Alma 170a
Scarry, John 70b
Schabrod, Klara 122a
Schachter, G. 99a
Schaefer, Philip A. 232b
Schappes, Morris U. 215b
Schapsmerer, Frederick H. 268b
Scharnberg, Carl 50a
Schaumann, H. 268b
Scheer, Robert 140a, 229b
Scheinbaum, Stanley K. 159a
Scheinberg, Stephen J. 171b
Schellinck, Jean 298b
Schenck, Harry P. 282b
Schenck, Marie 70b
Schenkelberg, Michael A. 291a
Schenker, Rozalia 99b, 110a, 129b
Schenker, Siegfried 129a
Robert Scher Community for New Politics 70b
Scherer, Hans 99b, 122a
Schermer, H. 70b
Scheurer, Paul 323a, 334a
Schick, Alan S. 70b
Schieber, Tilman 268b
Schiecke, Ulrich 232b
Schiefelbein, Anita 70b
Schiessel, R. 269a
Schild, J.E. 167b
Schillbach, Johannes 98b, 134b
Schiller, F.C.S. 9b
Schilling, Sonja 116a
Schilpp, Paul A. 200a, 221a, 269a
Schindtler, Edward 90b
Schippanoski, Ralph 172a
Schireson, Peter L. 269a
Schirmer, Sergio 70b
Schischkoff, G. 232b
Schlesinger, Jr., Arthur 77b
Schlesinger, Rudolph A.J. 70b, 117a, 132a
Schlick, Blanche 90b
Schmauss, A.K. 189b
Schmidt, Dieter 175a
Schmidt, Hans-Joachim 70b
Schmidt, Jürgen 323a, 334a
Schmidt, Michael 90b
Schmidt, Siegmund 70b
Schmidt, Waldemar 99a
Schmielewski, Yogi Alfred 275a, 334a
Schnapp, Simon 134b
Schneider, Aiziks 116a
Schneider, Dorothy L. 70b
Schneider, Georgia H. 90b
Schneider, J. 144a
Schneider, Morris D. 90b
Schneider, Sally Russell 269a
Schneier, Arthur 232b
Schneits, Pierre 321b
Schneps, Maurice 237b
Schnobel, Jane 146a
Schöchlin, Raoul 71a
Schoelm, Raymond E. 269a
Schoenbach, Victor J. 115a, 131b, 232b
Schoenberner, Gerhard 174b
Schoenfeld, Clara 129a
Schoenman, Edie 143b, 293a
Schoenman, Helen 269a, 293a
Schoenman, Ralph 143b, 148b, 184b, 185a-b, 188a-b, 189b, 232b, 269a, 334a
Schoenman, Theodore 119a, 150a, 232b, 269a, 293a
Scholarships Committee of South Africa 130a
Scholnick, Lewis Barnard 291a
Schon, Jennifer 174b
Schönbauer, Gina 174a
Schönfeld, T. 151a
Schönfeldt, Otto 98b, 174b
Schonfield, Hugh J. 334a
Schönholzer, Ernst 71a
School and College 351a
School of Living 71a
Schools' Conference 13a
Schools for Nonviolence 217a
Schorer, Sheldon 298b
Schott, Guenter 71a, 334a
Schott & Co. Ltd. 90b
Schou, August 147b
Schrag, Philip G. 52b, 71a
Schreiber, Isabelle Georges 71a
Schreiter, Helfried 174a
Schreyer, Lester 269a
Schrift für Architektur und Stadtbau 232b
Schröder 349b
Schroenen, Joseph 93b
Schroll, Susannah 71a
Schröter, Gertrud 121b
Schröter, Rudolf 121b
Schrut, Albert 167b
Schulburg, Budd 232b

Schüler ? 232b
Schuller, T.M. 240b
Schulz, Belle W. 90b
Schuster, David 111a
Schuster, M. Lincoln 149b, 234a
Schutz, Robert R. 334a
Schutzberger, Faye 269a
Schwab, Osmund 174b
Schwabach, Deborah 269a
Schwarcz, Ernst 170b
Schwartz, Itta 112b
Schwartz, J. 269a
Schwartz, J.A. 71a
Schwartz, Josef 111a
Schwartz, Laurent 71a, 93a, 119a, 131a, 148a, 157a, 161a, 185a-b, 192a, 298b
Schwartz, Lupa 112a
Schwartzburd, Leonard 135b
Schwarz, Günther 71a, 144a
Schwarz, Rudolf 288b
Schwarzenburger, Georg 167b, 232b
Schwarz-Otava, Rudolph 299a
Schweid, Leonardo César 167b, 207a
Schweig, Bruno 71a
Schweiger, Walter 71a
Schweitzer, Albert 99b, 133b, 149a, 206a, 212a, 269a
The Albert Schweitzer Fellowship 149a
Schweizerische Bundeskanzlei 71a
Scida, Louis 233a
Science 152a, 336a
Science and Humanity 233a
Science & Society 233a
Science & Times 233a
Science Reporter 334a
Scientia 338b
Scientist and Citizen 155b
Scientists' Appeal for Vietnam 91a, 167b
Scientist's [*sic*] Committee to End Chemical Warfare in Vietnam 167b
Scînteia 233a
Scînteia Tineretulin 233a
Scoop Press Agency Ltd. 233a
Scorer & Harris, Notaries Public 314a
Scotsman 13b, 96b
Scott, Bev 220b
Scott, Elizabeth 131b
Scott, Edward J. 71a
Scott, G. Michael 71a
Scott, Jack 183a
Scott, James A. 198a, 233a
Scott, Jim 179a
Scott, Joan 71a
Scott, Lawrence 167a
Scott, Margaret 269a
Scott, Michael 10b, 11a, 114a, 142b, 152a
Scott, R.P. 278a
Scott, Regan 230b
Scott, William R. 71a
Scott, Foresman and Co. 233a
Cyril Scott Presentation Fund 91a
Scottish National Conference on Vietnam 16a
Scwell, Frances 71b
"Sea Life" 154a
Seal, B.N. 330b, 334a
Seal, Brajendranath 334b
Seale, John R. 269a
Seaman, Gerald 91a
Search 233a
A Search for an Alternative to War and Violence 233a
Searle, Alan 177a, 288a
Sears, John L. 146a, 233a
Sears, M. 71b
Seary, William J. 71b
Seattle Peace Information Centre 71b
Seaver, Richard 220b
Sebai, Mr. 113b
Sechrest, Larry James 197b
Martin Secker & Warburg 233a, 332a
Second German Television Corporation 122b
The Second International Congress of Classical Studies 334b
Secretary-General to the Prime Minister's Conference 101b
Secreteriado Nacional da Informação, Cultura Populare Turismo 128b
Secrève, Leo H. 208b
The Security Council of the UN 115a, 118b
Sedgwick, Peter 132a, 167a
Seed, Philip 145b
Seeger, Peter 269a
Seeley, John R. 71b
Segal, Allen 71b
Segal, Iancu 110b
Segal, Ronald 129b
Segal, Zvi 135a
Segaram, G.S. 71b
Segefjord, Bjarne 233a
Segerstedt, Torgny 112b
Seginer, Bella 122a
Seginer, Salomon 122a
Segura, Felipe Tirado 297b
Segura, Ricardo Tirado 297b
Seidenschnur 175a
Seidler, Vojtech 96b, 121a
Seigle, Stacey 296a
Seikyo Shimbum 233b
Sekai 144b
Sel, Yilmaz 71b
Selby, D.A. 71b
Seldes, Gilbert 269b
Selection 233b
Selk, Merry 155b
Sellar, Helen 116a, 152a
Haile Sellassie 97a, 110b, 124a
Sellers, Peter 269b
Sellers, Sandi 139b
Selman, Gordon 172a
Selmer, Erik R. 74a
Sels, V. 91a
Selvablancos, Nicholas 46b
Selzer, Michael 25a, 107a
Semenass, Erika 111b
Semler, E.G. 198a
Sen, Alokemoy 153b
Sen, B.R. 71b, 115a
Sen, Krishna 269b
Sen, P.C. 294b
Senanayake, D.S. 95a
Sencer, Muammer 233b
Senchea, Gabriela 291a
Sencourt, Robert 269b
Sendles, R.L. 88b
Senegal 110b
Senegal Peace Movement 151b
Seng, Chau 94b
Senghor, Leopold S. 110b
Senkovic, Predrag 71b
Senoo, Y. 197b
Sensen-Verlag 170b
September Flag 171b
September, Reg 294a
Seragg, T.W. 91a
Sere, Beniamino 294a
Sereni, Emilio 204b
Serra d'Or 233b
Serrano, Carmen 120b, 149a
Servan-Schreiber, Denise 153a
Setina, Vladimir 71b
Sevitt, S. 159a
Seward, M. 71b
Sexton, J.H. 117a
Seyler, M. 91a
Sforsa, Francisco 141a, 299a
Shaalan, M.S̄. 107a
Shaber, Milton B. 71b
Shabsovitch, G.L. 111b, 134b
Shachman, Arthur O. 299a
Shackleton, James 71b
Shadan Hojin Correspondents Club of Japan 233b
Shaffer, Mrs. Robert 71b
Shafindder, Mr. 108b
Shah, F.P. 71b
Shah, H.M. Zahir, Afghanistan, 93a, 126a
Shah of Iran (*see* Pahlevi, Mohammed Reza)
Shahak, Israel 104a
Shaheen 233b
Shahn, Ben 91a
Shaikh, Z.H. 71b
Shainkman, Joseph 134a
Shakeri, Khosrow 106b, 125a
Shakespeare, William 335b
The Shakespeare Exhibition 91a
Shalam Light 153b
Shalit, Morris 288b
Shami, M.A. 233b
Shamlal, Vimle 219b
Shammout, A. 161a, 174a
Shamsuddoha 108b
Shanin, Teodor 71b
Shank, Paul 71b
Shanks, Bob 138b

Shanti, Farid 91a
Shapiro, Mr. 3a
Shapiro, Aliza 113a
Shapiro, Mark A. 71b
Shapiro, Pauline W. 71b
Shar, Zahir 95a
Shariff, S.M. 127b
Sharland, B.W. 334b
Sharma, Dhirendra 233b
Sharma, Kusum 71b
Sharon, Art 120b, 170b
Sharp, Miss 51b
Sharp, Gene 13b, 72a, 143b
Sharp, Jack 72a
Sharp, M.P. 10b
Sharp, Megan 171a
Sharp, Sheila 209a
Shastri, Lal Bahadur 102a, 124b
Shavers Place 114b
Shaw, Anne 72a
Shaw, G. Bernard 337b
Shaw, Denis 91a
Shaw, Grazia Deny 288b
Shaw, H.C.W. 72a
Shaw, Robert B. 118b
Shaw, W. 98b
Shawcross, Lord 121b
Shayegan, Dr. Ali 106b
Shea, Robert J. 202b
Shealy, Edwin A. 72a
Sheed and Ward Ltd. 233b
Sheen, Ena 206b
Sheffer, Henry M. 269b
Sheffield City Libraries 282b
Sheffield Telegraph 233b
Sheffield University Students' Union 167b
Sheikhmous, O. 72a, 125b
Anthony Sheil Associates Ltd. 233b
Sheldon, W.F. 72a
Shelford, Marian 291a
Shell 233b
Shelley, J. 218b
Shelley, Percy Bysshe 350b
Shenke, Edwin A. 198a
The Shenval Press 233b
Shephall Labour Party 167b
Shepherd, B.M. 146a
Shepherd, Jack 72a, 145b
Shepherdson, ? 216b
Sheppard, Barry 178b
Sheppard, F.A. 91a
Sheratte, I.V. 175b
Shereshevsky, Simon 72a, 103b
Sheridan, Jeanne 288b
Sheridan, Peter 288b
Sherman, Elna 72a
Sherman, M.N. 172a
Sherman, Paddy 334b
Sherwin, Larry 269b
Sheth H.P. Arts & S.M. Panchal Science College, India 299a
Shew, Ernest 269b
Shibata, Mrs. Sadato 341b
Shibata, Shingo 45a, 104b, 145b, 186b, 187a, 189a, 233b, 341a-b
Shick, Kim Hyan 225b
Shiel, James 266b
Shields, George 91a
Shiga, H. 175b
Shigeo, I. 144b
Shima, Yasuharu 72a, 144b, 145a, 167b, 299a
Shimabuko, Eduardo 72a
Shimamura, Yohane 144b
Shimizu, Gilda 171a
Shimizu, Ikutaro 145a
Shimizu, Takeo 17a
Shimizu, Toshio 242a
Shinar, Bluma 111a, 299a
Shinwell, E. 114b, 118b
Shioya, Shigeru 199b
Shipley, R. 309b
Shirazi, Ayatulah 125a
Shire and Spire 199b, 233b
Shirer, William L. 142b, 288b
Shirzad, N. 125a
Shishkin, I. 117a
Shively, Daniel 91a
Shloimovitz, Marcus 72a, 134a
Shlonsky, Avraham 72a
Shlyk, Anatoli Ilych 134a
Shmeli, Babanskaja 134b
Shmueli, Cilla 134b
Shneidman, Edwin S. 334b
Shnjakine, Victor 117b
Shodunke, M.O. 72a
Shoenfield, Jerome 234a
Shoner, Sarah 72a
Shoosmith, G.T. 309b
Shore, Donald P. 72a
Shoukair, Abdul Rahman 106b
Should India Make an Atom Bomb? Bertrand Russell Answers 144a
Shrapnell, Mike 72a, 148a
Shroff, A.D. 91a
Shtaadze, A.B. 134a
Shubart, Robert Franz 269b
Shudarsky, E. 134a
Shui, Chien-tung 233b
Shukla, Mukesh 299a
Shukla, R.C. 102a
Shukla, Shyam 72a
Shulgasser, Lew 117a
Shulman, Milton 211a
Shura, Shames 72a
Shute, G.J. 272a
Shwayder, D.S. 334b
Sibley, Mulford Q. 334b
Sibthorp, M.M. 233b
Siddiqi, Nazeer 233b
Siddiqui, Z.A. 196b
Siddiqur 229b
Sidenius, Henrik 173a
Sidgwick, H. 256a
Sie + er 334b
Siebens, Henry C. 72a
Sieff, John Henry 72a, 91a, 134a
Siegal, Gerald M. 334b
Siegel, Eli 72a
Max Siegel & Associates 233b
Siemens-Schuckertwerke 91a
Siempre 15b, 94a
Sierra, Francisco Díaz 72b
Sierra, Marta 167b
Sierra Leone **110b**
Sievers, John R. 299a
Siganos, Manolis 123b, 124a
Sigg, Walter 72b
Siggers, Marnie 12b
Siggs, Albert 91a
El Siglo Illustrado S.A. 233b
Sihanouk, Norodom 94a
Sik, Endne 290b, 295a
Sil, Arun Kumar 72b, 290a, 334b
Silburt, Beth 112a
Silcox, Lucy 269b, 310b, 353b
Silkin, Lord 142b, 176a
Silkin, John 116a
Sillars, James 72b
Sillitoe, Alan 116a, 152a, 177a, 288b
Silver, Ali 269a
Silver, James 76a
Silver, Michael M. 72b
Silveria, Enio 207b
Silverman, S.J. 72b
Silverman, Sydney 159a, 176b, 269b
Silver Pears Trophy for Achievement 154b
Silvers, Stuart 72b, 165a
Sim, James E.H. 170b
Simard, Albert 154b
Simich, Milutin 72b
Simizu, Takari 167b
Simmen, Jean-Louis 16b
Simmonds, Aubyn L. 72b
Simmons, III, Charles 135b
Simmons, Donald 72b
Simmons, Mr. and Mrs. G.B. 119a
Simmons, James R. 72b
Simmons, Peter 145b, 251a
Simon, Charles 72b
Simon, Edward J. 216a
Simon, Henry W. 322a
Simon, John J. 230a
Simon, Ruth B. 91a
Simon, Sidney 334b
Simon and Schuster, Inc. 149b, 234a, 322a
Simon of Wythenshawe, Lady 203a, 269b, 299a
Simon of Wythenshawe, Lord 10b
Simons, Enid 269b
Simons, G.L. 269b
Simons, Sheila 269b
Simonsui, I. 131a
"Simple, Peter" 205a
Simpson, D. 91a
Simpson, E.L. 91a
Simpson, F.A. 269b
Simpson, G.G. 327b
Simpson, John C. 72b
Simpson, M. 72b
Simpson, Mary W. 72b
Simpson, N.F. 232a
Simpson, Roger A. 72b, 269b
Sims, B.J. 72b

Simson, George 269b
Simson, W.A. 170a
Sinclair, Andrew 218b
Sinclair, Donald 269b
Sinclair, Geoffrey 184b
Sinclair, Hamish 240b
Sinclair, Jo 167b
Sinclair, Keith 147a
Singer, D. 72b
Singer, Esther 91a
Singer, Jacques 228b
Singer, Stanley 72b
Singh, D. 72b
Singh, Dirsh 102b
Singh, G. 270a
Singh, Iqbal 218a
Singh, Kalu J. 291a
Singh, Kewal 102a
Singh, Manjit 102a
Singh, P.P. 72b
Singh, Shambhri N. 72b
Singh, Surya Nath 270a
Singh, Yuvaraj Karan 270a
Singhgill, Dhanwant 72b
Singleton, Jack 38a
Sinh, Aditya V. 73a
Sinha, K.K. 73a
Sinha, K.P. 153b
Sinha, Murari 73a
Sinha, S.M. 234a
Siniansky, Elie 129a, 135a
Siniansky, Ilya 129a
La Sinistra 73a, 234a
Sino-India Conflict **110b**
Sirc, Ljubo 73a
Sirhan, Mary 299a
Siriwarnasingha, Wilson 234a
Sirota, H. 134b
Sirota, T. 135a
Sisc ?, Mme. Paul 299a
Sitnam, E. 270a
Sitwell, Edith 152a, 288b
Sitwell, Nigel 197a
Sitzungsberichte der Bayerischen Akademie der Wissenschaften Mathematisch-naturwissenschaftliche Abteilung 333b
Sixth Form Opinion 234a
Sixth Hungarian Peace Conference 73a
Siyavurgil, Sabri Esat 106b
Skarzynski, Janusz 73a
Skaug, Arne 108a
Skelly, [Alan] 280b, 281b
Skerl, Valerie 73a
Skilton, Charles 36b
Skinner, J. Allen 143b
Skinner, Jon 30b
Skinner, M.B. 73a
Sklar, Robert 234a
Skoglund, Bo 73a
Skolnick, Sol 73a
Skorpil, P.R. 73a
Skriver, Ansgar 99b
Skupnik, W. 127a
Slaghuis, Walter 170a
Slanson, J. Sayne 73a
Slater, John G. 172b, 270a
Slater, Rina 202a
Sleep, Philip 73a
Sliwka, Jon 109b
Sloan, Edward Martin 73a, 166a, 295b
Sloan, Pat 201a
Slobinsky, Emilio 270a
Slobodan Princip-Seljo School 157b
Slocombe, Charles H.A. 73a
Slonimsky, Nicolas 273b
Slough College Students Union 299a
Slovanski Porocevalec 243a
Slovin, L. 113a
Smailes, Julia 91a
Smallshaw, J.W. 201b
Smart, Colin 149a
Smart, Michael 73a
Smeaton, Jack 225a
Smedley, Frederic C. 73a
Smeets Weert 234b
Smets, Dore 116a
Smickowitch, Haim 111b
Smiley, T.J. 270a
Smit, H. 270a
Smith, A. 91b
Smith, Battle 79b
Smith, Mr. & Mrs. Charles 270a
Smith, David 301b
Smith, David M. 270a
Smith, Frank Penn 353b
Smith, Gloria 73a
Smith, Grover 270a
Smith, H. 270a
Smith, Iris 224b
Smith, Jr., J. Kellum 90b
Smith, J. Michael 73a
Smith, Jack 73a
Smith, Jessica 223b
Smith, Lewis 270a
Smith, Louise Pettibone 264b
Smith, Mamie 39a, 74a, 93b, 111a, 129b
Smith, Marilyn 67a
Smith, N.A. 335a
Smith, Mrs. P. 73a
Smith, P.L. 114b
Smith, P.R. 88b
Smith, Peggy 299a
Smith, Peter 73a, 91a
Smith, Peter R. 174b
Smith, Peter Wesley 170a
Smith, R.S. 270a
Smith, Robert 30a, 174b, 297b
Smith, Robert J. 175a
Smith, Roy 145b
Smith, Wayne A. 296b
Smith, William F. 234b
W.H. Smith & Son 234b, 308b
Smithback, John B. 73b
Smolski, Theresa L. 73b
Smythe, Samuel 297a
Smythe, Tony 59a, 81a, 114b, 131b, 135b, 297b
Snaith, Stanley 234b
S.N.C.C. 17a
SNCC Newsletter 139b
Snelling, O. 169b
Snelling, Richard 73b
Snellman, Benjamin 279a
Snobel, Alex X. 236a
Snow, C.P. 111b, 112b, 115b, 133b, 270a, 288b
Snowden, Elizabeth 215a
Snyder, Alice D. 270a
Sobani, Ishaque 24a
Sobel, Joseph 73b
Sobel, Samuel 42a
Sobell, Helen 140a, 290a
Sobell, Morton 10b, 73b, **133a**, 140a
Socec, A. 233a
Social Evils 329a
Social Research and Development Programs 73b
Social Surveys 131b
Socialist Attack 2 335a
Socialist Education Association 234b
Socialist International 62b
Socialist Labour League 178a
The Socialist Leader 146b, 234b, 335a
Socialist Party of Japan 11b
Socialist Party, Tokyo 299a
Socialist Review 234b
Socialist Society, Borough Road College, Ilseworth 73b
Socialist Society, University of Aston 178b
Socialist Union of Central-Eastern Europe 73b, 121a
Socialist Workers Party 73b, 115a
Socialist Zionist Party—Mapam 73b, 104a, 111a
Socialisten 234b
Socialistika Förbundet 73b
Sociedad Humanista 73b
Sociedad Mexicana de Geografía y Estadística 127a
Sociedade Amigos de Bertrand Russell 171a
Sociedade Amigos de Cuba 73b
Societas Scientiarum Fennica, Commentationes Physico-Mathematicae 337a
Société Britannique de Philosophie de Langue Française 335a
Société des Nations Service de la Republique de Chine 278a
Société Etudes Philosophiques 299a
Société Internationale de Prophylaxie Criminelle 73b
Société Radio-Canada 234b
Society for Aiding Victims of Miscarriages of Justice 73b
Society for Anglo-Chinese Understanding 73b, 95a
Society for Cultural Relations with the USSR 74a, 111b
Society for Defence of Law and

Liberty in Iraq 126b
The Society for Indian and Northern Education 234b
Society for Individual Freedom 234b
Society for Pollution and Environmental Control 234b
Society for the Cause of Mother's Lineage 74a
Society for the Prevention of World War III, Inc. 154b
Society of Democratic Action, Queensland University 169a
Society of Friends Peace Committee 74a, 232a
Society of Separationists, Inc. 270a
Socusson, B. 196a
Soebandrio, Dr. 107a, 124b
Soekarno, Dr. 288b
Soekarno, Achmed 102b
Sofiullah, M. D. 203b
Soiseth, L. 91a
Sokolinski, Joseph D. 335a
Solaiman, Lotfallah 159a
Soldatov, A. A. 111a, 112b, 116b, 117a-b, 134b
Soldo, John J. 270a
Soleillet, Maurice 31a
Soleyman-Irani, L. 135a
Solicitors' Law Stationery Society Ltd. 91a
Solidarité Fraternelle Mondiale 74a
Solidarité Pérou 109a
Solidarity Conference 95b
Soliongco, I. P. 109a
Solomcoe, Anna 94b
Solomon, Deborah 74a
Solomon, Golda 129a
Solomon, Luigi 129a
Solomon, Sarah 69b
Solstad, Ken 74a
Solti, George 288b
Somali Republic **110b**
Somerville, M. J. 74a
Sommer, M. Lloyd 74a
Sommer, Peter M. 212a
Sommerville, Brian 232a-b
Sommerville, John 335a
Somming, Léonie 288b
Somoza, Jose Antonio 74a
Søndergard, Vagn 173b
Soormally, A. M. 238b
Sopote, S. C. 169b
Soprano, Sacha 288b
Sorensen, Lord 116b
Sorensen, R. W. 74a, 91a
Sorlie, Wayne 74a
Sosialistik Ungdomsforbund 74a
Soskice, Frank 114a, 176b
Sosnen, Samuel 74a, 167b
Soubeyran, Charles 74a
Soucek, Sylvia 74a
Soumar, Robert B. 74a
Souphanouvong, Prince 159a, 187b
Sourâle, Agustina 167b
Souter, Gavin 236b
South Africa **110b-111a, 129b**
South Africa Protest and Defence and Aid 74a, 111a, 129b
South African Coloured Peoples Congress 130a
South African Journal of Science 338b
South Arabia **111a, 130a**
South Carolina SHICK 139b
South Coast Peace Committee 93b
South-East Asia Appeal **156a**
South Place Ethical Society 74a
The South Swedish Biafra Committee Operation Outrage 108a
South Vietnam Liberation Red Cross Society 118b, 167b
South Vietnam National Front for Liberation 153a
South Vietnam National Front for Liberation in Budapest 162b
South Vietnam National Liberation Front 167b, 176a
South Vietnam Peace Committee 163a, 299a
South Wales Nuclear Disarmament Campaign 74b
South West Committee for Peace in Vietnam 176b
South-West Essex Technical College and School of Art Students' Union 234b-235a
Southampton University Students Union 167b
Southern California Council for a Sane Nuclear Policy 288b
Southern Illinois University Press 234b
Southern Rhodesia **130a**
Southon, R. M. 74b
Souvanna Phouma, H. H. Prince 105b
Souvannarath, Kykeo 187b
Souyiah, Haouari 120a, 151b
Soviet Embassy 153a
Soviet Jews **111a-b-112a, 133a-135a**
Soviet News 352a
Soviet Peace Committee 74b, 104a, 116b, 118b, 136b, 167b, 291a
Soviet Peace Fund 15a, 74b, 117b, 335a
Soviet Press Agency 12b
Soviet Russia 235a
Soviet Scientists on the Danger of Nuclear Tests 155a
Soviet Writers' Union 112b
Sovietisch Heimland 14a, 111b, 112b, 117a
Sow, Alfâ Ibrâhîm 74b, 101b
Sowerby, G. S. 74b
Soyinka, Wole 74b
Sozialistische Hefte 235a
Sozialistische Jugend Deutschlands 99b
Sozialistischer Deutscher Studentenbund 16b, 174b
Spa, H. 235a
Spafford, Richard 217b
Spain **113a, 130a**
Spalding, D. B. 110a
Spanel, Abram N. 74b
The Spanish Ambassador to the United Kingdom 113a
Spanish Delegation 151b
Spanish Intellectuals in the U. S. S. R. 130b
Spanish Refugee Aid, Inc. 91a
Spanish Workers' Defence Committee 113a, 130a, 299a
The Spark 35a
Sparkes, T. Roy 299a
Spartacus 235a
The Spastics Society 91a
Spaziani, L. 74b
Speart-Binns, John 270a
The Spectator 108b, 235a
Spectorsky, A. C. 228a
Speegel, Armin 91a
Spence, Mrs. 353b
Spence, Patricia 213a, 233a, 282a-b
Spencer, Alec 75b
Spencer, Ann 74b
Spencer, E. M. 270a, 276b
Spencer Brown, G. (David) 270a, 335a
Spender, Stephen 117a, 150b, 231a, 270a
Spett Rai Radio Televisione Italiana 314a
Sphere Books 235a
Sphinx 235a
Der Spiegel 16a, 174b, 183b, 235a
Spieole, Mrs. M. 74b
"Spies for Peace" 12a
Spiess, C. 115b
Spillman, Martin 74b, 125a
Spilman, Ramona 74b
Spilsbury, David E. 251a
Spinks, J. W. T. 298b
Spivack, Morris Redman 335a
Spock, Benjamin 159a, 226b
Wolf Spoerl Ltd. 91a
The Spokesman 299a
Spokesman-Review 183a
Sponsors of the BRPF **149a**
Spooner, Heather 74b
Spreafico, Antonio 291a
Sprecher, Max 74b
Springer, D. H. 216a
Springer, M. R. 24a, 111b, 134a
Axel Springer & Sohn 235a
Sproul, Robert G. 256b
Squires, Vera M. 74b
Squitieri, Neal Paul 74b
Sramek, Ivo 173a
Srednicki, Jean 133a, 156a
Srenaski, Denis 74b
Sreshta, S. K. 291b
Sri Lanka Anti-Imperialist Youth

Front 172b
Srinivasan, Chakravarthi 153b
Srinivasan, T.V. 153b
Srivastava, Saurabh 235a
Srokola, Adalberto 169a
SSRS Newsletter 335a
Staatliche Bibliothek Regensburg 235a
Staatliches Sinfonie Orchester 175a
Stacey, Janine 196a
Stack, Jim 74b
Stackler, Susan 282b
Stadler, Ann 71b
Stadt Frankfurt-am-Main Oberbürgermeister Bockelmann 99a
Stafanovic, Alexander V. 205b
Stafford, Richard 335a
Stahl, Donald 74b
Staines, Bernard R.J. 91a
STAKE 75a
Stalder, Fred 75a
Stalin, J. 10a
Stallwitz, Walter 64a
Stallybrass, Oliver 233a
Stanciu, V.V. 73b
Standage, Joan 271a
Standard, Michael 142b, 149a, 150a
Standard, William L. 147b
Stanbury, B. 270a
Standen, R.N. 146b
Standen, W.G. 91a
Stander, Philip 235b
Ständiger Arbeitsausschus für Frieden 75a
Standish, Peter R. 75a
Stanford, John W. 75a
Stanford, Jr., John W. 137b
Stanford University Peace Caucus 118a
Stanich, Ray 291a
Staniger, W.L. 75a
Stankovic, Peter J. 75a
Stanley of Alderley, Fabia, Lady 314a
Stanley, D. 94b
Stanley, Maud 281b
Stanley, Pamela 75a
Stanley Relatives **304a**
Stanton, Charles E. 75a
Stanton, John 159a
Stanton, Margaret 101b
Stanton, Nile 75a
Stanton, R.W.B. 277b
Stanton, V.H. 304a
Stanton, Wm.F. 301b
Stanway, Brenda 145b, 146a
Stanworth, J.K. 236a
Stapleton, Syd 167b
Stapp, Andrew 25a
The Star-Bulletin 183b, 235b
Starcke, Viggio 75a
Starostin, E.V. 270b
Starr, Leon 129a
Starr, Martin K. 219b
Starrs, Robert J. 75a, 167b
State Bank of Pakistan 37b, 108a
The Statesman 81b, 153b, 235b
The Statesman (Pakistan) 15a, 109a
Stather, Ralph 126a
Statt, Réginald C. 49b
Steadman, John 91a
Steadman, Patricia H. 30b
Stebbing, A. Francis 335a
Steckler, Mr. 235a
Steckler, Doris 299a
Steckler, Eddie 299a
Steege, Ted 66a
Steel, A.J. 227b
Steel, Antony 75a, 100b, 122b
Steele, James 171b
Steen, Otto A. 75a
Steeples, Joe 218b
Steer, Gillian C.A. 87b
Steer, R.W. 167b
Stefan 299a
Steffens, Jr., Henrik 75a
Stefka, Eugen 121a
Steichen, Edward 335a
Stein, Mrs. 154a
Stein, Gordon 270b
Stein, M. 104a
Steiner, Helmut 170b
Steiner, Rudolf 75a, 167b
Steinfelder, Frank 75a
Steinhart, L. 130b
Steinhaus, Kurt 157a
Steinkraus, Warren E. 291a
Steinmann, Anne 91a
Steinmetz, Harry 137a, 282b
Steinweg, Gernot 75a
Stell, Karl H. 75a
Stelzenmuller, T. 122a
Stemmer, Karl 224a
Stenning, N. 60a
Stenzler ? 135a
Stenzler, J. 111b
Stephanopoulos, Stephanos 100b
Stephen, Judith 353b
Stephen, Karin 353b
Stephens, Bette 75b, 235b
Stephens, J.S.A. 100b
Stephens, Kenneth 75b
Stephens, Violet 293a
Stephenson, P. 270b
Sterchi, Roger 167a
Stern, Alfred 172b
Stern, Axel 335a
Stern, Lee 150a
Stern, Martha Dodd 173a
Sternberg, Vernon 234b
The Lawrence Sterne Trust 91a
Sternglass, Ernest J. 140a, 155a-b
Stersky, Attila (Sztersky) 124b
Stetler, Jr., Russell Dearnley 96a, 118a, 150b, 157b, 184b, 270b, 299a
Stetler, Sue 23a
Stettner, Louis B. 299a
Stetznmeyer, Bill 299a
Steuer, Arthur 138a
Stevenage Youth Peace Action 178b
Stevens, Jr., Herbert H. 270b
Stevenson, Adlai 12b, 55b, 137a, 138a, 142b
Stevenson, David 335b
Stewart, D.R. 201a
Stewart, Dorothy 91a
Stewart, Gloria 167b, 235b
Stewart, Iain 235b
Stewart, Leslie 153a
Stewart, Man 169b
Stewart, Mary 270b
Stewart, Michael 114b, 116b, 141b
Stewart, Ralph 270b
Stewart, Thomas William 266a
Stewart, W.M. 75b
Stfosis, Kostas 124a
Stibbs, Timothy 75b
Stickland, Irina 270b
Stickland, Nicholas 270b
Stickland, Stefan 270b
Stickland, Ursula 270b
Stichting Anti Atoobom Actie 75b
Stichting J'Accuse 75b
Stichting Werkgroep Wereldunie 75b
Stieger, Mr. & Mrs. 75b
Stierwaldt, Max 99b
Still, Joseph W. 75b
Stiller, Carlheinz 98b
Stillwell, Caro 293a
Stirling, Ian 75b
Stjärnskog, Hans 75b
Stockholm Conference on Czechoslovakia 96b
Stockholm Conference on Vietnam 18a, 167b, 185b
Stockholm International Peace Research Institute 75b
Stocks, Ian J.A. 235a
Stockwood, Mervyn 75b, 176b
Stodden, K.M. 30a, 169b
Stoff, Alois 48b, 166a, 174b
Stoke Newington and Hackney North Young Socialists 75b
The Stoke Newington Liaison Committee for Women's Peace Groups 75b, 130a
Stokowski, Leopold 270b
Stoll, Dennis Gray 288b
Stommel, Edeltrud 75b, 174b
Stone, Esther 354a
Stone, I.F. 95b, 115b, 137a, 149b, 159a, 235b, 354a
Stone, Keith 235b
Stone, M.K. 75b
The Stone Wall Press 235b
Stoneman, Margaret 233b
I.F. Stone's Weekly 94a, 95b, 183a, 235b, 335b
Stonor, C.R.P. 75b
STOP-WAR-VIP-TRIP 76a
Storch, Vergel Cook 76a
Storey, John A. 76a
Story, Richard W. 231a
Stovicék Iva 76a

Stowell, Robert F. 76a
Strandberg, Ole 166a, 173b
Strassburg, Richard C. 76a
Strategy and Conscience 212a
A Strategy for American Security–An Alternative to 1964 Military Budget 330b
Streatfield, Raymond 353b
Streatfield, Y. 47b
Streit, Dr. 99a
Streller, Herr 99a
Strelsky, Katharine 205a
Stricker, O. 76a
Strickland, Gerald 145b
Strickland, Kathleen 270b
Strike 18b, 235b
Strinitz, Werner 98b
Strobl, Lily 91a
Strong, Anna Louise 95a
Strong, Eithne 304a
Strong, J. 116a
Strong, Rupert 304a
Strowski, Steve 101b
Struelens, Louise 170b
Struelens, Stephanie 170b
Stuart, John 270b
Stuart, Maxine 76a
Stubbes, E.H. 272a
Stubbs, Mr. 307b
Stuber, Ernst 76a, 335b
Stücki, Alice 270b, 283a
Student 235b
The Student 235b
Student Mobilization Committee Benefit Fund 76a
Student Mobilization Committee to End the War in Vietnam 167b
Student Mobilizer 167b
Student Non-Violent Coordinating Committee 139b, 157a-b, 192a
Student Peace Movement 76a
Student Peace Union 76a
Student Struggle for Soviet Jewry 111b
Students for a Democratic Society 76a, 150a
Students' Front Against Aggression, Lahore 108b, 235b
Students of Nagaya University 157b
Students of University of California 291b
Students to Organize for Peace 167b
Students' Union (Autonomous), Calcutta University 167b
Students Union, L.S.E., Clare Market 114b
Students' Union President, Essex University 114b
Studie 235b
Studie en Aktie Komittee Camilo Torres 105b
Studies in the Cold War 153a
Studio Kievnauch-film 74a
Studio Neue Literatur 91a
Studio Radio Bern 235b
Stupin, Karl 76a, 98b
Sturgis, George 282b
Sturgis, Norman 150a
Sturla, Ana Maria 76a
Stüttgen, Wolfgang 76a
Style, Mrs. O-lan 203a
"S. Viet-Nam" 118a
Su, Han Duk 127a, 145a
Suarez, Armando Rodrigues 16b
Suárez, Eduardo 106a
Suberville, Gerald 109a
Subramanian, Bala 299a
Subramanian, M. 235b
Subramanian V. 102a
Subramanyam, B.K. 76a
Subrt, Miroslav 173a
Sucesos 235b
Such, Richard 118a, 167b
Sucker, I.E. 287b
Sucupira, Ney de Araripe 76b
Sud, Mohan 301b
Sudan **113a**
Sudbury Mine, Mill & Smelter Workers' Union 299a
Sueo, Muta 145a
Sugimoto, Atsushi 58b
Sugunasiri, S.H.J. 288b
Suhramin?, S. 212b
Suhrkamp Verlag 236a
Suirez, ? 76b
Sukarno, Dr. 124b
Sukartiko, R. 103a
Suleiman, Mohammed 159a
Suleimanova, Tova 135a
Sullhau, Hari Krishan 76b, 127b, 153b
Sullivan, Christopher J. 76b
Sullivan, Dan 335b
Sullivan, Marjorie 36b
Sullivan, Vicki M. 76b
Sultan, Paulette 301b
Sulzberger, C.L. 28b, 41b
Sumbuddhananda, Swami 270b
"Summary of Facts Concerning the War in Vietnam" 118a
Summers, John 236a
Summers, N. 141b
Summers, Orville E. 270b
Sun 14a, 114b, 220a, 236a
The Sun: Newspaper of the Guild Students 236a
The Sunday Citizen 236a, 335b
Sunday Dispatch 10b
Sunday Pictorial 325b
The Sunday School Board 236a
Sunday Sun, New Delhi 76b
The Sunday Telegraph 126b, 155a, 178a, 228b, 236a
The Sunday Times 13b, 37a, 101b, 114a, 118b, 123b, 146a, 148a, 156b, 183a, 200a, 220a, 236a, 264a
Sunday Times of Ceylon 236a
Sundra, Trisko 76b, 115b
Sung, Kim Il 105a, 189a
Sung, Vo Van 162b
Sunshine, Adrian 111b
Supek, Ivan 208a, 351b
Supek, Rudi 228b
Superintendent of Police 277a
Suraa Karya Samsad 236a
Surridge, L. 76b
Suryadarma, Utami 103a, 159a
Suryaprakasarao, P. 76b
Suryo-di-Puro, Suyoto 102b
Sussex Archaeological Collections 338a
Sussex Union, University of 18a
Susskind, David 149b, 270b
Sutch, W.B. 147b
Sutcliffe, Sara 76b
Sutherland, Elizabeth 157b
Sutherland, Graham 91a
Sutherlands, Keith 171b
Suttles, Wayne 270b
Suudi, Ann E.G. 211a
Suyin, Han 236a
Suzara, Ramon Carter 147b, 291a-b
Suzuki, Kazunaga 145a
Suzuki, Mary 65b
Suzuki, Shuken 144b
Svadost, Ermer 270b
Svahnström, Bertil 112a, 115b, 167b
Svantesson, Sven 335b
Sved, Ignacio 150a, 299a
Svenska Fräindustriarbetareförbundet 113a
Svensson, Gustav 270b
Sveriges Radio 236a
SVN Peace Committee 138b, 182a
Svobodova, I. Lubor 76b, 299a
Svobodova, Jirina 299a
Swaffer, David 155a
Swain, G.W. 76b
Swaine, Tom 100b
Swaminathan, Samaswati 206b
Swan, William H. 199b
Swann, Robert 76b, 121a, 127a, 128b, 129a, 164a
Swanwick, H.M. 79a
Swarajya 66a, 335b
Swartz, William 270b
Swaziland Progressive Party 96a
Sweden **113a-b, 130b**
Swedish Communist Party Congress 113b
Swedish Peace and Arbitration Society 299a
Sweeny, Kim 76b
Sweet, Ben 150a, 217a
Sweet, Colin 30b, 164b
Sweetman, Stella 101b, 117a
Sweezy, Paul M. 89b, 127a, 137a, 221a
Swepstone, Walsh, & Son 313a
Swift, Basil 335a
Swindells, Pauline 149a
Swindley, R.D.H. 76b
Swindon Public Libraries Philosophical Society 270b
Swinkels, C.H. 154a

Swiss Confederation 130b
Swiss Credit Bank 91a
Switzerland **113b, 130b**
Sydney Morning Herald 236b
Sydney "Save Our Sons" Movement 170a
Syed, Yehia M. 221b
Sykes, Hugh 236b, 299a
Sykes, Josephine 353b
Sykes, Manuela 96a
Sym, Kent 91a
Symonds, Ruth 91a
Symons, Janice 76b
Syndicalist Workers' Federation 95b, 130b
Syndikalistiska Foreningen 236b
Synge, R.L.M. 149b, 159a
Synic 236b
Syria **113b, 130b**
Systematics 323b
Szabó, Miklós 335b
Szaulski, Florian 335b
Szczesny, Gerhard 236b
Szczesny Verlag 236b
Szekeres, G. 322b
Szent-Györgyi, Albert 236b, 335b
Szilard, Leo 29a, 335b
Szondy, G.A. 76b
Szpakowski, Slawomir 76b
Szur, Leon 91a

T

Tabak, Salomão 120b
Tabata, I.B. 149a
Tabata, Shinobu 145b
Tabb, Eric 236b
Tabet, Antoine 106b, 126a
Tabibi, A. 271a
Tabibi, Sharahm 271a
Tabio, Alvarez 186a
Table Ronde pour les Libertés au Portugal 128b
Tacchi-Morris, Kathleen 76b-77a
Tacer, Yavuz 271a
Täckmark, Sven Erik 271a
Tagett, R.H. 91b
Taghi 215a
Taghizadeh, A. 124b
Tagliazucchi, Pino 167a
Tahri, Mohamed 77a, 97b
Tai, Abdullah 105a
Taieb, Lucien 114a, 121a
Taikan, Rosa 77a
Tait, Anne 282b, 283a
Tait, Charlie 281b, 282a, 283a
Tait, David 283a
Tait, Johnathan 283a
Tait, Katharine (née Russell) 276a, 277a-b, 280b-283a, 284a, 314a, 353b
Tajima, Shinzo 145a
Takata, Toyozo 77a
Takeda, Hiroyuki 144b
Takeda, Kiyoko 145a
Takeiri, Yoshikatsu 297a
Takemura, Keisui 144a
Takman, Jan 82a
Takman, John 160b, 162a, 185a
Talaat, ? 149a
Talabani, ? 159a
Talbot, D.A. 115b
Talbot, H.C. 143a
Talmage, D. 119a
Talmor, Ezra 103b
Taluka, D.D. 77a
Tamarin, N. 143b
Tambo, Oliver 129b, 159a, 160b
Tampoe, Bala 77a, 172b
Tamshead, V. 115b
Tan, Allen L. 148a
Tanabe, Koichiro 145b
Tañada, Lorenzo M. 159a
Tanasescu, Horia 110a
Tanasescu, Mircea 110a
Tandon, R.S. 222b
Tanesse, Georges 288b
Tanggaard, E. 236b, 287a
Tanghe, Fernand 171a
Tanikawa, Tetsuzo 104b, 145a, 271a
Tanjug 236b
Tanner, Cicely (née Young) 271a
Tanner, Jack 278a
Tanwir, Ghulam Rasul 236b
Tanzania **113b, 131a**
Tanzania High Commission 113b
Tanzi, Carla 196b
Tapies, Antonio 77a
Tappe, Horst 236b
Tarantino, P. Conti 225b
Tarbuck, Ken 143b
Targ, William 242a
Tarrant & Frazer Ltd. 91b
Tarrow, William 77a
Tarry, Paul B. 77a
Tarsis, Valery 77a, 116b, 132a, 133b
Tarski, Alfred 335b
Tarumoto, Mieko 143b
Tasopoules, Dimos 124a
Tass 13b, 190b, 236b
Tassé, Gérald 234b
Tate, Allen B. 271b
Tate, Brian 77a
Tate, Ernest 77a, 168a, 178a
Tate, Robert S. 77a
Tatlock, J.D. 271a
Taussig, H.C. 207a, 209a
Taussig, Michael 27a
Tautfest, Peter 175a
Tawfik, Yaqoob 225b
Tax Payers Against War 168a
Taylor, Dr. 13b, 138a
Taylor, Brian D. 77a
Taylor, D.M. 147a
Taylor, David K. 77a, 168a
Taylor, Davidson 222b
Taylor, Dora 113b, 143b, 299a
Taylor, Dorinda (Doreen) 271a
Taylor, G. 77a
Taylor, George 271a
Taylor, George R. 77a, 271a
Taylor, Jr., Greer M. 352b
Taylor, H.G. 288a
Taylor, Harold 149b
Taylor, Ian 37a
Taylor, Isabel 77a
Taylor, J.A. 143b
Taylor, J.D.R. 208a
Taylor, J.M. 251a
Taylor, Mr. & Mrs. K. 146b
Taylor, Karl 251b
Taylor, Kathleen 77a, 116a
Taylor, Lewis W. 309b
Taylor, M. 330b
Taylor, Margaret R. 271a
Taylor, Marjorie E. 145b
Taylor, Mary 32b
Taylor, Michael 236b
Taylor, Noel 143b
Taylor, Norman 77a, 170a
Taylor, Stuart 77a
Taylor, Vic 236b
Tchubine, T. 106b
Teaque, III, Walter D. 168a
Technical Assistance Board 115a
Tedesco, Mrs. 265a
Tedesco, Melanie 271a
Teichman, C. Joseph 77a
Teimourian, Hazhir 77a, 299a
Teitelbaum, Isidor 77a
Teitelbaum, Maureen 128b
Tejeda, M. 294a
Tejpal, Nautalal C. 236b
Tek?, Richon 281b
Tekva, Petah 135a
Telegraph House 310a, 312a
Telegraph-Journal 236b
Telephone House 77b
Telford, Michael 77b
Teller, Edward 324a
Teller, Eva 228a
Telmon, Sergio 229b
Telsey, S.W. 271a
Temoijnage Chrétien 17a
Temple, Robert 236b
Temple, W.H. 91b
Les Temps Modernes 236b
ten Cate, L.O. 77b, 210a
Tendulkar, D.G. 336a
Teoresi 329b
Terkel, Studs 336a
Terman, Mandel A. 112a
Terre des Hommes 174a
Terry, Belaunde 109a, 128a
Testro, Rex C. 77b
Teusaca 95a
The Texas Observer 136a, 137a-b
Tezel, Ilhan 168a
Thach, Colette 161a
Thach, Pham Ngoc 157b, 162a, 188b
Thailand **113b**
Tham, Le Dinh 160b, 162b
Thanh, Pham Duc 35a
Thank You, Bertrand Russell 152b
Thanning, Niels S. 77b, 173b
Thant, U 18b, 37a, 54b, 59a, 67a, 70b, 76a, 79a, 79b, 80a, 86a, 115a, 118b, 141a, 147a-b, 152b,

288b, 299a
Tharaldsen, Mary Ann 77b
Thatcher, David S. 271a
Thayer, H.S. 263a
Theatret Fiol 173a
Theilheimer, Edmundo Guerra 179a
Themerson, Franciszka 271a, 293a
Themerson, Stefan 116b, 210a, 271a, 288b, 293a
Theodorakis, Mikis 101a, 123a
Theoria 328b
Therborn, Göran 113b
Thero, U Saranankara 271a
Theta Upsilon Sorority 282b
Thetford, Philip Henry 77b
Thi, Dinh Ba 153a, 162b, 163a
Thi Yomiuri 236b
Thibaut, Marcel 171a
Thibaut, Roland 174a
Thiel, J. Christian 288b
Thieme, Dr. Walter 98b, 99a
Thien-Hoa, Thich 168a
Thier, Karl-Heinz 77b
Thiles, Sheila 30b
Thing, Bob 77b
Think 237a
Thinking in Front of Yourself and Other Plays 276a
The Third Force, Central Committee 104a
The Third Kyoto Conference of Scientists 105a
Third World Organizing Committee 168a
The Third World: The Unaligned Countries and the World Revolution 333b
Thirkell, Angela 271a
Thirring, Hans 77b, 288b
Thiruvalluvar House 237a
Tho, Nguyen Huu 118a, 162a, 163a, 176a, 186b, 187b, 188b, 299a
Thomas, A. 77b
Thomas, A.V. 299a
Thomas, Alfred J. 77b, 336a
Thomas, Bruce 77b
Thomas, David 79a
Thomas, Donald 303a
Thomas, E.A. 288b
Thomas, J. Morgan 208a
Thomas, James Carey 256a
Thomas, N. 237a
Thomas, Norman 77b, 124b, 133b, 136b, 288b
Thomas, W. Harford 141b
Thompson, ? 15b
Thompson, C. 91b
Thompson, David F.M. 77b
Thompson, Dorothy 293a
Thompson, Edward 143b
Thompson, Elsa Knight 216b
Thompson, Jr., H.K. 237a
Thompson, Joan Lee (*see* Braby, Joan "Gogi")
Thompson, John B. 171b
Thompson, John J. 231b
Thompson, Keith 207b
Thompson, L.H. 39a, 170b
Thompson, Manley 150a, 237a
Thompson, Marjorie 170a
Thompson, Michael 271b
Thompson, Ralph 200b
Thompson, W.S.K. 150a
Thomsen, Alexander 77b
Thomson, George 116b
Thomson, Gladys 271b
Thomson, John 225a
Thomson, Lord 176a
Thomson, Peter 271b
Thönnessen?, Dr. Werner 91b, 99a, 121b
Thorndike, Dame Sybil 271b, 287a
Thornhill, C. 77b
Thornton, Michael 238a
Thornton, J.C. 88b
Thorogood, Maura 77b
Thorpe, F.A. 237a
Thorpe, Jeremy 129b
Thorpe, R. 288b
F.A. Thorpe Publishing 237a
Thorsson, Leif 234b
Thorton, Dennison 44a
Thouroude, Jean-Claude 77b
The Three-Penny Review 144b
Thrlik, Z. 121a
Thuan, Cam Pham Ngoc 163a
Thuy, Xuan 56b, 162a, 299a
Tibol, Raquel 295b
Tibor, Asher 77b
Tidningarnas Telegrambyrå 237a
Tidsignal 143b, 154b, 237a
Tierney, J.C. 77b
Tierney, Penelope 77b
Tigar, Michael E. 226a
Tikhonov, Nikolai 74b, 116b, 118b, 136b, 167b, 291a
Tilakaratna, B.P. 95a
Tilden, Marian 220a
Till Eulenspiegel 77b
Tillich, Paul 328b
Tilmann, Klemens 175a
Time 220b
Time Incorporated 237a
Time Magazine 237a
The Times 11a, 12a, 13a-b, 17a-b, 18b, 30a, 35a, 44a, 45a, 63b, 93a, 94a, 96b, 100b, 101a, 103b, 109b, 112b, 114b, 115a-b, 118b, 119a, 123b, 124b, 129b, 135a, 146b, 153b, 156a, 176a, 183a, 185b, 203a, 231b, 237a, 278b, 304a, 314a, 334a, 351b
The Times Educational Supplement 237a
Times of India 50b, 62a, 67a, 153b, 336a
The Times of Karachi 237b
Timpany, Frederick P. 77b
Tinbergen, N. 336a
Tinh, Nguyen Duy 162a, 162b
Tinker, Jonathan 32a, 66a, 83b, 199a, 201b, 215a, 251b, 313a
Tinner, Dale R. 78a, 168a
Tippett, Michael 152a
Tirnoveanu, N. 237b
Tiselius, Arne 168a
Titchenor, ? 78a
Tito, Josip Broz 86b, 119a, 132a, 154b, 299a
Tiwar, Shesh Narayau 78a
To the Conscience of Humanity 172b
Tobal, Ibrahim 59b, 93a
Tobas, Jorge Albarnoz 172b, 237b
Tobey, Marjorie E. 209b
Tobin, Michael A. 237b
Today 11a, 237b
Today's Japan 237b
Todd, Luis 135b
Todd, Mich. O'Cleary 173a
Tofallis, Zannetos 14b, 78a, 96a, 124a, 237b
Togo, Republic of 113b
Tokarczyk, A. 332b
Tokkie, Rik 78a
Tokyo Conference of Scientific Technique Study (Executive Committee) 78a
Tokyo Junior Chamber of Commerce 144a
Tokyo Tribunal on U.S. Crimes of Agression and War in Vietnam 17b, 168a, 186b, 336a
Tolentino, Gustavo 160a, 184b
Leo Tolstoy's Message to Sir Bertrand Russell 271b
Tomalin, Nicholas 237b
Toman, Cyril 28a
Tomer, D.S. 214a
Tomes, W. Hartford 211a
Tomimori, Hidenao 145a
Tomkinson, Anne 271b
Tomkinson, C.M.H. 271b
Tomlin, Ian 78a
Tomonaga, Shinichiro 144b
Tompkins, Ann 149a
Tøndel, Torre 299a
Toni ?, Y.T. 278a
Tonki, Syed Mohammad 299a
Tonnies, J.E. 91b
Tonthaltung, Emues
Topchiev, A.V. 31a, 78a, 237b, 336a, 351b
Topeka State Journal 237b
Topham, A.J. 114b
Topham, Tony 148a, 154b, 271b, 291b, 299a
Topic Records 13b
Topley, Elizabeth 159a
Topolski, Feliks 226a
Topor, Doina 233a
Toren, Simona 110a
Torii, Kimihiro 144b
City Council of Toronto 299a
Toronto Daily Star 94b, 237b
Toronto Star Ltd. 183a
Toronto Star Weekly 12a, 37b,

118a, 183a, 237b
Torrado, President Osvaldo Dorticos 95b
Torres, Edelberto 78a
Torres, Fermín 73b
Toth, Robert C. 218b
Totterman, Richard 97a
Touias, Jean 39a
Touré, Sekou 101b
Towards Truer Democracy 330b
Towhidi, Nasser 175a
Town 237b
Townroe, Christopher 78a
Townsend, Tessa 283b
Towry Law (General Insurance) Ltd. 143b
Toynbee, Arnold 60a, 136a, 139b, 159a, 271b, 288b, 291b, 293a
Toynbee, Philip 271b
Toyoda, Toshiyuki 145a
Trabert, Dr. 121b
Trabulsi, Fawwaz 107a
Tractatus Logico-Philosophicus 334b
Tracy, I.I. 78a
Trade Union Committee for Defense of Maurice Paul 137a
Trade Union Congress Conference 15b
Trafalgar Square Rally 101b
Trafalgar Square Speech 129b
Trajtenberg, Mario 78a
Tran-Van-Tung, Mr. 190a
Trans World Airlines Inc. 91b
Transactions of the Cambridge Philosophical Society 322b
Transition 237b
Transport and General Workers' Union 78a, 129b
Transworld Circulation Co. 143b
Tran-Thiet, Jean-Paul 174a
Traverne, Dick 130a
Treadgold, Donald W. 237b
Trehern, Frank 203b
Trelleck Parochial Appeal Committee 271b
Tremlett, George 237b
Trent, Christopher 204b
Trent Park College Socialist Society 78a
Trepczynski, ? 109b
Trepra, Jauun Nekamoto ? 336a
Treuhaft, Robert 271b
Trevelyan, Charles 79a, 271b, 278a
Trevelyan, Elizabeth 271b
Trevelyan, G.M. 283b, 288b
Trevelyan, Julian 173a, 271b, 277a, 280a, 293a
Trevelyan, Mary 271b, 280a, 293a
Trevelyan, Raleigh 215b
Trevelyan, Robert 280b
Trevor-Roper, Hugh 95a, 271b, 288b
Trevor-Williams, Michael 262a, 279b
Trexler, Margaret P. 233a
Trhlik, Zdenek 96b
Triad 336a
Tribuna 237b
Tribunal 189b, 190b
Tribunal de Grande Instance de la Seine 175a
Tribunale per i Crimini di Guerra 16b
Tribune 95b, 154a, 176b, 183a, 184b, 336a
The Tribune 128b, 154b, 237b
Tribune: Ceylon News Service 238a
Tribune de Genève 323a, 334a
Tribune de la Jeunesse 120b
Tricontinental Committee 168a, 173a
Tricontinental Committee in Support of Vietnam 95b
Tri-Continental Information Centre 105b
Tricontinental Magazine 78a
Tricot, G. 230b
Trinidad/Tobago **113b**
Trinity College, Cambridge 353a
Trinity College Library, Cambridge 279a
Trinity Review 238a
Trio International 238a
Trionfera, Roberto 229b
Tripp, Mrs. Leslie M. 78a
Tri-Service Council, Proceedings of the 4th Annual 155a
Tristram, M.P.W. 78a
Trivedi, Purushottam N. 78a
Trivedi, Sudhir 78a
Troeller, Gordian 188a
Trofimenko, ? 146b
Troga, Awna 299a
Trombadori, Antonello 187b, 188b
Trondheim Student Union 78a
Trost, A.H. 271b
Trotman, Anthony F. 197b
Trotta, Avv. Arvena 78a-b
Trowell, Susan 291a
Trowsdale, David Howell 224a
True World Order 335a
The Trumpet, London 238a
The Trumpet, Long Island, N.Y. 238a
Trussler, Darian 301b
Trussler, M. 299a
Trust House Service Ltd. 91b
Truth Quest 336a
Tschernobilski, Josef Romaianasi 133b
Tschudi, Hans-Peter 113b
Tsendenbal, Yumzhagün 108a
Tsigmond, Anna 78b
Tsolakis, Mr. 96a
Tsamantanis, Constanten 122b
Tsukaguchi, Yoshiyuki 12b
Tsuneto, Dr. 145a
Tsung-ying, Lee 101b
Tsuru, Shigeto 145a
Tsuruaka, Misao 336a
Tsurushima, Setsure 78b, 160b, 175b, 187a
Tsushima, Toshiko 145a
Tubman, Marilyn J. 238a
Tubman, William 105b
Tuborg Breweries Ltd. 91b
Tucci, Niccolo 272a
Tucci, Vieni 272a
Tuck, David 186b, 188b
Tuck, Gene 272a
Tucker, Bill 78b
Tucker, John 238a, 336a
Tucker, O.R. 78b
Tudor-Hart, Beatrix 272a
Tufail, Mohammad 225a
Tuft, Patrick 299b
Tuft, Pauline 299b
Tuli, Kailash 272a
Tull, James L. 134b
Tull, T.S. 326a
Tunemi, Horikoshi 91b
Tung, H.F. 85a
Tung, Tont Hat 299b
Tunisia **113b-114a, 131a**
Tunisian Delegation 151b
Tunisian National Opposition 93a
Tuong, Tran Cong 164b
Turin Vietnam Committee 16b
Turk, M.A. 78b
Turkey **114a, 131a**
Turkish Teachers' Union Revolutionary Education Council 114a
Turnbull, Arthur 78b
Turnbull, E. 121b, 131b
Turnbull, Eddie 78b
Turnbull, Frances 78b
Turnbull, Mary 238a
Turner, Eileen 25b, 130a
Turner, H.H. 272a
Turner, Judith M. 91b
Turner, Margaret 78b, 131b
Turner, Martin 272a
Turpin, C.C. 78b
Turpin, R. 78a
Tusa, John 209b
Tusquets, Esther 207b
Tutino, Saverio 78b, 94a
Tuttle, Bert 91b
Charles E. Tuttle Co. 145a, 238a
Tvardovsky, Alexander 224b
Mark Twain Journal 219b, 297b
The Twentieth Century 238a
20th Century and Peace 238a
21st Atomic Bombing Anniversary International Conference 145b
Twin, Tom L. 78b
Twine, Fred 178a
Twinn, Stephen 78b
Tyler, F.J. 143a
Tyler, Mary 78b, 121a
Tylor, Louis E.P. 88a, 223b, 279a, 281a, 307b, 309a, 312a
Tynan, Kenneth 116a, 159a, 272a
Tynemouth CND 78b
Tyrrell, Barbara 78b
Tzakov, Boris 272a

U

Uchida, Shigeo 211b
Ude, Wilhelm 14a
Ueda, Teiji 78b, 145a
Uemura, Tamaki 145a
Uenaka, Sotaro 336b
Uffelmann, Erika 78b
Uganda **114a**
Újszó 238a
Ulanora, Galina 116b
Ulbricht, Walter 99a, 121b
Ulrich, E. 336b
Ulus, Feyzi 168a
Umlandt, Wolf-G. 78b, 174b
l'UNEF 16a
Unarmed Victory 7b, 19a, 95a, 103b, 152b, 349a, 351a
The Under Secretary of State 114a
Underdog 156b
Underhill, Marion 137a
Underwood, Austin 272a, 299a, 352b
Underwood, Christopher 205a
Underwood, R. D. 197b
Underwood Business Machines 278b
UNESCO 52a, 203a, 238a
The Unesco Courier 155a
UNESCO Secretariat 280b
Ungaretti, Guiseppe 133b
Unicrit 238a
Unidade Democratica Portuguesa 78b, 109b, 128b
Unified Buddhist Church of Vietnam 168a
Unilateral Initiatives and Disarmament 334b
Union d'Entraide en Favour de l'Hopital due Dr. A. Schweitzer 79a
Union de Escritores y Artistas de Cuba 78b
Union de Peruanos en Cuba 128a
Union des Architectes du Vietnam 79a
Union for the Protection of the Human Person by International Social and Economic Co-operation, Inc. 254b
Union Nacional de Mujeres Mexicanas 299b
Union of American Exiles in Britain 79a, 140a
Union of Australian Women 79a, 126b, 170a, 299b
Union of Democratic Control 79a, 271b
Union of Greek Political Refugees Great Britain 101a
Union of Greek Political Regugees in Poland 124a
The Union of Mauritian Students 238b
Union of Mutual Prosperity Headquarters 144b
Union of Relatives of Greek Political Refugees Abroad 124a
Union of Shop, Distributive and Allied Workers 79a
Union of Socialist Students of Austria 170b
Union Transport Finance Ltd. 314a
Union Voice 238b
Unione Tipografico-Editrice Torinese 238b
l'Unita 238b
Unitarian Church of Calgary 13a, 118a
Unitarian Extension Movement in Australia 79a
Unitarian Universalist Association 91b
United Arab Republic **107b, 114a, 131a, 155b**
United Arab Republic Ambassador to the U.K. 107b
United Arab Republic Branch of BRPF **149b**
United Arab Republic—Correspondence 156b
UAR Delegation 151b
United Arab Republic Peace Council 107b
U. A. R. Peace Committee 156b
United Association for the Protection of Trade (London Branch) 91b
United Coalition to Avert Pandemic and Biocide 168a
United Democratic Youth Organisation of Cyprus 96a
United Federation of Teachers 79a
United Kingdom **114a-115a, 131a-132a, 351a**
United Malaysian and Singaporean Students' Action Front 127a, 299a
United Nations 54b, 59a, 79a, 82b, 86a, 86b, 101a, 115a, 121a, 141a, 147b, 149a
United Nations Association 38b, 146b
United Nations Association, Hemel Hempstead Branch 291b
United Nations Association, Highgate 79a
United Nations Association in Canada, Hamilton Branch 91b
United Nations Association, London 79a
UN—Division of Human Rights 134b
U. N. London Information Centre 115a
United Nations Security Council 95a
United Nations Student Association 91b, 168a
United Nations Technical Assistance Board 79a
United News of India 238b
United Peace Front Party 79a
United Press International 238b
United Secretariat Fourth International 128a
United Workers Party of Israel—The Central Committee 104a
U. S. S. R. **116a-117b, 132a, 351a**
U. S. S. R. Embassy, London 116a
U. S. Air Force ROTC Air University 189a, 336b
U. S. A. **115a-116a, 135a-140a, 156b**
U. S. A. Office **149b**
U. S. Committee for Justice to Latin American Political Prisoners 105b, 109a, 127b, 150b
U. S. Committee to Aid the National Liberation Front 168a
United States Information Service 238b, 336b
US News and World Report 79b
United States Student Press Association 238b
United Tobacco Company 91b
United Towns Organisation 110b
United World Federalists 79a
Universal Brotherhood 79b
Universal Friendship Organisation 91b
Universal Knowledge Foundation 238b
Universal Medical Assistance 91b
Universal Peace Festival 79b
Universal Pictorial Press & Agency Ltd. 238b
Universidad Autonoma de Chihuahua Mexico 299b
Universidad Javeriana 79b
Universities' Committee for Soviet Jewry 112a
Universities Fight for Economic Development 91b
University College Library, London 272a
University College of North Wales 238b
University College of North Wales Humanist Society 238b
University College of Wales Humanist Study 272a
The University of Aston in Birmingham 272a
University of Bombay 238b
U. C. L. A. 281b
The University of Chicago Law Review 10b, 239a
University of Chicago Press 239a
University of Chile 288a
University of Exeter Socialist Society 178b
University of Ghana 100a
University of Hanoi Student Aid Fund 170a
University of Liverpool Guild of Undergraduates 239a
University of London Union 12a

University of London Vice Chancellor 131b
University of Michigan Press 239a
University of Sussex Joint Faculty-Student Committee on Vietnam 168a
University of Toronto 172a
University of Toronto Library 272a
University of Virginia 168a
Univeristy of Washington Vietnam Committee 81b
University of Waterloo, Department of Philosophy 294a
University of Wisconsin Student/Faculty Committee to End the War in Vietnam 168a
Unkel, Edna 231b
Unno, Shinkichi 145b, 175b
Unovirs 350a
Unterman, Iser J. 112a, 133b
Unwin, A.H. 272a
Unwin, Mary 293a
Unwin, Rayner 292a
Unwin, Sir Stanley 20b, 142b, 196a
Uomini e Idee 289a
Uphouse, Dr. Willard 137b
Uppman, Ingegerd 91b
Upton, J. Duane 272a
Urban, George 229b
Urch, Phyllis 263a, 283b
Urdu Digest 79b, 239a
Ure, P.N. 350a
Uribe, Angel Caamaño 106a
Uris, Norman Burton 239a
Urquhart, Clara 118a, 121b, 123a, 213a, 272a
Urrego, Agudelo Antonio M. 79b
Uruguay **115a, 132a**
Uruguayan Branch of BRPF **149b**
Usakov, A.T. 134a
Usborne, Henry 79b, 336b
Usdin, Emma 111b
Ushakov, Mr. 134a
Ushenko, Andrew 336b
Ushio 239a
Usmani, M.A. 272b
Utley, Freda 353b
Uzdánski, E. 51b
Uzdi, Muhammed bin Abdulla 131a
Uzzell, Thomas H. 239a

V

Vaab, Mihkel 111b
Vack, Klaus 50a, 80a, 100a
Vaish, R.N. 153b
Vaishnavi, Rugho Nath 79b, 108b
Valadão, Ramiro 128b
Valente, Pedro Soares 171a
Valente, Philip 272b
Valentino, Anna 353b
Valet, Roanne 239a
Van Ausdall, B.J. 239a
Van Bloemen, Sheila 96a
Van Bösllager, Ada ? 79b
Van Brantegem, Victor 112b
van Cung, Dr. Phung 119a, 138b, 167b, 182a
Van Cutsem, Pierre 239a
Van Damme, C. 111a
van de Coppello, N.J.C.M. Kappeyne 147b
van de Sande, Sara 170b
van den Boomen, G. 223a
van den Bosch, Baron Jean 94a, 170b
Van den Heuvel, Walter 79b
Van den Hooff, Arnold 352b
Van Dooren, L.A.T. 336b
Van Essen, Jac 336b
van Gelderen, Millie 128a
van Heerden, P.J. 336b
van Heesch, C.A. 79b
van Heijenoort, Jean 239b
van Kerkhoven, Jan 239b
Van Lan, Ha 157b
Van, Le Huu 163a
Van Meers, Mary Lou 201a
Van Meter, Jr., Robert H. 79b
Yan Noi, Huang 353b
D. Van Nostrand Company 239b
Van Olphen, H. 272b
van Rooy, Silvio E. 125b
van Rossum, Roger 337a
Van Stolk, C.R.A. 79b
Van Teslaar, Amiel 283b
Van Twyl, Myrth 79b
Van Wormer, Mrs. 79b
Wilfrid Van Wyck Ltd. 289b
Vancouver Sun 239a
The Vancouver Viet-Nam Day Committee 79b, 171b
Vande Velde-Schlick, Barbara 239b
Vandel, Mark 173b
Vandendries, Pierre 258b
Vanderbilt University 130a
Vandercom, Stanton & Co. 277b, 309a, 310b
Vanderhaeghen, Claude 35b, 79a, 120a
Vane, Raymond R. 79b, 168a
Vanguard 239b
Vanita Maha Vidyalaya 102a
Vanly, Ismet Cheriff 126b
Vanoss, S.F. 211b
Vardin, Catherine 299b
Vargas, Pedro E. Muñoz 168a
Vargas, Philip 79b
Várkonyi, P. 101b, 124b
Varley, Geoff 131a
Varnalis, Costas 122b, 123b
Varsity 137b, 239b
Varughese, P.N. 79b
Vasalos, Kostas 124a
Vasiliev, A. 258b
Vasilios, Doukaksis 123a
Vassev, Mr. V.M. 112b, 116a-b
Vastapane, Dino 94a
Vasudev, G.V. 60a
Vatra, Ardeleanu 299b
Vaughan, Edward 80a
Vaughan, James W.K. 80a, 239b
Vaughn, Sue A. 80a
v.d. Bergh-v.d. Meer, Marian 75b
Vaz, Benedito Teixeira 110a
Vazir, Mira 235a
Vazquez, Delores Soleto 299b
VEB Hochbauprojektierung, Schwerin 175a
Vecerni Praha 96b
Vecker, Jacques 58a
The Vedanta Movement 80a
Vèdele, Vittorio 289a
Vedin, John-Bertil 237a
Vega, Camilo Alonso 113a, 130b
Vega, Hilario Molina 173a
Vega, José María 113a, 239b
Vega, Nageswara Rao 239b
Velazquez, Carlos Maria 115a
Vélez, Fernando 95a
Velikovsky, Immanuel 272b
Veliz, Claudio 95a
Venezuela **117b, 132a**
Venezuelan Oil Concessions Stock Certificate 314a
Venezuela's Cuban Exiles 121a
Venis, Martin A. 337a
Verband der Kriegsdienstverweigerer 80a, 99b, 121b, **144a**, 289a
Verein Iranischer Studenten 125a
Verein Iranischer Studenten in Wien 125a
Vergelis, Aron 112b, 117a
Verlag der Philosophischen Akademie 239b
Verlag Kurt Desch GMBH 157b, 239b, 240a
Verlag Schnelle 144a
Verlon, André 239b
Verma, Gurdial 80a
Verma, R.P. 80a
Vernal, Jean-Luc 35b, 120a
Vernon, Hilda 80a, 118a, 153a, 178a, 180a
Verona, Sergiu 80a
Veroz, L. 80a
Verry, H.L. 147a
Vesey, Godfrey 353a
Vesper-Triangel, Bernward 80a, 122a, 174b, 207a, 240a
Vester, Bill 168a
Vestnik Akademii nauk SSSR 336a
Vetter, Hermann 80a
Vetter, O. 24a
Vettikattumattom, V.C. Mathew 153b
Vexler P., Erica 230b
Vezumi, Minoru 144b
Il Vice Presidente dei Consiglio dei Ministri 142a
Vicic, J. 272b
Victims of Repression in Peru 299b
Victoria Humanist 80a
Victoria, Queen 3a
Vidal i Sanfeliu, Ignesi 207a
Vidmar, Josip 157a

Vie Nuove 239b
Viennot, Jean-Pierre 125b
Vierra, Robert S. 337a
Viet, Hoang Quoc 168a
Viet Report 239b
Vietnam **117b-118b, 132a-b, 156b, 196b**
Vietnam—A Voice from the Villages 165a
Vietnam Action Committee 169a
Vietnam Action Group 168a
Vietnam Afroasian Solidarity Committee 132a, 162a
Vietnam-aktion 173a
Vietnam Bulletin 118a, 180a
Vietnam Committee for the Defence of World Peace 162b, 168a
Vietnam Co-ordinating Committee 170b
Vietnam Day Committee 80a, 168a
Vietnam Day Committee News 239b
Vietnam Federation of Trade Unions 168a
Vietnam Free Speech Petition 177a
Vietnam Friendship Committee (Finland) 16b
Vietnam North 16a
Vietnam Peace Committee 162a, 163a, 185a, 299b
Vietnam Peace Movement, Oxford 80a
Vietnam Peace Parade Committee 139a
Vietnam Pictorial Monthly 188b
Vietnam Solidarity Bulletin 178a, 345a
Vietnam Solidarity Campaign 50b, 52a, 67b, 80b, 171a
Vietnam Solidarity Campaign, Hull Branch 291b
Vietnam Study Group 169b
Vietnam Women's Union Standing Committee 45a
Vietnamese Lawyers 159a
View 239b
Views 185b, 239b
Vigier, Jean-Pierre 160b, 161a
Vigne, F. 48a
The Viking Press 240a
Villa, Carlos Escallon 240a
Villamil, Ricardo Bengoa 80b
Vincent, Jean-Marie 161a
Vincente, Andres Solari 168a
Vinden, Kathleen 240a
Viney, Janet 29b, 179a, 201b, 272b
Vinogradoff, Julian 283b
Viola, C.R. 80b
V.I.P. Newsletter Management Guide 80b
Visa Campaign 14b
Visa pour un Enfant 240a
Vishnu-devananda, Swami 336a
Vishva Manav Mandal 80b
Visvakala 330b
Vitarelli, William V. 91b
Viterbo, Enio 141a
Vlada, Kastich 291b
Vlahov, Ivan Stefanov 80b, 171b
VNA News Bulletin 171a
Vogel, Hellmut 98b, 99a
Vogel, Paul Ignaz 223a
Vogler, Anne 240a
Vogue 240a
Voice of the Unions 80b, 148b, 176a
The Voice of Vietnam 380a
Voice of Women 80b, 91b, 337a
Voice of Women/La Voix des Femmes, Quebec 299b
Voigt, Gerold D. 175a
Vokrouhlický, Zbynek 12b, 48a
Vole, W.J. 114b
Volkszeitung 291b
Vollrem, Kaare 80b
Vollset, Vigdis 74a
Voltaire Society 154b
Voltaire Verlag 240a
Volunteers' Organization for World Disarmament 80b
von Arb, Joseph K. 50b
Von Ardenne, Manfred 80b, 337a
Von Bruns, Günter 323a
von der Goltz, Michael 299b
von Etzdorf, Hasse 99b
von Glahn, Jeffrey 272b
von Grünigen, Heinrich 235b
Von Holzer, E. 287b
von Makal, Paul K. 240a
von Mannerheim, Karl Gustav 279a
von Nottbeck, Dr. Arvid 99a-b
von Ossietzky, Maud 272b
Von Samson, Armin 85a
von Schoen, Rolf 337a
von Schwarze, Klaus E.R. 80b, 121b, 272b
Von Thun, Mr. 75b
von Trott, Adam 353b
von Uexkull, Jakob 236b
von Westphalen, Karl Graf 80b, 100a, 121a-b, 122a, 291b
von Winthofen, Alexander 80b, 173a
von Wright, G.H. 240a, 337a
Von Zeppelin, Amethe 272b, 280b
von Zircz, Mr. 77b
Vorgänge 143b
Voroshilov, Klimentiy E. 117a, 121b, 134b
Vosnjak, Sergei 234a-b
Vosseler, Marion 272b
Votes for Youth Campaign 80b
Voutov, Peter 94a
Vowles, Joy 272b
Voz de Portugal 110a
Vrbrovska, Anca 196b
Vrhunec, Marko 119a
Vroland, Anna 83b
V.S.C. Conference 15b
V.S.C. Strathclyde University 179a
Vukovic, Catherine 272b
Vyas, R.N. 240a

W

W. "Occasional Verse" 337a
Wachter, Heinz 291b
Wade, Dyan 234a
Wade, Margaret 80b
Christopher Wade Ltd. 91b
Wadhams, Jack 80b
Wadia, H.R. 81a
Wadsworth, Art 217a
Wadsworth, Arthur J. 342a
Wadsworth, Geoffrey 299b
Waerland, Ebba 81a
Wagner, Audrey 30b, 128b
Wagner, John 272b
Wagstaff, E.W. 98b
Wagunyanya, J.G. 81a
Waheed, A. 127b
Wahlberg, U.M. 173b
WAIF—International Social Service 240a
Waih, Elisabeth 81a
Wainhouse, Austryn 173b
Wainright, Charles Anthony 240a
Wainwright, M. 74a
Waite, Tom 81a
Wajdani, Malik H. 81a
Wakabayashi, Hiroshi 144b
Wakely, P.G. 262a
Walczer, Theodore 272b
Wald, George 81a
Wald, Karen 24a, 166b, 168a, 222a
Waldeck-Rochet, W. 112a-b
Wales Against Apartheid 81a
Wales Rejects Apartheid Co-Ordinating Committee 81a
Waley, Arthur 273a, 281b, 353b
Walk for Peace Committee 156b
Walker, Aileen 91b
Walker, Alan 202a
Walker, Claire 81a
Walker, Eric 34b
Walker, Harold 176b, 273a
Walker, I.G. 147a
Walker, Ian 273a
Walker, Jan 81a
Walker, L.R. 91b
Walker, Phyllis Helen 299b
Walker, Samantha 81a
Walker, Scot 273a
Walker, Simon 301b
Walker, T. 81a
Wall, W.A. 352a
The Wall Street Journal 240a
Wallace, Delight S. 283b, 310b
Wallace, Derek 91b
Wallace, Frank 337a
Wallace, Irving 273a
Wallace, Lane 204b
Wallace, R.G. 234b
Wallas, May 274a

Waller, Ellen 289a
Walling, Mary 211b
Wallis, R.G. 81a
Walmsley, Margot 208a
Walrus 240a
Walsh, Maurice N. 273a
Walshe, Francis 309b
Walston, ? 114b
Walston, Lord 115b
Walter, Ivan 273b
Walter, Nicolas 81a, 273a, 337a
Walters, A. 53a
Walters, Margaret 81a
Walton, E.H.H. 81a
Wandersleb, Gottfried 36a
Wang, Hao 273a
Wang, Tze-Koong 269a
Wantuck, Julius O. 81a
War Crimes in Vietnam 8a
War/Peace Report 240a
War Resisters' International 81a, 102b, 121b, 124a, 132a, 135b, 150a, 168a, 173b, 299b
War Resisters League 81b
War Stock 314a
Warbey, William 14b, 81a, 118b, 147b, 168a
Warburg, Fredric 233a
Warburg, James P. 81b, 156b, 337a
Warby, H.M. 56a
Ward, A.J.B. 337b
Ward, Emily T. 212a
Ward, Harriet (née Barry) 283b
Ward, Dr. Harry F. 258b
Ward, Helen 128a, 273a
Ward, Hilda 82b, 128a
Ward ?, J.N. 281b
Ward, James 256a
Ward, Michael D. 81b, 240b
Ward, R.H. 282b
Ward, Robert 81b
Ward, Shirley 81b
Warda, Samuel S. 81b, 168a
Wardell, Gareth 273a
Wardey, Nicholas 92a
The Warfare State 219a
Warner, Harry A. 91b
Warpiuk, Douglas 60b-61a
Warren, Dennis M. 302a
Warren, Kenneth 17a, 171b, 172a
Warren Report 156a
Warth, Derek 81b
Washi, Y. 91b
Washington, George 257b
Washington, Walter 81b
Washington Evening Star 55b, 240b
Washington Newsletter 156b
The Washington Post 38b, 135b, 137b, 139b, 183a, 220a, 240b, 352a
Washington Square Press 240b
Wasserman, Ben 273a
Wasserman, Benno 146a
Wasson, M.J. 240b
Watan 240b
Waterlow, Mrs. Rupert 273a
Waterlow, Sidney 29b, 278a
L.E. Waterman Co. 283b
Waters, Doris W. 91b
Waters, Gilbert 42a
Waters, Timothy J. 240b
Waterworth, Hanson 273a
Watford, Ann V. 228a
Watkins, Eric 168a
Watkins, John M. 228b, 240b
Watkins, Peter R. 81b
Watney, Annette H. 273a
Watson, Barbara 273a
Watson, Dean? 81b
Watson, G.S. 322b
Watson, Gordon 81b
Watson, H. 273a
Watson, J.H.A. 326a
Watson, Luise 293a
Watson, Oliver 223a
Watson-Watt, Robert 81b, 142b, 149a
Watter, P. 34b, 204a
Watterson, Eleanor 353b
Watts, Frederick 218a
Watts, Julyan A. 91b
Watts, Stephen 240b
C.A. Watts & Co. 95a, 240b
The Way to World Disarmament–Now! 155b
Ways of Peace 240b
W.B.A.I.—F.M. Radio 82a
WBAI Radio Station 240b
We, The Peoples 240b
Weaver, Anthony 82a
Webb, Beatrice 273a, 337b
Webb, Colin 82a
Webb, N. 240b
Webb, Sidney 337b
Webber, Rollin 91b
Webbs 114b
Weber, Edward 52a
Weber, Helga 299b
Weber, Neil 82a
Webman, S. 52b
Webster, Adrian 165b
Webster, S.E. 273a
Wechselblatt, Paul 111b, 112b
Wedderburn, K.W. 159a, 176a
Wedgewood, Veronica 278b
The Week 14b, 118b, 128b, 138b, 240b
Weekend Telegraph 241a
The Weekly Graphic 128a
Weeks, Edward 198a
Weeks, W. 59b
Weeks, W.G. 170a
Weener, Martin 82a
Wegodsky, R. 82a
Weibringhaus, H. 70b
Weichert, Hildegard 48a
Weidenfeld, George 241a
George Weidenfeld & Nicolson 241a
Weidenfeld, Leon 110b
Weidner, Hansgeorg 82a
Weight, Ellen Comfort 91b, 337b
Weik, Mary H. 135b, 155b, 241b
Weil, Josef 134a
Weil, Robert 82a, 156a
Weiler, Heinrich 82a, 175a
Weinberg, Mindy 82a
Weinelberg, U. 133a
Weiner, Rachel 113a
Weiner, T. 273a
Weingarten, J. 85a
Weingarten, Samuel 241a
Weinman, Maryann 273a
Weinschenk, Jacob H. 337b
Weintraub, Stanley 273a
Weir, H.A. 273a
Weir, Ian G. 82a, 299b
Weisbart, Herr 91b
Weisberg, Harold 82a
Weis-Fogh, Torkel 141b
Weisman, Zena 112b
Weiss, Adnard 337b
Weiss, Arnold 91b
Weiss, John 91b, 337b
Weiss, Paul 337b
Weiss, Peter 82a, 96a, 136a, 155a, 157a, 161a, 192a
Weiss, Mr. and Mrs. Peter 148a
Weiss, Rita 91b
Weisselberg, Maximilian 110a
Weisselberg, Sidonia 110a
Weissman, Maryann 34a, 139b, 143b
Weitzner, Dorothea 91b
Welker, Nannie 291b
Wellborne, J.E. de Montfort 82a
Weller, Ken 91b, 143b
Wellisch, Ivanne 101b
Wells, Donald G. 337b
Wells, D.R. 82a
Wells, Dee 273a
Wells, Gip 273a
Wells, H.G. 273a
Wells Street Magistrates' Court 143b
Wellwood, R.E. 337b
Welsh, David 229b
Welsh Committee of 100 152a
Welsh Council for Peace in Vietnam 15a, 168a
Welsh Office 273b
The Welsh Party 82a
Weltert, Christopher 82a
Welwyn Garden City & District Trades Council 299b
Wemyss-Smith, W. Duncan 299b, 338a
Wener, Edward 172b
Wenger, Elisabeth 273b
Wenk, Juerg 82a
Wenner Gren, Mrs. 113a
Wennström, Gösta 157a
Wenting, A.W. 299b
Werbitzky, Susana 111b
Werbitzky, Teodoro 111b
Werbos, Paul J. 273b
Werkheiser, Don 215b
Werkmeister, Frank 121b
Werner, Ivar 157b

Werner, R. 82a
Werres, Johannes P. 273b
Werskey, Gary 273b
Werstein, Jacob J. 273a
Wertheimer, Robert G. 273b
Wesker, Arnold 112b, 152a, 168a, 181a
West, G.A. 273b
West, R.C. 92a
West, Dame Rebecca 273b
The West Australian 241a
West Australian University Labour Party 168a
West Birmingham Youth C.N.D. 82a
West European Conference for Amnesty 128a
West European Conference for an Amnesty for Greek Political Prisoners and for a Return to Normal 'Democratic Life' 123b
West European Conference for Amnesty for Portuguese Political Prisoners and Exiles 82a-b
West Germany **174a**
West German Ambassador 99b
West Indian Gazette 178a
West Indies Guiana Socialist Union 82b
West Indies News Bulletin 82b
West London Observer 241a
West of England Campaign against Factory Farming 242a
West Pakistan College Teachers Association 82b
West Riding Humanist Society 241a
Westby, Jill 178b
Westergaard, Anna 280a-b
Westergaard, John 92a, 165a
Westerholm, Kurt 97a
Western Australian Medical Students' Society 241a
Western Institute for Advanced Study 82b
Western Mail 241a
Western Review 241a
Westminster, City of 213a
Westminster Amnesty Group 131b
Westlands Committee of 100 122b
Westminster Bank Ltd. 92a, 232a
Westoby, Frank 241a-b
Weston, Grainger 273b
Weston, Mary 82b
Wewer, Heinz 206a
Weyditch, Ivan Walter V. 273b
Weyl, Richard 100a, 122a, 273b
Weyrauch, Wolfgang 116a
Whale, J.S. 196b
Wharton, Joan 224a
Wharton, Michael 205a
Wheaton, Donald 273b
Wheeldon, John 299b
Wheeldon, Mary 299b
Wheeler, Geraldine 225a
Wheeler, George 168a
Wheeler, Harvey 258a
Wheeler, J.G. 338a
Wheeler, John 82b
Wheeler, Romney 222b
Wheelwright, Alice 142a
Whelan, Joe 166b-167a
Whettam, Graham 131b, 273b, 299b
Whillier, Colin 53b
Whincop, Katherine E. 273b
Whisson, M.E. 82b
Whitaker, Ben M.D. 115a, 273b
Whitaker, Paul M. 168b
White, A. Fraser 29a
White, Alan R. 273b
White, Amber Blanco 353b
White, Cynthia 240b
White, D. 89b
White, Eirene 116b
White, George 92a
White, H.L. 169b
White, Jeffrey 171b
White, Louis A. 82b
White, Mary Anne 98b
White, Merit P. 82b
White, Robert O. 215b-216a
White, Robert Tyner 82b
White, W. Alan 273b
The White Cross Movement for Infantile Paralyses 82b
White Elephant Club 26b
The White House 118b
Whitechapel Bell Foundry 273b
Whitehead, A.N. 256b, 324b, 335b
Whitehead, John 299b
Whitehead, N. 82b, 116b
Whitehouse, M.D. 117a
Whiteman, Anne 293a
Whiteman, John B. 273b
Whitman, G. 92a
Whitman, George 143b
Whitman, Samuel 273b
Whitman, W.W. 204b
Whitten, Jacquelyn 53a
Whitten, Philip 274a
Whlie, Thomas D. 82b
Who Killed Kennedy? Committee 52a, **156b**
Who's Who 199b, 241b
Who's Who in America 241b
Who's Who in British Science 241b
Why I Am Not a Christian 333b
Whyte, L.L. 274a
Whyte, Quintin 46b
Whymant, Neville 338a
Wicken, Joan E. 113b, 147b
Wicken Fen Appeal 92a
Wickenden, Joanna 127b
Wickens, Keith 82b
Wicker, Tom 159a
Wicks, John 82b, 95b, 338a
Der Widerstandskämpfer 241b
Wieck, Fred 211b
Wielek, Harry 75b
Wielon, John J. 92a
Wieluch, Doman 274a
Wienand, W.G. 274a
Wiener, Martin J. 274a
Wiener, Norbert 9b, 150b, 328b
Wiener, Philip P. 241b, 289a
Wiener, S. 274a
The Wiener Library, Department of Contemporary Jewish History 112a
Wienhold, Leonhard 174b
Wiesenthal, Simon 241b, 338a
Wiffin, T. 122a
Wiggins, James Russell 240b
Wiggs, Richard 82b, 145b
Wigham, Wilfred 47a, 234b
P. Wigham-Richardson & Co. 92a
Wight, R. 274a
Wightman, G. 274a
Wighton, Charles 82b, 98a, 122a
Wijayatilake, Padmavarna 172b
Wijesna, P.K.D. 83a
Wildbolz-Dorman, Moura 83a
Wilder, Isabel 274a
Wildman, Louis 211a
Wiley, John C. 83a
Wilhelm, Wolfgang 100a, 338a
Wilhelmy, Jerry 83a
Wilk, Andrzej 241b
Wilkes, Mr. & Mrs. Owen 83a, 147b
Wilkes, R.G. 83a
Wilkie, Lloyd 214b
Wilkinson, Mrs. 147b
Wilkinson, M.G. 83a
Wilks, Helen 92a
Willcox, Bertram F. 83a
Willey, Arthur 134a
Willi, Ernst 274a, 289a, 291b
Williams, Mr. 282a
Williams, A.L. 52a
Williams, Anne M. 83a
Williams, Bennett L. 83a
Williams, Bryan 83a
Williams, Bryce 83a
Williams, Charles 299b
Williams, Charles St. E. 83a
Williams, Colin 31a
Williams, Donald 164a
Williams, Donald C. 338a
Williams, Eric 113b
Williams, Eva 83a
Williams, George 135b
Williams, Mrs. H. 39b
Williams, H.C.N. 88a
Williams, H.L. 278a
Williams, Ivor 130a
Williams, J.O. 277b, 308a
Williams, James Malcolm 33b, 165a
Williams, James T. 216a
Williams, Neville V. 83a
Williams, Norah 288b
Williams, Sir Osmond (Michael) 274a, 293a
Williams, Peter 223a
Williams, R. 92a
Williams, R.H. 131a
Williams, Raymond 168b, 299a

Williams, Reginald? 276b
Williams, Richard 83a, 291b
Williams, Robert L. 83a
Williams, Roger J. 13a, 118a, 338a
Williams?, Vivienne 293a
Williams-Ellis, Amabel 274a, 283b, 293a, 353b
Williams-Ellis, Cicely 274a
Williams-Ellis, Clough 274a
Williamson, H.A. 338a
Williamson, J.H. 83a
Willis, Lord Ted 115b, 116a
Willmann, Heinz 63a, 98a
Willms, Dr. 122a
Willoughby, George 167a
Wills, Michael 83a
Wills, Ruth 353b
Wills, T.T. 83a
Wills-Johnson, Alistair 338a
Wilmer & Broun 309b
Wils, Ingrid 83a, 122a
Wilson, ? 83a
Wilson, Barbara A. 179a, 299b
Wilson, Cora 150a
Wilson, Dagmar 25a, 84a, 138b, 171b
Wilson, David Q. 274a
Wilson, E.J. 170b
Wilson, Edmund 10b, 274a
Wilson, Edwin H. 197a
Wilson, F.W. 274a
Wilson, G. 90b
Wilson, G.H. 83a
Wilson, H.H. 149a, 150a
Wilson, Harold 8a, 60b, 67b, 100b, 114a, 117b, 147b, 185a, 189a, 293a
Wilson, M.H. 83a
Wilson, Margaret 312a
Wilson, Richard 299b
Wilson, Robin 289a
Wimbledon Town Hall 141b
Wimbledon Young Socialists 168b
Win, Ne 94b
Winbolt, S.E. 338a
Winchester, Gail 83a
Winckworth, Archie M. 92a
Windeyer, B.W. 131b
Windmiller, Marshall 217b
Window on the World 155a, 241b
Windrum, R.N. 229a
Windsor, Garith 230a
Wine, Sherwin T. 213b
Winiawsky, Clemens 83a
Wink, Walter 83b
Winkel, Victor W. 83b
Winkworth, A.S.W. 202b
Winocour, Jack 112a-b
Winser, Pearl 274b
Winslow, Calvin 81b, 136a
Winslow, Hank 83b
Winston, C. 274b
Winston, James 83b
Winter, Anne 279a
Winter, Ella 83b, 115b, 168b
Winter, Mike 274b
Winthofen, Alexander 85a
Winwood, A. 83b
Wirsig, Wolfgang 175a
Wirtanen, Atos 83b
Wisdom, J.O. 274b
Wisdom 241b
Wisdom of the West 209a, 260a, 349a
Wise, J. Hooper 241b
Wise, Robert E. 92a
Wissenschaftliche Buchgesellschaft 241b
Witchell, John B. 83b, 152a, 338a
Withers, Bernard 63a, 226a
Withers, John J. 309a, 309b, 310a
Withers & Co. 309a, 309b
Witlin, Frances 83b
Wittgenstein, Ludwig 10a, 274b
Wittig, Georg 83b
Wittkamp, William T. 83b
Wittmer, Sylvia ? 338a
Wittrock, John W. 274b
Wivel, Ole 83b, 159a, 173a
WNEW-TV 241b
Wobbe, Charles C. 83b
Wober, J.M. 83b
Woburn Trust 92a
Wocker, K.H. 224a
Wohlgemuth, A. 274b, 352b
Wojtaszek, E. 166a
Woker, Gertrude 120b
Wolf, Professor 83b, 175a
Wolfers, John 48a, 157b
Wolfgang, Walter 108a
Wolfman, Cyril 241b
Wolfson, Isaac 42a
Wolfson, Louis E. 42a
Wolin, Ron 83b
Wolins, Le Roy 168b
Wolkowska, Ruth A. 83b
Wollast, R. 165b, 170b
Wollheim, Richard 165a
Wolman, Benjamin B. 241b
Wolpin, Miles D. 92a
Wolsencroft, Frank 146b
Wolters, Adrien 117a, 135a, 152a
Woman Today 241b
Women Against War 83b, 138b, 142b
Women for Peace 83b, 118b
Women Strike for Peace 84a, 98a, 154a
Women's Association for Radiation Information 84a
Women's International Congress for Peace in Moscow 190a
Women's International Democratic Federation 174b, 299b
Women's International League for Peace and Freedom 14a, 84a, 155b, 168b, 169a
Wontner & Renwick 309a
Wood, A.M. 116b
Wood, Alan 274b
Wood, Alex 338a
Wood, Clive 215b
Wood, David 260b, 274b, 291b, 293a
Wood, Ernest 130a
Wood, G. 84a
Wood, Herbert 84a
Wood, Jonathan 260b, 274b
Wood, Marilyn Rose 84a
Wood, Marshall K. 338b
Wood, Mary 274b
Wood, Pamela 274b, 293a
Wood, Ralph W. 310b
Wood, Roman Kenneth 84a
Wood, Stuart L. 84a
Wood, Costa & Hardy 131b
Woodfall Films Ltd. 94a
Woodley, William L. 84a
Woodridge, Philip D. 198a
Woodruff, Virginia 241b
Woods, James H. 274b
Woods, P.A. 274b
Woods, R.A. 84a
Woods, William M. 92a
Woodson, E.A. 231a
Woodsworth, K.C. 251a
Woodward, M. 84a
Woodworth, Richard H. 84a
Woolf, Cecil 15b, 119a, 241b
Woolf, Ethel 92a
Woolf, Leonard 289a
Woolf, Sheila 274b
Woolfenden, D. 289a
Woolley, Geoffrey 123b, 153a, 237a
Wootton, Barbara 115b
Wooton, K.R. 92a
Worcester College for the Blind 84a
The Worcester Diocesan Messenger 241b-242a
The Word 124a, 130a
Worden III, Edward Chauncey 274b
Wordsworth, Christopher 283b
Workers Committee for the Defence of Freedom of Press and Freedom of Speech 84a
Workers Control Conference in Nottingham 18a
Workers of the World Party 168b
The Workers' Party of Turkey 106b
Workers Trade Union Alliance of Spain 130b
Working Group World Union 84a-b
Workman, Peter 226b
The World 242a
World Academy of Art and Science 84b, 242a
World Affairs Club, Tarsus 84b
World Affairs Council, Los Angeles 104a
World Assembly for Peace 84b, 155a
World Association for International Friendship, Peace, and Security 173a
World Association of World Federalists 84b

World Campaign for the Release of South African Political Prisoners 129b, 130a
World Citizens Information Communication Centre 92a
World Committee for a World Constitutional Convention 84b
World Conference Against Atomic and Hydrogen Bombs 12b, 84b
World Conference in Hiroshima and Nagasaki 144b
World Conference on Peace 14a
World Congress for General Disarmament and Peace 78a
World Congress for World Federation 84b, 299b
World Congress of Women 84b
World Congress of Women, British Delegation 168b
World Constitution Coordinating Committee 338b
World Council for the 'Righteous Gentiles' at the World Jewish Congress 134a
World Council of Peace 84b, 151a, 123b, 156a, 291b
World Council of Peace Presidential Committee 153a, 168b
World District Agency 85a
World Federation 338b
World Federation of Democratic Youth 101a, 102a, 126a
World Federation of Scientific Workers 168b
World Federalists of Canada 85a
World Festival of Youth and Students for Solidarity, Peace and Friendship 120a
World Forum 85a
World Government League 85a
World Government of Youth 85a
World in Action, Granada TV 274b
World Institute for World Peace 85a
World Internationalists 85a
World Jewish Congress 99a, 110b, 133a
World Jewish Congress, British Section 112a-b, 131a
World Jewish Congress, Department of International Affairs 112b
World Muslim Congress 85a
World Outlook 242a
World Parliament Association 289a
World Peace Association 85a
World Peace Brigade 85a, 102b
The World Peace Research Association 85a
World People's Television Offices 92a
The World Publishing Co. 242a
World Romany Community, Canada 126b
World Scientific Community 185a
World Union 242a
World Union of Freethinkers 85a, 274b
World Union of Jewish Students 112a, 117b, 134a-b, 156a, 242a
World Vietnam Committee 182a
World War III and the Southern Hemisphere 333b
World Wealth without War 255b
World Welfare Association 299b
World Wise 325a
World Youth 242a
World Youth Campaign of Action 168b
Wormald, Michael 85a
Worrall, Michael 85a
Worrall, T. 85b
Worsley, P.M. 142a
Worth, Arthur 121a
Worthington, Erika 299b
Worthy, J. 289a
Worthy, William 85b, 136b, 137a, 150a, 168b
Wright, Gregory 275a
Wright, Helen Rosita 299b
Wright, J.E.B. 265b
Wright, Miriam L. 338b
Wright, Olwen 114b
Wright, Mme. Richard 122b
Wrightson, Graham 85b, 174b
Wrightson, Rodger 85b
Wrinch, Dorothy 279a
Wrinch, Pamela N. 338b
Wulfsberg, Fredrik 242a
Wundt, W. 349b
Wyatt, Ena 275a
Wyatt, R.D. 128b
Wyatt, Winifred L. 85b, 291b
Wyatt, Woodrow 304a
Wyer, F.P.W. 145b, 289a
Wyeth, Jr., M.S. 212a
Wyly, III, L. David 85b
Wyly, L.T. 85b
Wyman, Daniel 85b
Wyncoll, Peter 168b
Wyneken, Gustav 122a
Wythenshawe (*see* Simon of Wythenshawe, Lady)

X

X, Malcolm 136a, 138b
Xien, Nguyen 118a, 132a, 162a, 295b
Xirotagaros, Theodore 123a
Xunhasaba 168b
Xynides, Tom 92a

Y

Yaari, A. 103b-104a
Yaari, Meir 104a
Yajima, Shuzo 144a
Yakovleva, Natasha 92a, 224b
Yale Political 242a
Yale University 330b
Yamada, Setsuo 85b, 105a, 145b, 299b
Yamagiwa, Masamichi 145a
Yamamoto, Sanehiko 275a
Yamazaki, E. 233b
Yamagishi-kai 144b
Yamagwa, Masamichi 145a
Yamed, Béchir Ben 215b
Yan, Law Wai 85b, 299b
Yanez, Alejandro 172b
Yano, Yutak 145a
Yapa, C.S. 85b
Yapp, Brian 236a
Yarham, E.R. 92a
Yasue, Ryosuke 144b
Yasui, Kaoru 12b, 49a, 104b, 144a, 215a
Yasuneba, Tanaka 144b
Yeager, Ruth G. 85b
Yeakel, Jesse 85b
Yearsley, John A. 242a
Yeh, C.H. 95a
Yehuda, Isser 112a
Yeldon, Judith 213b
Yelland, Leslie F. 85b
Yemen 118b
Yemeni Revolutionary Front 119a
Yen, Mrs. 120b, 168b
Yen, Leo K.T. 120b, 168b
Yen, Pham Thi 187b
Yerna, J. 171a
Yevonde 242a
Yevsei, Yevrienov 112b
Yevtushenko, Yevgeni 159a
Ying, Seto Kwok 85b
Yoga Forum of Canada 334a
Yogi, R.S. 36b
Yoken, Melvin B. 302a
Yokoi, Jinze 212a
Yomiuri Shimbun 242a
Yonekawa, Seikichi 144a
York Clinic 283b
York Committee to End the War in Vietnam 171b
York Gazette & Daily 137a, 242b
York University Magazine 242b
York Vietnam Group 168b, 242b
The Yorkshire Post 154b, 242b
Yoseloff, Thomas 198b
Yoshida, Kazuto 215a
Yoshida, Micko 85b
Yoshida, Yoskikiyo 49a
Yoshino, Genzaburo 144b, 215a
Yoshioka, S. 145a
Yoshiza, Hiroaki 186b
Youde, E. 117a
You'll See: Report from the Future 329b
Young, Mr. 310a
Young, A. Morgan 275a
Young, Allen 34a, 165b
Young, Amicia M. 30b, 181a
Young, Anthony 275a
Young, Denis 85b
Young, Douglas 92a
Young, Edgar P. 85b

Young, Fredric 85b
Young. L.C. 85b
Young, Kenneth 242b
Young, Tony 85b
Young European Left 85b
The Young Idea 308b
Young Japanese World Federalists 12a
Young Men's Progressive Association 86a
Young Rationalists' Club 242b
Young Socialist 242b
Young Socialist Alliance 136a
Young Socialist Forum 172a
Young Women's Christian Association of Great Britain 92a, 146b
Young Women's Christian Association of Zambia 242b
Susie Younger Korean Trust 92a
Youran, Chan 94b
Yourgrau, Bertrand 275a
Yourgrau, Wolfgang 275a, 338b
Yousuf, M. Shahid 195a
Youth Action for Peace 86a
Youth Against the Bomb 338b
Youth Against War and Fascism 14a, 86a, 103a, 150a, 168b, 291b
Youth Campaign for Nuclear Disarmament 14b, 154b, 299b
Youth for Peace in Vietnam 168b
Youth Forum 13b
Youth Movement 141a
Youth Peace Campaign 12b, 86a
Youth Society for Nuclear Disarmament "Bertrand Russell" Committee of 100 100b
Yueff, Mike 86a
Yugoslav League for Peace Independence and Equality of Peoples 299b
Yugoslav Pugwash Group 351b
Yugoslavia **118b, 132b**
Yugoslavian Ambassador 132a
Yukawa, Hideki 142b, 159a, 300a, 351b
Yule, Alastair 86a, 149a, 275a, 297a
Yusuf, I. 130a
Yusuf, S.M. 108b
Yusufzai, Farman 125a, 242b

Z

Zabara, Jacob 338b
Zachäi, Ingrid 142b, 156a
Zacielsky, M. 134b, 135a
Zacz, Sima 116a
Zahedi, Ardeshir 125a
Zaheer, S. Husain 204a
Zahn, Franklin 275a
Zajícek, Oldrich 86a
Zajonz, Herbert 98b
Zaki, Khalid 23b, 95a, 103b, 125a, 126b, 156b, 275a
Zaki, Mohd. 228b
Zakkas, Andreas 122b
Zaman, A. 86a
Zambia **119a**
Zamindar, N.C. 18b, 86a, 102a
Zamir, Shalom 86a
Zamoyski, Count 64a
Zandee, Pieter 86a, 175a
Zander, Anita 98a
Zaninovic, Lucas Seperiza 86a
Zápisník 63 242b
Zareifis, Stathis 123a
Zarodov, K. 235a
Zarogikas, G. 338b
Zasler, Bob 86a
Zatloukal-Williams, Richard 92a, 275a
Zaustinsky, Julia 242b
Zbrijer, Nathan 117a
Zeayen, Yossif 113b
Zeidler, Frank P. 92a
Zeigler, Harley H. 242b
Zeisler, Ernest B. 289a
Zeitschrift für math. Logik und Grundlagen d. Math. 323b, 334a
Zelenka, Paul 89a
Zeleznik, Carter 339a
Zeller, C.E. 113b
Zelluk, Graham J. 242b
Zemedelsko Zname 242b
Zemskov, V. 116b
Zengakuren (All Japanese Federation of Student Autonomies) 144a
Zeno 327a
Zenshin
Zerfas, A. 92a
Zhang, Xienf 275a
Zhelyaskov, L. 94a
Zhivkov, Todor 94a
Zhukov, Yuri 74b, 116b, 152b
Zia-un-Nabi, Syed 86a
Zidovec, Vesna 168b
Ziegler, Antoinette 86a
Ziegler, G. 175a
Zienau, Sigurd 275a, 299a
Ziferstein, Isidore 339a
Zikria, Faiz Ahmad 93a
Zilber, Jacob 229a
Zilinski, I. 111b
Zilliacus, Konni 86a
Zim, Marvin 237a
Zimmerman, Mrs. Jules 134a
Zimri 242b
Zink, Donna 24b
Zinner, A. 86a
Zis, Mr. 123a
Zissimos, C. 101a
Zivanović, Milisav M. 86b
Znanie 233a
Zo Haderekh 242b
Zoltick, Jerel 300a
Zonshtein, Lev 134a
Zook, Douglas-Paul 86b
Zorzoli, G.B. 203b
Zourek, Jaroslav 173a
Zu'bi, Abdul Aziz 104a
Zuby, Ozzir 86b
Zugaro, Ricardo 134b
Zukas, Simon B. 119a
Zukerman, William 154b
Zunic, Radovan 86b
Zuno Arce, Andrés 86b
Zupan, Milan 119a
Zusman, Salomon 86b
Zvezda 243a
Zwillinger, Frank 170b, 174a
Zyss, W. 238a
Zyzak, George 109b

Printed in Great Britain by
Antony Rowe Ltd, Chippenham, Wiltshire